THE

LIFE OF OUR LORD

UPON THE EARTH;

CONSIDERED IN ITS

HISTORICAL, CHRONOLOGICAL, AND GEOGRAPHICAL RELATIONS.

BY

SAMUEL J. ANDREWS.

NEW YORK:
CHARLES SCRIBNER, 124 GRAND STREET
1863.

JOHN F. TROW,
PRINTER, STEREOTYPER, AND ELECTROTYPER,
48 & 50 Greene Street,
New York.

TO

MY BROTHER,

WILLIAM WATSON ANDREWS,

GUIDE OF MY EARLY,

AND COMPANION OF MY LATER STUDIES,

THIS BOOK IS

Affectionately Inscribed.

ERRATA.

Preface, p. vii., 5th line from top—for "Life of Christ" read "Life of Jesus."

Do. Do. 16th line.

P. 22, Note 1—for "Usher says, two years and a half old," read "Usher, two years and a half before."

P. 27, 3d line from top—for "Hoffman" read "Hofmann."

P. 375, 4th line from top—for "He made no more circuits," read "He made no long circuits."

P. 384, 2d line from bottom—for "Ephraim" read "Ephron."

P. 513, 6th line from bottom—for "9th April" read "7th April."

PREFACE.

It may be well to state distinctly here that this book does not design to enter into any critical inquiries respecting the text of the Evangelists. In the few cases where a historical statement is affected by the different readings, Tischendorf is followed, use being made of his "Synopsis Evangelica," Lipsiæ, 1854. Reference is also made in such cases to Meyer and Alford, and occasionally to other authorities. Nor does it design to enter into any questions respecting the authorship of the Gospels, the time when written, or their relations to each other. Nor does it discuss the point of their inspiration, but assumes that they are genuine historical documents, and statements of facts; and deals with them as such. Nor does it aim to explain or interpret the Lord's parables, or discourses; or to discuss questions of mere archæology, or of verbal criticism. Those who wish information upon these points will consult the authors who have written specially upon them.

The simple purpose of this book is to arrange the

events of the Lord's life, as given us by the Evangelists, so far as possible, in a chronological order, and to state the grounds of this order; and to consider the difficulties as to matters of fact which the several narratives, when compared together, present; or are supposed by modern criticism to present.

As the necessary foundation for a chronological arrangement, the dates of the Lord's birth and death, and the duration of His public ministry, are discussed in brief preliminary essays. The geographical discussions are all limited to the sites of places directly related to the narratives. No more notice is taken of the general history of the time, than is necessary to explain the occasional references of the Evangelists.

In order not to avoid any points of real difficulty which the historical statements of the Gospels present, and, at the same time, not to weary the reader with discussions of the alleged discrepancies which some critics find, or affect to find, so thickly strewn upon their pages, I have selected, as the latest exponents of the critical tendencies of the times, the Commentaries of the German, Meyer, and of the Englishman, Alford. Both of these are ready, and over ready, as I think, to admit mistakes in matters of fact, and to affirm that the Evangelists, in certain points, cannot be harmonized; yet both admit the supernatural element in the Gospels, and expose and set aside many of the objections of the merely negative criticism. To these two commentators, therefore, very frequent reference is made, and whatever difficulties they present, as really such, are for the most part noticed.

From what has just been said, the reader will not be surprised that no notice whatever has been taken of Strauss, and his "Life of Christ." The principle upon which he proceeds, in his historical criticism, he thus states: "No just notion of the true nature of history is possible, without a perception of the inviolability of the chain of finite causes, and of the impossibility of miracles." If a miracle is impossible, it is plainly a work of supererogation to refute in detail a history, which, upon its face, professes to be a record of supernatural events. After striking out all that is ascribed to immediate divine agency, as incredible, the residuum is scarce worth the trouble of contending for. Besides, an attentive examination of Strauss' "Life of Christ" has made upon my own mind the impression that he deals with the evangelic narratives in a most unfair, not to say dishonest, spirit. Everywhere he finds discrepancies and contradictions; and one cannot help feeling, that whatever the Evangelists might have narrated, he would find as many objections to their statements as now. For the same reason that nothing is said of Strauss, no allusion is made to Hennell, or Bruno Bauer, or others of that school. The Commentaries of De Wette, and the Life of Jesus by Hase, have high literary merits, but the sceptical spirit in which they are written, gives them only a negative value in these inquiries.

It will be noted that the references are almost exclusively to recent writers. This is intentional. To notice the latest results of modern criticism and investigation, has been my purpose; but, at the same time, I have not neglected to examine the more prominent of the older writers in this department, so far as I have been able, from Augustine downward. While, in some cases, and chiefly those pertaining to chronology and geography, the wider scope of modern scholarship has given us new materials for judgment, yet it must be admitted that in regard to internal discrepancies, not unfrequently the old solutions are the best. No reader, familiar with their writings, will be surprised to find Lightfoot, Lardner, Baronius, Reland, and some others, here referred to as of high authority, even at this day, in their respective departments. That so many references are made to German writers, is owing to the fact that no other scholars have labored so diligently and successfully in this field.

That all will find the solutions of alleged discrepancies and contradictions here given, satisfactory, is not to be expected. Nor will the chronological order, or topographical results, be received by all. But it is a great point gained, to be able to see just what the amount of the discrepancy or contradiction, if it really exists, is. Those readers who have been accustomed to hear, through sceptical critics, of the numerous errors and mistakes of the Evangelists, will be surprised to learn how few are the points of real difficulty, and how often these are exaggerated by the misinterpretation of the critic himself. There are not a few commentators who adopt the rigid literalism of Osiander; not, like him, to defend the credibility of the Gospel narrative, but to destroy it.

In regard to the exact order of events, there is room for great differences of opinion, and positive statements are impossible. There are, however, certain well marked lines of division, and the precise arrangement of the details is comparatively unimportant, as not at all affecting the historical accuracy of the narratives, and must be left to the exegetical tact, or critical acumen of the student.

It will not be expected that I should present, upon a subject discussed for so many centuries by the best minds of the Church, anything distinctively new. Still, I trust that some points have been set in clearer light, and that the general arrangement will facilitate the inquiries of those who seek to know as much as is possible of the external history of the Lord's works and words, that they may the better penetrate into their spiritual meaning. I have given considerable prominence to the great divisions of His work, first in Judea, and then in Galilee, and to the character of His last journey to Jerusalem; both as explaining some peculiarities in the synoptical Gospels, and as showing that His work was carried on under true historic conditions. There is no fact more important to be kept clearly in mind in these studies than this, that Jesus was very man no less than very God. While recognizing the supernatural elements in the evangelic narratives wherever they exist, we are not so to introduce them as to make these narratives the records of a life neither human, nor divine. The Lord, in all His words and works, in His conduct toward the Jews, and His repeated efforts to make them hear and receive Him, acted as man, under those laws which God at the beginning established to guide human action. His life on earth was in the highest sense a human one, and it is this fact that gives us the key to the Gospels as real historic records.

It may properly here be said, that this work was ready for the press two years since, and that its publication has been delayed to this time by the troubled aspect of our political affairs. I cannot regret the delay, as it has given me the opportunity to examine several valuable works that have appeared in this interval. Among these are Ellicott's "Historical Lectures on the Life of our Lord;" vols. fifth and sixth of Sepp's "Leben Jesu;" Jones' "Notes on the Scriptures;" and Lewin's "Jerusalem." To the first of these, distinguished by its accurate scholarship and reverential tone, and which happily has been republished in this country, and is thus accessible to all, I have made frequent references. I cannot refrain from expressing my obligations to the Notes of the late Judge Jones, whose deep insight into the meaning of the Evangelists none can doubt, although he may, perhaps, at times be charged with over-subtlety and refinement. I must also make thankful mention of the Commentaries on Mark and Matthew, the latter unhappily unfinished, of the late Prof. J. A. Alexander, who, without any of the parade of learning, gives us its most solid results. Some recent works, as that of Tischendorf, "Aus dem heiligen Lande," Leipzig, 1862, came into my hands too late to be of use.

How poor and unworthy of Him, the external aspects of whose earthly life I have endeavored in some points to portray, my labors are, none can feel more deeply than myself. I can only pray that His blessing—the blessing that changed the water into wine—may go with this book, and make it, in some measure, useful to His children.

HARTFORD, CONN., *Oct.* 1862.

LIST OF AUTHORS CITED.

For the convenience of younger students, and because, in the notes I have generally, for the sake of brevity, referred to authors by their names, and not given the titles of their works, I add here a list of such of the more recent writers as are most frequently cited, with the titles in full. The elder writers, whose works are well known, it is not necessary to include in the list.

Alexander, J. A., Commentary upon Matthew and Mark. New York, 1858–1861.

Alford, H., The Greek Testament, vol. I., containing the Four Gospels. New York, 1859.

Barclay, J. T., City of the Great King. Philadelphia, 1858.

Baumgarten, M., Die Geschichte Jesu. Braunschweig, 1859.

Bleek, F., Beiträge zur Evangelien Kritik. Berlin, 1846.

Bleek, F., Synoptische Erklärung der drei ersten Evangelien. Leipzig, 1862.

Bloomfield, S. T., Greek Testament, with English Notes. Boston, 1837.

Browne, H., Ordo Sæclorum. London, 1844.

Bucher, J., Das Leben Jesu Christi. Stuttgart, 1859.

Clinton, Henry F., Fasti Romani. Oxford, 1845–1850.

De Costa, I., The Four Witnesses. New York, 1855.

De Saulcy, Dead Sea and Bible Lands, Trans. London, 1854.

Ebrard, J. H. A., Wissenschaftliche Kritik der Evangelischen Geschichte. Erlangen, 1850.

Ellicott, C. J., Historical Lectures on the Life of Our Lord. London, 1860.
Ewald, H., Drei ersten Evangelien. Göttingen, 1850.
" Die Alterthümer des Volkes Israel. Göttingen, 1854.
" Geschichte Christus und seiner Zeit. Göttingen, 1857.

Fairbairn, P., Hermeneutical Manual. Philadelphia, 1859.
Friedlieb, J. H., Archäologie der Leidensgeschichte. Bonn, 1843.
" Geschichte des Lebens Jesu Christi. Breslau, 1855.

Gams, Johannes der Täufer. Tübingen, 1853.
Greenleaf, S., Testimony of the Evangelists. Boston, 1846.
Greswell, E., Dissertations upon the Principles of an Harmony of the Gospels. Oxford, 1837.

Hackett, H. B., Illustrations of Scripture. Boston, 1857.
Hofmann, R., Das Leben Jesu nach den Apokryphen. Leipzig, 1851.
Hug, J. L., Introduction to New Testament. Trans. Andover, 1836.

Ideler, C., Handbuch der Mathematischen und Technischen Chronologie. Berlin, 1825–1826.

Jarvis, S. F., A Chronological Introduction to the History of the Church. New York, 1845.
Jones, J., Notes on Scripture. Philadelphia, 1861.

Kitto, J., Life of Our Lord. New York, 1853.
Krafft, C. H. A., Chronologie und Harmonie der vier Evangelien. Erlangen, 1848.

Lange, J. P., Leben Jesu. Heidelberg, 1847.
Lange, J. P., Bibel Werk: Matthäus, Markus, Johannes. Bielefeld, 1857–1860.
Lewin, Thomas, Jerusalem. London, 1861.
Lichtenstein, F. W. J., Lebensgeschichte des Herrn. Erlangen, 1856.
Lynch, W. F., Exploration of the Jordan and Dead Sea. Philadelphia, 1849.

Messiah, The. London, 1861.
Meyer, H. A. W., Commentar. Die Evangelien. Göttingen, 1855–1858.
Mill, W. H., The Mythical Interpretation of the Gospels. Cambridge, 1861.

MILMAN, H. H., History of Christianity. New York, 1841.
MORISON, J. H., Notes on Matthew. Boston, 1860.

NEANDER, A., The Life of Jesus Christ. Trans. New York, 1848.
NEWCOME, Bishop, Harmony of the Gospels, edited by Robinson. Andover, 1834.
NORTON, A., Translation of the Gospels, with Notes. Boston, 1856.

OOSTERZEE, J. J., Bibel Werk: Lukas. Bielefeld, 1859.
OSBORNE, H. S., Palestine, Past and Present. Philadelphia, 1859.
OWEN, J. J., Commentaries on Matthew, Mark, and Luke. New York, 1858–1861.

PATRITIUS, F. X., De Evangeliis: Friburgi, 1853.
PAULUS, H. E. G., Das Leben Jesu. Heidelberg, 1828.
PAULUS, H. E. G., Exegetisches Handbuch, über die drei ersten Evangelien. Heidelberg, 1842.
PORTER, J. L., Handbook for Syria and Palestine. London, 1858.

RAUMER, KARL VON, Palästina. Leipzig, 1850.
RIGGENBACH, C. J., Leben Jesu. Basel, 1858.
ROBINSON, E., Biblical Researches in Syria and Palestine. Boston, 1856.
ROBINSON, E., Harmony of the Gospels. Boston, 1845.
RITTER, CARL, Die Erdkunde von Asien. Band viii. 15th u. 16th Theile.

SCHAFFTER, A., Der ächte Lage des Heiligen Grabes. Berne, 1849.
SCHWARTZ, J., Geography of Palestine. Philadelphia, 1850.
SEPP, J. N., Das Leben Jesu. Regensburg, 1853–1862.
SMITH, W., Dictionary of the Bible, vol. I. London, 1860.
STANLEY, A. P., Sinai and Palestine. New York, 1857.
STEWART, R. W., Tent and Khan. Edinburgh, 1857.
STIER, R., The Words of the Lord Jesus. Trans. Edinburgh, 1855.
STRONG, JAMES, Greek Harmony of the Gospels. New York, 1854.
STROUD, W., Physical Cause of the Death of Christ. London, 1847.

THIERSCH, H. W. J., Versuch für die Kritik N. T. Erlangen, 1845.
THILO, J. C., Codex Apocryphus, vol. I. Leipsic, 1832.
THOLUCK, Commentary on St. John. Trans. Philadelphia, 1859.
THOMSON, W. M., Land and Book. New York, 1859.
TISCHENDORF, C., Synopsis Evangelica. Lipsiæ, 1854.
TOBLER, T., Bethlehem. Gallen u. Berne, 1849.

TOBLER, T., Golgotha. Seine Kirchen u. Kloster. Berne, 1851.
" Die Siloahquelle u. der Oëlberg. St. Gallen, 1852.
" Topographie von Jerusalem. Berlin, 1853.
" Denkblätter aus Jerusalem. Constanz, 1856.
" Dritte Wanderung nach Palästina. Gotha, 1859.
TOWNSEND, G., The New Testament, Arranged in Historical and Chronological Order. Revised by T. W. Coit. Boston, 1837.

VAN DER VELDE, C. W. M., Journey through Syria and Palestine. Trans. Edinburgh, 1854.
VAN DER VELDE. C. M. W., Memoir to accompany Map of Holy Land. Gotha, 1858.

WESTCOTT, B. F., Introduction to Study of the Gospels. London, 1860.
WICHELHAUS, J., Geschichte des Leidens Jesu Christi. Halle, 1855.
WIESELER, K., Synopse der vier Evangelien. Hamburg, 1843.
WILLIAMS, G., The Holy City. London, 1849.
WILLIAMS, I., Narrative of our Lord's Nativity. London, 1844.
WILSON, J., Lands of the Bible. Edinburgh, 1847.
WINER, G. B., Real Wörterbuch. Leipzig, 1847.
WINER, G. B., Grammatik des Neutestamentlichen Sprachidioms. Sechste Auflage. Leipzig, 1855.
WRIGHT, T., Early Travels in Palestine. London, 1848.

Occasional references are made to the valuable articles in the Real Encyklopädie für Protestantische Theologie und Kirche, von Dr. Herzog, Hamburg, 1854–1862; and in the Kirchen Lexicon, oder Encyklopädie der Kathol.scher Theologie, von Wetzer und Welte, Friburg, 1847–1857.

CHRONOLOGICAL ESSAYS.

[In the following Essays, and throughout this work, the dates are given according to the æra beginning with the building of Rome, or *ab urbe condita;* more briefly, U. C. Reckoning backward from Christ, the year 1 of Rome corresponded to the year 753 B. C. The year of Rome corresponding to the year 1 of the Christian æra, was 754. Hence, to obtain the year of Rome after Christ, we must add to 753 the number in question: thus the year 30 A. D. would correspond to 753 + 30, or 783. If we would obtain the year of Rome before Christ, we must subtract the number in question from 754: thus if Herod died 4 years before the Christian æra or 4 B. C., 754–4 would give 750 of Rome. Always, if not expressly stated to the contrary, the year of Rome is to be understood.]

DATE OF THE LORD'S BIRTH.

We take as our starting point in this inquiry the statement of Matthew, (ii. 1–9,) that Jesus was born before the death of Herod the Great. We must, therefore, first ascertain when Herod died. According to Josephus,[1] "he died the fifth day after he had caused Antipater to be slain; having reigned since he caused Antigonus to be slain, thirty-four years, but since he had been declared king by the Romans, thirty-seven." He was so declared king in 714. This would bring his death in the year from 1st Nisan 750 to 1st Nisan 751, according to Jewish computation, at the age of seventy.

But the date of his death may be more definitely fixed. Josephus relates[2] that he executed the insurgents, Matthias and his companions, on the night of an eclipse of the moon. This eclipse took place, as has been ascertained by astronomical calculations,[3]

[1] Antiq., 17. 8. 1. [2] Antiq., 17. 6. 4.
[3] Ideler, Handbuch Chronologie, 2. 391.

on the night of the 12th and 13th March, 750; yet he was dead before the 5th of April, for the Passover of that year fell upon the 12th April, and Josephus states[1] that before this feast his son and successor Archelaus observed the usual seven days' mourning for the dead. His death must therefore be placed between the 13th March and 4th April, 750. We may take the 1st of April as an approximate date.[2]

How long before Herod's death was the Lord born? The Evangelists Matthew and Luke relate certain events that occurred between His birth and Herod's death, His circumcision upon the eighth day, the presentation at the Temple on the fortieth, the visit of the Magi, the flight into Egypt, the murder of the Innocents. Whatever view may be taken as to the order of these events, they can scarcely have occupied less than two months. This would bring His birth into January, or February at latest, 750.

Having thus reached a fixed period in one direction, and ascertained that His birth cannot be placed later than the beginning of 750, let us consider the data that limit the period upon the other side. And the first of these we find in the statement of Luke, (ii. 1–6,) that He was born after the edict of Augustus that all the world should be taxed. In obedience to this edict, his parents went to Bethlehem to be taxed, and there He was born. If, now, we can ascertain when this edict went into effect in Judea we have another fixed period.

It is known from Suetonius and from the Ancyranian monument, that Augustus three times instituted a census, in 726, 746, and 767.[3] Of these the second only needs to be considered. But this seems to have been confined to the Italians or Romans, *cives Romani*, and thus a *census civium*,[4] and not to have extended to the provinces.[5] It cannot, therefore, have been the taxing of Luke. That Augustus did at different times take a census of the provinces is well established, but we know not the exact periods. As we

[1] Antiq., 17. 8. 4.

[2] Almost all chronologists agree in putting Herod's death in 750. So Browne, Sepp, Wieseler, Ammer, Ewald, Winer, Hales, Meyer. Jarvis puts it in March, 749; Greswell, April, 751; Clinton in 750 or 751.

[3] Sepp, 1. 139.

[4] Usher, 10. 458; Greswell, 1. 536 and 4. 22.

[5] This, however, is doubted by many. Browne, 45; Friedlieb, 53; Sepp, 1. 141. See Ewald, 5. 141.

cannot, then, bring the taxing of Luke into any direct and positive connection with the census of 746, it affords us no certain chronological datum.

Attempts have been made to reach a positive result in another way. According to Tertullian,[1] the census at the birth of Christ was taken by Sentius Saturninus. *Sed et census constat actos sub Augusto tunc in Judaea per Sent. Saturninum, apud quos genus ejus inquirere potestis.* It is said that this necessarily implies that Saturninus was governor of Syria. We have then only to inquire when he was thus governor. He is often mentioned by Josephus.[2] There is some difference of opinion as to the length of his administration. Greswell makes it to extend from 746–750, but most only to 748.[3] If, then, this census was taken by Saturninus as governor of Syria, it must have been before 748, and consequently the Lord's birth must be placed as early as 747.[4]

Against this it may be said that Tertullian stands quite alone in this statement, and is at variance, not only with St. Luke, but with many of the early writers, and is not here to be credited.[5] Or if it be admitted as correct, it by no means follows that Saturninus was governor of Syria at this time; he may have been a special commissioner for the purpose.[6] The supposition of Browne, (47,) that the census began under him while governor, and so before 748, is not probable. Patritius, iii. 168, makes Saturninus to have been governor and Cyrenius legate extraordinary, and both to have assisted in the work; but this conflicts with Luke's statement that the latter was governor of Syria. In either case we fail to fix the time for the taxing through its connection with him.

We now turn to the statement of Luke (ii. 2): "This taxing was first made when Cyrenius was governor of Syria." This language is susceptible of various constructions, which will be hereafter fully considered. We are concerned with it here only in its chronological bearing as connected with Cyrenius. If it be read "this taxing was before he was governor," or "this taxing first took effect when he was governor," it gives us no aid in our in-

1 Adv. Marc., 4. 19.

2 Antiq., 16. 10. 8; 16. 11. 3; 17. 1. 1; 17. 2. 1; 17. 3. 2. War., 1. 27, 2; 1. 29. 3.

3 Ideler, Zumpt, Sepp, Ammer, Browne.

4 Patritius and many. 5 So Friedlieb, 54. 6 So Ammer, 18.

quiry. We learn from Josephus[1] that after Archelaus was deposed, and Judea annexed to Syria, Cyrenius was sent by the Roman emperor as governor of this province, and then instituted a census. But this was not earlier than 758 or 760, and of course cannot be the taxing mentioned by Luke; for the Lord was born, as we have seen, before Herod's death in 750. If, however, the right interpretation of the Evangelist's words is that which makes this taxing to have been the first as distinguished from a second, and both during his governorship; or that he was governor when this very taxing took place, the question arises, was Cyrenius at any period earlier than 758, governor of Syria? That he was twice governor was asserted by Baronius; "but in this," says Lardner, "he is deserted by all learned men." [2] Recently, however, the matter has been more thoroughly discussed by Zumpt in his essay *de Syria Romanorum provincia.*[3] We shall, therefore, give a brief outline of the point as it now lies in the light of this investigation.

In Josephus the names of several persons who were governors of Syria about the time of the Lord's birth are mentioned, but they are mentioned only incidentally, nor is the list complete. Of S. Saturninus, whose administration ended in 747, we have already spoken. He was followed by P. Q Varus.[4] Varus was with Herod at the trial of his son Antipater, and afterward aided Archelaus against the insurgent Jews.[5] He was therefore in office at least till the summer of 750. After this time Josephus makes no mention of him, nor does history give us any positive information how long he continued in office. Of what took place during the ten years' rule of Archelaus, Josephus says very little, nor does he mention the name of any other Syrian governor till Cyrenius, who began his administration after Archelaus had been deposed and Judea annexed to Syria.[6] Archelaus was deposed in the tenth year of his reign,[7] or in 759. That Varus did not act as governor during all this interval, is probable from the fact that it was a fixed rule with Augustus that no one should govern a province

[1] Antiq., 18. 1. 1.

[2] 1. 336. For a full discussion of the grounds taken by Baronius, see Spanheim, Dubia Evangelica, Pars Secunda, Dubium v.

[3] In the 2d vol. of his *Comment. Epigr. ad Antiq. Rom. pertinent. Berol*, 1854.

[4] Antiq., 17. 5. 2.

[5] Antiq., 17. 10. 9 and 10.

[6] Antiq., 17. 13. 5; 18. 1. 1.

[7] Antiq., 17. 13. 2.

more than five years.[1] A coin of Antioch proves that in fact in 758 L. V. Saturninus was governor. But by whom was this office filled from 750–758?

It is at this point that the researches of Zumpt have for us special importance. In his list of Syrian governors, (ii. 149,) extending from B. C. 30 to A. D. 66, we find the interval from 748–758 thus filled: P. Q. Varus, 748–750 or 6–4 B. C. P. S. Qurinius (Cyrenius) 750–753 or 4–1 B. C. M. Lollius, 753–757 or 1 B. C. to 3 A. D. C. M. Censorinus 757–758 or 3–4 A. D. After Censorinus follows L. V. Saturninus, already mentioned, from 758–760 or 4–6 A. D., who is succeeded by P. S. Qurinius for the second time. This second administration extends from 760–765 or 6–11 A. D. If Zumpt be right in this order, Cyrenius was twice governor of Syria, but we are now concerned only with his first administration, or that from 750–753. Upon what ground does this statement rest?

Our chief knowledge of Cyrenius is derived from Tacitus.[2] He was of low origin, a bold soldier, and attained a consulship under Augustus in 742, and was afterward proconsul in the province of Africa. After this he conquered the Homonadenses, a rude people living in Cilicia, and obtained a triumph. He was subsequently made rector to Caius Cæsar when the latter was appointed governor of Armenia. At what time and in what capacity did he carry on the war against the Homonadenses? The time is thus determined: He was consul in 742. As it was a rule with Augustus to send no one sooner than five years after his consulship as legate to a province, he could not have been in Africa earlier than 747. But he was made rector to C. Cæsar in 753, after the war against the Homonadenses, so that this war was between 747 and 753. In what capacity did he carry it on? Probably as governor of Syria. It is important to bear in mind that at this time there were two classes of provinces, the one under the immediate control of the Emperor, the other under the control of the Senate. The governors of the imperial provinces were called Legates or Proprætors, and continued in office during the pleasure of the Emperor; those of the Senatorial provinces, Proconsuls, whose authority lasted only for one year. Syria and Cilicia were both provinces of the former kind, and administered by proprætors. The Homonadenses were a people living in Cilicia, but Cilicia be-

[1] Greswell, 1. 507. [2] Ann., 3. 48.

longed from 25 B. C. down to the time of Vespasian to the province of Syria. As Cyrenius had been proconsul in Africa, and as it was a rule that the same person should not be ruler over more than one of the consular or prætorian provinces under the care of the Senate, he could not have been governor of any of the provinces immediately adjacent—Asia, Pontus, Bithynia, Galatia; he must then have been acting as governor of the province of Syria and as legate of the Emperor.

We cannot here enter into an investigation of the many intricate questions which belong to this point, and which are fully discussed by Zumpt.[1] The result of all is that Cyrenius became governor of Syria as the successor of Varus toward the end of 750, and continued in office till 753.

It cannot be said that Zumpt demonstrates that Cyrenius was twice governor of Syria, but he certainly makes it highly probable.[2] It is indeed possible that he was acting in the East at the time of the Lord's birth as legate extraordinary, or as head of the census commission for Syria and the East.[3] As, however, Luke's language seems to mean that he did act as governor of Syria at this time, and as he is confirmed in this by many of the earliest Christian writers, the burden of proof lies upon those who dispute his accuracy. As the case now stands, we may assume that Cyrenius was so governor from the end of 750 till 753.

But the exact chronological value of this fact, in its bearing upon the date of the Lord's birth, still remains to be considered. If, as we have seen, Herod died in the spring of 750, and after Christ's birth, and Cyrenius was not governor till the autumn of that year, how can it be said that this taxing took place under him?

It must be admitted that the census began under Varus, 748–750, and before Herod's death; but if in consequence of this death and of the popular disturbance that followed, it was for a time suspended and its execution was reserved to Cyrenius, it would very naturally be connected with his name. It is not improbable also that so long as Herod lived he appeared as the chief agent

[1] An abstract of his argument may be found in Fairbairn, Her. Man., 507; in Friedlieb, Leben Jesu, 57; and a brief notice in Alford, vol. i., Proleg. p. 50.

[2] Merivale, however, (Roman Hist., 4. 456,) calls it "the demonstration, as it seems to be."

[3] See Ewald, 5. 140, note; Browne, 45.

in its execution; and only after his death did the Roman governor take a prominent part. It is also not improbable that, as Herod's death materially changed the relations in which Judea stood to the empire, Justin Martyr's[1] allusion to Cyrenius as first procurator of Judea may refer to his more active interference in Jewish affairs.[2] We conclude, then, that the taxing of Luke, and so the Lord's birth, was in the latter part of 749 or beginning of 750.[3]

The statement of St. Luke, (iii. 23,) "And Jesus himself began to be about thirty years of age," is to be considered.[4] This passage may be variously interpreted.[5] According to some it means, "Jesus was," at this time of His baptism, "beginning to be about thirty years of age," *i. e.*, He was almost but not quite thirty.[6] Greswell affirms that this was the universal interpretation of the words by the Greek fathers.[7] According to most modern interpreters the meaning is, "Jesus was about thirty when He began His ministry."[8] We have, then, taking the latter as the right construction, to ask how great latitude is to be given to the expression "about thirty." According to some it is to be understood as a round or indefinite number, embracing any age between twenty-five and thirty-five. But when we consider how short was the Lord's ministry, this is in the highest degree improbable. According to others, it permits a latitude of two or three years.[9] But even this latitude is hardly justified by Luke's use of language.[10] The more natural construction is that the Lord was some months or parts of a year more or less than thirty. He was not just thirty, nor twenty-nine, nor thirty-one. Still it cannot be positively affirmed that the Evangelist does not use it in a larger sense.

[1] Apol. 1, c. 34.

[2] Friedlieb, Leben Jesu, 60.

[3] So Merivale, 4. 457. "It would appear from hence that our Lord's birth was 750, or 749 at the earliest."

[4] The reading of Tischendorf, Και αυτος ην ο Ιησους αρχομενος ωσει, &c., does not materially affect the sense. See Wieseler, 123.

[5] See Jarvis, 524.

[6] So Lightfoot, 3. 35; Greswell, 1. 367; Bloomfield in loco.

[7] See, however, Patritius, iii. 388.

[8] So Meyer, Alford, Norton, De Wette, Wieseler, Tischendorf, Robinson.

[9] So Ammer, Alford.

[10] We give for comparison all the passages where ωσει is used by him in connection with numerals: Gospel, i. 56; ix. 14; ix. 28; xxii. 59; xxiii. 44; Acts of Apostles, i. 15; ii. 41; iv. 4; v. 36; x. 3; xix. 7.

The argument that He was thirty at this time, because the priests at this age began their ministry,[1] has little force. The law (Num. iv. 3) has reference only to Levites, and the age when the priests began to serve is not known.[2] Besides, Jesus was not a priest, although the Baptist was.[3]

If we assume that the Lord was about thirty at the beginning of His ministry, we must, to make this datum useful in our present inquiry, ascertain in what year this ministry began. This, it is said, we are able to do through the words spoken by the Jews at Jerusalem in reply to His parable respecting the temple of His body, (John ii. 20.) "Then said the Jews, Forty and six years was this temple in building, and wilt thou rear it up in three days?" This building, or rather rebuilding, of the temple was begun by Herod in the eighteenth year of his reign, or during the year from Nisan 734 to Nisan 735.[4] The forty-sixth year following was from Nisan 780–781. It is admitted that the temple was not finished till 818.[5] But from what point of time are the forty-six years to be reckoned backward? The words may be rendered as by Lightfoot, "Forty and six years hath this temple been in building."[6] Up to this time, the Passover, when the words were spoken, the work had continued and was not yet ended. But is the forty-sixth year to be taken as current, or as completed? If the latter, the Passover was that of 781;[7] if the former, it was that of 780.[8] Some, however, understand the words, "In forty and six years was this temple," all that is yet finished, "built." Tholuck (in loco) observes, "We may suppose that at this time, probably after the completion of some main part of the edifice, a cessation in the building had taken place."[9] If this interpretation be right the passage loses all its chronological value, as it is impossible to tell how long the forty-six years had been completed.

All, therefore, that this passage gives us is a probability that the Lord's first Passover was that of 780 or 781. The former is to be preferred. If, then, he was about thirty at this time, but not a year more or less, his birth would be about 750. The Passover of 780 fell upon the 9th April. His baptism was a few weeks earlier

[1] So Lightfoot, Jarvis. [2] Winer, 2. 269. [3] Gres., 1. 374.
[4] Josephus, Antiq., 15. 11. 1. [5] Josephus, Antiq., 20. 9, 7.
[6] So Greswell, Norton, Bloom. [7] So Meyer, Wieseler, Tisch., Lange.
[8] So Lardner, Licht., Friedlieb. [9] So Olshausen, Ewald.

than this, for there intervened the temptation of forty days, His return to Jordan, His visit to Cana and to Capernaum, and journey to Jerusalem. Allowing two or three months for all this, His baptism was in the last of 779, or beginning of 780. If we suppose Him to have been just thirty at His baptism, His birth must be placed in the last of 749, or beginning of 750. If, then, for reasons already given, we cannot interpret "about thirty" as a wholly indefinite expression, but must understand it as meaning that He was some months more or less than thirty, we cannot place His birth earlier than the middle of 749.

Still another datum is the visit of the Magi. This, as we learn from Matthew, (ch. ii.,) was before the death of Herod, and so before April, 750. How long an interval elapsed between their coming and his death is matter of inference. Their arrival at Jerusalem cannot, however, well be placed later than February, 750. At this time Herod was there, (Matt. ii. 1-7,) but at the eclipse of the moon,[1] March 12–13, he was at Jericho, where he subsequently died. If, then, the Magi came in February, the Lord's birth must have taken place some time earlier, as early at least as the beginning of 750.

The cause of the coming of the Magi to Jerusalem was the appearing of a star, which in some way, whether by astrology, or tradition, or by direct divine revelation, they knew to indicate the birth of the King of the Jews. If this star were a real star, subject to the ordinary laws which rule the heavenly bodies, and the time of its appearing could be determined astronomically, we should find in it a most valuable chronological aid. But many regard it as wholly supernatural, a luminous body like a star specially prepared by God for this end; and others as a new star, that, after shining awhile in the heavens, totally disappeared; and others still, as a comet.[2] If either of these suppositions be correct, it gives us no chronological datum. But a considerable number of modern commentators are inclined to regard it as a conjunction of planets, and its time thus capable of determination. This hypothesis was first advanced by Kepler, whose attention was turned to the matter by a similar conjunction at the close of 1603, A. D. In De-

[1] Josephus, Antiq., 17. 6. 4.

[2] Winer, 2. 523. Trench, Star of the Wise Men, 28. Spanheim, Dubia Evangelica, Pars Secunda.

cember of that year Saturn and Jupiter were in conjunction, and to them in the spring following Mars was added. In the autumn of 1604, a new star of distinguished brilliancy appeared, which, however, soon began to fade, and finally, at the end of 1605, vanished from sight. His attention thus aroused, Kepler found by computation that during the year 747 of Rome, the planets Jupiter and Saturn three times came into conjunction. These computations, as corrected by Ideler,[1] show these conjunctions to have taken place on 20th May, 27th Oct., and 12th Nov. of that year, all in the sign of Pisces. At the first conjunction they were only one degree removed, in the two latter were so near that both planets appeared to a weak eye as one.[2] In the spring of 748, to these conjunctions Mars was added, and from some Chinese astronomical records it has been affirmed that a comet was visible from February to April, 749, and again in April, 750.[3]

Those who regard these planetary conjunctions as the star of Matthew, are by no means agreed as to their chronological bearing. Kepler placed the Lord's birth in 748, reckoning from the conjunction of the three planets in the spring of that year, or from the supposed appearance of a new star in the autumn, whilst the two planets were still in the immediate neighborhood of each other. Ideler, rejecting the new star of Kepler and looking only to the conjunctions, puts His birth in 747. Ebrard, though adopting the same date, supposes with Kepler that the star of Matthew was a new star which appeared at the same time. Wieseler makes it to have been the Chinese comet which appeared in 749 and 750, and therefore places His birth early in 750.

It is not consistent with our present purpose to enter into a discussion of the many questions connected with the star of the wise men. The fact that such conjunctions should have taken place so near the time when we know from other sources that the Lord was born, and in that sign Pisces, which, according to the Jewish Rabbi, Abarbanel, who wrote half a century before Kepler,[4] was of special significance to the Jews, is in itself remarkable, but leads to no definite chronological results. It is at best doubtful whether any conjunction of planets could answer to the statements of Matthew respecting the star. Ideler's assertion that the

[1] Handbuch Chronologie, 2. 406.
[2] Ideler, 2. 407.
[3] See Wieseler, 69.
[4] Amsterdam, 1547.

two planets were so near together as to appear as one, is denied by Rev. C. Pritchard.[1] "Mr. Pritchard finds, and his calculations have been verified and confirmed at Greenwich, that this conjunction occurred not on Nov. 12, but early on Dec. 5; that even with Ideler's somewhat strange postulate of an observer with weak eyes, the planets could never have appeared as one star, for they never approached each other within double the apparent diameter of the moon." Alford, on the other hand, assuming that, on the last two conjunctions, "the planets were so near that an ordinary eye would regard them as one star of surpassing brightness," proceeds to show how they may have guided the Magi on their journey. "Supposing the Magi to have seen the *first* of these conjunctions, they saw it actually 'in the East,' for on the 20th May it would rise shortly before the sun. If they then took their journey, and arrived at Jerusalem in a little more than five months, (the journey from Babylon took Ezra four months,) if they performed the route from Jerusalem to Bethlehem in the evening, as is implied, the *November* conjunction, in 15° of Pisces, would be before them in the direction of Bethlehem, coming to the meridian about eight o'clock P. M. These circumstances would seem to form a remarkable coincidence with the history in our text." If these observations were well founded, the Lord's birth must be placed in 747. In this result Alexander agrees, (On Matt. ii. 2.) "The concurrence is in this case so remarkable, and the explanation recommended by such high scientific authority, that it would probably have been universally adopted but for the foregone conclusion in the minds of many that the birth of Christ took place in a different year. But that assumption is so doubtful, and the views of the best writers so discordant, that it can scarcely be allowed to decide the question now before us, but may rather be decided by it."

Notwithstanding the weighty names that may be cited in support of this explanation, it must, we think, be admitted that the whole tenor of Matthew's narrative points strongly to some extraordinary luminous appearance in the form of a star, which, having served its purpose of guiding the Magi to Jesus, vanished forever. That the use of αστηρ rather than αστρον indicates a single star is apparent.[2] But these conjunctions did not appear at any time as a single star, nor can we well apply to them the language which

[1] See Smith's Bible Dict., 1. 1072. [2] See Meyer.

the Evangelist uses of the movements of his star, (ii. 9.) If this be the correct interpretation of the narrative, it does not, however, exclude the astrological value of these conjunctions. The Magi were students of the heavens, and such remarkable phenomena would naturally attract their observation. Precisely what significance they would ascribe to them we cannot say, but doubtless in their astrology they indicated some remarkable event. Perhaps, also, the meeting of the planets in Pisces turned their attention especially to Syria and Judea. We may thus at least suppose that through the planetary conjunctions their attention was arrested, and they prepared to watch the heavens with deep interest for further signs, and to note the new star so soon as it appeared. How they knew it to be the star of "the King of the Jews," does not here concern us. All this still leaves undetermined the time of the appearing of the star, but indicates that it must have been after the conjunctions, or subsequent to Dec. 747. Yet it was some time before Herod's death in 750.

Many have found a more definite chronological datum in the statement of Matthew (ii. 16) that Herod, after the departure of the Magi, slew all the children of Bethlehem "from two years old and under, according to the time which he had diligently inquired of the wise men," (see v. 7.) It is said that the first appearing of the star marked the Saviour's birth; that the command to slay the children "from two years old and under," shows that more than a year had elapsed since its appearing; and that, consequently, He must have been at that time in His second year.[1] But this is by no means conclusive. It is not certain that the appearing of the star marked the Saviour's birth. It may have preceded it and marked the Incarnation, which the early church connected with the Annunciation, not with the Nativity. If so, the star may have been seen in 747, yet His birth have been in 748; or the star in 748, and His birth in 749. Nor does the fact that Herod slew all the children from two years and under, give us any exact result. This expression is in itself remarkable, and indicates that two years was the extreme beyond which the king did not think it necessary to go, and that in all probability Jesus was much younger. "This does not imply that Jesus was just two years old at this time, but rather that He was not, as appears from the word *under*."[2] He

[1] So Meyer. [2] Alexander.

would be sure that the child should not escape, and therefore enlarged the time, taking in those of greater age than he had any reason to suppose Him to be. It is plain that he did not learn from the Magi the date of His birth, or any close approximation to it, for if He had just been born, why kill the children of two years, and if He were now more than a year, why kill all of a less age? Thus from this expression we may infer that Jesus was only recently born.[1] This is confirmed by the scope of the narrative which implies that the Magi came soon after his birth. If we suppose that the star announcing the Incarnation appeared to the Magi early in 749, and place their visit in the beginning of 750, Herod, ignorant what relation the time of its appearing had to Christ's birth, might well have ordered that all the children of Bethlehem born in 749 and up to this time in 750, should be slain; and this would correspond to the "two years and under" of the Evangelist.

Whilst, then, we cannot reach any precise chronological results from the visit of the Magi, we may perhaps say that the conjunctions of the planets define the earliest period at which the Lord's birth can be placed. We thus gain the two termini between which He was born: the planetary conjunctions in 747, and the death of Herod in 750.

Still another datum on which some rely is the existence of general peace throughout the world at the Lord's birth. This peace is supposed to have been foretold by the prophets, and its realization announced by the angels in their song on the night of the nativity, (Luke ii. 14,) "Glory to God in the highest, and on earth peace, good will toward men." With this is joined the closing of the temple of Janus by Augustus, the sign of peace throughout the Roman Empire. It is known that this temple was twice closed by him, in 725, 729, and probably also a third time, though the year is not certainly determined. "We know no more concerning it than this: that 744 *sub finem*, it was intended to have taken place, but was delayed a little longer by some unimportant com-

[1] Greswell, 2. 135, would understand by children of two years those of thirteen months only. All older than this were exempt. But this is doubtful, and is unnecessary. Browne, Ordo Sæclorum, 52, explains Herod's order from the fact the star appeared two years before the nativity.

motions among the Daci and Dalmatæ."[1] In the absence of exact information, we can say no more than that there was a period of general tranquillity throughout the Roman world for five or six years, or probably from 746 to 752, during which period the Lord was born. We cannot, without building on conjecture, reach any more exact result.

To sum up the results of our inquiries, we find that the birth of the Lord was not later than April, 750, and probably not later than January. The time in this direction is limited by the death of Herod in April of that year, and the events immediately preceding it. On the other hand, if we give to the conjunction of planets in 747, as connected with the visit of the Magi, any chronological value, we cannot put his birth earlier than that year. Again, if Cyrenius was governor of Syria from the autumn of 750–753, we must put it as near as possible to the beginning of his administration. And as He was about thirty years of age at the beginning of His ministry, and the date of His first Passover after its beginning was 780, we reach the year 749. We have thus to choose between the years 747, 748, 749, and the beginning of 750. The probabilities are in favor of 749, and in our further examinations we shall assume this as the year of His birth.

We add the opinions of some of the leading chronologists and commentators.[2] For the year 747, Sanclemente, Wurm, Ideler, Münter, Sepp, Jarvis, Alford, Patritius, Ebrard; for 748, Kepler; Lardner hesitates between 748 and 749; for 749, Petavius, Usher, Noris, Tillemont, Lichtenstein, Ammer, Friedlieb, Bucher, Browne; for 750, Lamy, Bengel, Wieseler, Greswell, Ellicott. Clinton finds the earliest possible date the autumn of 748, the latest that of 750. The years 751, 752, and 753 have also their supporters, but not among the more recent writers, with one or two exceptions.

We proceed to inquire in what part of the year the Lord was born. The only direct datum which the Gospels give us, is found in the statement of Luke, (i. 5,) that Zacharias "was of the course of Abia." It is known that the priests were divided into twenty-

[1] Greswell, 1. 469. See Patritius, iii. 165. According to Sepp and Browne, it was closed from 746–752; to Ammer and Greswell from 748 or 749–752 or 753; to Jarvis from 746–758. Wieseler makes the order to shut it to have issued in 743, but its execution to have been delayed till 752.

[2] See Friedlieb, Leben Jesu, 91; Wieseler, 485.

four classes, each of which officiated at the temple in its turn for a week.[1] This order, originally established by David, was broken up by the captivity. The four classes that returned from Babylon were divided anew by Ezra into twenty-four, to which the old names were given. Another interruption was made by the invasion of Antiochus, but the old order was restored by the Maccabees. Of these courses that of Jehoiarib was the first, that of Abia the eighth. We need therefore only to know a definite time at which any one of the courses was officiating to be able to trace the succession. Such a datum we find in the Talmudical statements, supported by Josephus,[2] that at the destruction of the temple by Titus on the 5th August, 823, the first class had just entered on its course. Its period of service was from the evening of the 4th August, which was the sabbath, to the evening of the following sabbath, on the 11th August. We can now easily compute backward, and ascertain at what time in any given year each class was officiating.

If now we take the year 749 as the probable year of Christ's birth, the appearance of the angel to Zacharias announcing John's birth must be placed in 748. In this year we find by computation that the course of Abia, or the eighth course, officiated during the weeks from the 17–23 April and again from the 3–9 October.[3] At each of these periods, therefore, was Zacharias at Jerusalem. If the annunciation of the angel was made to him during the former, the birth of John may be placed near the beginning of 749, and the Lord's birth about six months later, or near the middle of 749; if the annunciation was made during the latter, John's birth was near the middle of 749, and the Lord's birth near its end.

The fact that we do not know how soon after the completion of the ministry of Zacharias the conception of John is to be placed, prevents any very exact statement of dates. Luke (i. 24) uses only the general expression "after those days his wife Elisabeth conceived." Yet the tenor of the narrative leads us to believe that it was soon after his return to his home, and may be placed in either of the months April or October. Counting onward fifteen months

[1] 1 Chron., 24. 1–19; Lightfoot, 9. 44.

[2] War, 6. 4. 5.

[3] So Wieseler, 143; Licht., 76; Friedlieb, 80; Browne, 35. Greswell, 1. 434, Sept. 30—Oct. 7.

we reach June and December, in one of which the Lord's birth is thus to be placed.

In choosing between these periods, some weight is to be given to the statement of Luke (ii. 8) that in the night when the Lord was born, shepherds were in the field keeping watch over their flock. Does not this rather point to the summer, than to the winter, to June than to December? To answer this we must make some inquiries respecting the climate of Judea. Travellers in Palestine differ widely in their meteorological accounts, nor is this to be wondered at, as the seasons vary greatly in different years, and each traveller can speak only of what falls under his own personal observation. Instead, therefore, of trying to reach some general conclusions from such isolated accounts, we shall take the statements of those who, having resided some time in Jerusalem, give us the results of their observations for several successive years. And we select as authorities Schwartz[1] and Barclay.[2]

The year is divided into two seasons, summer and winter, or the dry and the wet. The winter rains begin to fall in the latter part of October or beginning of November. The most rainy month is February. During the months of December, January, February, and March, there is no entire cessation of rain for any long interval; "yet an interregnum of several weeks' dry weather generally occurs between the middle of December and the middle of February, somewhat distinguishing the former rains of the season from the latter."[3] "The average monthly temperature during four years from 1851 was, for November, 63° 8′; December, 54° 5′; January, 49° 4′; February, 54° 4′; March, 55° 7′."[4] "The temperature of Palestine averages during the winter 50° to 53½°."[5] Of the month of December, the following account is given: "The earth fully clothed with rich verdure. Wheat and barley still sown, also various kinds of pulse. Sugar-cane in market. Cauliflowers, cabbages, radishes, lettuce, lentiles, &c. Ploughing still continues at intervals."[6] "Temperature same as preceding month. The sowing of grain in the field has already commenced. Although the oranges and kindred fruit have been long since ripe, they continue to mature on the trees till toward April and May."[7]

1 Descriptive Geography of Palestine, 325–331.
2 City of the Great King, 414–429.
3 Barclay. 4 Barclay. 5 Schwartz. 6 Barclay. 7 Schwartz.

January is the coldest part of the year, and fires are used by the Frank population, though little by the natives, and snow and ice are occasionally seen.

These statements are confirmed in general by the highest authorities.[1] Although they may have in part more special reference to Jerusalem, they apply equally well to Bethlehem, the climate of which is not unlike that of Jerusalem, though milder.[2] There seems then, so far as climate is concerned, no good ground to affirm, that shepherds could not have been pasturing their flocks in the field during the month of December. As we have seen, Barclay states that in this month the earth is fully clothed with rich verdure, and that there is generally an interval of dry weather between the middle of December and the middle of February. Schubert [3] says that the period about Christmas is often one of the loveliest periods of the whole year. Tobler says, the weather about Christmas is favorable to the feeding of flocks, and often most beautiful. "On the 27th December, 1845, we had very agreeable weather."[4] It is during this month that the wind begins to blow from the south or southwest, which, according to Schwartz, "brings rain and betokens warm weather," and thus hastens forward vegetation.

Unless, then, the climate of Judea has become in the lapse of years much warmer than of old, the flocks may have been feeding in the fields of Bethlehem in the month of December. But according to Arago,[5] there has been no important change for the last three thousand three hundred years. Nor do the incidental notices of Scripture conflict with this. The Lord's words, "Pray that your flight be not in the winter," are easily understood when we remember that winter is the rainy season, and most unfavorable for journeying. That a fire was made at a much later period of the year, (John xviii. 18,) is plainly an exceptional case, and for this reason mentioned. "Strong, and at times cold winds prevail in April." [6]

There remains to be noticed a saying of the Talmudists, that the flocks were taken to the fields in March and brought home in November. But this had reference to those pastures that were

[1] Winer, 2. 691; Raumer, 77; Robinson, 2. 428; Tobler, Denkblätter, 3, &c.
[2] Tobler, Bethlehem.
[3] Quoted by Wieseler, 148.
[4] So Ritter, Theil 16. 480.
[5] In Winer, 2. 692.
[6] Schwartz.

found in the wilderness far away from the cities or villages, and were resorted to by the shepherds during the summer months. "The spring coming on, they drove their beasts into wildernesses, or champaign grounds, where they fed them the whole summer. The winter coming on, they betook themselves home again with the flocks and herds."[1] That the flock was near Bethlehem would therefore show, that this was a winter rather than a summer month; and the autumnal rains beginning to fall in November, there would soon be abundance of grass. The inference drawn by many[2] that, the flock being kept through the night in the fields, it could not have been so late in the year as December, is without basis. How generally during the winter months the cattle were stalled, we cannot tell, but doubtless in this the shepherds were governed by the peculiar character of the season.

If, then, we have to choose between the months of December and June, the balance of probabilities is in favor of the former. As the spring rains cease in April, the whole country soon becomes dry and barren. Of May, Barclay (423) remarks: "Vegetation having attained its maximum, now begins rapidly to decline for want of rain;" and of June, "Herbage becoming parched, the nomad Arabs begin to move northward with their flocks."

As the early tradition of the Church designated this month as the time of the Lord's birth, it has been generally accepted, but not universally. Lightfoot makes it to have been in September, Newcome in October, Paulus in March, Wieseler in February, Lichtenstein in June, Greswell in April, Clinton in spring, Lardner and Robinson in autumn, Strong in August.

If we accept the month of December, the day of the month still remains undetermined. If we place the ministry of Zacharias in Jerusalem from the 2d to 9th Oct. 748, and the conception of John soon after, the sixth month of Elisabeth (Luke i. 36) would extend from the middle of March to the middle of April. During this period was the annunciation to Mary, and the Lord's birth must then be placed between the middle of December, 749, and the middle of January, 750. A more definite result we cannot reach, except we receive the traditional date of the 25th of December. The origin and value of this tradition we proceed to consider.

1 Lightfoot on Luke ii. 8.

2 So A. Clarke, Greswell.

It is now generally granted that the day of the nativity was not observed as a feast in any part of the Church, east or west, till some time in the fourth century.[1] If any day had been earlier fixed upon as the Lord's birthday, it was not commemorated by any religious rites, nor is it mentioned by any writers. The observance of the 25th December is ascribed to Julius, Bishop of Rome, A. D. 337–352. It is mentioned as observed under his successor Liberius, A. D. 352–366. In the Eastern Church till this time, the 6th January had been observed as the day of the Lord's baptism, and had been regarded also as the day of His birth, it being inferred from Luke iii. 23, that He was just thirty when baptized. It was only by degrees that a distinction began to be made between the date of His birth and that of His baptism, and that each began to be observed upon different days. Chrysostom[2] states that it was only within ten years that the 25th December had been made known to them by the Western Church as the day of His nativity, but asserts that through the public records of the taxing (Luke ii. 1–4) preserved at Rome it had long been known to the Christians of that city. From this time, about the end of the fourth century, this day was commemorated as the birthdav both in the east and west.

Thus we have in favor of the 25th December, the fact that the Eastern Churches were induced to adopt it, and to transfer to it the feast which they had before observed upon the 6th of January. We can scarce think this done without some good chronological grounds, real or supposed. But we do not know what these grounds were. Some[3] ascribe great importance to the statements of Justin Martyr, Tertullian, and Chrysostom, that in the public archives at Rome a registry existed of the census under Augustus, by which the Lord's birthday was conclusively established. Jarvis supposes Tertullian to give the very words of the enrolment as he found them in the Roman archives, in which Mary is mentioned as the mother of Jesus—*Maria ex qua nascitur Christus.* Thus the day being proved by the register at

[1] So Clinton. "Not only was the day unknown, but for 300 years after the ascension no day was set apart for the commemoration of the birth of Christ."

[2] Antioch, A. D. 386.

[3] So Jarvis, 370 and 537.

Rome, the knowledge of it gradually spread to the Eastern Churches. But most chronologists have regarded these statements as of little value.[1]

The fact that the tradition, which placed the Lord's birth on the 25th December, also placed the birth of John Baptist on the 24th June preceding, the annunciation to the virgin on the 25th March, and day of Elisabeth's conception on the 24th September, or on the four cardinal points of the year, has led many to suppose that these periods were selected with reference to their astronomical significance, rather than as the real dates of these events. It strengthens this supposition that so many of the Christian festivals were placed upon days remarkable in the Julian calendar. Noting these facts, Sir Isaac Newton[2] inferred that "these days were fixed in the first Christian calendars by mathematicians at pleasure, without regard to tradition, and that the Christians afterward took up what they found in the calendars." More probable is the supposition that these dates were in part selected as the times of Christian feasts, in order to serve as a counterpoise to the corresponding heathen festivals, and in part because of their typical meaning. It does not appear that the feast of the nativity can be directly connected with any heathen festival, for the connection between this day and the *dies natalis solis invicti*, cannot be proved; but as the winter solstice its bearings are often typically interpreted by the fathers.[3] Thus the words of John Baptist spoken of Christ, (John iii. 30) "He must increase but I must decrease," are applied to the fact that, at John's birth in June 24th, or the summer solstice, the days began to decrease in length, but at Christ's birth, December 25th, the days began to increase. Thus Augustine[4]: *Hodie natus est Johannes, quo incipiunt decrescere dies—eo die natus Christus, quo crescere.*

Whilst such typical applications naturally tend to beget doubts whether the dates so connected with the great astronomical epochs of the year have any historic foundation, yet on the other hand it should be borne in mind that if the 25th December were actually

[1] See Kingsley in New Englander, April, 1847, who says that they are not referred to by Baronius, or Pagi, or Causabon, or relied on by Usher or Newcome.

[2] Observations upon Daniel and Apoc.

[3] Sepp, 1. 200.

[4] Homil., 3.

the Lord's birthday, the events preceding it, the conception of John, the annunciation to Mary, and the birth of John, must have taken place nearly at the times which tradition has assigned. And it deserves to be considered, that the hour of His birth, who is Lord of all, was not matter of accident, but divinely appointed. What season of the year might be most fitting to so great an event, or whether, astronomically viewed, the winter solstice has any such fitness, are questions not necessary to be answered here. It is at least not unreasonable to believe, that the sun, in its course, may typify Him who is the Sun of righteousness, and the year in its seasons foreshadow the epochs of His life.

The strongest argument against the 25th December, if the birth be put in 749, is that it leaves too little space for the events that occurred before Herod's death. This death was about the 1st of April, 750; we thus have a little more than three months. In this period were the visit of the Magi, the presentation at the Temple, the flight into Egypt, and sojourn there. If, according to general tradition, the Magi came on the 6th January or 13th day after the Lord's birth, and the presentation was on the 40th, or early in February, He went down into Egypt about two months before Herod's death. Those who put the flight into Egypt immediately after the coming of the Magi, on the 6th January, and the presentation upon the return after Herod's death, gain another month. If, however, we follow the order of most modern harmonists, and put the visit of the Magi after the presentation on the 40th day, the time of the sojourn in Egypt up to Herod's death was a little less than two months.

Those who put the Lord's birth in 748 or 747, make the period spent in Egypt much longer—some three years, some two, some one, some six months. Those who put the birth later than the 25th December, 749, and Herod's death in April, 750, make the sojourn but three to four weeks, or less; Wieseler and Ellicott only about a fortnight. There is nothing in Matthew's narration, or the circumstances of the case, that makes it probable He was there more than a few weeks. There does not, therefore, appear any good reason why all the events he narrates may not have taken place between the 25th December and the following 1st of April.

Our inquiries lead us, then, to these general results. We find it most probable that the Lord was born near the end of the year 749. At this period all the chronological statements of the Evangelists seem most readily to centre and harmonize. In favor of December, the last month of that year, as much may be said as in favor of any other, and this aside from the testimony of tradition. As to the day, little that is definite can be said. The 25th of this month lies open to the suspicion of being selected on other than historic grounds, yet it is not inconsistent with any data we have, and has the voice of tradition in its favor. Still, in regard to all these conclusions, it must be remembered that many elements of uncertainty enter into the computations, and that any positive statements are impossible. It is well said by Spanheim: *Sed cum hac de re altum apud Evangelistas sit silentium, nec Apostolicæ Ecclesiæ vel sanctionem, vel praxin legamus, causæ nihil est, cur temere definiamus quod solide definiri non potest.*

DATE OF THE LORD'S BAPTISM.

If we assume, upon grounds stated in the essay upon the date of the Lord's birth, that the Passover following His baptism was that of 780, we have to determine how long an interval elapsed between them. Our only data to decide this are the statements of the Synoptists compared with those of John. The former relate how Jesus came from Galilee to Jordan unto John, and was baptized, and how He was immediately led up of the Spirit into the wilderness to be tempted of the devil, and was there forty days. Of His return to the Baptist at the Jordan, they say nothing, but John supplies the omission, (John i. 29.) Returning after the temptation to the Jordan, where the Baptist bears witness to Him as the Lamb of God, He begins to gather disciples, and with Simon and Andrew and others departs to Cana of Galilee. All this may have occupied six or seven days. After the wedding at Cana He went down to Capernaum, but made there only a brief sojourn, and then went up to Jerusalem to the Passover, which fell this year upon the 9th April. Supposing that he reached Jerusalem a month after the wedding at Cana, we find that the whole interval between the baptism and the Passover was from two to three months.[1] If this be admitted, the Lord was baptized some time in the month of January, 780.

Against this result, a very strong objection is brought, derived from the relation in which the Lord's baptism stands to John's ministry. From Luke (iii. 1–2) we learn that the word of God came to John in the wilderness in the 15th year of the reign of Tiberius Cæsar. If this year corresponds, as is said, to the year 782, and marks the beginning of his work, then John could not have baptized Jesus in 780. Here are two points to be examined: first, what is meant by the word of God coming to John; second, from what point of time is the 15th of Tiberius to be reckoned?

The obvious and natural interpretation of the Evangelist's language: "The word of God came unto John in the wilderness, and he came into all the country about Jordan preaching—as it is written;" is that it refers to the beginning of his ministry. But as Christ's work in Galilee, which only is mentioned by Luke, began after John's imprisonment, it is said that this imprisonment took place in the 15th year of Tiberius, and that his ministry immediately preceding it is that referred to. That it was early so understood, is said to be shown by Eusebius, (iii. 24,) when he says that the Synoptists "only wrote the deeds of our Lord for one year after the imprisonment of John Baptist, and intimated this in the very beginning of their history." In recent times, the denial that Luke's words refer to the beginning of the Baptist's ministry, has been defended by several eminent chronologists.[2] Sanclemente[3] attempts to show that the 15th year of Tiberius "*non ad initium ministerii Joannis, non ad baptismum a Christo in Jordane susceptum, sed ad ipsius passionis et crucifixionis tempus ipso evangelista duce atque interprete esse referendum.*" Brown (92) adopted this explanation in a modified form. "The heading of St. Luke's third chapter contains the date, not of the mission of St. John the

[1] Some chronologists would much enlarge this period. Hales puts the baptism six months before the Passover; Usher, says two years and a half old. See Clinton, 2. 234, note. But most agree that it was from two to four months.

[2] So Sanclemente, Browne, Wieseler; and following the latter, Tischendorf and Ellicott.

[3] As cited by Wieseler, 196, note.

Baptist, but of the year of our Lord's ministry, especially in reference to the great events with which it closed." Wieseler, (194,) referring the Evangelist's words to the imprisonment of John, has defended this view most ingeniously and elaborately. It is obvious, that in this way we avoid a great chronological difficulty, but we meet others as great. The 15th year of Tiberius, counting from the death of Augustus, on the 19th August, 767, was the year from August 781 to August 782. Wieseler puts the imprisonment of the Baptist about the middle of March, 782, and his death in April following. Thus the period of his imprisonment is limited to three weeks, which is manifestly too brief. Again, if the statements of Luke (iii. 3–18) have reference to a work of John immediately preceding his captivity, he must have returned from Ænon (John iii. 23) to the Jordan, and thus have begun anew his labors. But this is inconsistent with the fact, that his work had reached its culminating point at the baptism of Jesus. From that time he began to decrease. It could not be said of him in the last stage of his ministry, as Luke relates, (iii. 15,) that "all men mused in their hearts of John, whether he were the Christ or not."

We therefore conclude, in common with the great body of chronologists and commentators, that Luke designs to refer the 15th year of Tiberius to the beginning of the Baptist's ministry.[1] We must now turn to the second point, from what period is the 15th year of Tiberius to be reckoned? Tiberius was the step-son of the emperor Augustus, and was formally adopted by him in 757. After filling several high stations in the civil and military service, he was associated with him in the general administration of the empire in 764 or 765.[2] Upon the death of Augustus, on the 19th of August, 767, he became sole ruler. Thus there are two periods from which his rule or administration may be reckoned: that when he was associated with Augustus, and that when he began to rule alone. To which of these periods does Luke refer? If to the former, the 15th year of his government was that of 779–780; if the latter, from 19th August, 781–782. If we accept the latter date, and John began his ministry in August, the baptism of Jesus must be

[1] So Meyer, Lichtenstein, Ebrard, Winer, Krafft.

[2] According to Greswell, 1. 344, and most, in beginning or middle of 765. According to Sepp, 1. 231, in year from Aug. 763–764.

placed in 782. If He was born in 749 or beginning of 750, He must have been thirty-two or thirty-three years of age at this time, which it is difficult to reconcile with Luke (iii. 23) that He was "about thirty years of age." If born in 748 or 747, He was now thirty-four or thirty-five, which presents a still greater difficulty. Hence many have inferred that Luke, who could not well have overlooked the apparent discrepancy, must have reckoned the 15th year of Tiberius, from the time when he became colleague with Augustus.

The importance of this date, and the many difficulties connected with it, demand that we give to it a more particular examination. Three points claim our attention. 1st. The fact of Tiberius' association with Augustus in the government of the empire. This fact is beyond all doubt. The direct evidence is found in Tacitus, Suetonius, and Paterculus, and there are incidental allusions to it in several other writers.[1] Tacitus says[2] "that on him every honor was accumulated; he was adopted by Augustus for his son, assumed colleague in the empire, and presented to the several armies." He relates also that Tiberius, in reply to the request of the Senate to take the government, said that "Augustus only was capable of so mighty a charge, that for himself, having been called by him to a participation of his cares, he had learned by experience how difficult to bear, and how subject to fortune was the burden of the general administration"—*regendi cuncta.* In like manner, Suetonius[3] says that "Augustus ordered that Tiberius should be named as his colleague"—*collegam suum Tiberium nuncupare jussit.* He mentions also a law promulgated by the consuls, that "Tiberius, jointly with Augustus, should rule in the provinces and also take the census"—*ut provincias cum Augusto communiter administraret, simulque censum ageret.* Merivale (4. 367) observes: "This communication of proconsular power abroad could hardly admit of any other interpretation than that the son was thereby formally associated in the empire with his father." Paterculus, (103,) alluding to his adoption by Augustus, represents himself as unable to describe the joy of that day; the great concourse of all ranks of the people, and their hopes and prayers. He mentions also the triumph due him because of his victories in Pannonia and Dalmatia, and which was celebrated with great magnificence, after the Senate and people of Rome, on a request being made by his father that he might be

[1] See Lardner, 1. 355. [2] Ann., 1. 3. [3] August., 97.

invested with authority equal to his own—*ut æquum ei jus in omnibus provinciis exercitibusque esset, quam erat ipsi*, had passed a decree to that effect. Paterculus adds, as his own comment, that it would have been unreasonable if he could not have ruled what he had secured.

Thus the fact is abundantly established, that Augustus did formally associate Tiberius with him in the rule of the empire. At his request, a decree to this effect was passed by the Senate and people. Nor was Tiberius a colleague in name merely. Augustus, very aged, and now sinking under bodily infirmities, was almost wholly under the control of his wife, the mother of Tiberius, whilst the latter was in the prime of life, active and energetic. In the very nature of the case, Tiberius, from the time of his colleagueship the recognized successor to the imperial throne, must have been a most conspicuous and influential person, and, we may perhaps say, the emperor *de facto*, although the name and prestige remained with Augustus till his death. That upon this event he did not openly and immediately act as emperor, but paid court to the Senate, as if the Republic still existed, and as if he were irresolute about assuming the sovereign rule,[1] is attributable to the peculiar political circumstances of the times; and also to his haughty temper, that chose rather to ascribe his elevation to the voice of the people, than to the intrigues of his mother, and to the favor of a weak, superannuated old man.

2d. When was Tiberius thus made colleague with Augustus? Most chronologists agree in placing the decree of the Senate already alluded to, near the end of 764 or beginning of 765.[2] We may accept this as the true date. Taking then the year 765, from January to January, as the 1st of Tiberius, the 15th is the year 779. Some time, then, in 779, is the beginning of John's ministry to be placed.

3d. Is it probable, that Luke would compute the reign of Tiberius from his colleagueship? It is said that there is no proof that this mode of computation was known to any of the fathers, or that it was ever used by any historians.[3] Clemens of Alexandria does, however, mention that, according to one mode of computing,

[1] Tacitus, Ann., 1. 7.

[2] So Greswell, Wieseler, Lichtenstein, Robinson.

[3] See Browne, 67, note; Ammer, 75.

Tiberius reigned twenty-two years, according to another twenty-six years, which, if it be not a numerical error, indicates a twofold beginning of his reign. Hoffman[1] supposes that in Josephus[2] there is a reference to the colleagueship, where he states that "Tiberius died after he himself had held the government twenty-two years"—σχων αυτος την αρχην. The most obvious construction of this phrase, is that which refers it to his sole administration, in contradistinction to his colleagueship. That such a twofold computation took place in the case of some of the later emperors, is unquestioned. A coin exists bearing the inscription: "In the 11th holy year of the government of the emperor Titus."[3] As he himself lived only two years after his father's death, the other nine years must refer to his joint rule with his father as a colleague. And whether the fathers were ignorant that the reign of Tiberius might be reckoned from two epochs, is doubtful. Lardner reasons that they must have known it, because as they almost universally placed the crucifixion in the 15th year, they must have seen how inconsistent it was with Luke, who placed the beginning of John's ministry in that year.

We cannot, without doing St. Luke great injustice as a historian, suppose him to have been ignorant of a fact so public and notorious as that of the association of Tiberius with Augustus in the empire; and there is no good reason why, if knowing it, he should not have taken it as an epoch from which to reckon. If the Italians dated his reign from the emperor's death, that naturally follows from the fact that the imperial authority of Tiberius, during his colleagueship, was little felt in Italy; his administration being especially confined to the provinces. But it gives a good reason why those in the provinces, especially of Asia Minor and Syria, should reckon from the time when he became in regard to them the acting emperor. Whether by the choice of the word "reign," ηγεμονια, rather than Βασιλεια or μοναρχια, he designed to indicate this,[4] is uncertain, but the word is certainly applicable to a government administered by more than one person. The cases in all eastern countries where the sons of kings were associated with their fathers in the kingdom were so common, that the double reckoning of their reigns could not have been any thing

1 Cited by Lichtenstein, 129.
2 Antiq., 18. 6. 10.
3 Sepp, 1. 230.
4 So Sepp.

unusual. Indeed, the epoch from which to date a reign is often perplexing, and brings no little confusion into chronology. Greswell (1. 336) ascribes the Evangelist's statement to "that scrupulous regard to truth, which we should have a right to expect from an inspired historian. He could not deliberately call that year the 13th of Tiberius which he knew to be really his 15th."

These considerations will, we trust, exculpate the Evangelist from all charges of historical inaccuracy. It is plain that he might reckon the years of Tiberius' reign from that time, when, by his father's desire and the solemnly expressed will of the Senate and people, he entered upon the exercise of imperial power. But whether, in point of fact, Luke thus computes, continues to be matter of dispute.[1]

To sum up our investigations upon this point, we find three solutions of the chronological difficulties which the statements of Luke present. 1st. That the 15th year of Tiberius is to be reckoned from the death of Augustus, and extends from August 781 to August 782. In this year, the Baptist, whose labors began some time previous, was imprisoned, but the Lord's ministry began in 780, before this imprisonment, and when He was about thirty years of age. 2d. That the 15th year is to be reckoned from the death of Augustus, but that the statement the Lord was about thirty years of age is to be taken in a large sense, and that He may have been of any age from thirty to thirty-five, when He began His labors. 3d. That the 15th year is to be reckoned from the year when Tiberius was associated with Augustus in the empire, and is therefore the year 779. In this case, the language "He was about thirty" may be strictly taken, and the statement, "the word of God came unto John," may be referred to the beginning of his ministry.

Of these solutions, the last seems to have most in its favor; and we shall assume that during the year 779, or the 15th year of

[1] In favor of the computation from the colleagueship, Usher, Bengel, Lardner, Jarvis, Greswell, Lichtenstein, Sepp, Friedlieb, Bucher, Patritius; of the sole reign of Tiberius, Lightfoot, Wieseler, Meyer, Ebrard, Tischendorf, Ewald, Browne, Ellicott, Ammer. Clinton says, "We are compelled to conclude that St. Luke computed the years of Tiberius in a peculiar manner," but denies that there is any ground for selecting the year 765 as the year of the colleagueship.

Tiberius, reckoned from his colleagueship with Augustus, John began to preach and baptize. We have next to inquire in what period of the year his labors began.

From the fact that the Levites were not allowed to enter upon their full service till the age of thirty, (Numb. iv. 3,) it has been generally supposed, although there is no express law to that effect, that the priests began their labors at the same age. At this period the body and mind were deemed to have reached their full vigor.[1] Hence it has been inferred that John must have reached the age of thirty ere he began his ministry. If this inference be correct, he began to preach during the summer of 779, his birth having taken place, as we have seen, in the summer of 749. We may then conclude that he entered upon his work near the middle of 779, when he was about thirty. If so, he began to preach and baptize about July or a little later. How long his labors had continued before Jesus came to him to be baptized, we can but conjecture. That, however, he had been active for a considerable period, is apparent from the statements by the Synoptists respecting "the multitudes that came out to him from Jerusalem, and all Judea, and all the region round about Jordan," (Matt. iii. 5; Mark i. 5; Luke iii. 7.) Some months at least must have elapsed ere his fame could have spread so widely, and so many have been drawn to him. And if we suppose that the larger part of these crowds received the rite of baptism at his hands, a still longer period is required. A body of disciples, as distinguished from the multitudes, had already gathered around him. If we add to this, that at Christ's baptism, his work seems to have reached its highest point, and thenceforward began to decline, we cannot well estimate this period as less than six months in duration.

On the other hand, there are some considerations that prevent us from much enlarging this period. The general belief of the Jews that the coming of the Messiah was near, and their earnest desire for it, would naturally turn their attention to John as soon as he appeared in public. His ascetic life, his energetic speech, his boldness of reproof, and the whole character of his teachings, were adapted to produce an immediate and powerful impression upon the people at large. And the frequent gathering of the inhabitants from all parts of the land at the feasts, would serve

[1] Greswell, 1. 377.

rapidly to diffuse the tidings, that a new prophet had arisen. But as such a phenomenon as this preacher in the wilderness could not long escape the notice of the Pharisees and the ecclesiastical rulers at Jerusalem, so it could not long remain unquestioned. So soon as his popularity became wide-spread, and multitudes began to receive baptism at his hands, they would seek to know who he was, and by what authority he instituted this new rite. But, as appears from John, (i. 19–28,) no such formal inquiry was made by the Pharisees of the Baptist till after the baptism of Jesus. Hence we may infer that his ministry had not yet continued any very long period.

We may also add that John's message, "Repent ye, for the kingdom of heaven is at hand," was plain and easily understood. He was no teacher of abstract doctrines, but a herald of the Messiah, and his words took immediate hold of men's hearts. Thus his mission could be speedily fulfilled.

In view of the above considerations, we conclude that John's ministry may have continued about six months, when the Lord came to be baptized.[1] If he was already thirty when he began his work, and his birth be placed in June, 749, six months before that of the Lord, he began in July, 779, to preach and baptize. If about six months elapsed ere the Lord came to him at the Jordan, His baptism was near the beginning of 780. It confirms us in this result, that two or three months must have elapsed from the baptism of Jesus to the first Passover, (John ii. 13.) We rest, then, in the conclusion, that Jesus was baptized December, 779, or January, 780.

In the absence of all other data, we must here consider the tradition that puts His baptism on the 6th of January. It has already appeared in our inquiries into the date of our Lord's nativity, that both His birth and baptism, and also the adoration of the Magi, were originally commemorated on the same day, and that this day was the 6th of January. This feast was called the feast of the Epiphany, *επιφανεια* (Titus ii. 13), and commemorated His manifestation to the world. After the Roman Church had established the feast of the nativity upon the 25th December, it still continued to observe the 6th January in commemoration of the adoration of the Magi and of the baptism, giving, however, more

[1] So Lightfoot, Newcome, and many.

prominence to the former than to the latter.[1] The Greek Church, on the contrary, after it began to observe the 25th December as the day of the nativity, transferred to it also the adoration of the Magi, and commemorated only the baptism on the 6th January. Thus both the Roman and Greek Churches now agree in the observance of this day as that of the Lord's baptism.

If we now proceed to ask, on what grounds this day was selected as that of the baptism, we obtain no very satisfactory answer. The feast of the Epiphany seems to have been originally commemorative of the baptism as the time when the Lord was first manifested openly as the Son of God, (Matt. iii. 16–17;) and as He was supposed, through a too literal interpretation of Luke, (iii. 23,) to have been just thirty years of age, the day of the baptism was also that of the birth. The same feast, therefore, might well embrace both events. Afterward, other events, coming under the same general idea of manifestation, were included in the commemoration; the adoration of the Magi, the first miracle at Cana of Galilee, where "He manifested forth His glory," and, later still, the miraculous feeding of the five thousand.[2] As all these events could not have taken place on the same day of the year, it becomes doubtful whether any of them can be referred to the 6th of January. The observance of this day as that of the baptism, is first mentioned by Clemens, of Alexandria, as existing amongst the Gnostic Basilidians of that city.[3] Some have thought that, as the Egyptians celebrated at this time the feast *Inventio Osiridis*, the Basilidians adopted both the feast and date from them. But, aside from other objections to this Egyptian origin,[4] it is most improbable that the church at large would have borrowed any feast from the Gnostics. We may rather, with Neander,[5] suppose it to have originated with the churches in Palestine or Syria. If so, the selection of the 6th January may rest upon some good basis. There can be no question that the baptism, the *secunda nativitas*, was commemorated before the nativity itself. Beyond the simple fact that the Epiphany was put on this day, we have no knowledge. Sepp, (1. 243,) though in general a defender of tradition, here rejects it, and Jarvis, (467,) at the close of his investigations into the

[1] See Missale Romanum. In Epiphania Domini.

[2] See Dorner, Christologie, 1. 284

[3] Guericke, Archäologie, 201.

[4] See Wieseler, 136.

[5] Ch. Hist., 1. 302.

matter, simply says that, as there is no testimony against it, there is no impropriety in considering the 6th January as the true date.[1]

But there is an objection to the month of January drawn from the climate of Palestine that deserves to be considered. It is said that such multitudes could not have gathered to John in the midwinter, nor could the rite of baptism then have been performed in the cold and swollen Jordan.[2] We must then examine more closely the climatic peculiarities of Judea.

In the inquiry into the date of the Lord's birth, we have already had occasion to speak of the general character of the seasons. That during the winter, or rainy season, after heavy rains the travelling is difficult and fatiguing, all travellers testify.[3] But the rains are not constant. Beginning in October or November they fall gradually and at intervals, but become more copious and frequent in December, January, and February, and continue into March and April. It is stated by Barclay, that nine-tenths of all the rain falls in December, January, February, and March. In January, there are gushes of rain and sometimes snow, but in the southern parts of the land the sky clears up and there are often fine days.[4] The rain comes mostly out of the west, or west-northwest, and continues from two to six days in succession, but falls chiefly at night. Then the wind turns to the east, and several days of fine weather follow. The whole period from October to March is one continuous rainy season, during which the roads become muddy, slippery, and full of holes; but when the rain ceases, the mud quickly dries up, and the roads become hard,[5] though never smooth.

If, as we have supposed, John began to preach in the summer, perhaps in July, there is nothing in these statements to lead us to suppose that he suspended his labors when the rainy season began. During the intervals of clear weather, at least, the people continued to gather to him. Besides, we cannot tell what was the character of this particular season. According to Thomson, (1. 129,)

[1] So Bucher, Friedlieb, Browne. "About the last half of January," Greswell. In December or January, Lichtenstein. "In Tisri, about the feast of Tabernacles," Lightfoot. In November, Usher. In Spring, Clinton. The 7th of October, Sepp. Beginning of December, Patritius.

[2] So Robinson, Sepp.

[3] Thomson, 1. 329.

[4] Winer, 2. 692.

[5] Herzog's Encyc., 11. 23.

the climate is "extremely variable and uncertain. I have seen the rains begin early in November and end in February, but they are sometimes delayed until January and prolonged into May." We cannot, in a climate so changeable, undertake to say that John might not without any serious obstruction continue to preach and baptize throughout the whole rainy season. Greswell (1. 372) finds it specially fitting that he should commence his ministry at a time when water was so abundant, and affirms that "in Judea the winter season would be no impediment to the reception of baptism." So far as regards the valley of the Jordan, he is in this justified by the statements of travellers. This valley lies so low that the cold of winter can scarce be said to be felt there at all. Especially is this true of the lower part of it, where John baptized. Lying twelve or thirteen hundred feet below the level of the Mediterranean Sea, it has a tropical climate. Josephus,[1] speaking of the plain of Jericho, says: "So mild is the climate, that the inhabitants are dressed in linen when the other parts of Judea are covered with snow." Robinson also, (1. 533,) writing in May, speaks in like terms: "The climate of Jericho is excessively hot. In traversing the short distance of five or six hours between Jerusalem and Jericho, the traveller passes from a pure and temperate atmosphere into the sultry heat of an Egyptian climate." Porter describes the air as being "like the blast of a furnace."

It appears, then, that the mere chilliness of the water of the Jordan running through this deep hot valley, where snow or ice is never found, cannot be so great as to prevent baptism even in midwinter, except perhaps in some very rare instances. Nor is this river usually at its highest stage till April or May. As it was in Joshua's time so is it now. "Jordan overfloweth all his banks all the time of harvest," (Josh. iii. 15,) or, as explained by Robinson, was full up to all its banks, "ran with full banks, or brimfull." "Then, as now, the harvest occurred during April and early in May, the barley preceding the wheat harvest by two or three weeks. Then, as now, there was a slight annual rise of the river, which caused it to flow at this season with full banks, and sometimes to spread its waters even over the immediate banks of its channel where they are lowest, so as in some places to fill the low tract covered with trees and vegetation along its sides."[2]

[1] War, 4. 8. 3. [2] Robinson, 1. 540.

Thomson (2. 453) speaks to the same effect, and explains why the overflow of this river should be so late in the season as March or April after the rains are all over. This explanation he finds in the fact that its waters come from great permanent springs lying on the southern declivities of Hermon, and which are not at all affected by the early winter rains. "It requires the heavy and long-continued storms of midwinter before they are moved in the least; and it is not till toward the close of winter that the melting snows of Hermon and Lebanon, with the heavy rains of the season, have penetrated through the mighty masses of these mountains, and filled to overflowing their hidden chambers and vast reservoirs, that the streams gush forth in their full volume. The Huleh, marsh and lake, is filled, and then Gennesaret rises and pours its accumulated waters into the swelling Jordan about the first of March."

That there should be occasional floods in this river after long-continued rains, before the time of harvest, and during the rainy season, is to be expected, and will serve to explain the statements of those travellers who found it swollen during the autumn and early winter. Thus Seetzen [1] states, that in consequence of a storm accompanied with high cold winds, he was compelled to remain from the 8th to the 14th January on the bank before he was able to cross. Sepp, (1. 240,) who bathed in it on the 6th January, 1846, found the current swift and the water cold. But such occasional floods do not affect the general rule, that during the winter the water remains at its ordinary level, and begins to rise toward March, and is highest at the time of harvest. "All rivers that are fed by melting snows are fuller between March and September, than between September and March, but the exact time of their increase varies with the time when the snows melt." [2]

From what has been said, it follows that so far as the climate is concerned, and the overflowing of the Jordan, no reason exists why John may not have been baptizing in midwinter. That baptisms at this season of the year actually took place in later times, we learn from the testimony of Felix Fabri.[3] He says that the cloisters of St. John on the banks of the river at the time of the Abbot Zozima were inhabited by many monks, who about the

[1] Cited in Ritter, Theil, 15. 517. [2] Smith's Bib. Dict., 1. 1128.
[3] Cited in Ritter, Theil, 15. 539.

time of Epiphany—the 6th January—kept high festival there. The Abbot of Bethlehem, the Patriarch of Jerusalem, with many monks and clergy, walked down to the river in solemn procession, and after a cross had been dipped in the waters, all the sick through their baptism were healed, and many miracles wrought in behalf of the pious. So in the time of Antoninus Martyr and Willibaldus, "the annual throng of pilgrims to bathe in the Jordan took place at the Epiphany."[1] It is therefore perfectly credible that John may have baptized many, and with others the Lord, in the month of January.

We may now sum up the results of our inquiry. The first Passover after the Lord's baptism was that of 780, and fell upon the 9th April. The baptism preceded this Passover some two or three months, and so probably fell in the month of January of that year. John's ministry began soon after he was thirty years of age, or about July, 779. Allowing that his labors had continued six months before the Lord was baptized, we reach in this way also the month of January, 780. Tradition has selected the 6th of this month as the day of the baptism, but we have no positive proof that the tradition is well, or ill-founded. The climatic peculiarities of the country offer no valid objections to this date. Although there is good reason to believe that in December or January Jesus was baptized, yet the day of the month is very uncertain.

DATE OF THE LORD'S DEATH.

This point is so closely connected with the length of His ministry, that we shall consider the two together. And we first inquire what data do the Evangelists give to determine how long the interval from His baptism to His death? It has already been shown that about three months intervened between His baptism and the Passover following. This was probably the Passover of 780, and the first during His ministry, (John ii. 13.) Another Passover is mentioned, (John vi. 4,) and still another, (xi. 55.) It is universally admitted that the latter was the last Passover. If there be none other than these named by John, His ministry was

[1] Robinson, 1. 546. Early Travels, 17.

of two years' and two or three months' duration. But John speaks of a feast (v. 1) which he does not name, and which many regard as a Passover. If so, there would be four Passovers, and consequently His ministry embrace a little more than three years. We have then to determine what feast is meant by John (v. 1.) This will hereafter be fully discussed. We shall here assume that it is a Passover. We thus reach the result that the Lord's ministry, computing from His baptism, embraced three years and about three months, and that the Passover on which he died was that of 783.

The day on which the Lord died was Friday, as plainly appears from the Evangelists. Joseph went to Pilate to obtain the body of Jesus "when the even was come, because it was the Preparation, that is, the day before the Sabbath," (Mark xv. 42.) "And that day was the Preparation, and the Sabbath drew on," (Luke xxiii. 54.) "The Jews, therefore, because it was the Preparation, that the bodies should not remain upon the cross on the Sabbath day," (John xix. 31,) &c. That this Sabbath was the regular weekly Sabbath, appears from Matt. xxviii. 1; Mark xvi. 1; Luke xxiii. 56. Jesus was crucified on Friday, and buried the same day; was in the grave over the Sabbath, and rose on the morning of the first day of the week.

If thus the Lord died on Friday, as is almost universally admitted, what day of the month was this? Here we meet the much disputed point whether He was crucified on the 14th or 15th Nisan. This will be fully considered in its place, and we assume here that it was the 15th. We have then to determine upon what year following 780, the 15th Nisan fell on a Friday. According to Wieseler (389) this was the case only once from 782–786. In 783 the 15th was upon Friday. To those who make the crucifixion to have been on the 15th Nisan, the year 783 is therefore the year of His death. Others, who place the crucifixion on the 14th Nisan, find that in 786 this day was a Friday,[1] others still in 782.[2] It is admitted that too many doubtful elements enter these calculations to make them perfectly trustworthy.[3]

Some have thought to find a chronological datum in the fact of the darkening of the sun at the time of the Lord's crucifixion.

[1] So Ewald, 5. 136. [2] So Browne, 54. [3] Winer, 1. 562.

As this was upon the 14th or 15th of Nisan, and so at the time of a full moon, it could not have been an eclipse. But as mention is made of an eclipse which occurred near this time, some of the fathers, and some moderns have sought to establish a connection between the two events. Phlegon, of Tralles, who died about 155 A. D., and who wrote some historical works, of which only a few fragments remain, relates that, in the fourth year of the 202 Olympiad, or from July 785 to 786, a great eclipse of the sun took place, greater than any that had ever been known, so that at the sixth hour it was very dark and the stars appeared. There was also a great earthquake in Bithynia, and a great part of Nice was destroyed.[1] This statement presents several apparent points of resemblance to those of the Evangelists, but a brief examination shows that it cannot refer to the darkness at the crucifixion. Phlegon speaks of an eclipse; had he meant an extraordinary or supernatural darkness, he could scarcely have failed distinctly to mention it. The time also of this eclipse is uncertain, for some of those who have reported his statement refer it to the fourth, and some to the second year of the 202 Olympiad, or to the fourth year of the 201.[2] But the astronomer Wurm has computed that only one eclipse took place in this Olympiad, and that in November 24, 782.[3] It seems, therefore, that Phlegon has himself erred in the date, or that he wrote the first year of this Olympiad, which has been changed into the fourth. As it is not mentioned at all by most of the early fathers, it seems that they must have regarded it as an ordinary eclipse, and therefore without any special relation to the crucifixion.[4] Most moderns agree that it is of no chronological value.[5]

Some have found ground for a chronological inference as to the time of the Lord's death, in the assertion of the Pharisees before Pilate, (John xviii. 31,) "It is not lawful for us to put any man to death." Lightfoot (on Matt. xxvi. 3) gives, as a correct tradition of the Talmudists, "Forty years before the Temple was de-

[1] For some little differences in the versions, see Jarvis, 420.

[2] See Ammer, 41; Wieseler, 387.

[3] Winer, 2. 482.

[4] See Jarvis, 427.

[5] Winer, Lichtenstein, Meyer, Jarvis, Greswell. Sepp would prove from it that the crucifixion was in 782; Ammer, that it was in 786.

stroyed, judgment, in capital causes, was taken away from Israel."[1] It is generally agreed that the Temple was destroyed in August, 823. Computing backward forty years, we reach 783, as the year when the Jews lost the power of inflicting capital punishments. Hence it follows, that if Christ had been tried by them before the year 783, they would have had the power of punishing Him with death, according to their own laws. His crucifixion, therefore, could not have been earlier than this year.

As we have no knowledge how this judgment in capital cases was lost to the Jews, whether by the act of the Romans, or, as Lightfoot supposes, by their own remissness, we cannot tell how strictly the "forty years" is to be taken. They may be used indefinitely, forty being here, as often, a round number. Little stress in this uncertainty can be laid upon this result.

Some find in the parable of the barren fig-tree, (Luke xiii. 6–9,) an allusion to the length of the Lord's ministry—"Behold, these three years I come seeking fruit on this fig-tree, and find none."[2] It certainly cannot be without meaning that three years are mentioned. This is ascribed by some to the fact that so many years must pass after planting before the tree can bear fruit.[3] But the language shows that fruit is sought, not after, but during the three years. Some refer it to the whole period of grace before Christ.[4] But why designate it as three years? Perhaps some three epochs in Jewish history may be meant, although it is not clear what they are. It is not, however, improbable that Christ's ministry is referred to. If we suppose it to have been spoken late in 782, His ministry beginning in 780, this was the third year, and He was not crucified till 783. But it cannot be said that the tree was actually cut down after the expiration of the one year of grace. As a chronological datum, the mention of the three years has little value.[5]

From early times, many have found a prophetic announcement of the length of the Lord's ministry in the words of Daniel ix. 27, —"And He shall confirm the covenant with many for one week, and in the midst of the week He shall cause the sacrifice and the oblation to cease." Of the fathers, Browne says, (77,) "Others, comparatively late writers, were led by their interpretation of Daniel's

[1] See also Friedlieb, Archäologie, 22.

[2] So Bengel, Hengstenberg, Wieseler, Alford.

[3] So Bloomfield.

[4] So Grotius, McKnight.

[5] So Meyer, Trench.

prophecy to assign a term of three and a half years." This interpretation has all along to the present day had advocates. Thus Lightfoot, (3. 39,) "He had now three years and a half to live, and to be a public minister of the Gospel, as the Angel Gabriel had told that in half of the last seven of the years then named He should confirm the covenant." Barnes (in loco) says: "The meaning of the passage is fully met by the supposition that it refers to the Lord Jesus and His work, and that the exact thing that was intended by the prophecy was His death. Whatever difficulties there may be about the precise time of our Lord's ministry, it is agreed on all hands that it lasted about three years and a half, the time referred to here." It seems also to have been commonly believed by the ancients that the last week of the seventy includes the *prædicatio Domini* to the Jews for three and a half years before, and the same length of time after the Passion."[1] Greswell (4. 406) maintains the same interpretation. Vitringa, with whom Hengstenberg agrees,[2] says: "His death was undoubtedly to happen in the middle of the last hebdomad, after the seven and sixty-two years had already come to an end."[3]

Without denying that the prophecy has reference to the Messiah, it is questionable whether it is to be so pressed as to furnish a proof that the Lord's public work continued just three and a half years. The number of interpretations that have been proposed is very great, and there is far from being even now unanimity of opinion. Thus Lightfoot makes the Lord's own ministry to have been three and a half years. Greswell adds to three years of the Lord's ministry half a year of the Baptist; Browne to one year of the Lord's ministry two and a half years of the Baptist.[4] We cannot, under these circumstances, attach much chronological importance to it.—*Obscurum non probatur per obscurius.*

Computations as to the year when the seventy weeks ended, as bearing on the time of the Lord's death, can be but little relied on, and need not be considered here.

Into the mazes of patristic chronology we are not called to enter, nor could we thus attain any important results.[5] Still a brief survey of early opinions will not be without its value. We

[1] Browne, 385.
[2] Christology, 3. 163.
[3] See Sepp, 1. 284.
[4] See Ammer, 116.
[5] See the very full investigations of Patritius, iii., Diss. xix.

find three distinct views prevalent. First. That which makes the Lord's ministry to have continued but one year, and the whole length of His life to have been about thirty years. This view first comes to our notice among the Valentinians, a heretical sect, who said that there were thirty Æons corrresponding to the thirty years of His life before His ministry, and that He died the twelfth month after His baptism. Among the orthodox, Clemens, of Alexandria, († 220,) is the earliest defender of this view, and gave it wide currency. Among those who adopted it in substance were Tertullian, Origen, Lactantius, and perhaps Augustine, although the former is by no means consistent in his statements, Origen is confused, and Augustine doubtful. It is placed mainly upon Scriptural grounds, much stress being laid upon Isaiah lxi. 2, quoted by the Lord, (Luke iv. 19,) and by some upon Ex. xii. 5.

Second. That which makes His age at His death to have been between forty and fifty. Of this, Irenæus († 202) appears as the first defender, although it appears from Augustine that there were others later that held it. In proof, two passages in John's Gospel were cited, (viii. 57 and ii. 20.) From the former it was inferred that He was more than forty, and from the latter that He was just forty-six, as the temple of His body had been so long in building. Irenæus, arguing against the Valentinians, shows from the mention of three Passovers by this Evangelist, that the Lord's ministry was more than a year, but how long he does not determine.

Third. That which makes His ministry to have continued from two to four years, and His whole life from thirty-two to thirty-four years. Of this view Eusebius, Epiphanius, and Jerome were the earliest representatives.

If we now ask after the data upon which the early fathers based their opinions, we find the following the most important. Till the time of Tertullian († 243) there is mentioned no datum for determining the length of His ministry other than is given by the Evangelists. If, as is affirmed by some, the church at Jerusalem had preserved the knowledge of the year by tradition, there is no proof of the fact. Tertullian is the first, so far as we know, who connects the crucifixion with the consulship of the two Gemini. "He suffered under Tiberius Cæsar, R. Geminus, and P. Geminus, being consuls, on the eighth day before the calends of April," (25th March.) In this statement Tertullian was followed by Lactantius, Augustine, and others, especially of the Latin fathers.[1] Whence had Tertullian this information? This is not apparent. Some suppose that Pilate having sent to Rome an account of the Lord's crucifixion, which was placed in the archives, Tertullian thus learned its date. But on whatsoever basis it rested, this statement soon obtained general currency, and was almost universally received. If we assume its truth we must consider to what results it leads us.

The Gemini were consuls during the year beginning January, 782. Thus this consular year was contemporaneous with about eight months of the fifteenth year of Tiberius, and four months of the sixteenth year. The fifteenth year of Tiberius, if reckoned, as it seems to have been, from the death of Augustus, extended from August 19, 781, to August 19, 782, and the sixteenth to August 19, 783. But the crucifixion was, according to Tertullian, in March, 783, and was not, therefore, during their consular year, which ended with December, 782. Still, as only about three months elapsed from the end of their consulship, it might readily be connected with their names. It is also to be remembered that there was a threefold mode of reckoning the Roman year—the political, the civil, the historical.[2] The first was according to consulships, and from January to January; the second, from March to March; the third, dating from the time of founding the city, and from 21st April to 21st April. It is, therefore, possible that we may explain the discrepancies respecting the time of the crucifixion in the following manner: The year of the consulship of the Gemini, 782, reckoned from January to January, is not wholly identical with 782 of Rome, which was reckoned from April 21 to April 21, but has about eight months in common with it. We have thus three years, all bearing on the same event, the crucifixion, yet differently computed; first, the fifteenth of Tiberius from August, 781, to August, 782; second, the consular year of the Gemini from January, 782, to January, 783; third, the year 782 of Rome from 21st April, 782, to 21st April, 783. It is apparent how confusion may have arisen from neglect to mark accurately the dates as connected with these several modes of computation.[3]

[1] See full citations in Greswell, 1. 451; Jarvis, 376.
[2] Ideler, 2. 150. [3] See Greswell, 1. 456.

That the Lord did not suffer in the fifteenth year of Tiberius, is plain from St. Luke himself, as in this case John's ministry and that of the Lord must both have been embraced in the brief period of twelve months. If, however, His death be placed in the sixteenth year of Tiberius, the Baptist may have begun his labors in August, 781, the Lord have been baptized in January, 782, and suffered in April, 783, thus making His ministry to have continued one year and some months, but in this case He did not suffer in the consulate of the two Gemini. Greswell remarks, (1. 439,) "I am persuaded, that during the first two centuries, no Christian doubted of the fact that our Lord suffered in the fifteenth or sixteenth year of Tiberius."

That no value is to be ascribed to the tradition of the Lord's death in the fifteenth year of Tiberius, is apparent from the fact, that it plainly contradicts the statements of John, who mentions three Passovers; and it limits His ministry to a year and some months. Nor is it possible that He died during the consular year of the Gemini, for then His crucifixion was in the early part of that year or the spring of 782, which presents the same difficulty. Nor can this have taken place on the 25th March of that year. He was crucified on the 14th or 15th Nisan, but these days in 782 fell on the 16th and 17th of April.[1] The designation of the day and month is necessarily wrong, and this invalidates the accuracy of the whole tradition. Besides, this tradition was by no means universal or unquestioned. The early fathers were not wholly unaware of these difficulties, and several of them state that they had not the data for a conclusive judgment. Irenæus says: "We cannot be ignorant how greatly all the fathers differ among themselves, as well concerning the year of the Passion as the day." Again: "Concerning the time of the Passion, the diversities of opinion are infinite." Augustine says, that except the fact that He was about thirty at His baptism, all else was obscure and uncertain. Tertullian is inconsistent with himself, and now makes His ministry to have continued one year, and now three; now puts His baptism in the fifteenth year of Tiberius, and now in the twelfth. In regard to Tertullian, the bishop of Lincoln, in his account of his writings,[2] observes: "The correct inference appears

[1] Ideler, 2. 422. [2] London, 1845, p. 147.

to be that Tertullian believed that our Saviour's ministry continued for three years, but mistook the year in which He was revealed for the year in which He suffered." Some began early to put His death in the sixteenth, others in the seventeenth or eighteenth, and finally in the nineteenth of Tiberius. This tradition, so indefinite, and never finding general reception, has now no claim upon our attention.

From this survey of the several data respecting the time of the Lord's death, we conclude that none lead us to positive results. If it were certain that the Friday on which He was crucified, was the 15th Nisan, there would be strong probability, if not absolute certainty, that the year was that of 783. If, however, it was the 14th Nisan, as many affirm, this datum fails us, and we have to choose between the years 782 and 786. The computation of the length of His ministry, from the number of Passovers, has an element of uncertainty which forbids a definite judgment; and the computations based upon the darkening of the sun at His crucifixion, upon the loss of power to inflict capital punishments by the Jews, upon the parable of the barren fig-tree, upon the prophetic half-week of Daniel, and upon tradition, are all inconclusive.

We add a brief survey of opinions respecting the duration of the Lord's public life. The first is that which limits His ministry to a single year, or a year and some months. As has been said, this was a very early opinion in the church, many of the fathers finding in it a fulfilment of Isaiah lxi. 2, where mention is made of "the acceptable year of the Lord."[1] This early opinion has been recently defended by Browne in his *Ordo Sæculorum* (p. 92.) He thus meets the difficulties arising from the mention of three Passovers by St. John. That mentioned in John vi. 4, is not rightly found there, since it is not mentioned by some of the early fathers, who, in their notices of this subject, must have alluded to it, had it been in the text of the first two centuries. The feast (John vi. 1) was not Passover but Pentecost. Thus but two Passovers remain, and the following order is obtained: 1. Passover, John ii. 13; 2. Pentecost, v. 1; 3. Tabernacles, vi. 4 and vii. 2; 4. Dedication, x. 22; 5. Passover of the crucifixion. Thus the whole ministry extends from one Passover to another.

How insufficient are the grounds upon which the rejection of

[1] Others, however, applied this passage not to His whole ministry, but to the first year of it.

the Passover (John vi. 4) rests is apparent. Nor is it possible upon any grounds, external or internal, to defend this order, which thus crowds all the events of the Lord's public life into a single year.

If some find but two Passovers in the sacred history, others find five, or even six. McKnight supposes that the Lord's public work may have been prolonged more than five years complete.[1] "Nay, it may have been several years longer, on the supposition that there were Passovers in His ministry, of which there is neither direct mention made, nor any trace to be found in the history." This opinion has now no advocates, and needs no discussion.

Rejecting the extremes on either side, our choice must lie between a ministry embracing three, and one embracing four Passovers. The former has many advocates, but labors under many difficulties, which will be pointed out as we proceed. On both internal and external grounds we are led to choose the latter, and to give to His ministry a duration of a little more than three years. Placing His death in April, 783, His public life, if it be dated from the purgation of the Temple, continued just three years, if from His baptism, three years and about three months, or from January, 780, to April, 783.

We accept, then, as probable conclusions, that the Lord was born December, 749; baptized January, 780; crucified April, 7, 783; length of ministry, three years and three months. That the 25th December and 6th January were the days of the nativity and baptism rests wholly upon tradition.

For comparison, we add the various dates of the Lord's death, which have found recent advocates: 781, Jarvis; 782, Browne, Sepp, Clinton, Patritius; 783, Wieseler, Friedlieb, Greswell, Tischendorf, Bucher, Ellicott, Thomson, Riggenbach; 784, Hales, Paulus; 786, Ebrard, Ammer, Ewald.

[1] Har., Preliminary Obs.

THE LIFE OF OUR LORD.

PART I.

FROM THE ANNUNCIATION TO ZACHARIAS TO THE BAPTISM OF JESUS; OR, FROM OCT., 748, TO JANUARY, 780. 6 B.C.—27 A.D.

3–9 Oct., 748. 6 B.C.

Near the end of the reign of Herod the Great, King of Judea, an angel was sent by God to Zacharias, an aged priest of the course of Abia, whilst ministering in the Holy Place, to announce to him the birth of a son, who should be the forerunner of the Messiah. Luke i. 5–22.

The chronological value of this statement has been already considered in the essay on the date of the Lord's birth.

Some of the fathers supposed that Zacharias was the high priest, and that the services in which he was engaged were those of the great day of atonement, upon the 10th of Tisri.[1] But there is no ground for this. Zacharias is called only a priest, not high-priest, and was a member of one of the twenty-four courses, which the high-priest was not. He was also chosen by lot to burn incense upon the golden altar in the Holy Place; but the high-priest's duties upon this day, as at other times, were all prescribed by law, and could not be given him by lot. Besides, the latter must

[1] So Chrysostom, Ambrose; see Williams' Nativ., 23.

reside at Jerusalem, but the residence of Zacharias was in some neighboring city.[1]

OCT., 748—MARCH, 749. 6–5 B. C.

Returning after his course had completed its ministry, to his own house in the hill-country of Judah, his wife Elisabeth conceived a son, and spent the five months following in retirement. LUKE i. 23–25.

The home of Zacharias was in "the hill-country," or mountainous region of Judah, (Luke i. 39 and 65.) But as the name of the city is not mentioned, several cities have contended for the honor of John's birthplace. Many have supposed Hebron to be meant, a city very ancient, and very conspicuous in early Jewish history.[2] A Jewish tradition also gives this as John's birthplace.[3] Aside from this, its claims rest chiefly upon the fact that it was a priestly city; and upon the form of expression in Joshua, (xx. 7, xxi. 11,) where it is described as being "in the mountain," and "in the hill-country of Judah."

Some have contended for Jutta, the Juttah of Joshua, (xv. 55,) regarding Juda (v. 39) Ιουδα, as an erroneous writing of Jutta, Ιουθα, or Ιουτα. This view, first suggested by Reland, (870,) although wholly unsupported by any manuscript authority, has found many advocates.[4] The modern Jutta is described by Robinson, (ii. 206,) who saw it from a distance, as "having the appearance of a large Mohammedan town on a low eminence, with trees around." It is about five miles south of Hebron, and was one of the priestly cities. (Josh. xxi. 16.) But granting the identity of the Juttah of Joshua with the modern city, this adds nothing to the proof that it was John's birthplace; and the

[1] Greswell, i. 382; Patritius, iii. 8.

[2] So Baronius, Lightfoot, Ewald, Sepp, Townsend.

[3] Winer, i. 586. Ritter, Raumer, Robinson, Patritius.

fact that there is no tradition of that kind amongst the inhabitants, nor any local memorials, seems to make strongly against it.

Those who made Zacharias to be high-priest, and so necessarily resident near the Temple, supposed Jerusalem to be the city meant, but this has now no advocates.

An ancient tradition designates a small village about four miles west of Jerusalem, as the home of Zacharias.[1] It is now called by the natives Ain Karim, and is thus described by Porter (i. 233): "Ain Karim is a flourishing village, situated on the left bank of Wady Beit Hanina. In the midst of it, on a kind of platform, stands the Franciscan convent of St. John in the Desert. The church is large and handsome, and includes the site of the house of Zacharias, where St. John Baptist was born. It is in a kind of grotto, like all the other holy places, and is profusely ornamented with marble, bas-reliefs, and paintings. In the centre of the pavement is a slab, with the inscription, *Hic Praecursor Domini natus est.* About a mile distant is the place known to the Latins by the name of the *Visitation.* It is situated on the slope of a hill, where Zacharias had a country house. Tradition says that the Virgin Mary, on her visit, first went to Elisabeth's village residence, but not finding her there, proceeded to that in the country, where accordingly took place the interview related in Luke i. 39–55. The spot is marked by the ruins of a chapel, said to have been built by Helena. About one mile farther is the grotto of St. John, containing a little fountain, beside which the place is shown where he was accustomed to rest."

Ain Karim has found a recent supporter of its traditionary claim in Thomson, (ii. 537,) who finds no reason "why the home of the Baptist should be lost any more than the site of Bethlehem, or Bethany, or Nazareth, or Cana." Tobler, however, traces these traditional claims of Ain

[1] See Early Travels, 287 and 461.

Karim only to the beginning of the 16th century. According to Raumer, a still older tradition designated Beth Zacharias as the place of John's birth. The point is in itself of very little importance. We need not infer, as some have done, (so Meyer,) from the Evangelist's silence, that he was ignorant where Zacharias lived, but only that he did not think it important to mention it.

That Elisabeth left her own house, and went to some obscure dwelling, where she might be hidden from all observation for a time, is not improbable; yet the text is consistent with the supposition that, continuing at home, she withdrew herself from the eyes of visitors.

March—April, 749. 5 B. C.

In the sixth month of Elisabeth's conception, the Angel of the Lord was sent to Nazareth, a village in Galilee, to a virgin named Mary, who was betrothed to a man named Joseph, of the house of David, to announce to her that she should be the mother of the Messiah.

Luke i. 26–38.
Matt. i. 20.

The most important point that meets us here is the relation of Mary to the house of David. Was she of that royal family? But before we consider it, let us sum up what is known, either from the Gospels or from tradition, of the personal history of Joseph and of Mary.

Joseph is distinctly declared by Matthew to have been of the house of David through Solomon, and his genealogical register, going back to Abraham, is given. (Matt. i. 1–18.) In his dream the angel addresses him as "the son of David," (v. 20.) So by Luke (i. 27) he is said to be of "the house of David," (also ii. 4.) He was thus of royal descent, though occupying an humble position in society. His calling was that of a *τεκτων*, or carpenter, or, as the word may mean, any worker in wood.[1] He was generally

[1] Thilo, Codex Apoc., 368, note.

believed by the early Church to have been an old man at the time he was espoused to Mary, and is so represented in the earliest paintings of the Holy Family.[1] In later pictures he is represented as younger, and from thirty to fifty years of age. According to Epiphanius, he was more than eighty; whilst in the Apocryphal Gospel, "Historia Josephi," he is said to have been ninety, and his age at the time of his death 111 years.[2] It is not improbable that he may have been considerably older than Mary, as, though alive twelve years after Christ's birth, (Luke ii. 42,) his name is not afterward mentioned; a circumstance most easily accounted for upon the supposition that he was dead before the Lord began His ministry. Some have inferred from Luke's words, (ii. 51,) that He was subject unto His parents, that Joseph lived till He had reached manhood. Tradition also relates of him, that he was a widower, and the father of four sons and two daughters. This point of a prior marriage will be considered when we come to inquire who were the Lord's brethren.

Of Mary, the Gospels give us even less information than of Joseph. In Matthew, her name only is mentioned, and no allusion is made to her family or lineage. In Luke, she is simply spoken of as a virgin; and only incidentally is it mentioned that Elisabeth, the wife of Zacharias, was her "cousin," or relative, *συγγενης*, (i. 36.) But the silence of the Gospels is amply compensated by the fulness of tradition.[3] We thus learn that she was the daughter of Joachim (Eliachim or Eli) and of Anna, her father being of Nazareth, and her mother of Bethlehem. They seem, however, to have resided at Jerusalem, as the church of St. Anne is said to have been built over the grotto which was the birthplace of the Virgin.[4] Yet another tradition makes

[1] Jameson: "Legends of the Madonna."
[2] Thilo, Codex Apoc., 361, note; Hofmann, 62.
[3] Hofmann, 5.
[4] Robinson, i. 233.

them to have resided at Sef-furieh, a village a few miles north of Nazareth.[1] Many fables are related of the miracles heralding her birth, of her education at Jerusalem in the Temple, of her vow of perpetual virginity, and of her marriage to Joseph.[2] That she was young at the time of her marriage, we may infer from the fact that females were married in the East at a very early age, generally from fourteen to seventeen, and often earlier.[3] The Apocryphal Gospels make her to have been, some twelve, and some fourteen, when betrothed to Joseph. The latter was more generally received in later times, though a few theologians make her to have been twenty-four or twenty-five when Jesus was born, *ut perfecta mater perfectum filium gigneret.*[4] No allusion is made in any of the Evangelists to her parents, or to any brothers, but Mary the wife of Cleophas is spoken of as her sister, (John xix. 25,) though this relationship, as we shall hereafter see, has been called in question.

From the statements of Luke, (i. 26; ii. 4,) we naturally infer that both Joseph and Mary resided at Nazareth at the time of the Annunciation. But some have maintained (see Meyer) that this is inconsistent with the statements of Matthew, (ii. 22, 23,) which show that he then dwelt at Bethlehem. But there is no real discrepancy. None of the Evangelists tells us where Joseph lived before he was espoused to Mary. Matthew, relating the circumstances connected with the birth of Christ, (i. 18–25,) makes no allusion to the place where they occurred. He does not mention Nazareth or Bethlehem. Afterward, in connection with the visit of the Magi, (ii. 1,) he speaks of Bethlehem as His birthplace, and mentions that Joseph intended to return thither from Egypt after Herod's death, and that through divine direction he was made to change his purpose, and go and dwell at Nazareth. All this proves

[1] Robinson, ii. 346. [2] See Apocryphal Gospels, Baronius, Sepp.
[3] Greswell, i. 398. [4] Hofmann, 52.

nothing respecting his previous residence at Bethlehem. Matthew relates only the fact that the child was born there; Luke tells us how it happened that this was His birthplace. Matthew states that it was Joseph's purpose to return there from Egypt, but unable to do so he went to Nazareth; Luke states only that leaving Bethlehem he went to Nazareth. The only ground for supposing that Joseph had formerly resided there is found in his purpose to return thither; but this is easily explained as springing from the desire to rear the child of David's line in David's city. That he had no possessions there is apparent from Luke's statement respecting the circumstances of Mary's confinement. The only interest that Matthew takes in Nazareth or Bethlehem is from the connection in which these two cities stand to the Messianic prophecies, (ii. 5–6, and 23.) In itself it was of no moment to him where either Joseph or Mary had lived before the birth of Jesus, nor indeed after it, except so far as their residence was His.

We now turn to the question of the Davidic descent of Mary. If we set aside for the present the genealogical table in Luke (iii. 23–38) as of doubtful reference, there is no express declaration that she was of the house of David. The reference to her, (Luke i. 27,) though formerly defended by many, and lately by Wieseler,[1] is very doubtful.[2] Some have supposed that she went with Joseph to Bethlehem at the time of the taxing, (Luke ii. 5,) because she, like him, was a descendant of David.[3] This journey, however, may be explained, as will soon appear, on other grounds.[4] This silence respecting Mary, contrasted with the prominence

1 Stud u Krit, 1845:

2 Against it Bengel, Meyer, Patritius, Alford, Fairbairn.

3 So Robinson's Harmony, 186; Mill, 209: "The words distinctly indicate that Mary accompanied Joseph for the purpose of being enrolled herself."

4 Patritius finds in Mary's supposed vow of perpetual virginity a proof that she was an heiress, and married to Joseph as a kinsman.

given to the Davidic descent of Joseph, has led many to suppose that the Evangelists attached no importance to her lineage, but only to her conjugal relation to him. As his wife she became a true member of David's family. Her child belonged to him according to the principle which lay at the foundation of marriage amongst the Jews, that what was born of the wife belonged to the husband. As it had no human father, and as he adopted it, it became in fact his, and inherited whatever rights or privileges belonged to Davidic descent. Since then through His legal relationship to Joseph Jesus could truly be said to be of the house and lineage of David, it was wholly unimportant to specify the family of Mary.[1] That she was however in fact of David's line, is maintained by most who regard the fact as in itself unimportant, or not proved.

When we compare the very remarkable declarations of the prophets respecting the Messiah, as the son of David, with their historical fulfilment as recorded by the Evangelists, it may at first appear that they refer to Him rather as the adopted and legal son of Joseph than as the son of Mary. Had His descent through His mother been regarded as the true fulfilment of the prophetic predictions, and of the covenant with David, would the Evangelists have passed it by without distinct mention? We might therefore infer from their silence respecting Mary's relation to David, that they regard her royal lineage as not essential to the fulfilment of prophecy. Joseph had a good title to the throne; and Jesus as his son stood in his stead, the rightful Heir of all the Covenant promises.[2]

The question of the Davidic descent of Mary thus regarded becomes one of secondary interest, as no promise

[1] So lately Da Costa, Fairbairn.

[2] So Da Costa, who supposes Mary to have been of the tribe of Levi. See contra Spanheim, Dubia Evangelica, i. 128, against Antonius, who defends this view. See also an able paper on this side in Bibliotheca Sacra of April, 1861, by G. M'Clellan.

of God is made dependent upon it. But if we take higher ground and seek more than a legal relationship, there is good reason to believe that she was of the royal family, and that thus Jesus was in every sense the son of David. Peter upon Pentecost (Acts ii. 30) declared that in Him was fulfilled the oath which God sware to David "that of the fruit of his loins according to the flesh He would raise up Christ to sit on his throne." This language, taken in connection with the phraseology of the original promise, (2 Sam. vii. 12,) "I will set up thy seed after thee which shall proceed out of thy bowels," seems to point to Jesus as his lineal descendant. The words of Paul readily bear the same interpretation (Acts xiii. 23): "Of this man's seed hath God according to His promise raised unto Israel a Saviour, Jesus." Again, he says, (Rom. i. 3,) "Which was also made of the seed of David according to the flesh." (See also Isaiah xi. 1; 2 Tim. ii. 8; Heb. vii. 14; Rev. xxii. 16.) In the words of the angel to her, (Luke i. 32,) "the Lord God shall give unto Him the throne of His father David," it is intimated that as her son He was son of David, and so heir of the throne. (See also Luke i. 69.)

The prominence given by Matthew to the Davidic descent of Joseph, and his silence respecting the family of Mary, finds a ready explanation in the peculiarities of his Gospel as designed for the Jews. Its very first sentence gives the clue to its right understanding: "The book of the generation of Jesus Christ, the son of Abraham, the son of David." He aims to show that Jesus is the heir of the two great Jewish covenants, that with Abraham, and that with David. To this end he must establish first, that Joseph, Jesus' legal father, was of David's house and so a lawful heir of the dignity promised in the covenant; second, that Jesus stood in such relation to Joseph as Himself to have legal claim to all promises belonging to the latter. He therefore brings prominently forward in the beginning of his Gospel the fact that Joseph was of royal lineage, and cites his genealogical register in proof. To have said that Mary was of the house of David, and to have cited her genealogy, would have availed nothing, as it was a rule of the Rabbins, and one universally recognized, that "the descent on the father's side only shall be called a descent; the descent by the mother is not called any descent."[1] He could not therefore speak of Jesus as son of Mary, even had it been generally known that she was of David's line, for as such he had no royal rights. It was only as the son of Joseph that he could be the heir of the covenants. Matthew must therefore bring forth clearly the legal relation in which Jesus stood to Joseph as his adopted son, but for his purpose it was wholly unimportant who his mother was. Hence he says very little of Mary, mentioning only her name, and without any explanatory remarks except respecting her relation as a betrothed virgin, but says much of Joseph. His silence, therefore, so easily explained from the character of his Gospel, respecting Mary's lineage, proves nothing against her Davidic descent.

In our examination of this point it should be remembered that from the earliest period the testimony of the Church has been that Mary was of David's family.[2] This was a matter of fact about which the Apostles and early Christians could not well have been ignorant; and it is difficult to see how such a belief, if not well founded, could have become so early and universally prevalent.

The allusion (Luke i. 36) to kinship between Mary and Elisabeth determines nothing respecting the family of the former, as the term used denotes simply kindred, or relationship without defining its degree. As all the tribes might intermarry, Mary might have been of the tribe of Judah, though Elisabeth was of the tribe of Levi. It was early said that the Lord was both of kingly and priestly de-

[1] Da Costa, 474. [2] Meyer on Matthew, i. 17;

scent, by Joseph on the one side and Mary on the other.[1] But this has no foundation.

Thus we find sufficient grounds aside from the genealogical table of Luke to regard Jesus as the son of David through His mother. Yet the question, to whom does this table refer, is one of no little interest, as well as difficulty, and worthy of our careful examination.

The fact that there should be two genealogies of Jesus given is in itself a remarkable and perplexing one, and the most obvious explanation is that presented by the peculiar circumstances of His birth. As the legal son of Joseph, the genealogy of His father must be given; as the son of Mary and without any earthly father, her lineage becomes His. Yet in point of fact this explanation in early times found few, or no advocates; the general opinion being that both tables were those of Joseph.[2] But how could the same person have two such differing lines of ancestors? The most probable answer is that which refers the table of Matthew to the legal successors of the throne of David, and that of Luke to Joseph's paternal ancestors.[3] The former gives those who were the legal heirs to the kingdom. The line of Solomon failed in Jechonias, (Jer. xxii. 30,) and the right of succession then passed over to the line of Nathan in the person of Salathiel. From Joseph a younger son of Juda, or Abiud of that line, Joseph, the husband of Mary, traced his descent. The family of the elder son becoming extinct, Matthan, Joseph's grandfather, became the heir. This Matthan had two sons, Jacob and Heli. The elder Jacob had no son, but probably a daughter, the Virgin Mary. The younger Heli had a son Joseph, who thus became both heir to his uncle and to the throne.

[1] Testamentum 12 Patriarchum, in Lardner, ii. 330. Hofmann, 7.

[2] Mill, 196, says: "We find no tradition more clear, more perpetual and universal."

[3] So Hervey in Smith's Bible Dictionary, 666.

Thus Mary and Joseph were first cousins, and the genealogical tables have equal reference to both.

Both tables were referred to Joseph by Africanus, (220 A. D.,) whose solution of their difficulties is given by Eusebius, (i. 7.) It supposes that Melchi and Matthan, Joseph's grandfathers in the two genealogies, the one being of the family of Nathan, the other of the family of Solomon, had married successively the same woman, Estha, by whom the former had Eli, and the latter Jacob. Eli and Jacob were thus brothers uterine, though by their fathers of different families. Eli married and died childless, and Jacob according to the Jewish law married his widow, and had by her a son Joseph, who was in the eye of the law the son of the deceased Eli. According to Jewish custom the pedigree is recorded following both descents, the legal and the natural, that of Eli given by Luke in the line of Nathan, and that of Jacob given by Matthew in the line of Solomon.[1]

It deserves to be noticed that Africanus affirms that his account is not an idle conjecture, nor incapable of proof, but came from the relatives of the Lord, who "gloried in the idea of preserving the memory of their noble extraction." Whether his statement respecting the destruction of the Jewish family registers by Herod is historically true has been often doubted.[2] Of this mode of solution by reference to the ancient law of Levirate marriages, Lightfoot says, (on Luke iii. 23,) "There is neither word, nor reason, nor indeed any foundation at all."[3]

But whilst the early Church generally ascribed both tables to Joseph, many since the Reformation have strenuously maintained that Luke gives the genealogy of Mary. And this view has not a little in its favor. It is not im-

[1] Some, in later times, reversed this, making Joseph the natural son of Eli and legal son of Jacob.

[2] So Hervey in Smith's Bible Dictionary, 663; contra, Sepp, ii. 106.

[3] See, however, Mill, 201.

probable that the tables given by Matthew and Luke are to be regarded as copies of family registers to which they had access, and which they give as they found them. It is said that there is no reason to believe that they were guided by the Spirit to make any corrections, for only as exact copies would the Jews deem them of validity.[1] This must be taken with some limitations. It, however, would not forbid the insertion of an explanatory clause not affecting the order of the descent. Looking at the table in Luke in this light, we find it thus introduced (iii. 23): "And Jesus Himself began to be about thirty years of age, being (as was supposed) the son of Joseph—of Eli," &c. The text is thus given by Tischendorf: *ων υιος, ως ενομιζετο, του Ιωσηφ*, &c.—"being son, as was supposed, of Joseph," &c. The first point to be determined is respecting the explanatory statement here made by the Evangelist. Is it only "as was supposed," or rather "as was supposed, son of Joseph"? If the latter be taken, then the table proper would read, "being (as was supposed, son of Joseph) son of Eli," &c. If the former be taken it would read, "being (as was supposed) son of Joseph—of Eli," &c.

If now, to determine the construction of this clause, we consider the general scope of Luke's Gospel, we observe that he has already stated at length that Jesus was the son of Mary through the immediate power of God. None of his readers could therefore suppose that he here speaks of Joseph as His natural father. If, like Matthew, it was his purpose to found Christ's Messianic claims upon His legal relationship to Joseph, he would, like him, give Joseph's genealogical table. But such does not seem to have been his purpose. Had he designed to set forth Jesus as the Messiah he would in some way have designated the covenants with Abraham and David, which were the basis of all Messianic hopes. But no allusion is made to these cove-

[1] So Morrison.

nants, nor any prominence given to Abraham, or David, and the genealogy is continued upward to Adam. We do not therefore find grounds for believing that Luke had in view, like Matthew, the proof that Jesus as the legal son of Joseph was the promised Messiah. What then is his purpose? It is one in conformity with the general scope of his Gospel, which was designed for Gentiles, and takes little note of the special relations of the Jews to God. After giving a full narrative of the Lord's miraculous conception and birth, and a brief mention of His baptism, as preparatory to His public ministry, he proceeds to give His genealogy on that side only on which it could be really given, that of His mother. Through her He was made man, and through her should His descent from Adam be traced.

If upon these grounds we assume that Luke gives the genealogy of Mary, let us note the force of his explanatory statement. Why does he insert the clause, "as was supposed, son of Joseph"? Is it that, being about to give Joseph's genealogy as the legal father of Jesus, he thinks it necessary to insert a declaration that he was not His true father? This in view of the previous narrative seems superfluous, for he had already shown Him to be the son of God. And it is plainly incongruous to assert that He was not the son of Joseph, and then proceed to give Joseph's genealogy, unless he would make prominent His legal sonship, which, as we have seen, he has not done. If, however, we suppose that he designs to give the Lord's descent through His mother, the bearing of the parenthetical clause is obvious. By the Jews at large he was regarded as the son of Joseph, and some explanation therefore was necessary why, contrary to all usage, the mother's, not the father's, genealogy should be given. This explanation is made in the statement that He was supposed to be son of Joseph. "Jesus, generally but erroneously supposed to be son of Joseph, was the son of Eli, of Matthan, of

Levi," &c. That Mary's own name is not mentioned makes no difficulty, since the mention of female names was contrary to usage in such tables, and as she had already been distinctly mentioned as His mother, there was no danger of misapprehension. Her name being omitted, Jesus must be brought into immediate connection with her father, His grandfather. That He is called son, not grandson, is unimportant, the former term being often used to express the more distant relationship. That it is not strictly used throughout the table is apparent from v. 38, where Adam is called the son of God. That Eli is not expressly said to be Mary's father is not essential, since the form of the table implies the degree of relationship.[1]

Some, who regard the table in Luke as that of Mary, and Eli as her father, suppose that Joseph is brought into it as his son-in-law or adopted son.[2] If it be admitted that this degree of relationship may be thus expressed, it is doubtful whether it would, without express mention, find place in a table in which only the direct line of descent is given. Jesus, having no earthly father, may well be called the son of Eli, although strictly grandson, from the necessity of the case, but the same reason does not hold in the case of Joseph.

Thus the two tables given by Matthew and Luke, regarded as those of Joseph and of Mary, are in beautiful harmony with the scope of their respective Gospels. Through that of Matthew Jesus is shown to be the heir of David as the legal son of Joseph; through that of Luke, to be of David's seed according to the flesh by His birth of Mary. The former beginning with Abraham, the father of the chosen people, descends through David the king, to Christ the royal heir, in whom all the national covenants should be

[1] That the Jews so regarded him is shown by Lightfoot on Luke iii. 23; Sepp, ii. 8.

[2] Robinson's Harmony, 185. Alexander.

fulfilled; the latter beginning with the second Adam, the eternally begotten Son of God, ascends to the first Adam, the son of God by creation. Each Evangelist gives His genealogy in that aspect which best suits his special purpose; to the one He is the Messiah of the Jews, to the other the Saviour of the world.

The opinions of modern scholars upon this point are about equally divided. Among those who regard Luke's table as that of Mary, not of Joseph, are: Newcome, Robinson, Greswell, Lange, Wieseler, Riggenbach, Auberlen, Ebrard, Krafft, Bloomfield, Alexander, Oosterzee. Contra —Alford, Meyer, Winer, Bleek, Fairbairn, Da Costa, Friedlieb, Patritius, Mill, Ellicott, Westcott.

Our purpose does not lead us to consider further the special features of these genealogies. Regarding them as copies of family registers, documents for whose accuracy in every point the Evangelists are not responsible, any real or seeming discrepancies do not affect their credibility, unless disproving the fundamental fact of Christ's descent from Abraham and David. But in this fact both tables agree, and any minor inaccuracies, if there be such, are unimportant.[1]

That Joseph was the legal heir to the throne of David his relation to Jesus, the promised Messiah, sufficiently shows. Whether he and Mary were the only surviving descendants of David we have no positive data to decide; but it is not probable, for if they had been the sole survivors, this very fact, which could not have been unknown, must have made them conspicuous. Hegesippus[2] makes mention of the grandchildren of Juda, the brother of the Lord, who were brought before Domitian, as being of Da-

[1] Those who will see the questions respecting the divisions in Matthew's tables, his abridgments and omissions, and the relations of his table to that of Luke, will find all points fully treated by Mill, 147. See also Ebrard, 188, and the Dubia Evangelica of Spanheim, Pars Prima.

[2] In Eusebius, iii. 20.

vid's race. Not improbably there were many in more or less distant affinity to this royal family. It has been supposed by some, that the residence of Joseph and Mary, so far from their ancestral seat, in despised Galilee and in one of its most obscure villages, is to be explained by the fact that they were generally known to be of David's line, and so exposed to the jealousy of Herod.[1] But of this there is no proof. It is rather to be explained as a sign of the fallen state of that once royal house. Its members were now amongst the humblest of the people, too humble to arouse the jealousy of the Idumean usurper. We do not learn that in the course of his reign he took any precautionary measures against any of the descendants of David, looking upon them as claimants of the throne. They seem to have sunk wholly out of public sight. Yet, on the other hand, the expectation that the Messiah should spring from the house of David, was strong and general.[2] How can these facts be reconciled? If the people were really looking for a Messiah descended from that family, must not all who were known to be members of it have occupied a large space in public attention?

Perhaps the following may be the just solution of the difficulty. The promise made to David and his house respecting the throne of Israel was not absolute. (2 Sam. vii. 12, &c.) Its fulfilment was to depend upon the condition of obedience. Yet if the condition failed the promise was not withdrawn. His descendants were not reduced to the rank of private citizens, but its fulfilment was suspended, and their kingly claims were in abeyance. After the return from the captivity of Babylon, the house of David, at first prominent in Zerubbabel, fell more and more into obscurity.

[1] So Bucher.

[2] According to Mill, (285,) it was with the view to obviate this national expectation that Herod, two years before his death, imposed an oath of fidelity to Cæsar and himself. This is hardly warranted by the language of Josephus.

Other families began to be prominent. At last, the Maccabees through their wisdom and valor won the highest place, and became the acknowledged heads of the nation—both the civil and ecclesiastical chiefs. After their decay the family of Herod through Roman favor became dominant. During these 400 years no one of David's lineage seems to have been conspicuous, or in any way to have drawn to himself public attention; and probably little faith existed among the people at large that the Divine promise would have any fulfilment in that house. But the Messianic hopes of the Jews had, during the wars of the Maccabees, and under the usurpation of Herod, been constantly gaining in depth and strength. Everywhere they began to turn to their Scriptures, and to read them with new earnestness and faith. And as the expectation of the Messiah became more and more prevalent, it was naturally connected with the promise to David. Yet among his descendants there was no one to whom public attention was turned as in any way likely to fulfil their hopes. Hence, while a general belief existed that the Messiah should be of that family, its individual members continued to live in obscurity. And as it was also firmly believed that Elijah the prophet must personally come as the forerunner of the Messiah, this belief would naturally prevent any special attention being turned to them till that prophet actually appeared. Thus Joseph, the carpenter of Nazareth, might have been known to be of David's line, and even the legal claimant of the throne, and yet live unhonored and unnoticed.

Nazareth and its geographical position will hereafter be more particularly spoken of. It is disputed where Mary was when the angel visited her to announce the Lord's birth.[1] The Greek Church affirms that she was not at her own house when he came, but had gone to the fountain of the village,

[1] See Hofmann, 74.

and that he found her there.[1] Over this fountain, the source of the present one, to which its waters are conducted by a stone aqueduct, the Greeks have built a church which is called the Church of the Annunciation. The Latins affirm that the angel found her in a grotto, over which stood the house that was carried in the thirteenth century by angels, first to Dalmatia, and thence to Italy, where it still remains.[2] The exact places in this grotto where the angel and the virgin stood during their interview are marked out by two pillars. Over this grotto now stands a church, which is said to be, after that of the Holy Sepulchre, the most beautiful in Syria.[3] Tradition also points out the workshop of Joseph, now a Latin chapel. The time of Gabriel's appearance was, according to Bengel, (in loco), at evening, *vesperi, ut probabile est.* See Dan. ix. 21.

March—April, 749. 5 B. C.

Immediately after the visit of the angel Mary left Nazareth, and went to the home of Zacharias in the hill-country of Judah, and remained there about three months. Luke i. 39–56.

It has been supposed that Mary remained at Nazareth several weeks before visiting Elisabeth, and that during this period the events related by Matthew (i. 18-25) occurred.[4] But with this, Luke's statement, (i. 39,) that "she went with haste into the hill-country," is inconsistent; for going with haste cannot refer merely to the rapidity of the journey after it was begun, but to the fact that she made no delay in commencing it. Hug refers to a traditionary law that virgins should not travel, and that therefore Joseph must previously have taken her home as his wife. Al-

[1] See Protevangelium Jacobi, ch. ii.

[2] See Baronius, who affirms that no one should doubt respecting the reality of this miracle. In refutation, Stanley, 439.

[3] Porter, ii. 361. Stewart, 445.

[4] Ebrard, Alford.

ford says that "as a betrothed virgin she could not travel," but cites no authority. But if any such law were at this time in force, which is very doubtful, Mary may have journeyed in company with friends, or under the special protection of a servant, or with a body of neighbors going up to the Passover. That no unmarried female could journey even to visit her friends is incredible. "The incidental mention of women and children in the great assemblies gathered around Jesus is true to Oriental life, strange as it may appear to those who read so much about female seclusion in the East. In the great gatherings of this day, at funerals, weddings, feasts, and fairs, women and children often constitute the largest portion of the assemblies."[1] Ebrard's supposition (222) that Mary continued at Nazareth till certain suspicious women, the *pronubæ*, informed Joseph of her condition, and that then God made known to him what had occurred, has nothing in its favor. As little basis has the supposition that she told Joseph of the visit of the angel.[2] The narrative plainly implies that Mary, without communicating to him, or any one else, what had taken place, departed immediately to seek Elisabeth.[3] That under the peculiar circumstances in which she was placed she should greatly desire to see Elisabeth, was natural, and it is most improbable that she should wait several weeks, when all this time she could have no communication with Joseph except through these pronubæ. The whole narrative shows that neither Elisabeth nor Mary rashly forestalled God's action. Both, full of faith, waited in quietness and silence till He should reveal in His own way what He had done. Perhaps the expression, (Luke i. 56) "she returned to her own house," εις τον οικον αυτης, may imply that she had not yet been taken to the house of Joseph.

The distance from Nazareth to Jerusalem is about

[1] Thomson, ii.84. [2] So Lange.
[3] So Tischendorf, Robinson, Lichtenstein.

eighty miles,[1] and if Zacharias lived at Hebron seventeen miles south of Jerusalem, the whole journey would occupy four or five days. Several routes were open to Mary. The most direct was by Nain and Endor, and through Samaria and southward by Bethel. If for any cause Samaria was to be avoided, the Jordan could be crossed near Scythopolis, and the way followed through Perea along its eastern bank. This was the common route with the Jews in their journeyings to the feast, if they wished specially to avoid Samaria. Still a third way was by Dor on the sea-coast, passing through Lydda, and thence over the mountains of Ephraim.

JUNE, 749. 5 B. C.

A little before the birth of John, Mary returns to Nazareth; Joseph, seeing her condition, is minded to put her away privily, but is commanded by God, through an angel, to take her home as his wife, for that which is conceived of her is of the Holy Ghost. He obeys the word, and takes Mary as his wife. Elisabeth gives birth to a son, who is circumcised on the eighth day, and named John in obedience to angelic direction. — MATT. i. 18–25. LUKE i. 57–80.

Whether Mary left Elisabeth before or after John's birth, is not expressly stated, but the most natural construction of the narrative is that it was before.

The interval that had elapsed between the Annunciation and Mary's return from Judea, was sufficient to make manifest to Joseph her condition. That she at this time informed him of the visit of the angel, and of the divine promise, is not said in so many words, but is plainly implied. The position in which Joseph was now placed was one of great perplexity; and as a just man who desired to mete out to every one that which was his due, he was, on the one hand, unwilling to take her under such imputation of immorality, yet, on the other hand, unwilling to condemn her where there

[1] Kitto, Sepp, 80–90 Roman miles.

was a possibility of innocence. He therefore determines to put her away privately, which he could lawfully do, and so avoid the necessity of exposing her to public disgrace, or of inflicting upon her severe punishment. Whilst yet in doubt as to his proper course, the angel of the Lord, in a dream, confirmed the statement of Mary, and directed him to call her son by the name of Jesus, as the future Saviour of His people. Agreeably to the divine commandment, Joseph takes Mary at once to his own house as his wife.

While these things were taking place in Galilee, John was born in Judea, and was circumcised at the legal time. It was customary to join the giving of the name with the performance of this rite. This custom seems to have originated in the fact that Abraham's name was changed at the time he was circumcised.[1] (Gen. xvii. 23.) The name John, given the Baptist by the angel, is of importance, as showing the purpose of God in his ministry. It means "the Grace of God," or "one whom Jehovah bestows," and indicated that God was about to begin an economy of grace, in distinction from the economy of the law. His ministry, like that of Jesus, was for mercy, not for judgment.

Dec., 749. 5 B. C.

In consequence of an edict that all the world should be taxed, Joseph and Mary leave Nazareth to go to Bethlehem, the city of David, to be taxed there. — Luke ii. 1-5.

The chronological and other questions connected with this taxing are undoubtedly among the most perplexing which meet us in the whole Gospel narrative. The former have been already considered, but the latter demand a careful examination. Before we proceed to consider them, let us note the character of the Evangelist's statements, and his general purpose.

[1] Winer, ii. 133.

Turning to Luke's words, (ii. 1–3,) we find that he speaks in very brief and comprehensive terms. An edict had been issued by the Emperor Cæsar Augustus, "that all the world should be taxed, and this taxing was first made when Cyrenius was governor of Syria." In obedience to this edict, all went to be taxed, each into his own city. This is all the information the Evangelist gives. He does not say when this edict was issued, nor what were its peculiar features, nor give any account of its execution, except in Judea. Its only apparent value to him, and the only cause that leads him to mention it is, that it was the occasion that brought Joseph and Mary to Bethlehem. He therefore speaks of it only in the most general way, and we cannot learn from him whether it was a mere enrolment of persons, or also a census of property; whether it embraced all the provinces of the empire, or but a part; whether it was executed at once, or after a lapse of time, or in various provinces at various times. He is concerned only with its immediate relations to the birth of Jesus at Bethlehem, and does not mention even the manner of its execution in Judea, whether by Herod and his officers, in obedience to imperial direction, or by a special commissioner from Rome, or by the governor of some adjoining province. In the absence of definite statements in the Gospels, we turn to contemporary history, but here a like silence meets us. How little the historians of those times record of the period from 750–760, we shall soon see.

In our examination of this subject we shall consider: 1st. The nature and extent of this taxing; 2d. The proof that it actually took place; 3d. Its connection with Cyrenius.

First, the nature and extent of this taxing. The word translated taxing, *απογραφη*, means "properly transcription, then inscription, both of persons and things."[1] It may

[1] Alexander.

therefore denote simply an enrolment or enumeration of persons, a *descriptio capitum*; or may involve also a registration of property upon which taxes are to be assessed. For the latter, however, the Greeks had a special word, αποτιμησις.[1] To this corresponded the Latin term census, whose first object, according to Greswell,[2] was to ascertain the value of property; but, according to Winer, απογραφη was generally used by Grecian writers upon Roman matters as equivalent to census. That it is used by Luke in the latter sense in the only other passage of his writings, (Acts v. 37,) in which it is found, is plain.

From the term itself, then, no certain inference can be drawn. It may have been an enrolment of the people, with a view to learn the number of the inhabitants of the empire, and for general statistical purposes; or it may have had direct reference to taxation. If we turn, then, from the term itself to the context, to learn its meaning, it is said that no census of property can be referred to, as there is nowhere in the narrative any allusion to patrimony or inheritance, and that Joseph and Mary could have had no possessions at Bethlehem.[3] A more forcible argument upon this side is the fact that there was a rebellion of the Jews against the attempt to impose taxes upon them under Cyrenius, at a later period.[4] (Acts v. 37.) This implies that there had been no previous attempt to tax them, and that the registration now in question was one of persons only, with reference to the amount of population.[5] On the other hand, Meyer insists that Luke puts this taxing upon the same footing as that of Cyrenius, as an enrolment for taxation, and that not future but immediate. Most, however, take a middle view, supposing Augustus in his edict to have reference to taxation, but not designing that it should at once take effect.[6]

1 Winer, ii. 398. Ebrard, 169. 2 i. 541. 3 Greswell, i. 542.
4 Josephus' Antiquities, 18. 1. 1.
5 So Alford, and many. 6 So Ewald, v. 20.

It seems most probable, all things considered, that this enrolment had reference both to persons and property. That Augustus, now in the prime of life and undisputed master of the empire, should desire to establish a general and uniform system of taxation, finds support in his general character and policy. But he was far too wise a man to hasten matters prematurely, or to force disagreeable measures upon disaffected provinces. If, then, this enrolment was with reference to taxation, in its execution he would be governed by policy. The first step was to learn the number of the inhabitants, their names, tribes, families, &c., and together with this, to make a registration of property as the basis for the assessment of taxes. But considerable time may, and in many cases must have elapsed between the enrolment and the subsequent collection of such taxes. If, therefore, we suppose that Joseph and Mary went to Bethlehem, not simply to have their names registered, but also to give account of their possessions, it would by no means follow that taxes were then and there collected of them. If this had been so, we may well be surprised that no disturbance should then have taken place among the people at large, as did take place a few years later. The preliminary steps, though pointing to a future exercise of power in the actual assessment and collection of taxes, could give no tangible ground of offence.

It has been said by many, that this edict was confined to the Holy Land, and did not apply to the whole empire.[1] But the weight of authority is decidedly the other way.[2] The phrase πασα η οικουμενη, "all the world," when used in the Gospels, (Acts xi. 28, is in dispute,) beyond question refers to the Roman Empire as embracing at that time the greater part of the habitable world. But while the edict thus had application to the whole empire, and may have looked

[1] See Lardner, i. 267.
[2] So Meyer, Greswell, Wieseler, Ebrard, Alford.

forward to some general system of taxation as the final result, yet in a kingdom composed of so many heterogeneous and discordant provinces, its execution in each must have been governed by circumstances. A ruler wise as Augustus would, in a province like Judea, temporize and wait for a favorable opportunity, rather than meet the perils of rebellion. It is not improbable, therefore, that years may have passed before the edict was carried fully into effect.

Second, the proof that such a taxing actually took place confirmatory of the statement of the Evangelist. It is admitted that there is no express statement in any contemporary writer of such a taxing or census at this time, and embracing the whole empire, whether as a registration of persons, of property, or for general statistical purposes. Suetonius[1] relates that Augustus three times held a census, and from the Ancyran monument we learn that these were held in 726, 746, and 767; but it is probable that they were confined to Italy, and did not extend to the provinces.[2] But that the census did at times extend to particular provinces, is beyond question. Thus there was one in Gaul, one in Spain, and Strabo alludes to them as not uncommon.[3] If then Augustus held a census, now in Italy and now in the provinces, there is nothing improbable in the fact that he should hold one throughout the empire. And there are several circumstances mentioned by writers of that period that confirm this supposition. That there was a geometrical survey of the Roman Empire, which, if not commenced, was carried out by Augustus, seems to be well established.[4] Of the Roman chorographic maps, Merivale says (iv. 426): "They measured, we may believe, not only the roads, but the areas which lay between them; the labors of a quarter of a century produced no doubt a complete registration of the size, the figure, and the natural features of every prov-

[1] Aug. c. 27. [2] Wieseler, 91. Greswell, i. 535.
[3] Lardner, i. 263. Greswell, i. 536. [4] Wieseler, 77–81. Sepp, i. 136.

ince, district, and estate throughout the empire." And that with such a survey a general census should be connected is antecedently probable. The statement of Suidas, (Lex. απογραφη,) that "Augustus sent out twenty men of great probity into all parts of his empire, by whom he made an assessment of persons and estates," is indeed unsupported by any other author, but has no intrinsic improbability.[1] We know also from Tacitus[2] that Augustus had a little book which he had written out with his own hand, and which contained accounts of the numbers of soldiers, of the taxes, imposts, and the like: Opes publicæ continebantur. Quantum civium, sociorumque, in armis; quas classes, regna, provinciæ tributa, aut vectigalia et necessitates et largitiones, quæ cuncta suâ manu perscripserat Augustus. This *breviarium imperii* is mentioned also by Suetonius and Dio Cassius, and must have been based upon governmental surveys of all parts of the empire. As has been said by Prideaux, it was probably something of the same kind as the Doomsday Book of William the Conqueror.

If all the facts do not prove with absolute certainty that Augustus did ever order a general census, they go far, at least, to make it probable, and thus to confirm the Evangelist's statement. Lardner (i. 267) objects chiefly upon the ground of the silence of the Roman historians. But in the history of Dio Cassius there is a great gap from 747–757, the very period in which Luke states this taxing to have been held. Suetonius is very brief, as also Tacitus. The argument, therefore, from the silence of contemporary writers is of little force, and if pushed to its extreme would compel us to believe that no important event took place in the long reign of Augustus of which the few historians whose works remain to us in whole, or in part, have not made specific mention.[3]

Third. The connection of this taxing with Cyrenius.

[1] Greswell, i. 537. [2] Ann., i. 11. [3] See Ebrard, 171.

We have, already, in the essay upon the date of Christ's birth, examined the point whether Cyrenius was not twice governor of Syria, and found strong grounds to believe that this was the case. If so, his first administration was from the autumn of 750 to 753, and the taxing now in question was the first as distinguished from the second, which took place during his second administration, some ten years later. But as some degree of doubt, from the scantiness of our data, must necessarily rest upon this conclusion, let us suppose, as has usually been done, that he was not governor of Syria till 760, and examine Luke's statement from this point of view.

The first point that meets us is the right construction of the Evangelist's words: "this taxing was first made when Cyrenius was governor of Syria," *αυτη η απογραφη πρωτη εγενετο, ηγεμονευοντος της Συριας Κυρηνιου.* If this be read, this was the first taxing, in distinction from a second, and took place under him as governor of Syria, but in fact he was not so governor till 760, we must construe the term *ηγεμονευοντος*, "governing," in its wide sense as applicable to any one who fills a place of rule. Thus understood, Cyrenius, though not the governor, may have been a joint, or assistant ruler, as Josephus[1] speaks of Saturninus and Volumnius as the presidents of Syria. Or he may have been an extraordinary commissioner sent from Rome especially for this purpose.[2] In all this there is nothing intrinsically improbable, and it agrees with the fact that he was about that time in the East, and engaged in political affairs. It corresponds also to the statements of the fathers, except Tertullian, that this taxing was by Cyrenius. Still, on the other hand, the obvious import of Luke's words is, that he was then the governor over Syria, not an assistant, and still less a commissioner appointed to a special service in a neighboring kingdom.

[1] Antiq. 16. 9.

[2] Lardner, i. 329. Wieseler, 113.

According to another construction of Luke's words, taking πρωτη for πρωτερον, this taxing was before Cyrenius was governor of Syria.[1] So understood, it was the purpose of the Evangelist to distinguish between the two taxings, taking for granted that all knew that the second was under Cyrenius. But admitting that the Greek will bear this interpretation, still had this been Luke's meaning it would have been more naturally expressed another way.

Most English commentators have preferred the following construction; this taxing was first made—*i. e.* carried into effect, when Cyrenius was governor of Syria.[2] The enrolment was made at the time of the Lord's birth, but its actual execution was deferred some nine or ten years, or till Judea was made a Roman province. This is not inconsistent with Luke's words, since the enrolment was only preparatory to the assessment and collection of the taxes, and the latter may have been delayed by political difficulties till the time of Cyrenius.

Some, as Lardner, (i. 333,) would make ηγεμονυοντος της Συριας to be merely an official title, and to imply not that Cyrenius was then actually governor, but that he had at some previous period of his life filled the office. Having been governor, the title continued to cleave to him, and by it he was generally designated and best known. This, however, is forced.

But some objections still remain to be considered. First, that this taxing could not have taken place in Herod's lifetime, because inconsistent with the political relations of his kingdom to the Empire. It still had a nominal independence, and was not converted into a province till the banishment of his son Archelaus. In this, however, is little force.[3] The relations between Rome and her dependent kingdoms

[1] So Usher, Whitby, Tholuck, Wieseler, Ewald, Greswell.

[2] Middleton, Hales, Campbell, Norton. So among the Germans, Ebrard, Lange, Lichtenstein.

[3] Winer, ii. 399.

were constantly fluctuating; and what rights and privileges she should at any time give them, was a matter of policy.[1] Judea was well known to Augustus as full of discontent and sedition, and there can scarce be a doubt that it was his purpose even before Herod's death to reduce it, so soon as circumstances permitted, to the rank of a province. Besides, the personal relations of Augustus and Herod had a little before this become far from friendly,[2] and therefore the former was not likely to be governed in his actions by mere considerations of good will. And Herod could offer no effectual resistance to any measure the Emperor might propose. He was now old and greatly hated by the Jews, and without Roman assistance could not have been sure of his kingdom for a day.

If, then, Augustus designed this enrolment as only preparatory to taxation, and if Herod looked upon it as an infringement of his royal rights, he could only submit. Resistance would only have brought his own downfall and the downfall of his family. And it is most probable that the execution of the measure was given chiefly into his hands. Two facts are mentioned by Josephus, both of which have been supposed to have some relation to this taxing. He speaks[3] of an oath which all the Jews were obliged to take, giving assurance of their good will to Cæsar and to the king's government, and which was refused by six thousand of the Pharisees. This is supposed by Patritius (iii. 171) to refer to the taxing of Luke. But this took place under Saturninus and before the taxing. He speaks also of an insurrection a little before Herod's death.[4] This insurrection, though the ostensible cause of it was the erection of a golden eagle over the great gate of the temple, doubtless had far

[1] As to the tribute actually paid by the Jews to the Romans, see Greswell, ii. 375; and as to the autonomy of subject provinces, Merivale, iv. 400.

[2] Josephus, Antiq., 16. 9. 3.

[3] Antiq., 17. 2. 4.

[4] Antiq., 17. 6. 2.

deeper roots, and very probably stood in direct connection with the enrolment, which the insurgents, who were zealots for the law, regarded as only a preliminary step to their more complete subjugation to Rome.

We find also, in these statements of Josephus, an answer to a second objection that such an enrolment could not have taken place without popular disturbances, such as took place afterward, and are mentioned by Luke, (Acts v. 37.) Both just before and after Herod's death were commotions which showed that the people at large were much disquieted, although there was no general resistance to Roman rule. But there was a large party who wished that Judea might then be made a Roman province,[1] and those who were zealous for national independence were now by no means so numerous as a few years later. The enrolment, therefore, might have been carried into effect without producing any general rebellion, however a few excitable spirits may have been aroused to resistance.

The conspicuous part which Cyrenius played in this taxing, so conspicuous that Luke connects it directly with his name, will surprise no one who considers the peculiar state of political affairs. Archelaus, the successor of Herod, received but half of his father's territories, and that not under the name of king, but of ethnarch. He ruled only by sufferance, and was from the beginning both hated and despised by the Jews. In this condition of things, it was natural that the chief direction of public matters should fall into the hands of the governor of the adjoining province. Josephus gives ample proof how ready the Romans were under Varus, to interfere in Jewish quarrels, and with what contempt the Syrian governors treated the subject kings around them.[2] If, also, as there is good reason to believe, it was the purpose of Augustus at the first favorable oppor-

[1] Antiq., 17. 11. 2. [2] Antiq., 19. 8. 1.

tunity to depose Archelaus and to reduce Judea to a province, we shall find no difficulty in believing that Cyrenius, as governor of Syria, might then have conducted the taxing.

But how is the silence of Josephus in regard to this matter to be explained? Whatever may have been his motives, we find that, in point of fact, he does pass over the whole period of the rule of Archelaus almost in silence. He mentions no governor of Syria from Varus, 750, to Cyrenius, 760. So he wholly passes over the Parthian war under Caius Cæsar.[1] This cannot have been from ignorance. Wieseler (98) supposes that he concealed, so far as possible, all that testified to the Messianic hopes of the Jews and against their submission to Roman domination. His mention of Judas of Galilee, who headed the rebellion at the second taxing, is very brief.[2] Lardner, (i. 355,) alluding to this latter passage, supposes that Josephus avoids the mention of these contests between the Jews and Romans, because the principles of Judas were very popular, and he must offend his countrymen on the one hand, or the Romans on the other. Thus much is plain, that he passes over as lightly as possible every thing that testifies to the degradation of his people.[3]

Thus, in various ways, the difficulties connected with the taxing may be met (though it cannot be said that they are all yet removed), if we assume that Cyrenius was but once governor of Syria. But we have strong historical evidence that he twice filled this office. If this shall be confirmed by further investigations, all doubts as to the literal accuracy of Luke will be removed.

Why, in Joseph's journey to Bethlehem, Mary should have accompanied him, is not stated by the Evangelist. Some have supposed that she was obliged to go, in order to be enrolled; but neither, according to Jewish or Romish

[1] Zumpt, ii. 87. [2] Antiq., 18. 1. 6.

[3] See Journal Sac. Lit., vol. vi. 292, &c.

custom, was it necessary that she should be personally present.[1] Others suppose that she possessed a little inheritance in Bethlehem, and so must go thither.[2] But this is without proof and against probability; for, if she had had possessions there, she would scarce have been compelled to go to the inn. In all likelihood she went with Joseph because, at this delicate and trying period, she was unwilling to be left at Nazareth alone. That she was aware of the prophecy that the Messiah should be born at Bethlehem is not improbable; but that she journeyed there with a design thus to ensure its fulfilment,[3] is not consistent with the general tenor of her conduct.

Dec., 749. 5 B. C.

Upon the arrival of Joseph and Mary at Bethlehem, they could find no room at the inn, and took refuge in a cottage where the babe was born, and laid in the manger. — LUKE ii. 6–7

The village of Bethlehem, "house of bread," lies about six miles south of Jerusalem on the way to Hebron. There was another city or village of this name in Zebulon, (Josh. xix. 15,) whence this is called, to distinguish it, Bethlehem-Judah. It is not mentioned in the catalogues of the cities of Judah. In Genesis (xlviii. 7) it is called Ephrath, and in Micah (v. 2) Ephratah—an epithet given it because of its fruitfulness. It appears in Scripture chiefly in connection with the house of David, and seems never to have been a place of much importance. "The Jews are very silent of this city; nor do I remember that I have read any thing in them concerning it besides those things which are produced out of the Old Testament."[4] Micah speaks of it as little amongst the thousands of Judah. It was here that the

[1] See, however, Sepp, ii. 68.
[2] Olshausen, Michaelis.
[3] So Lange.
[4] Lightfoot, iii. 100.

fields of Boaz lay, in which Ruth gleaned, (Ruth, ii. 4;) and here the son of Obed was born. Hither came Samuel, and anointed the youthful David to be the successor of Saul. That the Messiah should be born here was expressly declared by the prophet Micah, (v. 2;) and the Jews seem to have had no question as to his meaning, nor ever to have doubted the literal fulfilment of the prophecy. (Matt. ii. 6; John, vii. 42.)

Bethlehem lies on the eastern brow of a ridge that runs from east to west a mile in length, and is surrounded by hills. From the highest point of the ridge there is an extensive view toward the south and east, in the direction of Jericho, the Dead Sea, and the mountains of Moab beyond. There are deep valleys both on the south and north; that on the north stretches toward Jerusalem, and in it olives, figs, almond-groves, and vineyards are found. The village has one street, broad, but not thickly built. The present inhabitants are chiefly occupied in the manufacture of holy trinkets and relics, beads, crosses, &c., for the pilgrims who visit Jerusalem.

The exact spot where the Lord was born, has been the subject of anxious investigation and of zealous controversy. All the information upon this point that the Scriptures give, is contained in the words of Luke, that when Joseph and Mary arrived at Bethlehem, they could find no place at the inn, or khan; and that, when Jesus was born, she was compelled to put the new-born babe in a manger, φατνη. From this statement some have inferred that the manger was in a stall connected with the inn itself;[1] but this is hardly consistent with other features of the narrative. That the place in which she took refuge was a stall, or room where cattle were lodged, may fairly be inferred from the mention of a manger.

The place now shown as the Lord's birthplace is a

[1] Wilson, Lands of the Bible, i. 392; Kitto, Life of Christ, 62.

cave southeast from the town, and now covered by the Latin convent. The tradition that connects this cave with His birth is very ancient.[1] Robinson (ii. 416) speaks of it as "reaching back at least to the middle of the second century." Justin Martyr (150, A. D.) mentions it; as also Origen about a hundred years later. Queen Helena erected a church over it, (325 A. D.) Here came Jerome, (400 A. D.,) and dwelt for many years. So far then as early tradition can authenticate a place, this seems well authenticated.[2] Yet there are objections which have led many to deny the truth of the tradition.[3] The point then demands some further examination.

The objection, that Luke says nothing of a cave, is not important. His purpose is simply to show the humble and friendless state of the infant child, and this is done by the mention of the circumstances that there was no room for his parents in the inn, and that when He was born He was laid in a manger. Any other particulars were for his purpose unnecessary.

A more important objection is that drawn from the fact, that tradition makes caves or grottoes to be the sites of so many remarkable events. That, as was long ago said by Maundrell, "wherever you go, you find almost every thing represented as done under ground," naturally awakens our incredulity. Yet, on the other hand, they could not have been so generally selected for such sites, unless there were some grounds of fitness in the selection. The scriptures, Josephus, and all travellers speak of the numerous caves that are found throughout Palestine. They were used for dwellings, for fortresses and places of refuge, for cisterns, for prisons, and for sepulchres. Travellers used them as inns, robbers as dens, herdsmen as stalls, husbandmen as

[1] See Thilo, Codex Apoc., i. 381, note.

[2] See a full statement of the evidence in Patritius, iii. 293.

[3] So Ritter, Robinson.

granaries. Many of these caves were very large. One is mentioned (Judges xx. 47) large enough for six hundred men. Bonar,[1] in reference to the cave of Adullam, says: "you might spend days in exploring these vast apartments, for the whole mountain seems excavated, or rather honey combed." Pococke speaks of one large enough for thirty thousand men.

These caves, so numerous in the light limestone formation of Judea, and easily wrought into any shape, and always dry, were naturally thus applied to many uses. We need not be surprised to find them connected with many remarkable events, and hallowed by sacred associations. The traditions that connect them with the history of Jesus are neither to be indiscriminately received, nor indiscriminately rejected. Whether a particular event did, or did not, take place in a grotto is to be judged of according to its intrinsic probability, and the amount of evidence. Whilst no unprejudiced person will be disposed to put the site of the Annunciation to Mary, or of the Agony, or of the Ascension, in a cave, yet all recognize the cave as a fitting place for the sepulchre. Whether a cave was, or not, the birthplace of the Lord, must be judged of by its own merits.

Thus looking upon this tradition, we find no sufficient reason why it should be wholly rejected. Probably there is some measure of truth in it. It is indeed hard to believe that the present cave, so deep down and inaccessible, could ever have been used as a stall for cattle. Perhaps the fact may be that this cave, in its original shape, was connected with a house forming its rear apartment, and used as a stable. To this house went Joseph and Mary, when they could find no room at the inn, and when the child was born, it was laid in the manger as the most convenient place. Arculf, (A. D. 700,)[2] describing the cave as it was in his day, says: "At the extreme eastern angle (of the ridge)

[1] Land of Promise, 246. [2] Early Travels, 6.

there is a sort of natural half-cave, the outer part of which is said to have been the place of our Lord's birth: the inside is called our Lord's manger. The whole of this cave is covered within with precious marble." Willibald (A. D. 722) says: "The place where Christ was born was once a cave under the earth, but it is now a square house cut in the rock, and the earth is dug up and thrown from it all around, and a church is now built above it." Thus the small cave that originally existed in the rear of the dwelling, and was used as a stable, has been gradually converted into its present shape.

This view of the matter is defended by Thomson, (ii. 533.) "It is not impossible, to say the least, but that the apartment in which our Saviour was born was in fact a cave. I have seen many such, consisting of one or more rooms in front of, and including a cavern where the cattle were kept. It is my impression that the birth actually took place in an ordinary house of some common peasant, and that the babe was laid in one of the mangers, such as are still found in the dwellings of the farmers of this region. That house may have stood where the convent does now, and some sort of a cave, either natural or made by digging the earth away for building, and for the roofs of houses, may have been directly below, or even included within its court." Elsewhere (ii. 98) he thus speaks of the manger, which he identifies with the "crib" mentioned by Isaiah (i. 3)—"It is common to find two sides of the one room, where the native farmer resides with his cattle, fitted up with these mangers, and the remainder elevated about two feet higher for the accommodation of the family. The mangers are built of small stones and mortar in the shape of a box, or rather of a kneading-trough, and when cleaned up and white-washed, as they often are in summer, they do very well to lay little babes in. Indeed our own children have slept there in our rude summer retreats on the mountains."

We may then conclude that tradition has not in this case erred. The site of the Lord's birthplace must long have been remembered by the shepherds, (Luke ii. 16,) and been generally known in the region round. But the present condition of the cave is doubtless very unlike its original condition. It has been greatly enlarged and deepened, and space made in various directions for the various accessory grottoes and sepulchres which are now shown. In this way all the statements of Luke can be easily reconciled with the tradition. Here was the cave in the rear of the house, and used for cattle. In a manger, as the most ready and fitting place, the babe was laid. Hither came the shepherds, to pay their adorations, and here probably still later came the Magi. These remarkable events would not easily pass from men's memories, and some knowledge of the spot where they occurred could not well have escaped the early disciples.

The church that now stands over the cave of the nativity was built by the Emperor Justinian upon the site of that built by the Empress Helena, A. D. 330.[1] Adjoining it are the Latin, Greek, and Armenian convents, whose monks have a common interest in it for purposes of worship. It is now much dilapidated, though, as the oldest Christian church in the world, it continues to possess great architectural interest. The cave of the nativity is 38 feet long by 11 wide, and a silver star in a marble slab at the eastern end marks the precise spot where the Lord was born. Here is the inscription: *Hic de virgine Maria Jesus Christus natus est.* Silver lamps are always burning around, and an altar stands near, which is used in turn by the monks of the convents. The manger in which the Lord was laid was taken to Rome by Pope Sixtus V. and placed in the church of St. Maria Maggiore, but its place is supplied by a marble one. A few

Tobler's Bethlehem, 104.

feet opposite, an altar marks the spot where the Magi stood. The walls are covered with silken hangings.

The usual exaggeration of tradition may be seen in the many apocryphal sites gathered around the central one. In adjoining grottoes are shown the chapel of Joseph and the chapel of the Innocents, where the children murdered by Herod were buried. A stone is also shown that marks the spot where, in the firmament above, the star stood still that guided the Magi in their journey. Of more interest to the Christian scholar is the cave, now converted into a chapel, where Jerome lived, studied, and prayed. It is said by Stanley, (436,) that during the invasion of Ibrahim Pasha the Arabs took possession of the convent, and found by the removal of the marbles, &c., with which it was encased, that the grotto of the nativity was an ancient sepulchre. If this were so, it is highly improbable that Joseph and Mary would have entered it. But the statement needs confirmation.

That the Lord was born very soon after their arrival at Bethlehem, may be fairly inferred from the fact that "there was no room for them in the inn."

DEC., 749. 5 B. C.

The same night upon which He was born, an Angel of the Lord appeared to some shepherds, who were keeping watch over their flocks, and announced to them His birth. Leaving their flocks, they hastened to Bethlehem to see the child, and finding Him, returned praising God. LUKE ii. 8-20.

The bearing of the fact that the shepherds were in the field watching their flocks, upon the date of the Lord's birth, has been already examined.

The residence of the shepherds is not mentioned, nor do we know the place where they were keeping watch. It appears to have been in the vicinity of Bethlehem, and yet some little distance removed. There is now, a mile or more east from the convent, a plain in which is a little village called the Village of the Shepherds. Not far from this village is pointed out the field where, it is said, they were feeding their flocks, and here is shown a grotto, called the Grotto of the Shepherds. In this field a church was built by the Empress Helena. In its neighborhood stood formerly a cloister, but now only ruins of a church or cloister are to be found. It is mentioned by Bernard, A. D. 867.[1] "One mile from Bethlehem is the monastery of the holy shepherds to whom the angel appeared at our Lord's nativity." Tradition makes the number of Shepherds three or four, and gives their names.[2]

JAN.—FEB., 750. 4 B. C.

Upon the eighth day following His birth, the Lord was circumcised, and the name Jesus given Him. Forty days after the birth, Mary presented herself with the child at the Temple in accordance with the law, and after the presentation returned again to Bethlehem. LUKE ii. 21. LUKE ii. 22–38.

The order of events following Christ's birth to the time He went to reside at Nazareth, is much disputed. The chief point of controversy is respecting the time of the visit of the Magi. If this can be determined, the other events may be easily arranged.

An early and current tradition placed the coming of the Magi on the 6th of January, or on the 13th day after His birth.[3] This day was early celebrated as the Feast of the Epiphany, or the manifestation of Christ, and originally had reference to His birth, to the visit of the Magi, and to His baptism. It is now observed both in the Greek and Roman Churches with reference to the latter two events, of which

[1] Early Travels, 29. [2] Hofmann, 117.
[3] See Thilo, Codex Apoc., i. 385, note.

the adoration of the Magi is made most prominent. This is also the case in the English and American Episcopal Churches. But the tradition did not command universal assent. Eusebius and Epiphanius, reasoning from Matt. ii. 16, put the coming of the Magi two years after His birth. And others have thought the 6th January selected for convenience, rather than as having any direct chronological connection with the event. The apocryphal gospel of the birth of Mary puts their coming on the forty-second day, or after the presentation, but some copies on the 13th.[1]

If we now ask the grounds upon which, aside from this tradition, the coming of the wise men is placed so soon after the birth, and before the presentation in the Temple, the more important are these: first, that the words *του δε Ιησου γεννηθεντος*, "Now when Jesus was born," (Matt. ii. 1,) imply that the one event speedily followed the other, the participle being in the aorist and not in the perfect; second, that directly after the presentation Jesus went with His parents to Nazareth, (Luke ii. 39,) and that therefore the presentation must have been preceded by their visit; third, that at the coming of the Magi Herod first heard of the birth of Jesus, but if the presentation at the Temple had previously taken place, he must have heard of it, as it had been made public by Anna, (Luke ii. 38.) But none of these reasons is decisive. There is nothing, as asserted, in the use of *γεννηθεντος*, "now when Jesus was born," that proves that they came so soon as He was born, or that an interval of two months may not have elapsed.[2] The opinion of many of the fathers that they found Him still in the manger, or stall, *in spelunca illa qua natus est*, may be true, if the manger was in a cave in the rear of the house. (See Matt. ii. 11.) The statement of Luke, that "when they had performed

[1] Hofmann, 126. [2] See Gal. iv. 29, and Meyer, in loco.

all things according to the law of the Lord, they returned into Galilee, to their own city Nazareth," has often been interpreted as affirming that they went directly from the temple to Nazareth without any return to Bethlehem.[1] But this interpretation is arbitrary. It is apparent that Luke does not design to give a full history of Christ's infancy. He says nothing of the Magi, of the murder of the children, of the flight into Egypt. Whatever may have been the motive of this omission, which Alford, in common with many German critics, ascribes to ignorance, nothing can be inferred from it to the impugning of Matthew's accuracy. His statement respecting the return to Galilee is general, and does not imply any strict chronological connection. Elsewhere in Luke like instances occur, as in iv. 14, where Jesus is said to have "returned in the power of the Spirit into Galilee," whence it would appear that this return followed immediately upon the temptation; yet we know that an interval of several months must have elapsed. It is the fact that His childhood was passed at Nazareth, which Luke brings prominently forward, not the precise time when He went thither, which was unimportant. It is not inconsistent with his language that Jesus should have returned to Bethlehem from the Temple, an afternoon walk of two hours, and have gone thence to Nazareth by way of Egypt, though had we this gospel alone, we could not infer this. Besides, it is apparent from Matthew's narrative (ii. 22–3) that Joseph did not design upon his return from Egypt to go to Galilee, and went thither only by express divine direction. Plainly he looked upon Bethlehem, not Nazareth, as the proper home of the child who should be the heir of David.[2] And finally the fact that Anna "spoke of Him to all them that looked for redemption in Jerusalem," by no means shows that her words came to the ears of Herod.

[1] So early, Chrysostom; and now, A. Clarke and Meyer.

[2] See Wieseler, 154.

The number of those who shared the faith of Simeon and Anna was doubtless few, and the birth of Jesus was not an event that they would blazon abroad before the Pharisees and Herod.

Those who thus place the visit of the Magi before the purification of Mary and the presentation of Jesus, are by no means agreed as to the time of the latter events. If the visit of the Magi was on the thirteenth day after His birth, and the murder of the children and the flight into Egypt took place immediately after, the purification must have been delayed till the return, and so in any event after the legal time on the fortieth day.[1] To avoid this, some suppose that, although the suspicions of Herod had been aroused by the inquiries of the Magi, yet he took no active measures for the destruction of the child, till the rumor of what had taken place at the Temple at the time of the presentation (Luke ii. 27–38) reaching his ears, stirred him up to give immediate order for the murder of the children.[2] Others still, making the departure to Nazareth to have immediately followed the purification, are compelled to make Nazareth, not Bethlehem, the starting point of the flight into Egypt.[3]

The obvious difficulties connected with this traditional view of the coming of the wise men on the thirteenth day after the Lord's birth, have led most in modern times to put it after the purification on the fortieth day. Some, who hold that Jesus went immediately after that event to Nazareth, suppose that after a short sojourn there He returned to Bethlehem, and there was found by the wise men.[4] But most who put the purification upon the fortieth day, make the visit of the Magi to have shortly followed, and prior to any departure to Nazareth.[5] And this order seems best to harmonize the scripture narratives. The language of Luke

[1] Friedlieb, Bucher. [2] Augustine, Sepp, Alford. [3] Maldonati.
[4] Epiphanius, and now Jarvis, and Patritius.
[5] Robinson, Tischendorf, Wieseler, Lichtenstein.

ii. 22, compared with v. 21, plainly intimates that as the circumcision took place on the eighth, or legal day, so did the presentation on the fortieth. Till this day, the mother was regarded as unclean, and was to abide at home, and it is therefore very improbable that the adoration of the Magi, and especially the flight into Egypt, should have previously taken place. Doubtless, in case of necessity, all the legal requisitions could have been set aside, but this necessity is not proved in this case to have existed. That the purification was after the return from Egypt, is inconsistent with Matthew's statements, (ii. 22), that after Joseph had heard that Archelaus was reigning in Judea, he was afraid to go thither. If, then, he dare not even enter the king's territory, how much less would he dare to go to Jerusalem, and enter publicly into the temple. The conjecture of some,[1] that Archelaus was then absent at Rome, is wholly without historic proof.

That Matthew puts the flight into Egypt in immediate connection with the departure of the Magi, (ii. 13,) is plain.[2] No interval could have elapsed after their departure, for it is said, v. 14, that he "took the young child and His mother by night, and departed into Egypt." He went so soon as the angel appeared to him, apparently the same night. We cannot then place the history of the purification after their departure, and before the flight into Egypt, as is done by Calvin and many. Nor could Herod, after his jealousy had been aroused by the inquiries of the Magi after the new-born King of the Jews, have waited quietly several weeks till the events at the purification awakened his attention anew. He doubtless acted here with that decision that characterized all his movements, and seeing

[1] So Hug.

[2] Alford. Ellicott says: "Probably on the same night that the Magi arrived." From the fact that they "were warned of God in a dream," it may, however, be inferred that the dream of Joseph was the night following.

himself mocked by the wise men, took instant measures for the destruction of the child.

The fact that Mary offered the offering of the poor, (Luke ii. 24,) may be mentioned as incidentally confirming this view; for if she had received previously the gifts of the Magi, particularly the gold, we may suppose that she would have used it to provide a better offering.[1]

We thus trace a threefold adoration of Christ: 1st, that of the shepherds; 2d, that of Simeon and Anna; 3d, that of the Magi; or a twofold adoration of the Jews, and then the adoration of the heathen.

FEB., 750. 4 B. C.

Soon after the presentation, came the wise men from the East to worship the new-born King of the Jews. This visit excited the suspicions of Herod, who made diligent inquiries of them, but being warned of God in a dream that they should not return to him, they departed to their own country another way. MATT. ii. 1–12.

The time of the appearing of the star which led the Magi to seek Jesus, has been already considered; and in the preceding note the reasons have been given why their coming should be placed after the purification on the 40th day.

It is not said whence the Magi came, except *απο ανατολων*, "from the east." In this phrase Arabia may be included, though lying rather to the south than east of Judea; but its more probable reference is to the regions beyond the Euphrates. Whether however of these, Persia, or Chaldea, or Parthia, may be meant, we have no data to determine. Some have preferred Persia, because this was the home of the Magian religion; others Arabia, because the gifts given were native to that country, and it was

[1] The whole subject of the coming of the Magi is elaborately discussed by Patritius, iii. 326 and 340.

near to Judea, and also because of the prediction of the Psalmist, (lxxii. 10,) that the kings of Seba and Sheba should offer gifts.

According to Rawlinson,[1] Magism was not the primitive religion of the Persians, but was received among them from the Scyths. Its chief feature was worship of the elements. The Magi, distinctively so called, were a tribe of the Medes, to whom were intrusted all the priestly functions connected with the practice of that religion, holding a relation to the other tribes similar to that of the tribe of Levi to the Jews. They were astrologers, and interpreters of dreams. The name, at first one of honor, lost in later times its significance, and was applied to all who made pretensions to supernatural knowledge, the itinerant conjurors, wizards, jugglers, often spoken of by the Roman writers, and mentioned by Josephus and Luke.[2]

That these astrologers may have had some knowledge of Balaam's prophecy of a star out of Jacob, (Num. xxiv. 17,) is not impossible.[3] Of the prophecies of Daniel, from the peculiar relation in which he stood to the wise men of Babylon, they could scarcely have been ignorant. That a general expectation pervaded the East that a king should arise in Judea to rule the world, seems well authenticated.[4] At least there were great multitudes of Jews in the East, and their Messianic hopes could hardly fail to come to the knowledge of the Magi. According to Ellicott,[5] it is most probable that they had learned of "prophecies uttered in their own country, dimly foreshadowing this divine mys-

[1] Herodotus, i. Essay v.

[2] See Trench, Star of the Wise Men. It is singular that Lightfoot should insist that it is used here, as well as elsewhere in the Scripture, in its bad sense.

[3] See, however, Kurtz, Gesch. des Alt. Bund., 492.

[4] Suetonius, Vesp., c. iv.; Tacitus, v. 13. It is, however, asserted by Giesseler, that both these historians copied Josephus. Neander speaks doubtingly.

[5] 72, note 1.

tery." Some suppose these wise men to have been themselves Jews, but their question, "Where is he that is born King of the Jews?" plainly implies that they were not of that people. Aside, then, from any immediate supernatural revelation to them, we may infer that they were in a position to interpret the appearing of the star as connected with the fulfilment of Jewish prophecies respecting the Messiah, and thus could speak of it as "His star." Still there is good reason to believe that they were taught of God by special revelation the meaning of the things they saw.

Of the supernatural character of this star we have already spoken. The part it plays in guiding the wise men on their way, its appearing and disappearing and reappearing, cannot well be explained by a reference to the conjunctions of planets, or to the ordinary movements of the stars. It has well been said by one: *Præter illam stellæ speciem quæ corporeum incitavit obtutum, fulgentior veritatis radius eorum corda perdocuit.* And Augustine calls the star *magnifica lingua cœli.*

Many traditions have been current in the Church respecting these Magi.[1] They were said to be three in number; they were kings, one of Arabia, one of Godolia or Saba, and one of Tharsis: their names Melchior, Balthasar, Caspar; they were baptized by St. Thomas, their bones were gathered by St. Helena and buried at St. Sophia in Constantinople, and were finally removed to Cologne, where they now lie.[2]

If the Magi came from beyond the Euphrates, they probably came by way of Damascus and thence to Jerusalem. In returning, they may have gone south of the Dead Sea to Petra, and thence have crossed the Euphrates.

[1] Hofmann, 120.

[2] Hildesheim, die Legende von den heiligen drei Königen, Hertzog Encyc., ii. 503. For a full discussion of all these traditions, see Spanheim, Dubia Evangelica, ii. 271, and Patritius, iii. 318.

FEB.—MAY, 750. 4 B. C.

Immediately after their departure, Joseph, warned by God in a dream, takes Mary and Jesus and goes down into Egypt. MATT. ii. 13–15. Herod, so soon as he finds himself mocked by the wise men, gives orders that all the children in Bethlehem of two years and under be slain. MATT. ii. 16–18. Joseph with Mary and Jesus remains in Egypt till he hears through an angelic messenger of Herod's death. MATT. ii. 19–23. He designs to return to Judea, but is directed by God to go to Nazareth, where the Lord remains during His childhood and youth. LUKE ii. 39–40.

The time of the sojourn in Egypt was not probably of long duration, although extended by some of the early writers to several years. In the Gospel of the Infancy it is stated at three years; in the History of Joseph at one year; in Tatian's Harmony at seven years; by Epiphanius at two years. Athanasius makes Jesus four years old when He came from Egypt; Baronius eight years. In modern times those who put the Lord's birth one or more years before Herod's death, prolong correspondingly the sojourn in Egypt, some one, some two, some three years.[1] But if his birth be placed late in 749, as we place it, His return from Egypt must have been in the early summer of 750. Lardner, (i. 358,) after Kepler, has attempted to show from the expression of the angel, (Matt. ii. 20,) "they are dead that sought the young child's life," that Antipater was included with Herod, and as he had been at enmity with his father for near a year, that the attempt upon His life, and the murder of the Innocents must have been so long before Herod's death. But this is doing violence to the expression.[2]

Joseph was to remain in Egypt till God should send him word, and this word was sent apparently so soon as Herod died. Considering how numerous were the Jews in

[1] Patritius, Sepp, Jarvis.

[2] See Trench, Star, 107; Meyer in loco.

Egypt, and the constant communication between the two countries, the news of Herod's death must soon have reached him in the ordinary way; but it was first made known to him by the angel, and no long interval, therefore, could have elapsed. That he made no delay but hastened his return, is implied in the fact that he did not know that Archelaus was Herod's successor till he came to the land of Israel. We infer, then, that the return was in the summer of 750, after a sojourn of three or four months.[1]

Tradition marks out the route which Joseph took into Egypt to have been by way of Hebron, Gaza, and the desert; which, as the most direct way, is very likely the true one. At Hebron is still pointed out upon a hill the spot where the family rested at night, and a similar one at Gaza. Probably near a fortnight was occupied in the journey. The place of their sojourn in Egypt was the village Metariyeh, not far from the city of Heliopolis on the way toward Cairo. An old sycamore is still shown as that under which they rested in their journey.[2] It is probable that many Jews dwelt at this time in the neighborhood of Heliopolis, which may explain the choice of a village in its vicinity as their place of refuge. Another tradition, however, makes them to have left Metariyeh, and to have dwelt at Memphis.[3] The temple built by Onias about 150 B.C. at Leontopolis still continued to be a much frequented place of worship to the Egyptian Jews, of whom Lightfoot says, "there was an infinite number at this time."

[1] According to Greswell, 7 months; to Lichtenstein, 4–5 weeks; to Wieseler and Ellicott, 2–3 weeks. Patritius, iii. 403, argues that the return was during the little interval when Archelaus ruled as king, or from the death of his father to his departure to Rome, whither he went to obtain the confirmation of Herod's will. This would make it to have been early in April, 750. It may, however, be doubted whether the expression of Matthew, ii. 22, that "Archelaus did reign," is not pressed too far.

[2] Kitto, Life of Christ, 139.

[3] Thilo, Codex Apoc., 93

From the nearness of Bethlehem to Jerusalem, Herod doubtless learned very early after the departure of the Magi that they had deceived him, and that through them he could not discover the new-born child. But as he had already diligently inquired of them what time the star appeared, he thought to accomplish his purpose by ordering that all the male children from two years old and under, in Bethlehem and its environs, should be put to death. The truth of the narrative has been often questioned, and on various grounds. The only important objection, however, is that springing from the silence of Josephus, who, it is said, must have mentioned an event so peculiar and cruel.[1] The common answer to this, that among the many insane and fiendish acts of cruelty that marked the last days of Herod, this might be easily overlooked, is amply sufficient.[2] The expression, "from two years old and under," is ambiguous. According to Campbell, "Only those beginning the second year are included." Greswell also limits it to the age of thirteen months. If it be thus confined, the number of the children murdered is much diminished. But under any circumstances it could not have been large. Sepp, supposing the whole number of inhabitants of Bethlehem and its coasts to be 5,000, would make the male children of this age about ninety; but this is a large estimate. Townsend, making the inhabitants to be 2,000, makes 50 children to have been slain. Some would reduce the number to ten or fifteen.[3] Voltaire, after an old Greek tradition, would make it 14,000. In peaceful times, such an act as this, even if executed as this probably was, in secrecy, would have excited general indignation when it became known; but now the Jewish people had so long "supped with horrors," and were so engrossed in the many perils that threatened their national existence, that this

[1] Meyer in loco. [2] Winer, i. 483. [3] Winer, i. 483; Morrison.

passed by comparatively unnoticed. Such a deed—from a man, of whom Josephus says, that "he was brutish and a stranger to all humanity," who had murdered his wife and his own children, and who wished in his dying rage to destroy all the chief men of his kingdom, that there might be a general mourning at his funeral—could have awakened no surprise. It was wholly in keeping with his reckless and savage character; but one, and by no means the greatest of his crimes. It is therefore possible that it may never have come to the knowledge of the Jewish historian, writing so many years after the event.

If, however, Josephus was aware of this atrocity, it by no means follows that he would have mentioned it. With the reasons for his silence we are not particularly concerned. It may be, as some say,[1] that he purposely avoided every thing that drew attention to the Messianic hopes of his people; or, as others,[2] that "he could not mention it without giving the Christian cause a great advantage." But whatever his motives, his silence cannot invalidate the statement of Matthew, except with those who will not credit an Evangelist unless corroborated by some Jewish or heathen author.

There are some[3] who think that the sedition of Judas and Matthias[4] occurred at this very time, and was connected with the visit of the Magi. The inquiries of these strangers for the King of the Jews, aroused into immediate activity the fiery zealots, and a report of the king's death finding credence, they attacked at noon day the golden eagle he had placed over the temple gate. About 40 of them being arrested were burned with fire. Exasperated at this bold sedition, and aware of the cause, the king gave orders for the slaughter of the children at Bethlehem. Of these two acts of this tragedy, Matthew relates

[1] Lichtenstein, 97. [2] Lardner, i. 351. [3] So Lardner, i. 348.
[4] Josephus, Antiq. 16. 6. 3 and 4.

only that with which he was concerned, that which took place at Bethlehem; and Josephus that which concerned the general history of affairs. The silence of the one is no disproof of the other.

The objection of Hase and Meyer, that this murder of the children was both superfluous and unwise, may be very true, but does not affect the historic truth of the event. The silence of heathen historians respecting it is wholly unimportant. Judea did not hold so high a place in their estimation that they should trouble themselves about its internal history, so little intelligible to a stranger. Herod's name is occasionally mentioned by them in connection with Roman matters, and there is in one a brief allusion to the trial and death of his sons, but nothing more. The well-known jest of Augustus, preserved by Macrobius,[1] might be cited if it could be shown that he had borrowed nothing from Christian sources. He says: "When Augustus had heard that among the children under two years old, *intra bimatum*, which Herod had commanded to be slain in Syria, his own son had been killed, he said it is better to be Herod's swine than his son." The expression, "two years old," points too directly to Matthew to allow us to suppose that it had an independent origin, although the words of Augustus may be literally given. Most agree that it is of no historical value.[2]

It would be strange indeed that while oriental history is full of such deeds of cruelty, which are believed upon the authority of a single writer, the statement of the Evangelist should be disbelieved, though confirmed by all that we know of the character of the chief actor, and of the history of the times. A like rule applied to general history would leave not a few of its pages empty.

[1] Sat., ii. 2.

[2] So Lardner, Meyer, Trench, Alford. See, however, Mill, 294; Ellicott, 78, note 2.

When directed to go into Egypt, Joseph was not told to what place he should return, (Matt. ii. 13,) nor afterward, when directed to return, was the place designated, (v. 20.) It is plain, however, that he did not design to return to Nazareth. He evidently regarded Bethlehem, the city of David, the proper place in which to rear the son of David. The province of Galilee was politically of little weight, and ecclesiastically it was despised; and Nazareth was one of its most inconsiderable villages, to say nothing of the bad name it seems to have borne. He naturally supposed that He who was of the tribe of Judah should dwell in the land of Judah, the most religious, most sacred part of Palestine; and, as the promised Messiah, should be brought as near as possible to the theocratic centre, where He might have frequent intercourse with the priests and rabbins, and be educated under the very shadow of the temple. Only through a special command of God, was he led to return with Jesus to Galilee; and that he made his abode in the obscure vale of Nazareth, can only be explained by the fact, of which Matthew is wholly silent, that this had been his earlier residence as related by Luke.

How diverse the opinions of harmonists have been, in regard to the order of events of the Lord's infancy, will appear by a comparison of their several arrangements. We give such as best present this diversity: EPIPHANIUS. Birth. Circumcision on 8th day. Presentation on 40th. Departure to Nazareth and sojourn there two years. Return to Bethlehem. Coming of Magi. Flight to Egypt and sojourn there three years. Return to Galilee. LIGHTFOOT. Birth. Circumcision on 8th day. Presentation, 40th day. Return to Bethlehem and sojourn there till two years of age. Coming of Magi. Flight into Egypt and sojourn there three or four months. Return to Galilee. CHEMNITIUS. Birth. Circumcision on 8th day. Coming of Magi just before the Presentation. Presentation on 40th day.

Flight into Egypt and sojourn there four years. Return to Galilee. SEPP. Birth. Circumcision on 8th day. Coming of Magi, 13th day. Presentation, 40th day. Flight into Egypt and sojourn there two years. Return to Galilee. FRIEDLIEB. Birth. Circumcision on 8th day. Coming of Magi on 13th. Flight into Egypt and sojourn there three or four months. Return to Judea. Presentation. Departure to Nazareth. WIESELER. Birth. Circumcision on 8th day. Presentation on 40th. Coming of Magi. Flight into Egypt and sojourn there two or three weeks. Return to Galilee.

In the village of Nazareth the Lord spent the larger part of his earthly life, and it therefore deserves our special notice. His residence here being brought by Matthew into direct connection with the Old Testament prophecy, the etymology of the name has been much discussed.[1] By many it is derived from Netser, the Hebrew for sprout, or twig, either because of so many thickets upon the adjoining hills, or because the village itself was small and feeble, like a tender twig.[2] So Jesus is called (Isaiah xi. 1) a Branch. Others derive it from Notser, that which guards or keeps; hence Nazareth, the protecting city.[3] Others still derive it from Nezer, to separate.[4] Jerome interpreted it as meaning a flower. *Ibimus ad Nazareth, et juxta interpretationem nominis ejus, florem videbimus Galilæ;* referring, as would appear from his language elsewhere, to Jesus as the Branch, or Flower from the roots of Jesse. It is noticeable that travellers speak of the great quantity of flowers now seen there.[5] The present name in Arabic is En Nâsirah.

Nazareth lies in a small valley a little north of the great

1 See Meyer in loco. 2 Winer, ii. 142; Hengst, Christology, ii. 109.
3 See Riggenbach, Stud. u. Krit, 1855.
4 Lightfoot and Bengel in loco.
5 Stanley, 359. The subject is discussed by Mill, 335.

plain of Esdraelon, from which it is reached by very rocky and precipitous paths. Its elevation above the plain is estimated to be from 300 to 350 feet. Bonar (398) speaks of the main road "as little better than a succession of rocky slopes or ledges, rugged with holes and stones. Yet this was the old road to Nazareth. There could be no other from this side, so that one travelling from the south must have taken it." The valley runs northeast and southwest, and is about a mile long and a quarter of a mile broad. Around it rise many small hills of no great height, the highest being on the west or southwest. They are of limestone, and give to the scenery a grayish tint, and are covered thickly with shrubs and trees. "The white rocks all around Nazareth give it a peculiar aspect. It appears dry and tame, and this effect is increased by the trees being powdered over with dust during the summer season. The heat was very great, and the gleam from the rocks painful to the eye."[1] "The upper ridges of the hills were, as is usual in this worn-out land, gray and bare, but the lower slopes and dells and hollows were green, sprinkled not scantily with the olive, the fig, the prickly pear, and the karub; while in the gardens the usual oriental fruit trees showed themselves."[2]

The village itself lies on the western side of the valley upon the side of the hill. The houses are in general of stone, and more substantially built than most of the towns of the region, and from their whiteness it has been called the white city;[3] the streets or lanes are, however, narrow and filthy. Porter (ii. 359) speaks of it "as built on the side of the highest hill; on the north the side of the hill is steep, and where it joins the plain is seamed by three or four ravines, and on the lower declivities of the ridges between them stands the village of Nazareth. This therefore is 'the hill

[1] Mission of Inquiry, 306. [2] Bonar. [3] See Schwartz, 178.

whereon the city was built,' (Luke iv. 29.) The houses in some places seem to cling to the sides of the precipices, in others they nestle in glens, and in others again they stand boldly out overlooking the valley." The present number of inhabitants is variously estimated: by Robinson at 3,000, by Porter at 4,000, by Lynch, 5,000, by others much less.

Nazareth is not mentioned in the Old Testament, nor by Josephus, from which we may conclude that it was a place of no importance. Although so intimately connected with the life of Jesus, and therefore so prominent in the Gospels, it is not mentioned by any Christian writer prior to Eusebius in the 4th century, nor does it seem to have been visited by pilgrims till the sixth.[1] After this time it became one of the most famous among the holy places. In the 7th century two churches are mentioned, one on the site of Joseph's house, and the other on the site of the house where Gabriel appeared to Mary.[2] During the Crusades it was made the seat of a bishopric. It was destroyed about A. D. 1200, by the Saracens, and for 300 or 400 years seems to have been inhabited chiefly by Mohammedans, and very little visited by pilgrims.[3] One of the churches was rebuilt in 1620 by the Franciscans, who added to it a cloister. Nazareth was for some time, and is now, the seat of a Greek titular bishop.

All travellers agree in praising the extent and beauty of the prospect from the top of the hill northwest of Nazareth. It is surmounted by the tomb of a Mohammedan saint, and is about 400 or 500 feet above the valley.[4] To the north is seen the wide plain of el Buttauf, running from east to west, having Cana of Galilee upon its northern,

[1] Robinson, ii. 341.
[2] Arculf, Early Travels, 9.
[3] Early Travels, 46 and 298.
[4] So Robinson, ii. 333, note. Schubert makes it 700 or 800 feet above Nazareth.

and Sepphoris upon its southern border, and beyond it rise in parallel ridges the hills, one behind another, to the heights of Safed. To the northeast Hermon is seen, and eastward the ranges of Bashan beyond the Sea of Galilee, whilst Tabor lies between it and the sea. To the southeast stretch Little Hermon and Gilboa in parallel lines. On the south lies the great plain of Esdraelon, bounded southward by the hills of Samaria and the long line of Carmel. Over the broken ridges that join Carmel to Samaria, is seen the Mediterranean far to the southwest, and the eye following the summits westward reaches the high promontory where Carmel ends upon the shore; from this point is seen the unbroken expanse of water many miles to the north. This view is said by Porter (ii. 263) to be the richest, and perhaps also the most extensive, which one gets in all Palestine, and to surpass that from Tabor.[1]

That Nazareth, from some cause, had at the time when the Lord resided in it an evil name, appears plainly from John i. 46.[2] The objection of Nathanael was not merely that it was in Galilee, and that the Messiah could not come out of Galilee, (John vii. 41,) but he refers specially to Nazareth. Nor was it that it was a little village, for so was Bethlehem. The obvious import is, that Nazareth was in ill-repute throughout the province, and of this Nathanael, who was from Cana but a little way distant, was well aware. This is confirmed by the revengeful and cruel treatment of the Lord when he first preached to the inhabitants, (Luke iv. 28, 29.)

April 8, 761. A. D. 8.

From Nazareth, at the age of twelve, the Lord goes up for the first time to Jerusalem to keep the Passover. After the expiration of the feast He remained behind to converse — Luke ii. 41-52.

[1] See Robinson, ii. 336; Stanley, 357. [2] See Kitto, Life of Christ, 27.

with the doctors, and was found in the temple three days after by His parents. Returning to Nazareth, He dwelt there in retirement till the time came that He should enter upon His public work. LUKE ii. 41–52.

Supposing the Lord to have been born in seven hundred and forty-nine, the year when He went up with His parents to the Passover was seven hundred and sixty-one, and the feast began on the 8th April. His presence at the Passover at the age of twelve, was in accordance with Jewish custom. At that age the Jewish boys began to be instructed in the law, to be subject to the fasts, and to attend regularly the feasts, and were called the sons of the Law.[1] This, however, is called in question by Greswell, (i. 396,) who asserts that boys did not become subject to ordinances, till they had reached the age of fourteen years, and that the purpose for which Jesus was now taken up was not to celebrate the Passover, but to be "made a disciple of the Law, and to undergo a ceremony, something like to our confirmation." He sees in this the explanation of the Lord's presence in the midst of the doctors. It is not probable that up to this time Jesus had accompanied His parents to Jerusalem to any of the festivals. Of all that passed between Him and the Rabbis, a full account may be found in the Apocryphal Gospel of the Infancy.[2] It needs no proof that on this occasion He was not taking upon Himself the part of a teacher, nor asking questions for disputation, but was seeking to learn the truth from those who were appointed of God to be the teachers of the Law. Where He was sitting with the doctors is uncertain. Lightfoot, (in loco,) after discussing the point, says: "There is nothing absurd in it if we should suppose Christ gotten into the very Sanhedrim itself. Thither Joseph and His mother might come, and seeking Him, might find Him on the benches of the fathers of the coun-

[1] Meyer in loco; Sepp, ii. 172. [2] See Hofmann, 259.

cil for that time, they having found Him so capable both to propound questions and answer them."

The three days that elapsed before His parents found Jesus, may be thus computed: the first, that of their departure from Jerusalem; second, the day of their return; third, the day when He was found: or, if we exclude the day of departure—first, the day of their return; second, the day of search in Jerusalem; third, the day when He was found. Some, with much less probability, count three days from the day of their return. That He might very easily be separated from them without any culpable carelessness on their part, appears from the great multitudes that were present, and the confusion that would necessarily prevail at such a time. Tradition makes Beer or El Bireh to have been the place where His parents spent the first night, and where they missed their son. "The place where Christ was first missed by His parents is commonly shown at this day to travellers, by the name of Beer, but ten miles from the city."[1] As is well known, the first day's journey of a company of eastern travellers is always short. "On that day it is not customary to go more than six or eight miles, and the tents are pitched for the first night's encampment, almost within sight of the place from which the journey commences."[2] That, leaving Jerusalem in the afternoon with the crowd of Galilean pilgrims, Mary and Joseph should have lost sight of Jesus for three or four hours, and yet not have felt any alarm, supposing Him to have been somewhere in the company, presents no difficulty.[3]

How the eighteen years of the Lord's life passed at Nazareth were spent, we have no means of determining. The Evangelists have maintained upon this point entire silence. It is most probable that He was taught His father

[1] Lightfoot. [2] Hackett, Scrip. Ill., 12.

[3] As to the more distinguished Rabbis whom the Lord may have met at this time, see Sepp, ii. 178.

Joseph's trade, according to the settled custom of the Jews to bring up their sons to some trade or art.[1] This is very plainly taught in the question of the inhabitants of Nazareth, "Is not this the carpenter?" which, as Alford remarks, "signifies that the Lord had *actually worked* at the trade of His reputed father." Justin Martyr (100–150 A. D.) says that "Christ being regarded as a worker in wood, did make, while among men, ploughs and yokes, thus setting before them symbols of righteousness, and teaching an active life."[2] That this was His occupation seems to have been generally believed by the early fathers. Some in later times, thinking bodily labor derogatory to Him, made this time of retirement at Nazareth to have been spent in contemplation and prayer. The traditions that He made a journey to Persia to visit the Magi, or to Egypt to visit her sages, need no notice.[3]

It is an interesting inquiry, and one that may properly be considered here, Who constituted the household of Joseph and Mary at Nazareth? Was Jesus the only child in the family circle, or were there other children? and if there were others, in what relation did they stand to Him? Reference is several times made by the Evangelists to His brothers and sisters. (Matt. xii. 46–50; xiii. 55, 56; Mark iii. 31; vi. 3; Luke viii. 19; John ii. 12; vii. 3; Acts i. 14.) St. Paul refers to "the brethren of the Lord," (1 Cor. ix. 5;) and calls James "the Lord's brother," (Gal. i. 19.) Who are these? The answer to this question is confessedly one of the most difficult that meets us in the whole range of our inquiries. It has been in dispute from very early times, and opinions are as much at variance now as ever. All that can be attempted here is to set the matter in its most important bearings fairly before the reader.

Let us first sum up what we know from the New Testa-

[1] See Lightfoot on Mark vi. 3.

[2] See contra Mosheim, Com., i. 85.

[3] See Hofmann, 264.

ment of these brothers and sisters of the Lord. The names of the former are given by Matthew xiii. 55, and by Mark vi. 3, as James, Joses, Simon, and Judas.[1] Both Evangelists mention His sisters, but neither their number nor names are given. From the language of the Nazarenes, (Matt. xiii. 56,) "His sisters, are they not all with us?" there must have been at least two, who were probably married and resident at Nazareth. His brethren are spoken of as going with him to Capernaum, (John ii. 12,) and afterward appear in company with His mother again in the same city, (Matt. xii. 46; see also John vii. 3–10.)

In all these references to the Lord's brethren, several things are noticeable: first, that they are always called brothers and sisters, *αδελφοι* and *αδελφαι*, not cousins or kinsmen, *ανεψιοι* or *συγγενεις*; second, that they are called always His brothers and His sisters, not sons or daughters of Mary; third, that they always appear in connection with Mary, as if her children and under her direction.

We may thus classify the various theories respecting them: First, that which makes them to have been the children of Joseph by a former marriage, or by adoption, and so Christ's brothers and sisters. Second, that which makes them to have been children of a sister of His mother, and so His cousins-german. Some make them His cousins by His father's as well as His mother's side. Third, that which makes them to have been His own brothers and sisters, the children of Joseph and Mary. Each of these theories will be briefly examined.

First, that they were children of Joseph by a former marriage or by adoption. That Joseph at the time of his marriage to Mary was a widower, is often and expressly said in the Apocryphal Gospels. In the "History of Jo-

[1] Tischendorf has in Matthew Joseph for Joses; in Mark Ιωσητος: so Alford. As to the bearing of this diversity of readings, see Wieseler, Stud. u. Krit, 1842, p. 75.

seph," ch. ii., the names of his children by his first wife are given: Judas, Justus, Jacobus, and Simon; Assia and Lydia. In the "Gospel of James," ch. ix., Joseph says, "I am an old man, and I have sons." According to Hofmann,[1] it is generally agreed that he had but four sons, but their names are variously given. There is no general agreement as to the names, or number of the daughters.[2] It is said by Thiersch[3] that this was the only tradition respecting the parentage of these brothers and sisters of the Lord that existed during the second and third centuries, and was the ruling one till the time of Jerome. This father, writing against Helvidius, first gave currency to the view that they were cousins of the Lord, and hence is called by Baronius *fortissimus adstipulator, vel potius auctor* of this theory.[4] The object of Jerome, in denying that they were the children of Joseph, was to exalt celibacy. Not only had Mary continued all her married life a virgin, but Joseph also; and hence his former marriage must be denied, and another parentage given his reputed children. In the Latin Church the view of Jerome, supported by Augustine, became, and continues to be, the ruling one; but in the Greek Church, the old tradition still continues current.[5]

This theory, that makes them the children of Joseph by a former marriage, has, in itself, nothing intrinsically improbable; though regarded by some as a mere fiction, devised to save Mary's virginity.[6] If Joseph had had children by an earlier wife, these would properly be the Lord's brothers and sisters, and their presence with His mother would be readily explained. That they are not called Joseph's children, might be accounted for by his death before they appear in the gospel narrative. But there are still very weighty objections. If children by a former marriage,

1 Leben Jesu, 4.
2 See Thilo, Codex Apoc., i. 363.
3 Versuch., 361 and 431.
4 See Pearson on the Creed, art. iii.
5 See Schaff, die Brüder des Herrn., 80; Hofmann, Leben Jesu, 4.
6 So Stier, Greswell.

they must have been born before Jesus, and some of them been much older, and this seems inconsistent with their relations to him, and their continued attendance upon Mary. If also He was not the eldest, but youngest son of Joseph, how could He be called the legal heir to the throne? Nor can it be shown that the tradition, however ancient, was ever universally received.

There is a modification of this view, which makes the Lord's brethren to have been the adopted children of Joseph. Joseph had a brother, Clopas, or Alpheus,[1] who married a certain Mary, not the sister of the Lord's mother, and had by her four sons and some daughters. Clopas dying, Joseph took these children to his own house, and became their father. Thus by birth they were the legal cousins of Jesus, children of His father's brother, and now become His brothers and sisters by their adoption. Mary, their mother, came with them, and was an inmate of Joseph's house, and a member of the family. Thus her presence at the cross and sepulchre finds a ready explanation, (Matt. xxvii. 56 and 61.) As the adopted sons of Joseph they could well be called by the Evangelists the Lord's brethren. Still, being bound by no ties of blood to Mary, His mother, and having a mother of their own, He could upon the cross commend her to the care of John, who was her nephew, the son of Salome, her sister.[2] According to Lichtenstein, 124, the two brothers, Joseph and Clopas, married two sisters, both named Mary. Clopas dying, Joseph took his wife Mary and her children into his family.' Thus, the children were the Lord's cousins, both on His mother's and father's side, and brothers and sisters by adoption.

This explanation, though not without its advantages, rests upon no certain historic basis. There may be no good reason to question the assertion of Hegesippus,[3] that Clopas

[1] Eusebius, iii. 11. [2] So Lange, in Herzog, vi. 409.
[3] In Eusebius, iii. 11.

was the brother of Joseph, though it does not appear whether he uses the term brother strictly, or as meaning that the two married sisters. And it may also be admitted that Alpheus and Clopas are one and the same person. But there is no proof of the early death of Alpheus, nor that Joseph adopted his children; and the absence of all allusion in the Evangelists to Mary, the real mother of these children, when they are collectively mentioned, is very surprising.

A tradition that makes Joseph to have married the wife of his brother Alpheus, according to the law regulating Levirate marriages, to raise up seed to his brother, and that the fruit of this marriage was four sons and two daughters, needs no confutation.[1]

Second, that these brothers and sisters of the Lord were His cousins, the children of Alpheus and Mary. This view rests upon the supposition that His mother and Mary, wife of Alpheus, were sisters. Of this Mary we have little knowledge. It is generally supposed that she stood in the relation of wife to Alpheus, though some have questioned it.[2] She is also spoken of as mother of James the Less, and of Joses, (Matt. xxvii. 56; Mark xv. 40.) Was she also sister to Mary, mother of the Lord? This has been generally inferred from John xix. 25: "Now there stood by the cross of Jesus, His mother, and His mother's sister, Mary, wife of Clopas, and Mary Magdalene." But are three or four persons mentioned here? Many maintain that there are four, the sister of the Lord's mother being a distinct person from the wife of Clopas.[3] In favor of this construction is the fact that two sisters would otherwise have the same name.[4]

[1] Schaff, 13; Greswell, ii. 113.

[2] See John xix. 25. *Μαρια η του Κλωπα*, which some understand to mean daughter of Clopas. Winer, ii. 58.

[3] So Meyer, Alford, Wieseler, Lange, Tischendorf, Da Costa.

[4] See, on the other side, Ebrard, 555, note 23; Stier, vii. 467; Olshausen and Luthardt, in loco.

In this uncertainty respecting the relationship of Mary, wife of Clopas, to the Lord's mother, it cannot be positively affirmed that her children were His cousins, or relatives at all. If, however, this be admitted, the question remains, can these sons of Alpheus and Mary be identified with His brothers? The names of the former were James and Joses. Two of the latter have the same names. That James, son of Alpheus, was an apostle is expressly said. (Matt. x. 3, and elsewhere.) Of Joses we know nothing.[1] It is affirmed that beside Joses, Alpheus and Mary had another son, named Jude or Judas. In the list of the apostles as given by Luke, (vi. 16; Acts i. 13,) a Judas is mentioned as standing in some relation, not defined, to a James; Ιουδας Ιακωβου, Judas of James. Many suppose the fraternal relation to be meant, as in our version, Judas brother of James.[2] Others suppose the paternal relation, Judas son of James.[3] This latter construction finds some confirmation in the fact that Judas is not anywhere brought into relationship to Alpheus and Mary. If the latter was really his mother, why should not his name be mentioned in connection with that of his brother James, both being apostles? She is called the mother of James and Joses, not of James and Judas. It does not then appear at all certain that Alpheus and Mary had more than two sons, James and Joses, of whom the former was an apostle. The language in the epistle of Jude, where the writer speaks of himself as "brother of James," decides nothing till we have learned whether he is the same person as the apostle Judas. The inference from verse 17 that he was not an apostle, is not conclusive.

Supposing it, however, to be shown that Jesus had three cousins german, James, Judas, and Joses, of whom

[1] Sepp, ii. 248, would identify him with Barsabas, Acts i. 23, but without a particle of evidence.

[2] So Norton, Alford.

[3] Meyer, Oosterzee, Ewald.

the first two were apostles, can what is said of the Lord's brethren by the Evangelists be applied to them? That they should be uniformly called His brothers, never His cousins, is, as has been already observed, remarkable, but not decisive. Still more remarkable is it that they never appear in connection with their own mother, but always with His mother, as if her constant companions, (John ii. 12; Matt. xii. 46.) A stronger objection to their identity is found in the fact that the Lord's brothers are spoken of as not believing in Him till the end of His ministry, or perhaps, till after His resurrection, while two of the sons of Alpheus and Mary were early called into the ranks of the apostles. It is difficult to believe that His brethren, who came with His mother desiring to speak with Him, (Matt. xii. 46; Luke viii. 19,) could have been at that time apostles, and so His constant attendants. Their language at a later period, as given by John, (vii. 3, 4,) when they desired him to go up to Jerusalem, and the express testimony of the Evangelist, (v. 5,) for "neither did His brethren believe on Him," seem most plainly to disprove their apostleship. Moreover, a line of distinction between His disciples and apostles, and His brethren, is kept up in the evangelical narratives, from the beginning of His ministry till its close, and nowhere appears more marked than after His ascension, (Acts i. 13–14.) It is also recognized by St. Paul many years later, (1 Cor. ix. 5.)

Upon the other hand, much stress is placed by many upon the words of Paul, (Gal. i. 19,) "But other of the apostles saw I none, save James, the Lord's brother."[1] From these words it is inferred that James, the Lord's brother, was an apostle and must have been James the son of Alpheus, as it is agreed that James the son of Zebedee could

[1] See also ii. 9, where James, Cephas, and John are spoken of as pillars. Wieseler asserts that the James of ch. i. is the Lord's brother, the James of ch. ii. the son of Alpheus. Most, however, maintain that the same person is meant in both.

not be meant. It follows that the term brother is equivalent to cousin, and thus that by the Lord's brethren we are to understand His cousins, the sons of Alpheus and Mary.

The value of this argument rests upon the grammatical construction of St. Paul's words. Does he mean to designate James as an apostle, or, on the contrary, to distinguish him from the apostles? His language is by no means clear. It may be read, "I saw none other of the apostles, but only (I saw) James, the Lord's brother." [1] In this way, James is brought into direct contrast with the apostles. But the other construction, that identifies James as an apostle, in the stricter or wider sense, has much in its favor.[2] It finds some confirmation in Acts ix. 27, where mention is made of "apostles," with seeming reference to Peter and James. His apostleship appears also to be proved by the mention of his name (ii. 9) before those of Cephas and John, who were undeniably the leading apostles among the Twelve, for could such a preëminence be given to any one not an apostle?

It is in this high position given to James, the brother of our Lord, that we find our strongest argument for his identification with the apostle James, the son of Alpheus. There is little doubt that he is the same person mentioned, (Acts xii. 17, xv. 13, xxi. 18,) and the author of the epistle bearing his name. From all the Evangelists say of him, it is plain that he was a man very conspicuous in the Church, and of great influence and authority. This, however, is greatly exaggerated by some, who make him the superior of Peter.[3] Some would explain the eminence ascribed to

[1] See Winer, Grammatik, 557. Wieseler, Stud. u. Krit., 1842, 92, who cites Fritzsche: alium apostolum non vidi, sed (ει μη) vidi Jacobum, fratrem Domini. Schaff, 17; Thiersch, Kirchen Gesch., 80; Riggenbach, 296. Compare Rev. xxi. 27; Matt. xii. 4; Luke iv. 26–7. Very early, Victorinus, in his commentary, in loco, cited by Mill, 252, said: "Paul disclaims James as an apostle, saying that he saw no other apostle beside Peter, but only James."

[2] See Ellicott, commentary, in loco, who refers to 1 Cor. i. 14.

[3] So Fitch, *The Lord's Brother*, New York, 1858, who, although he denies him to be one of the Twelve, exalts him to the rank of a Pope, whose word is

him, and the importance attached to his opinion in all points respecting the observance of the law by the Gentiles, to the peculiar position which he occupied as the first bishop and head of the mother and central church at Jerusalem, identifying him with James the Just, of whom Eusebius speaks, (ii. 1 and 23,) "He was the first who received the episcopate of the church at Jerusalem." It is not, then, necessary to suppose him to have been an apostle, or to have exercised any special apostolic functions, in order to explain why he should be placed upon an apparent equality with the apostles. As the Lord's brother, a more than ordinary degree of respect would naturally be paid him, and to him, when alone, Jesus appeared after His resurrection, as he had done to Peter, (1 Cor. xv. 7.) Rigidly observant himself of the law, and a strenuous defender of the Mosaic institutions, his counsels had great weight when the relations of the circumcision and the uncircumcision were in question.[1]

Into a more particular consideration of this point it would be foreign to our purpose to enter. We conclude that James, the Lord's brother, was not necessarily an apostle and bishop, but may have been simply bishop, and therefore is not to be identified with James the son of Alpheus. If, then, these were distinct persons, the former must be identified with that James mentioned with Joses, Simon, and Judas, (Matt. xiii. 55,) as one of Christ's brethren. If so, there can be little doubt that Judas, the author of the Epistle, who calls himself brother of James, was also one of these four brethren, and not a son of Alpheus and Mary.

If then, for the reasons now given, the theory that these brethren of the Lord were his cousins german, the children of Alpheus and Mary, be rejected, we come to the third

final: "Paul did not hesitate to speak his mind to Peter; but however much Paul or Peter may differ from James, and they be in the right, when once James has spoken, never is there a word in reply."

[1] See Thiersch, Kirchen Gesch., 80; Schaff, 61.

explanation—that these were the sons and daughters of Joseph and Mary, and His own brothers and sisters. But here we meet dogmatic difficulties. It is an article of faith with the Roman and Greek Churches that Mary had no children beside the Lord, and the same opinion rules in the Lutheran symbols. In the Helvetic confession Jesus is spoken of as *natus ex Maria, semper virgine.* A large number of Protestant writers in all the religious bodies strongly maintain the perpetual virginity. Pearson[1] says that the Church of God in all ages has maintained that she continued in the same virginity.[2] It has been well remarked by Alexander (on Mark vi. 3) "that multitudes of Protestant divines and others, independently of all creeds and confessions, have believed, or rather felt, that the selection of a woman to be the mother of the Lord carries with it, as a necessary implication, that no other could sustain the same relation to her; and that the selection of a virgin still more necessarily implied that she was to continue so. After all, it is not so much a matter of reason or of faith as of taste and sensibility; but these exert a potent influence on all interpretation, and the same repugnance, whether rational or merely sentimental, which led fathers and reformers to deny that Christ had brothers in the ordinary sense, is likely to produce the same effect on multitudes forever, or until the question has received some unequivocal solution."

The early belief in the perpetual virginity of Mary may perhaps be explained as springing in part from a desire to separate Christ, as widely as possible, from other men. He had no brothers or sisters; His mother had no other child. Thus, not only in His essential personality, but in the outward circumstances of His life, a broad line of distinction was to be drawn between Him and all beside. To suppose that He had brothers according to the flesh was to degrade Him by bringing Him into too close relationship with weak

[1] Upon the Creed, art. iii. [2] So Mill, 274.

and sinful men. The special honor paid to Him would naturally cause high honor to be paid to his mother. To this was added the admiration of celibacy springing from Gnostic principles, that began very early to prevail. Both His parents were thought to be honored by being presented to the world as virgins. Occasionally from time to time, and especially for a few years past, the tendency has manifested itself to bring more distinctly forward the humanity of Christ, and to give prominence to the truth expressed by the Apostle, (Heb. ii. 11,) "For both he that sanctifieth and they who are sanctified are all of one." Not to remove Him from the pale of human sympathies, but to bring Him in as many points as possible into contact with the experiences of human life, has seemed to many best to correspond to the historical statements of the Gospel, and the doctrinal statements of the Epistles. Hence perhaps there is now felt less reluctance to regard Him as having been in the truest sense a member of the family, having brothers and sisters bound to him by ties of blood, and as a partaker of the common lot in all the relationships of life which were possible to Him, that thus "He might be touched with a feeling of our infirmities." [1]

Leaving all theological considerations on one side, the more natural and obvious interpretation of the language of the Evangelists leads to the belief that the Lord's brothers and sisters were such in the ordinary meaning of the words. In the case of another no hesitation could be felt. Not only are they always called His brothers, but are always found in company with His mother. They are, indeed, not called her sons, but this is explainable from the fact that they are spoken of only in their relations to Him, who everywhere in the Gospel is the one great central figure.

The expression in Matt. i. 25, "And knew her not till

[1] See Herder, quoted in Schaff, 30, note.

she had brought forth her first-born son,"[1] certainly implies that afterward they lived together as husband and wife. Still this is not decisive. Alexander, (in loco,) after referring to some examples of the use of "till" in other parts of the Scriptures, observes: "These examples are sufficient to establish the position that the inference in question from the use of the word *till*, however natural, is not conclusive; or, in other words, that this expression cannot prove the fact of subsequent cohabitation in the face of cogent reasons for disputing it." Nor does the term "first-born" (Luke ii. 7) show that other children were subsequently born. As primogeniture brought with it under the law certain privileges, the term "first-born" acquired a technical meaning, and was applied to all who had a right to those privileges, without regard to the fact that they were, or were not, the only children of their parents.

The existence of two households having so many names in common as those of Joseph and Mary, and Alpheus and Mary, are supposed to have had, is regarded by some as highly improbable. As we have seen, however, it is not certain that Mary and Alpheus had but two sons, James and Joses; and that these two very common names should be found among the Lord's brethren is not at least more surprising than that, according to the view that makes them His cousins, the Lord's mother and her sister should both have the name of Mary.[2] Others regard it as a decisive proof that Mary had no other son, that Jesus upon the cross should have commended her to the care of John, (John xix. 26–27.) But why, if James and Judas were apostles and His cousins, sons of her sister and long inmates of her family, and it was a question of kinship, did he not commend her to their care? If His brethren were at this

[1] Tischendorf omits "first-born;" Alford retains it.

[2] According to Smith's Bib. Dict., i. 231, Josephus mentions 21 Simons, 17 Joses, and 16 Judes.

time, as we may suppose, unbelieving, and thus in a most vital point without sympathy with her, we can well understand why He should give John, the disciple whom He loved, to be her son, not so much to supply her mere bodily needs, as to comfort and strengthen her in the peculiar trials through which she would be immediately called to pass.

It is evident from this brief survey of the chief opinions respecting the Lord's brethren and their relations to Jesus, that the data for a very positive judgment are wanting.[1] There can be no doubt that the very general, not universal, opinion in the church, has been in favor of the perpetual virginity of Mary. In regard to the Lord's brethren, there were some in very early times who thought them the children of Joseph and Mary, but most thought them to be either His cousins, or the children of Joseph. It is difficult to tell which of the latter two opinions is the elder, or best supported by tradition. The words of Calvin on Matt. i. 25, deserve to be kept in mind: *Certe nemo unquam hac de re questionem movebit nisi curiosus; nemo vero pertinaciter insistet nisi contentiosus rixator.*

[1] Of the more recent writers, many affirm that they were the children of Joseph and Mary, and His own brothers and sisters. So Neander, Greswell, Wieseler, Alford, Stier, Schaff, Meyer, Winer, Ewald, Lechler, Owen; contra, Lange, Olshausen, Lichtenstein, Friedlieb, Norton, Sepp, Hug, Thiersch, Alexander, Mill, Ellicott. See upon the subject, Das Verhältniss des Jacobus Bruders des Herrn zu Jacobus Alphäi, von Philipp Schaf. Berlin, 1842. Wieseler in Stud. u. Krit, 1842. Lange in Herzog, vi. 409; Lichtenstein, 100; Alford on Matt. xiii. 55; Winer, i. 525; Smith, Bib. Dict., i. 231 and 920; Mill, Mythical Interpretation, 219.

PART II.

FROM THE BAPTISM TO THE BEGINNING OF THE MINISTRY IN GALILEE; OR FROM JANUARY, 780, TO APRIL, 781. 27, 28 A. D.

The Divisions of the Lord's Ministry.

In order to understand the scope of the Lord's ministry in its external aspects, as narrated by the Evangelists, it is necessary to keep in mind certain great facts that gave it form and character. We shall thus be prepared to understand the significance of particular events, and to assign them their proper places in the history.

First, The Lord came to a nation in covenant with God—His elect people. He had chosen for them a land in which they might dwell apart from the nations, and in a wonderful manner had given them possession of it. He had given them laws and institutions, which, rightly used, should secure their highest national well-being. He had established His temple in their chief city, in which He revealed Himself in the Visible Glory, and which was appointed to be "a house of prayer for all nations." How highly they had been honored and blessed of God is seen from His words (Exod. xix. 5–6): "If ye will obey my voice indeed, and keep my Covenant, then ye shall be to me a peculiar treasure above all people, and ye shall be unto me a kingdom of priests and a holy nation." And from among them should the Great Deliverer, the Seed of the woman, come. The Messiah should reign at Jerusalem, and from thence establish justice and judgment throughout the earth. He was to be of the tribe of Judah, of the family of David, and His birth-place at Bethlehem; and many other things respecting Him had been foretold by the prophets.

To a people thus in covenant with God, and awaiting the Messiah, Christ came. There was a general expectation that He was about to come, and a general desire for His coming. The appearing of the Baptist, and his message, gave a new impulse to the common feeling, and doubtless in the minds of many changed what had been but an indefinite expectation into an assured hope. But how should the nation discern the Messiah when He came? Should there be such wonderful signs attending His birth that it should at once be known? Or should His infancy and youth be passed in obscurity? How should His public career begin? what His acts as Messiah? Here was a large field for differences of opinion among the people, according to differences in spiritual character and discernment. But the great part of the nation, including most of the ecclesiastical rulers and teachers, seems to have had no doubt that He was to appear, not primarily as a religious reformer, but as a political leader and warrior, and that one of His first Messianic acts would be to cast off the Roman yoke and set the nation free. This done, He would proceed to restore the Mosaic institutions to their primitive purity, and fulfil the prediction that "out of Zion should go forth the law, and the word of the Lord from Jerusalem."

It is apparent that, thus mistaking the character and work of the Messiah, the very intensity of their desire for His coming would but the more certainly insure His rejection. They had formed conceptions of Him which Jesus could not realize. Their ideal Christ was not the Christ of the prophets. To be at once received by them, Jesus must act in a manner corresponding to their preconceived opinions, and thus fulfil their expectations. But this He could not do, since these expectations were based upon misconceptions of their own moral needs, and of God's purpose. They felt deeply their political servitude, but were unconscious of the spiritual bondage into which they had fallen. They knew not how utterly unprepared they were for the coming of their Deliverer. Hence it was, that Jesus could not openly assume the name of Messiah, because it had become the exponent of so many false hopes, and would have gathered around Him a body of followers, moved more by political than spiritual impulses.

A *second* fact to be noted is, the wish and will of God that the Jews should receive His Son. Here, indeed, we meet the same problem that we meet everywhere in human history—the foreknowledge and purpose of God, and the freedom and responsibility of man. According to the eternal purpose of God, Christ was "the Lamb slain from the foundation of the world," and without the shedding of blood is no remission of sin. "Known unto God are all His works from the beginning of the world." But the Jews knew not of this purpose, although, as we now see, it was not dimly intimated in their sacrificial rites. The Jews knew not that they should crucify their Messiah. They had not learned this from their prophets. The Baptist said nothing of His death; Jesus Himself, till near the close of His ministry, said nothing of it; the Apostles, down to the week of His Passion, did not comprehend it. When, therefore, Jesus presented Himself to the nation as the Messiah, it acted without knowledge of the secret counsel of God, and with entire freedom. He desired that they should receive Him. All that God had done for them from the days of Abraham was with the intent that they might be a people ready for the Lord at His coming. The end of all the institutions He gave them was so to develop faith and holiness in them that they should discern and receive His Son. And Jesus during His ministry gave them every possible proof of His divine character, and reproved and warned and beseeched them, that He might save them from the guilt of His rejection; yet all in vain. "He came unto His own, and His own received Him not." How touching are His farewell words to Jerusalem, (Matt. xxiii. 37): "How often would I have gathered thy children together, even as a hen gathereth her chickens under her wings, and ye would not."

Still a *third* fact is, that as the covenant of God with the Jews was a national one, so must also Christ's acceptance or rejection be. From the beginning of their history God had dealt with the people as a corporate body. Their blessings were national blessings, their punishments national punishments. All their institutions were so devised as to deepen the feeling of national unity: one high priest, one temple, one altar. What was done by the heads of the nation was regarded as the act of all, and involving common responsibility. Only in this way could the purpose of God in their election to be His peculiar people, be carried out. Hence, in this greatest and highest act, the acceptance or rejection of His Son, the act must be a national one. It must be done in the name of the whole people by those who acted as their rightful representatives. If those who sat in Moses' seat should discern and receive Him, the way for the further prosecution of His work was at once opened, and under His Divine instruction the nation might be purified for the glorious kingdom, so often sung by the psalmist and foretold by the prophets. But if, on the other hand, He was rejected by the nation, acting through its lawfully constituted heads, this national crime must be followed by national destruction. A few might be saved amid the general overthrow, but the people, as such, could be no more the holy and elect of God.

It was under the conditions imposed by these great historic facts that the Lord began His ministry among the Jews. He came to a people in covenant with God, a people that God desired to save, and that must as a people, accept or reject Him. All the details that are given us of that ministry by the Evangelists must therefore be viewed in the light of these facts.

The first event that meets us in the evangelic narrative, is the mission of John the Baptist, the forerunner of the Messiah. His work was threefold. First, he was to announce that the kingdom of God was at hand, and the Messiah about to appear. In this announcement he especially displayed his prophetic character. Second, he was to bring the nation to repentance, and "make ready a people prepared for the Lord." Here he especially manifested himself as a preacher of righteousness. Of this righteousness the law was the standard, and by the law must the nation be judged. Hence, John was a preacher of the law. The burden of his message was, "Repent, for the kingdom of God is at hand." As a wicked, disobedient people, they were not ready for that kingdom. True, they were "Abraham's children," and "sons of the kingdom," but this did not suffice. They had broken the Holy Covenant, they had not hearkened to God's voice, and He had punished them terribly in His anger. The Baptist came to awaken them to a sense of their guilt, to make them see how by their unbelief and sin they had frustrated the grace of God; and thus move them to repentance. Comparing the promises of God with their fulfilment, they might see how little He had been able to bestow upon them, how little they had answered to the end for which He chose them. How glorious the promises, how melancholy the history! Their national independence was gone; the covenant with the house of David was suspended, and that royal family had sunk into obscurity. Their high priest was appointed by the Roman governor for political ends, and was a mere tool in his hands; the priesthood, as a body, was venal and proud; the voice of prophecy had long been unheard, and for the teachings of inspiration were substituted the sophisms and wranglings of the Rabbis; the law was made, in many of its vital points, of none effect by traditions; the nation was divided into contending sects; a large party, and that comprising some of the most rich, able, and influential, were infidels, open or secret; some, aspiring after a higher piety than the observance of the law could give, wholly ceased to observe it, and withdrew into the wilderness to follow some self-devised ascetic practices; still more were bigots in their reverence for the letter of the law, but wholly ignorant of its spirit, and bitter and intolerant toward all whom they had the power to oppress. The people at large still continued to glory in their theocratic institutions, in their temple, in their priesthood, and deemed themselves the only true worshippers of God in the world. They were unmindful that almost every thing that had constituted the peculiar glory of the theocracy was lost by sin; that the Visible Glory that dwelt between the cherubim had departed, that there was no more response by the Urim and Thummim, that the ark, with its attendant memorials, was no more to be found in the Holy of Holies, that all those supernatural interpositions that had marked their early history had ceased; in short, that the whole nation "was turned aside like a deceitful bow."

To the anointed eye of the Baptist, the unpreparedness of the nation for the Messiah was apparent. He saw how in it was fulfilled the language of Isaiah: "The whole head is sick, and the whole heart faint. From the sole of the foot even unto the head, there is no soundness in it, but wounds, and bruises, and putrefying sores;" and he would, if it were possible, awake the people to a sense of their real spiritual condition. Unless this were done, they could not receive the Messiah, and His coming could be only to their condemnation and destruction. Deliverance was possible only when, like their fathers in Egypt, they became conscious of their bondage, and began to sigh and cry for deliverance, (Exod. ii. 23.) And as the elders of the people gathered themselves together unto Moses and coöperated with him, so must now the priests and Levites, and all who, by God's appointment, held any office among the people, be co-workers with Jesus. In this way only was it possible that the promises of the covenant could take effect, and the predictions of the prophets be fulfilled.

To awaken in the hearts of the Jews a deeper sense of their sins, and of the need of cleansing, John established the rite of baptism in the Jordan. He taught that this rite was only preparatory, a baptism of repentance, and that the higher baptism of the Spirit they must still receive at the hands of the Messiah Himself, who was speedily to come. All whom he baptized came confessing their sins. Thus, the extent of his baptism was an index how general the repentance of the people, and consequently how general the preparation for the Messiah.

Third, John was to point out the Messiah personally to the nation, when He should appear. This was the culminating point of his ministry, and would naturally come at the close of the preparatory work.

Let us now survey for a moment the Baptist's ministry as narrated by the Evangelists, and see how far its purpose was accomplished. First, he aroused general attention to the fact that the Messiah was at hand. Second, his preaching brought great numbers to repentance. Multitudes from every part of the land came to his baptism. But of these it is probable that many did not understand the significance of the rite, or truly repent of their sins. Perhaps with comparatively few was the baptism with water a true preparation for the baptism with the Holy Ghost. And it is to be specially noted, that those thus coming to John to be baptized were mostly, if not exclusively, of the common people, and not of the priests, or Levites, or members of the hierarchical party. Many of the Pharisees and Sadducees came to be spectators of the rite, but only with hostile intent; or if some received baptism at his hands, we find few or no traces of them in the subsequent history, (Matt. iii. 7; Luke vii. 29–30.) In the hearts of those who sat in Moses' seat, the spiritual rulers and guides of the nation, no permanent sense of sin was awakened, and they could not submit to a baptism of which they felt no need. To all his exhortations they had the ready, and, as they deemed, sufficient reply, "We have Abraham to our father." Thus John did not effect national repentance. The highest proof of this is seen in the deputation that was sent him from Jerusalem to ask him who he was, and by what authority he acted, (John i. 19–27.) It is plain from the narrative that he was wholly unable to satisfy the Jewish leaders that he was divinely commissioned, or that his baptism had any validity. It followed of course, that they paid no heed to his prophetic or personal testimony to the Messiah.

As his last official act, he pointed out Jesus in person to the nation as the Messiah. He whom he had foretold was come. Henceforth they must see and hear Him.

Turning now to the ministry of the Lord, let us consider it in its relations to that of the Baptist, and as under those historic conditions that have been already mentioned. His first work was to present Himself to the Jews as their Messiah, in whom the covenants of God with Abraham and David should find their fulfilment, all the predictions of the prophets be accomplished, and for whom the Baptist had prepared the way. Of His Messiahship He must give proof, first and chiefly, by His words, which should show Him to be the Truth of God; and second, by His works, which should show Him to be the Power of God. All the scriptural expectations created by the announcement of John were to be realized in Him. Thus, presenting Himself to the people, and especially to its ecclesiastical rulers, and having shown by the evidence of His own works and words, corresponding to the testimony of the Baptist, that He was the Messiah, He must await the action of the nation.

The obstacles that stood in the way of His acceptance are obvious. The nation was morally unprepared for Him. Whilst so many were looking for Him, few were looking for Him in such a guise. To say nothing of the obscurity in which He had hitherto lived, and of His supposed birth at Nazareth, His present conduct in no degree corresponded to their expectations. His wisdom and eloquence could not be questioned, nor the fact that He wrought miracles; but all this did not suffice. He might be a teacher sent from God, or a prophet, but the Messiah must be much more than this. He might perhaps be, as John declared himself to be, a forerunner of the Messiah. A few, mostly or wholly from the ranks of John's disciples, at once received Him as the Messiah, but, as afterward appeared, with most imperfect conceptions of His person and work; the people at large, and its rulers, discerned Him not. It is plain, from the account of Nicodemus, (John iii. 1–2,) that the presentation of Himself at Jerusalem, and His words and works there, had called forth no response from the ecclesiastical leaders. Even now their incredulity was shown in a demand for a sign, which He would not give.

Whatever hostility had manifested itself at this His first public appearing in Jerusalem, still there was hope that it might be removed by greater knowledge of His character and work. The Lord, therefore, still remaining in the province of Judea, and thus directly under the eyes of the priests, begins the work of baptizing. Many gather around Him, and receive baptism at the hands of His disciples. But it does not appear that any of the Pharisees, or of the higher and more influential classes, were among them, and still less any of the rulers. After a summer thus spent, His enemies endeavoring to sow dissensions between His disciples and those of John, He gives up His baptismal work, and retires into Galilee. Near a year had now passed since He had been pointed out as the Messiah to the nation, and yet very few had received Him as such, and all who bore rule, or certainly most of them, manifested an increasing hostility. He found no general, much less a national reception.

After a few weeks spent in Galilee, Jesus goes up the second time to Jerusalem to a feast, and heals the impotent man at the pool of Bethesda, (John v.) The charge is at once made against Him that He had broken the Sabbath by this work of healing, and His defence, based upon His Divine Sonship, so offended the ruling party that His life was in danger. This open manifestation of hostility marks the first great turning-point in the Lord's ministry. It was now apparent that the rulers at Jerusalem would neither listen to His words, nor be convinced by His works. So far from recognizing in Him the Messiah, His acts were violations of the law, and His defence blasphemy. Henceforth they stood to Him in an attitude of avowed hostility, and waited only for a sufficient pretext to arrest Him and put Him to death. How far in this they represented the sentiment of the people at large, it is impossible for us to say, but it appears from the subsequent history, that although many came to Christ's baptism, yet that He had not at any time a large body of adherents in Judea. So far as appears, the people acquiesced in the decision of their rulers.

Forced to flee from Jerusalem, the Lord goes into Galilee. And now the second stage of His ministry begins. His work in Galilee seems to have had a twofold purpose. It was first directed to the gathering of disciples, such as hearing His words felt their truth, and seeing His works recognized in them a Divine power. To Him, the true Light, all who loved the light would come. Thus He gathered around Him the most receptive, the most spiritually minded from every rank and class, and teaching them, as they were able to hear, the mysteries of His Person and of His Kingdom, prepared them to be His witnesses unto the nation. Through the testimony of a body of faithful disciples, the rulers at Jerusalem might yet be led to hearken to His words, and their own faith be quickened by the faith of others, and thus the nation be saved. But if this were in vain, and neither the words of the Baptist, nor the teachings of Jesus Himself and His works, nor the testimony of the disciples, could convince them, these disciples would still serve as the foundation of that new and universal church which God would build if the Jews rejected His Son. If, because of unbelief, the natural branches should be broken off, and the heathen be grafted in, in that body of followers the Lord had those who could serve Him as the builders and rulers of the new household of God.

Thus the gathering of disciples, whilst, on the one hand, it looked toward the acknowledgment by the nation of Christ's Messianic claims, and regarded such acknowledgment as still possible, yet, on the other, looked forward to the hour when He, whom the Jewish builders rejected, should be the corner stone of a church, in whose blessings Jews and Gentiles should alike participate. Of this future service the disciples themselves knew nothing, nor could they till Christ had ascended. For the present, he would teach them such truth as immediately concerned Himself and His work. He must deliver them from the false and narrow notions in which they had been educated by their

Rabbis, and, so far as they had ears to hear, open to them the purpose of God, as revealed in the Law and the Prophets.

Into the details of the Lord's work in Galilee this is not the place to enter. Suffice it to say that He gathered many disciples, and that His fame spread throughout all the land. But the favor which was showed Him in Galilee did not propitiate His enemies at Jerusalem. They very early sent spies to watch His movements, and in concert with the Pharisees, who were found in greater or less numbers in all the villages, they organized a systematic opposition to the progress of His work. Every thing was done to poison the mind of the people against Him, as a transgressor of the law, and even as in alliance with evil spirits. The fact that a large number believed in Him as the Messiah, was so far from proving the reality of His Messiahship, that it only stimulated them to new efforts for His destruction. Thus, more and more, the hope that the nation, as represented by its rulers, could be brought to receive Him, faded away. His journey to the feast of Tabernacles and reception at Jerusalem, showed in the plainest way that their hostility was undiminished, (John, chs. vii.–x.) It was apparent to Him that the "Kingdom of God must be taken from them and given to a nation bringing forth the fruits thereof," and as preparatory to this, He began to teach His disciples of His approaching death, resurrection, ascension, and coming again.

The false conceptions entertained by the Jews respecting the person and work of the Messiah, had to this time prevented the Lord from publicly assuming this title and proclaiming Himself as the Son of David and rightful King of Israel. He spoke of Himself habitually as the Son of Man. But, as it became evident that His death was determined upon, He will not permit the nation to commit so great sin without the distinct knowledge of His Messiahship. They shall not reject Him as a simple prophet, or as a forerunner of the Messiah, but as the Messiah Himself. In the third or last stage of His ministry, therefore, we shall find His Messianic claims made prominent, both in His own teachings and in the testimony of His disciples, who, to the number of seventy, were sent two and two before Him as He journeyed to Jerusalem. In this city only could He die, for this was "the City of the Great King," and His death could not be by lawless violence, or in secret, but must be in the most public manner, and by a solemn and judicial act, and here He must announce Himself as the true King, the Son of David, the long-promised Deliverer. This He did when He entered the city, fulfilling the prophetic word, "Behold, thy King cometh, sitting on an ass's colt." He accepted, as rightfully belonging to Him, the homage of the multitude, who spread their garments and branches of palm trees in the way, and cried, "Hosanna to the Son of David." "Blessed is the King of Israel, that cometh in the name of the Lord."

Thus in the Lord's public life we seem to find three stages distinctly marked. The first is that period extending from the first Passover (John ii. 13) to the feast when the impotent man was healed, (John v. 1,) and embraced about a year. It began with the purgation of the Temple, and ended with the attempt of the Jews to kill Him because He made Himself equal with God. During this time His labors were confined mainly to Judea. Near the close of this period we may place the imprisonment of the Baptist. The second stage is that period following His return to Galilee immediately after the feast, (John v. 1,) and embraces the whole duration of His ministry there, or about a year and six months. This period may be divided into two, of which the death of the Baptist will serve as the dividing line. The third stage begins with His final departure from Galilee, and ends with His death at Jerusalem, and embraces five or six months. The peculiarities of these several stages of ministry will be noticed more in detail as each shall come before us.

The Lord's Ministry in Judea.

A careful consideration of the Lord's Judean ministry shows the following characteristics. It was begun by an open assertion of His Messianic character, in the cleansing of the Temple. In this act He assumed an authority based upon His relation to God as His Son, (John ii. 16,) and in it He brought His claims directly to the knowledge of the priests and of all who had any supervision of the Temple service. This act he follows by miracles, perhaps wrought in the Temple, and which could not have been unknown to the hierarchy. As none of the rulers acknowledge Him, or perhaps even visit Him, except the doubting Nicodemus, He leaves the city, and begins somewhere in the province the work of baptizing, which He performed by the hands of His disciples. He does not, so far as we know, go about preaching in the synagogues; He works no new miracles. All this is in harmony with His position as one waiting for the recognition of the nation. The Baptist had pointed Him out as the Messiah. In the Temple, before the priests and elders, in the most open and significant way, He had asserted His Messianic authority, and given miraculous proof of His divine commission. He had thus presented Himself before those whom God had appointed to rule the nation, and into whose hands it was given to receive or reject Him. As He finds no recognition, He still seeks to draw them to His baptism, and thus lead them to a right knowledge of His work.[1] In all that He does during this period there is apparently no step looking forward to the abrogation of the Mosaic institutions, and to the formation

[1] The nature of this baptism, and its relations to the baptism of John, will be hereafter fully considered.

of a church on a new foundation. Although assisted in His work by a few who early discerned in Him the Messiah, He seems to have organized no body of disciples, and to have done nothing that indicated a purpose to gather out a few from the nation at large. The whole Judean ministry is an appeal to the people to receive Him as the Messiah through the divinely constituted heads.

Summer of 779. 26 A. D.

In the fifteenth year of the reign of Tiberius Cæsar, John enters upon his work of preaching and baptizing. The people throng to him from all parts of the land, whom he baptizes, and to whom he bears witness	Luke iii. 1–18. Matt. iii. 1–17. Mark i. 4–11.
of the coming Messiah. After his ministry had continued several months, Jesus comes from Nazareth to the Jordan, and is baptized, and immediately the Holy Spirit descends upon Him.	John i. 32–34. Luke. iii. 21–22.

The chronological questions connected with this date have been already discussed in the essay upon the time of the Lord's baptism. The mention by Luke (iii. 1, 2) of Pontius Pilate as governor of Judea, of Herod as tetrarch of Galilee, of his brother Philip as tetrarch of Iturea and of Trachonitis, of Lysanias as tetrarch of Abilene, and of Annas and Caiaphas as high priests, brings before us some historical points which demand our attention.

The will of Herod, dividing his territories amongst his sons, was, after a time, confirmed by Augustus. Archelaus became ruler of Judea, Idumea, and Samaria, with title of ethnarch, and with the promise of the title of king if he should rule to the satisfaction of the emperor.[1] Herod Antipas became tetrarch of Galilee and Perea; and Herod Philip tetrarch of Gaulonitis, Trachonitis, and Paneas.

[1] Josephus, Antiq., 17. chaps. 8, 9, and 11.

The cities of Gadara, Gaza, and Hippo, Grecian cities, were joined to the province of Syria.

The rule of Archelaus was short. In the tenth year of his government, (759,) upon the accusation of his brethren, and of the chief men of Samaria and Judea, he was summoned by the emperor to Rome, and, unable to defend himself against his accusers, he was deposed from his dignity and banished to Vienna in Gaul.[1]

After the deposition of Archelaus, Judea and Samaria were united to the province of Syria, of which P. S. Quirinius (Cyrenius) was made president. The immediate direction of affairs in Judea and Samaria was, however, given to an officer called a procurator. The powers of this officer were not exactly defined,[2] and although subject in general to the president, yet in districts lying removed from the main province, large discretionary authority was necessarily put into his hands. A considerable number of troops were placed at his command, and in certain cases he had the power of life and death. The sixth in order of these procurators, or governors, was Pontius Pilate. He entered upon his office at the end of 778, or beginning of 779, and was removed 789.[3]

Herod Antipas ruled over Galilee and Perea for more than 40 years, (750–791,) and seems to have kept these districts in comparative peace. After his nephew, Herod Agrippa, had received from the Emperor Caligula the title of king, (790,) he was incited by his wife to go to Rome and seek the same dignity, but instead of obtaining it, he was banished to Lyons, in Gaul. His territories were subsequently given to Herod Agrippa. Nothing is recorded of Herod Antipas by Josephus that sets him before us in

[1] Antiq., 17. 13. 2.

[2] Winer, ii. 276.

[3] Winer, ii. 261. Greswell, i. 345, makes him to have become governor in the middle of the summer of 779, and to have continued in office ten years and two or three months.

any very favorable light. After he had been tetrarch a considerable period, and when well advanced in years, he fell in love with the wife of his brother, Herod Philip, who was living as a private citizen at Jerusalem, (Matt. xiv. 3,) and married her, his former wife fleeing to her father, King Aretas. Not only for this act was he reproved by John the Baptist, "but for all the evil which he had done," (Luke iii. 19.) By our Lord he was called "a fox." He seems to have been of an easy, selfish temperament, fond of pleasure, unscrupulous, cunning, and superstitious. That he should have ruled so long in such stormy times shows at least that he had some political tact, and artfully managed to keep on friendly terms with his subjects on the one hand, and with the Romans on the other. He had a taste for building, and erected Tiberias upon the site of an older city, and named it in honor of the Emperor Tiberius. He rebuilt Sepphoris, a few miles north of Nazareth, and made it one of the most beautiful cities of Galilee.[1]

Herod Philip, to whom was assigned Batanea, Gaulonitis, Trachonitis, and the region around Paneas, was a prince of mild character, who devoted himself to the good of his subjects.[2] He reigned thirty-seven years, (750–787,) and leaving no child at his death, his territories were annexed to the province of Syria. He also was fond of building, and rebuilt Paneas, and gave it the name of Cæsarea, in honor of the emperor. He enlarged the city of Bethsaida, upon the sea of Galilee, and named it Julias, from Cæsar's daughter.[3]

In connection with Lysanias and the tetrarchy of Abilene, we meet with some historical difficulties. It was formerly said by some critics that Luke had fallen into error, and referred to a Lysanias who, according to Josephus, had long before died, as contemporary with Pilate

[1] Josephus, Antiq., 18. 2. 1.
[2] Antiq., 18. 4. 6.
[3] Antiq., 18. 2. 1; War, 2. 9. 1.

and Antipas and Philip. The accuracy of the Evangelist is now generally admitted;[1] but a careful comparison of his statements with those of Josephus will show us why the name of a ruler is mentioned who did not rule in Palestine, nor stand in any apparent connection with the Gospel history.

Herod the Great came into possession of his territories by degrees. He became king in 717 by the conquest of Jerusalem, but subsequent additions were made to his kingdom through the good will of Augustus, comprising Trachonitis and the region between it and Galilee. It is in connection with these additions that mention is made of one Zenodorus, who had farmed the domain of Lysanias,[2] and who ruled over Trachonitis. This Lysanias was son of Ptolemy, king of Calchis, under Lebanon, and became himself king about 714. This prince was put to death by Antony, at the instigation of Cleopatra, about 720, and a part of his dominions given to her, and subsequently farmed by her to Herod.[3] Other parts were farmed by Zenodorus. This man, plundering the Damascenes from the district of Trachonitis, Augustus deprived him of it, and gave command of it to Herod in 724. After the death of Zenodorus, he also gave to him the region between Trachonitis and Galilee, and some other of his possessions.[4]

Of the extent of this kingdom of Lysanias, or the names of its provinces, we have little knowledge. Calchis seems to have been its chief city. Robinson identifies this city with the present Anjar in the Bakaa, south of Baalbek, where considerable ruins still exist. Lichtenstein infers from a comparison of the several statements of Josephus, that beside Calchis, the kingdom embraced Trachonitis Iturea, and Batanea. Whether Abila was also embraced in it is doubtful, as it is not mentioned by Josephus. This

[1] See Meyer in loco.
[2] Josephus, War, 1. 20. 4.
[3] Antiq., 15. 4. 1.
[4] Antiq., 15. 10. 3.

city lay upon the Barada, some 20 miles from Damascus, and between the latter city and Calchis, and in part upon the site of the present village Es Suk. Robinson (iii. 484) says: "The site is very definitely assigned by the ancient itineraries; it lay upon one of the great roads from Damascus to the sea coast; and the place was marked by ruins, attesting its ancient splendor, and by a necropolis, perhaps more extensive and remarkable than any other in Syria." This position of Abila between Calchis and Damascus makes it probable that it was subject to Lysanias, as he is spoken of as a neighbor to the latter city,[1] which would be inconsistent with the existence of a distinct principality between it and his own capital.

That part of the territories of Lysanias came into the possession of Herod, has been already stated. It is certain, however, that Calchis did not, nor, so far as we can judge, did Abila. Perhaps the latter and its territory remained under the rule of the family of Lysanias till it was made the seat of an independent tetrarchy. Of the formation of this tetrarchy Josephus gives us no notice. Whether it took place soon after the death of Herod, when his dominions were divided among his sons, or at a later period, is matter of conjecture. Its existence, however, a little later than the time spoken of by Luke, is distinctly recognized by Josephus in connection with Herod Agrippa. This prince, grandson of Herod the Great, and the Herod of the Acts of the Apostles, received from Caligula, 790, the tetrarchy of Philip, now dead, and also the tetrarchy of Lysanias.[2] Thus these two tetrarchies, only some ten years after the period of which Luke speaks, had a contemporaneous existence, and were now brought together under the rule of Agrippa. Whether the tetrarch Lysanias was now dead without heirs, or had been deposed, we know

[1] Josephus, Antiq., 13. 16. 3. [2] Antiq., 18. 6. 10.

not; but it appears that his territory was at the disposal of the emperor. Thus Abilene became for the first time a part of the Jewish kingdom, and continued such for several years. To the two tetrarchies of Philip and Lysanias, Caligula added that of Herod Antipas, and subsequently Agrippa received from Claudius, Judea and Samaria, so that he reigned not only over all Palestine, but also over Abilene. As he died early, leaving a son, Herod Agrippa II., only 17 years old, his kingdom was again reduced to a Roman province.[1] To this Agrippa II. was first given Calchis, and afterward he was transferred to the tetrarchy of Philip, comprising Batanea, Trachonitis, and Gaulonitis. "To these he added the dominions of Lysanias, and the province of which Varus had been president."[2] Thus, for the second time, the tetrarchy of Lysanias became part of Jewish territory. Of its subsequent history nothing certain is known.

We can now see clearly the reason why Luke, writing after Abilene had been made a part of the Jewish kingdom, should have mentioned the fact, having apparently so little connection with Gospel history, that at the time when the Baptist appeared this tetrarchy was under the rule of Lysanias. It was an allusion to a former well known political division that had now ceased to exist, and was to his readers as distinct a mark of time as his mention of the tetrarchy of Antipas, or of Philip. This statement respecting Lysanias shows thus, when carefully examined, the accuracy of the Evangelist's information of the political history of his times, and should teach us to rely upon it even when unconfirmed by contemporaneous writers.[3]

Having mentioned the civil rulers, Luke proceeds to mention the ecclesiastical. "Annas and Caiaphas were the

[1] Josephus, War, 2. 11. 6. [2] Josephus, War, 2. 12. 8.

[3] See, in reference to this point, Wieseler, 174; Lichtenstein, 130; Winer, i. 7; Robinson, iii. 482.

high-priests."[1] Let us, therefore, consider the personal and official relations of these two men to each other.

Annas was made high-priest by Cyrenius, the Roman governor of Syria, in 760, but was deposed by Gratus 767. He was succeeded in office by Ismael, by his own son Eleazar, by Simon, and then by his son-in-law, Joseph Caiaphas.[2] The latter was appointed 778, and held the office till 790. Afterward, several other sons of Annas became high-priests, and one of them, named Ananus, was in power when James, brother of the Lord, was slain.[3]

It thus appears that although Annas had been high-priest, yet that Caiaphas was actually such when the Baptist appeared, and that he continued in office during all the public life of Christ. According to the Mosaic institutions there could be but one high-priest at a time. The office was hereditary, and was held for life. As was to be expected after the Jews had fallen under bondage to the heathen nations, the high-priests, though nominally independent, became tools in the hands of their masters, and this high dignity was transferred from one to another, both by Herod and by the Roman governors, as their political interests demanded. Hence there were often living at the same time a number who had filled this office, and been deposed. Probably other ex-high-priests besides Annas were now living, and upon that ground equally well entitled as himself to the name. That he should be distinctively so called in the passage before us, does not then seem sufficiently explained by the fact that he had been high-priest some years before, and that he still retained the title among the people at large. Some ascribe the prominence given him to the fact that he stood high in popular estimation,

[1] Tischendorf reads επί αρχίερεως Αννα καὶ Καιαφα, "Annas, high-priest, and Caiaphas." So Alford. Compare Acts iv. 6, where a like form of expression is used.

[2] Josephus, Antiq., 18. 2. 2.

[3] Euseb., ii. 23.

and still exerted great influence; or that, as father-in-law of Caiaphas, he continued to direct public matters. Against this it may be said that Luke would scarcely have mentioned him in connection with the emperor, the governor, the tetrarchs, and the high-priest, unless he also was filling some high official position.

If, then, we conclude that Annas is not mentioned merely as an influential private person who had once been high-priest, what office did he fill? The word ἀρχιερευς, high-priest, does not decide it, as it is itself of indefinite signification. Hug (followed by Friedlieb)[1] supposes both Annas and Caiaphas to have held office at the same time, and to have officiated as high-priests in turn, one at one feast and the other at the next; or, more probably, one during one year and the other during the next. For this supposition there is no good ground, and it implies a tenure of office inconsistent with facts.[2] Others therefore make Annas to have been the Nasi, or president of the Sanhedrim. Others, the vice-president, the office of president belonging to the high-priest. Others still suppose that he was the sagan, or vicarius of the high-priest, "in his absence to oversee, or in his presence to assist in the oversight of the affairs of the temple, and the service of the priests."[3] "The vicar of the high-priest, the next in dignity to him, and the vice-president of the Sanhedrim."[4] But the existence of such a deputy is doubtful.[5] Some, finally, as Alford, referring to the fact that the Law directed the office to be held during life, suppose that Luke speaks of Annas as the lawful high-priest, one who, having held it, could not be legally deposed. Meyer thinks the Evangelist to have been ignorant who was the real high-priest, and therefore erroneously ascribes this title to Annas.

It seems, from the manner in which Annas is mentioned,

[1] Archäologie, 73. [2] Josephus, Antiq., 18. 2. 2.
[3] Lightfoot, ix. 38. [4] Greswell, iii. 200. [5] Winer, i. 507.

not only by Luke but by John, that he did in fact hold some high official position, and this probably in connection with the Sanhedrim. This point will be further examined when we consider the part he took in the trial of the Lord. That, in times of such general confusion, when the laws of Moses respecting the high-priesthood were very little regarded, and offices became important according to the political capacity of those that filled them, the exact relations of Annas and Caiaphas to each other can be determined, is not to be expected. A like difficulty seems to exist in explaining the relations of Ananus and Joshua, mentioned by Josephus.[1]

The year during which John began his ministry was probably a Sabbatic year, (Ex. xxiii. 11.) According to Wieseler, such a year was that from Tisri 779 to Tisri 780. Greswell makes from 780–781 a Sabbatic year. (He admits, however, that the received principles of the modern Jewish reckoning would require him to place it a year earlier.) If this year was now observed by the Jews according to its original intent, it was a most appropriate time for the Baptist to begin his labors, the people having no burdensome agricultural tasks to occupy them, and being thus at liberty to attend upon his instructions.[2]

It is not improbable that John may have begun his labors as a preacher of the kingdom some time before he began to baptize. Some instruction as to the nature of the rite, and some exhortation to convince of its necessity, would naturally precede its administration. His preaching then need not have been confined to the banks of the Jordan, but may have begun in the wilderness, and only after he began to baptize did he remain in one place, (Luke iii. 3.) From the expression in Mark i. 4, "John did baptize in the wilderness," some have inferred that he baptized

[1] Life, 38. 2; War, 4. 3. 9.

[2] Ewald, Alterthümer, 414.

before he came to the Jordan.[1] But the Jordan was included in the well-known designation "the desert." This desert, called in Matt. iii. 1 "the desert of Judea," and which is mentioned in Judges i. 16, seems to have comprised all the region between the mountains of Judea on the one side, and the Dead Sea and the lower parts of the Jordan on the other. According to some, this wilderness of Judah stretched along on the west side of the Jordan, from the end of the Dead Sea to Scythopolis.

The place where John baptized was Bethany, on the east side of Jordan, (John i. 28.) The *textus receptus* says Bethabara, but Bethany is generally admitted to be the right reading.[2]

The site of the place having been early forgotten, Origen conjectured that Bethabara must be meant, and thus this reading found its way into the text.[3] Some suppose that at different times the same place may have had both names. Bethany means, according to some, *domus navis*, "a house of ships," or "ferry-house."[4] Its position is uncertain. According to Stanley, it was the northern ford near Succoth, which is some thirty miles north of Jericho, (Gen. xxxiii. 17, Judges vii. 24.) It is strangely placed by Lightfoot between Lake Merom and the Sea of Galilee. It was doubtless at one of the fords of the Jordan, not far from Jericho, and thus in the great eastern line of travel, as the people came to the feasts. It could not have been at the ford nearest the mouth of the river, as the depth is too great to allow a passage, except by swimming;[5] but was probably that nearly east of Jericho at the mouth of Wady Shaib, and which is now the ordinary ford. Below this is the ruined convent of St. John the Baptist, near which the Latin pilgrims bathe; and two or

1 So Lightfoot.
2 So Tischendorf, Alford.
3 See Alford's note in loco; contra, Stanley, 304, note 3.
4 Winer, i. 167.
5 Robinson, i. 156.

three miles lower still is the bathing place of the Greek pilgrims. Both affirm that their respective bathing places were hallowed by the baptism of the Lord, and by the passage of the ark of the covenant.[1] Arculf (A. D. 700) says: "A wooden cross stands in the Jordan on the spot where our Lord was baptized. The river here is about as broad as a man can throw a stone with a sling. A stone bridge, raised on arches, reaches from the bank of the river to the cross where people bathe. A little church stands at the brink of the water, on the spot where our Lord is said to have laid His clothes when He entered the river. On the higher ground is a large monastery of monks, and a church dedicated to St. John."[2] Willibald also speaks of the cross as "standing in the middle of the river, where there is small depth of water, and a rope is extended to it over the Jordan. At the feast of the Epiphany the infirm and sick come hither, and holding by the rope, dip in the water."

Many in modern times have desired to place the Lord's baptism at the spot where the Israelites under Joshua crossed the Jordan, (Josh. iii. 16.) Thus Lightfoot says: "There is reason to believe that John was baptizing in the very place where the Israelites passed over; and that our Lord was baptized in that spot where the ark rested in the bed of the river." But it is generally agreed that it is impossible to determine the precise spot where they crossed. Such exact local coincidences are unimportant. It is enough that the places were not far removed from each other. Ffoulkes[3] supposes John to have baptized at three distinct fords of the Jordan: first, at the lower ford near Jericho, to which the people of Judea and Jerusalem would naturally come; second, higher up the river at Bethabara, to which the people of Galilee and the northern parts of the land came, and where Jesus was baptized; third, still

1 Lynch, 255; Ritter, Theil xv., 536. 2 Early Travels, 8.
3 Smith's Bib. Dict., i. 1127.

higher up, at Ænon, a ford less frequented, but where was abundance of water. It is more likely, however, that an abundance of water should have been found at the lower than the upper ford.

The recognition of Jesus by John, when the former came to be baptized, is to be explained, not by the fact of prior acquaintance,[1] for such acquaintance is by no means certain,[2] but by the immediate revelation of God. John knew the nature of his own mission, as the herald of the Messiah, but he did not know who the Messiah was, nor when He should appear. The mark by which he should recognize Him was one to be given at a fitting time, the supernatural descent of the Spirit upon Him, (John i. 33.) How far John may have had knowledge of the events connected with Jesus' birth, or been brought into personal intercourse with Him, does not appear.[3] It is, however, very much to be questioned, even if he knew Him personally, whether, either through his own parents, or Joseph and Mary, he had learned any thing of His miraculous conception, or Divine character. Such mysteries were too sacred to be prematurely revealed. It does not follow, as Alford supposes, (Matt. iii. 14,) "from the nature of his relationship to the Lord, that he could not but know those events which had accompanied His birth," nor is there any proof that, prior to the time when they met at the Jordan, John looked upon Him as the Messiah. At this interview, the whole appearance of Jesus, His demeanor and language, so manifested His exalted character to the discerning eye of the Baptist, illumined by the Spirit, that he had an immediate presentiment who He was, and could say to Him, "I have need to be baptized of thee." Such supernatural discernment of character was sometimes given to the old prophets. So Samuel discerned the future king in Saul, and afterward in David.[4] Still it

[1] So Hales, Townsend.

[2] Ewald, Christus, 162; Krafft, 68; Ellicott, 107.

[3] Ebrard, 258.

[4] 1 Sam. ix. 17; xvi. 12. Compare also Luke i. 41, when John, yet a

was not till John had seen the appointed sign, the descent of the Spirit, that he could bear witness to Jesus as the Messiah.[1]

The placing of the Lord's baptism, not at the beginning, but during or at the end of His Judean ministry,[2] is wholly arbitrary.

Some have inferred from Luke iii. 21, that the descent of the Spirit was in the presence of the multitude, and visible to all.[3] But it was a sign peculiar to John, for he was to bear witness to others, who should receive his witness. And thus he says, (John i. 32–34,) "I saw the Spirit"— "And I saw, and bare record that this is the Son of God." Others were to believe, not because they saw, but because he bare record.

JAN.—FEB., 780. A. D. 27.

Immediately after His baptism Jesus was led by the Spirit into the wilderness to be tempted of the devil, and continued there forty days. After the temptations were ended He returned to the Jordan. Just before His return, John was visited by a deputation of priests and Levites from Jerusalem, to inquire who he was, and by what authority he baptized. In reply, he announces himself as the forerunner of the Messiah. The next day he sees Jesus coming to him, and bears witness to Him as the Lamb of God. The day following he repeats this testimony to his disciples. Two of them follow Him to His home, and, joined by others soon after, go with Him to Galilee.

MATT. iv. 1–11.
MARK i. 12, 13.
LUKE iv. 1–13.
JOHN i. 19–28.
JOHN i. 29–37.
JOHN i. 38–51.

The Synoptists do not mention the visit of the deputation to the Baptist, nor does John mention the temptation, but it is plain that the latter preceded the former. The

babe in his mother's womb, leaps for joy at the salutation of the Virgin Mary.

1 Meyer in loco; Ebrard, 259.
2 So Pilkington and Whiston.
3 So Meyer.

temptation followed immediately upon the baptism, (Mark i. 12,) and during the forty days of its continuance John remained in the same place preaching and baptizing. His reputation seems now to have reached its culminating point, and attracted the attention of the Pharisees and ecclesiastical rulers at Jerusalem. So popular a religious reformer could no longer be left unnoticed, and accordingly, acting probably in an official manner as the Sanhedrim, they sent a deputation of priests and Levites to ask him certain questions. As he denied that he was "the Christ," or "Elias," or "that prophet," his answers gave them no sufficient ground of accusation against him, however much they might have sought it. The next day he sees Jesus, apparently now returning from the temptation, and for the first time points Him out as He that should come after him, the Lamb of God, and Baptizer with the Holy Ghost. This he could not have done till after the baptism, for after it was the sign given, and immediately after the descent of the Spirit, Jesus departed into the wilderness. This was, therefore, the first opportunity of the Baptist to testify to Him personally, as the Christ. If the baptism had not taken place before the coming of the priests and Levites, there is no room for it in the subsequent narrative. Some suppose that Jesus had returned from the temptation before the deputation came, upon the ground that v. 26 implies His personal presence.[1] Most, however, place His return upon the next day, (v. 29.)

John's testimony to Jesus was, up to this time, general. He knew that one should come after him, but who, or when, he could not say; and this is the character of his witness, as given in the Synoptists. But after the baptism he could bear a definite witness. He had seen and recognized the Messiah by the divinely-appointed sign, and could say, This is the man, he is come, he is personally present be-

[1] So Alford in loco.

fore you. To whom the testimony (vs. 29–34) was spoken, is not certain. Perhaps it was spoken before his disciples only, though the multitude, and also the deputation from Jerusalem, may have been present. As, however, the Pharisees generally rejected John's baptism, as without authority, and did not acknowledge his office as a divinely-appointed herald of the Messiah, it was plainly idle for him to point out Jesus to them as such, (Luke vii. 29, 30.) But to his own disciples, and to all the people who, by being baptized of him, had acknowledged his prophetic character, such a designation of Him was valid, and they would recognize His Messianic character upon his testimony.[1]

The next day (v. 35) John repeats his testimony in the presence of two of his disciples.[2] One of them was Andrew, and there is no doubt that the other was the Evangelist himself, though with the reserve that characterizes him he does not mention here, or elsewhere in his gospel, his own name, or that of his mother, or brother. "It was about the tenth hour" that the two disciples went with Jesus to His abode, (v. 39.) If we adopt the Jewish computation, which divides the day from sunrise to sunset into twelve hours, the tenth hour would be that from 3–4 P. M.[3] This, however, would leave but a brief space for their interview, and seems inconsistent with the statement that "they abode with Him that day." Some, therefore, refer this to the time when Andrew brought his brother Simon to Jesus. All the day had the two disciples been with Him, and did not leave Him till the tenth hour. Others say that the two going late in the afternoon remained with Him during the night. Many, not satisfied with these explanations, prefer the Roman computation,

[1] As to the view of Origen, that there were three different missions from Jerusalem, distinguished in vs. 19, 21, 25, see Williams' Nativity, 264.

[2] Sepp supposes these two to have been witnesses of the Lord's baptism, according to a Jewish law respecting the baptism of proselytes.

[3] Winer, ii. 560.

which began at midnight. So reckoned, the tenth hour would correspond to our 10 A. M., and the disciples had the whole day for their interview.[1] Whether, however, the Roman computation of the hours of the day really differed at all from the Jewish is doubtful;[2] nor, if so, does the Evangelist seem to have ever used it.[3]

The finding of Simon (v. 41) by his brother Andrew, and his coming to Jesus, was upon the same day spoken of, (v. 35.) It is probable, from the form of expression, "He first findeth his own brother Simon," that as Andrew brought his brother Simon to the Lord, so John also brought his brother James.[4] But Alford explains it as "implying that both disciples went together to seek Simon, but that Andrew found him first."

The next day (v. 43) Jesus departs to Galilee. There seems no good reason to doubt that He was accompanied by Simon, and Andrew, and John, who had recognized in Him the Messiah. Some, however, suppose that they remained with the Baptist, and did not join Jesus till a much later period.[5] This is intrinsically improbable. Whether Philip was called by the Lord before His departure, or upon His way, is doubtful.[6] Nor is it certain that the calling of Philip was founded upon a previous acquaintance with the Lord; it may have been through the agency of Simon and Andrew, who were of the same city, (v. 44.) Philip now brings to the Lord another disciple. Where he found Nathanael is not said, but most probably upon the journey.

[1] So Ebrard, 276; Ewald, Christus, 248.

[2] See Becker's Gallus, 315; Pauly, Real Encyclopädie, ii. 1017.

[3] Against it, Meyer, Lichtenstein, Luthardt, Alford. See the following passages, iv. 6 and 52; xi. 9; xix. 14, which will each be examined in their order. Greswell, ii. 216, admits that the Jewish and Roman modes of computation were alike, but supposes John to have used the modern—from midnight to noon, and noon to midnight.

[4] Meyer, Lichtenstein.

[5] So author of "The Messiah," 73.

[6] For the former, Meyer, Alford; for the latter, Tholuck.

As the home of Nathanael was at Cana of Galilee, (John xxi. 2,) it has been thought by some that there he was brought to the Lord.

The place of the Lord's temptation was in the wilderness of Judea already spoken of, and cannot be more particularly designated. Tradition points to a high mountain a little west of Jericho, overlooking the plain of the Jordan, and which was the "exceeding high mountain" from which the Tempter showed the Lord all the kingdoms of the world. This mountain, in allusion to the forty days' fast, was called the Quarantana. Thomson says that "the side facing the plain is as perpendicular and apparently as high as the rock of Gibraltar; and upon the very summit are still visible the ruins of an ancient convent." Robinson speaks of it as "a perpendicular wall of rock, 1,200 or 1,500 feet above the plain." He does not think the name or the tradition to be older than the crusades, the mountain being first mentioned by Saewulf about 1100 A. D., and its name a hundred years later. Stanley makes the scene of the temptation to have been on the eastern side of the Jordan, among "the desert hills whence Moses had seen the view of 'all the kingdoms' of Palestine." [1] An old tradition makes the trial of Adam and Eve in Paradise to have been forty days.

Matthew and Luke differ in the order of the three temptations; but on internal grounds, which cannot here be given, that of Matthew is to be preferred.[2]

That Jesus returned at once from the wilderness to the Jordan, is apparent from the whole order of the narrative. Wieseler, however, (258,) makes a period of 5–7 months to have intervened, during which nothing respecting Him is narrated. This is in the highest degree improbable.

[1] See Ellicott, 109; Greswell, ii. 202. Sepp also puts it on the eastern shores of the Dead Sea.

[2] As to the relation of the fast to the temptations, see Greswell, ii. 206; Williams, Nativ., 244.

Feb.—April, 780. A. D. 27.

Arriving at Cana of Galilee, the Lord, at a marriage feast, changes water into wine. Afterwards He goes down with His mother, and brethren, and disciples, to Capernaum, but remains there only a few days, as the Passover was at hand. From Capernaum He goes up to Jerusalem to attend this feast.

John ii. 1–11.

John ii. 12, 13.

"And the third day there was a marriage," (v. 1.) It is disputed from what point of time this third day is to be reckoned. Some would make it the third day after His arrival in Galilee;[1] others, as Alford, the third day from the calling of Nathanael, but one day intervening; and others, as Lange, identify it with the day last mentioned, (v. 43.) Blunt[2] supposes the Evangelist to have some event in his mind from which he dates, but which he does not mention. But most count from the day of the departure to Galilee, (v. 43.)[3] The order of events may be thus given (John i. 19—ii. 1): the 1st day, verse 19, the visit of the deputation from Jerusalem; the 2d day, verse 29, Jesus returns from the temptation, and John bears witness to Him; the 3d day, verse 35, the two disciples visit Him; the 4th day, verse 43, He begins His journey to Galilee; the 5th and 6th days are spent upon the way. According to Luthardt, on the third day the two disciples visit Jesus; on the fourth Simon is brought to Him; on the fifth Philip and Nathanael; on the 6th He is on His way; on the seventh He reaches Cana. Thus, the Lord's ministry begins as it ends, with seven days, whose events are specifically mentioned. At least two days must have

[1] So Friedlieb, Leben Jesu, 189; Trench, Mir., 83.

[2] Script. Coincidences, 261.

[3] So Robinson, Meyer, Lichtenstein, Ellicott.

been spent on the way, as the distance from Bethabara to Nazareth was not far from 60 miles.[1]

It is probable that the Lord passed through Nazareth on His way to Cana. Ewald supposes that the family of Joseph had at this time left Nazareth, and were already settled at Cana.[2] But it seems conclusive against this that Philip should speak to Nathanael of Jesus as Jesus of Nazareth, (John i. 45,) and that Nathanael, who was of Cana, should know nothing of Him. The mother of Jesus seems to have been intimate in the family where the wedding took place, from which it has been inferred that she was a relative of one of the parties. One tradition makes Alpheus and Mary, the sister of the Lord's mother, to have resided at Cana, and the marriage to have been that of one of their sons. According to Greswell, it was the marriage of Alpheus and Mary themselves. Another tradition, current among the Mohammedans, and maintained by some in the Church, makes John the apostle to have been the bridegroom; another that the bridegroom was Simon the Cananite, the latter epithet being a designation of his residence, not of his character. As no allusion is made to Joseph, the most obvious inference is that he was already dead. From the fact that His disciples were invited with the Lord, it would appear that they were friends of the married pair, or that they were present as friends of Jesus. It is not certain that all the disciples are here included; perhaps only Philip and Nathanael went with Him.[3] Some, however, find in the six water pots an allusion to the Lord and His five disciples.[4]

The marriage took place at "Cana of Galilee." The name signifies, in Hebrew, a "place of reeds," and is once

1 Epiphanius puts the miracle at the wedding on the 6th January, but this is rightly rejected by Baronius.

2 So Stanley, 359, note.

3 Trench, Mir., 84.

4 See Luthardt, i. 77

used in the Old Testament as the name of a stream on the borders of Ephraim and Manasseh, (Josh. xvi. 8,) and of a city in Asher, (Josh. xix. 28.) With this city of Asher Greswell identifies the Cana of the Gospels. The addition "of Galilee" here seems designed to distinguish it from some other Cana. There are now two Canas in Galilee; one Kana el Jelil, north; the other Kefr Kenna, north-east from Nazareth, and it is disputed which is meant. Robinson (ii. 347) shows that upon etymological grounds the former is to be preferred, the present Arabic name Kana el Jelil being identical with Cana of Galilee, while Kefr Kenna "can only be twisted by force into a like shape." He shows also that the former was by early tradition pointed out as the true site of the miracle, and that only since the 16th century, and for the convenience of monks and travellers, was the latter selected. In this view of Robinson most now agree.[1] De Saulcy, however, (ii. 376,) maintains the claims of Kefr Kenna, affirming that the present name of Kana el Jelil does not mean Cana of Galilee, but Cana the great, or illustrious. He also objects that this village is too far from Nazareth, and in the wrong direction, to answer to the narrative.[2] Stanley speaks of the claims of the two Canas as "being about equally balanced." Thomson speaks hesitatingly. Making inquiries, when in the neighborhood, of all he met, where the water was made wine, "with one consent they pointed to Kefr Kenna. Some of them knew of a ruin called Kanna on the north side of the great plain of Bŭttauf, but only one had ever heard of the word 'Jelil' as a part of the name, and from the hesitancy with which this one admitted it, I was left in doubt whether he did not merely acquiesce in it at my suggestion. It is certain that very few, even of the Moslems,

[1] So Winer, Raumer, Ritter, Meyer, Porter, Van de Velde, Sepp.

[2] See Robinson's Reply, iii. 108, note. Ewald, Christus, 170, note, decides against De Saulcy.

know the full name of Kana el Jelil; and yet I think Dr. Robinson has about settled the question in its favor." Osborne says that at Kefr Kenna he inquired its name of his guides and Arabs, who said it was also called Kenna el Jelil. Also one of the natives called it Jelil. He considered it, however, a new name, devised to preserve the character of the place as Cana of Galilee.

This village lies 12 or 15 miles north of Nazareth, on the southern declivity of a hill that overlooks the plain El Bŭttauf. According to Robinson: "The situation is fine. It was once a considerable village, of well-built houses, now deserted. Many of the dwellings are in ruins; we could discover no traces of antiquity." Thomson says that there is not now a habitable house in the village, though some of them may have been inhabited within the last fifty years. There are many ancient cisterns about it, and fragments of water-jars in abundance, not, however, of stone, but of baked earth. Not only is the village deserted, but the near neighborhood is so wild, that it is the favorite hunting ground for the inhabitants of Kefr Kenna.

Kefr Kenna lies 4 or 5 miles north-east of Nazareth, in a small valley upon the border of a plain. At the entrance of the village is a fountain made out of an ancient sarcophagus, which the inhabitants show as the fountain from which the water-pots were filled. A Greek church is built upon the site of the miracle, but is a modern structure. In this church are shown two enormous stone vases, as two of the six water-pots. De Saulcy maintains that they are as old as the period at which the miracle took place. There are some ruins apparently ancient, and among them is shown the house of Simon the Cananite.

The marriage festivities among the Jews usually continued six or seven days, and it is not certain upon which of these days the miracle was wrought, but probably toward the last. At their expiration Jesus went with His mother and brethren and disciples to Capernaum. The occasion of this journey is not mentioned; perhaps, because invited by Peter and Andrew, who seem now to have resided there. Friedlieb (191) suggests that, as the Passover was now not distant, they might have desired to join a party of pilgrims going up to the feast from that city. The fact that He did not remain there many days, is mentioned as indicating that His public ministry had not yet begun. There is no intimation that He taught, or made any public manifestation of Himself while at Capernaum. Probably His time was spent in private intercourse with His disciples. Lightfoot, (iii. 44,) who makes four months to intervene between the temptation and first Passover, supposes Him to have spent this interval in a "perambulation of Galilee." Of this there is no hint in the narrative. As the Passover drew nigh, He went up to Jerusalem. Whether the disciples accompanied Him is not stated; but as they would naturally attend the feast, and as afterward they are found with Him, (John ii. 22,) we infer that they did so.

Passover, April 11-18, 780. A. D. 27.

At this feast Jesus with a scourge drives out of the temple the sellers of animals for sacrifice, and the money-changers. To the Jews, demanding His authority to do such things, He replies in a parable. During the feast He wrought miracles which led many to believe on Him. He is visited at night by Nicodemus, to whom he explains the nature of the new birth. Afterward He departs from Jerusalem into the land of Judea, where He tarries with His disciples, and they baptized.

John ii. 14–22.
John ii. 23–25.
John iii. 1–21.
John iii. 22.
John iv. 2.

This Passover, according to Greswell, was on the 9th April. Friedlieb makes it to have been on the 11th. We follow the latter. If the Lord's baptism was, as we have supposed, early in January, between the baptism and the

Passover was an interval of some three months.[1] The exact length of this interval depends, of course, upon the date of the baptism. With this Passover His public ministry may properly be said to begin.

This purification of the Temple is plainly a different one to that mentioned by the Synoptists, (Matt. xxi. 12–16; Mark xi. 15–19; Luke xix. 45–48.) This occurred at the beginning; that at the end of His ministry. The act, in all its essential outward features, must have been the same; but its significance varied with the time. As now performed, it was a plain and open avowal of His Divine authority, and a public reproof of the wickedness of the priests and rulers, who permitted His Father's house to be made a house of merchandise. Nothing could have brought Him more publicly before the ecclesiastical authorities and the multitudes who thronged to the feast, than this act; nor have shown more distinctly the nature and extent of His prophetic claims. He was the Son of God, jealous of His Father's honor, and to whom it especially belonged to see that His courts were not defiled.

As the chief sacrifice, that of the Paschal Lamb, was offered on the first day of the feast, it is probable that this purification took place before or on that day. Although the act must have drawn to Him popular attention, and awakened general inquiry who He was, no hostile measures seem to have been taken at this time by the Jewish authorities. They asked for a sign (v. 18) as a voucher for His Divine commission, which He declined to give, and answered them in an enigmatical manner. Still He wrought afterward, during the feast, miracles which caused many to believe in Him. But their faith resting merely upon the exhibitions of power which they saw, not upon any perceptions of the moral character of His works, He did not com-

[1] Paschale Chronicon, 76 days; Friedlieb, 87 days; Greswell, 64 days.

mit Himself to them, or enter into any intimate relations with them, as with His disciples from Galilee. But in Nicodemus, whom Lightfoot calls "one of the judges of the great Sanhedrim," He found one in whom were the germs of a true faith, and to whom He could reveal Himself, not only through work, but through word. That Nicodemus should come secretly by night, shows that there was, even now, among the priests and rulers with whom he had most intercourse, a feeling of dislike to Jesus, and that some degree of odium attached to all who were known to visit Him.

After the feast was over, Jesus, leaving the city, went into some part of the territory adjacent, or into the province of Judea, as distinguished from its chief city. The part of the land to which He went is not mentioned, but we may infer that, as His purpose was to baptize, He went to the Jordan, or to some one of the streams running into it. Sepp (ii. 100) supposes Him to have gone from place to place in southern Judea, baptizing at all the principal fountains, which He could do, as His baptism was by sprinkling, as that of John was by immersion. This is pure conjecture. Perhaps we may infer from John, (iv. 4,) "And He must needs go through Samaria," that He was at this time in the northern part of Judea.[1] That He began the work of baptizing by His disciples soon after the feast, and before He returned to Galilee, seems fairly inferable from the narrative. It has, however, been said[2] that a considerable interval (from April to October) elapsed, during which the Lord and His disciples returned to Galilee, and lived in retirement, engaged in their usual pursuits. In support of this it is claimed that the baptismal activity of Jesus must have been very brief, since the Baptist's disciples speak of it as recent, (John iii. 26,) and it was given up so soon as His work

[1] See Meyer in loco. [2] Lichtenstein, 157.

began to awaken the jealousy of the Pharisees, (John iv. 1–3.) Supposing that the Lord left Judea, upon grounds to be hereafter stated, in November or December, He must have been there about six months. We cannot certainly determine whether He was so long actually engaged in the work of baptizing. Greswell makes the time so spent to have been less than a month; Norton only two or three weeks. But we need not suppose Him to have commenced immediately after the Passover, though we have no data to determine the exact time. Nor can we tell when John left the Jordan and began to baptize at Ænon, (v. 23.)[1] That Jesus had been for some time carrying on His work before the complaint made by John's disciples, (v. 26,) appears from the great numbers that thronged to His baptism.

We see, then, no good grounds for believing that Jesus after the Passover went into Galilee, and returning after some months, began to baptize. Yet we may, on the other hand, admit that His baptismal work was not of very long duration. There is nothing in the note of time, (v. 22,) "after these things," μετα ταυτα, that forbids us to suppose that a few weeks may have elapsed between the feast and the beginning of this work.[2]

Whilst Jesus was baptizing, John was also prosecuting his work. He had, however, left the Jordan and gone to Ænon, (v. 23.) The site of this place is not known. The Evangelist speaks of it as near to Salim, and gives as the reason of its selection that there was "much water," or "many fountains," υδατα πολλα, there. The word Ænon means fountains, but it is doubtful whether it denotes here,

[1] See Greswell, ii. 215, who thinks the statement that there was much water there, "a proof that the rainy season had been some time over, and water was beginning to be scarce," and thus showing that it was near midsummer. Little reliance can be placed on this.

[2] Compare the parallel expressions, John v. 1; vi. 1; vii. 1. "The sequence is not immediate," Alford in loco.

a village, or fountains near a village. The latter seems most likely, as its position is defined by saying that it was near to Salim, "Baptizing near the waters of deep-waved Salim."[1] But the position of this Salim is also undetermined. Jerome speaks of a town called in his day Salem, not far from Scythopolis, where the ruins of a palace of Melchizedek were shown. He speaks also of a Salumias, which he apparently identifies with Salem, as lying in the plain or valley of the Jordan, eight miles south of Scythopolis. He places Ænon in the same locality, near Salem and the Jordan.[2] Here it is now placed by Van de Velde, at the base of Tell Ridghah, where there are some ruins and a spring.[3] If this be correct, Ænon would have been within the bounds of Samaria. But it is difficult to believe that John, the preacher of the Law, could have entered Samaria to baptize, when, at a later period, the Lord forbade the Twelve to preach in any of its cities, (Matt. x. 5.) Nor is there any trace, in the conversation of the Samaritans with Jesus, of any such ministry of the Baptist among them, (see John iv. 9.) Salim and Ænon have therefore been looked for in other directions. Some, as Wieseler, have found them in the wilderness of Judah, referring to Josh. xv. 32, where a city Ain is mentioned in connection with Shilhim. Lichtenstein (160) finds an Ænon in Wady el Khulil, a little west of Hebron. Sepp, in Beit Ainun, north of Hebron. Barclay (558) thinks he finds it in certain fountains in Wady Farah, six miles north-east from Jerusalem, of which he speaks as of all the fountains in the neighborhood of Jerusalem, by far the most copious and interesting. One is capable of driving several mills as it gushes forth from the earth, but is intermittent. The Wady in which they lie he heard also called Salim, and his guide conducted him to the site of an ancient city near by. Below, the stream is

1 Nonnus in Lightfoot, x. 337. 2 Raumer, 142; Robinson, iii. 333.
3 Memoir, 345; so Ellicott.

called the Kelt, and is generally supposed to be "the brook Cherith that is before Jordan," (1 Kings xvii. 1–7.) In his second journey, Robinson (iii. 298) made special search for Salim in the Jordan valley, but could find no ruins, nor trace of the name. He mentions, however, a plain of Salim east of Nablous, and a small village of the same name, which was "said to have two sources of living water, one in a cavern, and the other a running fountain." Many, as Greswell, follow Jerome.

Among so many discordant opinions, the true site of Ænon must be left undecided. Most agree in placing it on the west side of the Jordan, as it is contrasted (v. 26) with John's former place of baptism at Bethabara. That he should have gone so far from the earlier scene of his labors as the south of Judea, is improbable. We best meet the scope of the narrative if we suppose that Jesus and John were not very far distant from each other, and both in the region of the Jordan. Some have supposed a contrast to be drawn between "the land of Judea," and "Ænon," (vs. 22 and 23,) as if the latter was not in the former.[1] But the contrast was not between the place of John's ministry and that of Jesus, but between the labors of Jesus in Jerusalem and His labors in the country. That John was not immediately upon the Jordan is rightly to be inferred from the statement that there was much water there, a statement superfluous if he had been on the banks of that river.

In the act of baptizing Jesus personally took no part. It was done by His disciples. The names of these disciples are not mentioned, but they were doubtless the same whose names had been already mentioned, (John ch. i.,) and who came with Him to the Passover from Galilee. As the former disciples of John, and perhaps his assistants, this rite was not new to them. Having also been for some time in company with Jesus, they were prepared by His teach-

[1] So Winer, i. 34

ings to understand the meaning of the service He required from them. As yet, however, their relations to Him were much the same, as their former relations to John, and very unlike what they afterward became.[1]

These contemporaneous baptismal labors of the Lord and of John present many interesting questions, but most of them lie out of the pale of our inquiry. As the former did not Himself baptize, it is a question how His time was spent. Probably He taught the crowds that came to His baptism, but there is no hint that He healed the sick, or wrought any miracles. We can scarce doubt that He went up to Jerusalem to attend the two great feasts during this period, that of Pentecost and of Tabernacles, and here He must have come more or less into contact with the priests and Pharisees. It does not appear, however, that He went about from place to place to teach, or that He taught in any of the synagogues. Still it is not improbable that before He began to baptize, or at intervals during His labors, He may have visited many parts of Judea, and have noted and tested the spiritual condition of the people. It may be, also, that at this time He formed those friendships of which we later find traces, as that with Joseph of Arimathea, and that with Mary and Martha.

Dec., 780—March, 781. A. D. 27–28.

The Pharisees sowing dissensions between the disciples	John iii. 25, 26.
of John and those of Jesus, the latter gives up His work	John iv. 1–3.
of baptizing and goes back to Galilee. The Baptist, in re-	John iii. 27–36.
ply to the complaints of his disciples, bears a fresh testi-	
mony to Jesus as the Messiah. Jesus takes His way to	John iv. 4–42.
Galilee, through Samaria, and abides there two days teach-	
ing, and many believed on Him. Upon reaching Galilee	
His disciples depart to their respective homes. He is re-	John iv. 43–45.

[1] See Greswell, ii. 284.

ceived with honor by the Galileans, because of the works which He did at Jerusalem at the feast. Coming to Cana, He heals the nobleman's son at Capernaum. He afterward lives in retirement till called to go up to Jerusalem at the following feast.

JOHN iv. 46–54.

JOHN v. 1.

Before entering upon the examination of the several points which this section presents, it will be well to take a brief preliminary survey of the several stages of John's ministry, and their relations to corresponding stages in the Lord's work.

The first labor of the Baptist was to announce the near approach of the Messiah, and through the baptism of repentance to prepare His way. He demanded of the people that they should believe in Him that should come after him, and who should baptize with the Holy Ghost, (Acts xix. 4.) When, after a considerable time thus spent, and multitudes from all parts of the land had been baptized, Jesus appeared and was recognized by him as the Messiah, his ministry necessarily took a new form. He could no longer testify to his auditors of one to come, but must point out Jesus as the Messiah already come. This he did, when, in the presence of his disciples and of the people, he pointed to Jesus as the Lamb of God. This witness to the personal Christ was the culminating point of his work. It was now a question for the Jews, how they would receive and treat Him to whom he had thus borne witness. Jesus henceforth became the chief figure on the stage, and John sank to the position of a subordinate.

With the coming of Jesus it might have been supposed that the mission of the Baptist would cease, its end being accomplished. As we have seen, however, it did not wholly cease, but it changed its form. And it is probably from this point of view that we are to explain the departure of John from the Jordan to Ænon. And as the place of baptism was changed, so also in some degree the rite. His baptism could no more have a géneral and indefinite reference to one still to come. Having declared Jesus of Nazareth to be the Messiah, the undefined Messianic hopes of the nation were now to be concentrated upon Him. All the teachings and labors of the Baptist pointed to Him, and all tended to prepare the people to receive Him. Whether there was any change in the baptismal formula may be doubted, but the immediate and personal reference to Jesus as the Messiah was that which distinctively characterized the last stage of John's work.

To this form of John's ministry the ministry of Jesus, at its beginning, corresponded. The former had borne his witness to Him, and He must now confirm that witness; must show Himself to be the Messiah through His own words and acts. This He does. He gathers a small body of disciples, to whom He manifests His glory through the miracle at the marriage in Cana. Afterward, before the priests and the people, He asserts His Messianic claims by the purifying of the temple, and the miracles He subsequently wrought at the feast. But why should He establish, or rather continue the rite of baptism? In what relation did this rite stand to His Messianic character? The answer to this question may be found in its nature as the baptism of repentance. It was an indispensable condition to the reception of the Christ, the Holy One of God, that sin should be repented of and put away. Upon this John had insisted in his preaching, "Repent, for the kingdom of God is at hand." But this preaching, and this rite, both pointing to repentance, were no less important now that the Messiah had actually come. Without holiness of heart they could not receive Him, could not even discern Him as the Messiah. John had already baptized many into the hope of His coming, but others had equal need to be baptized into the reality of it.

We can now see why John should have continued baptizing after the Lord came, and why Jesus should Himself, through His disciples, adopt the rite. It was not enough that He had personally come. Would the Jews receive Him? None could do so but the repentant. All those that, with hearts conscious of guilt, both personal and national, and truly penitent, were waiting for the consolation of Israel, were willing to be baptized, confessing their sins; but the unrepentant, the unbelieving, the self-righteous, all who justified themselves, rejected the rite, (Luke vii. 29, 30.) Hence it was a most decisive test of the spiritual state of the people. And tried by this test, the nation, as such, was condemned. Neither the baptism of John, nor that of the Lord, brought it to repentance. True, great numbers went at first to John, and afterward many resorted to Jesus, and were baptized; but these were the common people, those without reputation or authority. Those who ruled in all religious matters and gave direction to public opinion, the priests, the scribes and Pharisees, the Sadducees, and the rich and influential, held themselves almost wholly aloof. Hence, as regarded the nation at large, the baptismal work failed of its end. The true and divinely-appointed representatives of the people, the ecclesiastical authorities, who sat in Moses' seat, were not brought to repentance, and therefore could not receive the Messiah.

Thus Jesus began His work as the Baptizer with water unto repentance. It was this baptism that gave to His Judean ministry its distinctive character. It was an attempt to bring the nation, as headed up in its ecclesiastical rulers, to repentance. Had these come to Him, or to John, confessing their sins, His way would have been prepared, and He could then have proceeded to teach them the true nature of the Messianic kingdom, and prepared them for the baptism of the Holy Ghost. But as they had "frustrated the counsel of God within themselves, being not baptized of John," so they continued to frustrate it by rejecting the baptism of Jesus. To continue, therefore, to baptize was to expose God's ordinance to contempt, and discontinuing His labors in Judea, He retired into Galilee. How long after this John continued to baptize, we are not told. He must have felt that, as regarded the rulers and the body of the people, little could be done, (John i. 19–25 ; and iii. 32 ;) and perhaps he may now have gone from place to place, seeking out and baptizing all who had humility to confess their sins, and faith to receive his witness. Not improbably, as the novelty of his first appearance was over, his popularity was already on the wane, although the people at large continued to hold him in high esteem as a teacher and prophet.

Many have placed the imprisonment of John by Herod (Matt. iv. 12 ; Mark i. 14 ; Luke iii. 19 and 20) just before this departure of Jesus into Galilee, and regard the latter as determined by the former. But for this there are no sufficient grounds. There is nothing in the language of the fourth Evangelist that implies this ; but, on the contrary, a fair construction of his words (iv. 1) shows that John was yet baptizing when Jesus left Judea. "When, therefore, the Lord knew how the Pharisees had heard that Jesus made and baptized more disciples than John—He left Judea." Translated more strictly, it would read, "that Jesus is making and baptizing more disciples than John." This plainly implies comparison between the two, and therefore their contemporaneous activity. Both are making and baptizing disciples, but more come to Jesus than to John.[1] There is, beside, no allusion to Herod, or intimation that the Baptist's labors were now suspended because of his imprisonment. Nor, unfriendly as the Pharisees doubtless were to him, is there mention anywhere made of any overt acts of hostility against him. They were satisfied with de-

[1] So Greswell, ii. 212; Wieseler, 161.

nying his authority to baptize, for his reputation was too high among the people to permit them to take any active steps against him. His imprisonment was not their act, nor do they seem to have had any part in it, (Matt. xiv. 3.)

But if John was not now imprisoned, why did Jesus now cease baptizing and retire into Galilee? Some ascribe this to His fear of the Pharisees.[1] But there is no proof that this party was ready at this early period to hinder Him in His work by any active opposition, much less that His life and personal safety were endangered. When a few months afterward they sought to slay Him, because by healing on the Sabbath He had, as they said, broken the Law of God, (John v. 16,) there was a plausible reason for their hostility; but this did not now exist. Others, on better grounds, ascribe this departure to the fact that the Pharisees were availing themselves of the jealousy of John's disciples to the injury of Jesus.[2] It appears from John iii. 25–27, that there was a dispute between the disciples of John and the Jews, or a Jew, respecting purification. This may have had reference to the nature of baptism as a purifying rite; to the authority of John to administer it; or, more probably, to the respective values of the baptisms of John and Jesus. That the baptismal work of the latter gave umbrage to John's disciples, upon some ground, is apparent; for they complain to their master that He was baptizing, and that all the people were thronging to Him. They seem to have considered this act on His part as one that needed explanation, perhaps as an interference with John in his peculiar work, or as unsuitable to His Messianic character.

If, however, we admit that the Pharisees did attempt to arouse the jealousy of John's disciples to the injury of

[1] So Greswell, Alford, Meyer.

[2] So Lichtenstein, 162; Luthardt, i. 391.

the work in which he and Jesus were jointly engaged, this alone does not explain why the latter should have ceased to baptize. The true reason has been already intimated. The increasing popularity of Jesus, as shown by the numbers that came to His baptism, only brought out more strongly the envy and dislike of the Pharisees, and confirmed them in their hostility. To have continued His work could, therefore, have answered no good end, since it was not now the gathering of a body of disciples around Him at which He aimed, but the repentance of the priests and leaders of the people. We conclude, therefore, that He now left Judea because the moral conditions for the successful prosecution of His baptismal labors were wanting.

The only datum we have by which to determine the time of the year when Jesus went into Galilee, is found in His words to His disciples when seated by the well in Sychar: "Say not ye there are yet four months and then cometh harvest? behold I say unto you," &c., (John iv. 35.) Some, however, deny that this reference to the harvest, as yet four months distant, is of any chronological value, because the expression is a proverbial one, based upon the fact that there is an average interval of four months between the sowing and harvesting.[1] But the form of the expression seems to forbid that we regard it as a proverb, "Say not ye there are yet four months," &c.; here "yet," ετι, obviously refers to the time when the words were spoken. From this time, not from the time of sowing, are four months, and then the harvest.[2] We are then to determine the time of the harvest, and counting backward four months, reach the time when the words were spoken. Upon the 16th Nisan, a sheaf of the first fruits of the harvest was to be waved before the Lord in the Temple.

[1] Norton, Krafft, Greswell, Alford.

[2] Lightfoot, Baronius, Lichtenstein, Wieseler, Stier, Meyer, Robinson.

Till this was done, no one might lawfully gather his grain.[1] From this legal commencement of the harvest about the first of April, we obtain the month of December as that in which the words were spoken.[2] Tholuck (in loco) regards the expression as proverbial, yet reaches nearly the same result. "As our Lord points them to the fields, it is highly probable that it was just then seed-time, and we are thus furnished with the date, to wit, that Jesus had remained in Judea from April, when the Passover occurred, till November."[3]

A very different result is reached by some, who take the Lord's words: "Lift up your eyes, and look on the fields; for they are white already to the harvest," as not figurative, but literal, and expressive of an actual fact. The harvest, then, was not four months distant, but just at hand. Upon this ground Greswell (ii. 229) decides "that the time of the journey coincided with the acme of wheat harvest, or was but a little before it," and puts it two or three weeks before Pentecost, or about the middle of May.[4]

The direct route from Judea to Nazareth led through Samaria by Sichem, and was generally taken by the companies attending the feasts from Galilee, although the enmity of the Samaritans to the Jews seems especially to have manifested itself on such occasions.[5] Josephus says[6] that it was necessary for those that would travel quickly to take that route, as by it Jerusalem could be reached in three days from Galilee. Sychar is regarded by many as another reading for Sychem, (Acts vii. 16,) which stood upon the site of the present Neapolis, or Nablous,

1 Levit. xxiii. 10, &c.; Deut. xvi. 9, &c.; Josephus, Antiq., 3. 10. 5.

2 Lightfoot, Lichtenstein, Meyer, Ellicott.

3 A. Clarke and Stier, putting the harvest in May, make the departure to have been in January. Stanley, in January or February.

4 So Townsend in loco, "The Messiah," 101. Alford regards all chronological inferences built on this passage, as unwarranted.

5 Josephus, Antiq., 20. 6. 1.

6 Life, 52.

and is often mentioned in biblical history.[1] For a time after the return from the captivity, Samaria (1 Kings xvi. 24) was the chief city, but Sichem soon gained the ascendency. The change from Sichem to Sychar is supposed to mark the contempt of the Jews toward the Sichemites, the latter word meaning the "toper city," or the "heathen city." Alexander calls it "a later Aramaic form." It is not to be supposed that this change was made by John in his narrative to express his own dislike, or that, as said by Stier, "it was an intentional intimation of the relation and position of things between Judea and Samaria." Unless the name Sychar was in common use, we can scarce suppose him to have employed it; for, in a simple historical statement, the intentional use of any mock name or opprobrious epithet would be out of keeping.

Some make Sychar a village near Sichem, but distinct from it.[2] This was the early opinion. They were distinguished by Eusebius, and in the Jerusalem Itinerarium.[3] Raumer supposes that the village of Sichem was a long straggling one, and that the east end of it, near Jacob's well, was called Sychar. There is now a village near the well called El Askar, which some have supposed to be Sychar. Thomson (ii. 206) says: "This is so like John's Sychar that I feel inclined to adopt it."[4]

Jacob's well, where Jesus was resting Himself when He met the Samaritan woman, "is on the end of a low spur or swell running out from the north-eastern base of Gerizim; and is still 15 or 20 feet above the level of the plain below."[5] It is dug in the solid rock to the depth of 75 or 80 feet, and is about 9 feet in diameter, and the sides hewn smooth and regular, and perfectly round.[6] The quantity of water in it

[1] So Meyer, Weiseler, Raumer, Robinson, Ritter, Alford.

[2] Hug, Luthardt, Lichtenstein.

[3] See Raumer, 146, note.

[4] See contra Robinson, iii. 133; see also Wieseler, 256, note.

[5] Robinson, iii. 132.

[6] Porter.

greatly varies. Maundrell found it 5 yards in depth. Sometimes it is nearly or wholly dry. Dr. Wilson (1842) found so little water in it, that a servant, whom he let down to the bottom, was able, by means of dry sticks thrown to him, to kindle a blaze which distinctly showed the whole of the well from the top to the bottom. Osborne[1] says: "There was no water at the time of our visit, near the close of December." "Formerly there was a square hole opening into a carefully-built vaulted chamber, about 10 feet square, in the floor of which was the true mouth of the well. Now a portion of the vault has fallen in, and completely covered up the mouth, so that nothing can be seen but a shallow pit half filled with stones and rubbish."[2] A church was built near this spot, of which few traces remain.

It has been much questioned why a well should have been dug here, since there are several springs within a little distance giving an abundance of water. Some suppose that earthquakes may have caused the springs to flow since the well was dug. More probable is the supposition that Jacob found the springs in the possession of others, who were unwilling to share the water with him, and therefore, as matter of necessity, he must obtain it from a well. Why the woman should have come to this well to draw water, which was so much more easily attainable near by, cannot now be explained. If the city itself was at some distance, and the language seems to imply this, (vs. 8, 28–30,) she may have lived in the suburbs, for it is not said that she resided in the city; but if she did so, she may have had special reasons for wishing the water of this well, because of its coolness or other qualities; or as especially valuable because of its association with Jacob. Porter (ii. 342) speaks of those at Damascus, who send to a par-

[1] Palestine, 335. [2] Porter, ii. 340.

ticular fountain a mile or more distant from their homes, although water is everywhere very abundant.

It was about the sixth hour that Jesus sat on the well. This, according to Jewish reckoning, would be 12 M. or noon; if reckoned according to Roman computation, 6 P. M., or as some say,[1] 6 A. M. Ebrard (296) contends that John always uses the Roman computation, and prefers the evening here, on the grounds that the noonday was an unfit time to travel, and that wells were usually visited for water at evening. But if we remember that this was in December, travelling at mid-day will not appear strange. Noon was not indeed the time for general resort to the well, but such resort must be determined in particular cases by individual need; and that the woman was alone, and held so long a private conversation uninterrupted, shows that it was an hour when the well was not generally visited. There seems, then, no reason to depart from the common opinion that it was about noon. At this hour the Jews were accustomed to take their principal meal.[2]

The reception which the Lord met with among the Samaritans was in striking contrast with His reception in Judea; yet among the former He seems to have wrought no miracles, and to have been received because the truth He taught was the convincing proof of His Messianic character.

Arriving in Galilee, Jesus was honorably received by the Galileans, for they had been at the Passover, and had "seen all the things that He did at Jerusalem at the feast," (John iv. 43–45.) But in face of this honorable reception, how are His words (v. 44) to be understood, "that a prophet hath no honor in his own country," and which are apparently cited as explaining why He went into Galilee. There are several interpretations: 1. Galilee is to be taken

[1] Greswell, ii. 216; McKnight. [2] Winer, ii. 47.

in opposition to Nazareth. In this city, His own country, Jesus had no honor, but elsewhere in Galilee He was received as a prophet.[1] 2. Galilee is to be taken in opposition to Judea. Judea was His birthplace, and so His own country, and it was also the land of the prophets; but there He had found no reception, and had been compelled to discontinue His ministry. In Galilee, on the contrary, all were ready to honor Him.[2] 3. Galilee is His own country where, according to the proverb, He would have had no honor, except He had first gone into Judea and distinguished Himself there. It was His miracles and works abroad that gave Him fame and favor at home.[3]

The last interpretation appears best to suit the scope of the narrative. The connection between vs. 43 and 44 is this; in v. 43 the fact is stated that He went into Galilee, and in v. 44 the reason is assigned why He went. As, according to the proverb, a prophet is without honor in his own country, by retiring into Galilee He could avoid all publicity, and find retirement. But in v. 45 the fact is stated that the Galileans, notwithstanding the proverb, did receive Him, and the reason is also added, because they had been at Jerusalem, and had seen what He did there. And in verses 46–53 a particular instance is given, showing how high His reputation in Galilee, and what publicity attended His movements. His arrival at Cana was soon known at Capernaum, and a nobleman from the latter city, supposed by many to be Chuza, steward of Herod, coming to Him, desires that He would return with him, and heal his son. Without leaving Cana, Jesus heals him. This was His second Galilean miracle.

From the time of this miracle at Cana, we lose sight of the Lord till He reappears going up to a feast at Jerusalem (John v. 1.) If, as we have supposed, He left Judea in De-

[1] Lightfoot, Krafft. [2] Ebrard, Norton. [3] Meyer, Alford.

cember, this miracle must have been wrought soon after His arrival in Galilee. As the first feast which He could attend was that of Purim, in March, an interval of some two or three months must have elapsed. If this feast were the Passover, or any of the later feasts, this interval was correspondingly prolonged. How was this time spent? Those who make the imprisonment of the Baptist to have taken place before He left Judea, suppose that He now entered upon His Galilean work. But, upon grounds already stated, we conclude that John was not yet imprisoned, and therefore His Galilean work could not now begin, as the two are closely connected by the Synoptists, (Matt. iv. 13, Mark i. 14, Luke iii. 20, and iv. 14.) Several additional considerations induce us to think that this period was not spent in any public labors. 1. When, after the imprisonment of John, Jesus went into Galilee to teach and to preach, His disciples were not with Him, and not till He had begun His labors at Capernaum did they rejoin Him, (Matt. iv. 18, Mark i. 16; Luke v. 2–11.) There was, then, an interval after He had ended His baptismal labors in Judea, in which they were His helpers, and before the beginning of His ministry in Galilee, during which His disciples were separated from Him, and seem to have returned to their accustomed avocations. But if His Galilean work began as soon as His Judean work ended, there was no time for them to have thus returned to their homes, and, therefore, no opportunity to recall them to His service.

2. The Lord gave up baptizing, as we have seen, because of the hostility of the Pharisees, and their rejection of the rite. But, so long as John was able, both in word and act, to bear witness to Him as the Messiah, He could Himself seek retirement, and wait the issue of John's ministry. He could not, till the Baptist was imprisoned and his voice thus silenced, finally leave Judea and begin His work in Galilee. To Galilee He went, therefore, as a place

of seclusion, not of publicity; of rest, not of activity. The proverb, that a prophet has no honor in his own country, did not indeed prove true in His case. He was honorably received, and immediately besought to heal the sick. Still there is no record that He entered upon any public labors, that He preached or taught in the synagogues, or wrought any miracles. How or where His time was spent, can only be conjectured. From the fact that no mention is made of Nazareth, it has been inferred that He purposely avoided that city, and took another route to Cana.[1] That He is spoken of as being at Cana, gives a show of confirmation to the supposition already alluded to, that Mary and her children had now left Nazareth, and were dwelling at Cana. But we may as readily suppose that He was now visiting at the house of the friends or relatives, where he changed the water into wine.

Passover, March 30—April 5, 781. A. D. 28.

From Galilee Jesus goes up to the feast of the Pas-	John v. 1.
sover, and at the pool of Bethesda heals an impotent	John v. 2–9.
man. This act, done on the Sabbath day, arouses the	John v. 10–16.
anger of the Jews, who conspire against His life. He	John v. 17–47.
defends His right to heal on the Sabbath upon grounds	Matt. iv. 12.
that still more exasperate them. At this time He hears	Mark i. 14.
of the imprisonment of the Baptist, and retires to Galilee,	Luke iv. 14.
to begin His work there.	

"After this there was a feast of the Jews; and Jesus went up to Jerusalem." Which feast was this? Opinions are divided between Purim in March, Passover in April, Pentecost in May, and Tabernacles in September. Before considering the arguments used in favor of each by their respective advocates, let us examine the statement of John.

[1] So Newcome.

There is much doubt as to the true reading, whether a feast or the feast, εορτη or η εορτη. Tischendorf[1] retains the article, Meyer and Alford reject it. The weight of authority seems against it, and at any rate the reading is so doubtful that we can lay no stress upon it.[2] But if it were "the feast," η εορτη, this would not, of itself, as some suppose,[3] decide in favor of the Passover, as it might refer either to Passover or to Tabernacles, the two most prominent feasts. Of the latter Josephus speaks,[4] as "a feast most holy and eminent;" and again,[5] as "a festival very much observed amongst us." But if the article would not limit this feast to the Passover, it would certainly exclude the lesser feasts, as that of Purim.

But, if the article be wanting, it is said that the feast is still defined by the addition to it of the explanatory words "of the Jews," των Ιουδαιων.[6] It is given as a rule of Hebrew, and so transferred to Scripture Greek, that the "noun before a genitive is made definite by prefixing the article, not to the noun itself, but to the genitive."[7] Thus the phrase before us should be rendered "the feast of the Jews," or "the Jews' festival," which must be understood of the Passover. But the rule is given with an important qualification by Winer,[8] "The article is frequently omitted, when a noun, denoting an object of which the individual referred to possesses but one, is clearly defined by means of a genitive following."[9] As there was but one feast of Tabernacles, the phrase εορτη των σκηνων would be properly ren-

[1] Synopsis, xxvi., note 2.

[2] It is found in the newly discovered Sinaitic manuscript, but the value of that MS. is not yet settled.

[3] Hengstenberg, Robinson.

[4] Antiq., 8. 4. 1.

[5] Antiq., 15. 3. 3.

[6] Hug, Int., 449.

[7] Robinson, Har., 190. See in the Septuagint, Deut. xvi. 13; 2 Kings, xviii. 15; also Matt. xii. 24; Luke ii. 11; Acts viii. 5.

[8] Gram., 107.

[9] See also Lücke in loco, who agrees that only where the governing noun exists singly in its kind, is it rendered definite by a noun following.

dered "the feast of Tabernacles;" but as there were several feasts kept by the Jews, ἑορτη των Ιουδαιων, "feast of the Jews," may mean any feast. The passages cited by Robinson come all under the above rule.

From the form of the expression, then, nothing can be determined. We learn simply that Jesus went up to Jerusalem at one of the Jewish feasts. We do not even learn whether it was one of the greater or lesser feasts. It seems to be mentioned only as giving the occasion why He went up to Jerusalem. He would not have gone except there had been a feast, but its name was unimportant to the Evangelist's purpose.[1] Let us then enquire what light is thrown upon it from the general scope of this Gospel.

It is apparent that John does not design, any more than the other Evangelists, to give us a complete chronological outline of the Lord's life. But we see that he mentions by name several feasts which the Lord attended, which the Synoptists do not mention at all.[2] The last Passover all the Evangelists mention in common. But these were by no means all the feasts that occurred during His ministry. That of Pentecost is nowhere mentioned, nor does John say that those mentioned by him were all that Jesus attended. During the first year of His labors, or whilst baptizing in Judea, there is good ground to believe that He was present at the three chief feasts, though the Passover only is mentioned. On the other hand, one Passover is mentioned which it is probable He did not attend, (John vi. 4.) Upon examination, we see that the feasts which are alluded to stand in some close connection with the Lord's words or acts, so that it is necessary to specify them. Thus in ii. 13, the mention of the Passover explains the purification of the temple, or driving out of the sellers of oxen and sheep; in vi. 4 it explains how such a great company should

[1] See Luthardt in loco.

[2] See ii. 13; vi. 4; vii. 2; x. 22.

have gathered to Him in so lonely a region across the sea; in vii. 2 His words take their significance from the special ceremonies connected with that feast; in x. 22 His presence in Solomon's porch is thus explained. In each of these cases the name of the feast is mentioned, not primarily as a datum of time, but as explanatory of something in the narrative; and as the mention of the other feasts was unimportant to his purpose, John passes them by in silence. But the feast before us he mentions, yet does not give its name. What shall we infer from this? Some infer that it must have been one of the minor feasts, for had it been one of the chief feasts it would have been named. But as he specifies (x. 22) one of the minor feasts, there seems no sufficient reason why he should not specify this, had it been such. All that we can say is, that there was no such connection between this feast and what Jesus said or did while attending it that it was necessary to specify it. The healing of the impotent man, and the events that followed, might have taken place at any feast.

The silence, then, of John determines nothing respecting the nature of this feast. We cannot infer because he has mentioned three Passovers beside, that this was a fourth; nor, on the other hand, that he would so specify it had it been a Passover.

Let us now pass in review the various feasts, and consider what may be said in favor of each. We have seen that in December the Lord left Judea for Galilee. The first feast was that of Dedication, which was observed in Kislev, or about the middle of December. It is generally agreed that this feast cannot be meant. The next in order was Purim, which fell in March. That this feast was the one in question was first suggested by Kepler, but has since found many eminent supporters.[1] But before we con-

[1] See Meyer in loco.

sider the arguments in its favor, let us examine its origin and history. Purim was not a Mosaic feast, or of divine appointment, but one established by the Jews whilst in captivity, in commemoration of their deliverance from the murderous plans of Haman, (Esther iii. 7; ix. 24.) It is derived from "pur," the Persian word for lot. Haman sought to find an auspicious day for the execution of his design by casting lots. The lot fell on the 14th Adar. Failing in his purpose, this day was kept thereafter by the Jews as a festival. It seems, however, to have been first observed by the Jews out of Palestine, and eighty-five elders made exceptions against it as an innovation against the Law.[1] It is mentioned in Maccabees (2 Mac. xv. 36) as Mordecai's day. It is also mentioned by Josephus,[2] who says "that even now all the Jews that are in the habitable earth keep these days festival." It is often alluded to in the Talmud.[3]

Such was the origin of the feast. It was commemorated by the reading of Esther in the synagogues, and by general festivity, with plays and masquerades. Maimonides says it was forbidden to fast or weep on this day. It was rather a national and political, than religious solemnity,[4] and as no special services were appointed for its observance at the temple, there was no necessity of going up to Jerusalem, nor does it appear that this was their custom. Each Jew observed it as a day of patriotic rejoicing and festivity, wherever he chanced to be.[5] Lightfoot (on Mark i. 38) remarks that if the feast did not come on a

[1] Lightfoot on John x. 22.
[2] Antiq., 11. 6. 13.
[3] Winer, ii. 289.
[4] Ewald, iv. 261.
[5] Of the mode of its observance in this country at the present time, a recent New York journal gives the following account: "The day is devoted to mirth and merry-making. In the evening and morning the synagogues are lighted up; and the reader chants the book of Esther. It is a custom among the Jews on this occasion to visit each other's house in masked attire, and exchange joyful greetings."

synagogue day, those living in a village where was no synagogue, need not go to some other village to read the book of Esther, but could wait till a synagogue day.[1]

From this brief survey of the history, and the manner of observance of this feast, it is highly improbable that it is the feast meant by John. It was not one of their divinely appointed feasts, nor was there any legal obligation to keep it. It was not a feast specifically religious, but patriotic; a day, making due allowance for difference in customs and institutions, not unlike the day that commemorates our own national independence. There were no special rites that made it necessary to go up to Jerusalem, and even those residing in villages where was no synagogue were not obliged to go to a village where one was to be found. Why then should Jesus go up from Galilee to be present at this feast? It was not a time in which men's minds were prepared to hear spiritual instruction, nor could He sympathize with the rude and boisterous, not to say disorderly and drunken manner in which the day was kept. Stier, (v. 75,) who defends Purim, admits "the revengeful and extravagant spirit which animated it," and "the debauched manner in which these days of excess were spent." Yet he thinks motives of compassion disposed the Lord to visit once "this melancholy caricature of a holy festivity." But we can see no sufficient motive for such a journey. The tenor of the narrative naturally leads us to think of one of the greater and generally attended festivals. If it be said of a Jew that he went up to Jerusalem to a feast, the obvious understanding would be that it was a feast that he was legally bound to attend, and which could be rightly kept only at Jerusalem.

The chief argument in favor of Purim is that it is brought by John into such close connection with the Pass-

[1] See generally Hengstenberg, Christ, iii. 240 Hug, Int., 449; Wieseler, 222; Brown, Jew. Antiq., i. 574.

over, (vi. 4,) and that if it be not Purim, then a year and a half, at least, must have elapsed ere Jesus visited Jerusalem again, the next recorded visit being that to Tabernacles, (John vii. 2.) It certainly, at first sight, seems improbable that a year should intervene between v. 1 and vi. 4, as would be the case if the former were a Passover. But this is not the only instance in which John narrates events widely separated in time, without noting the interval. Thus, ch. vi. relates what took place before a Passover, and ch. vii. what took place at the feast of Tabernacles, six months later. In like manner, in x. 22, is a sudden transition from this feast of Tabernacles to that of Dedication. Why the intervening events are not mentioned finds explanation in the peculiar character of this gospel. That Jesus should have absented Himself for so long a time from the feasts, is explained by the hostility of the Jews, and their purpose to slay Him, (John v. 16–18; vii. 1.)

On the other hand, if this feast be Purim, and the Passover, vi. 4, the first Passover after, or the second of the Lord's ministry, then the interval between them, about three weeks, is not sufficient for all the events that must have taken place. And still less is the interval between December, when most of the advocates of Purim suppose the Lord's Galilean work to have begun, and the following Passover (vi. 4) sufficient to include all that the Evangelists relate. The feeding of the five thousand, as is generally agreed, and as will be hereafter shown, marks the culmination of His work in Galilee; yet this took place, according to this view, in three or four months after His work began, for it was a little before the Passover, (vi. 4.) And into this short space are crowded two-thirds, at least, of all that He did in Galilee, so far as recorded. This would be very improbable, even if, as is supposed, His labors there extended only through a year. In the highest degree improbable is the view of Wieseler, followed by Ellicott, that for all this, the little interval between Purim and Passover was sufficient.[1]

Upon these grounds we think the feast of Purim is to be rejected. It was a feast which it is not at all probable Jesus would go up to Jerusalem to attend, and whose introduction here brings chronological confusion into the gospel history.

The next feast in order is that of the Passover. In favor of this feast it may be said, that it was one which Jesus would naturally attend, as having for Him a special significance. It was also the feast that had the most distinctly religious character, and it was very generally attended by the people, especially the most serious and devout. According to Hengstenberg, "it was the only one at which it was a universal custom to make a pilgrimage to Jerusalem."[2] We may thus infer that He would certainly go, unless prevented by the open hostility of the Jews. But no such hostility appears. It was aroused by the healing of the impotent man (John v. 16–18) into activity, but till this event He was unmolested.

But the objection is taken that if this be a Passover, and another is mentioned, (vi. 4,) which apparently He did not attend, then He was not present at any feast till the feast of Tabernacles, (vii. 2,) a period of a year and a half.[3] This objection has been already alluded to. Whether the Lord did actually go up to any feast between that of v. 1 and that of vii. 2, cannot be determined.[4] We know, at least, that He would not, after the rulers at Jerusalem had sought to slay Him, needlessly expose His life to peril. To the laws of God respecting the feasts He would render all obedience, but with the liberty of a son, not with the ser-

[1] See Lichtenstein, 174; Riggenbach, 406.

[2] See Luke ii. 41, where this feast is specially mentioned.

[3] Hug, Int., 448.

[4] Jarvis, Int., 570–576, makes Him to have attended them all, even that of Dedication. This is in the highest degree improbable.

vile scrupulosity of a Pharisee. As He was Lord of the Sabbath, so He was Lord of the Feasts, and He attended them, or did not attend them, as seemed best to Him. From John, (vii. 21 and 23,) where He refers to a work which He had previously done at Jerusalem, and which we must identify with the healing of the impotent man, (John v. 5,) it appears obvious that He had not, during the interval, been publicly teaching there, and therefore had not attended any feast. Still the point is not certain, as He might have been present as a private worshipper, and without attracting public attention; yet this is improbable.[1]

Another objection to identifying this feast with the Passover is that John relates nothing as having occurred between v. 1 and vi. 4, an interval of a year. This objection has already been sufficiently noticed.

Pentecost is the feast next in order, and occurred this year on the 19th May. This feast is not mentioned by any of the Evangelists. Though it has had some able advocates, as Calvin, Bengel, and lately Townsend, and was adopted by many of the ancients, it has no special arguments in its favor. It was not so generally attended as Passover or Tabernacles, and no reason appears why Jesus should have omitted Passover and gone up to Pentecost.

The feast of Tabernacles followed upon the 23d of September. The chief argument in its favor is that it brings the feast of v. 1 into close connection with that of vii. 2, only a year intervening, and thus best explains his words, vii. 21–23.[2] But some months more or less are not, under the circumstances, important, for the miracle with its results must have been fresh in their minds even after a much longer interval. If He had not in the interval between these

[1] See Greswell, ii. 247, who maintains that the five instances recorded by John "embrace all the instances of our Saviour's attendance in Jerusalem at any of the feasts."

[2] So Riggenbach, 408.

feasts been at Jerusalem, as is most probable, His reappearance would naturally carry their minds back to the time when they last saw Him, and recall both His work and their own machinations against Him. Lichtenstein (175) defends this feast, but it is in connection with the view which we cannot adopt, that our Lord spent the summer of 780 in retirement.

The great objection to identifying the feast before us with that of Tabernacles, is that it puts between the end of chap. iv. and the beginning of chap. v. a period of eight or nine months, which the Evangelists pass over in silence.[1]

Comparing these various feasts together, that of the Passover seems to have most in its favor, and that of Purim least. Some incidental points bearing upon this question will be discussed as we proceed. We give the following order as the result of our inquiries: Jesus ceases baptizing and leaves Judea in December, 780. His disciples depart to their homes, and He lives in retirement till March, 781, when He goes up to this feast, the Passover. At this time, on His way or after His arrival, He hears of the imprisonment of John, and returns to Galilee to begin His work there.

The name of the pool, Bethesda, *locus benignitatis*, "house of mercy," indicates that it was a place of resort for the sick, and that its waters had, naturally or supernaturally, healing virtue.[2] Its position is mentioned as being near the sheep gate, for so επι τη προβατικη is generally understood. About the pool were five porches or arches, where the sick might be sheltered.

A pool has long been shown at Jerusalem as the pool of Bethesda. It lies near St. Stephen's gate, along the

[1] Ebrard avoids this objection, but falls into another as great by supposing nothing recorded between the two feasts, (John v. 1, and vii. 2), but the sending of the twelve and the feeding of the five thousand.

[2] As to other etymologies, see Herzog, Encyc. ii. 118; Riggenbach 406, note.

north wall of the Temple, and is 360 feet long, 130 broad, and 75 deep.[1] There are still to be seen at the southwest corner two arched vaults, one of which Dr. Robinson measured 100 feet westward. He infers that this excavation is part of the deep trench that once separated the temple enclosure from the adjoining hill,[2] and that it extended to the northwest corner of Antonia. It was afterward used as a reservoir, its walls within being cased over with small stones, and these covered with plaster, but bearing no special marks of antiquity.[3] Ferguson, however,[4] affirms that from "the curiously elaborate character of its hydraulic masonry it must always have been intended as a reservoir of water, and never could have been the ditch of a fortification."[5] The traditional site is defended by Williams, and approved by Ellicott. According to Wilson, it was both the "fosse" and the "pool." De Saulcy, (ii. 285,) following Jerome and some of the early travellers, maintains that the language of the Evangelist should be understood, "Now there is in Jerusalem by the Probatica (pool) a pool called Bethesda," &c. Thus there were two pools, *piscinæ gemillares*, "twin fish pools," one called Probatica and one Bethesda, of which the latter is the same as that now known by this name, and the two were connected together by the arches still to be seen. Stewart, (278) also, supposes that two separate pools lay along the northern wall of the Temple enclosure, the sheep gate being between them, one of which was the Struthius of Josephus, the other the pool of Bethesda. Robinson (i. 342; iii. 249) would identify the pool of Bethesda with the present fountain of the Virgin. The waters of this fountain flow irregularly or intermittently, and thus "the moving of the water," v. 3, may be

1 Robinson, i. 293.

2 Josephus, War, 5. 4. 2.

3 With Robinson, Porter, i. 115, and Barclay, 324, agree.

4 Smith's Bib. Dict., i. 1028.

5 See also Idem, art. Bethesda, 200; Stewart, Tent and Khan, 277.

accounted for. The fountain is thus described by Porter (i. 139): "The water springs up at the bottom of an artificial cave some 25 feet deep, excavated in the rock of Ophel. Descending by a flight of 16 steps, we reach a chamber 18 feet long by 10 wide and 10 high. Thence going down 14 steps more into a roughly hewn grotto, we reach the water." Barclay says (516) "the stream ebbs and flows quite irregularly, but generally three or four times a day in Autumn, and oftener in Spring, running from two to four hours in the twenty-four, and appearing perfectly quiescent during the remainder of the day, although a little water always runs." It is plain that this fountain, a deep excavation in the rock, difficult of access, and without any space in its narrow chamber for the five porches, cannot have been the place where "lay a great multitude of impotent folk." Barclay also objects that there is no proof that it was intermittent in the time of the Lord, and derives an argument from the silence of Josephus, and of the Roman writers. The narrative seems plainly to imply supernatural agency.[1] Lightfoot makes the pool of Bethesda to be that of Siloam. To the waters of Siloam he ascribes supernatural virtues. In regard to Bethesda he says (v. 238): "The general silence of the Jews about the wondrous virtue of this pool is something strange, who, in the abundant praises and privileges and particulars of Jerusalem which they give, yet speak not one syllable, that I have ever found, toward the story of Bethesda." Barclay (326) finds another site for this pool on the lower side of the sheep quarter, to the east of the Temple. By some it has been held to be a tank just north of St. Stephen's gate.

[1] It should, however, be remembered, that verse 4, "For an angel went down at a certain season into the pool," &c., is of doubtful genuineness. It is rejected by Tischendorf, Meyer, and Alford, but defended by De Wette and Stier. See Alford in loco; Trench, Mir. 203.

As the healing of the impotent man took place on the Sabbath, it gave the Jews the desired opportunity of accusing Him of a breach of the law; and it seems indeed as if the Lord desired to judge their whole system of legal righteousness, by an emphatic condemnation of the interpretation they gave to one of the most important of the commandments. Lightfoot (*in loco*) observes: "It is worthy our observation that our Saviour did not think it enough merely to heal the impotent man on the Sabbath day, which was against their rules, but farther commanded him to take up his bed, which was much more against that rule." A rigid observance of the Sabbath, even to the prohibition of the healing of the sick on that day, (Luke xiii. 14,) was a main element of Pharisaic righteousness, and therefore on this point He took issue with them. According to the order we follow, it was the first time that He had healed on the Sabbath, and the question how such a work should be regarded, whether as lawful or unlawful, came before the ecclesiastical authorities at Jerusalem for their decision. That they decided it to be unlawful, appears from the angry opposition which subsequent cases of healing on that day called forth.

With this miracle, the healing of the impotent man, the Lord's Judean work, or the first stage of His ministry, came to its close. It brought out the enmity of the Jews at Jerusalem into full manifestation, and showed how unprepared were the rulers, the priests and scribes, and elders, to receive Him. In vain John bore witness to Him, in vain He Himself taught and wrought miracles. They had neither eyes to see, nor ears to hear. It is apparent that from the very first they had regarded Him with great suspicion, arising from His peculiar relations to John the Baptist, whom they disliked and rejected. His assumption of authority at the purification of the temple, and the sharp reproof which that act implied, of their own criminal remissness, must have been in the highest degree offensive to them; nor did any miracle that He subsequently wrought remove their dislike, or convince them of His divine commission. Although they took no active measures to stay Him in the work of baptizing, yet it is evident that they were annoyed and angry at the numbers that flocked to His baptism. But there was yet no sufficient ground for open opposition, and they seemed to have gained a victory, in that He had given up His work of baptizing and retired into Galilee. But now that He comes to Jerusalem, and violates the Sabbath by working in public a miracle on that day, the way is open to proceed against Him as a breaker of the law. There can be little doubt that He was now brought before the Sanhedrim, and that the discourse given (John v. 17–47) was spoken before that tribunal. This appears from His allusion to the deputation from Jerusalem to the Baptist, (verse 33,) "Ye sent unto John, and he bare witness unto the truth;" a deputation sent by those He was then addressing.[1] Whether any judicial action was now taken, does not appear, but the Evangelist a little later explains the fact of His ministry in Galilee, by saying that He could not walk in Judea, "because the Jews sought to kill Him," (vii. 1.) From this we may infer that it was formally determined upon to seize Him and put Him to death if found in Judea.[2] From this province He was thus, by the act of the ecclesiastical rulers, excluded.

The ground of defence in the Lord's discourse before the Sanhedrim, based upon His divine Sonship and His equality with God, only the more inflamed the anger of His enemies. Not only did He claim to be the Messiah, but more; He made Himself equal with God. Regarded as the last appeal to them to receive Him, the closing words of His Judean ministry, this discourse has a special signif-

[1] So Meyer, Lange, Tholuck.

[2] Compare John vii. 25–32.

icance. It states first the relation between the Father and the Son, and the threefold evidence by which His own mission was confirmed. The Baptist bare witness; His own works, wrought in the power of the Father, bare witness; and finally, the Scriptures bare witness.[1] But even this "threefold cord" did not bind them, and nothing now remained but to turn away from a people that received Him not, (verse 43,) and enter upon a new stage of His work in despised Galilee. It is well said by Ellicott, (141,) "This is the turning point in the Gospel history. Up to this time the preaching of our Lord at Jerusalem and in Judea had met with a certain degree of toleration, and in many cases even of acceptance; but after this all becomes changed. Henceforth the City of David is no meet or safe abode for the son of David; the earthly house of His Heavenly Father is no longer a secure hall of audience for the preaching of the Eternal Son."

As Jesus now left Judea and only returned to it after a considerable interval, and then only for very brief periods at the feasts, His enemies in that province had little opportunity to arrest Him. We know, however, that in point of fact they attempted to do so at the very first feast He attended, (John vii. 32.) So long as He was in Galilee, all they could do was to watch His proceedings there, and seize upon every occasion that presented itself to destroy His reputation, and hinder His work. How zealously they labored to this end will appear as our history proceeds.

[1] See "The Messiah," 153.

PART III

FROM THE IMPRISONMENT TO THE DEATH OF JOHN THE BAPTIST; OR, FROM APRIL, 781, TO MARCH, 782. A. D. 28, 29.

Upon the Lord's Ministry in Galilee to the Death of the Baptist.

Of the general character of the Lord's work in Galilee, as distinguished from His work in Judea, we have already spoken, when considering the divisions of His ministry. It is in the light of this distinction that certain remarkable, and to some perplexing, features of the synoptical Gospels find their explanation. As is patent upon their narratives, they relate nothing that the Lord did prior to John the Baptist's imprisonment. Only from the Evangelist John do we learn that His field of labor, till the Baptist was imprisoned, was Judea. Here His time was spent from the Passover of 780 till the December following, and if He resided in Galilee a few weeks till the feast, (John v. 1,) as He seems to have done, this was in consequence of the enmity of the Jews, and the time was apparently spent in seclusion. So far as the narratives of Matthew, Mark, and Luke go, the beginning of His public labors is to be dated from the time when, the Baptist being cast into prison, He went from Judea into Galilee. They all assume that He was in Judea up to this time, this being the province to which His early labors were confined. The reasons why they pass over in silence this first year of His ministry, and why they bring His work in Galilee into such close connection with the Baptist, we now proceed to consider.

The silence of the Synoptists respecting the Judean work of the Lord, will not appear strange if we recall the purpose and result of that work. As we have seen, John, after the baptism of Jesus, was visited by a deputation of priests and Levites from Jerusalem, to whom he bore formal witness that the Messiah had come, (John i. 19–28.) Perhaps, also, he pointed out Jesus to them in person. It was now a question distinctly before the ecclesiastical rulers, Would they receive Jesus thus pointed out to them as the Christ, or reject Him? As they took no steps to seek Him, thus showing their disregard of the Baptist's testimony, He Himself will bring the matter to an open and speedy test. At the first feast after this testimony, He appears in the temple, and there assumes authority as the Son of God, to purge it. He also works miracles, and many believed in Him as one sent from God. Still the ecclesiastical rulers did not receive Him. He therefore begins to baptize; but they did not come to His baptism; and the gathering to Him of the people only augments their hostility, and they seek to cast impediments in His way by sowing dissensions between His disciples and those of John. As they will not come to receive baptism, no further step could be taken in the regular development of His Messianic work. He therefore ceases to baptize, and retires from Judea. Still the time is not yet come for Him to begin His work in Galilee, for the Baptist is at liberty, and through his witness and labors the rulers may yet be brought to repentance, and the nation be saved. He will wait till His forerunner has finished his work in Judea, ere He commences His work in Galilee. But John's ministry comes to a sudden and untimely end, (Mark ix. 13.) He is shut up in prison, and can bear no further witness. Once more the Lord presents Himself in Jerusalem, and works a miracle, but is called a blasphemer, and His life endangered. There is now no place for Him in Judea. All the labors of the Baptist, and His own labors had been unavailing to turn the hearts of those in authority, and ensure His reception as the Messiah. By their own unbelief, those who sat in Moses' seat, the priests and Levites, made it impossible that He could use them in His service, and continuing to reject Him, they themselves must be rejected. The Mosaic institutions must be set aside, and their priesthood cease.

It is here that we find the essential distinction between the Lord's work in Judea and that in Galilee. The former had reference to the Jewish people in their corporate capacity, a nation in covenant with God; and aimed to produce in them that sense of sin, and that true repentance, which were indispensable to His reception. The latter was based upon the fact that the ecclesiastical rulers of the Jews would not receive Him, and had sought to kill Him, and that therefore, if they persisted in their wickedness, God was about to cast them out of their peculiar relations to Him, and establish a church, of which the elect of all nations should be members, (Matt. viii. 11, 12.) Going into Galilee, the Lord will gather there a body of disciples, who shall bear witness to Him before the nation, but who, if this testimony is unavailing, shall serve as the foundations of the new institutions resting upon the New Covenant. Thus the departure from Judea into Galilee does not imply that the Lord regarded this rejection of Himself by the Jews as final, and that nothing remained but to lay new foundations and choose a new priesthood. He will leave Judea, but after a time He will return. His work in Galilee still has reference to national salvation, through the faith of those who should believe on Him there. If, however, the nation will not hear them, then from among them He will select those who shall take the place of the priesthood of the Aaronic line, and be builders and rulers under Him, the Stone which the builders had refused, but now become the Head of the corner.

Thus, it will not appear strange that the Synoptists, writing after all these events had developed themselves, should pass over in silence the Lord's Judean work. Regarded in its relations to the Christian Church, its mention was comparatively unimportant; and they could well commence their narratives with that work in Galilee, which, looking forward to the future, was already developing itself so widely and powerfully.[1] It was comparatively of little moment that their readers should know, in detail, that the Lord first began His labors in Judea, and that, after a few months, He was compelled to abandon them, through the enmity of the rulers; since all knew that He was finally rejected by them, and suffered death at their hands. But the Galilean work was of the highest moment, as it marked where the dividing line began between the old and the new, between Moses and Christ. And this may also explain their silence in respect to the feasts which the Lord attended while in Galilee. Any transient work at Jerusalem,

[1] Some find difficulty in reconciling the Synoptists with John, because the former say that Jesus went to Capernaum to begin His ministry after the imprisonment of the Baptist, while John relates two visits to Capernaum and Galilee before this imprisonment. (John ii. 12; iv. 46.) But these visits they might well pass over in silence, as not at all affecting the general fact that the field of labor during the first part of His ministry was Judea, and not Galilee. The first of these visits to Galilee was before the first Passover, and of short duration; the second was after the work in Judea had been interrupted, and was also brief, and neither of them was marked by public labors. He began to preach in Galilee only when He had ended for the time His work in Judea, and this was after the imprisonment of the Baptist and the attempt of the Jews on His own life. (John v. 18.)

addressing itself especially to the hierarchy, had no important bearing upon the great result.

On the other hand, the mention of the Lord's ministry in Judea by John, and his silence respecting much that was done in Galilee, follow from the special purpose of his Gospel, which is to show that Jesus is the Christ, the Son of God, (xx. 31;) and, as incidental, how faith on the one side and unbelief on the other were developed among those who, from time to time, were brought into contact with Him. He draws no sharp line of distinction between what Jesus did in Judea and in Galilee, nor makes any particular mention of John's imprisonment. He selects from the many acts of His life such as will best answer his purpose, wherever they took place, and the events seem, for the most part, to be narrated that he may give the discourses that stand in connection with them.[1] It is thus incidentally and not formally, that he mentions what was done in Judea, and it is only by a careful comparison of his narrative with those of the Synoptists, that we reach our general result.

It is to be remembered that Galilee had been spoken of several centuries before the Saviour's birth, by the prophet Isaiah, (ix. 1, 2,) as that part of the Holy Land to be especially blessed by His labors. It had been the part least esteemed, not only because in the division of the kingdom it was joined to Israel in opposition to Judah, but as also especially exposed to foreign invasion, and which had in fact been repeatedly conquered. Here was the greatest admixture of foreign elements, the natural result of these conquests, and hence the name, "Galilee of the Gentiles." The prophet mentions the two tribes of Zebulon and Napthali as peculiarly despised; and within the

[1] Compare the visit of Nicodemus, the incident at Jacob's well, the visit to the feast, (v. 1,) the feeding of the five thousand, the visit at the Feast of Dedication, and many others.

bounds of the first was Nazareth, and within the bounds of the second was Capernaum. How wonderfully this prophecy, so dark in its literal interpretation, was fulfilled, the history of the Lord's ministry shows. His own in Judea and Jerusalem would not walk in His light, and thus it was that, in "Galilee of the Gentiles, the people which sat in darkness saw great light."

To this prediction of Isaiah, the Evangelist Matthew, according to his custom, calls the attention of his readers, and affirms that in Galilee, thus prophetically marked out, the preaching of the Lord actually began, (iv. 17.) "From that time," that is, from the imprisonment of John, and the departure into Galilee, that immediately followed it, "Jesus began to preach," &c. "His earlier appearance in Judea, though full of striking incidents and proofs of His divine legation, was preliminary to His ministry or preaching, properly so called, which now began."[1] Luke seems plainly to intimate that the first teaching of the Lord in the synagogues was that which he records at Nazareth. That His enemies at Jerusalem regarded His labors as first taking positive form and character in Galilee, appears from their accusation, (Luke xxiii. 5,) "He stirreth up the people, teaching throughout all Jewry, beginning from Galilee to this place." (See also the words of Peter, Acts x. 37, "That word which was published throughout all Judea, and began from Galilee.") And as God had ordered that Galilee should be the chief theatre of His teaching, so He providentially overruled the political arrangements of the time, that there He could labor without hindrance, since the tetrarch Herod Antipas did not trouble himself concerning any ecclesiastical movements that did not disturb the public peace. And here, also, the people were less under the influence of the hierarchy, and more open to His words.

[1] Alexander in loco; so Greswell, ii. 274; Stier on Luke iv. 18.

Thus the silence of the Synoptists, respecting the work of Jesus in Judea, is satisfactorily explained; and we also see why the imprisonment of the Baptist is made so prominent in their narratives. It marks the time when He left Judea for Galilee, and is thus a great turning point in His ministry. So long as John was free to prosecute his work of calling the nation to repentance, He could take no steps looking forward to the establishment of new institutions. He could not begin to preach or teach in Galilee. But John in prison could no more prepare His way, could no more testify of Him to the nation, or administer the baptism of repentance. The voice of the forerunner thus silenced, Jesus, departing to Galilee, can there begin Himself to preach, and to gather disciples, and prepare them for their future work.

As the primary object of the ministry in Galilee was to gather disciples, the Lord directs His teachings and works to that end. Hence His visits to all parts of the land, His use of the synagogues for preaching, His teachings in the streets, in the fields, upon the sea-shore, wherever the people gather to Him. He speaks to all, that whosoever has ears to hear may hear. Hence, also, His readiness to heal all who may come unto Him, that the faith which the word could not draw forth might be drawn forth by the work. Thus by degrees He gathered around Him the most spiritually minded and receptive of the Galileans, and of the adjacent regions. From these He chooses a small body whom He keeps near Himself, and to whom He explains what is obscure in His public discourses, as they are able to hear; and these, after He had instructed them, He sends forth to be witnesses to the people at large.

This work of Jesus in Galilee, gathering and educating His disciples, continued from the Passover of 781 till the Feast of Tabernacles in 782, or a period of about one year and six months. The death of the Baptist, which we place in the spring of 782, had an important bearing upon His labors, and divides this Galilean ministry into two parts, which are easily distinguishable from each other. The grounds of this distinction will be noted hereafter. Our present period ends with the Baptist's death. The important events that mark its progress will be noticed as we proceed.

April, 781. A. D. 28.

Hearing whilst in Jerusalem of the imprisonment of	Matt. iv. 12.
John the Baptist, the Lord leaves Judea and goes into	Mark i. 14, 15.
Galilee to begin His ministry there. In His progress He	Luke iv. 14, 15.
comes to Nazareth and teaches in its synagogue. His	Luke iv. 16–32.
words enraging the people, and His life being in danger,	
He leaves Nazareth, and going to Capernaum there takes	Matt. iv. 12–17.
up his abode.	

An important and difficult point here meets us: When was John imprisoned?

We first inquire what data we have bearing upon it, other than the statements of the Evangelists. In Josephus [1] we find mention made of the imprisonment of John by Herod the Tetrarch, at the castle of Machærus, where he was subsequently put to death. This imprisonment and death of the Baptist Josephus connects with the defeat of Herod in battle by Aretas, king of Arabia; the defeat being regarded by many of the Jews as a just punishment sent by God upon Herod for this act of injustice and cruelty. He does not mention that John reproved Herod for his marriage of Herodias, and seems to place the arrest solely on political grounds.

It appears, from these statements of Josephus respecting the origin and history of the war, that the death of

[1] Antiq., 18. 5. 1.

John was before the defeat of Herod by Aretas, and that this defeat was before the death of Tiberius. This emperor died in March, 790. It was also probably before the death of Philip the Tetrarch.[1] Thus we reach only the indefinite result, that John was beheaded before, or in 787. And we have no data in Josephus to come to any more exact conclusion. Some have sought to obtain a more definite result by determining the time when Herod made that journey to Rome in which he met Herodias, but without success.

If, then, only the general conclusion can be drawn from the statements of Josephus, that John was put to death before 787, let us turn to the Evangelists. We learn from John, (iii. 23, 24,) that while Jesus was baptizing in Judea, John was baptizing at Ænon. This was during the summer of 780. Jesus discontinued His baptismal work, probably in December of that year, and retired into Galilee. We have already seen that John continued to prosecute his work later. In John (iv. 1) there is no assertion that the Baptist's work had ended, but rather a plain intimation that it was still in progress, for there is a comparison between them, and the result is that Jesus is baptizing more than John.[2] We may then conclude that John was still at liberty, and engaged in his work about the beginning of December, 780.

The grounds upon which the many harmonists and commentators, who make the cessation of the Lord's baptismal work contemporaneous with John's imprisonment, reach this conclusion, are various and by no means concordant. But most agree that the Lord was afraid of a like imprisonment. Thus Lightfoot, on John iv. 4, says: "Herod had imprisoned John Baptist under pretence of his growing too popular. Our Saviour, understanding this,

[1] See Greswell, iii. 414. [2] Wieseler, 224.

and that the Sanhedrim had heard of the increase of His disciples, withdrew too from Judea into Galilee, that He might be more remote from that kind of thunderbolt St. John had been struck with." But the arrest of John was not because of his baptism, but because of his reproof of Herod, and there is no reason to believe that the Pharisees had any thing to do with it. That Jesus did not fear any arrest from Herod, is apparent from the fact that He now leaves a province under Roman rule to go into one ruled over by Herod himself, and moreover, takes up His abode in the near vicinity of his capital. Nor, as has been already shown, was He in any bodily danger from the Pharisees. So long as Jesus simply permitted his disciples to baptize He was guilty of no crime, although the validity and value of His baptism might be denied.

Greswell, (ii. 212,) who admits that the words of the Evangelist imply, that when Jesus set out on His return to Galilee, John was not yet cast into prison, (John iv. 1,) supposes that before He reached there he was imprisoned. This, however, contradicts the Synoptists, who say that Jesus was in Judea when He heard of John's imprisonment, and that this was the cause of his departure into Galilee, (Matt. iv. 12.)

If we compare the account of what followed the return of Jesus to Galilee, as given by John (iv. 43–54) with that given by the Synoptists, we find full proof that they refer to different periods. According to the former, Jesus went to Galilee, not to begin public labors, but to find retirement. The prophet, as a rule, having no honor in his own country, He might well hope to pass the time there in seclusion, without attracting public attention, till the issue of John's ministry was determined. He did not indeed find the privacy which He sought, because the Galileans had been eye-witnesses of what He had done at Jerusalem, and were favorably inclined toward Him. Very soon after His return the nobleman from Capernaum sought His aid; but aside from this, there is no indication that He performed any miracles or engaged in any teaching. No disciples are spoken of as with Him, nor any crowds of people. Nor when He goes up to the feast (v. 1) does He appear to have been attended by any disciples. On the other hand, according to the Synoptists, (Matt. iv. 12–25; Mark, i. 14–21; Luke, iv. 14, 15), so soon as He heard of John's imprisonment He began His labors in Galilee, very early gathering again His disciples, and working miracles, and teaching in all the synagogues. His fame spread immediately through the whole region, and wherever He went crowds followed Him.

The manner in which John relates what the Lord did in Galilee up to the time of the feast, (v. 1,) shows that he regarded Judea as the proper field of His labors during this period, and His works in Galilee as only exceptional. Only two miracles were wrought in Galilee during this period, and both at Cana, (John ii. 1; iv. 46.) Of the first, the Evangelist says: "This beginning of miracles did Jesus in Cana of Galilee, and manifested forth His glory." Of the second: "This is again the second miracle that Jesus did, when He was come out of Judea into Galilee." Both these miracles were wrought under peculiar circumstances, and for special ends, not in the ordinary course of His ministry. Those wrought by Him in Jerusalem at the first Passover (John ii. 23, compare iii. 2) are merely alluded to, although they seem to have been of a striking character; but these are specified as wrought by Jesus coming out of Judea, the proper place of His ministry, into Galilee where His ministry had not yet begun, John being not yet imprisoned.[1]

We thus find confirmatory evidence that the Baptist was not imprisoned till after December, 780. But on the

[1] See Wieseler, 271, note 2.

other hand, this imprisonment was before the feast, (John, v. 1.) The proof of this we find in the words of the Lord spoken at this feast, (v. 35,) referring to John, "He was a burning and a shining light, and ye were willing for a season to rejoice in his light." Here John's work is spoken of as something past. "He was," and "ye were willing for a season." Alford remarks, "This 'was,' ἦν, shows, as Stier rightly observes, that John was now cast into prison, if not executed." Tholuck says, "'He was,' implies that John had already left the stage." But the feast at which these words were spoken, we have already identified as the Passover of 781. Some time, then, between December, 780, and April, 781, the Baptist was imprisoned.

But we may fix the time still more definitely. When Jesus heard of John's imprisonment He was in Judea, and there is no reason to suppose that, after He gave up baptizing and retired into Galilee, He came again into Judea till the feast, (v. 1.) It was at this time (April, 781) that He heard at Jerusalem of John's imprisonment, to which, as we just saw, He alluded in His address to the Jews. We may then place this event a little before this feast, say in March, 781.

St. John, who has been our sole informant in all relating to the work of the Lord in Judea, narrates nothing that occurred between the feast (v. 1) and the feeding of the 5,000, (vi. 1,) an interval of a year. We must therefore turn to the Synoptists, whose narrative commences at this point.

By Matthew (iv. 12) it is said that Jesus, "when He heard that John was cast into prison, departed into Galilee, and leaving Nazareth came and dwelt in Capernaum." This implies that on leaving Judea He went first to Nazareth and afterward to Capernaum. Mark (i. 14) speaks only in general terms of His coming into Galilee. Luke (iv. 14, 15) gives a brief outline of His ministry there, that He taught in their synagogues, that His fame spread abroad, and that He was glorified of all. It is not wholly clear whether this Evangelist here gives by anticipation a summary of His work and its results, or means to state that Jesus began preaching in the synagogues of Galilee previous to His arrival at Nazareth, and was everywhere favorably received. The latter is in itself not improbable, but the former is most in keeping with the narrative. Some have supposed that He went to Nazareth by way of Capernaum, and that in the latter city He wrought some miracles which are not directly mentioned, but to which He is thought to allude when He speaks at Nazareth of works which He had done at Capernaum, (Luke iv. 23.)[1]

But it is not impossible, as said by Ebrard, that He refers to the earlier healing of the nobleman's son, who was sick at Capernaum, though Jesus Himself was at Cana. This is confirmed by the manner in which the teaching of the Lord in the synagogue at Capernaum and His miracles are spoken of, (Mark i. 21–34 ; Luke iv. 31–42,) as if He then for the first time began His labors there.

As Matthew (xiii. 53–58) and Mark (vi. 1–6) both speak of a visit of Jesus to Nazareth, but apparently at a later period, it is a question whether this visit can be identified with that mentioned by Luke, (iv. 16–30,) or whether they are to be regarded as distinct.[2] There are several points of likeness, but not more than would naturally exist in two visits made under such peculiar circumstances. In both His words excite the astonishment, not unmixed with envy, of His fellow-townsmen ; and recalling to mind His origin, and His education amongst themselves, and His family, whose members they knew, they are offended at His prophetic claims. In both He repeats the proverb, so strikingly

[1] Krafft, Alford, Riggenbach.

[2] Opinions of recent inquirers are about equally divided. In favor of their identity are Lange, Alford, Bucher, Friedlieb, Lichtenstein ; against it, Meyer, Stier, Robinson, Tischendorf, Wieseler, Krafft, Townsend, Ellicott.

applicable, that "a prophet is not without honor save in his own country;" but with this difference, that at the second visit He adds, with apparent reference to His brothers and sisters, "and among his own kin and in his own house." On the other hand, the points of difference are more numerous, and more plainly marked. In the former visit He is alone; in the latter He is accompanied by His disciples, (Mark vi. 1.) In the former He is attacked by the enraged populace, and escapes through supernatural aid the threatened death; in the latter, though He marvelled at their unbelief, He continues there for a time, and heals a few sick folk. In the former, "passing through the midst of them He went His way, and came to Capernaum, a city of Galilee;" in the latter He "went round about the villages teaching." The mention of the healing of the sick by Mark clearly shows the visits to have been distinct, for it could not have taken place before His first teaching in the synagogue on the Sabbath, and immediately afterward He was obliged to flee from their rage.

The wrath of the people, so unprovoked, and their effort to kill Him, seem sufficiently to justify the opinion of Nathanael in regard to Nazareth. From this incident it is plain that they were fierce and cruel, and ready from mere envy to imbrue their hands in the blood of one who had lived among them, a neighbor and friend, all His life. It is not improbable, however, that they may long have been conscious that, though dwelling among them, He was not of them, and thus a secret feeling of dislike and ill-will have been slumbering in their hearts. This is the only instance recorded of the Lord's reading in a synagogue, and He may have been asked so to do as having been for so many years a member of the congregation, or because of the reputation He had already acquired. Elsewhere He preached in the synagogues, permission being everywhere given Him, apparently in virtue of His prophetic claims. (Compare Acts xiii. 15.)

The city of Nazareth, being built upon the side of a steep hill, presents several precipices down which a person might be cast. That which has for many years been pointed out as the place where the attempt was made on the Lord's life, and called the Mount of Precipitation, lies some two miles from the village. It is a conspicuous object from the plain of Esdraelon, which it overlooks. Its distance from the village is a sufficient proof that it cannot have been the real scene of the event. The cliff which travellers have generally fixed upon as best answering to the narrative lies just back of the Maronite church, and is some thirty or forty feet in height.[1]

A chronological datum has been found by Bengel in the fact that the passage of Isaiah read by the Lord (Luke iv. 18, 19) was that appointed to be read on the morning of the great day of Atonement.[2] But it is by no means certain that such was the order at this time; nor does it appear whether Jesus read the passage appointed for the day, or that to which He opened intentionally or under divine direction. Some of the fathers, from v. 19, where mention is made of "the acceptable year of the Lord," inferred that His ministry continued but a single year. That no definite period of time is meant sufficiently appears, however, from the context, (Is. lxi. 2.)

Thus rejected at Nazareth, Jesus departs to Capernaum. We know not whether private and personal reasons had any influence in the selection of this city as the central point of His labors in Galilee. Some, as Lightfoot and

[1] Robinson, ii. 235; Ritter, Theil xvi. 744. Van De Velde, Journey, ii. 385, thinks that this cannot be the place, and supposes that the precipice where the Saviour's life was threatened, has crumbled away from the effect of earthquakes and other causes.

[2] See also McKnight, Har. in loco.

Ewald, have supposed that Joseph had possessions there, and that the family, the Lord's mother and brethren, were now residing there, (John ii. 12.) More probably, in the selection of Capernaum He was determined chiefly by its local position and relations. Lying upon the sea of Galilee, and the great roads from Egypt to Syria running through it, and in the direct line from Jerusalem to Damascus,[1] it gave Him such facilities of intercourse with men as He could not have had in secluded Nazareth. Not only could He readily visit all parts of Galilee, but by means of the lake He had ready access also to the region upon the other side, and to the towns both north and south in the valley of the Jordan. From it he could easily make circuits into Galilee on the west, into Trachonitis on the north, and into Decapolis and Perea on the east and south. Besides this local fitness for His work, it was also the residence of Simon and Andrew, and but a little way from Bethsaida, the city of Philip.

It does not appear from the Gospels whether the Lord had a house of His own at Capernaum, or dwelt with some relative or disciple. His own words, (Matt. viii. 20,) "the Son of Man hath not where to lay His head," seem decisive that He did not own any dwelling, but was dependent upon others even for a place where to sleep. He is spoken of as entering the house of Peter, (Matt. viii. 14,) and the form of expression, (Mark ii. 1,) "it was noised abroad that He had come home," (compare iii. 19,) implies that He had a fixed place of abode. Norton, in common with many, supposes that He resided in the house of Peter; Alexander (on Mark i. 29) suggests that Peter may "have opened a house for the convenience of his Lord and master in the intervals of His itinerant labors." If, however, His mother was now living at Capernaum, which is by no means certain, He

[1] Robinson, ii. 405; Ritter, Theil xv. 271.

would naturally take up His abode with her. "The change of abode," says Alford, " seems to have included the whole family, except the sisters, who may have been married at Nazareth." Greswell asserts that the incident respecting the tribute money (Matt. xvii. 24) proves indisputably that He was a legal inhabitant of Capernaum.

The sea of Galilee is formed by the waters of the Jordan, which enter at the northern, and flow out at the southern extremity. *Its shape is that of an irregular oval*, somewhat broadest at the upper part, and is about fourteen miles in length, and six or seven in width. The water is clear and sweet, and used for drinking by the inhabitants along its shores, many of whom ascribe to it medicinal qualities. It is 650 feet lower than the Mediterranean, and probably may fill the crater of an extinct volcano. The west shores of the lake are more precipitous than those of the east. Being surrounded with hills, those on the east nearly 2,000 feet high, which are seamed with deep ravines down which the winds sweep with great violence, it is very much exposed to sudden and furious storms.[1]

Nearly midway on the western side of the lake is " the land of Gennesaret," (Matt. xiv. 34; Mark vi. 53.) It is made by a recession of the hills from the shore, and forms a segment of a circle, being about four miles long and three broad. It begins on the south, just above the village of Mejdel, or Magdala, and extends northward to the point where the promontory of Khan Minyeh stretches down to the water. It is well watered, though better in the southern than in the northern part, several fountains arising in it, large and copious, and several streams from the hills westward pouring their waters through it to the lake in the rainy season.[2]

In or near the land of Gennesaret was the city of Ca-

[1] See Stanley, 361; Robinson, ii. 416; Porter, ii. 418.
[2] See Josephus, War, 3. 10. 8; and Robinson, ii. 402.

pernaum. The interest which all feel in a place which was so long the Lord's residence, and the central point of His labors, leads us to inquire with some minuteness respecting its site. This has long been the subject of dispute. Neither the statements of the Evangelists, nor of Josephus, nor of the fathers, are so definite that we can determine the exact spot; and modern travellers who have carefully examined all probable sites along the lake, are by no means agreed in their conclusions. All, therefore, that we can now do is to give a summary of the question as it stands in the light of the most recent investigation. As Bethsaida and Chorazin were adjacent cities, joined with Capernaum in the same high privileges and falling under the same condemnation, (Matt. xi. 20; Luke x. 13,) and their sites are also subjects of dispute, we shall embrace them in this geographical inquiry.

It is known from the Gospels, (Matt. iv. 13, ix. 1, xiii. 1; Mark ii. 13; John vi. 17,) that Capernaum was seated upon the sea-shore, and it appears from a comparison of John vi. 17 with Matt. xiv. 34, and Mark vi. 53, that it was either in or near "the land of Gennesaret." More distinct information is given us by Josephus,[1] who, speaking of the plain of Gennesaret, says: "It is irrigated by a highly fertilizing spring, called Caphernaum by the people of the country. This some have thought a vein of the Nile, from its producing a fish similar to the coracin of the lake of Alexandria." If, then, Capernaum lay upon or near the plain, as all admit, the position of this spring must determine its position, for we cannot doubt that the fountain took its name from the city, and the two were near each other. But how shall we determine which of the several fountains watering that plain is the one in question? Let us pass them all in review, and test them by the description of Josephus.

[1] War, 3. 10. 8.

The southernmost fountain, lying near the western range of hills, and a mile and a half distant from the lake shore, is that known as the Round Fountain, from a circular inclosure of hewn stones, and is described by Robinson as "forming an oval reservoir more than fifty feet in diameter; the water is perhaps two feet deep, beautifully limpid and sweet, bubbling up and flowing out rapidly in a large stream to water the plain below. Numerous small fish are sporting in the basin." This, however, cannot be the fountain, as no ruins are to be found around it. Robinson, who made search for them, says, "there was nothing that could indicate that any town or village had ever occupied the spot." In this opinion Thomson concurs.

On the other hand, the claims of this fountain to be the fountain of Caphernaum are strenuously defended by De Saulcy, (ii. 423,) who asserts that he found distinct traces of the ruins of the city upon the adjacent hills. His facility, however, in finding ruins is so great, that his judgment here needs corroboration.[1]

Aside from the absence of all indications that a city ever stood near it, the Round Fountain would answer well to the description of Josephus. A large stream of water flows from it to irrigate the plain, and numerous fish are found in its basin, though it does not appear that they are of a species different from those found in the lake. It is not clear how the particular mentioned by Josephus respecting the fountain of Caphernaum, that it produced a fish like the coracin of the lake of Alexandria, and hence was supposed to be a vein of the Nile, is to be understood. If the fish in the lake and in the fountain were the same, it is not easy to see why the fountain should have been thought a vein of the Nile. This would then imply that there was no such connection between the fountain and the lake as to

[1] See Robinson, iii. 350.

allow the fish to pass and repass. The fish in the fountain were like those in the lake of Alexandria, and unlike those in the lake of Galilee. This circumstance points to the Round Fountain, which is too far distant to allow "fish of any size to pass between it and the lake." Robinson, however, draws directly the opposite inference, that the fish in the fountain and the lake were the same, and that the former must have been on the shore, so that the fish "could pass and repass without difficulty." As the language of Josephus is thus susceptible of such opposite interpretations, no particular stress can be laid upon this circumstance.

Dismissing, then, the claim of the Round Fountain, because of the absence of any ruins in its neighborhood, we proceed to the next fountain which presents its claim. This is called Ain et Tin, and rises near Khan Minyeh, at the point where the western hills approach the lake shore at the north-eastern extremity of the plain. Robinson thus describes it, (ii. 403,) "Between the Khan and the shore a large fountain rushes out from beneath the rocks, and forms a brook flowing into the lake a few rods distant. Near by are several other springs. Our guides said those springs were brackish, but Burckhardt describes the waters of the main source as sweet. Along the lake is a tract of luxuriant herbage occasioned by the springs." And elsewhere, "The lake, when full, as now, sets up nearly or quite to the fountain." Thompson speaks of it as "coming out close to the lake and on a level with its surface," and of its waters as not good to drink. Porter says: "From the base of the cliff, not far from the water line, springs a large fig tree, which spreads its branches over a fountain called from this circumstance Ain et Tin, 'the Fountain of the Fig.'" From these descriptions it seems plain that this cannot be the fountain spoken of by Josephus. He says, "the plain is irrigated by a highly fertilizing spring called

Caphernaum." The fact that Ain et Tin lies close to the lake, and almost upon a level with it, makes it impossible that its waters could ever have been used for purposes of irrigation. "It is very improbable," says Norton, "that Josephus would have spoken in the terms which he uses of this latter fountain, the fertilizing effects of which are so confined." That the few yards or rods lying between it and the shore should be watered and fertilized, is unimportant. Nor are there any ruins of importance near this fountain, such as would naturally mark the site of a city like Capernaum. They are thus spoken of by Robinson: "A few rods south of the khan and fountain is a low mound or swell, with ruins occupying a considerable circumference. The few remains seemed to be mostly dwellings of no very remote date, but there was not enough to make out anything with certainty." Upon his second journey the ruins appeared to him more extensive (iii. 345): "The remains are strewed around in shapeless heaps, but are much more considerable and extensive than my former impressions had led me to anticipate. Indeed, there are here remains enough not only to warrant, but to require the hypothesis of a large ancient place." Thomson (i. 545) on the contrary speaks of "the few foundations near Khan Minyeh as not adequate to answer the demands of history. No one would think of them if he had not a theory to maintain which required them to represent Capernaum." Porter (ii. 430) speaks of "many vestiges of ruins between the fountain and the shore, but it requires a careful scrutiny to find them." Bonar (437) says: "The ruins to the south of the Khan on a small rising ground are inconsiderable, so much so that we should not have noticed them had not our attention been called to them. No large town surely stood here, else it would have left some traces of itself." These differing and somewhat conflicting statements show at least that, whatever may be the cause, whether by the transportation of the stones to Tiberias or elsewhere, as said by Robinson, or as the more direct result of the doom spoken against it, almost all traces of the city, if it stood here, have disappeared.

If, then, neither the Round Fountain nor that of Ain et Tin, answers to the description of Josephus, and are the only fountains lying in the plain, we must seek it away from the plain, and yet so near it that its waters may irrigate its fields. Such a one Thomson thinks he finds about 15 minutes north of Khan Minyeh, and which is called Et-Tabiga. The grounds of his opinion will be best shown by some quotations from Robinson and Porter. In going northward along the shore from Khan Minyeh, says Robinson (iii. 345), "we struck up over the rocky and precipitous point of the hill above the fountain, toward the northeast. There is no passage along its base, which is washed by the waters of the lake. A path has been cut in ancient times along the rock, some twenty feet above the water, and we found no difficulty in passing. One feature of the excavation surprised us, namely, that for most of the way there is a channel cut in the rock, about three feet deep and as many wide, which seemed evidently to have been an aqueduct once conveying water for irrigating the northern part of the plain El-Ghuweir (Gennesaret.) There was no mistaking the nature and object of this channel; and yet no waters were near which could be thus conveyed except from the fountains of Et-Tabighah. The fountains issue from under the hill, just back of the village. We went thither, and found built up solidly around the main fountain an octagonal Roman reservoir, now in ruins. Like those at Ras-el-Ain, near Tyre, it was obviously built in order to raise the water to a certain height for an aqueduct. The head of water was sufficient to carry it to the channel around the point of the opposite hill into the plain El-Ghuweir; but whether this was done by a canal around the sides of the valley, or whether even it was done at all, there are now no further traces from which to form a judgment. The water has a saltish taste, but is not unpalatable." We add Porter's description (ii. 429): "Et-Tabighah is situated in a little nook or bay close upon the shore. The first thing that attracts attention is the abundance of water; streams, aqueducts, pools, and fountains are all around us. The large fountains burst out from the base of the hill, a few hundred yards to the north, and here, around the principal one, is an ancient octagonal reservoir, something like those at Ras-el-Ain, near Tyre, probably constructed to raise the water so that it might be carried to the plain of El-Ghuweir westward, for irrigation."

Here then at Et-Tabiga, is a fountain sufficiently copious to irrigate the plain of Gennesaret, and at no great distance. That its waters were actually used for that purpose appears from the fact that a reservoir was built to raise them to the requisite height, and that an aqueduct was cut through the rock at the north-eastern extremity of the plain to convey them there. It seems impossible to account for this reservoir and this aqueduct, except as constructed for purposes of irrigation, and Robinson speaks of the northern part of the plain lying back from the shore as "apparently fertilized by water brought by the aqueduct around the point of the northern hill."

In this point, then, Et-Tabiga answers fully to the description of Josephus, and the great abundance of water bursting out from beneath the hill would much better justify the popular fancy that it was a branch of the Nile, than the lesser fountains already mentioned.

Assuming for the present with Thomson, that at Tabiga is the fountain Capharnaum of Josephus, let us now look for the city. But in its immediate vicinity are no ruins of importance; the nearest are those of Tell Hum, lying northeasterly upon the shore. "Here," says Robinson, (ii. 246,) "are the remains of a place of considerable extent, covering a tract of at least half a mile in length along the shore, and about half that breadth inland. They consist chiefly of the fallen walls of dwellings and other buildings, all of unhewn stone, except two ruins." Thomson (i. 540) thus describes them: "The shapeless remains are piled up in utter confusion along the shore, extend up the hill northward for at least fifty rods, and are much more extensive and striking than those of any other ancient city on this part of the Lake." Keith[1] says: "They form no inconsiderable field of ruins, at least a mile and a half in circumference." Robinson does not speak of any ruins as lying between Tabiga and Tell Hum, a distance of twenty or thirty minutes, but Thomson says that "traces of old buildings extend nearly all the way along the shore." As there are no indications that a large city was ever situated directly at Tabiga, those who regard this fountain as that of Caphernaum must place the city itself at Tell Hum. Let us consider the arguments in favor of this site.

A principal argument is the similarity of name, the last syllable being the same in both. Caphernaum is Kefr Nahum, "the village of Nahum," who was some well-known person; or "the village of consolation," *vicus consolationis*.[2] Thomson asserts that it is "a very common way of curtailing old names to retain only the final syllable." The substitution of Tell, meaning hill, for Kefr, village, he explains by the fact that the village became a heap of ruins or rubbish, and to such a heap the Arabs apply the term Tell. Thus Kefr Nahum was changed into Tell Nahum, and then abbreviated into Tell Hum.[3]

Another argument in favor of Tell Hum is drawn from

1 Evidence of Prophecy, 1860, 155.
2 Herzog, Encyc., vii. 369; Winer, i. 210.
3 Winer, i. 210; Wilson, ii. 139; Ewald Christus, 257, note.

the narrative of Josephus.[1] Being bruised by a fall from his horse in a skirmish near the mouth of the Jordan, he was carried to a village named Cepharnome. Here he remained during the day, but was removed by medical direction that night to Tarichea, at the south end of the lake. From this the inference may be drawn that Capernaum was the first city of importance from the entrance of the Jordan southward, as the soldiers would not have carried a wounded man further than was necessary. Hence Capernaum was Tell Hum rather than Khan Minyeh.[2] This is not improbable, but as we know not whether special reasons may not have led Josephus to prefer Capernaum to any other city on that part of the shore, irrespective of distance, the argument is not at all decisive.[3]

In favor of Tell Hum Thomson also appeals to tradition: "So far as I can discover, after spending many weeks in this neighborhood, off and on, for a quarter of a century, the invariable tradition of the Arabs and the Jews fixes Capernaum at Tell Hum, and I believe correctly."

To this view two strong objections are made: First, that Tell Hum is too remote from the fountains at Tabiga. The exact distance is in dispute. Robinson took thirty-five minutes in passing from the latter to the former. Elsewhere he speaks of them as an hour apart; Porter as forty minutes, Thomson as thirty minutes. The distance must be a mile and a half or two miles. Robinson insists, in reply to Ritter, that the city and fountain, both bearing the same name, must be adjacent to each other. It is doubtless generally true, that the site of the fountain determines the site of the village, and both lie in close proximity; but the rule would not hold in case of those cities which were built along the lake, and thus amply supplied with water. Here the selection of a site would naturally be governed by other

[1] Life, 72. [2] So Stanley, 376, note 2; Wilson, ii. 139.
[3] Ritter, Theil xv. 340; Robinson, iii. 352; Van de Velde, Memoir, 301.

considerations. We are not then to think it impossible that a considerable distance should intervene between the city and its fountains. If the latter were within the territory of the former, and their waters used by its citizens for mills or other purposes, they would naturally be called by its name. As we have seen, the quantity of water at Et-Tabiga is very abundant. Robinson speaks (ii. 405) of "a very copious stream bursting forth from immense fountains. The stream drives one or two mills, and double the same quantity of water runs to waste. Several other mills are in ruins." It was not then merely to supply water for drinking and general domestic uses that these fountains were valuable. Thomson regards Tabiga as "the great manufacturing suburb of Capernaum," where were clustered together the mills, potteries, and tanneries, and other operations of this sort, the traces of which are still to be seen. "I even derive this name Tabiga from this business of tanning." If Tabiga were thus a suburb of Capernaum, we should naturally expect to find remains of former habitations scattered along between them. Thomson states that "traces of old buildings extend all the way along the shore from Tabiga to Tell Hum," thus connecting them together as city and suburb. Robinson, on the other hand, speaks of "other fountains and a town" as lying between. In this we have Thomson's personal assurance that he is in error.[1]

But the second and more important objection is that Capernaum, according to the Evangelists, was situated in the land of Gennesaret, and cannot, therefore, have been at Tell Hum.[2] The consideration of this point necessarily involves a consideration of the site of Bethsaida.

It is said by Luke (ix. 10) that after the return of the apostles from their mission, and the announcement of the

[1] As to the statement of Arculf, Early Travels, 9, see Wilson, ii. 147; Thrupp in Journal Class. and Sac., Phil. ii. 290.

[2] See Robinson, iii. 349 and 358.

death of the Baptist, the Lord "went aside privately into a desert place belonging to the city called Bethsaida." All now agree that this was Bethsaida on the east of Jordan, or Bethsaida Julias. In this neighborhood took place, probably within a few hours, the feeding of the five thousand. After this, toward night, He sends His disciples away in a ship, "to go unto the other side before unto Bethsaida," or over against Bethsaida, (Mark vi. 45.) John says (vi. 17) that "they entered into a ship and went over the sea toward Capernaum." Bethsaida and Capernaum, therefore, lay in the same general direction. The wind being contrary, they toiled all night, and had made but 25 or 30 furlongs, when in the early morning Jesus came to them walking upon the sea, and "immediately the ship was at the land whither they went," (John vi. 21.) This was the land of Gennesaret, (Matt. xiv. 34; Mark vi. 53.) From this it has been inferred that Bethsaida and Capernaum were near each other on the shore of the lake, and both in, or near the land of Gennesaret.

Before examining these accounts of the Evangelists, let us sum up all that we know from other sources respecting Bethsaida. In Josephus[1] we find mention made of a village of this name. "Philip the Tetrarch also advanced the village Bethsaida, situate at the lake of Gennesaret, unto the dignity of a city, both by the number of inhabitants it contained, and its other grandeur, and called it by the name of Julias, the same name with Cæsar's daughter." Elsewhere he states that it was "in the lower Gaulonitis,"[2] and in describing the course of the Jordan, he says[3] that it "divided the marshes and fens of the lake Semechonitis; when it hath run another hundred and twenty furlongs, it first passes by the city Julias, and then passes through the middle of the Lake Gennesaret." Thus Josephus places Bethsaida

[1] Antiq., 18. 2. 1. [2] War, 2. 9. 1. [3] War, 3. 10. 7.

at or near the entrance of the Jordan into the Sea of Galilee. It is placed, also, by Pliny, upon the east side of the Jordan, and by St. Jerome upon the shore of Gennesaret.[1] No other Bethsaida than this seems to have been known, down to the time of Reland,—at least no other is mentioned.[2] Reland, (653,) pressed by the difficulty of harmonizing the Evangelists, conjectured that there were two Bethsaidas, one on the east of Jordan, in Gaulonitis, and one on the west side of the lake, in Galilee, (John xii. 21.) And this conjecture has been almost universally received as the true solution. But he himself was aware of the improbability that two towns of the same name should lie upon the same lake only a few miles apart, and adopted this solution only because he had no other to give. *Atque ita, quamvis non sim proclivis ad statuendas duas pluresve urbes ejusdem nominis, (quod plerumque ad salvendam aliquam difficultatem ultimum est refugium,) hic tamen puto id necessario fieri oportere.* He does not, however, allow that there is any mention in the Gospels of the Bethsaida east of Jordan. *Christus de Bethsaida loquens non potuit nisi de sola Galilaica intelligi.*

The grounds upon which is based the view of two Bethsaidas were: 1st. That the Bethsaida of Josephus was in Gaulonitis, whereas John (xii. 21) speaks of a "Bethsaida of Galilee." 2d. That from the statements, (Mark vi. 45; John vi. 24–25,) Bethsaida must have been on the west shore of the sea, since, being on the east side, they entered a boat to cross to the other side.[3] We are, therefore, led back to an examination of the accounts of the feeding of the 5,000, and the subsequent crossing of the lake.

It is generally agreed that the place in which the 5,000 were fed, was on the east side of the lake in the territory

[1] See Ritter, Theil xv. 280.
[2] Raumer, 109, note; Robinson, ii. 413, note 6.
[3] Raumer, 109, note 20.

of Bethsaida, (Luke ix. 10.) Thomson (ii. 29) thinks he finds the exact spot at the point where the hills on the east side of the plain Butaiha come to the edge of the lake. No other spot than this answers to all the conditions of the narrative. From this point the mouth of the Jordan lies three or four miles north-west, and Tell Hum, nearly directly west across the lake; the land of Gennesaret lying to the south of Tell Hum. The narratives, then, may be thus explained. According to Mark, (vi. 45,) the Lord "constrained His disciples to get into the ship, and to go to the other side before unto Bethsaida, while He sent away the people." They should go before Him unto Bethsaida, and He would follow after He had sent away the people.[1] Here Bethsaida appears as the point of destination. John says (vi. 17) that "the disciples entered a ship and went over the sea toward Capernaum." Here Capernaum appears as the point of destination. Let us suppose that Bethsaida was, as stated by Josephus, at the mouth of the Jordan, and that Capernaum was at Tell Hum, and, as the Lord's own residence, the point at which they aimed. The relative positions of the two places are such, that to reach Capernaum from the point where the Lord then was, a boat would naturally go in a north-westerly direction, and so pass near Bethsaida.

If the disciples, according to His request, left the Lord alone at night upon the eastern side, and returned to Capernaum in the only boat they had, how could He follow them? They were naturally, therefore, unwilling to leave Him in that desert place; but He "constrained" them to go. They directed their course toward Bethsaida, both as on their way, for they would naturally row along the northern shore,[2] and as also hoping that after He he had sent the multitude away, He would rejoin them there.[3] But the

[1] Alexander in loco. [2] Robinson, iii. 354.

[3] See Wieseler, 274, note 1. Newcome, 263, who quotes Lamy to the same effect.

wind being contrary, or blowing from the north-east, they were driven southward, away from the northern shore, and could not make Bethsaida, and toiled all night, and when Jesus joined them in the morning, were nearly in the middle of the lake. After He joined them, they came to the land of Gennesaret, (Matt. xiv. 34,) or "the land whither they went," (John vi. 21.) This implies that Capernaum, their point of destination, was near Gennesaret; but that they did not land immediately at that city is evident from Mark vi. 54–56. He seems to have gone thither the same day, healing the sick by the way.

If there were two Bethsaidas, upon which of them did the Lord pronounce a woe? The only "mighty works," which are recorded to have been done by Him in any Bethsaida, are the healing of a blind man, (Mark viii. 22,) and the feeding of the five thousand, (Luke ix. 10.) That this was the Bethsaida Julias is generally admitted.[1] Upon this, therefore, the woe was pronounced, and not upon the Bethsaida west of the lake.

Thomson, examining the narratives of the Evangelists, upon the very spot where he supposes the Lord to have stood when He sent away His disciples, finds no necessity of placing a Bethsaida on the west side of the lake to satisfy their conditions. The examination made by one so familiar with their localities, and with the sea spread out before him as a map, and so well acquainted with all the points of difficulty involved in the question, may be regarded as turning the balance of probability in favor of a single Bethsaida, and that situated at the mouth of the Jordan.

But there stills remains an objection to be noted; how can Bethsaida at the mouth of the Jordan be called Bethsaida of Galilee? This may readily be answered if we accept the very probable supposition of Thomson, that the

[1] Meyer, Oosterzee, Alford.

town was built upon both banks of the river, and thus a part was in Gaulonitis, and a part in Galilee.[1] As the river is narrow, it is almost certain that if the main part of the city was upon one bank, the other would also be inhabited. Philip the Tetrarch, in enlarging and ornamenting it, doubtless confined himself to the eastern side, or that part which lay in his own dominions, and this would thus become, if it were not at first, distinctively the city, to which the western side would stand as the suburbs. Philip, the disciple, living on the west bank, may thus have been from Bethsaida of Galilee, which the Evangelist thus designates in order to distinguish it.

There are no ruins indicating antiquity by which to determine the site of Bethsaida Julias. Robinson places it on a hill, two or three miles above the mouth of the Jordan. "The ruins cover a large portion of it, and are quite extensive, but so far as could be observed, consist entirely of unhewn volcanic stones, without any distinct trace of ancient architecture." Porter says: "Heaps of unhewn stones, and a few rude houses, used as stores by the Arabs, are all that have hitherto been seen on the spot." Neither of these travellers speak of any remains at the mouth of the river. Thomson, however, says that "the only ruins of any importance are below, along the foot of the hills bordering the vale of the Jordan, and at its debouchure on the west side." Here he mentions as still to be seen, some remains of ancient buildings. He supposes that as the city derived its name from its fisheries—house of fish—"it must have been located on the shore, and not several miles from it at the Tell, to which the name is now affixed."

It would be useless to dwell upon the conjectures that have been made for the purpose of harmonizing the Evan-

[1] So Röhr, Palestine, 154. "Bethsaida Julias lay on the north-east shore of the lake near the influx of the Jordan, and probably on both sides of the river." So Calmet and others.

gelical narratives without resorting to the supposition of two Bethsaidas. The most probable was that of Lightfoot, who made Galilee to have extended beyond the Jordan so as to embrace Bethsaida Julias. Recently, De Saulcy, on the other hand, would make Gaulonitis to have extended westward of the Jordan, and thus bring Bethsaida within its limits.

If we rest in the conclusion that there was but one Bethsaida, and that at the mouth of the Jordan, the question respecting the site of Capernaum is somewhat simplified. If we place the latter city at Tell Hum, the distance between them is about three miles. Robinson was an hour and five minutes from Tell Hum to the banks of the Jordan just at its entrance into the lake. There is nothing in the Gospel which makes it necessary to bring them into close proximity, and their relative positions conform to the Evangelical notices and to the statements of travellers. Willibald, proceeding northward from Tiberias, "went by the village of Magdalene to the village of Capernaum, and thence he went to Bethsaida." So Robinson, from a comparison of Mark vi. 45 and John vi. 17 infers that Bethsaida lay north of Capernaum. As Tell Hum lies about an hour north of Khan Minyeh, it better fits the narrative, (Mark vi. 33,) since it was much easier for the crowds, that followed Him on foot to the desert place on the east side, to go from the former than the latter.[1] The little distance of Tell Hum from the land of Gennesaret presents no difficulty. "The position of Tell Hum seems to us to agree in every respect with the Gospel narrative, being *near*, not *in* the land of Gennesaret, and not too far from the east side of the lake to allow people to follow Jesus on foot while He was crossing the water with His disciples."[2] When, after the Lord joined them upon that memorable night,

[1] So Wilson, ii. 145

[2] Van de Velde, Memoir, 302.

they landed upon the plain, it is obvious from the following statements that they did not land directly at Capernaum, but some distance southward, and that, going to Capernaum in the course of the day, He was there found by the people that followed Him (Mark vi. 53–55 ; John vi. 24.)

We have still to inquire respecting the site of Chorazin. Two or three miles northwest from Tell Hum are some ruins called Khirbet Kerazeh. They were visited by Robinson, who describes them as "a few foundations of black stones, the remains evidently of a poor and inconsiderable village," and regards them as "too trivial ever to have belonged to a place of any importance. Chorazin too, according to Jerome, lay upon the shore of the lake, but the site is an hour distant, shut in among the hills, without any view of the lake, and remote from any public road, ancient or modern." While Robinson thus rejects Kerazeh as the site of Chorazin, Thomson is equally decided in its favor. "I have scarcely a doubt about the correctness of the identification, though Dr. Robinson rejects it almost with contempt. But the name Korazy is nearly the Arabic for Chorazin; the situation, two miles north of Tell Hum, is just where we might expect to find it; the ruins are quite adequate to answer the demands of history, and there is no rival site." With Thomson Keith agrees:[1] "There seems no reason for questioning that Korazy is the Chorazin of Scripture, in which it is not said to stand on the *shore* of the lake of Tiberias, as Capernaum and Bethsaida are. We reached it in fifty-five minutes from the chief ruin of Tell Hum, from three to four miles distant. It lies almost directly to the west of the point where the Jordan flows into the lake. It retains the name and is known by it still among the inhabitants of the country round, and, as we repeatedly enquired, especially at Safet, by no other. Ko-

[1] Evidence of Prophecy, 160.

razy, of which not a house now stands, consists of fallen walls lying in heaps of no defined form, intermixed with lines of ruined buildings, and some squares whose form is still entire, filled with ruins. A small field of tobacco amidst the ruins was the only sign of industry about it, and, though in a hilly region, a few poor tents were the only dwellings near it. The ruins were at least a mile in circumference, possibly more." That the ruins of Kerazeh do not lie directly upon the lake is not in opposition to Jerome. "Jerome in his translation of Eusebius says that Chorazin stood at the second milestone from Capernaum, that is, north of Capernaum, the milestones being reckoned from Tarichaea."[1]

This topographical discussion, extended as it is, by no means exhausts the subject.[2] Certainty as regards these sites is at present unattainable, but as the question now stands it is most probable that Capernaum was at Tell Hum; that there was but one Bethsaida, and this at the entrance of the Jordan into the lake, and lying on both sides of the river. Chorazin may be left undetermined, being but twice spoken of in the Gospel narratives, and only in connection with its doom. As to the size and population and business of Capernaum, the Evangelists give us no definite information. It is, with Bethsaida and Chorazin, called a city, (Matt. xi. 20,) and often elsewhere. But Norton refers to Josephus, who calls it a "village;" and to the statement, (Luke vii. 5,) "For he loveth our nation and he hath built us a synagogue," as showing that the city had but one, and that one built by a Roman centurion.

We have thus far left unnoticed the ground recently taken by some Biblical critics, that "the land of Gennes-

[1] Norton, notes, 115. See Winer, i. 228; Van de Velde, Memoir, 304. Greswell makes Chorazin the same as Chor Ashan. 1 Sam. xxx. 30.

[2] The reader who desires to examine it further, will find ample materials in Robinson, Thomson, Raumer, Ritter, and others.

aret" is to be identified with the plain El Batihah at the mouth of the Jordan.[1] The arguments by which it is supported are briefly these, that the political divisions, which assigned the Jordan as the eastern limit of Galilee, had no existence prior to the will of Herod partitioning his dominions among his sons; that there was but one Bethsaida, and that Bethsaida Julias at the mouth of the Jordan; that the Scriptures show that Capernaum and Bethsaida were but a step apart, and therefore Capernaum was in the plain El Batihah; and that this site best corresponds to the language of Josephus.[2] Admitting that there is some force in these considerations, still they are by no means so weighty as to lead us to change the position of the land of Gennesaret from the west to the north of the lake. That there was but one Bethsaida has been already shown.[3]

April—May, 781. A. D. 28.

Arriving at Capernaum the Lord begins to gather about Him His former disciples that they may accompany and assist Him in His work. He enters the Synagogue and there heals a demoniac. Thence he goes to the house of Peter, and heals his wife's mother of a fever, and in the evening He heals many sick persons who were brought to Him.	Matt. iv. 18–22. Mark i. 16–34. Luke v. 1–11. Luke iv. 33–41. Matt. viii. 14–17.

The arrival of the Lord at Capernaum, there to take up His abode, offers us a fitting place in which to speak of His Galilean work in its general practical features. In many

[1] For an account of this plain, see Robinson, ii. 409.

[2] See article by Tregelles, in Journal of Classical and Sacred Philology, vol. iii. p. 145. See also article, vol. ii. p. 290, by Thrupp, who regards Gennesaret as El Batihah, but identifies Capernaum with Tell Hum, and finds no trace or tradition of a Bethsaida on the western side of the lake.

[3] See Ewald, Jahrbuch, 1856, p. 144, who also places Gennesaret on the north of the sea.

points it was very unlike His earlier work in Judea. So far as we can learn, He did not then go from place to place baptizing, nor does He seem to have made any use of the synagogues for the purpose of teaching. Like the Baptist, He did not seek the people in their cities and villages, but made the people seek Him, (Matt. iii. 5 ; xi. 7.) In Galilee the Lord began immediately to visit the people in all their cities and villages, making Capernaum the central point of His labors, and this He did in a systematic manner. He went round about the villages teaching, (Mark vi. 6.) "In a circle," says Alexander, "or circuit, that is, not merely round about, but on a regular concerted plan of periodical visitation." We have not sufficient data to determine the local order of these visitations ; but it is natural to suppose that He would first visit the places near Capernaum, and then those more remote, (Mark i. 38.) From this city as a centre He would go forth to preach in the adjoining towns, and extend His labors to those more distant by degrees. And His course would be directed rather to the west than to the east, both because Galilee lay to the westward, and because of the semi-heathenish character of the people who lived beyond the lake. It was, in fact, a considerable time, as we shall see, ere He visited the regions of Cæsarea Philippi and of Decapolis.

During these circuits we find the Lord journeying from place to place, remaining for the most part only a little while in a place. In these journeys He was attended by His disciples; at first by those who had before been with Him, and whom He recalled, and then by others, and afterward by the body of the Apostles, who were His constant attendants. At a later period of His ministry, His mother and other women accompanied Him in some of His circuits, (Luke viii. 2,) and He was followed by crowds, who were drawn to Him by various motives. His common mode of procedure was apparently this: on entering a city where was a synagogue, He availed Himself of the privilege which His reputation as a rabbi and prophet gave Him, to teach the people from the Scriptures. This He did upon the Sabbaths and synagogue days. At other times He preached in the streets or fields, or sitting in a boat upon the sea; in every convenient place where the people were willing to hear Him. His fame as a healer of the sick caused many to be brought to Him, and He appears in general to have healed all, (Mark vi. 56; Matt. ix. 35.) His sojourn in any single village was necessarily brief, and therefore those who had been really impressed by His works or words, and desired to see or hear Him more, followed Him to the adjoining towns, or sought Him at Capernaum. The disciples do not appear to have taken any public part as teachers, but may privately have aided Him in various ways to disseminate truth among the people. The expenses of these journeys were probably borne by the contributions of the disciples, and by the voluntary offerings of the grateful who had been healed, and of their friends. After the Twelve had been chosen, one of their number seems to have acted as treasurer, taking charge of the moneys designed for the common use, (see John xii. 6.)

A specimen of the daily activity of the Lord may be found in the narrative of His early work in Capernaum. He enters upon the Sabbath into the synagogue, and teaches, filling all His hearers with astonishment at His words. He then heals a demoniac, probably immediately after the discourse. Leaving the synagogue, He enters Peter's house and heals a sick woman, and crowds coming to Him at evening, He heals many others. The next morning, after a time of meditation and prayer, He departs to another city. Similar, doubtless, in their main features to this, were His labors upon subsequent Sabbaths. In mentioning these circuits, none of the Evangelists give them in regular order, or relate the events in chronological succession.

Each has his own principle of selection and of arrangement, with which we are not now concerned; but it is obvious when we remember how great the Lord's activity, how many His works and words, that within the limits of their narratives only very brief outlines can be given.

The stages of progress in the Lord's labors in Galilee will be noticed as we meet them. Yet it should be noted as characteristic of the beginning of His ministry, that we do not find any open avowal of His Messianic claims. He wished the people to infer who He was from His words and works, rather than learn it from any express declarations of His own. He preached the kingdom of heaven as at hand, and illustrated it by His miracles. If the people had sufficient spiritual discernment to see the true import of what He said and did, this was all the proof that was needed that He was the Messiah.

We give at this point, for the sake of convenient reference, an outline of the Lord's Galilean work, divided into periods of sojourn in Capernaum, and of circuits in the adjacent territories. The grounds for the order will be stated as the particular periods come under consideration.

First Sojourn in Capernaum.

Rejected at Nazareth He comes to Capernaum. In its neighborhood He calls the four disciples while fishing upon the lake. On the following Sabbath He preaches in the synagogue, and heals the demoniac, and afterward heals the mother of Peter's wife. In the afternoon, after the sun had set, He heals many others. Early the next morning He rises to pray, and then departs to preach and heal in the adjacent cities and villages.

FIRST CIRCUIT.

He visits the "next" villages, probably those lying nearest Capernaum, as Chorazin and Bethsaida. No particulars of this circuit are given, except that He heals a leper "in one of the cities." This being noised abroad, He is for a time unable to enter any city, and retires to secluded places, where the people gather to Him.

Second Sojourn in Capernaum.

Crowds begin to gather to Him so soon as it is known that He is at home. A paralytic is brought to Him, whom He heals, forgiving his sins. This awakens the anger of the scribes, who regard it as an assumption of the Divine prerogatives. He goes forth again by the seaside, and teaches. Walking along the shore, He calls Levi. He goes upon a Sabbath through a field in the neighborhood of Capernaum with His disciples, and on the way plucks and eats the ears of corn. This is noted by the Pharisees of the city, who were watching Him. He enters the second time into the synagogue, and heals the man with a withered hand. The Pharisees and Herodians now conspire against Him. He departs to the seaside, and is followed by crowds.

SECOND CIRCUIT.

Leaving Capernaum, He goes to a mountain in the neighborhood, and after a night spent in prayer, calls His disciples, and from them chooses the twelve apostles. Great multitudes now gathering to Him, He delivers the Sermon on the Mount, and returns, apparently the same day, to Capernaum, still followed by the multitudes.

Third Sojourn in Capernaum.

He heals, immediately upon His return, the Centurion's servant. The people so throng Him, and His labors are so incessant, that He has not time even to eat, and His friends fear for His sanity.

THIRD CIRCUIT.

The day following He goes to Nain, and raises from death the widow's son. He continues His ministry in the adjacent region. John Baptist sends a message to Him from his prison; to which He replies, and addresses the people respecting John. He dines with Simon, a Pharisee, and is anointed by a woman, who is a sinner. He returns again to Capernaum.

Fourth Sojourn in Capernaum.

He heals a blind and dumb possessed; whereupon the Pharisees blaspheme, saying that He is aided by Beelzebub. His mother and brethren come to Him, but He rejects their claims. He goes to the sea-shore and teaches in parables.

FOURTH CIRCUIT.

The same day at even, He crosses the sea with His disciples, and stills the tempest. He heals the Gadarene demoniacs, and the devils, entering into, destroy a herd of swine. The people of the country entreat Him to depart, and He returns to Capernaum.

Fifth Sojourn in Capernaum.

Here Levi makes Him a feast. He heals the daughter of Jairus, and the woman with an issue of blood.

FIFTH CIRCUIT.

He goes to Nazareth, and is a second time rejected. He teaches in the villages of that part of Galilee, and sends out the twelve apostles on their mission. About this time Herod puts the Baptist to death, and now hearing of Jesus and His miracles, wishes to see Him. Jesus returns to Capernaum, and the apostles gather to Him there.

Sixth Sojourn in Capernaum.

No event is narrated as having occurred during this sojourn. Probably it was very brief—a mere passage through the city.

SIXTH CIRCUIT.

He crosses the sea with the Twelve to seek retirement, but the multitude immediately follow Him. He feeds the 5,000, and sending away the apostles by ship, He rejoins them the next morning, walking on the sea. Landing on the plain of Gennesaret, they return to Capernaum.

Seventh Sojourn in Capernaum.

He discourses in the synagogue upon the bread of life. His discourse causes many of His disciples to forsake Him. He addresses the Pharisees, and heals the sick.

SEVENTH CIRCUIT.

He goes to the coasts of Tyre and Sidon to find retirement. Here He heals the daughter of the Syro-Phœnician woman. Crossing the northern part of the Jordan, He goes to Decapolis. He heals a deaf man, and feeds the 4,000, and returns by Dalmanutha to Capernaum.

Eighth Sojourn in Capernaum.

He is tempted by the Pharisees, who seek a sign.

EIGHTH CIRCUIT.

He crosses the sea and visits Bethsaida, where He heals a blind man. He goes toward Cæsarea Philippi, and is transfigured. He heals the lunatic child, and returns to Capernaum.

Ninth Sojourn in Capernaum.

He pays the tribute money, and discourses to the disciples. His brethren would persuade Him to go up to the feast of Tabernacles, and work miracles at Jerusalem. He rejects their counsel.

NINTH CIRCUIT.

He goes up in secret to Jerusalem during the feast of Tabernacles, and teaches the people. Afterward, a woman taken in adultery is brought before Him. He heals a blind man, and addresses the people. He returns to Capernaum.

Final Departure from Capernaum and Galilee.

The first notice we have of the Lord, after leaving Nazareth, (Matt. iv. 18; Mark i. 16; Luke v. 1,) brings Him before us standing on the shore of the lake, and surrounded by people that pressed upon Him to hear the word of God. How long an interval had elapsed since He left Nazareth, we have no data to decide, but this gathering of the people to Him presupposes a period, longer or shorter, during which He had been teaching. Not improbably He may have been several days upon the journey, and His growing reputation as a prophet, joined to rumors of what had taken place at Nazareth, would procure Him audience in whatever village He entered. Especially as He came near the lake, the numerous cities and villages would furnish crowds of listeners to hear one who spake as never man spake.

It was as He thus approached Capernaum that He met upon the lake His former disciples, Simon, Andrew, James, and John, and called them again into His service. We have already seen that on leaving Galilee, His baptismal work ceasing, His disciples left Him and returned to their homes and usual pursuits. To the feast (John v. 1) He seems to have gone unattended, nor apparently were any disciples with Him at Nazareth. But now that John's imprisonment had determined the character of His future ministry, He proceeds to gather around Him those who had already been workers with Him, that they might enter upon this new sphere of labor. Heretofore their relations to Him had been similar to their previous relations to John the Baptist, involving only a temporary absence from their families and business. "These disciples, hitherto," says Lightfoot, "were only as private men following Christ." But now the Lord sought to engage them in a work which should be life-long, and which was incompatible with other pursuits. They should now be His constant attendants, going with Him wherever He went, and thus necessarily separated from their families and friends. This call to follow Him, was not, indeed, as Alford and others suppose, a call to the apostleship, but to a preliminary service; and those thus called had as yet little understanding what labors, dangers, or dignities, it involved.

To one who considers the essentially different character of Christ's work in Judea and in Galilee, it will not appear surprising that, beginning the latter, He should give to these disciples a new and distinct call. Only neglect to note this difference permits any one to speak of a want of harmony between John and the Synoptists upon this ground.

From the narratives of Mark, (i. 16–35; see also Matt. iv. 18–23,) we should infer that the call of Peter and Andrew, James and John, was His first act after the Lord came to Capernaum. Luke, however, (iv. 31–42,) places the preaching in the synagogue, the healing of the demoniac, and of Peter's wife's mother and others, and His first circuit, before this call; which order some follow. But we shall find abundant proof that Luke does not follow the chronological order, and that nothing decisive can be inferred from the fact that he places the call after the miracles and teaching. Still, as his accounts of this call differ somewhat from those of Mark and Matthew, many have been led to regard them as distinct, and as happening at different times.[1] The peculiarity of the call in Luke, according to this view, is, that it was later than that in Matthew and Mark, and that now "the disciples forsook all, and followed Him." Now they became fishers of men, (Luke v. 10,) in fulfilment of His previous promise, (Matt. iv. 19.) This involved the entire relinquishment of their secular callings, and to convince them of His ability to take care of them and supply every temporal need, the Lord works the miracle of the draught of fishes. But the words of both Matthew (iv. 20) and Mark (i. 18) are express that "they straightway forsook their nets and followed Him." How, then, should they be found several days after engaged in their usual occupations? That, whenever the Lord was at Capernaum, these disciples were wont to follow their calling as fishermen, as said by Alford, is plainly inconsistent with their relations to Him, and with the service He sought from them. Certainly they could have had little time for such labors amidst the pressure of the crowds, which seem to have ever gathered around Him when He came to Capernaum.[2]

The circumstances attending the call of the disciples, as related by the several Evangelists, may be thus arranged: As Jesus approaches the plain of Gennesaret from Nazareth, teaching by the way, many flock round Him to hear His wonderful words. Passing along the level and sandy shore, where the fishermen's boats were drawn up, He sees amongst them the boats of Simon and Andrew, and of

1 So early, Augustine, and recently, Krafft, Stier, Greswell, Alford.
2 See Ebrard, 307.

James and John, who having been fishing, were now washing their nets. As the people pressed upon Him, He requests Simon to push off his boat from the shore a little way, that from it He may teach the multitude as they stand before Him. After His discourse is ended, He directs Simon and Andrew, and perhaps also others with them, to push out into the deep waters and let down the net. This, after a little hesitation arising from the ill-success of their labors the previous night, Simon does, and they take so great a number of fish that the net begins to break. He now beckons to those in the other boat, James and John, and their companions, who had doubtless been watching the whole proceeding, and who now come to their help, and both boats are so filled as to be in danger of sinking. This unexpected success, and all the attendant circumstances, make such a powerful impression upon Simon's mind, that acting with his usual impetuosity he casts himself at the Lord's feet, saying, "Depart from me for I am a sinful man, O Lord." All are astonished to see a Divine hand in what had happened. Soon after this, probably so soon as they reached the shore, He calls Simon and Andrew, in whose ship he still was, to follow him, for He will make them fishers of men. During this time James and John had gone a little distance from them, and were engaged in repairing the net that had been broken. Walking upon the shore He goes to them and calls them also to follow Him, and they, leaving their father and servants, follow Him.

In this way may we find a natural and easy solution of the apparent discrepancies between Matthew and Mark on the one hand and Luke on the other. Luke alone relates that Jesus spake to the people from Simon's boat, and afterward directed him to fish, and shows in what relation this fishing stood to the subsequent call of the fishermen. Matthew and Mark omit all but the fact that they were engaged in their usual work of fishing when thus called. There is then no such opposition in the accounts as to make it necessary to refer them to different events.[1]

On the first Sabbath following the call of the four disciples, he enters the synagogue and teaches. His teaching excited general astonishment, but not the envy that manifested itself at Nazareth. Present in the synagogue was a man possessed with a devil, whom He heals, and through this miracle, thus publicly performed, His fame spreads rapidly through all Galilee, (Mark i. 28.) It is to be noted that he did not here, or subsequently, permit evil spirits to bear witness to His Divine character or Messianic claims, (Mark i. 34; Luke iv. 41.) The ground of this imposition of silence may have been, that the intent with which such witness was offered was evil, and that it would also have tended to evil by awaking premature and unfounded expectations as to His future work.

From the synagogue the Lord proceeds to the house of Simon and Andrew, where He heals Simon's wife's mother. As mention is made by John (i. 44) of Bethsaida, as the city of Peter and Andrew, it has been conjectured that the house at Capernaum was that of the parents of Simon's wife; but against this is the expression "house of Simon and Andrew," which implies the joint ownership of the two brothers. It is therefore more probable that they had now left Bethsaida and taken up their residence at Capernaum.[2] The healing of Peter's wife's mother seems to have been at the close of the synagogue service, and before evening, for at evening all that were diseased and possessed were brought to Him. The synagogue service closed at or be-

[1] In this general result agree Lightfoot, Newcome, Townsend, Robinson, Wieseler, Tischendorf, Lichtenstein, Ebrard. For an answer to objections, see Blunt, Scriptural Coincidences, 256, note.

[2] This may be a slight confirmation of the supposition that there was but one Bethsaida, and that east of the Jordan.

fore noon, and it may be inferred from the fact that she "ministered unto them," that she served them at the table at the midday meal. According to Josephus,[1] the hour of this meal was, on the Sabbath, the sixth, or twelve o'clock. That the sick should wait till the sun was gone down, (Mark i. 32,) may be referred to the great scrupulosity of the Jews in regard to the Sabbath.[2]

May, 781. A. D. 28.

The next morning, rising up early, Jesus goes out into	Mark i. 35.
a solitary place to pray. Simon and others go out to seek	Luke iv. 42.
Him because the multitude waited for Him. He replies,	
that He must also preach in the neighboring towns. He	Mark i. 38.
goes preaching in the synagogues and working miracles.	Luke iv. 43.

This quick departure from Capernaum may perhaps be explained from the Lord's desire that a period of reflection should follow the surprise and wonder which His words and works had excited in the minds of the people. Their astonishment at the supernatural power He manifested, and their readiness to come to Him as a healer of the sick, did not prove the possession of true faith. He therefore will leave them to meditate on what they have seen and heard, and depart to visit the other cities and villages of Galilee, probably, as has been suggested, following some fixed order of visitation. Galilee at that time, according to Josephus,[3] was very populous. "The towns are numerous, and the multitude of villages so crowded with men, owing to the fecundity of the soil, that the smallest of them contains above 15,000 inhabitants." Elsewhere he incidentally mentions[4] that there were 204 cities and villages in Galilee, thus giving a population of more than three millions. This

[1] Life, 54.
[2] See Lightfoot on Matt. viii. 16; and xii. 10.
[3] War, 3. 3. 2.
[4] Life, 45.

statement is confirmed in general by Dion Cassius, who says, that under Hadrian 985 villages of the Jews were laid waste.[1] Making all necessary allowance for the exaggeration of Josephus in regard to the populousness of each village, still it is apparent that the land was crowded with people, and that the Lord, with all His activity, could, during the brief period of His ministry, have visited but a part of the towns. We see also whence came the multitudes who seem to have followed Him wherever He went.[2]

That this, the Lord's first circuit with His disciples, must have continued some time, appears from the statements of the Evangelists, (Mark i. 39—ii. 1; Luke iv. 44; Matt. iv. 23,) though their language may perhaps describe His general activity rather than any particular period of it. The expressions in Mark ii. 1, δι' ημερων "after some days," is indefinite, and its length must be otherwise determined. The attempt of Greswell to show, from the number of places He would visit, and the length of the stay He would make in each, that the duration of a circuit would never be less than three months, and probably never less than four, rests upon no sound basis. Ellicott, (168,) going to the other extreme, makes this circuit to have lasted only four or five days. It is intrinsically improbable that, as Greswell supposes, Jesus should have journeyed now wholly around Galilee, keeping on its boundary lines. What particular parts of the province He at this time visited, we have no data to decide, but it is certain that early in His ministry He visited the cities of Bethsaida and Chorazin, adjacent to Capernaum, and labored much in them, though of these labors there is little or no mention, (Matt. xi. 21.) His fame rapidly spread, and soon the people from the regions adjacent to Galilee began to gather to him.

[1] Raumer, 81. [2] See Greswell, iv. 486.

Of His works of healing during the first circuit, no instance is given, unless the healing of the leper (Matt. viii. 2; Luke v. 12; Mark i. 40) took place at this time. Matthew places it immediately after the Sermon on the Mount. Luke introduces it with no mark of time: "And it came to pass when He was in a certain city," &c. Mark connects it with the first circuit in Galilee, but with no mention of place. That this healing is not chronologically placed by Matthew, appears from the whole arrangement of chapters viii. and ix. The first verse of chapter viii. more properly belongs to the conclusion of the history of the Sermon on the Mount; verse second begins the narrative of healings and other miracles, of which ten particular examples are successively recorded, but without regard to the exact order of time in which they occurred. After healing the leper, Jesus commands him to go and show himself to the priests, and to say nothing to any one else of the miracle, (Matt. viii. 4.) This command of silence plainly implies that the miracle had been done privately, and not in the presence of the multitude, and could not have been, therefore, as He came from the Mount, for great crowds then followed him. Nor in the presence of the people could a leper have approached Him.[1] This command to keep silence the leper disobeys, and every where publishes abroad what Jesus had done. This wonderful cure, for leprosy was deemed incurable, made the people to throng to Him in such crowds, that He could no more enter into any city.[2] He was obliged to retire to the desert, or uninhabited places, to avoid them; but even then they gathered to Him from every quarter.

If then the healing of the leper be placed during this circuit, it was probably during the latter part of it. As He

[1] Greswell, ii. 296, note, infers that Jesus was in some house apart when the leper applied to Him, and that his cure took place in private.

[2] Or into *the* city—i. e., Capernaum. So Norton.

proceeded from place to place, He healed such sick persons as were brought to Him, and the reports of these cures spreading in every direction, all in every city would be brought so soon as His presence was known. The leprosy may have been one of the last forms of disease He healed, partly because of want of faith on the part of the lepers, and partly because it was difficult for them, amidst such crowds, to get access to Him. But why in this case should silence be enjoined? And why, after He had wrought so many other cures, should this have aroused so much attention as to make it necessary for Him to avoid the cities and go into uninhabited places? The most probable answer is, that the public proclamation of this miracle gave the people such conceptions of His mighty power to heal, that all thronged to Him to be healed, and thus His teachings, the moral side of His work, were thrust into the shade. It was the word which He wished to make prominent, and the work was but subsidiary. He would not that the people should merely wander after Him as a miracle worker, but should learn through His works the true nature of the redemption He came to proclaim.

SUMMER, 781. A. D. 28.

After some time the Lord returns to Capernaum. So soon as it is known that He is returned, the multitudes begin to gather, bringing their sick, whom He healed. The Pharisees and doctors of the law from all parts of the land, came to Capernaum to see and hear the new prophet. A paralytic is brought to His house upon a bed, whom He heals, forgiving his sins. This awakens the indignation of the Pharisees, who regard him as a blasphemer. Leaving the city, He goes to the seaside and there teaches. Afterward walking on the shore, He saw Levi, the publican, sitting at the receipt of custom, whom He calls to follow Him.

MARK ii. 1–12.
LUKE v. 17–26.
MATT. ix. 2–8.
MARK ii. 13, 14.
MATT. ix. 9.
LUKE v. 27, 28.

The order of Mark, who places the healing of the paralytic after the return to Capernaum, is plainly the right one.[1] Matthew, in his grouping of the miracles in chapters viii. and ix., does not follow the order of time. Luke narrates it after the healing of the leper, but without specifying time or place. He mentions, however, the fact, that there were "Pharisees and doctors of the law sitting by, which were come out of every town of Galilee, and Judea, and Jerusalem; and the power of the Lord was present to heal them." It is not wholly clear who these persons were, or why they were now present. Greswell (ii. 298) cites Josephus to show that they were "a sort of village schoolmasters, or a class of inferior municipal magistrates, who might consequently be met with everywhere." They are to be distinguished from the scribes, who came down from Jerusalem at a later period, with evil intent, and who were sent apparently by His enemies to watch Him, (Mark iii. 22.) These, on the contrary, came to be healed, or to see and hear Him whose fame had gone so widely abroad. There is no distinction taken by the Evangelist between those from Galilee and those from Judea and Jerusalem, as if the latter were present from any special cause. At this period of the Lord's career the nature of His work was very imperfectly understood; and many in every part of the land and of every class, looking for the Messiah, would be naturally attracted to one who showed such wonderful power in word and deed. But in a little time, as His teachings became more distinctly known, His disregard of merely legal righteousness, His neglect of their traditions, His high claims as a Divine Person, awakened great and general hostility. We see here how these scribes, who came, perhaps hoping to find in Him their Messiah, perhaps to judge by personal observation how far the popular

[1] So Robinson, Tischendorf, Alford, Greswell.

reports respecting Him were true, were turned into enemies and accusers when He said to the paralytic, "Thy sins be forgiven thee," which was to speak blasphemy, because implying an equality with God.

There are several allusions to the Lord's teaching by the seaside. Whether He now stood upon the shore or entered a boat, does not appear. It was not however till afterward (Mark iii. 9) that He commanded that a small ship should wait on Him. Thomson (i. 548) speaks of the small creeks or inlets near Tell Hum, "where the ship could ride in safety only a few feet from the shore, and where the multitude, seated on both sides, and before the boat, could listen without distraction or fatigue. As if on purpose to furnish seats, the shore on both sides of those narrow inlets is piled up with smooth boulders of basalt."

The road from Damascus to the cities along the coast passed by "Jacob's bridge" over the Jordan, and thence along the shore of the lake. It is probable that the place of toll, where Levi sat, was upon this road, near its entrance into the city.[1] The manner of this call, like the call of Simon and Andrew, and James and John, presupposes a prior acquaintance of Jesus with Levi. The tax-gatherer, from his occupation and local position, must have been aware of all that was taking place in the neighborhood, and could not easily have been ignorant of the Lord's person and work. Not improbably also, he was already a disciple in the wider sense of the term, this not involving the giving up of his usual calling. It would appear that the call was given on the same day in which Jesus taught the people, and soon after His discourse was ended.[2]

By some this call to Levi is placed after his election to the Apostleship. Having been already chosen one of the

[1] See Lichtenstein, 280; Herzog, Encyc., xv. 161.

[2] Bleek, Synoptische Erklarung. i. 384. As to the identity of Matthew and Levi, see Winer ii. 61.

Twelve, he returns to his ordinary labors; and now is called to enter upon his apostolic duties, to leave all and follow Christ. But this in itself is exceedingly improbable, and we shall soon see that the election to the apostleship is later.

The call of Levi to stand in such intimate relations to the Lord, must have been a great stumbling-block to all the Pharisaic party, and to all those in whose hearts national pride and hatred of foreign rule were ardent. The occupation of the publican was odious, if not in itself disgraceful, as a sign and proof of their national degradation; and the selection of disciples from this class to be His constant attendants, by one who claimed to be the Messiah, must have strongly prejudiced many against Him and His work.[1] Such selection implies, also, that already the Lord was turning away from the legally righteous, the Pharisees, because His words found so little entrance into their hearts, and was turning to those who, though despised as publicans and sinners, were nevertheless ready to receive the truth. Unable to draw the priests into His service, He calls fishermen; and what He cannot accomplish because of the unbelief of Pharisees, He will do through the faith of publicans.

Many bring the feast which Levi made for the Lord (Luke v. 29; see, also, Matt. ix. 10; Mark ii. 15) into immediate connection with his call.[2] Still there is nothing in the language of the Evangelists that implies immediate sequence, and as Capernaum doubtless continued to be his residence, and to which he frequently returned, the feast may with equal likelihood have taken place at a later time, and be here related, in order to bring together all that concerned him personally.[3]

[1] "The Talmud," says Lightfoot, iii. 61, hath this canon: "'A Pharisee that turns publican, they turn him out of his order.'"

[2] Lichtenstein, Tischendorf, Stier.

[3] So Lightfoot, Newcome, Townsend, Robinson. Newcome, 259, refers to the Harmony of Chemnitius, "where it appears that Levi's call and feast

The chronological connection between this feast and the healing of the daughter of Jairus (Matt. ix. 18–25) will be examined when we reach this miracle.

Greswell (ii. 397) attempts to show that the feast of Matthew (Matt. ix. 10) was different from that mentioned by Mark and Luke; that the former was later, and not in the house of Levi; and that at this feast, only the disciples of John were present. This view removes some difficulties, but the arguments in its favor are more ingenious than convincing.

SUMMER, 781. A. D. 28.

During this sojourn in Capernaum, the Lord with His disciples walked through the fields upon a Sabbath and plucked and ate the ears of corn. This was observed by some of the Pharisees who were watching Him, and who complained of it to Him as a violation of the Sabbath. He answers them by referring to what David did, and asserts His power as Son of man over the Sabbath.	MATT. xii. 1–8. MARK ii. 23–28. LUKE vi. 1–5.
Upon another Sabbath He heals a man with a withered hand, which leads the Pharisees to conspire with the Herodians to destroy Him.	LUKE vi. 6–11. MATT. xii. 9–14. MARK iii. 1–6.

Both the time and place of this event have been much disputed. It is mentioned by all the Synoptists, by Matthew in one connection, by Mark and Luke in another; but by none in such a way as to determine its chronological succession. All agree that it took place upon a Sabbath, and Luke (vi. 1) defines this Sabbath by the epithet "second Sabbath after the first," or "second first"—ἐν σαββάτῳ δευτερο-πρώτῳ.[1] But what was this second first Sabbath?

were separated in the most ancient harmonies from Tatian in A. D. 170 to Gerson A. D. 1400."

[1] The right rendering is "first after the second." So Campbell, Norton, Robinson, Greswell. For other renderings see Meyer in loco.

No certain answer can be given. Many doubt the correctness of the reading.[1] If, however, we receive it as the right reading, we have no positive key to its meaning, as the word, so far as is known, is used by no other writer than Luke. A great number of different interpretations have been suggested.[2] That of Scaliger has found many advocates.[3] We give it as stated by Lightfoot on Matt. xii. 1. Provision was made by the Law that the sheaf of first-fruits should be offered on the second day of Passover week, (Levit. xxiii. 10, 11,) not on the morrow after an ordinary Sabbath, but the morning after the first day of Passover week, which was a Sabbatic day. From the second day were numbered seven weeks to Pentecost—for the day of the sheaf and the day of Pentecost did mutually respect each other. The offering of the sheaf was supplicatory, beseeching a blessing on the new corn, and leave to eat and to put in the sickle into the standing corn. Some weeks intervened, and the calculation of the Sabbaths was by numbering them; *σαββατον δευτερο-πρωτον*, the first Sabbath after the second day of Passover; the second Sabbath after the second day; the third Sabbath after the second day, and the like. Lightfoot therefore concludes that this was the Sabbath mentioned John v. 9, or that next after it.

Wieseler (231) defends the view that the Jewish years were reckoned by a series, or cycle of sevens, and the first Sabbath of the second year of one of these cycles is meant, or the first Sabbath in Nisan.[4] Others have understood a Sabbath of the second rank, or a feast day immediately fol-

[1] So Alford, who says: "It is not altogether clear that the word ought to be here at all." Meyer rejects it, and Lichtenstein, Browne, Bleek; Tischendorf rejected it at first, but restored it in his Synopsis, 1854. Winer defends it.

[2] See Meyer in loco.

[3] So A. Clarke, Bloomfield, Robinson, De Wette.

[4] With Wieseler, Tischendorf, Oosterzee, Ellicott; contra, Winer, ii. 348.

lowing a Sabbath; others a Sabbath preceded by a feast day; others the first week Sabbath in a Passover week; others the first Sabbath of the second month; others the first week Sabbath after the great feasts. The last view[1] makes the first week Sabbath after Passover to be the first-first; the first after Pentecost to be the second-first; the first after Tabernacles the third-first. In like manner, we have now in common use the designations, first Sunday after Epiphany, the first after Easter, the first after Trinity. Browne (657) remarks: "Of all the explanations known to me this seems the best, indeed the only likely one." Clinton calls it "equally probable" as that first mentioned.[2]

In this chaos of interpretations, the mention of this Sabbath as the second-first gives us no chronological aid. The circumstance, however, that the disciples plucked the ears of corn and did eat, defines the season of the year as that when the corn was ripe. The kind of grain is not mentioned, whether barley, which was earliest, or wheat, which was later. Barley harvest was regarded as beginning from the second day of the Passover, and hence it has been inferred that this incident was after this, as no one was permitted to gather any corn till the sheaf of first-fruits had been waved. The wheat harvest was ripe and gathered in May or June. Robinson speaks of seeing the wheat ripening upon the 9th May; and he also speaks of the people near Tiberias as engaged in gathering the wheat harvest upon the 19th June. We have, then, April, May, and June, in either of which months this plucking and eating of the corn may have taken place. It is erroneously said by A. Clarke that it cannot "be laid after Pentecost, because then the harvest was fully in." Thomson states that the Syrian harvest extends through several months, and "the wheat

[1] Grotius, Hammond, Norton.

[2] For a brief statement of opinions, see Winer, ii. 348; also Greswell, ii. 300.

is suffered to become dead ripe, and as dry as tinder before it is cut." Even if the harvest generally was reaped, particular fields may still have been ungathered, or this been that which was left for gleaners.

Without attaching any importance to a conclusion, confessedly so dubious, we are inclined to regard this second-first Sabbath, as the first after Pentecost, which was this year the 19th May. If this be correct, the ministry of the Lord in Galilee had now continued about two months.

Where did this event take place? It is narrated by all the Synoptists as occuring just before the healing of the man with the withered hand, and this healing was in the synagogue at Capernaum. "And He entered again into the synagogue," (Mark iii. 1,) that is, the synagogue already mentioned.[1] This appears also from the mention of His withdrawal to the sea after the healing, (Mark iii. 7; see also Luke vi. 6.) That the field where the ears were plucked was not far distant from Capernaum, appears from Matthew xii. 9, for the Pharisees who had blamed the disciples for that act, are spoken of as members of that synagogue. "He went into their synagogue."[2] They were, therefore, the Pharisees of Capernaum, and the field of corn was in the neighborhood of that city, and within the limits of a Sabbath day's journey.

We may, then, give the following order of events as one intrinsically probable. The Lord, after His return from His first circuit, remained some days, or weeks, at Capernaum, and upon a Sabbath walked out with His disciples through the fields in the vicinity of the city. As He had already, in the opinion of the Pharisees, broken the sanctity of the Sabbath by healing upon it, (Mark i. 23 and 30,) they followed Him to watch Him, perhaps to note whether His walk upon that day was longer than the law

[1] Alexander, Meyer. [2] Meyer, Norton.

permitted, (Acts i. 12.) Seeing His disciples plucking and rubbing the ears of corn in their hands, they fancied the act a violation of the law. It has sometimes been said that the Pharisees did not think it sinful to pull and eat the grain, but it was so to rub it in their hands, all preparation of food being forbidden. This is doubtful. Lightfoot says: "The plucking of ears of corn on the Sabbath was forbidden by their canons, *verbatim:* 'He that reapeth corn on the Sabbath, to the quantity of a fig, is guilty. And plucking corn is as reaping.'"[1] If done presumptuously, or without necessity, the punishment was death by stoning, and hence the Lord's defence of the disciples. His answer to their complaints could only have angered them still more, and when, therefore, He entered the following Sabbath into the synagogue, (Luke vi. 6,) it was to be expected that they would carefully watch all that He did to find some sufficient ground of accusation against Him. His renewed violation of the Sabbath by healing the man with a withered hand, added to their indignation, and they now began to plot how they might destroy Him.

Luke (vi. 6) defines the time of this work of healing as "on another Sabbath." Whether this was the Sabbath immediately following that on which He walked through the corn-field, is not said, though it is probable.[2] The alliance of the Herodians with the Pharisees, does not imply that Herod himself had at this time any knowledge of Jesus, or took any steps against Him. The Herodians were those among the people who, though hating the Roman rule, favored the pretensions of Herod's family to kingly power. In case of national independence this family should

[1] See also Meyer on Matt. xii. 1.

[2] Wieseler (237) conjectures that it was a feast Sabbath and the day following that mentioned in verse 1st. This seems to have little or no basis. Meyer's assertion, that Matthew (xii. 9) puts the two events on the same Sabbath in opposition to Luke, is wholly baseless.

reign rather than the house of the Maccabees, or any other claimants. They were never numerous, for the great body of the nation looked upon that family as foreigners and usurpers. "Why the Pharisees and Herodians," says Alford, "should *now* combine, is not apparent." The Herodians would, however, be naturally jealous and watchful of any one whom they supposed to be a claimant of the throne in opposition to the house of Herod; and the Pharisees, being angry at Jesus on religious grounds, a union of the two for His destruction was very easily made. We need not suppose that this conspiracy against Him as yet included others than the Pharisees and Herodians of Capernaum and its immediate vicinity, (see Matt. xii. 14; Mark iii. 6.) Doubtless, very soon after this, His enemies here took counsel with His enemies at Jerusalem, and the conspiracy against Him became general.

It appears from these narratives that, almost from the very beginning of His Galilean work, the Lord encountered the active hostility of the Pharisees of that province. At the feast (John v. 1) He had aroused the anger of the Pharisees at Jerusalem by healing the impotent man on the Sabbath, (verses 16 and 18;) and at Capernaum He continued again and again to heal upon that day, and in the synagogue itself. Their fanatical zeal could not allow such violations of the law to pass unnoticed, and as Jesus defended them on the ground of His divine right to work, even on the Sabbath, He seemed to them not only a Sabbath breaker, but also a blasphemer. At first they plotted secretly against Him, the people at large being friendly to Him. Whilst in the full flush of His popularity they dared take no steps openly against Him, but waited till some imprudence, or error, or folly on His part, or the fickleness of the multitude, should put Him in their power. There was early an active and constant correspondence between the scribes and Pharisees in Galilee and those in Jerusalem; and at intervals deputations from the latter came down to consult with the former, and to devise means to hinder Him in His work, and to bring Him to punishment. As yet the fact that He had broken the Sabbath by healing upon it, does not seem to have turned the popular feeling at all against Him, nor even the assertion of His power to forgive sins.

MIDSUMMER, 781. A. D. 28.

After healing the man with a withered hand Jesus withdraws to the sea-shore. Here great multitudes from all parts of the land resort to Him, and He heals many. As they press upon Him to touch Him, He directs that a small ship be prepared to wait upon Him.	MATT. xii. 15–21. MARK iii. 7–12. MATT. iv. 25.
Leaving the seaside He goes up into a neighboring mountain and spends the night in prayer. In the morning He calls the disciples to Him, and from them chooses the twelve Apostles.	LUKE vi. 12–16. MARK iii. 13–19.
The multitudes now gathering to Him He proceeds to deliver the discourse called the Sermon on the Mount.	MATT. v. vi. vii. LUKE vi. 17–49.

From Matthew (xii. 15) it would appear that Jesus was aware of the purpose of the Pharisees, and therefore avoided them. He would not, except so far as was necessary, come into collision with them nor expose His work to injury through their opposition. It was for this reason that, having healed all the sick among the multitudes that followed Him, He charged them that they should not make Him known, (v. 16.) He was now seeking for the humble and repentant, all in whom He could discern any sense of sin or germs of faith, and He would not for their sakes suffer Himself to be forced into a hostile attitude to the spiritual leaders of the people. This was the rule of His conduct, as it had been prophetically laid down by the prophet Isaiah (xlii. 2): "He shall not strive nor cry, neither shall any man hear His voice in the streets."

The withdrawal from the city to the sea-shore, (Mark iii. 7,) whilst it had thus for one end, to avoid His enemies, seems also to have been to find a more convenient place for teaching and healing. In the city He was exposed to constant interruption through the eagerness of the sick and their friends, who pressed upon Him to touch Him; and to secure personal freedom He was compelled to order a boat to attend upon Him, that He might, when necessary, use it as a pulpit to address the multitude standing before Him on the shore, and perhaps also to withdraw Himself wholly from them by crossing the lake.

The fame of Jesus seems at this time to have reached every part of the land. Crowds came, not only from Galilee and Judea, but also from Idumea and from beyond Jordan, and from the territories about Tyre and Sidon. That so great numbers, and from such remote regions, should gather at Capernaum, shows that He remained at that city for some time after His return from His first circuit. It was, doubtless, not His teachings, but His miracles of healing, that awakened such general attention, and drew such multitudes after Him. Most came attracted by His reputation as a healer of the sick. After making all allowance for the degraded condition of the present inhabitants of Palestine, the following remarks of Thomson (ii. 84) would not be inapplicable to the Jews of the Lord's day: "Should a prophet now arise with a tithe of the celebrity of Jesus of Nazareth, there would quickly be immense assemblies about him from Galilee, and from Decapolis, and from Jerusalem, and from Judea, and from beyond Jordan. Bad, and stupid, and ignorant, and worldly, as the people are, their attention would be instantly arrested by the name of a prophet, and they would flock from all parts to see, hear, and be healed. There is an irresistible bias in Orientals of all religions to run after the mere shadow of a prophet, or a miracle worker."

That the choice of the Twelve took place at this time, appears from the mention in Mark and Luke of the various parts of the country from which the multitudes came. According to Luke, (vi. 17,) they that heard the discourse upon the mount were from Judea and Jerusalem, and from the sea-coast of Tyre and Sidon. Mark (iii. 7, 8) mentions Galilee, Judea, Jerusalem, Idumea, beyond Jordan, and about Tyre and Sidon. Matthew, (iv. 25,) who does not mention the choice of the apostles, but gives the Sermon on the Mount, speaks of the great multitudes that followed Him from Galilee, Decapolis, Jerusalem, Judea, and beyond Jordan. It was at this point, when He had special need of their services, that He selected twelve out of the body of His disciples "that they should be with Him, and that He might send them forth to preach, and to have power to heal sicknesses and to cast out devils," (Mark iii. 14, 15.)

Whether some particular mountain is designated by the use of the article by the Synoptists, *το ορος*, "the mountain," or generally the ridges of hills on the sides of the Lake of Galilee, as distinguished from the low shores, we cannot easily decide. The Jews distinguished the face of the country into mountains, plains and valleys. According to Middleton,[1] by the mountain is here signified "the mountain district as distinguished from the other two."[2] It is most natural to refer it to some specific and well-known locality; but it is plain that the mountain here is not the same mentioned in Matt. xiv. 23, Mark vi. 46, John vi. 3, where the five thousand were fed, or that in Matt. xv. 29, where the four thousand were fed. We may then rather infer that in each of these cases the mountain is defined by the article, because supposed to be already well known as the site of the event. Where this mountain was is now only matter of conjecture. Tradition has chosen

[1] Greek article, 103. [2] See Ebrard, 349; Meyer on Matt. v. 1.

the hill known as the Horns of Hattin from its peculiar shape, and called by the Latins the Mount of Beatitudes. It is a ridge not far from Tell Hum, about a quarter of a mile in length, running east and west. At each end rises a small cone or horn. Its peculiar shape attracts the attention of the traveller, and is probably the cause of its selection. Robinson contends that there are a dozen other mountains in the vicinity of the lake which would answer the purpose just as well; and that the tradition which has selected this as the site goes no further back than the 13th century, and is confined to the Latin Church. As the same tradition placed here also the feeding of the five thousand, which is certainly an error, we are the more inclined to reject it.[1] Stanley, however, (360,) says: "The situation so strikingly coincides with the intimations of the Gospel narrative as almost to force the inference, that in this instance the eye of those who selected the spot was for once rightly guided."

We may arrange the events preparatory to the delivery of the Sermon on the Mount in the following order: the Lord leaving Capernaum in the evening goes to the mount, which cannot have been at any great distance, and spends the night alone. Very early in the morning His disciples, probably according to His direction, came to Him, and from them He selected the Twelve. By this time the multitudes who had lodged in Capernaum or in its neighborhood, learning whither He had gone, followed Him, and then He addresses them.

As Matthew (chs. v., vi., vii.) and Luke (vi. 17–49) introduce their reports of the Sermon on the Mount by the mention of differing circumstances, and as their reports differ in many points, it has been questioned whether both can refer to the same discourse. The various opinions may

[1] Raumer, 32, note.

be reduced to three · 1st. That which regards them as reports of discourses wholly distinct, and spoken at different times, and perhaps also at different places.[1] 2d. That which regards them as reports of distinct discourses, but spoken successively: the one before the choice of the apostles, the other after it; the one to the disciples, the other to the multitude; the one sitting upon the mountain, the other standing upon the plain.[2] 3d. That which regards them as abstracts of one and the same discourse.[3]

To determine which of these views is correct, or how the respective discourses of Matthew and Luke stand related to each other, we must examine in detail the several points of likeness and unlikeness. And 1st, the difference of place. Matthew (v. 1) says: "And seeing the multitudes He went up into a mountain, and when He was set His disciples came unto Him. And He opened His mouth and taught them." Luke (vi. 17–20) says, that after the choice of the Twelve "He came down with them, and stood in the plain, (επι τοπου πεδινου,) and the company of His disciples and a great multitude of people,... which came to hear Him and to be healed of their diseases; and they that were vexed with unclean spirits: and they were healed. And the whole multitude sought to touch Him, for there went virtue out of Him and healed them all. And He lifted up His eyes on His disciples, and said," &c. Thus, according to Matthew, the discourse was delivered by the Lord sitting upon the side or top of a mountain; according to Luke, after He had chosen the Twelve He descended to the plain, and having healed the sick, addressed those present. But the latter does not say that the discourse was spoken on the plain, although He does not mention any re-ascent. Such a re-ascent is however very probable, for it is said "that the whole multitude sought to touch Him;" and as,

[1] Krafft, Greswell. [2] Augustine, Lange.
[3] Robinson, Tischendorf, Stier.

when similarly pressed upon the sea-shore, (Mark iii. 9,) He entered a boat and taught from it; so now He would naturally ascend to a point where they could not reach Him, and from which He could easily be seen and heard by all.[1] Some would understand the "plain" of Luke of a level spot on the side of the mountain, or at its foot, where the multitude could sit or stand, this plain itself being, in reference to the sea-shore from whence they came, a part of the mountain. Thus Stanley, speaking of the hill of Hattin, says: "The plain on which it stands is easily accessible from the lake, and from that plain to the summit is but a few minutes' walk. The platform at the top is evidently suitable for the collection of a multitude, and corresponds precisely to the 'level place' mistranslated 'plain,' to which He would 'come down,' as from one of its higher horns, to address the people."[2] In this way all seeming discrepancy between Matthew and Luke as to the place, disappears. The choice of the Twelve was made upon the mountain before the multitude gathered, which choice Matthew does not mention. As the Lord beheld the people gathering to Him, He goes down with His disciples to meet them upon some level place, and after healing the sick, He seats Himself in a position, probably higher up upon the hill, where He can be seen and heard by the great crowds, and proceeds to address them.[3]

2d. Difference of time. Following his report of the sermon, Matthew relates (viii. 2–4) the healing of the leper as having immediately taken place. Luke (vii. 2–10) relates the healing of the centurion's servant as immediately following. As these events were separated by a considerable interval of time, so, it is said by Krafft and others,

[1] So Robinson, Har. 193.

[2] So Tholuck, Sermon on the Mount, 53, "a level place, not a plain."

[3] See Ebrard, 350; Stier, i. 327; Lichtenstein, 247. Alford, after Meyer, finds the two Evangelists in contradiction.

must have been the discourses which they respectively followed. But we have already seen that Matthew is not narrating events in chronological order, and that the healing of the leper took place before the Sermon on the Mount. We are not therefore obliged to suppose the discourses distinct upon this ground.

3d. Difference of audience. Matthew (iv. 25) describes the multitudes present as from Galilee, Decapolis, Jerusalem, Judea, and from beyond Jordan; Luke (vi. 17) as from all Judea, Jerusalem, and the sea-coast of Tyre and Sidon. From this partial difference of names Krafft (83) infers that those who heard the discourse reported by Matthew were mostly Jews, with perhaps a few Syrians; but that those who heard the discourse reported by Luke were mostly from the eastern side of Galilee and the coasts of Tyre and Sidon. But this inference is not warranted. In this enumeration neither of the Evangelists designs to discriminate between Jewish and heathen lands. This appears from Mark, (iii. 7, 8,) who mentions Galilee, Judea, Jerusalem, Idumea, beyond Jordan, and about Tyre and Sidon. If heathen were present, according to Luke, from Tyre and Sidon, so might they be also, according to Matthew, from Decapolis. The Evangelists plainly all intend to say, that the crowds who were present came from every part of the land; and any difference in the enumeration of the regions whence they came is unimportant. On the other hand, the very particularity of the mention of so many provinces by each, sufficiently shows that all point to one and the same period.

4th. Difference of contents. "Of 107 verses in Matthew, Luke contains only 30; his four beatitudes are balanced by as many woes; and in his text parts of the sermon are introduced by sayings which do not precede them in Matthew, but which naturally connect with them."[1] But

[1] Alford on Matt. v. 1. See also Greswell, ii. 429; Krafft, 83.

these differences are few when compared with the resemblances. The beginning and ending of both are the same; there is a general similarity in the order, and often identity in the expressions. Often in the Evangelists, when their reports are in substance the same, there are many variations.[1] That the two discourses should have so much in common if they were distinct, spoken at different times and to different audiences, is most improbable. That many of the shorter proverbial expressions might be used at various times is natural, but not that such similarity should prevail throughout.[2]

The supposition that the Lord first addressed the apostles and disciples, which address Matthew gives, and then the multitudes, which address Luke gives, was advocated by Augustine, and has been the ruling one in the Latin Church. It has been also adopted by most of the Lutheran harmonists, though Calvin calls this view light and frivolous. That there is something esoteric in the former and exoteric in the latter may be admitted; but this is owing not to the different audiences to whom the discourses were spoken, but to the different classes of readers for which the two Gospels were designed. It may be that neither Matthew nor Luke gives us the exact discourse as it was spoken. Without entering into the vexed question of inspiration, its nature and degrees, we may say that each Evangelist, writing under the direction of the Holy Spirit, made such selection of the Lord's words, as well as of the events in His history, and so arranged them, as best to meet the wants of those for whom he wrote. That Luke

[1] Compare the Lord's Prayer as given Matt. vi. 9–12, and Luke xi. 2–4; and His discourse concerning the Pharisees, Matt. xxiii. and Luke xx. 46.

[2] Neander's explanation, 224, that the original document of Matthew of Hebrew origin, "passed through the hands of the Greek editor, who has inserted other expressions of Christ allied to those in the organic connection of the discourse, but spoken on other occasions," is one of those arbitrary assumptions, whose frequency makes so much of German criticism worthless.

should omit those portions of the discourse having special reference to the Jewish sects, and to the Mosaic laws, was in accordance with the general scope of his Gospel as designed for heathen Christians; whilst Matthew, on the other hand, writing for Jewish Christians, would retain them. To this Alford and others object that in some cases Luke is fuller than Matthew, (compare Matt. vii. 1, 2, and Luke vi. 37, 38.) But, as has been said, Matthew may not give the words of the Lord in all their fulness; and it is not at all inconsistent with the fact of an epitome that certain thoughts should be more fully expanded than in the original, when this original is itself but an epitome.

There is still another argument against the identity of these two discourses, based upon the fact that Matthew does not relate his own call (ix. 9) till he had recorded the sermon. But it is so abundantly established that Matthew does not follow chronological order, that this is of no importance.

We conclude, then, that Matthew gives this discourse substantially, if not literally, as it was spoken, and that Luke gives the same, but modified to meet the wants of that class of readers for whom he especially wrote.

MIDSUMMER, 781. A. D. 28.

After the sermon was ended Jesus returns to Capernaum, still followed by the multitudes. Immediately after His return he heals the centurion's servant. The crowds continuing to follow Him so that He has no time even to eat, His friends become alarmed at His incessant labors, and thinking Him beside Himself, attempt to restrain Him.

MATT. viii. 5–13.
LUKE vii. 1–10.
MARK iii. 20, 21.

The form of expression, (Luke vii. 1,) "Now when He had ended all His sayings in the audience of the people, He entered into Capernaum," shows that He was at no great distance, and that no long interval elapsed between the discourse and the entry. Mark, (iii. 19,) after mentioning the election of the Twelve, merely adds, "And they went into a house," or more literally, "went home," εις οικον, that is, to His house in Capernaum.

Matthew (viii. 1) speaks of the great multitudes that followed Him descending from the mountain; and Mark (iii. 20) of "the multitude coming together again," as if after a temporary dispersion, such as was natural in coming down from the mountain, they had re-assembled in the city, and doubtless before His dwelling. So earnest were they to see and hear Him, and to bring to Him their sick, that He found no time even to eat, (Mark iii. 20.) This intense activity in teaching and working, without any intervals for repose, alarmed His friends. It is not certain who are here meant by "His friends," οι παρ' αυτου. The translation in the margin, "His kinsmen," is adopted by many.[1] Some suppose His unbelieving brothers to be especially meant.[2] Some, as Lichtenstein, make them to be the disciples other than the Twelve; and others still, as Ebrard, the strangers or people of the house, with whom He was staying. Probably they were His relatives, His mother and brethren, who, if still resident in Nazareth, had heard of His great labors, and now came to seek Him. Their affection would naturally make them anxious about Him; and their near relationship to Him would permit them to say, "He is beside Himself," which any of His disciples would scarcely do. This however does not indicate that in their opinion He was actually insane, but merely that He was prosecuting His work with too great zeal and energy. As expressed by Stier, "He does too much; forgets all moderation—is out of His senses, knows not what He is

[1] So Alexander, Stier, Alford.

[2] Meyer makes them to have recently arrived from Nazareth; compare v. 31; Lange to be already settled at Capernaum.

doing, so that we have to interfere." This language did not so much refer to the matter as to the manner of His work. Perhaps they may have had in mind that He had spent the night alone upon the mountain, and so had been for a time without food and sleep.

It appears from Luke, (vii. 1) compared with Matt. (viii. 5,) that the healing of the centurion's servant was on the day of His return from the mount. As the centurion seems to have been a resident of Capernaum, for he built them their synagogue, (Luke vii. 5,) it is not improbable that a Roman garrison was stationed there.[1] That the elders should come to make the request is wholly in accordance with oriental usage.[2] That they were willing to make this request, shows that at this time no general hostility had yet developed itself against Him in Capernaum.

Midsummer, 781. A. D. 28.

The day following the healing of the centurion's servant He goes to Nain, accompanied by the disciples and many people. He there restores to life the son of a widow as they were bearing him to the grave. Whilst continuing His ministry in that part of Galilee, John the Baptist, who hears of His works, sends from his prison a message to Him by two of his disciples. Jesus answers their question, and addresses the multitude respecting John.	Luke vii. 11–17. Matt. xi. 2–19. Luke vii. 18–35.

The order of events here will depend upon the reading, Luke vii. 11, whether εν τῃ εξης, or εν τω εξης, "the day after," or "afterward." The weight of authority is in favor of the former.[3]

The Lord gives Himself no rest, but enters immediately upon new labors. From this time the Twelve were con-

[1] Trench, Mir. 184. [2] Thomson, i. 313.
[3] Tischendorf, Robinson, Wieseler, Alford; contra, Meyer, Stier.

stantly with Him till sent forth upon their mission. Beside them many of the other disciples now accompanied Him, as well as much people.

Nain lies on the northwest declivity of the hill of Little Hermon, commanding an extensive view over the plain of Esdraelon, and the northern hills. It is now an insignificant village, with no remains of any importance. "No convent, no tradition marks the spot. But under these circumstances, the name is sufficient to guarantee its authenticity."[1]

As the Jews usually buried the dead upon the same day they died and before sundown,[2] it has been questioned how He could have reached Nain from Capernaum so early in the day as to meet the funeral procession. But as the distance is only about twenty-five miles, and probably less, it might be walked in seven or eight hours. As the orientals walk rapidly, and commence their journeys early in the morning, He might have reached Nain by noon, or a little after.

The restoration to life of the widow's son was the first work of this kind the Lord had wrought, and naturally produced a most powerful impression on all who heard of it. All saw in it the mighty hand of God, who alone could bring the dead to life. The Evangelist mentions (Luke vii. 16) that "there came a fear on all, and they glorified God, saying, That a great prophet is risen up among us." No such miracle had been wrought since the days of Elisha; the fame of it "went forth through all Judea, and throughout all the region round about," and thus coming to the ears of some of John's disciples, was told by them to their master. Luke says, (vii. 18,) "And the disciples of John showed him of all these things." This may mean that they told him of all that Jesus had recently done, His works of

[1] Stanley, 349. [2] Winer, ii. 16, note 1.

healing, the choice of the Twelve, the Sermon on the Mount, as well as of this work at Nain; and also of His great popularity, and of the crowds that continually followed Him. If we assume that the place of John's imprisonment was Machaerus,[1] a fortress in the southern part of Perea, just on the confines of Arabia, some days at least must have elapsed between this miracle and the coming of John's messengers.[2] Perhaps our Lord continued during this interval at Nain, teaching all who had been so impressed by His mighty work that they had ears to hear; or He may have visited the adjacent cities and villages; or He may, after a brief circuit, have returned to Capernaum, and hither, as the place of His residence, John's disciples have come.

Some place this miracle after the raising of the daughter of Jairus, chiefly because the former is a greater exhibition of the powers of Christ. Thus Trench[3] says of the three miracles of raising the dead, that "they are not exactly the same miracle repeated three times over, but may be contemplated as an ever-ascending scale of difficulty, each a greater outcoming of the power of Christ than the preceding." But this is more plausible than sound. If there be such "an ever-ascending scale of difficulty," we should find the Lord's first works of healing less mighty than the later; but this is not the case. If we compare the two miracles of feeding the multitude, the first is the more stupendous. The impression which the raising of the widow's son made on all, seems plainly to show that it was the first of its kind, (Luke vii. 16, 17.)

Perhaps the message of the Baptist may stand in close connection with the great miracle at Nain. Such a work must have convinced him, had he before had any doubts, that Jesus was divinely sent, and that the mighty power of God was indeed with Him. The question then, "Art thou

[1] Josephus, War, 7. 6. 1–3. [2] See Greswell, ii. 327. [3] Mir. 152.

He that should come, or look we for another?" may be an intimation that Jesus should now put forth in direct act that resistless power of which He had just shown Himself to be possessed. Art thou the Messiah? Act then as the Messiah. Thou canst raise the dead. Thou canst fulfil all the covenant promises to the patriarchs and prophets. Purge thy floor; gather the wheat into thy garner; and baptize with the Holy Ghost.

The answer of the Lord to the messengers meets this state of mind. He refers to His daily works as being truly Messianic, and such as befitted Him to perform. Not acts of judgment, but of mercy, belonged to His office. His work was now to heal the sick, to preach the Gospel to the poor, to raise the dead. He adds, as a caution to John, "Blessed is he whosoever shall not be offended in me." Blessed is he who shall understand the work I now do, and not stumble at it.

This question of John gives Jesus an opportunity to bear His direct witness to him as a prophet, and more, as the herald of the Messiah, (Matt. xi. 9, 10.) He declares also to the people, that if they will receive him, he is the Elias that was for to come; and reproaches them that they would not receive John or Himself in either of their different modes of working or teaching, (Matt. xi. 16–19; Luke vii. 31–35.) His testimony to John was well received by the people and the publicans, all those who had been baptized by him; but not by the Pharisees and lawyers, who had rejected his baptism, (Luke vii. 29, 30.)

This testimony of Jesus to John as the herald of the Messiah, was a plain assertion, though an indirect one, of His own Messianic character. But John was now in prison. How was this compatible with his being Elias? How could he prepare the Lord's way? Did not this very fact of his imprisonment conclusively disprove all his claims to be the forerunner of the Messiah? This tacit objection Jesus meets by showing that it depended on them, whether or no, he was the Elias. If they received him, if they hearkened to his words, and permitted him to do his work, then he would be to them that prophet, and fulfil all that was said of Elias. But they had not so received him; they had said of him that he had a devil; and now he was shut up in prison; and thus the Jews were made clearly to understand the connection between John's ministry and that of Jesus, and how the rejection of the former involved that of the latter.

Immediately upon these words concerning John, follows in Matthew (xi. 20–24) an address to the cities Bethsaida, Chorazin, and Capernaum. It is given by Luke later, and in connection with the mission of the seventy disciples, (Luke x. 13–16.) We shall discuss its right position when we consider that mission.

AUTUMN, 781. A. D. 28.

Jesus dines with a Pharisee named Simon, and while at the table is anointed by a woman who is a sinner. In reply to Simon's complaint He relates the parable of the two debtors.	LUKE vii. 36–50.
He continues His circuit in Galilee with the Twelve, and also accompanied by certain women.	LUKE viii. 1–3.

This dining with a Pharisee, and anointing, are mentioned only by Luke, (vii. 36–50,) and are not to be confounded with later events of a like kind mentioned by Matthew xxvi. 6–13, Mark xiv. 3–9, John xii. 2–9. The fact that both persons at whose houses these feasts took place bore the name of Simon, is not strange, when we remember how very common this name was. They are sufficiently distinguished by the addition in Luke of "Pharisee," and in the other Evangelists of "leper." Where this Simon lived is uncertain. Some have supposed at Nain, as the city last named,[1] others at Capernaum.[2] Those who make this Simon the same as Simon the leper, place the feast at Bethany; Romish tradition, which holds the woman to have been Mary Magdalene, gives the place as Magdala, where Jesus was on His return toward Capernaum.[3]

The identification of this woman, who was a sinner, with Mary Magdalene (Luke viii. 2) rests upon no sufficient grounds. Lardner argues[4] that Mary was a woman of quality on the ground that she is twice mentioned before Joanna, (Luke viii. 3 and xxiv. 10,) who was wife of Herod's steward. So the first place is often given her by the Evangelists, (Matt. xxvii. 56 and 61; xxviii. 1; Mark xv. 40 and 47; but see John xix. 25.) This was noticed by Grotius, who inferred from it that she was of higher rank than the other women. She seems also to have been at the expense of the spices for the Lord's burial. The mention of her name with those of the other honorable women who attended the Lord in His journeys, and ministered to Him of their substance, is inconsistent with the fact of a previous loose life; for such an one the Lord would not have permitted to be an attendant, or the other women have consented to it. Lardner adds: "I conceive of her as a woman of fine understanding and known virtue and discretion, with a dignity of behavior becoming her age, her wisdom, and her high station." It is generally admitted that this woman, described as a sinner, was of unchaste life. The text, as given by Tischendorf and Alford, changes somewhat the meaning: "a woman which was in the city, a sinner." Alford remarks: "We must either render 'which was a sinner in the city,'

[1] Greswell, Wieseler. [2] Robinson, Meyer.

[3] Friedlieb, 216, note, who supposes that the place of John's imprisonment was in the neighborhood of Magdala.

[4] See Lardner's letter to Hanway on Magdalen Houses, vol. x. 237; also Townsend, part iii., note 58.

i. e., known as such in the place by public repute, carrying on a sinful occupation in the place; or regard it as parenthetic, 'which was in the city a sinner.' The latter seems preferable." Lightfoot (in loco) maintains that this woman was Mary Magdalene, who was the same as Mary sister of Lazarus. He therefore identifies Magdala with Bethany, as very near to Jerusalem, and affirms that it was distinguished for the unchastity of the inhabitants. Thus Mary Magdalene twice anointed the Lord, now and at the beginning of His Passion.[1] This is without proof.

Whether the journey (Luke viii. 1–3) made in company with "the Twelve and certain women," was a continuation of the circuit from Nain is not certain, though most probable. If, however, the anointing was at Capernaum, this may refer to a new circuit. The remark of Ellicott (184) that "this circuit could not have lasted much above a day or two after the miracle at Nain," is plainly at variance with the Evangelist's language, (viii. 1,) that "He went throughout every city and village preaching," which upon its face implies a circuit of considerable duration.[2] This circuit is distinguished from His former ones by the attendance of these women, whose names are mentioned: Mary Magdalene, Joanna, wife of Chuza Herod's steward, and Susannah, and many others. Nothing is historically known of any of these persons more than is here related. Their attendance on the Lord may perhaps be regarded as marking an onward step in His ministry. Whether from this time they generally accompanied Him in His journeys is not stated, but is not improbable. (See Luke xxiii. 55.)

[1] In favor of the identity of Mary Magdalene with this sinner, see Baronius; Sepp, iii. 243; Oosterzee in loco; contra, Meyer, Winer. For a general discussion of the point, see Herzog's Encyc., vol. ix. 102.

[2] It is impossible, without great violence to language, to compress so much of the Lord's work into the brief interval between Purim and the Passover following, as Ellicott is compelled to do by assuming that the feast (John v. 1) is Purim.

AUTUMN, 781. A. D. 28.

Returning to Capernaum, the Lord heals one possessed with a devil, blind and dumb. The Pharisees hereupon charge Him with casting out devils by the help of Beelzebub, and some, tempting Him, ask a sign from heaven. He replies to their charge, and while	MATT. xii. 22–45. MARK iii. 22–30.
speaking it is announced to Him that His mother and brethren stand without, desiring to see Him. He points to His disciples, and says, Behold my mother and my brethren.	MATT. xii. 46–50. LUKE viii. 19–21. MARK iii. 31–35.

There is not a little difficulty in the arrangement of these events. We have first to inquire whether the healing in Matt. xii. 22 is identical with that in Luke xi. 14?[1] There are two cases of healing of dumb possessed persons related by Matthew. first in ix. 32, second in xii. 22. These have much in common, and at both did the Pharisees make the charge that Jesus cast out devils through the prince of the devils. There is, however, this important difference, that in the former the possessed was dumb only, in the latter, both dumb and blind. In the healing related by St. Luke the possessed was dumb. Some, as Greswell, find here three distinct cases of healing; others identify that in Luke with that in Matt. ix. 32;[2] but most with that in Matt. xii. 22. The chief ground for this identity is the great similarity of the Lord's reply, as given by the two Evangelists to the charge that He cast out devils by Beelzebub. (Compare Matt. xii. 25–45 with Luke xi. 17–36.) Against this identity is the position in which it is placed by Luke, as if occurring during the Lord's last journey to Jerusalem. Matthew also calls the possessed "blind and dumb;" Luke only "dumb." But this difference is un-

[1] So many, Robinson, Meyer, Lange, Bloomfield.
Krafft, Neander.

important. All depends upon the point whether Christ's reply to the Pharisees is identical in the two Evangelists. In favor of this is the general similarity in thought and expression, making it improbable that we have the reports of two distinct discourses. On the other hand, Luke brings it into immediate connection with a dinner at the house of a Pharisee, (v. 37,) which seems upon internal grounds to have been at a later period.[1] Some, however, do not think this dinner with the Pharisee to have followed immediately upon the preceding discourse, and render the phrase "And as He spake," εν δε τῳ λαλησαι, as meaning simply, "at some time when He was teaching," and thus find in it no chronological sequence.[2] This is hardly satisfactory. Shall we then say that all that Luke relates (vs. 14–54) is in chronological order? It is not impossible that all from v. 29 may be referred to a later period, as he seems to bring together, (vs. 15, 16,) the charges of the Pharisees, which Matthew keeps distinct. Krafft (85) attempts to show that the discourse given by Matthew (xii. 25–45) was not all spoken at once, nor has reference to the same miracle. In chapter ix. 32–34 mention is made of the healing of a dumb possessed man, when a like charge was made by the Pharisees that He cast out devils through the prince of the devils. It is in connection with this miracle that Krafft would place what Matthew narrates in xii. 38–46. But this division seems arbitrary. It is by no means impossible that this healing of the dumb possessed man in Luke is to be identified with the healing in Matt. ix. 32.[3] It is however very difficult to reach any satisfactory conclusion.

[1] See His words to the Pharisees present at the dinner, vs. 39–54, which indicate that the breach between Him and them was irreparable.

[2] Norton, notes, 268.

[3] So Tischendorf, who makes Luke xi. 17–26 = Matt. xii. 43–45; Luke xi. 29–36 = Matt. xii. 38–42.

According to many harmonists, the two Evangelists refer to two distinct cases of healing, and give two distinct discourses.[1] It is remarked by Greswell that cures of dispossession were among the earliest and commonest of the Saviour's miracles, and that Matthew himself gives two alike in almost every feature, and in both the same charge of being aided by the prince of the devils, was brought against Him. It is not, therefore, to be thought strange that His reply upon different occasions should be substantially the same. There is much force in this, and notwithstanding the strong objection that two distinct discourses should have so much in common, we shall, in the absence of all definite data, assume that Matthew and Luke refer to different cases of healing, and give different discourses.

That the healing of the dumb and blind possessed man took place at Capernaum, may be inferred from the mention of "the scribes which came down from Jerusalem," (Mark iii. 22,) and who would naturally seek Him in the place of His residence. Their presence at this time may be ascribed to the powerful impression which the raising of the widow's son at Nain had made upon all who heard of it, and the consequent necessity on the part of His enemies of taking some steps to counteract it. The cure of the possessed, it is said, amazed the people, and led them to ask, "Is not this the Son of David?" So far as we know, this was the first time that this specially Messianic title had been given Him; nor does it clearly appear what there was in this miracle that should lead them thus to speak. It would, however, naturally arouse the jealousy of the Pharisees, and make them the more eager to oppose Him. As the fact of the healing was beyond dispute, they could only assert that it was done through the aid of the prince of the devils. This ascription of His miracles to Satanic agency marks a decided progress in Pharisaic hos-

[1] McKnight, Greswell.

tility. Heretofore they had said of Him that He was a Sabbath-breaker and a blasphemer; now they say that He is in league with evil spirits. And this charge reached much farther than this particular miracle. It was virtually ascribing all that He said and did to a diabolical origin, and made the Spirit of God that rested upon Him to be the spirit of Beelzebub; and hence the severity of His language in reply, (Matt. xii. 34.)

It appears from Mark (iii. 22) that those who made this charge were the scribes which came down from Jerusalem. Luke (xi. 15) uses the indefinite expression, "some of them said." Matthew (xii. 24) refers it to the Pharisees. These scribes were doubtless themselves Pharisees, perhaps also priests, or Levites. Alexander well remarks: "It is a serious error to suppose that these descriptive titles are exclusive of each other, and denote so many independent classes, whereas they only denote different characters or relations, which might all meet in one and the same person, as being at the same time a priest and Levite by descent and sacred office, a scribe by profession, and a Pharisee in sentiment and party connection." It is not improbable that they came as a formal deputation to watch His proceedings, and to organize His enemies against Him throughout Galilee. Doubtless their calumny that He was aided by Beelzebub, was caught up and reiterated by the Pharisees of Capernaum.

The visit of His mother and brethren is mentioned by all the Synoptists; and that it occurred during, or immediately after, the reply to the Pharisees, appears from Matt. xii. 46. Luke (viii. 19) has it in another connection, but without any note of time. It is, perhaps, fairly inferrible that they now resided at Capernaum.[1] It is evident that Mary and His brethren were presuming too much on

[1] Greswell, ii. 270, admitting this, still affirms that "they had no house of their own, or none in which our Lord was living along with them."

their near relationship to Him, and that He wished to teach them that when engaged in His Father's work, merely human bonds must give place to higher obligations. Mary here showed the same spirit that twice before He had rebuked, (Luke ii. 49; John ii. 4.)

Autumn, 781. A. D. 28.

The same day He left His house and sat by the seaside, and as the multitudes gathered to Him, He entered a ship and taught them in parables. At the close of the day He gives commandment to depart to the other side. As they were preparing to go, He holds a conversation with a scribe, and with one of His disciples about following Him. He enters the ship with the disciples, and crosses the sea. Upon the way a violent tempest arises; Jesus rebukes the wind and waves, and there is a great calm.	Matt. xiii. 1–52. Mark iv. 1–34. Luke viii. 4–15. Matt. viii. 18–27. Luke ix. 57–60. Mark iv. 35–41. Luke viii. 22–25.

There is no reason why the language of Matthew "in the same day," εν ημερᾳ εκειvῃ—should not here be taken strictly, although sometimes used indefinitely, (Acts viii. 1.) It was the same day as that on which His mother and brethren visited Him, and on which He healed the blind and dumb possessed. Mark (iv. 1) has the same order. Luke (viii. 4–19) narrates the teaching in parables before His mother's visit. The similarity of statement is so marked in Matt. viii. 19–22, and Luke ix. 57–60, that we can scarce doubt that they are describing the same incidents. Their repetition is indeed possible, as affirmed by Stier, but improbable. They seem most fittingly arranged in the order in which they are placed by Matthew.

It is a question whether all the parables given by Matthew (xiii.) were spoken at once; and if not, when and where? Mark, although he gives only those of the Sower and the mustard seed, implies that there were others, (iv. 2,) "And

He taught them many things by parables;" language almost the same as that of Matthew, (xiii. 3,) "And He spake many things unto them in parables." After He had spoken the parable of the Sower, it is said (Matt. xiii. 10) that His disciples came to ask Him why He spake in parables. Mark (iv. 10) says: "When He was alone," they asked of Him the parable. Whether He was yet in the ship, or had gone to the shore, does not appear. Greswell attempts to show that the disciples did not ask any explanation of the parable of the Sower at this time, but only why He spake in parables at all. Afterward, when He had gone into the house, (Matt. xiii. 36,) they asked Him the meaning of this particular parable, and also of the tares. This involves more difficulties than it removes. Krafft makes the teaching in parables to have occupied at least two days. (See Luke viii. 22, who makes a distinction between the day of the visit of His mother and brethren, and that when He spake the parable of the Sower.) In this case, Mark (iv. 35) refers not to the day when He went down to the sea-side, but to the day following. Stier supposes the seven parables of Matthew to have been spoken on one day; the first four to the people on the shore, the last three to the disciples in the house. After several parables had been spoken, there was a pause, (Mark iv. 10; Matt. xiii. 10,) and then the questions following were asked.

It must remain doubtful whether this teaching in parables did not occupy more than one day. If, however, we limit it to one, we may give the following order of events as a probable one. After Jesus had spoken the parable of the Sower, He paused for a while, perhaps to give His hearers time to reflect upon it. During this interval, the Twelve and other disciples asked Him, first, why He taught in parables, and second, what this parable was? Where these questions were asked, is uncertain. Two circumstances only define it: that "He was alone," (Mark iv.

10,) or separated from the multitude; and that "the disciples came to Him," (Matt. xiii. 10.) All this may have taken place while He was still in the boat, in which with Him were doubtless the Twelve, and others may have joined them. By withdrawing a little way from the shore, they would be strictly alone. Greswell (ii. 440) objects that the multitude could not be called "those that are without," (Mark iv. 11,) unless Jesus and the disciples were somewhere within, that is, in a house; but the distinction is more subtle than solid. After His explanations to the disciples, Jesus again teaches the people, and adds the parables of the tares and wheat, the mustard seed, and the leaven. At this point, dismissing the multitude, He returns to His house, and His disciples coming to Him, He expounds to them the tares and wheat, and adds the parables of the hid treasure, the pearl, and the net. Going again at even to the shore, and the multitudes gathering around Him, He gives order to pass to the other side. The disciples, therefore, send away the people, and take Him as He was in the ship.[1]

This teaching in parables plainly marks an onward step in the Lord's ministry. He had now testified of Himself both in word and deed, had manifested Himself as the Messiah; and it was becoming apparent to Him that the great body of the people had no discernment of His divine character and mission, and would not receive Him, however they might for a time be personally attracted to Him, and marvel at His words and works. The Pharisees, the spiritual leaders both at Jerusalem and in Galilee, had taken decided steps against Him; and though with the common people His popularity seemed now at its height, He discerned that there was no root of faith, and that most followed Him through motives of wonder, or idle curiosity. He could, therefore, well speak of them (Matt. xiii. 13–15) as hearing

[1] See Newcome, Har. 256.

His words, and yet not understanding them, as seeing His works and not perceiving their significance. To them He could not explain the mysteries of the Kingdom. He must use the form of the parable which, hiding its meaning from the careless and foolish, opened it to the diligent and wise seeker after truth.

The motive of the Lord in crossing the lake is not stated, but apparently it was to escape the crowds never satisfied with hearing Him, and to find rest, (Matt. viii. 18.) His disciples "took Him as He was in the ship," or without any preparation for the journey; which implies that it was not premeditated, but suddenly determined on, (Mark iv. 36.) It was "even," probably near sundown, when they left the shore, and wearied by the labors of the day the Lord soon fell asleep. Whilst thus sleeping a fierce storm burst upon them. How exposed is the Sea of Galilee, from its peculiar position, to these storms, all travellers have remarked, but few have had any personal experience of their fury. Thomson, (ii. 32,) however, was for several days upon its shores during one of them, the character of which he thus describes: "To understand the causes of these sudden and violent tempests we must remember that the lake lies low, six hundred feet lower than the ocean; that the vast and naked plateaus of the Jaulan rise to a great height, spreading backward to the wilds of the Hauran, and upward to snowy Hermon; that the water-courses have cut out profound ravines, and wild gorges converging to the head of the lake, and that these act like gigantic funnels to draw down the cold winds from the mountains. And moreover, these winds are not only violent, but they come down suddenly, and often when the sky is perfectly clear. I once went in to swim near the hot baths, and before I was aware a wind came rushing over the cliffs with such force that it was with great difficulty I could regain the shore." Of another storm, when on the eastern side, he says: "The sun had scarcely set when the wind began to rush down toward the lake, and it continued all night long with constantly increasing violence, so that when we reached the shore next morning, the face of the lake was like a huge boiling caldron."—"We had to double-pin all the tent ropes, and frequently were obliged to hang with our whole weight upon them to keep the quivering tabernacle from being carried off bodily into the air."

The attempts to determine at what season of the year the parables were spoken, through the natural analogies upon which they are based, as Newton inferred that it was seed-time, or about November, because of the reference to the sowing of seed, lead to no substantial result. So also the storm does not, as said by Newton, define the time as winter; or as an equinoctial quarter of the year, as said by Greswell. That it was during the late autumn or early winter is upon other grounds probable.

Autumn, 781. A. D. 28.

After the stilling of the tempest He comes to the country of the Gergesenes. As He landed He was met by two men possessed by demons, whose dwelling was in the tombs near by. Beholding Jesus they run to meet Him, and He casting out the demons permits them to enter a herd of swine that was feeding near. The swine so possessed run down the hill-side into the sea, and so perish, and the inhabitants coming to Him desire Him to depart from their coasts. After directing the healed demoniacs to proclaim through Decapolis what had been done for them, He returns to Capernaum.	Matt. viii. 28–34. Mark v. 1–18. Luke viii. 26–39. Mark v. 19, 20. Matt. ix. 1.

As the Lord left the shore at even, and afterward fell asleep, we may infer that the storm came on in the night. The landing at Gergesa on the eastern side must then have been the next morning, as there is no mention that He returned that night to Capernaum, or landed elsewhere. He was met by the demoniacs so soon as He came out of the ship; and that it was broad daylight appears from the fact that He was seen by them afar off, (Mark v. 2–6.)[1]

The exact spot where Jesus met the demoniacs is uncertain. The first point of difficulty is to harmonize the various readings of the Synoptists. Without entering into a discussion upon this point, which could lead to no definite result, we find mentioned three distinct places, Gadara, Gerasa, and Gergesa. Of the two former we have some knowledge. Gadara is mentioned by Josephus[2] as the capital of Perea, and as destroyed by Vespasian. It is generally admitted that it stood upon the site now known as Um Keis, where very considerable ruins are still visible. Um Keis lies some six or eight miles southeast of the Sea of Galilee, and about sixteen miles from Tiberias, and three south of the Jarmuk, or ancient Hieromax. Gerasa is also mentioned by Josephus[3] as lying upon the eastern border of Perea, and as captured by a lieutenant of Vespasian. "In the Roman age no city of Palestine was better known than Gerasa. It is situated amid the mountains of Gilead twenty miles east of the Jordan, and twenty-five north of Philadelphia, the ancient Rabbath Ammon."[4] Gergesa is mentioned by Origen as an ancient city lying upon the Lake of Tiberias, and near the shore, and he adds that the precipice was still pointed out from which the swine rushed into the sea.[5] Alford, however, doubts whether there ever was a town named Gergesa near the lake; still, as he thinks that "Gergesenes" in the text could not, as a conjecture of Origen, have found its way into so many ancient versions

1 See Greswell, ii. 335.
2 War, 4. 7. 3.
3 War, 3. 3. 3; 4. 9. 1.
4 Smith's Dict. Bible, i. 678.
5 Origen quoted in Alford on Matt. viii. 28; see Reland, 806.

and manuscripts, he adopts it as the true reading.[1] He adds: "We cannot say that a part of the territory of Gadara may not have been known to those, who, like Matthew, were locally intimate with the shores of the lake, by this ancient and generally disused name."

Regarded merely as a question of topography, Gerasa must be at once rejected as the place of this meeting with the demoniacs, because too distant; unless indeed we suppose it to have been the name of a province so large as to embrace Gadara and all the region to the lake. So also Gadara, if the city be meant, is too remote to answer to the conditions of the narrative, for this plainly implies that the city was upon, or near the shore. Mark (v. 2) says: "And when He was come out of the ship immediately there met Him out of the tombs," &c. Luke (viii. 27) says: "And when He went forth to land there met Him out of the city a certain man," &c. These statements cannot well be explained otherwise than that the demoniacs met Him, as observed by Alexander, "as He landed, not merely after He had done so, which would admit of an indefinite interval; whereas the landing and the meeting were simultaneous, or immediately successive." It is not indeed said that the place of landing was close to the city, but Jesus does not seem to have left the spot where the demoniacs met Him upon the shore, and to which "the whole city came out to meet" Him; from which circumstance it may fairly be inferred that the city was at no great distance. Besides, although the place where the swine were feeding is spoken of as "a good way off," yet it was obviously near the lake, for it is simply said that after their possession they ran down a steep place into the sea. Thomson (ii. 35) satisfactorily shows that this city could not be Gadara. "I

[1] Bleek (Synoptische Erklärung i. 365) thinks Origen's words show that there was such a place in his day, the traditional site of the miracle, and one answering to its conditions.

take for granted, what I believe to be true, that Um Keis marks the site of Gadara, and it was therefore about three hours to the south of the extreme shore of the lake in that direction. There is first a broad plain from Khurbet Sarura to the Jarmuk; then the vast gorge of this river, and after it an ascent for an hour and a half to Um Keis. No one, I think, will maintain that this meets the requirements of the sacred narratives, but is in irreconcilable contradiction to them. It is true that a celebrated traveller, from his lofty stand-point at Um Keis, overlooks all intervening obstacles, and makes the swine rush headlong into the lake from beneath his very feet. But to do this in fact, (and the Evangelists deal only in plain facts,) they must have run down the mountain for an hour and a half, forded the deep Jarmuk, quite as formidable as the Jordan itself, ascended its northern bank, and raced across a level plain several miles before they could reach the nearest margin of the lake, a feat which no herd of swine would be likely to achieve, even though they were possessed."

If upon these topographic grounds, which are substantially those of Origen, we reject the claims of Gadara, we turn back to Gergesa. We have already referred to the testimony of Origen to Gergesa as an ancient city near the lake, and having a precipice hard by, which tradition in his day pointed out as the place where the swine ran down into the sea. Eusebius says that at his day, a village was shown upon the mountain near Lake Tiberias, where the swine ran down.[1] There is then no reason to doubt that at the time of Origen, and afterward, a town existed by the name of Gergesa near the lake, and which tradition made the scene of this miracle; and the absence of all later mention of it shows only that it had fallen into decay. The site of this city Thomson finds on the eastern shore directly

[1] Raumer, 218, note 331.

opposite the plain of Gennesaret, and near the point where Wady es Samak enters the lake. Here he found some ruins, and the name as given him by the Bedouins was Kerza or Gersa. "It was a small place, but the walls can be traced all round, and there seem to have been considerable suburbs. I identify these ruins with the long lost site of Gergesa."—"In this Gersa or Chersa we have a position which fulfils every requirement of the narrative, and with a name so near that in Matthew as to be in itself a strong corroboration of the truth of this identification. It is within a few rods of the shore, and an immense mountain rises directly above it, in which are ancient tombs, out of some of which the two men possessed of the devils may have issued to meet Jesus. The lake is so near the base of the mountain, that the swine rushing madly down it could not stop, but would be hurried on into the water and drowned. The place is one which our Lord would be likely to visit, having Capernaum in full view to the north, and Galilee over against it, as Luke (viii. 26) says it was. The name, however, pronounced by Bedouin Arabs is so similar to Gergesa, that to all my inquiries for this place they invariably said it was at Chersa, and they insisted that they were identical, and I agree with them in this opinion." Thomson strengthens this result by describing the topography of the shore of the lake to the south of Chersa, the mountains receding from the shore, and the plain between them becoming broader. "There is no bold cliff overhanging the lake on the eastern side, nor indeed on any other, except just north of Tiberias. Everywhere along the northeastern and eastern shores a smooth beach declines gently down to the water. There is no 'jumping off' place, nor, indeed, is any required. Take your stand a little south of this Chersa. A great herd of swine, we will suppose, is feeding on this mountain that towers above it. They are seized with a sudden panic, rush madly down the almost perpendicular declivity, those behind tumbling over and thrusting forward those before, and as there is neither time nor space to recover on the narrow shelf between the base and the lake, they are crowded headlong into the water and perish. All is perfectly natural just at this point, and here I suppose it did actually occur."

This discovery of the site of Gergesa removes all topographical difficulties from the sacred narratives. It is therefore unnecessary to mention in detail the other solutions that have been proposed, as that of Ebrard, (324,) who in answer to De Wette attempts to show that Gadara was but an hour distant from the sea. Stanley (372) places the scene of these events in Wady Feik, nearly opposite Tiberias.

The difficulties connected with the various readings in the texts of the Synoptists belong to another department of criticism. If, however, "Gergesenes" (Matt. viii. 28) was the reading of some manuscripts of Matthew before the time of Origen, we may readily suppose that this Evangelist mentioned the name of the city, although small, as one not unknown to his Jewish readers. The Evangelists, Mark and Luke, mention only the name of the larger and more important city, as more likely to be known to their distant readers, to whom exact topography was unimportant.[1]

We may then thus picture this incident to ourselves. The Lord, leaving Capernaum at even to avoid the ever-thronging multitude, directs his course southeasterly toward Gergesa. The storm bursting suddenly upon them during the evening, He, by His word, calms the sea. Very early in the morning He lands upon the coast of Gergesa, a little way south from the city. Here He is met, as He lands, by the demoniacs. Upon the steep slopes of the adjacent mountain the swine were feeding, and to

[1] Meyer in loco; Ebrard, 325; Ewald, Christus, 338; Porter, ii. 319.

Him upon the shore came out the inhabitants of the city, beseeching Him to depart from their coasts.

Matthew mentions two demoniacs; Mark and Luke but one. How shall this discrepancy be explained? Lightfoot, (on Mark v. 1,) who supposes that Gergesa was the name of a district embracing within it Gadara, which was a heathen city, makes one of the two to have been a Gadarene, and the other a Gergesene. Matthew mentions both, but Mark and Luke mention only him from Gadara as a heathen demoniac, "that so they might make the story more famous." Some, as Ebrard, make Matthew to have blended this case with that of the possessed healed at Capernaum, (Mark i. 23.) Da Costa supposes that Matthew knew that there was in fact but one, but that he might have seen a man attacked by the demoniac, and so gives the impression upon his mind as if there were two!

The common and most probable explanation is, that there were indeed two, but that one was much more prominent than the other, either as the fiercer of the two, or as of a higher rank and better known, and therefore alone mentioned by Mark and Luke.[1] That their silence respecting one of the demoniacs does not exclude him, Robinson thus illustrates:[2] "In the year 1824 Lafayette visited the United States, and was everywhere welcomed with honors and pageants. Historians will describe these as a noble incident in his life. Other writers will relate the same visit as made, and the same honors as enjoyed, by two persons, viz., Lafayette and his son. Will there be any contradiction between these two classes of writers? Will not both record the truth?" Greswell (i. 210) thinks that one of those thus healed became a disciple, and that the other did not. The former being thus better known, and his case

[1] So early, Augustine; and recently, Alexander, Krafft, Stier, Greswell, Ellicott.

[2] Har., 195.

invested with a personal interest, Mark and Luke speak of him only, and in much detail; whilst Matthew, who desires only to illustrate the power of Christ over evil spirits, mentions the healing of both, but says nothing of their subsequent history. He prefers, however, the conjecture based on Luke viii. 27, that this one demoniac was an inhabitant, and probably a native of Gergesa; but not the other.

Meyer, on the other hand, rejects all attempts to explain away the discrepancy; and Alford, who supposes that there was but one demoniac, thinks that perhaps his words, "My name is legion, for we are many," (Mark v. 9,) may have given rise to the report of two demoniacs in Matthew.

The request of the Gergesenes that Jesus would depart from their coasts, shows how material interests ruled in their minds, and how unprepared were they to understand the real significance of His work. The healing of the demoniacs, so mighty a miracle, and their restoration to sound mind, and to their families and friends, were of less value than the loss of their swine.

The direction to the healed to go to their homes, and proclaim what the Lord had done for them, so contrary to His general custom, shows that it was His desire to call attention to Himself in this section of the land; and, by making this miracle widely known, prepare the way for subsequent labors. Perhaps, also, something in the moral condition of the healed made this desirable for them.

AUTUMN, 781. A. D. 28.

Immediately upon His return to Capernaum He was	LUKE viii. 40–56.
surrounded by the multitude, which had been waiting for	MARK v. 21–43.
Him. Being invited by Matthew to a feast at his house,	MARK ii. 15–22.
He there held conversation with some Pharisees, and	LUKE v. 29–39.
afterward with some of John's disciples. Whilst yet	MATT. ix. 10–17.

speaking with them, came Jairus, a ruler of the synagogue, praying for the healing of his daughter. As Jesus was on His way to the house of Jairus, He heals a woman with an issue of blood. A messenger meeting Him announces the death of the girl, but He proceeds, and, entering the house, restores her to life. MATT. ix. 18–26.

We may put His arrival at Capernaum about midday. The crowds that for several days had been following Him, were awaiting eagerly His return, and now gladly received Him. That the first event following this return was not the healing of the paralytic, which succeeds in the order of Matthew's narrative, (Matt. ix. 2,) appears from Mark (v. 21, 22) and Luke, (viii. 40, 41,) who both narrate the healing of the daughter of Jairus. Besides, we have seen that the healing of the paralytic is to be placed earlier, immediately after the Lord's return from His first circuit. (See Mark ii. 1–12.)

The grounds upon which the feast of Levi is placed immediately before the healing of the daughter of Jairus, are found in the statements of Matthew, (ix. 10–19.) From these we learn that Jairus came to Jesus while speaking to certain disciples of John: "While He spake these things unto them, behold, there came a certain ruler," &c.[1] Jairus "came in," as if into a house. It is said also, (v. 19,) "and Jesus arose and followed Him." These expressions most naturally refer back to the mention of the feast, (v. 10,) where it is said that "Jesus sat at meat in the house." To the house of Levi came Jairus, and from it Jesus went forth with him. That the conversation between Him and the Pharisees in regard to eating with publicans and sinners, took place at the same time is probable, though not certain. The language of Matthew, "And when the Pharisees saw it they said," &c., does not prove that they were

[1] The received text has αρχων ελθων; Tischendorf gives αρχων εισελθων, so Meyer, Alford; Bleek, after Knapp, αρχων εἷς ελθων.

present as spectators, or addressed their question to the disciples during the feast. It may have been after the lapse of days, or even weeks. "The very circumstances related *show that this* remonstrance cannot have taken place *at* the feast. The Pharisees say the words to the disciples, our Lord hears it. This denotes an occasion when our Lord and the disciples were present, but not *surely intermixed with the great crowd of publicans*."[1] Nor does the language of Matthew, "Then came to Him the disciples of John," determine whether His conversation with them was at the same time and place. Alexander, who supposes that the Pharisees had intruded themselves upon Jesus while at the feast as spectators or spies, finds no ground for the presence at the same time of John's disciples. "It by no means follows from the consecution and connection of the narratives, even in Luke and Matthew, that the account of Matthew's feast is there continued; while in Mark another instance of the same kind seems to be added, without any reference to the date of its occurrence."

Admitting that none of the Synoptists show conclusively that the Pharisees, or the disciples of the Baptist were present at Matthew's feast, still this is the impression which the narratives make upon us. We, therefore, place the events before us in the following order, as taking place upon the same day: Matthew's feast; conversation with the Pharisees; conversation with the disciples of John; coming of Jairus. It is plain from Mark (v. 21, 22) and Luke, (viii. 40, 41,) that the healing of the daughter of Jairus was after the return from Gadara; and we therefore put the feast of Matthew or Levi after the return. As has been already said, there is nothing to show that Levi made the feast for Jesus upon the day when he was called to follow Him; and

[1] Alford in loco; Bleek, Synoptische Erklärung, i. 388.

we suppose that a few days did elapse between them, during which several events occurred; the plucking of the ears of corn; the choice of apostles; healing of the centurion's servant; journey to Nain; return to Capernaum; visit to Gadara. Still, it is admitted that the coming of Jairus to Jesus may have been some time subsequent to the feast of Levi. It is not clear that the conversation with the Pharisees took place at the feast; or if it did so, that the conversation with John's disciples was at the same time; or if this was so, that Jairus came during this conversation.

As there is much difference of opinion among harmonists, where this feast of Levi and related events should be placed, we give some of the more probable arrangements. And first, that which connects together the call of Levi; his feast; the conversation with the Pharisees and John's disciples; and the coming of Jairus.

1*st Arrangement.*—The Lord teaches in parables; crosses the sea and heals the demoniacs at Gergesa; returns to Capernaum; heals the paralytic; calls Matthew; attends Matthew's feast; heals the daughter of Jairus; chooses apostles, and delivers Sermon on the Mount.[1] This order is open to the invincible objection that the teaching in parables precedes the Sermon on the Mount, and the choice of apostles.

2*d Arrangement.*—The Lord chooses apostles; teaches in parables; crosses the sea and heals the demoniacs; returns to Capernaum; heals the paralytic; calls Matthew; attends his feast; heals the daughter of Jairus.[2] But it is a strong objection against this order that the choice of Matthew as an apostle precedes his call to follow Christ.

3*d Arrangement.*—This places the healing of the daughter of Jairus before the feast of Matthew. Jesus teaches in parables; crosses the sea; returns from Gergesa; holds the conversation with John's disciples respecting fasting; heals the daughter of Jairus, the woman with an issue of

[1] Lichtenstein. Stier.

blood, the blind, and the dumb possessed, and the paralytic borne of four; He calls Matthew and attends his feast; He elects the apostles; and delivers the Sermon on the Mount.[1] Here the conversation with the disciples of John is placed earlier than the feast of Levi and the conversation with the Pharisees, and is connected with the coming of Jairus. This is open to the same objection as the first arrangement, that it puts the speaking in parables before the choice of the Twelve and the Sermon on the Mount.

4th Arrangement.—Jesus heals the paralytic; He calls Matthew; attends his feast; holds a conversation with the Pharisees and John's disciples respecting fasting; plucks the ears of corn; (passing over the intervening events) He crosses the lake and heals the demoniacs at Gergesa; returns to Capernaum and heals the daughter of Jairus.[2] Here the coming of Jairus is separated from the conversation with John's disciples.

5th Arrangement.—Jesus heals the paralytic; He calls Matthew; attends Matthew's feast; holds a conversation with the Pharisees, but not with John's disciples. Here follow many events, the choice of the Twelve; Sermon on the Mount; teaching in parables; healing of demoniacs at Gergesa. On his return from Gergesa He meets John's disciples, and holds the conversation respecting fasting; heals the daughter of Jairus. Here the conversation with John's disciples is connected with the coming of Jairus, but is separated from the conversation with the Pharisees. Of all those arrangements that connect the feast of Matthew immediately with his call, this seems the preferable one.

That order, however, which separates the feast from the call, and places the former directly after the return from Gergesa, thus bringing it into connection with the conversations with the Pharisees and with John's disciples, and with the healing of Jairus's daughter, seems to have most in its favor.

[1] Ebrard. [2] Krafft.

The object of this feast, which was a great one, (Luke v. 29,) seems to have been both to honor the Lord, and to give Him an opportunity to meet in social intercourse many of Matthew's own class, the publicans and sinners. These plainly constituted the great body of invited guests; and for the Lord thus publicly to eat with them was a high mark of His regard for them, as it was also an open rebuke of Pharisaic self-righteousness. It seems, from the question of the Pharisees, "Why eateth your master with publicans and sinners?" that this was the first instance of the kind which they had known. It is not probable that any Pharisees were invited, nor that they would have accepted an invitation had one been given them, but with oriental freedom on such occasions, may have come in as spectators; or the language "seeing Him eat," (Mark ii. 16,) may refer only to their knowledge of the fact, and not to their personal observation. We may suppose that some of John's disciples were present with the Pharisees, and thus the seeming discrepancy between Matt. ix. 14, and Luke v. 33, is easily explained, (see Mark ii. 18.) The mention of John's disciples at Capernaum is to be noted as showing that there were some there who did not follow Jesus, and their affinity with the Pharisees.

The selection of Peter, James, and John, to go with Him to the house of Jairus, is the first instance recorded of special preference of these three above the other nine apostles. It is hardly to be questioned that this selection was determined by the personal peculiarities of these three, that made them more ready than the others to understand the real meaning of Christ's words and works, and to sympathize with Him in His trials and griefs. But why they should have been selected to be present at this particular miracle is not apparent. It was not, according to the order which we follow, the first case of raising the dead; and therefore they were not present, as Trench supposes, on this ground. But, unlike the raising of the widow's son at Nain, which was in public, before all the funeral procession, the Lord will here have no witnesses but His three apostles, and the father and mother of the maiden. Nor will He allow the wonderful work to be proclaimed abroad: "He charged them strictly that no man should know it." The grounds of these differences in the Lord's actings are probably beyond our knowledge, and cannot be explained.

Autumn, 781–782. A. D. 28–29.

Returning homeward from the house of Jairus He is followed by two blind men, saying, "Son of David, have mercy on us." They enter His house and are healed, and He charges them that they should not speak of what He had done; but they, going forth, everywhere proclaim it. As they departed, a dumb possessed was brought to Him, whom He healed, to the astonishment of the multitude. This gave the Pharisees new occasion to say that He cast out devils through Satan.

Matt. ix. 27–31.
Matt. ix. 32–34.

These cases of healing are mentioned only by Matthew, and by him in immediate connection with the raising to life of the daughter of Jairus. We assume that he here narrates in chronological order.[1] Some[2] identify Matt. ix. 32–34 with Luke xi. 14, 15; and as the healing of the possessed was immediately after that of the blind, place all these miracles at a much later period, and after the sending of the Seventy.

By these blind men was Jesus for the first time ad-

[1] Robinson, Greswell, Lichtenstein, Lange, Ebrard. Alford, however, observes that "παρ' εκειθεν is too vague to be taken as a fixed note of sequence; for εκείθεν, 'thence,' may mean the house of Jairus, or the town itself, or even that part of the country, as v. 26 has generalized the locality, and implied some pause of time."

[2] Krafft, Tischendorf.

dressed as "the Son of David." This shows that His descent from that royal house was known and recognized. Already the people had asked of Him, (Matt. xii. 23,) "Is this the Son of David?" and the use of the title by the blind men shows their disposition to honor Him whose help they sought.[1]

The impression which the miracle of healing the dumb possessed made upon the multitude, was very great, and explains why the Pharisees should repeat the charge that He cast out devils through the prince of the devils.

WINTER, 782. A. D. 29.

Leaving Capernaum Jesus goes, accompanied by His disciples, into lower Galilee, and again visits Nazareth. Rejected here the second time, He goes about through the cities and villages in that region. During this circuit He commissions and sends out the Twelve. In their absence He continues His work. About this time John is beheaded in prison, and the news of his death is brought to Jesus by some of John's disciples. Herod now hears of Christ, and expresses a desire to see Him. Jesus returns to Capernaum, and the Twelve gather to Him there.	MATT. xiii. 53–58. MARK vi. 1–6. MATT. ix. 35–38. MARK vi. 7–11. MATT. x. 1–42. LUKE ix. 1–9. MATT. xiv. 1–12. MARK vi. 14–30.

In the order of events we follow Mark: "And He went out from thence, and came into His own country; and His disciples follow Him." The place of departure was the house of Jairus, (Meyer,) or Capernaum and its neighborhood, (Alexander.) Matthew (xiii. 53–58) narrates this visit to Nazareth immediately after his account of the teaching in parables: "And it came to pass when Jesus had finished these parables He departed thence. And when He was come into His own country," &c. Here it is not

[1] Compare (Matt. xx. 30) the healing of the two blind men at Jericho, when the same title was used; as also by the woman of Canaan, (xv. 22.)

said that this coming to Nazareth was immediately subsequent to the departure after the parables were spoken. That departure was not to Nazareth, but across the sea to Gergesa, (Mark iv. 35.) We must then place between vs. 53 and 54 the healing of the demoniacs, of Jairus's daughter, of the woman with issue of blood, of the two blind men, and of the dumb possessed. All these may have taken place on the day of the return from Gergesa; and thus, between the teaching in parables and the departure to Nazareth, only an interval of two days have elapsed.

The grounds upon which this visit at Nazareth is to be distinguished from the earlier one mentioned by Luke, (iv. 16,) have been already stated. The circumstances under which He now returns to His early home are very unlike those of that former visit. Then He had but newly begun His public labors, and was comparatively but little known; and great surprise was felt that one, who only a few months before had been a resident among them, should make so high pretensions. How could He, whom they had known from childhood up, be a prophet, and possess such powers? Now His fame was spread throughout the whole land, and His character as a prophet was established. Crowds followed Him from all parts of the land. His miracles were familiar to all. He had, in the immediate neighborhood of Nazareth, raised a dead man to life. But His now enlarged and confirmed reputation did not weaken the feeling of surprise. All His life was familiar to them, and they could not believe that He was in aught greater than themselves. Jesus, therefore, could now well, and even with greater emphasis, repeat the proverb, "A prophet is not without honor but in his own country;" adding, with reference to the continued unbelief of His brethren, "and among his own kin, and in his own house." (See John vii. 5.) The Nazarenes do not now take any violent measures against Him, though "offended at Him;" and after teaching in the synagogue and healing a few sick folk, He made a circuit through the adjacent villages, (Mark vi. 6.) It is probable that Matthew (ix. 35–38) has reference to this circuit.

That the sending of the Twelve upon their mission was during this journey, appears from the order in which it stands in all the Synoptists. Matthew (ix. 35, &c.) connects it with the journey following the healing of the blind men, and the dumb possessed; and Mark (vi. 7) with that following the departure from Nazareth. Luke does not mention this visit at Nazareth, but narrates the sending of the Twelve (ix. 1–6) directly after the healing of Jairus's daughter.[1] How long this circuit continued, or at what point in it the Twelve were sent out, we have no data to determine. That it was extensive and occupied a considerable period may be fairly inferred from Matthew's language, (ix. 35,) that "He went about *all* the cities and villages." Nor can we tell from what place they were sent. Greswell (ii. 342) supposes it to have been Capernaum, and that therefore the sending was just at the close of the circuit. "It is certain that after their mission they rejoined our Lord at Capernaum; and it is not probable that they would be sent from one quarter and be expected to rejoin Him at another." On the other hand, Alford observes that no fixed locality can be assigned to their commission. "It was not delivered at Capernaum, but on a journey." The view of Krafft, (99,) that they were sent from Jerusalem when Jesus was at the feast of Tabernacles (John v. 1) is in every point of view unsatisfactory, and is refuted by the fact that the theatre of His activity was now Galilee, and not Judea.

The work of the Twelve in their mission corresponded in its main features to that of the Lord. He was still engaged in going "round about the villages teaching;" "en-

[1] So Tischendorf, Robinson, Alford, Greswell.

tering into all the synagogues, and healing every sickness and every disease amongst the people." The work of the apostles must be correspondent to this. They also must preach the Gospel, and illustrate its nature by their works. This they were directed to do, (Matt. x. 1–8,) and this they did. "And they went out and preached that men should repent. And they cast out many devils, and anointed with oil many that were sick, and healed them," (Mark vi. 12, 13; see Luke ix. 6.)

Thus their work had the same general character as that of Jesus. It was not so much to draw attention to Jesus personally, and to proclaim Him the Messiah, as to announce the approach of the Messianic kingdom, and to teach men its nature, and to prove it at hand by their miracles. If men had faith in the words of the apostles, they would soon come to Jesus to be taught by Him. The powers given them were large, and perhaps special to this mission. There is no mention that up to this time they had wrought any miracles, nor that they did so after their return, so long as Jesus was with them.[1]

It is apparent upon its face that the commission of the Twelve had a larger scope than these mere temporary labors.[2] It had prospective reference to their larger work after the Lord's ascension; and also in some measure to all the missionary work of the Church till His return. Some directions in it are plainly temporary, as those not to visit the heathen or Samaritans, and to make no provision of money or clothing. The prediction of persecutions and scourgings, on the other hand, had, at this time, no fulfilment.

Where did the Twelve labor? Luke (ix. 6) says, "they departed and went through the towns." It has been sup-

[1] See, however, Matt. xvii. 19, 20, which implies that the power to work miracles was not withdrawn, but was dependent upon their faith.

[2] Jones, Notes on Scripture, 100; Stier, ii. 2.

posed that this expression "towns," κωμας, may be used here in opposition to cities, implying that the Twelve visited only the smaller places. But the same expression is used of the Lord Himself, (Mark vi. 6.) Probably their labors were confined to Galilee. They were forbidden to enter Samaria, and it is not likely that they would enter Judea, from which the Lord was excluded. As they journeyed two by two, this would enable them to visit many towns in a few days. How long they were absent upon their mission does not appear. Wieseler, followed by Tischendorf, would limit it to a single day; Ellicott to two days; Krafft extends it to several months; Greswell makes them to have been sent upon their ministry in February, and to have returned in March, an interval of one or two months. That they were engaged in their labors several weeks at least, is plainly implied in the terms of their commission; for although this, as we have seen, had reference also to their future ministry, it had more immediate reference to the present. This is confirmed by the brief statements of their actual labors. (See Luke ix. 6; Mark vi. 12, 13, and 30.)

The commission of the Twelve is remarkable, as containing a much fuller declaration respecting the hatred they should meet, and the persecutions they should suffer, than was at any other time uttered by the Lord previous to the transfiguration. This must have been in striking contrast to the opinions the apostles were yet cherishing respecting the reign of the Messiah, and His general reception by the people. By speaking of their sufferings and persecutions, He announced, by implication, His own sufferings and rejection, although it is apparent that they did not understand the import of His words.

That Jesus continued His own personal labors during the absence of the Twelve, appears from Matthew, (xi. 1,) that "when He had made an end of commanding His Twelve disciples, He departed thence to teach and preach in their cities." In these journeyings He was probably accompanied by other disciples, doubtless by some of those who were afterward chosen among the Seventy, (Luke x. 1;) and perhaps also by the women who had before been with Him. If, as is probable, He had given direction to the Twelve to rejoin Him at Capernaum at some fixed time, He would now so direct His own course as to meet them there.

It was during the mission of the Twelve that the death of John the Baptist occurred. The news of it seems to have been communicated to Jesus by John's disciples, (Matt. xiv. 12,) but this must have been some days at least after the event. As the death of John had an important bearing upon the Lord's work, and to a great degree determined its subsequent character, we must examine the data that define the time of its occurrence.

The chief datum in this inquiry is the statement of John (vi. 4) that a Passover took place a little after the feeding of the five thousand. This Passover, the third of our Lord's ministry, was, as we have seen, that of 782, and fell on the 17th April. The death of John was then a few days before this. The exact date we cannot tell, as we do not know how long it preceded the feeding of the five thousand, nor how long this feeding preceded the Passover. If John was beheaded at Machaerus, on the southern border of Perea, some days must have elapsed ere his disciples could bury his body, and come to inform Jesus. So far as these data go we may place his death at the latter part of March, or the beginning of April, 782.

Wieseler (292) has attempted to reach a more definite result from the statements of Matt. xiv. 6, and Mark vi. 21, that Herod gave order for the death of John at a feast held upon his birthday. The word translated "birthday," γενεσια, is generally interpreted in its later and New Testament usage, as meaning birthday festivals, or celebrations.[1]

[1] Robinson, Meyer, Olshausen.

If it be so used here by the Evangelists, it gives us no chronological datum, since we do not know the time of Herod's birth. Wieseler, however, after Grotius and others, would make it refer to the feast kept in honor of his accession to the throne, and in this way obtains a known date, the 8th Nisan, or 11th April, 782, as the day of John's execution. Greswell, (iii. 425,) who also supposes that Herod was celebrating his accession, on the grounds that "the day of a king's accession was both considered and celebrated as his birthday;" and that the magnificence of his entertainment (Mark vi. 21) shows that he was commemorating something more than his birthday, reaches the result that John was put to death about the feast of Tabernacles, Sept. 22, 781.[1] Still this interpretation of "birthday" is too uncertain to allow any great weight to be placed upon it.[2]

We rest, then, in the conclusion that John was beheaded in the latter part of March, or beginning of April, 782.[3]

From Mark vi. 13, 14, and Luke ix. 6, 7, it appears that it was not till after the death of John that Herod heard of Jesus. But how could He have been so long active in one of Herod's provinces, followed by great multitudes, performing daily the most wonderful works, and His residence only a very few miles from Tiberias, where the king kept his court, and yet His fame never reach the royal ears? The most ready explanation would be, that during His ministry Herod had been absent from Galilee, either on a visit at Rome, whither he went about this time; or had been engaged in hostilities with Aretas, and thus re-

[1] Tischendorf, xxxiii., agrees with Wieseler; so Ebrard, 186; Ellicott, 195.

[2] See Alford and Meyer, notes on Matt. xiv. 6.

[3] So Güder, Herzog Encyc., vi. 770; Lichtenstein, 252; Lange. Winer, i. 590, finds no satisfactory data to determine the time of his imprisonment, or execution.

mained in good measure ignorant of what was taking place.[1] There is much probability in this supposition of Herod's absence, but decisive proof is wanting. If, however, he were in Galilee during this period, his ignorance of Jesus finds a sufficient explanation in his own personal character. We know from Josephus that he was a lover of ease and pleasure; and a man who occupied himself more in erecting fine buildings than in public affairs. Like all the Herodian family, he treated the Jewish religion with respect as a matter of policy, but did not interfere with ecclesiastical matters, except he saw movements dangerous to the public peace. The disputes of contending sects, or the theological discussions of the Rabbins, had no attractions for him; and provided the Jews were orderly and peaceful, he cared not to interfere in their religious quarrels. John's ministry continued a considerable period without any interruption on his part; and when he at last imprisoned him, it was on personal, not on political or religious grounds. Hence we can understand how Jesus might prosecute His work in Galilee, in the vicinity of Herod, without the latter learning any thing definite respecting it, or having his attention specially directed to His character or designs. As a new religious teacher, the founder of a new sect, an opponent of the Pharisees and scribes, the matter was unimportant, and beneath the royal notice. Unless the public tranquillity was actually disturbed, or seriously threatened, Herod, like Gallio, cared for none of these things.

During the imprisonment of the Baptist, Herod seems to have had several interviews with him, and learned to appreciate his bold and fearless honesty, (Mark vi. 20.) He did many things that John recommended, and heard him gladly. Hence, when in his drunken revelry he had given up the Baptist to the malice of Herodias, he was troubled in conscience; and his ears were open to any tidings that

[1] Greswell, iii. 428.

had connection with the departed prophet. It was a short time before this that Jesus had sent out the Twelve; a step that would naturally turn public attention to Him, and which might easily be misinterpreted. It would arouse His watchful enemies to action, for it apparently indicated a purpose to disseminate His doctrine more widely, and to make disciples in larger numbers. It might thus easily, through them, reach the ears of Herod, who would be led to inquire more particularly into the character and works of the new Rabbi. But his informants gave him different answers, (Mark vi. 14, 15; Luke ix. 7, 8.) Some said that He was Elias; others that He was a prophet, or as one of the prophets; and others still, ignorant of His earlier work, said that He was John the Baptist risen from the dead. This last account, to the uneasy and superstitious mind of Herod, was most credible, and explained how He wrought such mighty works as were ascribed to Him. Returned to life, he could do what could be done by no one in mortal flesh, (Matt. xiv. 2; Mark vi. 14.) All this awakened in Herod a lively desire to see Jesus, but no intimation is given us that he designed to arrest Him, or to hinder Him in His work. Thus far the Messianic claims of the Lord had been purposely kept in the background; and there was nothing in His teachings or actings, to awaken Herod's jealousy of Him as a claimant of the throne. At no period does the king seem to have looked upon Him with any dislike, or fear, as a political leader. The threatenings of the Pharisees at a later period, that Herod would kill Him, (Luke xiii. 31,) seem to have been a device of their own to frighten Him from His labors.

According to Josephus,[1] John was put to death at Machaerus, a fortress at the southern extremity of Perea on the borders of Arabia. When the first wife of Herod, learning his design to marry Herodias, fled from him to her

[1] Antiq., 18. 5. 2.

father Aretas, king of Arabia, this fortress belonged to the Arabians.[1] At what period did it come into the hands of Herod? Greswell (iii. 423) supposes that John reproved Herod, when he knew that a marriage with Herodias was intended, and before its completion. Having imprisoned John, he departed to Rome, and on his return beheaded him. According to this order of events, Herod now had possession of Machaerus, but it very soon fell into the hands of Aretas, and was in his hands when his daughter fled from Herod. But the common interpretation of the Evangelists, that Herod had taken Herodias as his wife before he was reproved by John, is most probable. Very soon, therefore, after his first wife's return home, this fortress must have been captured by Herod, but when or how we have no knowledge.[2] It has been questioned whether Herod would have made a birthday feast at the southern extremity of his dominions, where it would be difficult for the courtiers and noblemen of his court to attend. Still, if we remember that the Jews generally were in the habit of going up from the most remote parts of the land to Jerusalem, once or more every year to the feasts, the journey of a few courtiers to Machaerus will not seem strange. Besides, if Herod was detained there through the war, or other cause, the feast must follow his pleasure; and if Machaerus was not convenient to his guests from Galilee, it was more convenient to those from Perea.

Some, however, have supposed that the feast did not take place at Machaerus, although John was beheaded there, but at Tiberias, or at Julias. But although possible that the head of the Baptist should have been taken from Machaerus to Tiberias before the feast ended, yet the obvious interpretation of the narrative is, that he was beheaded

1 Antiq., 18. 6. 1 and 2.

2 Gams, der Täufer, 47. This supposed inconsistency in Josephus has led some to doubt whether indeed the Baptist was imprisoned at Machaerus.

the same night in which the daughter of Herodias danced before the king, or at least that no long interval elapsed. If the feast was not at Machaerus, where most place it,[1] it was most probably at Julias, as said by Wieseler, which was at no great distance, and where Herod had a summer palace.

[1] Meyer, Alford, Gams.

PART IV.

FROM THE DEATH OF THE BAPTIST TO THE FINAL DEPARTURE FROM GALILEE, OR FROM APRIL TO OCTOBER, 782. A.D. 29.

Upon the Lord's Ministry in Galilee from the death of the Baptist till its close.

THE connection between the imprisonment of the Baptist and the commencement of the Lord's ministry in Galilee, has been already considered. The same moral causes that determined this connection, make the death of the Baptist important in its influence upon the subsequent character of that ministry. It appears from the notices of the Evangelists that when this event occurred, the popularity of Jesus, if we may use this word, was at its height in Galilee. Great multitudes follow Him wherever He goes, and so throng Him that He has no leisure even to eat. From every part of the land they come to listen to His teachings and to be healed. Nor may we ascribe this concourse merely to curiosity and selfishness. These doubtless ruled in many; but that there was also at this period a large measure of faith in Him as one sent from God, appears from the fact that "whithersoever He entered, into villages or cities, or country, they laid the sick in the streets, and besought Him that they might touch if it were but the border of His garment; and as many as touched it were made whole." As His healing power seems now to have been manifested in its greatest activity, so now He performs one of the most stupendous of His miracles, the feeding of the five thousand. At no period of His ministry did He stand in such high reputation with the people at large as a Teacher and Prophet; and to the human eye, His labors seemed about to be crowned with great results.

It was at this stage of His ministry that He hears of the Baptist's death. To His clear-seeing eye the fate of His forerunner was prophetic of His own. As the Jews "had done unto the Baptist whatsoever they listed, as it was written of Him," so He knew that He also "must suffer many things and be set at naught," (Mark ix. 12, 13.) However well disposed toward Him individuals among the people might be, there was no longer hope that the nation, as such, would receive Him. The more clearly He revealed His Messianic character in its higher features, the more all the worldly minded, the unspiritual, turned away from Him. His popularity rested upon no solid or permanent basis, as there was no recognition of His divinity, and He was deemed merely the equal of John or Elijah. From this time, therefore, He begins to act as in view of His approaching death. More and more He withdraws Himself from the crowds that follow Him, and devotes Himself to the instruction of His disciples. It is not now so much His purpose to gather new adherents, as to teach those already believing on Him the great mysteries of His person and work. As yet the knowledge of even the Twelve was very imperfect; and He could not be personally separated from them till He had taught them of His divine origin, and, as subsequent to this, of His death, resurrection, ascension, and of His coming again in glory.

As the Lord seemed thus to shun public observation, it

was natural that the popular favor which had followed Him should suffer, at least, a temporary diminution; and that this should have been the signal for increased activity on the part of His enemies. As He made no distinct assertion of His Messianic claims before the people at large, and, so far from assuming royal dignity, seemed rather to take the position of a mere Rabbi, the fickle multitude was the more easily affected by the accusations and invectives of His foes. His teachings also seem to have gradually assumed a more mysterious and repellent character. He speaks of Himself as "the bread of life;" of the necessity of "eating His flesh and drinking His blood;" language so incomprehensible and so offensive, that many, even of His disciples, forsook Him. To the scribes and Pharisees He addresses reproaches of unwonted severity. Up to this time He had been engaged in gathering disciples, and for their sake He would not willingly array against Himself those whom all the people had been taught to honor as their ecclesiastical rulers and teachers. Such open hostility on their part, and a corresponding severity of rebuke on His, would have been a stumbling block to the tender conscience, and half enlightened mind. But the time is come that the line of separation must be clearly drawn, and the truth respecting Himself and His enemies be openly spoken; and His disciples learn that to follow Him involves the fierce and persistent enmity of their spiritual rulers and guides—an enmity which should follow them even after His own death.

That which specially characterizes the second part of the Lord's ministry in Galilee, or that from the death of the Baptist onward, we thus find to be, a gradual withdrawal of Himself from the multitude and from public labors; and the devotion of Himself to the instruction of His disciples. When by these instructions He has prepared them to understand His Divine Sonship and what should befall Him at Jerusalem, His Galilean ministry comes to its end.

April, 782. A. D. 29.

After the return of the Twelve to Him at Capernaum, Jesus prepares to go with them across the sea to find seclusion and rest. They desire to go privately, but the multitudes seeing them departing by ship, follow them on foot along the shore, and come to the place where He had gone. He heals their sick, and the	Mark vi. 30–44. Luke ix. 10–17. John vi. 1–4. Matt. xiv. 13, 1
same evening feeds 5,000 men besides women and children. Immediately after, He compels the disciples to return in the ship to Capernaum, and remains to dismiss the people. He spends the night alone, and early in the morning walks upon the sea to rejoin the disciples who had been driven from their course by the wind, and were unable to make the land. Having	Matt. xiv. 15–27. John vi. 5–14. Mark vi. 45–53. John vi. 15–21.
rescued Peter, who attempts to walk upon the water to meet Him, they both enter the boat, and immediately come to the shore in the land of Gennesaret.	Matt. xiv. 28–34.

It is not said where Jesus was when the disciples of John came to Him to announce their master's death, (Matt. xiv. 12,) but it was natural that they should seek Him at Capernaum. About the same time the Twelve, who had been absent on their mission, rejoined Him. Perhaps their return at this juncture may have been determined by the tidings of the death of the Baptist, which must very soon have become widely and generally known. As usual, whenever Jesus after one of His circuits returned to Capernaum, the people of the surrounding cities and villages flocked to see Him, bringing with them their sick. "Many were coming and going, and they had no leisure so much as to eat," (Mark vi. 31.) Jesus therefore determines to cross the sea and find repose in the uninhabited hills upon the eastern shore. Some attribute this departure to fear of Herod's hostility, and this has some countenance in the language of Matt. xiv. 13. But a more careful examination shows us that this could not have been His motive. Mark (vi. 31) gives the Lord's own words to the apostles, "Come ye yourselves apart into a desert place, and rest awhile;" adding the explanatory remark that "they had no leisure so much as to eat." He desired to separate the apostles from the multitude; and to give them, after their labors, a little period of repose, such as was not possible for them to obtain at Capernaum. Perhaps, also, He Himself desired a few hours for solitary communion with God, for the refreshment of His own spirit, agitated by the death of John, whom He mourned as a faithful friend; and in whose untimely and violent end He saw the sign and foreshadowing of His own approaching death.

That the departure across the sea was not through fear of personal violence from Herod, appears also from the fact that Jesus the next day returned, landing publicly upon the shore of Gennesaret; and thence attended by crowds went to Capernaum, where He taught openly in the synagogue, (Mark vi. 53–55; John vi. 22–59.) And after this, as before, He continued to make Capernaum His abode, and was not molested by Herod. Norton suggests that the death of John had produced a sudden excitement among the people; and that public attention began to be turned to Jesus as one who might avenge his murder, and become Himself their king. It was to escape the people, rather than Herod, that He crossed the sea. But the desire to make Him king, (John vi. 15,) seems to have been rather the effect of the miracle He wrought than of any popular indignation because of John's death.

The place to which the Lord directed His course across the sea, was "a desert place belonging to the city called Bethsaida," (Luke ix. 10.) The position of this city has been already discussed. According to the conclusion then reached, it was situated just at the entrance of the Jordan into the sea, and upcn both banks of the stream. Upon the east side lies the rich level plain of Butaiha, (Batihah,) forming a triangle, of which the eastern mountains make one side, and the river bank and the lake shore the two other. This plain, with its bordering hills, probably belonged to Bethsaida. It was at the southeastern angle of this plain, where the hills come down close to the shore, that Thomson (ii. 29) places the site of the feeding of the five thousand. "From the four narratives of this stupendous miracle, we gather, 1st, that the place belonged to Bethsaida; 2d, that it was a desert place; 3d, that it was near the shore of the lake, for they came to it by boats; 4th, that there was a mountain close at hand; 5th, that it was a smooth, grassy spot, capable of seating many thousand people. Now all these requisites are found in this exact locality, and nowhere else, so far as I can discover. This Butaiha belonged to Bethsaida. At this extreme southeast corner of it, the mountain shuts down upon the lake, bleak and barren. It was, doubtless, desert then as now, for it is not capable of cultivation. In this little cove the ships (boats) were anchored. On this beautiful sward, at the base of the rocky hill, the people were seated."[1]

We see no reason to doubt that Thomson has rightly fixed upon the site of the miracle. Tradition, indeed, placed it upon the west side of the lake, near the city of Tiberias. Arculf (A. D. 700) was shown "a grassy and level plain, which had never been ploughed since that event." But the tradition, though old, has no basis.[2]

There is a slight seeming discrepancy in the statements of Matthew and Mark respecting the meeting of Jesus with the multitude that followed Him. Matthew relates that "Jesus went forth and saw a great multitude, and was moved with compassion," &c.; implying that He had al-

[1] See also Porter, Hand Book, ii. 426.

[2] It has, however, been recently defended by Thrupp, Journal of Class. and Sac. Philology, vol. ii. 290.

ready reached the place He sought ere the crowds came. Mark relates that the crowds "outwent them, and came together unto Him. And Jesus, when He came out," i. e., from the ship, "saw much people, and was moved with compassion toward them," &c. Whether any discrepancy exists depends upon the meaning of "went forth," ἐξελθων, in Matthew. Meyer refers it to His coming forth from His place of retirement.[1] In his note on Mark, (vi. 34,) Alford remarks: "There is nothing in Matthew to imply that He had reached His place of solitude before the multitudes came up." There seems to be no good reason why the "went forth" in Matthew, should be differently understood from the "came out" of Mark; the word in both cases being the same, and in both may refer to His coming out of the ship. Lichtenstein reconciles the discrepancy by supposing that a few came before Jesus reached the shore, but unwilling to intrude upon Him, waited till the others came; so that He had a little interval of retirement ere He went forth to heal the sick and teach.

Some have supposed that John (vi. 4) mentions the fact that "the Passover was nigh," to explain why so great a company should have gathered to Him of men, women, and children. They were composed, at least in part, of those that were journeying toward Jerusalem to keep the feast.[2] Alexander, on the other hand, objects that, from the fact that they had nothing to eat, they could scarcely be a caravan of pilgrims, but were probably just come from their own homes. It would seem that the people were mostly from Capernaum and the towns adjacent. (See Mark vi. 33.)

It was, as has already been shown, the Lord's desire to go privately with the apostles, and thus escape the multitudes, but as His preparations to depart were necessarily made in public, and the departure itself was in sight of all,

[1] So Norton, Bengel, Trench.

[2] So Trench, Mir., 214; Bengel, Meyer. Alford doubts.

He could not prevent them from following Him. It strikingly marks the strong hold He now had upon the people at large, that so great a number should follow Him so far. That they should be able to keep pace with those in the boat, will not appear strange if we remember the relative positions of Capernaum and Bethsaida, as already defined. From the former city, which we identify with Tell Hum, to the entrance of the Jordan, where we place Bethsaida, is, according to Robinson, one hour and five minutes, or about two and a half geographical miles. The distance from the entrance of the Jordan along the eastern shore to the point where the mountains approach the lake, is also about an hour. The whole distance, then, which the people had to travel, was not more than six or eight miles, and from the conformation of the coast, could be as rapidly passed by those on the shore as those in the boat. Greswell,[1] who puts this Bethsaida at the southeastern angle of the lake, supposes that Jesus set out from Capernaum in the evening, and landed at Bethsaida in the morning, and that the people, who ran before on foot, travelled all night, a distance of about sixteen Roman miles. This needs no refutation.

The presence of this multitude, that had followed Him so far, awakened the Lord's compassion; and receiving them He "spake unto them of the kingdom of God, and healed them that had need of healing," (Luke ix. 11.) From John's language, (vi. 5,) it would seem that the Lord first addressed Philip with the inquiry, "Whence shall we buy bread that these may eat?" According to the Synoptists, it was the disciples who proposed to Him that He should send them away that they might buy themselves victuals. But none of the Evangelists narrate all the conversation that passed between Jesus and the disciples. Probably the disciples first proposed to send the people away to get

[1] ii. 344, note.

food, and He replies, "Give ye them to eat," (Mark vi. 35–37.) This leads to a general conversation in which He specially addresses Philip, and asks where bread could be bought. He then directs them to make inquiry how many loaves they had. After making inquiry, Andrew reports that there were five barley loaves and two small fishes; and hereupon He proceeds to feed the multitude. Why the question was addressed particularly to Philip, does not appear, except that the Lord would prove him. As a resident of Bethsaida, he would, however, naturally know how food could be procured in that region better than the other apostles.

The effect of this miracle upon the minds of those present was very great. So mighty and wonderful an exhibition of power, reminding them perhaps of the feeding of their fathers in the wilderness by Moses, led them to say, "This is of a truth that prophet that should come into the world." We can scarce doubt from the context that they meant the Messiah, for so great was their enthusiasm that they proposed among themselves to take Him by force and make Him king, (John vi. 14, 15.) Thus the effect of the miracle was to confirm them in their false Messianic hopes; for they interpreted it as a sign and pledge of the highest temporal prosperity under His rule, who could not only heal the sick of all their diseases, but feed five thousand men with five loaves of barley bread. Hence He must immediately dismiss them. It appears from Matthew and Mark that He sent away the disciples first, perhaps that the excitement of the multitude might not seize upon them. That they were unwilling to leave Him, and that He was obliged to "constrain" them to depart, is not strange if we remember that they knew no way by which He could rejoin them but by a long walk along the shore, and this in the solitude and darkness of the night, for it was evening when they left the place. (Compare Matt. xiv. 15 and 23, where both evenings, the early and late, are distinguished.) Aside from their reluctance to leave Him alone at such an hour, there may also have been fear upon their own part of crossing the lake in the night, remembering their great peril, from which He had a little while before delivered them, (Matt. viii. 24.)

After His disciples had departed, the Lord proceeds to dismiss the multitude, perhaps now more willing to leave Him that they saw His special attendants had gone. So soon as all had left Him, He went up into the mountain alone to pray—the second instance mentioned of a night so spent; the first being the night prior to the choice of apostles, (Luke vi. 12, 13;) and both mark important points in His life.

The details of the voyage of the disciples in their topographical bearings, have been already considered, and need not be re-stated here. We assume that the place where the people were fed, was the southern angle of the plain of Butaiha, where the mountains meet the lake. From this point the apostles, to reach Capernaum, would pass near Bethsaida at the mouth of the Jordan; and as Jesus, proceeding along the shore, must necessarily pass through it, we find no difficulty in supposing that they directed their course toward it with the design of stopping there, and taking Him with them into the boat when He should arrive. This is plainly intimated by Mark vi. 45;[1] and is wholly consistent with John vi. 17. This latter passage is thus translated by Alford: "They were making for the other side of the sea in the direction of Capernaum." He adds: "It would appear as if the disciples were lingering along shore, with the expectation of taking in Jesus; but night had fallen and He had not yet come to them,

[1] See Wieseler, 274, note 1; Newcome, 263. "They were to make Bethsaida in their passage, at which place it was understood that Jesus was to meet them by land, then embark with them."

and the sea began to be stormy." "The great wind that blew" and the tossing waves made all their efforts to reach Bethsaida useless. Nor could they even make Capernaum. In spite of all their endeavors, they were driven out into the middle of the lake and southerly, down opposite the plain of Gennesaret.

Thomson, (ii. 32,) referring to this night voyage of the disciples, says: "My experience in this region enables me to sympathize with the disciples in their long night's contest with the wind. I spent a night in that Wady Shukaiyif, some three miles up it, to the left of us. The sun had scarcely set when the wind began to rush down toward the lake, and it continued all night long with constantly increasing violence, so that when we reached the shore next morning the face of the lake was like a huge boiling caldron. The wind howled down every wady, from the northeast and east, with such fury that no efforts of rowers could have brought a boat to shore at any point along that coast. In a wind like that the disciples must have been driven quite across to Gennesaret, as we know they were. We subsequently pitched our tents at the shore, and remained for three days and nights exposed to this tremendous wind. No wonder the disciples toiled and rowed hard all that night, and how natural their amazement and terror at the sight of Jesus walking on the waves. The whole lake, as we had it, was lashed into fury; the waves repeatedly rolled up to our tent door, tumbling on the ropes with such violence as to carry away the tent pins." The width of the sea opposite the plain of Gennesaret is about six miles; and the disciples, who "had rowed about five and twenty or thirty furlongs" when Jesus met them, were thus something more than half the way over. As this was "about the fourth watch of the night," (Mark vi. 48,) or from 3–6 A. M., the disciples must have been struggling against the wind and waves some eight or ten hours.

The incident respecting Peter's attempt to walk on the water to meet Jesus, is mentioned only by Matthew. That after he had been rescued they entered the ship is expressly said: "And when they were come into the ship the wind ceased," (Matt. xiv. 32.) In like manner Mark, (vi. 51:) "And He went up unto them into the ship; and the wind ceased." But with this John's narrative has been thought by some to be in contradiction, (vi. 21:) "Then they willingly received Him into the ship, ηθελον ουν λαβειν αυτον εις το πλοιον; and immediately the ship was at the land whither they went." It is said that the disciples willed or desired to take Him into the ship with them, but did not, because the ship immediately came to the shore.[1] Tholuck, however, defends the translation of Beza, "they received Him with willingness," which is the same as our English version.[2] Some deny that the ship came to the shore by miracle, but suppose that it came rapidly in comparison with the earlier part of the voyage, the wind having subsided and the sea become smooth.[3] On the other hand, Luthardt, and we think rightly, regards it as supernatural.

April, 782. A. D. 29.

The people of Gennesaret, so soon as they knew that Jesus had landed upon their coasts, bring unto Him their sick, who are healed by only touching the hem of His garment.	Matt. xiv. 34–36. Mark vi. 53–56.
Those whom He had fed, and who had spent the night upon the eastern shore, now returning seek Him at Capernaum, whither He goes. In answer to their question how He came over the sea, He discourses to them concerning the bread of life.	John vi. 22–59.
His words are so offensive to many of His disciples	John vi. 60–66.

[1] So Meyer in loco; Bleek, Beiträge, 28.
[2] Alford; see Winer, Gram., 363; Trench, Mir., 228, note.
[3] Alford, Tholuck.

that they henceforth forsake Him. The Twelve continue with Him, but He declares that one of them is a devil. JOHN vi. 67–71.

The language of Matthew and of Mark is so express in connecting these miracles of healing with the return after the feeding of the five thousand, that there is no room for doubt that they then took place. It is not, however, necessary to regard their statements as descriptive of an activity confined to that one day, but rather embracing the whole period after His return till He again departed. All the accounts of this period indicate that He had now come to the culminating point of His labors. Never was His popularity so great, and never His mighty power so marvellously displayed. He could go nowhere, into country, or village, or city, that they did not bring the sick into the streets, that they might at least touch the hem of His garment; "and as many as touched were made perfectly whole." The fact that the men of Gennesaret "sent out into all that country round about, and brought unto Him all that were diseased," (Matt. xiv. 35,) indicates their great confidence in His ability and willingness to heal all that should be brought to Him; and perhaps also that, according to His custom, He would soon depart to other fields of labor.

Of those who had been present among the five thousand, some, and probably many, remained in the villages and towns on the eastern shore during the night. These, knowing that His disciples had departed the evening before for Capernaum, and left Him behind, naturally expected to find Him in the morning somewhere on that side of the lake. Not finding Him, they take boats, apparently boats that had been sent over by the boatmen from Tiberias for passengers, (John vi. 23,) and go to Capernaum, as His usual residence, to find Him. As He had landed very early upon the plain of Gennesaret, for it was about the fourth watch when He met the disciples, He had probably, ere their arrival, reached the city. The discourse concerning the bread of life was spoken in the synagogue at Capernaum, (John vi. 59,) and most probably upon the Sabbath. Still, no certain inference can be drawn from this mention of the synagogue, as it was used for teaching upon other days than the Sabbath.[1] Wieseler (276) makes the feeding of the five thousand to have been on the 14th Nisan or 16th April, at the same time when the paschal lamb was eaten at Jerusalem; and this day, therefore, was the 15th Nisan, or the first feast Sabbath.[2] But this is inconsistent with the notice of John, (vi. 4,) that the Passover was nigh, which implies that an interval of a day at least, if not of days, intervened.

This discourse of the Lord so offended many of His disciples that from this time they walked no more with Him. The answer of Peter to the question addressed to the Twelve, "Will ye also go away," marks a crisis in their relations to Him. Now for the first time, so far as we know, there was a defection among His disciples. His teachings were too hard for them, even when confirmed by such great miracles. But it was His words, not His works, that held the Twelve faithful. "Thou hast the words of eternal life," said Peter. The right reading of the confession of Peter immediately following is, according to Tischendorf,[3] "And we believe and are sure that thou art the Holy One of God." This confession is to be distinguished from that made later, (see Matt. xvi. 16,) which displays a higher knowledge of the mystery of the Lord's person.

Summer, 782. A. D. 29.

Whilst still at Capernaum, some of the scribes and Pharisees, who had come from Jerusalem, see His disciples eating with unwashed hands, and find fault.	Matt. xv. 1–20. Mark vii. 1–23.

[1] Winer, ii. 549.
[2] So Tischendorf, xxxiii.
[3] So also Meyer and Alford; Ellicott undecided.

This leads to a discussion of Pharisaic traditions, and sharp reproofs of their hypocrisy. Leaving Capernaum, He goes with the Twelve into the coasts of Tyre and Sidon, avoiding all publicity. But He could not be hid; and a woman of that region coming to Him with urgent request, He heals her daughter. From thence He departs to the region of Decapolis, where he heals many, and one with an impediment in his speech, and afterward feeds a multitude of 4,000 persons. Re-crossing the sea He returns to Capernaum.

MATT. xv. 21–28.
MARK vii. 24–30.
MATT. xv. 29–39.
MARK vii. 31–37.
MARK viii. 1–10.

How long, after the feeding of the five thousand, the Lord continued at Capernaum we cannot tell, but it is plain that He was found there by the Pharisees and scribes which came down from Jerusalem. That this was, as Wieseler maintains,[1] upon the 15th Nisan, the day when he supposes the discourse in the synagogue to have been delivered, is highly improbable. It is not likely that they would leave Jerusalem till the Passover was fully over.[2] Much earlier in the Lord's ministry, as we have seen, a deputation of scribes had been sent from Jerusalem to watch and oppose Him. The presence of this new deputation may be ascribed to the reports that had been borne to that city by the pilgrims going to the feast, of the feeding of the five thousand, and of the wish of the people to make Him king. So great a miracle, and its effect on the popular mind, could not be overlooked; and they hasten to counteract, if possible, His growing influence. Arriving at Capernaum, and watchful to seize every possible ground of accusation against Him, they notice that some of His disciples did not wash their hands in the prescribed manner before eating; a sign that they were already in some degree becoming indifferent to Pharisaic traditions. The words of the Lord in reply to the Pharisees are full of severity, and show that He knew that they were, and would continue to be, His enemies. Now for the first time He

[1] 311, note 1.
[2] Tischendorf, Greswell.

addresses them openly as hypocrites, and reproaches them, that they set aside by their traditions the commandments of God. He proceeds to address the people upon the distinction between internal and external defilement; and afterward, when He was alone with the disciples, He explains to them more clearly what He had said.

It has been questioned whether the Lord went merely to the borders of Tyre and Sidon, or actually crossed them, (Matt. xv. 21; Mark vii. 24.)[1] Some light may be cast on this point if we consider His motive in the journey. That it was not to teach publicly seems plain from Mark's words, (vii. 24,) "He would have no man know it." He desired that His arrival should be kept secret. As He had directed the Twelve, when upon their mission, not to "go into the way of the Gentiles" to preach, it is not probable that He would now do so. Nor is there any mention of teaching or healing, except in the case of the woman and her daughter. His motive in this journey obviously was to find seclusion and rest, which He had sought, but in vain, to find on the east side of the lake; and could not find in Capernaum. He hoped on the remote frontiers of Galilee to escape for a time popular attention, and to be hid from the crowds that followed Him. We see no evidence that any fear of the hostility of Herod or of the Pharisees actuated Him.[2] It is for the Twelve that He seeks a temporary retirement, and to them will He address His teachings.

It would not then be inconsistent with His purpose that He should enter the heathen provinces of Tyre and Sidon. Here at least He may obtain a little interval of repose.

[1] In favor of the latter, Alford, Alexander, Bleek, De Wette, Greswell; of the former, Stier and Meyer, who refer to Matt. xv. 22, as showing that the Phœnician woman came out of the coasts of Tyre and Sidon to meet Jesus, so that He was not within them.

[2] Greswell, (ii. 354,) who thinks His motive in this journey was concealment, makes the final end of this concealment to escape the observation of His pertinacious enemies, the scribes and Pharisees.

But He cannot be hid, and after healing the daughter of the Syrophenician woman in answer to her importunity, He is compelled to leave that region, and directs His steps to Decapolis. The route He followed is uncertain. It is said by Mark, (vii. 31 :) "And again departing from the coasts of Tyre and Sidon, He came unto the Sea of Galilee through the midst of the coasts of Decapolis." "As most of the cities of the Decapolis were situated near the valley of the Jordan, south of the Sea of Tiberias, it is not improbable that our Lord, having gone to the east of Phœnicia through Upper Galilee, returned thence, by way of Lower Galilee through the plain of Esdraelon, to Bethshean, (Scythopolis,) the only city of Decapolis which is to the west of Jordan. Here He would cross the river, perhaps at the bridge now called Jisr Majumah, then possibly make a circuit about the district of Pella and Philadelphia to the south, about Gerasa to the east, and Gadara, Dios, and Hippo to the north. Thus He would 'come unto the Sea of Galilee through the midst of the coasts of Decapolis.'"[1] But according to the reading of Tischendorf,[2] "departing from the coasts of Tyre He came through Sidon to the Sea of Galilee," δια Σιδωνος; He went therefore northward from Tyre, and, passing through Sidon, probably proceeded along the Phœnician border line to the Jordan, near Dan, (Laish,) and journeying along its eastern bank came to Decapolis. He may thus have visited Cæsarea Philippi, and the province of Herod Philip, although no special mention is made of it. "He went first northward (perhaps for the same reason of privacy as before) through Sidon, then crossed the Jordan, and so approached the lake on its east side."[3]

What part of Decapolis the Lord visited is not mentioned by any of the Evangelists. Under this title were

[1] G. Williams in "The Messiah," 268, note.

[2] So Meyer and Alford.

[3] Alford; see Lichtenstein, 284.

included ten cities, eight or nine of which were on the east side of the Jordan, and east or southeast of the Sea of Galilee. It is spoken of by Josephus as a well-known territorial designation, embracing towns and villages. After Syria had been conquered by the Romans, ten cities seem, on some grounds not well known, to have been placed under certain peculiar municipal arrangements, and brought directly under Roman rule. It is probable that their population was chiefly heathen. The names of the ten cities are differently given. To the original ten cities others were probably added, though at no time do they seem to have constituted a distinct province.[1]

It is impossible to tell where the healing of the deaf man with an impediment in his speech, took place, (Mark vii. 32.) If it was one of the cures mentioned by Matthew, (xv. 29–31,) it was near the sea; but from the fact that Jesus enjoined silence upon the deaf man and his friends, we infer that it was wrought before He came to the shore of the lake. The injunction of silence was not heeded: "The more He charged them, so much the more a great deal they published it." The effect of this was, as related by Matthew, a great gathering to Him of "the lame, blind, dumb, maimed, and many others," whom He healed. Both Matthew and Mark speak of the wonder and astonishment of the multitude as they saw these healings, as if they now saw them for the first time. It is to be remembered that Jesus had not visited this region at all, except for the few hours when He healed the demoniacs of Gergesa, and afterward when He fed the five thousand; and the great body of the people now saw Him for the first time. The expression, (Matt. xv. 31,) "they glorified the God of Israel," may indicate that part of the multitude were heathen, and now glorified Jehovah in contrast with their own deities; or it may have reference to the Jews as dwelling among

[1] See Winer, i. 263; Smith's Dict. of Bible, i. 419.

the heathen, who saw in these miracles new proofs of the power of their God, before whom all others were but idols.

Three days this great concourse of people continued with the Lord, beholding His works, and listening to His words. The place where they were assembled was, beyond question, on the east side of the lake, and some suppose at the same place where He had fed the five thousand.[1] Matthew (xv. 29) relates that "He came nigh unto the Sea of Galilee, and went up into a mountain and sat down there." The use of the article, το ορος, "the mountain," does not determine the spot, as it may be used to denote the high land in distinction from the lake shore. It seems, however, more probable that it was at some point near the south end of the lake, as several cities of the Decapolis were in that vicinity. Ellicott[2] suggests that its site may have been "the high ground" in the neighborhood of the ravine nearly opposite to Magdala, which is now called "Wady Semak." Whilst there are several points of resemblance between this miracle and that of the feeding of the five thousand, there are many of difference: as the number of persons fed, the quantity of food, the quantity of fragments gathered up, the time the multitude had been with Jesus, and the events both preceding and following the miracle. It is probable that many of the four thousand were heathen, or those who had come from the east side of the sea, whilst most of the five thousand seem to have followed Him from the western shore.[3]

After sending away the multitudes, He took ship, perhaps the ship kept specially for His use, and crossed the sea. He came, according to Matthew, (xv. 39,) "into the coasts of Magdala;"[4] according to Mark, (viii. 10,) "into the parts of Dalmanutha." Magdala is generally identified

[1] So Trench, Mir., 285; Greswell, ii. 357.

[2] 221, note 1.

[3] Trench, Mir., 286.

[4] For Magdala in the received text, Tischendorf and Alford substitute

with El Mejdel, a miserable village on the south side of the plain of Gennesaret, near the lake.[1] Dalmanutha is generally supposed to have been a small town or village in the neighborhood of Magdala, perhaps in its territory, and upon the shore. Porter places it about a mile south of Magdala, by the fountain Ain-el-Barideh. Thomson (ii. 60) speaks of a Dalhamia, or Dalmamia, on the east side of the Jordan, a little below its exit from the Sea of Galilee, which he supposes may be intended. The matter is in itself unimportant.

SUMMER, 782. A. D. 29

So soon as Jesus returns to Capernaum, the Pharisees and Sadducees begin to tempt Him by asking a sign from Heaven. He reproves their hypocrisy, and declares that no sign should be given them but the sign of the prophet Jonas.	MATT. xvi. 1-4. MARK viii. 11, 12.
Leaving them, He enters a ship, and again departs across the lake toward Bethsaida. Upon the way He discourses to the disciples respecting the leaven of the Pharisees.	MATT. xvi. 5-13. MARK viii. 13-21.
Arriving at Bethsaida, He heals a blind man and sends him privately home.	MARK viii. 22-26.

It is not expressly said that Jesus went from Magdala or Dalmanutha to Capernaum, and it is possible that He may have met Pharisees and Sadducees at either of the former places; yet as the latter city was His home, to which He returned after all His circuits, and was but few miles from Magdala, we have no reason to doubt that He went thither as usual. Here, also, He would more probably meet the Pharisees and Sadducees, for this meeting does not seem to have been accidental, but premeditated on their part. It is the first time the latter are named in conjunction with the former, as acting unitedly in opposition to

Magadan. Magdala is retained by Meyer. Of Magadan, if distinct from Magdala, nothing is known.

[1] Rob. ii., 397; Porter, ii. 431. See, contra, Norton, notes, 153.

Him. Apparently as a party, the Sadducees had up to this time looked upon Him with indifference if not contempt. But as His teachings began to expose their errors, their hostility was aroused; and from this time they seem to have acted in unison with the Pharisees against Him.

The peculiarity of the sign which His enemies now sought from Him, was that it should be from Heaven, or something visible in the heavens; perhaps some change in the sun or moon, or a meteor, or fire, or thunder and lightning. Denouncing them as hypocrites, who could discern the face of the sky, but could not discern the signs of the times, He refuses to give them any other sign than one too late to profit them, His own resurrection.

The departure from Capernaum across the sea seems to have followed close upon this temptation of the Pharisees and Sadducees. That the Lord was greatly grieved at this new instance of their unbelief, appears from Mark viii. 12, where it is said: "He sighed deeply in His spirit." Alexander also observes that the expression, (v. 13,) "'He left them,' suggests the idea of abandonment, letting them alone, leaving them to themselves, giving them up to hopeless unbelief." According to Matthew, He admonishes His disciples to beware of the leaven of the Pharisees and Sadducees; according to Mark, of the leaven of the Pharisees and of Herod. This slight discrepancy is generally explained by saying that Herod was a Sadducee. This is in itself probable, for none of the Herodian princes seem to have imbibed the true Jewish spirit; and though fearing the Pharisees, because of their great influence over the people, yet favored the Sadducees, and gave office so far as possible to men of that party. But it may be that the Lord speaks of hypocrisy in general as leaven, and so the same in whatsoever person or party it appeared.

If Bethsaida were, as we suppose, at the mouth of the Jordan, its position would correspond with all the conditions of the present narrative. From this point He could easily reach the town of Cæsarea Philippi. Although we know from the Lord's own words (Matt. xi. 21) that He had wrought many mighty works in Bethsaida, yet the healing of the blind man is the only one recorded, except the feeding of the five thousand which took place upon its territory. For some reason not stated, (Mark viii. 23,) the blind man was healed without the city. There are many points of resemblance between this miracle and that of the healing of the deaf man with an impediment in his speech, (Mark vii. 32–37.) In both the Lord is besought to touch them; He takes them aside from the people; He uses spittle; He enjoins silence.

Summer, 782. A. D. 29.

Leaving Bethsaida, He goes with His disciples to Cæsarea Philippi. Whilst upon the way, He asked them "whom do men say that I am?" He then asks them their own opinion of Him, and Peter replies that He is the Christ, the Son of the living God. This truth He commands them to tell to no one; and now begins to teach them respecting His approaching rejection by the Jews, His death, and resurrection after three days. Peter would rebuke Him for these words, but is himself rebuked.	Mark viii. 27–33. Matt. xvi. 13–23. Luke ix. 18–22.
Jesus afterward addresses the disciples and the people, and teaches them what is involved in following Him, and speaks of the rewards He would give to all when He should come again in the glory of His Father.	Mark viii. 34–38. Matt. xvi. 24–28. Luke ix. 23–27.
He adds, that some standing before Him should see Him come in the glory of His kingdom. Six days after He goes to a high mountain, taking with Him Peter, James, and John, and is transfigured before them.	Mark ix. 1–10. Matt. xvii. 1–9. Luke ix. 28–36.

It is much disputed whether the journey to Cæsarea Philippi, and the Transfiguration, followed immediately upon the miracle at Bethsaida, or whether an interval elapsed during which He may have journeyed in other directions. The connection of the narratives does not decide it. It is said by Matthew (xvi. 13) that, "When Jesus came into the coasts of Cæsarea Philippi, He asked His disciples," &c. This leaves the time of His coming indefinite. Mark (viii. 27) says: "And Jesus went out—εξηλθεν—and His disciples into the towns of Cæsarea Philippi." The phrase "went out," naturally, though not necessarily, refers to a departure from the place before mentioned, which was Bethsaida. "Neither Evangelist assigns the date of this transaction, even by connecting it expressly with the previous context as immediately successive. Into the villages or towns dependent upon this important city, Jesus came with His disciples; when or whence is not recorded. 'Went out' throws no light upon this point, as it may refer to any going forth for any purpose, even from a private house, upon a journey, or from Capernaum as the centre of His operations on a new official circuit."[1]

If, then, the Evangelists do not decide the point by their language, it must be decided by other considerations. It is said on the one side, that the Transfiguration most fittingly finds its place at the end of the Lord's Galilean ministry, and therefore at a later period. As at His baptism, when about to begin His work, there was a voice from heaven, saying: "This is my beloved Son in whom I am well pleased;" so now at its close the Father gives a like testimony.[2] The announcement, also, (Matt. xvi. 21,) that He must go up to Jerusalem to die, implies that His next journey thither would be His last. Some, therefore, as Lichtenstein, place the journey to Jerusalem to the feast of Tabernacles (John vii. 2) after the miracle at Bethsaida,

[1] Alexander in loco. See the same word, v. 11. "The Pharisees came forth," whether from their homes, or from the surrounding villages, or from Capernaum, is matter of conjecture.

[2] Hofmann in Lichtenstein, 307.

and before the journey to the coasts of Philippi. Stier, who makes Jesus to have returned to Galilee after the feast of Dedication, (John x. 22,) places the Transfiguration after that return. But on the other side, the natural inference, as we have seen from the narratives of Matthew and Mark, is that the Lord journeyed directly from Bethsaida toward Cæsarea Philippi, and that there was no return to Capernaum or visit to Jerusalem before the Transfiguration.[1]

It deserves, however, to be noticed that the Transfiguration was, in any event, very near the close of the Lord's ministry in Galilee. His labors after this, as indeed for some time previous, seem to have been devoted chiefly to His disciples, till He commenced His last journey, when they again assumed a public character.

From the direction given to the blind man at Bethsaida, not to speak of his cure, as well as from the statement (Mark ix. 30) that He desired to pass secretly through Galilee after the Transfiguration, we infer that this circuit, like the preceding, was not so much to teach the people at large as to escape the crowds that followed Him, and to find opportunity to teach His disciples.[2]

The apostles, in their answer to His question, "Whom do men say that I am?" give the opinions most current among the people generally in Galilee. It is not certain whether He was, through ignorance, confounded with John the Baptist, as if the latter were still living, or was thought to be the Baptist raised from the dead. The latter is most probable, and perhaps reference may be made to the opinion of Herod and his party. How intimate was the connection in the Jewish mind between the resurrection, and the kingdom of heaven and the advent of the Christ, is shown

[1] So most harmonists, Tischendorf, Robinson, Krafft, Friedlieb, Greswell, Newcome.

[2] From Mark viii. 34, Ellicott infers that His object was public teaching and preaching.

by Lightfoot, (on John i. 25:) "The Jews believed that at the coming of the Messiah the prophets were to rise again. The nearer still the 'kingdom of heaven' came, by so much the more did they dream of the resurrection of the prophets."

It is to be noted that no important part of the people seem to have regarded Jesus as the Christ, or else it would have been mentioned by the apostles. It is apparent that He was regarded rather as a forerunner of the Messiah than as the Messiah Himself, though public sentiment may have changed from time to time in regard to His Messianic claims.[1] On the one hand, He had been pointed out as the Messiah by John, and His mighty works manifestly proved His divine commission; yet, on the other hand, He did not openly avow Himself to be the Messiah, and His whole course of conduct was in striking contrast to their Messianic expectations. Whilst a few here and there said, "He is the Christ," the general voice was that He was but a forerunner. After the feeding of the five thousand, there was a desire to make Him king; but this does not show any real belief in His Messiahship. It was the natural effect of so stupendous a miracle upon the restless Jewish mind, eager to cast off the Roman and Idumean yoke; and the next day many of His disciples, and perhaps those most zealous to make Him a king, repelled by His words, "went back and walked no more with Him." This confession of Peter, which was that of all the apostles, was therefore a great turning point in their history. To others He was only the Baptist, or Elias, or one of the prophets; to them "He was the Christ, the Son of the living God." This confession involves much more than that at Capernaum a little earlier, (John vi. 69.) The latter was but an expression of their belief that "He was the Holy One of

[1] Lange on Matt. xvi. 14.

God."[1] "This," says Alford, "brings out both the human and the Divine nature of the Lord." This mystery of the Lord's person as both Divine and human, was something not to be known through any exercise of the understanding. If known, it must be through the revelation of God. That Peter should have discerned it, Jesus thus ascribes immediately to the revelation of His Father in heaven, (Matt. xvi. 17.)

This truth, so far surpassing all the common Jewish conceptions of the Messiah, of the united Divinity and humanity of the Lord, being known and confessed, Jesus could begin to open to them other truths till this time concealed. Now He could teach them that His first work in the flesh was to suffer; that He must be rejected by the Jews and be put to death; that He must rise from the dead, and afterward establish His kingdom. These truths, so new and strange to the disciples, so foreign to all their modes of thinking, they could not for a long time comprehend. The very fact of the Divinity of Jesus made it still more incomprehensible how He could suffer and die, nor could the plainest words of the Lord make it intelligible. How repugnant to their feelings was the announcement of His sufferings, is graphically shown in the language of the impetuous Peter, "Be it far from thee, Lord; this shall not be unto thee:" language which brought upon him the severest rebuke.

From this time the teaching of Jesus to His disciples, and also to the people at large, (see Mark viii. 34; Luke ix. 23,) assumed a new character. Gradually, as they were able to bear it, He showed them how the great purpose of God in the Messiah must be effected through His death, and how His sufferings had been foretold by the prophets. So far from establishing any earthly kingdom, in which

[1] Reading approved by Tischendorf, Alford, Meyer.

they should have distinguished places, He must be put to a most ignominious death, and all who received Him as the Messiah, should do it at the peril of their lives. Yet, as a counterpoise to the gloomy picture, He speaks of an hour when He would come again, and then every disciple should have His reward. Thus He confirmed to them the great fact that He was to establish a kingdom in power and glory. To prevent the disciples from seizing upon this fact, and indulging in dreams of a reign corresponding to that of earthly kings, the Lord was pleased to show certain of the apostles, by a momentary transfiguration of His person, the supernatural character of His kingdom, and into what new and higher conditions of being both He and they must be brought ere it could come. The promise that some then standing before Him should not taste death till they had seen "the Son of man coming in His kingdom," (Matt. xvi. 28,) or had seen "the kingdom of God come with power," (Mark ix. 1,) was fulfilled when, after six days, He took Peter, James, and John into a high mountain apart, and was transfigured before them. These apostles now saw Him as He should appear when, having risen from the dead, and glorified, He should come again from heaven to take His great power and to reign. They saw in the ineffable glory of His person, and the brightness around them, a foreshadowing of the kingdom of God as it should come with power; and were for a moment "eye-witnesses of His majesty," (2 Peter i. 16.) Many errors still remained to be removed from their minds, especially respecting the time of its establishment, (Acts i. 6,) but the great fact of its supernatural character they could not mistake. Henceforth the phrase "kingdom of God" had to these apostles a significance which it probably had not had to any of the prophets, and certainly had not to any of the Rabbis or priests.

The three apostles were commanded to tell no one of

the vision till Jesus had risen from the dead. It therefore remained for a considerable period unknown to the other apostles and disciples. It was natural that they should question one with another, as they descended the mount, what the rising from the dead should mean, (Mark ix. 10.) They had just seen the Lord transfigured. He had not died, yet had His body been invested with heavenly glory. It was not then necessary to die and to rise again in order to be glorified. What, then, should the death and resurrection of which He had spoken mean? Not a literal death and resurrection, but a spiritual death—some act of suffering, or self-sacrifice, upon which supernatural glory should follow. And thus the resurrection from the dead, as a preliminary to the kingdom, became still more incomprehensible.

The statements of the Evangelists do not enable us to decide where the Transfiguration took place. Matthew and Mark speak of it as "a high mountain;" Luke as "the mountain," *το ορος*. A tradition, dating back to the fourth century, gives Tabor as the site. So generally received for many centuries was this tradition, that Lightfoot (Mark ix. 2) says: "I know it will be laughed at if I should doubt whether Christ was transfigured on Mount Tabor, for who ever doubted of this thing." According to Robinson (ii. 358) the first notice of Tabor as the place of the Transfiguration is as a passing remark by Cyril of Jerusalem, and afterward by Jerome. Before the close of the sixth century three churches were builded there, and afterward a monastery was founded. Arculf, A. D. 700,[1] says: "At the top is a pleasant and extensive meadow surrounded by a thick wood, and in the middle of the meadow a great monastery with numerous cells of monks. There are also three handsome churches, according to the number of taberna-

[1] Early Travels, 9.

cles described by Peter." Robinson and Stanley think it conclusive against this tradition, that at the time of the Transfiguration "the summit of Tabor was occupied by a fortified city." Thomson, however, (ii. 139,) does not regard this as presenting any difficulty. "There are many secluded or densely wooded terraces on the north and northeast sides, admirably adapted to the scenes of the Transfiguration. After all that the critics have advanced against the current tradition, I am not fully convinced." Admitting that much may be said in favor of Mount Tabor as "the high mountain" of the Evangelists, still their narratives lead us to place this event in the neighborhood of Cæsarea Philippi rather than on the west of the lake, and so near Capernaum. "The Evangelists," says Lightfoot, "intimate no change from place to place." The expression of Mark, (ix. 30,) that "departing thence He passed through Galilee," would imply that He was not then in Galilee. We are therefore made to look for some mountain in the vicinity of Cæsarea, and Mount Hermon at once rises before us.[1] "Standing amid the ruins of Cæsarea we do not need to ask what that 'high mountain' is. The lofty ridge of Hermon rises over us, and probably on one or other of those wooded peaks above us that wondrous event took place."[2]

The difference in the computation of Matthew and Mark on the one side, who say, "After six days He taketh Peter, James, and John into a high mountain apart," and of Luke, who says, "About an eight days after these sayings, He took," &c., is easily reconciled if we suppose that the latter included, while the former excluded, both the day on which the words were spoken, and the day of the Transfiguration. Some, as Meyer, prefer to take Luke's phrase "about an eight days" as indefinite, but this is contrary to the use of

[1] Lightfoot, Reland.
[2] Porter, ii. 447; so Stanley, Lichtenstein, Ritter.

ὡσεὶ, with numerals by this Evangelist. The six days, according to Lange, are probably to be counted from the day of Peter's confession. Others, as Lightfoot, count from the day the words of Matt. xvi. 28 were spoken. Not improbably the days were identical. It is not certain at what period of the day the Transfiguration took place, but most probably during the night, or at the early dawn. Darkness was not indeed, as some have supposed, necessary that the glory of the Lord's person might be plainly visible, for when He appeared to Paul, (Acts xxvi. 13,) it was midday, yet the light that shone around Him was brighter than the sun. Nor does the fact that the apostles slept, show that it was night, for their sleep seems to have been not so much natural sleep, the result of fatigue, as stupefaction caused by the marvellous apparition, (Rev. i. 17.) Nor does the fact that He was at that time engaged in prayer (Luke ix. 29) determine it. But as He did not descend from the mount till the day following, it is not probable that He ascended upon one day, was then transfigured, remained after this during the night, and the next day returned to the disciples. It is most reasonable to suppose that the Lord went upon the mount at even, that He was transfigured at the early dawn, and soon after descended.

SUMMER, 782. A. D. 29.

Descending from the mount Jesus explains, in answer to a question from the apostles, how Elias must be the forerunner of the Messiah.	MATT. xvii. 10–13. MARK ix. 11–13.
At the foot of the mountain they meet the other apostles surrounded by a multitude, among whom were scribes questioning with them. The Lord heals a lunatic child, whom the apostles had not been able to heal.	MATT. xvii. 14–21. MARK ix. 14–29. LUKE ix. 37–42.

That Elijah must personally precede the Messiah, was one of the firmest and most undoubted convictions of the

Jews; and the fact that the Baptist denied himself to be Elijah, was a circumstance that went far to discredit his mission. If he was not Elijah then Jesus could not be the Christ. If he was a prophet, and so all the people regarded him, it by no means followed that the Messiah must immediately follow him; for there might be many prophets who should act as forerunners, and yet Elijah alone should prepare His way. As we have seen, most of the people seem to have regarded Jesus Himself only as one of the prophetic forerunners of the Messiah. Educated in the current belief respecting the office of Elijah, the three apostles could not reconcile it with his appearance upon the mount. The Lord clears up this great difficulty by explaining to them the truth, so strange, that there should be two comings of the Messiah, and so two forerunners. Thus the mystery of two Elijahs was cleared up so soon as the mystery of the two comings was known. It is remarked by Alford: "The double allusion is only the assertion that the Elias (in spirit and power) who foreran our Lord's first coming, was a partial fulfilment of the great prophecy, which announces the real Elias, (the words of Malachi iv. 5, 6, will hardly bear any other than a personal meaning,) who is to forerun His greater and second coming."

The other apostles and disciples had remained at the foot of the mount, probably in some town or village, during the absence of the Lord. In the morning, before He descended, a crowd had gathered around them, doubtless seeking Him, and in the crowd a man who had brought his lunatic son to be healed. In the absence of Jesus, he presented him to the disciples, who could not heal him. Among those present were certain scribes, who, apparently taking occasion from their ill success, began to question with them, and plainly with an evil intent. Whilst they are disputing with the disciples Jesus appears, and is gladly received by the multitude. In answer to the father's prayer He heals the child, after a severe rebuke of the general unbelief. The question afterward addressed to Him by the disciples when alone, "Why could not we cast him out?" shows that they supposed the power to work miracles, which had been given the Twelve when they were sent forth upon their mission, was still continued to them.

AUTUMN, 782. A. D. 29.

Departing from the place where He had healed the lunatic child, He passes through Galilee, avoiding, as far as possible, public attention, and giving Himself to	MARK ix. 30–32. MATT. xvii. 22, 23.
the instruction of His disciples. He repeats the announcement respecting His death and resurrection, but they do not understand Him, and are afraid to ask.	LUKE ix. 43–45.
After some time thus spent they come to Capernaum; and He here discourses to them of their equality as brethren, and teaches them who shall be regarded as	MARK ix. 33–50. MATT. xviii. 1–35. LUKE ix. 46–50.
the greatest in the Kingdom of Heaven. Peter, having declared to the tax gatherer that his master is liable to pay tribute, goes by Christ's direction to the sea, and finds the tribute money in the mouth of a fish.	MATT. xvii. 24–27.
Soon after this Jesus goes up secretly to Jerusalem to attend the feast of Tabernacles.	JOHN vii. 2–10.

If the healing of the lunatic child was, as we have supposed, in the neighborhood of Cæsarea Philippi, the Lord, crossing the Jordan near its sources, would enter the northern parts of Galilee, and thus journey toward Capernaum. That this circuit was not for the purpose of public teaching is expressly said by Mark, (ix. 30:) "And they departed thence, and passed through Galilee; and He would not that any man should know." And the reason is added why He would not be known, "for He taught His disciples," &c. To instruct them more fully in the truths He had just opened to them of His approaching death and resurrection, now occupied Him, and the presence of large crowds would have hindered Him in His purpose. How long this circuit continued we do not know, nor what particular parts of Galilee He visited. Matthew's language, (xvii. 22,) "And while they abode in Galilee," or more literally, "while they were going about in Galilee," implies that some time was spent there. The continued inability of the disciples to understand the Lord's words respecting His death and resurrection, will surprise no one acquainted with the Messianic expectations of the Jews. They found it impossible to give a literal interpretation to His words, but they were afraid to ask Him what He meant.

During these journeyings, and probably just before their arrival at Capernaum, a dispute had arisen among the disciples, who should be the greatest in the kingdom. That He was about to reveal Himself as the Messiah and set up His kingdom, was a belief still firmly rooted in their minds, and which His mysterious words about His death and resurrection seemed only to confirm. They knew that some great event was approaching; what should it be but this long hoped for manifestation of the kingdom, when David's son should sit on David's throne? It, therefore, naturally became now a question of deep personal interest to those most ambitious among them, who should fill the highest places under the new government. Perhaps the preference shown by Jesus to the three whom He took with Him upon the mount, and whom He had before specially honored, may have provoked envy and occasioned this dispute. It was not till after His arrival at Capernaum that Jesus took notice of it. From Matthew (xviii. 1) it seems that the incident of the tribute money had some connection with the strife, as some of the disciples coming to Him immediately after asked Him directly, "Who is the greatest in the kingdom of heaven?"[1] In the most ex-

[1] Greswell (ii. 462) attempts to show that the question in Matthew to Je-

pressive way, through a little child, He teaches them that only those like little children, trustful, humble, unambitious, could even enter the heavenly kingdom.

The tax demanded of Jesus was the temple tax, which all Jews were obliged to pay yearly, (Ex. xxx. 13.)[1] Some, as Wieseler, (265,) have understood a civil tax, payable to the Romans; but against this is the use of "didrachma" for the tribute, a sum equal to the half shekel, the legal due. Besides this, the scope of the Lord's reply shows that the temple tax is meant. As the Son of God, He was exempt from the payment to which others were bound for the support of ecclesiastical services. Had it been a civil tax, this reply would not have been so directly to the purpose.[2]

According to the Rabbins this temple tax was due between the 15th and 25th Adar.[3] This would be about the time of the Passover. Greswell, however, maintains, upon the same authority, that it was paid at each of the three great feasts. We cannot then determine at what period of the year this demand of the tax gatherer was made. If payment was legally due at the Passover, still it may not have actually been demanded till a later period. It may be that, being regarded as a prophet, up to this time no tax at all had been demanded of Jesus, and that now, at the instigation of His enemies, and for the first time, the demand was made.[4] Some suppose that the Rabbins were exempt from taxation; and the question of the tax gatherer seems to show that he had not previously collected it of the Lord. That he should ask the question of Peter, may be explained from his prominent position as a disciple, or because, as a resident in the city, he was well known. The

sus was subsequent to His question to the apostles in Mark (ix. 33) and in Luke, (ix. 46.)

[1] Josephus, Antiq., 18. 9. ..

[2] Meyer; Winer, ii. 588, note 3; Trench, Mir., 299; Alford; Ellicott, 229.

[3] See Winer, i. 4.

[4] See Lightfoot in loco.

inference of Bengel from the fact, that the Lord paid the tax for Himself and Peter but for none other of the apostles, that the others were too young to be taxed, is wholly improbable and unnecessary. A better basis has the inference of some early commentators, that the honor here shown to Peter gave edge to the dispute about preëminence.

It is at this period that we put His journey to Jerusalem to the feast of Tabernacles recorded by John, (vii. 2–10.) By many this journey and that mentioned by Luke (ix. 51–53) are regarded as identical. But a careful comparison shows so many points of difference that it is very difficult to believe them the same. These will be hereafter examined. For the present it will be assumed that the journeys are distinct.

In what place Jesus met His brethren, (John vii. 3,) and whence He departed to the feast, is not certain, but most probably it was Capernaum.[1] His brethren appear not wholly as unbelievers, but as those who, recognizing His works as wonderful, do not understand His course of conduct. Sharing the common opinions respecting the Messiah, they felt that if His Messianic claims were well founded, there could be no general recognition of them so long as He confined His labors to Galilee, (see vs. 41 and 52.) In advising Him to go and show Himself in Judea, their motives were friendly rather than evil. They knew that Jerusalem was the ecclesiastical centre, and that if He desired to be received by the nation at large, He must first find reception there. His works in Galilee, however great they might be, could avail little so long as the priests and scribes did not give Him their countenance and aid. The disciples He had already made were men of no reputation. Their adhesion gave Him no strength, for they were but Galilean fishermen and publicans, and, with few exceptions,

[1] Greswell, ii. 482.

poor and obscure people. He must then stay no longer in that remote province, but go up to Jerusalem, and there in the temple, and before the priests and rulers, do His works. If once recognized there, He would be everywhere received. Had Jesus been such a Messiah as they supposed was to come, their advice was good. It is plain that they did not in any true sense believe on Him, but in a spirit of purely worldly wisdom attempted to guide Him in His conduct. Their advice was in its nature a temptation like that of the devil, (Matt. iv. 5;) a temptation to reveal Himself before the time, and in a presumptuous way.

To the counsel of His brethren Jesus replies in substance, that His time is not come; that they were always sure of a friendly reception from the world, but Him it must hate, because He testified against it. Go you up to the feast. I do not go up to it, for my time is not yet come. Some think to find a contradiction here, since, saying "I go not up to this feast," He afterward went.[1] One solution makes Him to have had no intention at this time to go, but afterward He changed His mind and went. Another lays weight upon the use of the present tense, "I go not," which means "I go not now, or yet;" or, as given by Alford, "I am not at present going up." Another lays weight upon "this feast," which it is said He did not in fact attend, except in its last days. Still another thus defines His words: "I go not up with you, or in public with the company of pilgrims," or "I go not up in such way as you think or advise." The matter to one who considers the scope of Christ's reply to His brethren, presents no real difficulty. They had said: "Go up to this feast and manifest thyself. Show thyself to the world, and work thy miracles in Judea." He replied: "My time to manifest myself is not yet come. I go not up to this feast with such

[1] For the reading in the received text, "I go not up yet," *ουπω αναβαινω.* Tischendorf has, "I go not up," *ουκ αναβαινω.* So Alford, Meyer.

intent. At some subsequent feast I shall manifest myself." As He had said so He acted, going up to Jerusalem in a secret way, avoiding all publicity, nor arriving there till the feast was partially past. At the following Passover He acted in substance as His brethren had advised, showing Himself to the world, and entering the holy city as a King, amid the shouts of the multitude.

The feast of Tabernacles was preceded by the fast of the Atonement, upon the 10th Tisri, or the 6th October of this year, the feast itself beginning on the 15th Tisri, or 11th October. The Lord probably reached Jerusalem on the 12th or 13th October. That He had reached the city earlier, and only now first showed Himself in the temple, is not implied in the narrative. We know not whether the apostles waited for Him, or went up at the usual time, but the latter is more probable. He went "as it were in secret," which may imply not only that He went unattended, but went by some unusual and obscure route. That there was anything supernatural in His journey, or in His appearance in the temple, as some have supposed, does not appear in the narrative.

11th-18th Oct. 782. A. D. 29.

During the first days of the feast there was much inquiry among the people concerning Jesus, and His probable appearance at the feast, but no one spake openly through fear of the Jews.	John vii. 11-13.
After His arrival at Jerusalem, He went into the temple and taught. His enemies wish to arrest Him but do not, and many people believe on Him.	John vii. 14-31
Upon a subsequent day of the feast the Pharisees make an attempt to arrest Him, but it fails, and the officers they had sent return declaring, "never man spake like this man." Nicodemus makes an useless effort to induce them to act with equity.	John vii. 32-53.

Here, as elsewhere in the Gospel of John, a distinction is to be noted, although not always preserved, between the "Jews" and the "people." By the former he means the nation as headed up in its rulers, and represented by them, and ever hostile to the Lord. Thus he says, (v. 11,) "the Jews sought Him at the feast, and said, Where is He?" Again, (v. 13,) "no man spake openly of Him, for fear of the Jews." By the latter He means the people, (literally "crowd," "multitude," οχλος,) regarded as an assemblage of individuals, amongst whom there were many differences of opinion, some favorable and some unfavorable to Jesus. (See v. 12.) A large portion of the crowd on this occasion was composed of pilgrims to the feast, and these are distinguished from the citizens of Jerusalem, (v. 25.) But there was no public expression of opinion in His favor, all His friends being afraid of the hierarchy. His sudden appearance in the temple at so late a period of the feast surprised all; and the power of His speech, not the truths that He uttered, made His enemies to marvel. It will serve to the understanding of the present narrative to keep in mind that at the time of the healing of the impotent man the Jewish rulers determined, perhaps formally in full Sanhedrim, to put Him to death, (John v. 16–18;) that this determination was known to some at least of the citizens of Jerusalem; and that Jesus had not, from that time to the present, entered Judea. He can now, therefore, refer back to that miracle, and to the purpose to kill Him, as to things well known to the rulers and to some of the people, although some of the multitude, doubtless the feast pilgrims, (v. 20,) were ignorant of this purpose. Thus we readily see why the citizens were surprised that He should be allowed to speak at all in the temple.

It is not plain when the Pharisees and chief priests (v. 32) sent officers to take Him. It was perhaps, as said by Stier, upon the day following His appearance in the temple, and before the last day of the feast. Greswell supposes that for prudential reasons they deferred the attempt till the last day. It was plainly an act not of individuals but of the Sanhedrim, which probably was assembled specially for the purpose. They were induced to take this step by the great impression his teachings had made upon the people. But, if the officers were sent before the last day, they seem to have waited for a more favorable hour, perhaps fearing to attempt an arrest, and contented themselves with watching Him till the conclusion of the feast. Upon the last day some of the multitude (v. 44) would have taken Him, but the officers, who had been greatly moved by His words, made no effort to do so, much to the vexation of those who had sent them, and to whom they now made their report.

It is disputed whether "the last great day of the feast" (v. 37) was the seventh or eighth. Most maintain the latter.[1] According to the law, (Numb. 29, 35,) upon the eighth day a solemn assembly should be held and special sacrifices offered. This day seems to have become in popular estimation the great day of the feast. Lightfoot, (in loco,) after stating the Jewish opinions as to the meaning of the several sacrifices, adds: "On the other seven days they thought supplications and sacrifices were offered, not so much for themselves as for the nations of the world; but the solemnities of the eighth day were wholly in their own behalf. They did not reckon the eighth day as included within the feast, but a festival day, separately and by itself."[2] It is questioned whether the drawing of water, to which the Lord is supposed to allude, (vs. 37, 38,) and which took place upon each of the seven days, took place also upon the eighth.[3] But if it did not, as Alford rightly

1 So Meyer, Alford, Tholuck, Lichtenstein; contra, Greswell.
2 See Josephus, Antiq., 3. 10. 4.
3 See Winer, ii. 8, note 2; Alford in loco.

remarks, it would not exclude a reference to what had been done on the preceding days. Many, however, maintain that water was also poured out on the eighth day; and that Christ's words were spoken as the priest who bore it entered the court.[1]

The haughtiness of the priests and Pharisees, and their contempt for all not of themselves, are strikingly displayed in their remarks upon the return of the officers; and their rejection of the manifestly just and legal proposition of Nicodemus, shows that they were bound by no considerations of equity. It is possible that others agreed with Nicodemus, and that there were internal dissensions in the council.

Oct. 782. A. D. 29.

The Lord spends the night following at the Mount of Olives, and returning early next morning to the temple, teaches the people. An adulteress is brought before Him, whom He directs to go and sin no more. He answers the Pharisees from the treasury, and continues	John viii. 1–10.
to speak to the people. Many believe on Him, but others are angry, and take up stones to cast at Him.	John viii. 12–59.
As He goes He meets and heals a blind man, who had been blind from birth, and it was the Sabbath. So soon	John ix. 1–12.
as this miracle was reported to the Pharisees, they call him and his parents, and examine him and cast him out.	John ix. 13–34.
He afterward meets Jesus, and believes and worships	John ix. 35–38.
Him. Some Pharisees who are present ask Him a question, to which He replies in the parable of the Good	John ix. 39, x. 18.
Shepherd. There is great division of sentiment among the Jews in regard to Him.	John x. 19–21.

The exact order of the events given above is not certain. Many critics reject as not genuine the account of the

[1] See Tholuck in loco.

adulterous woman.[1] If this be rejected, commencing vii. 53, and extending to viii. 12, there seems ground to suppose that the words from viii. 12–20, were spoken in the treasury upon the last day of the feast, and perhaps also the subsequent words to v. 59. If it be not rejected, a day or more must have elapsed. We give the probable order in either case. The feast began on the 15th Tisri, and ended on the 21st. The eighth day was the 22d, which was observed as a Sabbath. We cannot tell whether Jesus appeared in the temple and taught (vii. 14) on the 17th, 18th, or 19th day. According to Wieseler (309) it was the 18th, which he makes to have been a Sabbath; according to Greswell (ii. 491) it was the 19th. It may, with equal probability, have been the 17th. Assuming that the last great day of the feast was the 22d, an interval of three or more days must have elapsed. Upon the first of these days occurred what is narrated in vii. 14–31, or, as some prefer, in 14–28. The next event mentioned, (v. 32,) the sending of officers, was probably on the last day, as on this day they made their report, (v. 45,) though it is possible that vs. 45–52 described what had occurred earlier. There are then two or three days of the feast during which Jesus was present, of which nothing is related. Upon the last day He speaks of Himself as giving living water (vii. 37–38.) Whether His words in viii. 12–20 and 21–59, omitting here the account of the adulterous woman as not genuine, were all spoken afterward upon the same day, or upon successive days, it is difficult to decide. Some infer from the mention of the "treasury," v. 20, and the use of "again," v. 21, that these words were spoken after the eighth day, and upon different days.[2] Some, on the other hand, making the healing of the blind man (ix. 1–7) to have taken place on the last day of the feast, which was a Sabbath, refer all His

[1] So Tischendorf, Meyer, Alford, Tholuck, Trench.

[2] So Meyer.

words (ch. viii.) to this day. The former is most probable, and fromviii. 21–59 we find but the events of a single day. Was the blind man healed on this day? So say many, bringing the attempt to stone Him and the miracle into immediate connection.[1] But it is more probable that some interval elapsed.[2] It is not likely that Jesus, when "He hid Himself and went out of the temple," was accompanied by His disciples; yet they were with Him when He saw the blind man, (ix. 2.) Nor would they in such a moment be likely to ask speculative questions respecting the cause of the man's blindness. We conclude then that the Sabbath upon which the blind man was healed (ix. 14) was not the eighth day of the feast, but the first week Sabbath following.

If we include the account of the adulterous woman, this interview with her was the day after the eighth of the feast, or upon the 23d Tisri. The healing of the blind man was then upon the Sabbath following. Against this it is objected that the Lord had no motive to remain in Jerusalem after the feast was ended, and that the narrative implies that the feast pilgrims were still present.[3] But on the other side, the mention that it was the Sabbath, (ix. 14,) implies that it was another day, and therefore so distinguished; and the Lord may, for special reasons, have remained after most of the pilgrims had gone.

The effect of Christ's words (viii. 21–29) was such, that "many believed on Him." It is questioned whether these believers are meant, (v. 33,) and whether to them, in common with others, are addressed the subsequent words, (34–38.) "The Lord mingles them indiscriminately in the general mass of the people, in spite of the transient and indistinct impulse of faith."[4] But it seems more probable that He speaks to the Jews generally, and does not include

[1] Meyer, Luthardt, Trench.
[2] See Alford in loco.
[3] So Lichtenstein, 299.
[4] Stier; so Alfo.

them; for how could those in any sense be said to believe on Him to whom He immediately addresses the reproach, "Ye seek to kill me because my word hath no place in you."

The attempt to stone Him was the fruit of sudden rage. It is denied by many, as Meyer and Alford, that the Lord's escape from their violence involved anything supernatural. The language may be construed either way; but, as said by Winer,[1] the supernatural interpretation is to be preferred as more correspondent with the character of this Evangelist. Tholuck does not find the intimation of a miracle in the strict sense of the word, but of a special providence.

The position of the pool of Siloam, where the blind man was sent to wash, has been much disputed, but most modern writers agree that it lies at the mouth of the valley of the Tyropoeon, near the base of Ophel.[2] The waters of this pool come from the fountain of the Virgin, which lies on the west side of the valley of Jehosaphat, through a subterranean passage cut in the rock. It is a current belief that the water of the fountain comes from a living spring beneath the temple. Barclay, (523,) however, asserts that the subterraneous canal derived its former supply of water, not from Moriah, but from Zion.[3] It is still in dispute whether any of the water of Siloam comes from the temple.

The effect of this miracle was to make a division among the Pharisees. Some said that it was a violation of the law, being done on the Sabbath; others, that no sinner could do such miracles. At first there was a general disposition to doubt the reality of the miracle. As this, however, is established by the testimony of his parents, they revile the man, and cast him out. This may refer to his

Gram., 264; see Bengel in loco. [2] Robinson, i. 333; Raumer, 296.
[3] See Robinson, i. 343; Porter, i. 138.

being thrust from the room where they were assembled,[1] or to the sentence of excommunication.[2] Some suppose that he was now before the great Sanhedrim; others, that he was before the lesser; others still, that he was not before any judicial tribunal, but before some of the chief Pharisees informally assembled. From the manner of the examination, and their action at its close, it is most probable that they were clothed with some ecclesiastical authority.

How soon after the blind man was cast out the Lord met him, is not stated. Not improbably, He may have met him the same day toward evening. The words (v. 39) seem to be addressed to the disciples, and probably after His meeting with the blind man, and the words to the Pharisees immediately followed. The effect of these words was again to work a division of opinion respecting Him, some saying that He had a devil, others, that neither His words nor works were those of a man who had a devil.

From Jerusalem the Lord returns to Galilee. Of His return the Evangelist gives us no information. Many suppose that He did not return to Galilee at all, but spent the interval between the feasts of Tabernacles and of Dedication at Jerusalem or in its vicinity.[3] Some suppose a return to Galilee after the latter feast. It has been assumed that the journey to the feast of Tabernacles (John vii. 10) is not identical with that in Luke ix. 51, but that the latter was subsequent. A full discussion of the point is reserved to the Part following.

[1] Meyer, Lichtenstein. [2] Alford. Trench embraces both.
[3] So Meyer, Alford, Tholuck, Robinson, Tischendorf.

PART V.

THE LAST JOURNEY FROM GALILEE, AND THE ARRIVAL AT BETHANY. NOV. 782, TO APRIL, 783. A. D. 29, 30.

Upon the Lord's Last Journey from Galilee.

If the views that have already been presented in regard to the divisions of the Lord's ministry are correct, we are in a position to judge rightly the statements of the Evangelists respecting the period that intervened between the departure from Galilee and the commencement of Passion Week, a period of about five months. In Galilee the Lord had accomplished His work. He had gathered about Him a considerable body of disciples, (1 Cor. xv. 6,) who saw in Him, with more or less clearness of vision, the Christ of the prophets, and Son of the living God; and there was also a much larger number, who, unable to see in Him the Messiah of their hopes, still believed that He was a prophet sent from God, and heard His words with reverence. Besides, there must have been very many in all parts of the land, who had seen His works, and been more or less impressed by them, and yet had not felt the power of the truths He taught. His labors had by no means been in vain, although, as set forth in His own parable, but little of the seed He had so diligently sown, fell into good ground.

There are two circumstances that seem to have marked, if not determined, the conclusion of the Galilean ministry; first, that the apostles, not to speak of other disciples, had learned the mystery of the Lord's person as the Son of God, divine and human; second, that the machinations of His enemies at Jerusalem were arousing great hostility against Him in Galilee, and making the further prosecution of His labors there full of difficulty and danger. Both of these points demand attention.

It needs no argument to show that the Lord's ministry must primarily aim at the recognition, on the part of His disciples, of the great fact that in His person "God was manifest in flesh." Until they were able to rise above the ordinary Jewish conceptions of the Messiah, and to see in Him the Son of God, He could open to them but little of the divine purpose. He could say nothing to them in distinct terms of His death, resurrection, and ascension. He must continue with them in person till, through their communion with Him, they should learn who He was, and what His relations to the Father. And, as we have seen, when Peter, in the name of all the apostles, made the confession that He was "the Christ, the Son of the living God," He for the first time announced to them His approaching death, (Matt. xvi. 21.) This announcement it was still very hard for them to understand, and perhaps the more that they now knew Him to be the Son of God, for what had death to do with Him? But, however imperfectly held, the germ of this great truth of His divinity was in their hearts, and they were now in a state to receive those teachings of Jesus which had reference to a heavenly kingdom, and implied His divine nature. Thus the foundation was laid of that high knowledge of God's purpose in Him, which they needed in their subsequent work, and for which they were further prepared, first by the teachings of the Lord Himself after His resurrection, and then by the descent of the Spirit at Pentecost.

Thus we see that the recognition on the part of His disciples of His divine Sonship, and the consequent announcement to them of His approaching death, mark the end of His Galilean ministry. Yet a little time must elapse, that these truths might get more firmly rooted in their faith, ere the terrible hour of His sufferings should come.

That, as His disciples grew in knowledge and love, the darkness and bitterness of His enemies should increase, was but what Jesus Himself had foretold. All who loved the light gathered around Him, the true light. His words were the test by which the thoughts of all hearts were revealed; and as His ministry was prolonged, and the truths He taught were more distinctly apprehended, the line of separation between His friends and His enemies became more and more marked. His popularity among the people seems to have been at its height about the time of the Baptist's death. Immediately after the feeding of the five thousand, many wished to take Him by force and make Him a king. But the nature of His teachings soon repelled not a few who had been counted among His disciples, (John vi. 66;) and the Pharisees at Capernaum, and elsewhere in Galilee, became daily more open and virulent in their opposition. Gradually the great crowds, that at first thronged around Him, diminished; the novelty of His first appearance passed away; His calls to repentance were by most disregarded; His miracles, wonderful as they were, were not of a kind to satisfy the populace that He was the expected Messiah; His enemies were active and unscrupulous in representing Him as a blasphemer; His nearest and most trusted disciples were uninfluential and obscure men, publicans, fishermen, and the like. It is not, therefore, in itself at all strange that there was not in Galilee at the end of His ministry any general belief in His Messianic claims. Outside of the circle of the disciples He was regarded by many as a prophet, but not as the Messiah, (Matt. xvi. 14; compare also xxi. 11.) The great body of the Galileans turned away from Him. Against those cities which He had often visited, and where He had wrought His mightiest works, He pronounced a fearful judgment. Thus in Galilee as in Judea, Jesus was despised and rejected of men.

But the Lord did not yet forsake His people. He will make one more, and a final appeal. Up to this time He had not openly and expressly declared Himself to be the Messiah, either in Judea or in Galilee. He left the Jews to judge for themselves, from His teachings and His works, who He was. But they did not for the most part discern Him. Their preconceived opinions of the Messiah prevented them from recognizing Him in the obscure, humble, peaceful Galilean, mighty as were His miracles, and sublime as were His teachings. Yet, while thus not answering to the popular apprehensions of the Messiah, He seemed in His discourses to claim higher rank and power than even the Messiah could claim; a mysterious relationship to God which was blasphemous. Thus, on the one side, His silence respecting His Messiahship caused many, who were astonished at His works and words, to look upon Him only as a prophet; and on the other, His repeated allusions to His divine Sonship drew upon Him the enmity of many as a blasphemer.

But while it was the will of God that His people should be left at first to recognize His Son by His words and works, yet He willed also that there should be borne clear and full testimony to His Messianic character, that all might be without excuse. Such testimony John the Baptist had borne, and to this was now added that of all His disciples, who in the very fact of their discipleship proclaimed Him to be the Messiah. He had not indeed permitted the apostles to proclaim Him by name, (Matt. xvi. 20,) because He then for their sake avoided publicity. But the time had now come when His Messianic character must be publicly asserted, that the whole nation might know that He was the Christ, the Son of David, the King of Israel; and if rejected, He must be rejected as such. The people should not be left in doubt whether He asserted Himself to be more than a simple prophet, or, like the Baptist, a forerunner of the Messiah. He will go up to Jerusalem; for if it cannot be that a prophet perish out of Jerusalem, how much more is this true of the Son of God; and He will go with every circumstance of publicity, to be received or finally rejected by those whom God had set to be the heads of the people. It must be a national act, and cannot be done in ignorance. In Judea, He had testified of Himself as the Son of God, but in vain. Now He will return thither, and His disciples shall bear witness to Him, if perchance the nation will hear them. To this end His messengers shall go before Him into every place where He designed to go, and announce the kingdom of God at hand in the person of the King.

Here, then, we find the grand peculiarity of the Lord's last journey to Jerusalem. As He knew, and had declared to His apostles, He went up to die; but to the Jewish people the issue of His journey was not known, and the secret purpose of God did not hinder this last appeal to them to repent and receive their Lord.

It is thus the mission of the Seventy, who were sent "two and two before His face into every city and place whither He Himself would come," that gives to this last journey its distinctive character. Going before Him, they announced that He was about to follow them on His way to Jerusalem, and thus prepared all who heard them to see in Him, not a mere prophet, the risen John, or Elijah, or any other; but the Christ. They were His heralds or forerunners, and their work was to announce His approach, and to prepare His way.

This large deputation, seventy in number, thus preceding Him, must of necessity have given great publicity to all the Lord's movements, and gathered crowds around Him in the various places He visited. As they were to confirm their message by healing the sick, this also would excite general interest and attention. It necessarily follows that He pursued some fixed order in the journey, going only where His messengers had preceded Him, and where they had found reception. As they were to go two and two, it follows also that the visitation of these cities must have occupied considerable time on His part, and that the journey may have been very circuitous, though always having Jerusalem as its goal. Being the last journey, and so the last opportunity to address those whom He met, His teachings would adapt themselves to the time; and the purpose for which He sought public attention through His heralds, would naturally give a peculiarly Messianic character to all His discourses. This fact would also arouse, in a marked degree, the jealousy of His enemies, who would not fail to see in His conduct fresh proof of His ambition, and new grounds of fear. Thus the Lord would be brought more and more into collision with them, and His reproofs become more severe as they displayed more openly their hate.

How far the last journey from Galilee is marked by these characteristics, we shall see when we come to the examination of the several evangelic narratives. It will not, however, be questioned by any one who attentively examines them, and especially that of Luke, which is most full, that He was attended by multitudes; that He came very often into collision with the Pharisees; that His reproofs of their hypocrisy were very severe; that His teachings to the people made prominent the need of self-denial on the part of those who would become His disciples; that

His parables taught very clearly the approaching rejection of the Jews, the appointment of new stewards, His departure to His Father, and His return in glory; and that He aimed to keep His approaching death clearly before the eyes of the apostles.

If the character of the Lord's last journey to Jerusalem be correctly stated, it is apparent that to the mission of the Seventy a much greater importance must be given than has usually been done by commentators and harmonists. Perhaps the fact that Luke alone mentions this mission, has led many to think it unimportant. But when we read the terms of their commission, and remember that it has had no other fulfilment than that here recorded, that there has never been, so far as we know, any body of men since to perform such a work;[1] we cannot believe that their duty was trivial, and its results insignificant. The labors of the Seventy must have been of an importance corresponding with the breadth and dignity of their commission, and have exerted a powerful influence upon the people in this last stage of the Lord's ministry.

Nov. 782. A. D. 29.

The time when He should be received up approaching, the Lord prepares to go to Jerusalem. He sends messengers before Him, who, entering into a Samaritan village, are rejected by the inhabitants. He reproves His angry disciples James and John, and departs to another village. He replies to one who proposes to follow Him. He now sends out seventy of His disciples, to go two and two into every city and place where He Himself would come. They depart, and re-

Luke ix. 51–56.
Luke ix. 61, 62.
Luke x. 1–24.

[1] Some, indeed, have affirmed, that as bishops answer to apostles, so do presbyters to the Seventy; but this view has found no general reception.

turn from time to time as they fulfil their commission. He follows in their steps, journeying through Perea toward Jerusalem. MATT. xix. 1, 2. MARK x. 1.

To reconcile the various statements of the Evangelists respecting the Lord's final departure from Galilee, and the course of His journeys till He reaches Bethany, six days before the Passover, is one of the most difficult tasks that meet the harmonist. That we may see clearly the points of difference, it will be well to consider, first, the statements of each Evangelist separately; and as John gives us the most distinct notices of time, we begin with his account.

Jesus goes up, "not openly, but as it were in secret," to the feast of Tabernacles, (vii. 1–14,) and continues at Jerusalem till the end of the feast, and perhaps longer, (vii. 14—x. 21.) He is present in the temple at the feast of Dedication, (x. 22–39.) He goes from Jerusalem beyond Jordan, and abides there and teaches, (x. 40–42.) He returns to Bethany, near Jerusalem, at the request of Mary and Martha, and raises Lazarus from the dead, (xi. 1–46.) He retires from Bethany to Ephraim to escape His enemies, and "there continued with His disciples," (xi. 54.) He leaves Ephraim, and reaches Bethany six days before the Passover, (xii. 1.) It thus appears that John does not mention any return to Galilee after Jesus left it for the feast of Tabernacles. Still, his narrative does not exclude it. If such a return took place, it may have been in the interval from Tabernacles to Dedication, a period of about two months, of which he gives no account; or it may have been after Dedication, and before the return to Bethany for the raising of Lazarus; or after the sojourn at Ephraim, and before the last arrival at Bethany.

In Matthew we find but a very brief mention of the departure from Galilee, (xix. 1, 2:) "And it came to pass that when Jesus had finished these sayings, He departed from Galilee, and came into the coasts of Judea beyond

Jordan: and great multitudes followed Him, and He healed them there." The language of Mark (x. 1) is very similar: "And He arose from thence, and cometh into the coasts of Judea by the farther side of Jordan; and the people resort unto Him again, and as He was wont He taught them again."[1] The direction of this journey is plain. Leaving Galilee, Jesus crosses the Jordan, and passing southward through Perea, thus comes to the borders of Judea, probably near Jericho. That the place of departure was Galilee, appears from its express mention by Matthew, and also from the "thence" in Mark, which obviously refers to Capernaum, mentioned ix. 33.[2] That this was the final departure, appears from the fact that no other is mentioned after it. Indeed, it is the only departure mentioned by them.

In Luke (ix. 51) we find mention made of a journey, which, upon the face of it, seems to have been the last to Jerusalem. "And it came to pass, when the time was come that He should be received up, He steadfastly set His face to go to Jerusalem." That reference is here made to His ascension into heaven, *της αναληψεως αυτου*, admits of no reasonable doubt.[3] We cannot, from the phrase, "when the time was come," *εν τῳ συμπληρουσθαι τας ημερας*, infer that the ascension was immediately at hand. It is well translated by Norton: "When the time was near for His being received into heaven." The end of His earthly career, His death, His resurrection, and His ascension, were

[1] For the *δια του περαν του Ιορδανου*, Tischendorf has *και περαν του Ιορδανου*. So Alford, Meyer.

[2] Meyer, Alexander.

[3] So Meyer, Robinson, Lichtenstein, Alford. The view of Wieseler, (324,) followed by Lange, that His being received up, refers to His favorable reception by the Galileans; and that the meaning of the passage is, when He no longer found Himself received in Galilee, He left that province and went up to Jerusalem to labor there, is very arbitrary, and finds no general support.

now constantly before Him. "He steadfastly set His face to go to Jerusalem." This was the goal of His journey. If He visited other cities, it was only transiently, and on His way thither. And the great object of His journey, as revealed unto Himself, was not to teach in the temple, or be present at a feast, but to finish His work, to die, and then ascend to God.

These words, then, seem plainly to refer to a final departure from Galilee. They are inconsistent with the supposition that the Lord returned again, to resume His labors, after a brief visit at Jerusalem. But here great difficulties meet us. Is all that Luke narrates, from ix. 51 to xviii. 15, when his narrative meets those of Matthew and Mark, an account of one and the same journey to Jerusalem? This seems to be so, because there is no mention of any other departure from Galilee, and Jerusalem is everywhere mentioned as the goal toward which His steps are steadily directed. It is said, in the only distinct notices of His movements during this period, (xiii. 22,) that "He went through the cities and villages, teaching, and journeying toward Jerusalem." Again, (xvii. 11:) "And it came to pass, as He went to Jerusalem, that He passed through the midst of Samaria and Galilee." This express mention of the fact that He was going to Jerusalem, taken in connection with the earlier statement, (ix. 51,) that "He steadfastly set His face to go to Jerusalem," strongly implies that the same journey is meant. If this be so, it is plain that the Evangelist does not follow a chronological order, as, early in the narrative, (x. 38,) He enters the village of Martha and Mary, which we know was Bethany, in Judea, and very near to Jerusalem.[1] Still later in the narrative,

[1] The elaborate dissertation of Greswell, (ii. 545,) to show that this was not Bethany, but some village of Galilee not named, is far from convincing. The main argument is drawn from a "singular idiom in St. John, affecting the use of the prepositions *απο* and *εξ*;" but the distinction taken is not generally recognized. See Meyer in loco; Winer, Gram. 326, note 1.

(xvii. 11,) the Lord appears passing through the midst, or along the border line, of Samaria and Galilee. These local notices show that two or three distinct journeys are embraced; or that if one only be meant, and that continuous *from Galilee to Jerusalem, the Evangelist arranges its* events by another order than that of time. Both these suppositions have their advocates, and we will consider, briefly, each of them.

First. Does Luke here include several distinct journeys? Many harmonists find three, but are not wholly agreed as to the way in which these several journeys of Luke should be connected with those mentioned by the other Evangelists. The first of these is, according to some, that mentioned in ix. 51 to the feast of Tabernacles, whose starting point was Galilee, and the same mentioned in John vii. 10. The second is that mentioned in xiii. 22, when He went up some two months later to the feast of Dedication, whose starting point was Perea, and to be placed in John x. between vs. 21, 22. The third is that mentioned in xvii. 11, when He went up to the last Passover, whose starting point was Ephraim, (John xi. 54.) Wieseler (321) makes Luke ix. 51 identical with John vii. 10; Luke xiii. 22, with John xi. 1–17; and Luke xvii. 11, with the last journey to the Passover, beginning at Ephraim, John xii. 1, and referred to by Matt. xix. 1, Mark x. 1. Krafft (107) identifies Luke ix. 51 with John vii. 10. After the feast of Tabernacles, Jesus sends out the Seventy from Jerusalem, and follows them Himself, in a circuit through Galilee and back to Jerusalem, before the feast of Dedication. To this circuit the notices in Luke xiii. 22 and xvii. 11 refer. To Luke xvii. 11, correspond Matt. xix. 1 and Mark x. 1. Robinson (Har. 198) also identifies Luke ix. 51 with John vii. 10, but refers all, from xiii. 22—xix. 1, to the last Passover journey, beginning at Ephraim, and to this journey refers Matt. xix. 1, and Mark x. 1.

As we see, all of these suppositions identify Luke ix. 51 and John vii. 10. But this is at best very doubtful. Let us note some of the points of difference: 1st, In Luke, Jesus leaves Galilee for the last time, going to Jerusalem to suffer. In John, He goes thither to a feast, some six months before His death. 2d, In Luke, He goes with an unusual degree of publicity, accompanied by the apostles, and sending messengers before Him to make ready for Him. In John, He "went up unto the feast, not openly, but as it were in secret." 3d, In Luke, He goes slowly, and apparently made a wide circuit, passing through many villages. In John, He goes rapidly and directly, not leaving Galilee till His brethren had gone, nor showing Himself in Jerusalem till "about the midst of the feast." The only important argument in favor of their identity is, that according to Luke, Jesus proposed to go through Samaria, which is supposed to explain John's statement that He went up "as it were in secret." It is said that the common route was through Perea on the east side of Jordan, and He therefore went on the west side, through Samaria.[1] But Josephus[2] says expressly, that it was the custom of the Galileans to pass through Samaria on the way to the feasts. No inference, therefore, that this was a secret journey, can be drawn from this fact. We conclude, then, that Luke and John refer to different journeys.[3]

If not the journey to the feast of Tabernacles, to what subsequent journey mentioned by John does Luke refer? Was it to the feast of Dedication, a few weeks later? (John x. 22.) As nothing is said by John of any return to Galilee after the feast of Tabernacles, it is inferred by many[4] that He must have remained till Dedication at

[1] Wieseler, 320. [2] Antiq., 20. 6. 1.

[3] So Meyer, Alford, De Wette, Riggenbach, Greswell, Neander, Baumgarten.

[4] Robinson, Meyer, Alford. The latter, however, expresses himself doubtingly

Jerusalem, or in its vicinity. But this silence respecting a return to Galilee by no means shows that none took place. The Evangelist is not giving a chronological outline of events, but the Lord's discourses, and adds only those historical facts that are necessary to explain them.[1] It is said again, that at the feast of Dedication (John x. 26) He alludes to His words spoken at an earlier period, (x. 1–5,) from which it is inferred that no long interval could have elapsed, and that His auditors must have been in both cases the same.[2] But two months is not so long an interval that His words could have been forgotten, especially if He had immediately after left the city; and His auditors at both feasts were in part the inhabitants of Jerusalem.[3] There seems, then, no need to suppose that His discourse respecting the sheep (x. 1–18) was spoken just before the feast of Dedication, and that He had therefore continued at Jerusalem since Tabernacles.

Against the supposition that He spent this interval in Jerusalem or in Judea, is the statement (John vii. 1) that "He would not walk in Jewry because the Jews sought to kill Him." The hatred of the Jews did not permit Him to remain in Judea to teach; and on this ground He appears to have passed by several of the feasts. It is highly improbable, then, that after the reception He had met at the feast of Tabernacles, when a formal attempt was made to arrest Him, and the populace had taken up stones to stone Him, He should have remained in Judea till the next feast, exposed to their machinations.[4]

Again, the Lord carried on no public work in Judea after He left it to begin His Galilean ministry. So far as we learn, He had not yet entered it for any purpose since the feast, (John v. 1.) That He had not been into Judea and manifested Himself there, was the basis of the com-

[1] Riggenbach, 421.
[2] Stier, v. 485; Meyer.
[3] See Luthardt in loco
[4] Luthardt, ii. 74; Lichtenstein, 299.

plaints of His brethren, (vii. 3, 4.) He did indeed teach the people at the feasts of Tabernacles and of Dedication, but, so far as appears, only in the temple. If, then, Judea was not now the scene of His labors, and nothing is said of any work now done in Perea, we conclude that He returned to Galilee, where His work was not yet fully ended.

If, then, Jesus returned to Galilee after the feast of Tabernacles, and the journey of Luke (ix. 51) was subsequent to this feast, can we identify it as the journey to the feast of Dedication? But before this point can be considered, it will be necessary to examine what is said of the mission of the Seventy, (Luke x. 1–17,) in its bearings upon the Lord's own labors during this last journey.

We are told that, "After these things the Lord appointed other seventy also, and sent them two and two before His face into every city and place, whither He Himself would come." This plainly shows that they were to act as His forerunners or heralds upon the journey He was about to undertake; and this journey can be no other than that mentioned, (ix. 51,) or His last journey from Galilee. It shows, also, that the route was determined upon; for where He designed to come, they should precede Him, and whither they went and found reception, there He should follow them. Thus their movements were arranged with reference to His. As they were to go two and two, they could easily in a short time visit a large number of cities. If each couple visited but one, this would make thirty-five, and it therefore follows that His journey, following on their steps, must have occupied a considerable period of time.

The end for which this large deputation was sent forth, was, as expressed in their commission, to heal the sick, and to proclaim the kingdom of God at hand; and thus prepare the way for the Lord, who was to follow them. But what was the significance of this proclamation? Was it merely a repetition of what had been preached by John the Baptist, by the Lord, and by the apostles? Did it not rather derive a peculiar character from the relations in which the mission stood to the Lord's subsequent journey? They were not to go to every part of the land, but only to those cities "where He Himself would come." We may, therefore, well infer that they did not merely announce in general terms the Messianic kingdom, but made specific mention of Jesus, who was to follow them, as the Messiah. "They were only to give notice that the Messiah was coming, and that in those places only to which He was to come."[1] It was not merely the proclamation of the kingdom, but also the proclamation of the King. Jesus was soon to follow on His way to Jerusalem, and thus the eyes of all were turned to Him, not as a great Teacher, or Prophet, but as the long promised Son of David and Redeemer of Israel.

Some, however, have questioned whether this sending of the Seventy can be brought into immediate chronological connection with the journey of Luke, (ix. 51.) It is said that the latter refers to His journey to the feast of Tabernacles, and that the Seventy were not sent till after His return from this feast to Galilee. But this is wholly untenable. We cannot suppose that after the Evangelist had said in so emphatic a manner, that He steadfastly set His face to go to Jerusalem, and sent messengers before Him, he should pass over in entire silence its further prosecution, His arrival at Jerusalem, and His return to Galilee, and then, without the least hint of it, begin the recital of another journey. We conclude, then, that the sending of the Seventy was very soon after the rejection of the messengers whom He had sent into Samaria.

We may now ask what light this mission casts upon the direction and time of the Lord's last journey. And

[1] Lightfoot in loco.

first, as to its direction. Where were the Seventy sent? Some say to Samaria.[1] This destination has some support in the fact that they, unlike the Twelve, were not forbidden to enter Samaria and the heathen cities; and also that the number seventy may have had some symbolic reference to the heathen nations. But it is, nevertheless, intrinsically improbable. It was to give the largest publicity to His own Messianic claims that Jesus now sent them forth. They were simply to announce the kingdom of God at hand, and thus the very nature of their mission limited it to those who were already familiar with the ideas which that announcement involved. Besides, He had been already rejected in Samaria by the rejection of His former messengers, (Luke ix. 53,) whose office it was not, indeed, to preach or to heal, but who had preceded Him, as servants precede a prince, to see that all is ready for His fitting reception.

Did He send them into Judea? This is in itself very probable. Although for a considerable period He had not walked in Jewry, because the Jews sought to kill Him, yet this would not prevent Him from now sending to that province His messengers, that perchance it might yet repent. If His life had been repeatedly threatened at Jerusalem, still other cities might be more favorably disposed, and through the proclamations of His heralds, the way be prepared for Himself. The number seventy, also, seems to have some symbolic reference to the seventy elders of Israel, (Ex. xxiv. 9; Num. xi. 24,) implying a general visitation. Still, it is not said by any of the Evangelists that He visited any part of Judea except that lying between the Jordan and Jerusalem. It may be that His purpose at first was to enter Judea by Samaria, but being rejected upon the border, He journeyed into Perea, designing thus to enter it; but His life being endangered when He reached

[1] Wieseler, 326, note 1; Lange.

Jerusalem, He turned back again to Perea. In the absence of all definite statements, great uncertainty rests upon the point whether any of the Seventy actually visited Judea; and if they did so, what reception they met, and whether they were followed by the Lord.

Did He send them into Galilee? This is possible, if we suppose Him to have sent them from Capernaum, and in such direction that, in following them, He should be going toward Jerusalem. Most parts of Galilee, however, He had doubtless already visited, and that He did not design to visit them again may be inferred from the woes He pronounced upon Chorazin, Bethsaida, and Capernaum, (Luke x. 13–15;) nor is there mention made of any Galilean village.

That the chief scene of the labors of the Seventy was in Perea, is apparent.[1] This province was under the jurisdiction of Herod, and here was offered them the same freedom of action that Jesus had had up to this time in Galilee. It was also a part of the country that He had but little visited, and the road along the Jordan was a much-travelled thoroughfare to Jerusalem.

The names of none of the cities visited by the Seventy, and afterward by the Lord, are given, and we cannot therefore tell how wide a circuit He may have taken. It is probable that they were sent to the larger towns, perhaps to those lying nearest the ordinary route to Jerusalem.

Second. When were the Seventy sent? Many, identifying Luke ix. 51 and John vii. 10, say, just before the feast of Tabernacles, and before Jesus had left Galilee.[2] Others, after He had left Galilee and while on His way to Jerusalem to this feast.[3] But, as we have seen, the character of that journey to the feast of Tabernacles forbids that He could have been preceded by such a deputation; some,

[1] So Lichtenstein, Robinson.

[2] Newcome, Townsend, Robinson, Strong.

[3] Lightfoot Friedlieb, Wieseler.

therefore, would make them to have been sent from Jerusalem, or from Judea, soon after the feast of Tabernacles, and before that of Dedication. But this implies that the interval between the feasts was spent in Judea, which is untenable; nor is it at all consistent with the object of the mission that the Lord should follow them away from Jerusalem. Many, who make Him to have returned to Galilee after the feast of Tabernacles, place the sending before the following feast of Dedication, and while He was on the way to Jerusalem through Perea.[1] This period has much in its favor. The last journey was through Perea, (Matt. xix. 1; Mark x. 1.) He was attended by great multitudes, (Matt. xix. 2; Luke xii. 1.) He resumed there the work of teaching the people, which for a time He had suspended, (Mark x. 1.) He goes not directly forward, but in a circuit through cities and villages, yet always making progress toward Jerusalem, (Luke xiii. 22.) Reaching the borders of Judea as the time came to celebrate the feast of Dedication, He goes up to Jerusalem. His appearance there seems to have been unexpected, perhaps from the fact that it was winter, when few journeyed from a distance; but the rumor that He was now more openly presenting His Messianic claims through the mission of the Seventy, had apparently reached the Jews, for they immediately demand of Him that He should tell them plainly whether He is the Christ. They would learn it from His own lips. Forced to flee from their wrath, He recrosses the Jordan, and in that part of the district of Perea, where John at first baptized, He took up His abode. As many had followed Him upon His journey, so many resorted to Him here, till He was called to Bethany, near Jerusalem, by the death of Lazarus. After the resurrection of Lazarus, He is compelled to hide Himself at Ephraim till the Passover came. Thus

[1] Tischendorf, Lichtenstein, Neander, Alford, Milman, Oosterzee, Riggenbach.

this last journey was not wholly continuous. It was interrupted by a period after the Dedication spent in Perea, which, however, seems to have been a period of activity, and later by a sojourn at Ephraim, where He apparently devoted Himself wholly to His disciples. But leaving Ephraim as the pilgrims begin to gather to attend the Passover, He joins them in the neighborhood of the Jordan, and the journey ends with the same publicity with which it began. Attended by the multitude, He enters Jericho, and from hence He goes to Jerusalem in triumphal procession. Thus the last journey of the Lord preserves its uniformity of character, from the commencement to the close.

Some, however, would place this journey after the feast of Dedication. But when, after this feast, did Jesus return to Galilee? Was it when, the Jews having sought to take Him, He escaped out of their hand? (John x. 39.)[1] When, however, we consider how continuously the narrative proceeds, there is no place for a return to Galilee. The Evangelist says: "He escaped out of their hand, and went away again beyond Jordan, into the place where John at first baptized, and there He abode." To insert between this escape and the departure beyond Jordan, a journey to Galilee and a return, is very arbitrary; and the more, that the syntax suggests immediate chronological sequence, the verb, v. 40, finding its subject in v. 39. It was not from Galilee that He went away beyond Jordan, but from Jerusalem, so far as appears from the narrative. Beyond Jordan He abides, till summoned by the sisters of Lazarus to Bethany. Immediately after the miracle there He retires to Ephraim.

Can we, then, place this last journey after the sojourn in Ephraim, as is done by Greswell? We are told that "He there continued with His disciples," (John xi. 54.) The

[1] Stier, Baumgarten.

retirement of Jesus thither being to escape the notice of the chief priests and Pharisees, who had determined to put Him to death, (vs. 47–54,) and who "had given a commandment that, if "any man knew where He were, he should show it, that they might take Him," there is a strong improbability that He would attract public attention to Himself by making excursions to teach, or to heal. While nothing is said of the nature of the Lord's labors in Ephraim, the mention of the fact that He continued there with His disciples, intimates that to them was His time devoted. It is not distinctly said when He left Ephraim for Jerusalem, but the impression made by the narrative, is that it was a very short time before the Passover. Of the route, the Evangelist says nothing, except that six days before the Passover He came to Bethany, (xii. 1.) If, however, He went first to Galilee, and then, sending out the Seventy, awaited their return, and followed upon their steps through Perea to Jericho and Bethany, He must have left Ephraim a considerable time before the Passover. Greswell (ii. 529) finds in this no difficulty, as he supposes Him to have reached that city about the end of December, and to have remained there a month, or to the end of January. Two months would thus remain for the last journey.[1]

Against this attempt to show that the Lord went from Ephraim back to Galilee, the language of Luke (ix. 51–53) forms a strong objection. The Samaritans "did not receive Him because His face was as though He would go to Jerusalem." The answer, that this does not refer to the direction of His journey, but to His purpose in undertaking it, is forced and unsatisfactory. It is plain that He was in Galilee when He sent messengers to the Samaritan village. He must, then, previously have left Ephraim, and gone into Galilee, of which journey nothing is said. This is not

[1] See also Robinson, Har. 202.

impossible, but it does not find any support in John or Luke.

If, then, we cannot, with Greswell, put all the Lord's last journey, beginning with Luke ix. 51, after the sojourn at Ephraim, can we thus put any part of it? Robinson here inserts all following Luke xiii. 10. But this arrangement, which he supposes to be presented, "perhaps, for the first time," meets none of the difficulties arising from the neglect of chronological order by Luke; nor is there anything in the narrative that leads us to suppose any such change of place. The view that Luke (xvii. 11) refers to His departure from Ephraim, is much better supported. The statement of the Evangelist: "And it came to pass as He went to Jerusalem that He passed through the midst of Samaria and Galilee," may be variously interpreted. Jerusalem was the goal, but what was the starting point? If the language means that He passed across these provinces, first Samaria and then Galilee, journeying northward, He could not have been in Galilee, or in Perea, or in Samaria; He must then have been in Judea. But to reach Jerusalem from Judea, why pass through Samaria? If we make Ephraim the starting point, and assume that this city was near the south border line of Samaria, we can suppose that He passed northward till He reached the frontier of Galilee, and proceeding along the frontier eastward, crossed the Jordan, and entered Perea.[1] In this case the Lord did not travel in Galilee, or perform any ministry there, so that His former departure (ix. 51) may be said to have been the last. But can this passage along the frontier be identified with that departure, of which Matthew (xix. 1) and Mark (x. 1) speak? From the very definite notice of place which the latter gives, "And He arose from

[1] That the expression, "Through the midst of Samaria and Galilee," δια μεσου Σαμαρειας και Γαλιλαιας, may be thus understood, is generally admitted. So Bengel, Meyer, Norton, Alford, Lichtenstein, Trench.

thence," we infer that this departure was from Capernaum, not from Ephraim. Jesus must then have gone from Ephraim back to Capernaum, and thence have commenced His journey. But the language (Luke ix. 51) implies that He then left Galilee for the last time. The words, also, of Matthew and Mark plainly intimate, that the Lord had continued His labors in Galilee down to the departure of which they speak. Thus, we conclude that Luke ix. 51 (not xvii. 11) is parallel with Matt. xix. 1, and Mark x. 1. The latter Evangelists, omitting most that took place during the journey, come again (Matt. xix. 13; Mark x. 13) into unison with Luke, (xviii. 15;) and from this point the narratives mention, for the most part, the same particulars. If we make Matt. xix. 1, and Mark x. 1, parallel with Luke ix. 51, it is not, however, necessary to refer the narratives of the former to what took place in the beginning of the journey. All that they tell us, may have taken place after the Lord left Ephraim, and while in Perea.

We come, then, to the conclusion that Luke's words, (ix. 51,) "He steadfastly set His face to go up to Jerusalem," refer to the Lord's final departure from Galilee; and that most of the events he relates from this point to chap. xviii. 15, where his narrative becomes parallel with those of Matthew and Mark, took place during this journey. We find no ground to believe, that after this departure He again visited Galilee. He did not, indeed, go directly to Jerusalem, as He was preceded by the Seventy, and His course was determined by the reception they met; nor, when He reached Jerusalem, could He abide there, but was forced to flee, first to Perea, and afterward to Ephraim. These flights the Synoptists do not mention, and we learn from them no more than that He went to Jerusalem by way of Perea.

If, then, all of Luke's account refers to one and the same journey, it follows that he does not relate in exact chronological order; nor does it appear by what principle he is governed in his arrangement. The various theories which have been presented, we must here pass by. That in the main the order is historical, is probable.

Comparing Luke with the other Evangelists, we mark the following points of identification: Luke ix. 51, and Matt. xix. 1, and Mark x. 1; Luke xvii. 11, and the journey from Ephraim, John xi. 55. Where, in Luke's account, the visit to the feast of Dedication (John x. 22) is to be placed, is not apparent. In the absence of all definite data, we shall assume that his statement (xiii. 22) is to be referred to the period immediately preceding this feast, and that all from chap. xiv. to xvii. 10 may have taken place after Jesus' return to Perea, (John x. 40.)

What determined the Lord to take the route through Samaria rather than through Perea, upon this His last journey, we cannot tell. Perhaps it may have been the favorable reception which He had before met from the Samaritans, (John iv. 39–42,) or that He desired to take the most direct route into Judea. That He should send messengers before Him, is to be explained from the fact that this journey was of great publicity. Whether "to make ready for Him," ετοιμασαι αυτῳ, means simply to prepare lodgings for Him, as most suppose, may be questioned. It seems much more to have had reference to the announcement that the Messiah was at hand, and that the inhabitants of the village should prepare themselves to receive Him with all the external marks of respect that befitted His high dignity. But a Messiah going up to Jerusalem, was a stumbling-block to the Samaritans, and they would not receive Him, ουκ εδεξαντο αυτον. (Compare John iv. 45.) This rejection of Himself in the persons of His messengers, was perhaps a divine intimation to Him that He should not go to Jerusalem through Samaria, but through Perea.[1] Who these

[1] See Lichtenstein, 316.

messengers were, is not known. The anger manifested by James and John, has led some, as A. Clarke, to suppose that Jesus had sent them, and that they felt the rejection as a personal insult; but for this there is no sufficient ground. The lofty and impetuous language of the two, "Wilt Thou that we command fire to come down from Heaven and consume them?" clearly intimates, however, that a new stage in the Lord's work had come; and that these disciples, elated with the hope that He was now about to assert His kingly claims, were ready to punish in the severest manner all who refused Him Messianic honors.

From this village they went to another, (Luke ix. 56.) It is not wholly clear whether the latter was in Samaria, or Galilee. The presumption is that it was in Galilee.[1] There is no mention of any new messengers, nor any further allusion to the Samaritans. The village where He was rejected is conjectured by Lichtenstein (318) to have been Ginnea or Jenin, situated upon the border of Samaria and Galilee, and overlooking the plain of Esdraelon. It is mentioned by Josephus.[2] From thence the Lord would pass eastward to the Jordan, and thus enter Perea.

Luke (vs. 57–60) mentions, in connection with this journey, the incidents which Matthew (viii. 19–22) mentions as taking place just before the journey to Gergesa; and adds also another of like kind. As it is very improbable that events, so remarkably similar, should have occurred twice; and as it is impossible to tell which of the Evangelists relates most accurately,[3] we have followed the order of Matthew in regard to the incidents which he and Luke

[1] Meyer, Lichtenstein. [2] Antiq., 20. 6. 1.

[3] In favor of Matthew most, as Meyer, Bleek, Lange, Lichtenstein; of Luke, Tischendorf; Alford, undecided. That the followers of Jesus here spoken of were Judas Iscariot, Thomas, and Matthew, is a mere fancy of Lange.

relate in common, and insert here what Luke alone relates, (vs. 61, 62.)

Nov. 782. A. D. 29.

During the journey through Perea, the Lord is attended by great multitudes, whom He teaches and heals. Upon the way He is tempted by a lawyer, who asks Him how he shall inherit eternal life. In reply, He relates the parable of the good Samaritan. One of His disciples asks for a form of prayer. He gives Him the form, and adds some remarks on the right method of prayer.

MATT. xix. 2.
MARK x. 1.
LUKE x. 25–37.
LUKE xi. 1–13.

It is not improbable, as has been already observed, that the popularity of the Lord had somewhat diminished in Galilee before His final departure, in part through the open and active hostility of the Pharisees, in part that the novelty of His appearance had passed by, and in part through the increasingly repellent character of His teachings. But He was now entering upon a field of labor almost new, and yet prophetically foretold—*περαν του Ιορδανου*, "beyond Jordan." Comparatively few in Perea, we may believe, had seen or heard Him; and the announcement of the Seventy that He was about to follow them, would naturally call general attention to His movements, and gather great crowds around Him. It is apparent, also, that the peculiar character of this journey gave new impulse to the prevalent Messianic expectations. It is mentioned by Matthew, (xix. 2,) in general terms, that He healed, but no specific cases are given. Mark speaks only of teaching.

We have no data to determine when the inquiry of the lawyer was made. It may have been early in the journey, whilst the Lord was yet on the border of Samaria; and His reply derives a special significance from the fact that He

Himself had just been rejected by the Samaritans. Still, the bitter hostility of the Jews to the Samaritans would have given point to the parable, wherever He may have been.

Luke (xi. 1) introduces the request for a form of prayer, with the remark, that "as He was praying in a certain place, when He ceased, one of His disciples said unto Him," &c. From this it has been inferred by some, as Oosterzee, that the incident stands here in its historical connection, and is inserted by Matthew out of its place in the Sermon on the Mount, (vi. 9–13.) It certainly appears more probable that it should be given in answer to a disciple than to the multitude; and if it had been spoken on that occasion, it might have simply been referred to here. Still, many, as Meyer, make it to have been original in Matthew, and repeated here; and others, as Alford, that it stands in close connection with what goes before in both Evangelists. Tholuck takes the distinction, that in the first instance it was generally given, but in the latter as a specific form. The difference of expression in the two cases is explained by the fact that Luke gives here, as often, a less complete report of Christ's words.

Nov.—Dec. 782. A. D. 29.

The Lord heals a dumb possessed man. The Pharisees accuse Him of casting out devils through Beelzebub. He replies to them, and while He is speaking a woman in the crowd blesses Him. He continues to discourse to the multitude on the desire for signs. He dines with a Pharisee, and sharply rebukes Pharisaical hypocrisy. The Pharisees are greatly enraged, and He proceeds to address the disciples, admonishing them to beware of the leaven of the Pharisees, and to fear God only. One of those present desires of Him that He will make his brother divide the inheritance with him. He denies his

Luke xi. 14–26.
" xi. 27–36.
" xi. 37–54.
" xii. 1–12.
" xii. 13–22.

request, and speaks the parable of the rich fool. He admonishes the disciples to watch for the coming of the Son of *Man*, *and*, *after answering* a question of Peter, proceeds to address the people respecting their inability to discern the signs of the times. LUKE xii. 22–53. " xii. 54–59.

The relation of this miracle of the dumb possessed, and of the discourse following it, to the healing mentioned by Matthew, (xii. 22,) and the discourse there given, has been already discussed. Most agree that Luke has placed them here out of their historical connections.[1] Tischendorf identifies this healing with the miracle in Matt. ix. 32–34, but regards it rightly placed here. Greswell strongly insists that this account is wholly distinct from those in Matthew and Mark. It being impossible to come to any certain result, we shall follow Luke's order, assuming that Matthew relates other cases of healing and another discourse. In regard to the rebukes of the Pharisees by the Lord, spoken at the house of a Pharisee, (vs. 37–52,) we cite the just observation of Alford, that He "spoke at this meal parts of that discourse with which He afterward solemnly closed His public ministry."

That Jesus should have been invited by a Pharisee to dine with him, or rather to breakfast with him, when the sect in general was so hostile to Him, may have been owing to the desire to have one so famous for a guest, or perhaps to a true impulse of hospitality. The severity of His language seems directed rather against Pharisaism than against the individuals then present, except so far as their consciences should compel a self-application. The sins are rebuked which were characteristic of that party. The lawyer (v. 45) seems to make a distinction between his class and the Pharisees in general, as if the former were a kind of higher order, a learned aristocracy. That the Lord

[1] So Robinson, Alford, Lichtenstein.

touched his hearers to the quick, is apparent from their vehement attempts to entangle Him by their questions.

It would seem that immediately after the rebuke of the Pharisees, the Lord admonished His disciples to beware of their hypocrisy, and added other injunctions, (xii. 1–12.) But as His words are given by Matthew in other relations, which seem historical, we must suppose either that He repeats sayings earlier spoken, or that Luke connects them with this occasion, disregarding the order of events. This remark also applies to all from v. 22 to the end of the chapter.[1]

The request of one of the company, that the Lord should speak to his brother to divide the inheritance with him, and the following parable of the rich fool, are mentioned only by Luke. The request shows how much the attention of men was turned to Jesus as the Messiah, and this fact doubtless greatly inflamed the hostility of the Pharisees.

Nov.—Dec. 782. A. D. 29.

Being told of the murder of the Galileans by Pilate, He replies, and adds a parable respecting the fig tree.	Luke xiii. 1–9.
Whilst teaching in the synagogue upon the Sabbath, He heals a woman who had been sick eighteen years. He is rebuked for this by the master of the synagogue, but puts him to shame. He continues His journey toward	Luke xiii. 10–17.
Jerusalem, and replies to the question of one who asked Him, Are there few that be saved? The same day He is warned by certain Pharisees against Herod.	Luke xiii. 22–35.

Of these Galileans, so murdered by Pilate, we have no other mention, and cannot tell when the event occurred. There can be little doubt that it was at Jerusalem, and during a feast.[2] The relations of Pilate to the Jews were

[1] See Oosterzee in loco; also Alford.

[2] See analogous cases in Josephus, Antiq. 17. 9 and 10.

such as to make this act of cruelty highly probable. He was no respecter of places, and did not hesitate upon occasion to violate the sanctity of the temple. Some have supposed these Galileans to be the followers of Judas of Galilee, (Acts v. 37,) but without any good grounds. Probably it was some sudden outbreak at one of the feasts, and they, perhaps taking part in it, perhaps only mere spectators, were slain by the Roman soldiers in the outer court. That the event was recent, and that it excited great indignation, are apparent from the narrative. The attempt of Greswell (iii. 26) to connect it with the sedition of Barabbas, (Luke xxiii. 19,) and to place it at the beginning of the last Passover, and thus to find in it a note of time, is more subtle than forcible. Hengstenberg,[1] supposing the parable of the fig tree was spoken a year before the Lord's death, makes the murder of these Galileans to have been at the last Passover but one, or that mentioned in John vi. 4, which the Lord did not attend. Of the tower that fell in Siloam, we have no knowledge.

The parable of the fig tree has been regarded by many as giving a chronological datum to determine the length of the Lord's ministry.[2] Some refer the three years to the whole period before Christ, during which God was waiting for the Jews;[3] some to the three polities, judges, kings, and high priests. But it is doubtful whether it has any chronological value.[4]

The healing of the sick woman is mentioned by Luke, without any mark of time or place, except generally, that it was in a synagogue and upon the Sabbath. The decided manner in which the ruler of the synagogue expresses himself against the lawfulness of healing on this day, indicates that the Pharisaic party had determined to treat such works of healing as a violation of its sanctity. There is no

[1] Christ, iii. 249.
[2] Bengel, Krafft, Wieseler, Stier.
[3] Grotius.
[4] So Meyer, Lichtenstein, Trench.

expression of sympathy with the woman, of sorrow at her sickness, or joy at her recovery. That in this condemnation of the Lord's act he was supported by others, appears from v. 17. Such a literal adherence to the law, and violation of its spirit, awaken Christ's just indignation, and He denounces him as a hypocrite. Perhaps, the parable of the mustard seed and leaven may have been repeated here.[1]

The account of the Lord's progress, (v. 22,) that "He went through the cities and villages, teaching, and journeying toward Jerusalem," is too indefinite to determine what stage of His journey He had now reached. Some would refer it to His going up from Perea to Bethany at the resurrection of Lazarus, (John xi. 1–17.)[2] Some support is thought to be found for this in the Lord's words, (vs. 32, 33:) "Behold, I cast out devils, and I do cures to-day, and to-morrow, and the third I shall be perfected. I must walk to-day, and to-morrow, and the day following." The three days are said to refer to the time necessary to go up from Perea to Bethany, and are to be literally taken. The meaning of His words then is, "In three days I perfect this part of my work, and not till then do I leave Herod's dominions." But even if the language is capable of this interpretation, it is certain that v. 22, which speaks of a journey to Jerusalem, would not be applied to a journey to Bethany, which was rather a turning aside from His fixed route, in answer to a special request.

The time when the Pharisees came to Him, to warn Him to depart or Herod would kill Him, is designated as the same day when the question was asked Him, "Are there few that be saved?" This was one of the days during which He was teaching and journeying toward Jerusalem, (v. 22.) That Herod should be spoken of, shows that Jesus was now either in Galilee or Perea, and so under his jurisdiction and exposed to his anger. Meyer supposes

[1] McKnight, Meyer, Alford. [2] Wieseler, Oosterzee.

Him to be still in Galilee, and that His reply to the Pharisees (v. 32) is to be understood: "I have yet three days in which to labor in Galilee and to complete my work of casting out devils and of healing, and then I must go up to Jerusalem." On the third day He comes to the border, as related in xvii. 11. But are the Lord's words to be understood of three literal days?[1] This literal interpretation is not to be pressed. There is no good reason why the language may not be understood as a general statement, that His labors must be continued till He should perfect them at His death in Jerusalem.[2]

The motive of the Pharisees in thus warning the Lord to depart, is not clear. It is possible that they were His friends, and that their message was based upon some information which they possessed of the purposes of Herod, who may have been in Perea, at Livias, or Machaerus. Had he been, the great publicity with which the Lord journeyed, could scarcely have failed to draw the king's attention to Him, and to awaken some suspicion of His designs. If not His friends, some suppose them to have been sent by Herod in order to frighten Him from his territories.[3] This supposition finds some support in His reply, "Go ye and tell that fox," &c. Less probable is the supposition that they feign themselves to be Herod's messengers, in order to drive Him into Judea, where He can be more readily arrested by the priests and rulers. Perhaps the simpler explanation is that, without being sent by Herod, or having any special knowledge of his plans, they gratify their malice by uttering the threat that he will kill Him if He does not depart.

The apostrophe to Jerusalem (vs. 34, 35) is found also in

[1] So Meyer, Alford. This, however, makes it necessary to render τελειουμαι, "I perfect my works;" not, as in our version, "I shall be perfected."

[2] So Lichtenstein, Stier, Owen. [3] McKnight, Meyer, Alford.

Matt. xxiii. 37–39, where it was spoken after the Lord left the temple for the last time. From its nature, and from the connection in which it stands in both Evangelists, it is probable that it was twice spoken.[1] Most who think it to have been spoken but once, find its most fitting place in Matthew.[2]

It has been questioned how the words, "Ye shall not see me, until the time come when ye shall say, Blessed is he that cometh in the name of the Lord," are to be understood. The most obvious meaning is, that they are to be taken in the large prophetic sense, and refer to His departure into Heaven, and to His joyful reception by the nation when He should come again in His kingdom. And this also best fits the connection of the thought. No prophet could perish out of Jerusalem. There He must die, and afterward ascend to God, to be seen no more till the hearts of the people should be made ready for Him. Till then their house was left unto them desolate. The supposition that He foretold His purpose to go up to the coming Passover, and that it there found its entire fulfilment,[3] is erroneous. That some of the people did then say, (Luke xix. 38,) "Blessed be the king that cometh in the name of the Lord," was no general, much less national, acceptance of Him, and no real fulfilment of His words. Still, some allusion to the shouts of the multitude at His triumphal entry. need not be denied.[4]

DEC. 782. A. D. 29.

From Perea He goes up to Jerusalem, to be present at the feast of Dedication. Upon the way He passes through the village of Bethany, and visits Mary and Martha. Reaching Jerusalem, the Jews demand that He declare plainly whether He is, or is not, the Messiah. JOHN x. 22–24. LUKE x. 38–42.

[1] So Stier, Alford, Ellicott

[2] Meyer, Lange, De Wette.

[3] Wieseler, 321.

[4] Meyer in loco.

He answers them by referring to His past words and works. The Jews, thinking His answer blasphemous, take up stones to stone Him. He continues His discourse to them, but as they seek to arrest Him, He escapes from them, and goes beyond Jordan to Bethany, (Bethabara,) and abides there. Many resort to Him, and believe on Him. JOHN x. 25–42.

It is at this point that we would insert the narrative of John, (x. 22–42,) embracing the visit to the feast of Dedication, and the return to Perea. These events are omitted by the Synoptists, as not falling into the scope of their narratives, which leads them to mention no visit at Jerusalem but the last.

That the visit at Bethany, mentioned by Luke only, took place at this time, cannot be positively affirmed, but it cannot well be put earlier. Not improbably it is placed by the Evangelist in its present position in the narrative upon other than chronological grounds.

The journey, as it has been traced, brings Him into the neighborhood of Jerusalem. His presence at the feast of Dedication is often ascribed to the fact of His proximity to the city, rather than to any design, on leaving Galilee, to be present.[1] It is not indeed probable that He would go up simply because of the feast, which He might have observed elsewhere. The three great feasts, says Lightfoot, "might not be celebrated in any other place; but the Encenia was kept everywhere throughout the whole land." As one of the minor feasts, His presence implies some special motive. May we not find this in the character of the Lord's last journey? For a considerable period He had avoided Jerusalem; at the feast of Tabernacles, He went up secretly. Now He seeks publicity. Wherever the Seventy go they proclaim Him, and all understand that He appears as the Messiah. Perhaps, as has been already

[1] Lichtenstein.

intimated, He may have designed to send His messengers into Judea; and if they found a favorable reception, to follow them. There is then no reason why He should longer avoid Jerusalem. He will present Himself before the priests and scribes and rulers, that they may show forth what is in their hearts; show whether they can yet recognize in Him the Messiah. And the feast of Dedication had special significance as the time of such a visit. It was appointed in commemoration of the national deliverance by the Maccabees from the oppression of the Syrians, (B. C. 164,) and of the cleansing of the temple and restoration of the appointed worship.[1] It should not only have reminded the Jews of the sins that brought them under the tyranny of Antiochus and of the goodness of God in their deliverance, but have taught them the true cause of their present bondage, and awakened in them hopes of a more glorious deliverance through the Son of David. Had the Lord found them conscious of sin, and humbling themselves under the punishments of God, the way would have been opened for a new cleansing of the temple, and the bringing in of a new and nobler worship. But the feast served only to feed their pride, to foster their hate of Roman rule, and to turn their hearts away from the true deliverer. A Judas Maccabeus they would have welcomed; but Jesus, whose first work must be to deliver them from sin, found no favor in their eyes.

It is possible that some of the Seventy may have preceded Jesus at Jerusalem, announcing His coming. The manner in which the Jews gather around Him, and the character of their question, "How long dost thou make us to doubt? If Thou be the Christ, tell us plainly," clearly indicate that in some way their attention had been especially drawn to Him as something more than a prophet, as indeed the Christ. If we compare this language with

[1] 1 Macc. iv. 52-59.

that uttered but two months earlier at the feast of Tabernacles, it appears evident that His Messianic claims had now become prominent. That the Jews asked the question with the intent to make an affirmative answer the basis of accusation,[1] is not improbable; but it may also have been an honest expression of doubt. It is to be noticed that no mention is made of any preliminary teaching or healing, nothing to call forth the question. He is silent till it is addressed Him by the people, and this was as soon as He appeared in the temple.

The Lord's reply, "I told you, and ye believed not," must refer to the general sentiment and scope of His teachings; for we nowhere have on record any express avowal to the Jews that He was the Messiah. Such an avowal He seems purposely to have avoided. His own words were: "If I bear witness of myself, my witness is not true. There is another that beareth witness of me," (John v. 31, 32.) In conformity to this general rule, He here refers the Jews to His works. "The works that I do in my Father's name, they bear witness of me;" and that this evidence was not sufficient He ascribes to their unbelief. This was not what they wanted, and they must have thought it very remarkable, that if He were the Christ, He did not explicitly and openly affirm it. They did not consider that "with the heart man believeth unto righteousness," and that the evidence that was convincing to a Nathanael, was wholly unsatisfactory to a Caiaphas. That in their question they had no other than the current conceptions of the Messiah, appears from the effect of His reply upon them. So soon as He began to speak of His relations to God as His Father, and said, "I and my Father are one," they sought to stone Him. This was open blasphemy, and the blasphemer must be stoned.

His reference to the figure of the sheep, (v. 26,) as it

[1] So Meyer after Luther.

had been used by Him at the feast of Tabernacles, (x. 1–18,) is not strange, for probably most of those now present, priests, scribes, and Pharisees, were residents in Jerusalem, and had heard His words at that time. The interval was but two months, not so long that they could have forgotten what He then said, especially if they had not heard Him since.

This attempt to take His life, compared with that at the feast of Tabernacles, (viii. 59,) may perhaps show less of hasty passion, but indicates a fixed purpose to destroy Him.[1] The attempt to take Him (v. 39) may have been with design to keep Him in custody till He could be formally tried; or that removing Him from the Temple, they might immediately stone Him. That His escape was miraculous, is not said, though so regarded by many.[2] If He had designed to send His messengers into Judea, this new manifestation of hostility may have prevented it; for if His life was in danger at Jerusalem, He could not have journeyed safely into other parts of the province. No other place of refuge was open to Him than Perea. Thus the Seventy may but partially have completed their intended circuit, Judea being shut against them; and this will explain why their labors are so briefly noticed by the Evangelist.

The Lord, now leaving Judea, goes beyond Jordan, "into the place where John at first baptized." There is no doubt that this was Bethabara or Bethany, (i. 28.) Its position has already been considered. The motives that led to its selection are wholly conjectural. That He sought it merely as a place of safety from the Jews, is possible; but here, on the other hand, He was exposed to the anger of Herod, (Luke xiii. 31, 32.) Aside from considerations of His personal safety, there is much significance in this return to the place of His baptism. He might expect to find there,

[1] Luthardt, ii. 190. [2] So Luthardt; contra, Meyer.

as He did, many whose hearts had been prepared by the teachings and baptism of John for the reception of His own words. It is said that "there He abode." This implies that He made no more circuits through the surrounding towns. He abode in the town or district of Bethany, where many resorted unto Him, and where Mary and Martha sent to Him during the sickness of Lazarus.[1] How long He sojourned here ere He went up to Bethany, near Jerusalem, to raise Lazarus, does not clearly appear. It is inferred by some, from the language of His disciples, after He had proposed to return to Judea, (xi. 7, 8,) "The Jews of late sought to stone Thee"—*νυν εζητουν*, &c., that He had but just come from Jerusalem.[2] Much stress, however, cannot be laid on this. (See Acts vii. 52.) From the feast of Dedication to the Passover was about four months, and it is not improbable that half of this, or more, was spent "beyond Jordan," in the neighborhood of Bethany. Many would place during this time much that Luke relates. Upon grounds already stated, we shall assign to this period all from chap. xiv. to xvii. 10.

Dec. 782. A. D. 29.

The Lord is invited to feast with one of the chief Pharisees on the Sabbath day, and there heals a man who had the dropsy, and defends the lawfulness of the	Luke xiv. 1–6.
act. He addresses the guests, reproving them for choosing the highest seats, and reminds His host of his	" xiv. 7–14.
duty to the poor, and speaks the parable of the great	" xiv. 15–24.
supper. As He journeyed on, great multitudes went with Him, and He addresses them upon the self-denial	" xiv. 25–35.
required in disciples. Publicans and sinners coming in	" xv. 1–32.

[1] As to the use of "abode," *μενειν*, see John ii. 12; iv. 40; vii. 9; xi. 6.
[2] Meyer.

large numbers to hear Him, the scribes and Pharisees murmur that He should receive them, and eat with them. He, therefore, utters several parables, that of the lost sheep, of the lost piece of silver, and of the prodigal son; and to His disciples that of the wasteful steward, adding admonitions against covetousness. The Pharisees deriding Him, He rebukes them, and utters the parable of the rich man and Lazarus. He addresses the disciples upon offences, and forgiveness, and faith.

LUKE xv. 1–32.
" xvi. 1–13.
" xvi. 14–31.
" xvii. 1–10.

The Pharisee by whom the Lord was invited to eat bread, is described as "one of the chief Pharisees." This may denote that he was of high social position, but probably includes some official distinction, as that he was chief of a synagogue, or member of the Sanhedrim. His motive in thus seeking the Lord's society, does not clearly appear; and it is possible that, unlike most of his sect, he wished to show him some mark of respect, perhaps as a prophet, perhaps as the Messiah. Still the Lord's words (v. 12) imply that he made the feast in a self-seeking, ostentatious spirit, and under the pretence of hospitality he may have hidden an evil design. It appears that there were many invited, and that they were of the richer and better class. It was customary for the Jews to entertain their friends upon the Sabbath, although they cooked no food. "The Jews' tables were generally better spread on that day than on any other.[1]"

The appearance of the dropsical man at such a feast, it is not easy to explain. He could hardly, if severely ill, have been invited as a guest; and it is said that after the Lord had "healed him He let him go," as if he were only accidentally present. Nor is it probable that he came merely as a spectator, although eastern customs permit strangers to enter houses at all hours with great freedom, and they are often present at feasts merely to look on.

[1] Lightfoot; see Trench, Mir. 263.

Some have therefore supposed that he was intentionally brought in by the Pharisees, to see if the Lord would heal him on that day.[1] But it is more probable that he came in faith to be healed, and unable, perhaps, to approach the Lord before He entered into the house, now forced himself into the room where He was. Had he been a mere tool in the hands of the Pharisees, it may well be doubted whether the Lord would have healed him.

McKnight supposes the parable of the great supper to be the same as that mentioned by Matt. xxii. 2–14, and to have been spoken a second time in the temple. But the parables are wholly distinct, as a comparison of the details plainly shows.

As the end of His ministry drew nigh, and the hostility of His enemies became more open, the Lord's words became more and more plain in showing how much of self-denial was involved in becoming one of His disciples. The same remarks in substance He had before made, (Matt. x. 37;) but He here adds new illustrations. He compares Himself to a man who wishes to build a tower, His Church; and to a king who goes to make war with another king, with the prince of this world; and they who would aid Him in this building, or in this warfare, must be ready to sacrifice all.

The great concourse of publicans and sinners to Him cannot be explained from any thing in His language (xiv. 25–35) as especially applicable to them, nor as springing from their exclusion from the feast. It rather marks the fact that, now that His words had become more sharp against the Pharisees, and the breach between them and Him more apparent, this class rallied around Him and thronged to hear Him. Much to the disgust of the Pharisees, He did not disdain even to eat with them. Such an act they deemed in the highest degree unbecoming in one who claimed to be the Messiah; and it was also a keen reproof

[1] McKnight, Oosterzee, Stier.

to themselves, who so scrupulously excluded all publicans and sinners from their society.

It is disputed whether the parable of the lost sheep, as here given by Luke, is the same as that given by Matt. xviii. 12, 13. From the relation in which it stands to the other parables which Luke has recorded, we cannot well doubt that it was spoken at the same time. But such an illustration, so natural and apt, may have been used more than once, and been spoken earlier in Galilee, as Matthew relates. Perhaps, both in form and in meaning, some distinction may be drawn between them.

The parables of the lost sheep, of the lost piece of silver, and of the prodigal son, seem to have been all uttered at once to the Pharisees and scribes, who murmured at His reception of publicans and sinners. That which immediately follows, of the unjust steward, was spoken to the disciples; but whether immediately or after a little interval, we have no data to decide.

It is not easy to see how the words addressed to the Pharisees in v. 18, respecting divorce and adultery, are to be connected with the verses immediately preceding; but the parable that follows, of the rich man and Lazarus, has plain reference to that sect. Whether the words to the disciples (xvii. 1–10) followed at once upon the parable, we cannot determine.

Jan.—Feb. 783. A. D. 30.

Lazarus, the brother of Mary and Martha, being sick, they send a messenger to the Lord in Perea to inform Him of his sickness. After receiving the message He abides still two days in the place where He was. Taking the disciples with Him, He then goes to Bethany and raises Lazarus from the dead. Many of the Jews present believed on Him, but others departing to Jerusalem tell — John xi. 1–46.

what had occurred to the Pharisees. A council is summoned, and Caiaphas the high priest advises that He be put to death. Jesus, learning this, goes with His disciples to a city called Ephraim, and His enemies give a commandment, that, if any man know where He is, he should show it, that they might take Him. JOHN xi. 47–57.

At this point in Luke's narrative we insert the account given by John of the journey of Jesus to Bethany to raise Lazarus, and of His subsequent departure to Ephraim and sojourn there. The Lord waits two days after receiving the message of the sisters ere He departs for Bethany. It is not certain how long after the death of Lazarus He arrived there. It is said (v. 17) that "when He came He found that he had lain in the grave four days already." We may then count as the first, that on which the message was sent and received; the two following days of waiting, and on the fourth He departs from Perea and arrives at Bethany If we suppose Lazarus to have died on the same day that the message was sent, and to have been buried the same day, as was customary, (see Acts v. 6 and 10,) the day of the Lord's arrival was the fourth after the interment. Reckoning a part of a day as a whole, we have thus the four days. Lardner[1] supposes that his burial was the day following his death. "If he died on the first day of the week, he was buried on the second, and raised on the fifth. He had been dead four days complete, and buried four days incomplete."

Tholuck (in loco) thinks it improbable that Jesus could have made the journey (perhaps 23–29 miles) in one day, and yet arrive in Bethany in season to do all that is recorded of Him. He must have spent parts of two days upon the road. He supposes, therefore, that Lazarus died the night following the arrival of the messenger and was buried the next day, and that Jesus reached Bethany the

[1] Works, x. 26, note.

fifth day. The first day was that of the burial; the second and third were spent in waiting; the fourth in journeying; on the fifth He reaches Bethany and raises Lazarus.

Some place the death of Lazarus on the last of the two days of waiting, referring in proof to Christ's words vs. 11 and 14.[1] He had waited till the death should take place, and, so soon as it did, He announced it to the disciples, saying, "Lazarus is dead." Thus He is made to reach Bethany on the sixth day.[2]

That the Lord, after He commenced this journey, went directly to Bethany, lies upon the face of the narrative.[3] Yet, some suppose that much related by the Synoptists finds here its proper place. Krafft (117) identifies the beginning of the journey with Mark x. 17: "And when He was gone forth into the way," &c.; and Mark x. 32, Matt. xx. 17, and Luke xviii. 31, with its progress. An enumeration of the events which he here brings together will show the great improbability of his arrangement: the discourse upon the danger of riches, the reward of the apostles, the third announcement of His approaching death, the strife of the apostles for supremacy, the entrance into Jericho attended by crowds, healing of the blind men, interview with Zaccheus, parable of the pounds; all this on the way to Bethany. Ebrard does not follow Krafft, yet supposes that, as He was two or more days on the way, He may have made several circuits. All suppositions of this kind are wholly untenable. The Lord went to Bethany for a special purpose, attended only by His followers, and without publicity.[4]

[1] Bengel, Krafft.

[2] See Greswell, ii. 513; Ebrard, 456; Stud. u. Krit., 1862, p. 65.

[3] So Meyer, Tischendorf, Lichtenstein, Robinson.

[4] The arrangement of McKnight is extraordinary. Placing Bethany, where He was sojourning, on the Jordan in northern Perea, he supposes Jesus to have gone through Samaria and Galilee, and on the way to have healed the ten lepers, (Luke xvii. 11,) and thence to Jerusalem, and from Jerusalem to Bethany of Judea.

A very slight examination shows that Krafft's order is without basis. It is scarcely possible that the Lord, going up to Bethany for a special purpose, and this a considerable period before the Passover, should have taken the Twelve, and said unto them: "Behold, we go up to Jerusalem, and all things that are written by the prophets concerning the Son of man, shall be accomplished," (Luke xviii. 31.) Did the great multitude that followed Him from Jericho go on with Him to Bethany? (Matt. xx. 29.) It is besides apparent that the journey through Jericho, made with such publicity, had Jerusalem as its goal, and that there was no delay, save for a few hours at Bethany, preparatory to the triumphal entry, (John xii. 1–12.)

Bethany lies on the eastern slope of the Mount of Olives, some fifteen furlongs (one and a half miles) southeast from Jerusalem. The etymology of the name is uncertain. According to some it means "a low place," *locus depressionis*, as lying in a little valley; according to others, a "house of dates," or "place of palms," *locus dactylorum*.[1] It is not mentioned in the Old Testament. Its chief interest to us is in connection with Lazarus and his two sisters. Its proximity to Jerusalem, and its retired position, made it a convenient and pleasant resting place for the Lord upon His journeys to and from the feasts, although there is mention made but once of His presence there (Luke x. 38–42) prior to the resurrection of Lazarus. It is now a small village of some twenty houses, occupied by Bedouin Arabs. "A wild mountain hamlet, screened by an intervening ridge from the view of the top of Olivet, perched on its broken plateau of rock, the last collection of human habitations before the desert hills which reach to Jericho—this is the modern village of El-Lazarieh."[2] Little that is ancient is now to be found. A tradition, that dates back to an early period, points out the sites of the houses of Simon and of Lazarus,

[1] Lightfoot, x. 85; Winer, i. 67. [2] Stanley, 186.

and the sepulchre of the latter. "This," says Porter,[1] "is a deep vault, partly excavated in the rock, and partly lined with masonry. The entrance is low, and opens on a long, winding, half ruinous staircase, leading down to a small chamber, and from this a few steps more lead down to another smaller vault, in which the body of Lazarus is supposed to have lain. This situation of the tomb in the centre of the village scarcely agrees with the Gospel narrative, and the masonry of the interior has no appearance of antiquity. But the real tomb could not have been far distant." Thomson says, (ii. 599 :) "By the dim light of a taper we descended very cautiously by twenty-five slippery steps to the reputed sepulchre of Lazarus, or El-Azariyeh, as both tomb and village are now called. But I have no description of it to give, and no questions about it to ask. It is a wretched concern, every way unsatisfactory, and almost disgusting." Robinson denies that the sepulchre now shown could have been that of Lazarus.

The impression which the miracle of the resurrection of Lazarus made upon the people at large, was very great. It was in all its circumstances so public, and so well authenticated, that it was impossible for the most sceptical to deny it, even if it did not lead them to faith in Jesus. It is said (vs. 45, 46,) "Then many of the Jews which came to Mary, believed on Him. But some of them went their ways to the Pharisees, and told them what things Jesus had done." From the grammatical construction, Meyer infers that those who went to the Pharisees were of those who believed, and that they went that they might testify to them of the miracle.[2] As all did not believe on Him, it is more probable that some of these unbelievers went to the Pharisees, and that their motive was evil. The ecclesiastical rulers felt that it was now high time that something should be done, and

[1] Hand Book, i. 188.
[2] See, contra, Luthardt and Alford in loco.

they proceed at once to call a council to determine what steps should be taken. Their deliberations ended with the resolve that He should be put to death. This may be regarded as the decisive and final rejection of Jesus by the Jewish authorities. Much earlier the Jews at Jerusalem had sought to slay Him as a Sabbath breaker and blasphemer, (John v. 16–18;) the Pharisees and Herodians in Galilee had taken counsel how they might destroy Him, (Mark iii. 6;) the Sanhedrim had agreed to excommunicate any one who should confess that He was Christ, (John ix. 22;) on one occasion officers had been sent to arrest Him, (John vii. 32;) and there was a general impression that His enemies would not rest till He was removed out of the way, (John vii. 25.) But it does not appear that to this time there had been a determination of the Sanhedrim, in formal session, that He should die. The miracle at Bethany, and its great popular effect, brought the matter to a crisis. The nation, in its highest council, presided over by the high priest, decided in the most solemn manner that the public safety demanded His death. All that now remained to be done was to determine how His death could be best effected.

It is to be noticed how, in the deliberations of the Sanhedrim, truth and justice were made wholly subservient to selfish policy. That Jesus had wrought a great and wonderful miracle at Bethany, was not denied. Indeed it was admitted, and made the basis of their action against Him: "If we let Him thus alone, all will believe on Him." But on what ground rested their fear that "the Romans would come and take away both their place and nation"? It seems plain that they did not look upon Jesus as one who, under any circumstances, would fulfil their Messianic hopes, and establish a victorious kingdom. Even if all were to believe on Him, and He should set up Himself as King, He could not resist the Romans. His undeniable miracles could not authenticate His Messiahship. This strikingly shows how little the impression made by the character of Jesus, His works and teachings, corresponded to the prevalent conceptions of the Messiah. It was to the Pharisees impossible that He, the teacher, the prophet, should become the leader of armies, the assertor of their national rights, the warrior like David. They felt that in Him their hopes never could be fulfilled. His growing popularity with the people, if it led to insurrection, could only bring upon them severer oppression. In this point of view, it was better that He should die, whatever might be His miraculous powers, than that all through Him should perish.

If, as the narrative plainly implies, the Sanhedrim held its session as soon as possible after the knowledge of the resurrection of Lazarus reached it, the Lord's departure to Ephraim could not have been long delayed. He could not remain in Bethany without each hour putting His life in peril. That He went secretly to Ephraim, appears from the commandment given by the chief priests and Pharisees that "if any man knew where He were, he should show it, that they might take Him." Yet the Twelve seem to have accompanied Him, or, which is more probable, to have gathered to Him there. It is not improbable that others, also, may have resorted to Him. Of the city Ephraim, in which He took refuge, little is known, and different sites have been assigned it. In 2d Chronicles xiii. 19, mention is made of an Ephraim in connection with Bethel and Jeshanah. Josephus[1] speaks of Ephraim in connection with Bethela, or Bethel. It was a small town lying in the mountainous district of Judah, and conquered by Vespasian. Eusebius mentions an Ephraim as lying eight Roman miles north of Jerusalem. Jerome,[2] who mentions

[1] War, 4. 9. 9. [2] Raumer, 171.

the same place, puts it at twenty miles. Lightfoot identifies the Ephraim of Chronicles, of Josephus, and of the text.[1] That the Ephron of Eusebius and Jerome is the same place, can scarcely be questioned; and their conflicting statements as to its distance from Jerusalem may be explained, as Robinson does, by the supposition that the latter corrects the former. Wieseler maintains that Eusebius is right. Proceeding upon these data, Robinson thinks that he finds the site of Ephraim in the modern Taiyibeh, which is situated about twenty Roman miles northeast of Jerusalem, and some five or six miles northeast of Bethel, upon a lofty hill, overlooking all the valleys of the Jordan. This identification is accepted by many.[2] Ebrard, however, denies that the Ephraim of Josephus can be identified with that of the Evangelist, and places the latter southeast from Jerusalem; because that Jesus, on His way from it to Jerusalem, passed through Jericho. Sepp places it in the land of Gilead; Luthardt regards its position as doubtful.

Feb.—March, 783. A. D. 30.

In Ephraim the Lord abides with the disciples till the approach of the Passover. A little before the feast, many went up out of the country to Jerusalem, to perform the necessary purifications, and there was much discussion as to the probability of His presence. He leaves Ephraim, and begins His journey toward Jerusalem, passing along the border line of Samaria and Galilee. Upon the way He meets and heals ten lepers. Being asked by the Pharisees when the kingdom of God should come, He replies, and adds the parable of the unjust judge. To certain self-righteous persons He spake the parable of the Pharisee and

John xi. 54–57.
Luke xvii. 11–19.
Luke xvii. 20–37.
Luke xviii. 1–14.

[1] So Tischendorf, Wieseler.

[2] So Ritter, Porter, Lange, Lichtenstein, Smith's Dict. of Bible, Ellicott.

17

publican. He replies to the question of the Pharisees respecting divorce. Little children are brought to Him, whom He blesses. As He is journeying, a young man follows Him, to know how he may inherit eternal life. Jesus bids him sell all that he has, and follow Him, and proceeds to address the disciples upon the dangers incident to riches. In answer to Peter, He speaks of the rewards that should be given the Twelve, and to all faithful disciples. He adds the parable of the laborers in the vineyard.

MATT. xix. 3–12.
MARK x. 2–12.
MATT. xix. 13–15.
MARK x. 13–16.
LUKE xviii. 15–30.
MATT. xix. 16–30.
MARK x. 17–31.
MATT. xx. 1–16.

Supposing the Lord to have gone to Bethany, beyond Jordan, immediately after the feast of Dedication, or in the latter part of December, and that He remained there several weeks before He heard that Lazarus was sick, we may put His departure to Ephraim in the latter part of February, or early in March. Here He continued till the Passover, which fell this year on the seventh of April. He was thus at Ephraim about six weeks. How was this time spent? It is said by some,[1] that He may have made excursions to the neighboring villages, or even to the Jordan valley. But, as His object in seeking this secluded spot on the edge of the wilderness, was to avoid the observation of His enemies, till the appointed hour had come, how could He go about the country, teaching and preaching? The place of His retreat must thus have come very speedily to the knowledge of the Pharisees. How little the people at large knew where He was, appears from the fact that those who went up early to the feast, sought Him at Jerusalem. Besides the position of Ephraim, though well fitted for seclusion, was not so for teaching. We conclude, then, as the narrative plainly implies, that He was spending the few days that remained to Him, not amidst crowds, nor renewing in some scattered villages the labors of His early ministry; but in the society of His disciples, teaching them such truths as they could receive, and preparing them for their labors,

[1] So Robinson, Har. 201.

after He should Himself be taken from them. Doubtless, also, this period gave Him many opportunities of solitary communion with His Father.

The fact that He had been present at the last two feasts in Jerusalem, led the people to expect that Jesus would also be present at the Passover. But, on the other hand, as He had withdrawn from public observation, and as the Jews had endeavored to learn the place of His concealment in order to arrest Him, it was doubtful whether He would dare to come and brave their enmity. That many should assemble before the feast, was made necessary by the laws respecting purification.[1]

Identifying Ephraim with the modern Taiyibeh, the distance to the border line of Galilee and Samaria was not great. If He left the former early in the morning, He may have reached the latter in the afternoon. That He was accompanied by others than the Twelve, appears from the statement (Matt. xx. 17) that "He took them apart in the way;" and from the mention of Salome, (v. 20.) As the time for concealment was now past, and it was His purpose to enter Jerusalem with all publicity, it is probable that He directed His course to the Jordan with a view to meet the pilgrims from Galilee, who took this way to the feast. So soon as He came into the valley of the Jordan, He would meet the larger processions that came from the neighborhood of the Sea of Galilee, by the road down the west bank of the river; and in the neighborhood of Jericho would meet those who crossed the ford from the eastern side. What multitudes attended the feasts, especially this feast, appears from Josephus.[2] From actual count, it appears that at a given Passover 256,500 paschal lambs were slain; and, allowing ten persons to each lamb, which was the smallest allowable number, the participants amounted to 2,565,000

[1] See Numbers ix. 10, and Ainsworth's note; 2 Chron. xxx. 17.

[2] War, 6. 9. 3.

persons. Admitting that this number is greatly exaggerated, there is no question that immense multitudes were always present; and all the roads leading to Jerusalem, for several days before and after the feasts, were thronged with passengers.

As to the name or position of the village where the ten lepers met Him, we know nothing more than that it was on the border of Samaria. It would seem, from the gathering together of so many lepers in one place, that the Lord's journey was widely known. The title by which they address Him, "Jesus, Master," indicates faith in Him as a prophet rather than as Messiah.

When or where the question of the Pharisees (v. 20) respecting the coming of the kingdom of God, was addressed to Him, we have no data to determine. The point of the question concerns the time: When wilt thou, announcing thyself as the Messiah, visibly set up thy kingdom? Probably it was asked in mockery; but, if honestly meant, it could not be answered as a matter of mere chronology. His words that follow, to the disciples, (vs. 22–37,) contain many expressions almost identical with those afterward employed by Him in His discourses respecting the destruction of Jerusalem, (Matt. 24,) giving some reason to believe that they are here recorded out of their order.

The parable of the unjust judge stands in obvious connection with the discourse immediately preceding; but that of the publican and Pharisee may have been spoken later.

The question concerning divorce is found both in Matthew and Mark, and is the first event related by them in their account of the last journey from Galilee to Judea. Whether it should be inserted here, or took place earlier, we have no data to determine. Being mentioned, however, by them both just before the incident of the blessing of the children, which Luke also mentions, this seems the most fitting place. Perhaps this question may refer to the disputes of the Jewish schools, one of which permitted divorces for many causes, even very slight ones; the other only for adultery.[1]

All the Synoptists mention the blessing of the children. It is plain that their parents were those who honored the Lord, and valued His blessing. Perhaps it may point to His near departure from this scene of labor.[2] The demand of Jesus upon the young ruler to sell all that he had and give to the poor, was something unexpected. Such a demand was totally at variance with the popular conceptions of the Messianic kingdom, in which all Jews confidently believed that every form of temporal blessing would abound. The question of Peter indicates how much his thoughts were engrossed with the rewards and honors of that kingdom, which all now thought to be near at hand.

March, 783. A. D. 30.

Upon the way to Jerusalem, the disciples were amazed and filled with fear, beholding Jesus going before them. He announces to the Twelve privately His approaching death and resurrection, but His words were not understood.	Mark x. 32–34. Matt. xx. 17–19. Luke xviii. 31–34.
Afterward James and John, with their mother Salome, come to Him, asking for the seats of honor in His kingdom. He denies their request. The jealousy of the other apostles.	Matt. xx. 20–28. Mark x. 35–45.

Upon the way, and probably soon after reaching the valley of the Jordan, He took the Twelve apart, and announced to them, for the third time, His approaching death,

[1] Lightfoot on Matt. v. 31, and xix. 3.
[2] See Oosterzee on Luke xviii. 15.

but with greater particularity than before. He now speaks of the mode of His death: that it must be by crucifixion; that He should be delivered into the hands of the Gentiles, and by them be mocked and scourged. That this announcement was made early in the journey, appears from the use of the present tense: "Behold we go up to Jerusalem."[1] Mark adds, "And Jesus went before them; and they were amazed; and as they followed they were afraid." As this amazement and fear were previous to His informing them what was about to befall Him, it indicates that there was something unusual in His manner, something that awed and appalled them.[2] Luke informs us that, notwithstanding the Lord's words were so plain and express, "they understood none of these things, and this saying was hid from them, neither knew they the things which were spoken." An undefined sense that some great and awful event was impending, seems for a little while to have had possession of their minds; but, even now, of its real nature they had no just conceptions. They knew why He had sought refuge in Ephraim, and that to go to Jerusalem was to expose Himself to the malice of the Pharisees, (John xi. 8 and 16,) and momentary doubts of the result troubled and depressed them. Yet, on the other hand, they had seen so many proofs of His mighty power in Galilee, and the resurrection of Lazarus was so fresh in their memories, that they could not believe that His life could be taken by violence, or against His will. That He should voluntarily yield Himself up as a victim, was wholly inconceivable, and His plainest words could not change their long preconceived and deeply-rooted opinions as to the nature of the Messianic kingdom. All His predictions respecting His suffer-

[1] See Lichtenstein, 370.

[2] Meyer, following a different reading, makes two parties: some who remained behind in their amazement, and others who followed Him, but with fear. The received text is followed by Tischendorf and Alford.

ings and death, though explicit in the letter, they so interpreted as to harmonize with a victory over all His enemies, and a triumphant reign.

A striking commentary upon Luke's statement, that the disciples understood none of the Lord's words, is found in the request of Salome, that her two sons, James and John, might fill the *highest places* in His kingdom. It has already been noted, that the sending out of the Seventy, and the peculiar character of this journey to Jerusalem, had awakened very strong expectations that the day was very near when He would openly and successfully assert His claims to the throne of His father David. Perhaps Salome and her sons may have had in mind His promise, spoken several months earlier, (Matt. xix. 28,) that the twelve apostles should sit in the regeneration on twelve thrones, judging the twelve tribes of Israel; and believed that the time for its fulfilment was near. The request was made by her in person, but her sons were also present, and the Lord's reply was addressed to them. Probably it was made some few hours after He had spoken to the Twelve of His sufferings and death; perhaps when they were drawing near to Jericho, and had already been joined by troops of the pilgrims on their way to the feast. The excitement of the occasion, the tumult of the multitude, and the joy and honor with which the Lord was greeted, would naturally drive from their minds the sombre impression of the earlier part of the journey. What the expectations of most of those who accompanied Him were, clearly appears from Luke's words, (xix. 11:) "They thought that the kingdom of God should immediately appear." Under these circumstances, it was not strange that Salome and her sons should present their request.

MARCH, 783. A. D. 30.

As in company with the crowd of pilgrims He approaches Jericho, two blind men, sitting by the way side begging, address Him as the Son of David, beseeching Him to restore their sight. He heals them, and they follow Him.	LUKE xviii. 35–43. MATT. xx. 29–34. MARK x. 46–52.
Entering Jericho, He meets Zaccheus, and goes to his house, where He remains during the night.	LUKE xix. 1–10.
In the morning, when about to depart, He speaks to the people the parable of the pounds. He leaves Jericho, and the same day reaches Bethany, near Jerusalem.	LUKE xix. 11–28.

The account of the healing of the blind men is differently related by the Synoptists, both as to the place and the number of persons. Matthew and Mark make it to have taken place as Jesus was leaving Jericho; Luke, as He was entering it. Matthew mentions two blind men; Mark and Luke mention but one. Of these discrepancies there are several solutions:

1*st.*—That three blind men were healed; one mentioned by Luke, as He approached the city; two mentioned by Matthew, (Mark speaks only of one,) as He was leaving the city.[1] Some, as Osiander, make four to have been healed.

2*d.*—That the cases of healing were two, and distinct; one being on His entry into the city, the other on His departure.[2] According to this solution, Matthew combines the two in one, and deeming the exact time and place unimportant, represents them as both occurring at the departure of the Lord from the city.

3*d.*—That two were healed, and both at His entry; but

[1] Kitto, Augustine, Morrison.

[2] Lightfoot, Ebrard, Krafft, Tischendorf, Wieseler, Greswell, Bucher, Lex, Neander.

one being better known than the other, he only is mentioned by Mark and Luke.[1]

4th.—That one of the blind men sought to be healed as the Lord approached the city, but was not; that the next morning, joining himself to another, they waited for Him by the gate, as He was leaving the city, and were both healed together. Luke, in order to preserve the unity of his narrative, relates the healing of the former, as if it had taken place on the afternoon of the entry.[2]

5th.—That only one was healed, and he when the Lord left the city. Matthew, according to his custom, uses the plural where the other Evangelists use the singular.[3]

6th.—That Luke's variance with Matthew and Mark, in regard to place, may be removed by interpreting (xviii. 35) "as He was come nigh to Jericho," εν τῳ εγγιζειν αυτον εις Ιεριχω, in the general sense of being near to Jericho, but without defining whether He was approaching to it, or departing from it. Its meaning here is determined by Matthew and Mark: He was leaving the city, but still near to it. Luke, like Mark, mentions only the more prominent person healed.[4]

Other solutions of the discrepancy in regard to place, have been given, as by Newcome,[5] that Jesus spent several days at Jericho, that He went out of the city, as mentioned by Matthew and Mark, for a temporary purpose, and that on His return He healed the blind men; by McKnight,[6] that there were two Jerichos, old and new; and the blind men, sitting on the road between them, were healed as the Lord was departing from one and entering the other; by

[1] Doddridge in loco. Newcome, Lichtenstein, Friedlieb.

[2] Bengel, Stier, Trench, Ellicott. See a modification of this view in McKnight, and another in Lange on Matt. xx. 30.

[3] Oosterzee on Luke; Da Costa.

[4] Grotius on Matt. xx. 30; Clericus, Diss. ii., Canon vi.; Pilkington, cited in Townsend v. 33; Robinson, Jarvis, Owen.

[5] Har., 275.

[6] Har., ii. 93.

Paulus, (iii. 44,) that there was a multitude of pilgrims with Jesus, and that the front ranks of the procession were leaving the city as He was entering it.

Olshausen and Riggenbach decline to attempt to harmonize the accounts, regarding the differences as unimportant. Meyer and De Wette suppose the Evangelists to have followed different traditions, and find the discrepancies invincible. With them Alford agrees in substance: "The only fair account of such differences is, that they existed in sources from which each Evangelist took his narrative." The supposition that two were healed separately, or that there were two distinct miracles combined by Matthew in one, he characterizes as "perfectly monstrous; and would at once destroy the credit of Matthew as a truthful relator." Norton (ii. 302) observes: "The difference in the accounts of the Evangelists is entirely unimportant, except as serving to show that they are independent historians; and it is idle to try to make them agree by the forced suppositions, to which some commentators have resorted." It is most probable that two were healed, though one only is mentioned by Mark and Luke.

None of the Evangelists state at what time of the day Jesus reached Jericho, but it was probably in the afternoon. The distance to Jerusalem, and the nature of the country through which the road passed, may have made it difficult or impossible to go on to Bethany that night, and there was no intervening village where they could encamp. That Jesus did spend the night at Jericho, appears from His words to Zaccheus, (Luke xix. 5,) "To-day I must abide at thy house;" and from the murmurings of the people, (v. 7,) "That He was gone to be a guest, (καταλυσαι,) with a man that is a sinner."[1] This visit of the Lord to the house of a publican, although a chief among his class, and

[1] For this usage of καταλυσαι, see Luke ix. 12; so Meyer, Alford, Greswell, Lichtenstein.

rich, did not escape strong animadversion. It was regarded by the people at large, and perhaps also by some of His own disciples, as an act unworthy of His high claims. In popular estimation, publicans, whose calling so odiously reminded them of Roman domination, were no fit hosts for Him whom they fondly believed to be now on His way to Jerusalem to proclaim Himself the king. The conversation between the Lord and Zaccheus (vs. 8–10) apparently took place in the court of his house, or near the entrance, where the crowd had followed. Olshausen supposes it to have been on the morning of His departure, but there is no good ground for this. It is not certain where the parable of the nobleman (vs. 11–27) was spoken, but it would seem from the connection that He was still standing by the door of Zaccheus' house.[1] Some, who suppose that He merely passed a few hours with Zaccheus, and then journeyed on toward Bethany the same day, make all from vs. 8–27 to have been spoken at His departure.[2] We need not, however, understand v. 28 as meaning that, immediately after He had uttered the parable, He went up to Jerusalem.

Of Zaccheus little more is known than is here related. He was not, as some have said, a heathen; but, as appears both from his name and from v. 9, of Jewish descent.[3] He was a chief publican, or head collector of the taxes, having the other publicans of that region under him. Jericho was rich in balsams, and therefore much toll was collected here. According to tradition, Zaccheus became bishop of Cæsarea. A tower, standing in the modern village of Riha, is still shown as the "house of Zaccheus."

[1] So Meyer, Lichtenstein. [2] Oosterzee in loco; Stier, iv. 318.
[3] So Meyer, Alford.

PART VI.

FROM THE ARRIVAL AT BETHANY TO THE RESURRECTION; OR FROM MARCH 31ST (8TH NISAN) TO APRIL 9TH (17TH NISAN) 783. A.D. 30.

FRIDAY, 31ST MARCH—SATURDAY, 1ST APRIL.

Arriving at Bethany, He abides there for the night.	JOHN xii. 1–9.
The next day He sups with Simon, a leper,—Lazarus,	MATT. xxvi. 6–13.
Martha, and Mary being present. Here He is anointed	MARK xiv. 3–9.
by Mary, while Judas and others are angry at so great waste. At even, many come out of Jerusalem to see	
Him and Lazarus. The rulers in the city hearing this, consult how they may put Lazarus also to death.	JOHN xii. 10, 11.

THE date of the arrival at Bethany is to be determined from the statement of John, (xii. 1,) that He came "six days before the Passover." But how shall these six days be reckoned? Shall both extremes, the day of His arrival and the Passover, be included, or both excluded? or one included and one excluded? The latter mode of computation is more generally received. Adopting this mode, we reckon from the Passover exclusive to the day of arrival inclusive. But here a new question meets us. What day shall be reckoned as the Passover, the 14th or 15th Nisan? The language of Moses is express, (Levit. xxiii. 5,) "In the fourteenth day of the first month at even is the Lord's Passover." Counting backward from the fourteenth and excluding it, the sixth day, or the day of the arrival at Bethany, was the 8th Nisan.[1] What day of the week was this? If the fourteenth fell on Thursday, the eighth was on Friday preceding; if on Friday, the eighth was on Saturday, or the Jewish Sabbath.

Owing to these differences in the modes of computation, very different results are reached by harmonists. Robinson, including both extremes, and counting from the fourteenth, or Thursday, makes Him to have arrived on Saturday the ninth. Strong, computing the same way, but making the fourteenth to fall on Friday, makes the arrival on Sunday the tenth. Greswell, including one extreme, and placing the Passover on Friday, makes it to have been on Saturday. Luthardt, counting Thursday the 15th as the Passover, makes it to have been on Sunday. Most, however, making the fourteenth Thursday, place it on Friday the eighth.[2] And this seems, on other grounds, the most likely. That Jesus would, without necessity, travel on the Sabbath, we cannot suppose; much less that He would go on that day from Jericho to Bethany, a distance of twelve or fifteen miles.[3] Some, as Robinson, suppose that He went on that day only a Sabbath day's journey; but that He should have come on Friday so near, and then have encamped, to finish the journey after sunset of the Sabbath, is not probable. The supposition of Greswell, that He spent that night at the house of Zaccheus, who lived between Jericho and Bethany, and went on to Bethany the next day, is wholly without proof, and, besides, does not meet the difficulty. We infer that He did journey

[1] So Meyer, Alford.

[2] Friedlieb, Bucher, Wieseler, Lichtenstein, Tholuck.

[3] Wieseler, 378.

directly from Jericho to Bethany · first, from the fact that the whole intervening country is a wilderness, without city or village, where no one would, without necessity, spend the night; second, that He was with the crowd of pilgrims, whose course was direct to Jerusalem, and who would naturally so arrange their movements as to reach it before the Sabbath.

We can easily understand why the Lord should desire to stop at Bethany rather than go on to the city. Here He found repose and peace in a household, whose members were bound to Him by the strongest ties; and here, in seclusion and quiet, He could prepare Himself for the trials and anguish of the coming week; and here continued to be His home till His arrest.

The distance from Jericho to Jerusalem is, according to Josephus,[1] a hundred and fifty furlongs; and from the Jordan to Jericho, sixty. Porter estimates the former at five and a half hours, and the latter at two hours. From Jericho to Bethany is about fifteen miles; and all travellers agree in describing the way as most difficult and dreary.

It is much disputed when the supper was made for the Lord. John merely says: "Then Jesus, six days before the Passover, came to Bethany—there they made Him a supper." This does not determine whether the supper was upon the day of His arrival, or the next, or even later; still the more obvious interpretation is, that it was that day or the next. He also gives us another note of time, in v. 12: "On the next day much people . . . took branches of palm trees," &c. But to what is this "next day" related; to the events immediately preceding (vs. 9, 10) the visit of many of the Jews to Bethany, and the consultation of the chief priests, or to the day of His arrival at Bethany? If to the latter, as by Meyer, the supper must have been in the evening of the day of His arrival; if to the former, as by

[1] War, 4. 8. 3.

Friedlieb, it is left undetermined. Those who put His arrival at Bethany on Saturday, or Sunday, put the supper on the evening of the same day; but most of those who put the arrival on Friday, put the supper on the following evening, or the evening of the Sabbath. And this seems most probable; for the language, "there they made Him a supper," implies that it was a feast given specially in His honor, and not an ordinary repast.[1] The presence of the Jews from Jerusalem, at Bethany, is thus, too, most easily explained; the sojourn of Jesus over the Sabbath giving ample time for His arrival to become known, and for all who wished to visit Him.

That the supper mentioned by Matthew (xxvi. 6–13) and Mark, (xiv. 3–9,) is identical with this of John, has been questioned, but without good grounds.[2] But if identical, why do the former place it in such direct relation to that assembling of the chief priests which took place two days before the Passover? From this relation many have inferred that Matthew and Mark narrate it in chronological order, and that John mentions it by anticipation.[3] If so, it was upon the evening following Tuesday. But the arguments for this order, are not convincing. A close examination of Matt. xxvi. and Mark xiv., shows us that the account of the supper is brought in parenthetically. Two days before the feast of the Passover, the chief priests and elders hold a council at the palace of Caiaphas, the high priest, and consult how they may kill Jesus. They dare not arrest Him openly, and with violence, but will do it by subtlety; yet, even this they fear to do during the feast. The result of their consultation thus was, that the arrest be postponed till the feast was past. But the Lord had

[1] As to feasts upon the Sabbath, see Luke xiv. 1; Winer, ii. 47 and 846.

[2] Lightfoot, Clericus, A. Clarke, McKnight, Whitby, make them distinct. See, contra. Michaelis in Townsend, part v. note 37.

[3] Bynaeus, Newcome, Robinson, Da Costa, Wichelaus, Owen.

declared, that after two days was the Passover, and then He should be betrayed to be crucified. Matthew and Mark, therefore, proceed to show how the Lord's words were fulfilled through the treachery of Judas, and the priests and elders made to change their resolution. This apostate, coming to the priests, offers to betray Him into their hands, and will do it so soon as an opportunity presents. Thus the matter is left between Judas and them, and they await his action.

Turning now to the account of the supper, we ask why it is thus interposed between the consultation of the priests and the action of Judas? Plainly that it may explain his action. He was offended that so much money should be wasted at the anointing of the Lord, and in his covetousness, as here revealed, we find the explanation of his subsequent treachery. But it is said that neither Matthew nor Mark make any special mention of Judas at the supper, and, therefore, give no explanation of his treachery. They say only that certain of the disciples were displeased. It must be admitted, that had we not the narrative of John, it would not be obvious why they should mention this supper in this connection. There may be some reason, unknown to us, why they omit the name of Judas, as the one chiefly offended. Yet, even with this omission, an impartial reader could hardly fail to infer that Matthew and Mark design to say that Judas, the one of the Twelve who went to the priests to betray Jesus, was one of those that had indignation; and that to the supper at Bethany we may trace the immediate origin of the treachery they relate. Some, however, think the supper to be mentioned here upon other grounds.[1] There is nothing in the language of Matthew or Mark, which necessarily implies that this supper took place two days before the Passover; for the

[1] Ebrard, 474; Strong, Har., note 51.

statement of the former, (v. 14,) "Then Judas . . . went unto the chief priests," does not connect the time of his visit with the supper, but with their council, (vs. 3–5.) All between vs. 5–14, comes in parenthetically as an explanatory statement. But against this it is objected,[1] that Judas would not have cherished a purpose of treachery four days in his heart without executing it. But the betrayal of his Lord was not a hasty, passionate act, done in a moment of excitement. It was done coolly, deliberately; and this is what gave it its atrocious character. Greswell remarks (iii. 129) that "this history is divisible into three stages, each of which has been accurately defined; the first cause and conception of his purpose; the overt step toward its execution; and lastly, its consummation. The consummation took place in the garden of Gethsemane; the overt step was the compact with the Sanhedrim; the first cause and conception of the purpose, if they are to be traced up to any thing on record, must be referred to what happened at Bethany."

Although Matthew and Mark speak of Jesus as being in the house of Simon the leper, yet many have supposed that the supper was made by the family of Lazarus, principally from the fact that "Martha served." But against this is the fact that Lazarus appears not as the master of the feast, but as a guest. According to some, it was a feast prepared in common by the disciples and friends of the Lord at Bethany, and held at the house of Simon. Of Simon we have no knowledge; but it is probable that he was a leper, and had been healed by the Lord. One tradition makes him to have been the father of Lazarus.[2] Another makes him to have been the husband of Martha.[3] We may readily believe that, although the supper was at the house of Simon, Martha and Mary may

[1] Robinson, Har. 210.
[2] See Ewald, v. 401, who defends it.
[3] Winer, ii. 464.

have been active helpers in its preparation. It is not necessary to suppose any kindred to explain Martha's service, for she would gladly honor her Lord, to whom she was so deeply indebted, by every act of personal attention it was in her power to render.

How often the Lord was anointed, and by whom, has been much discussed by harmonists and commentators from the earliest times. Some have affirmed that Luke (vii. 37) mentions one anointing; Matthew (xxvi. 7) and Mark (xiv. 3) another; and John (xii. 3) a third. But most have affirmed two anointings; some identifying the narratives of Luke and John,[1] but more identifying that of John with those of Matthew and Mark.[2] A few, as Grotius, affirm that He was but once anointed, making the narratives of the Evangelists all to refer to the same event. It is now generally held that there were two anointings; that mentioned by Luke, and that mentioned by the other Evangelists.[3] In regard to the persons by whom the Lord was anointed, there has been like difference of opinion. It is plain from John, (xi. 2,) that Mary the sister of Lazarus anointed Him once; and we cannot doubt that she is the person alluded to by John, (xii. 3,) and by Matthew and Mark. By whom was He anointed upon the occasion mentioned by Luke? Many affirm that this was also done by the same Mary.[4] This opinion is the ruling one in the Romish Church, being sanctioned in her ritual. The Greek Church, on the other hand, holds them to be different persons.[5] We can scarcely believe that the sister of Lazarus, a member of that family whose society the Lord seems

[1] Jerome, chiefly because both mention the anointing of the feet.

[2] Augustine, Calvin, Bynaeus.

[3] So Newcome, Trench, Tischendorf, Robinson, Meyer.

[4] So Augustine, who refers to John xi. 2, as showing that Mary would not be thus spoken of had there been another person who had done a like act.

[5] Origen and Chrysostom.

often to have sought, whom He loved, and whose name is associated in our minds with His words of praise, (Luke x. 42,) could have been ever a professed harlot, for such it would appear was "the sinner" of whom Luke speaks, (vii. 37.)[1] As the anointings must be distinguished from each other as to time and place, there is also no sufficient reason why the persons anointing should be identified.[2]

We give the following as the probable order of events. Jesus, leaving Jericho on the morning of Friday, reaches Bethany in the afternoon, perhaps about sunset. He leaves the pilgrims with whom He has journeyed, and who go on to Jerusalem, and with His apostles, stops till the Sabbath should be past; they being probably received by some of His friends, and He Himself doubtless finding a home in the dwelling of Lazarus and his sisters. The next day, being the Sabbath, is spent at Bethany, and in the afternoon Simon the leper makes Him a supper, at which His disciples, and Lazarus and his sisters, were present. During the afternoon the Jews of Jerusalem, who had heard through the pilgrims of His arrival, go out to see Him and Lazarus, and some of them believe on Him. This, coming to the ears of the chief priests, leads to a consultation how Lazarus may be put to death with Jesus.

SUNDAY, 2D APRIL, 10TH NISAN, 783. A. D. 30.

Leaving Bethany, He sends to Bethphage for an ass upon which to ride, and sitting upon it He enters Jerusalem amidst the shouts of His disciples, and of the populace. As He looks upon the city from the Mount of Olives He weeps over it. All the city is greatly moved, and the Pharisees desire Him to rebuke His	MATT. xxi. 1–11. MARK xi. 1–10. LUKE xix. 29–44. JOHN xii. 12–19.

[1] See note upon this passage, p. 259.

[2] As to the opinion of some that this Mary is the same as Mary Magdalene, see page 260.

disciples. He visits the temple; but, after looking around Him, leaves it, and goes out with the Twelve to Bethany, where He passes the night. MARK xi. 11.

Placing the Lord's arrival at Bethany on Friday, the supper and anointing on Saturday, His solemn entry into the city took place on Sunday.[1] As to the hour of the entry nothing is said, but from Mark xi. 11 it appears that it was late in the afternoon when He entered the temple; and, as no events intermediate are mentioned, the entry into the temple seems to have been soon after the entry into the city. It was, then, probably near the middle of the day when He left Bethany. Luthardt, who puts the supper on Sunday, makes the entry to have been still later upon the same day; but this would have brought it to the verge of evening. Greswell puts His departure from Bethany about the ninth hour, or 3 P. M.; his arrival in the temple before the eleventh, His departure before sunset.

The position of Bethphage, "house of figs," which is mentioned by the Synoptists in connection with Bethany, is much disputed. It may be inferred from Mark, (xi. 1,) "And when they came nigh to Jerusalem, unto Bethphage and Bethany, at the Mount of Olives," and the like expression in Luke xix. 29, that they were two distinct yet adjacent villages; but their relative positions to each other are not defined. From the fact, however, that Bethphage is first mentioned, the journey being from Jericho to Jerusalem, or from east to west, it is supposed that it was first reached, and therefore east of Bethany.[2] Others, however, maintain that the Evangelists in their narratives take Jerusalem as the centre, and mention Bethphage first, because first reached by

[1] So Lichtenstein, Robinson, Wieseler, Bucher, Friedlieb, Wichelhaus, Meyer.

[2] Winer, i. 174; Robinson, Meyer.

one going to the east.[1] Another reason for this order is given by Greswell, (iii. 75 :) " Bethphage lay upon the direct line of this route, but Bethany did not; so that one travelling from Jericho would come to Bethphage first, and would have to turn off from the road to go to Bethany." Lightfoot, (x. 76,) relying upon Talmudical authorities, would put Bethphage just under the city walls, and ascribe to it the same privileges as if actually within them. " The first space from the city, toward the Mount of Olives, was called Bethphage." He also speaks of " Bethphage within the walls and Bethphage without the walls." In like manner Alford speaks of it: " A considerable suburb, nearer to Jerusalem than Bethany, and sometimes reckoned part of the city."[2] A late tradition marks its site as about 100 paces below the top of the Mount, toward the east; but no traces of ruins, according to Robinson, exist there. Some suppose that Bethphage and Bethany are only designations for different parts of the same village.[3]

In his recent investigations in the neighborhood of Jerusalem, Barclay (65) found a site which he imagines to answer all the demands of the narrative. It is upon " a spur of Olivet, distant rather more than a mile from the city, situated between two deep valleys, on which there are tanks, foundations, and other indubitable evidences of the former existence of a village." This seems to be the same site to which Porter refers, upon the projecting point of a ridge, and marked by " scarped rocks, cisterns, and old stones."

Without attempting to define the exact position of Bethphage, we may thus arrange the circumstances connected with the Lord's departure from Bethany: Leaving this village on foot, attended by His disciples and others,

[1] Lichtenstein, Ellicott. [2] So Wieseler, 435, note.

[3] So Porter, (i. 188,) who refers to the similarity of their names, "house of figs" and " house of dates."

He comes to the place where the neighboring village of Bethphage is in view, over against them, perhaps separated from them by a valley. At this point He arrests His march, and sends two of His disciples; to find and bring to Him an ass tied, and her colt with her. When her owners demanded of them why they took the ass, they had only to say that the Lord had need of it, and the sight of Jesus, with the attendant crowds, would at once explain why He needed it. It is not, therefore, necessary to suppose that the owners were His disciples; much less that any previous arrangement had been made with them. Some would make the village where the ass was found, a village in the vicinity, distinct from Bethphage.[1] But there is no necessity for this. The animal being brought to Him, He is seated upon it, and, amidst the acclamations of the multitude, ascends to the top of the Mount.

As both the ass and her colt were brought, it has been questioned upon which the Lord rode. But Mark and Luke are express that it was the colt.[2] The multitude that accompanied the Lord was composed, in part, of those going up to the city from the neighborhood, and of the pilgrims from Galilee and Perea on their way thither; and, in part, of those who, hearing of His coming, had gone out from the city to meet Him, (John xii. 12, 13.) It is probable that most of the latter were pilgrims, not inhabitants of the city, and are spoken of by John as "people that were come to the feast." The priests, and scribes, and Pharisees, stood as angry or contemptuous spectators, and not only refused to join in the rejoicings and hosannas, but bade Him rebuke His disciples, and command them to be silent, (Luke xix. 39.)

The road by which the Lord passed over Olivet was probably the southern or main road, which passes between

[1] Ebrard, 477; Greswell, iii. 78.
[2] See Ebrard, 480; Meyer in loco.

the summit which contains the Tombs of the Prophets, and that called the Mount of Offence. This was the usual road for horsemen and caravans; a steep footpath leads over the central peak, and a winding road over the northern shoulder, neither of which could He have taken. Stanley (187) thus describes the procession: "Two vast streams of people met on that day. The one poured out from the city, and, as they came through the gardens whose clusters of palm rose on the southeastern corner of Olivet, they cut down the long branches, as was their wont at the feast of Tabernacles, and moved upward toward Bethany with loud shouts of welcome. From Bethany streamed forth the crowds who had assembled there the previous night. The road soon loses sight of Bethany . . . The two streams met midway. Half of the vast mass, turning round, preceded; the other half followed. Gradually the long procession swept up over the ridge where first begins 'the descent of the Mount of Olives' toward Jerusalem. At this point the first view is caught of the southeastern corner of the city. The temple and the more northern portions are hid by the slope of Olivet on the right; what is seen is only Mount Zion . . . It was at this precise point, 'as He drew near, at the descent of the Mount of Olives,' (may it not have been from the sight thus opening upon them?) that the shout of triumph burst forth from the multitude: 'Hosanna to the Son of David! Blessed is He that cometh in the name of the Lord!' Again the procession advanced. The road descends a slight declivity, and the glimpse of the city is again withdrawn behind the intervening ridge of Olivet. A few moments, and the path mounts again; it climbs a rugged ascent; it reaches a ledge of smooth rock, and in an instant the whole city bursts into view. It is hardly possible to doubt that this rise and turn of the road, this rocky ledge, was the exact point where the multitude paused again; and 'He, when He beheld the city,' wept over it."

Tradition makes the Lord to have crossed the summit of the Mount of Olives, and puts the spot where He wept over the city about half-way down on its western slope.[1]

This entry of Jesus into Jerusalem, "the city of the great king," was a formal assertion of His Messianic claims. It was the last appeal to the Jews to discern and recognize His royal character. He came as a king, and permitted His disciples and the multitude to pay Him kingly honors. He received, as rightly belonging to Him, the acclamations, "Hosanna to the Son of David! Blessed is He that cometh in the name of the Lord." "Blessed be the kingdom of our father David, that cometh in the name of the Lord." "Blessed be the king that cometh in the name of the Lord: peace in heaven and glory in the highest." "Hosanna! Blessed is the King of Israel, that cometh in the name of the Lord." He was the Son of David, the King of Israel, coming in the name of the Lord. But, although this triumphal entry excited general attention—"all the city was moved," (Matt. xxi. 10,) yet it is plain from the question put by the citizens, "Who is this?" that, as a body, they had taken little part in the matter. "And the multitude said, This is Jesus, the prophet of Nazareth of Galilee," (v. 11.) This multitude, thus distinguished from the citizens, consisted doubtless of those who had escorted Him from Bethany, and who were mostly Galileans; and their answer, as remarked by Meyer, seems to show a kind of local pride in Him as from Galilee, their own prophet. But this very answer was peculiarly adapted to set the people of Judea against Him. (See John vii. 52.)

The visit to the temple, and its purification, are put by Matthew (xxi. 12) as if immediately following the entry;

[1] See Van de Velde's Map of Jerusalem; Ellicott, 288, note 1.

but Mark (xi. 11) states that He merely entered the temple, and, looking around Him, went out because the even had come, and returned to Bethany with the Twelve. Luke (xix. 45) gives us no mark of time. The statement of Mark is so precise, that we cannot hesitate to give it the preference.[1] Some suppose the Lord to have twice purified the temple; on the day of His entry, and again the next day.[2] Others, that He began it on one day and finished it on the next, cleansing first the inner and then the outer court. Patritius makes Him to have healed the blind and lame, to have answered the priests and scribes, (Matt. xxi. 14–16,) and to have heard the request of the Greeks, (John xii. 20–22,) on this first entry. Alford's supposition,[3] that Mark relates the triumphal entry a day too soon; that Jesus, in fact, first entered the city privately, noticed the abuses in the temple, and, returning to Bethany the next day, made His triumphal entry; has no good basis. A private entry before the public one conflicts with the whole tenor of the narrative.

After looking about the temple, ("round about upon all things," Mark,) as if He would observe whether all was done according to His Father's will, He goes out, and returns to Bethany. Greswell (iii. 100) remarks: "It is probable that the traders, with their droves of cattle and their other effects, had already removed them for the day." But, if so, He saw by plain marks that His Father's house was still made a house of merchandise. There can be little doubt that He spent the nights during Passion week in this village, and probably in the house of Lazarus. Matthew says, (xxi. 17:) "He went out of the city, into Bethany, and He lodged there." Luke, speaking in general terms, says, (xxi. 37:) "And in the day-time He was teaching in

[1] Wieseler, Lange, Alexander, Robinson, Tischendorf, Bucher, Meyer, Ellicott.

[2] Lightfoot, Townsend; see Greswell, iii. 99.

[3] Note on Matt. xxi. 1.

the temple, and at night He went out and abode (lodged) in the mount that is called of Olives." Probably Bethany is here meant as a district embracing a part of the mount, for He could not well, at this season of the year, without a tent, lodge in the open air. Alexander supposes that Luke would suggest, that "a part of these nights was employed in prayer amidst the solitudes of Olivet." Some would put the request of the Greeks to see Jesus, and His answer to them, (John xii. 20–36,) upon this day; but it may better be referred to Tuesday, upon grounds to be there given.

Many would bring this visit of Jesus to the temple on the 10th Nisan into connection with the divine command to choose this day a lamb for the paschal sacrifice and supper, (Ex. xii. 3–6,) and thus find in it a mystical significance. He was the true Paschal Lamb, and was now set apart for the sacrifice.[1]

Monday, 3d April, 11th Nisan, 783. A. D. 30.

Jesus, leaving Bethany early with His disciples, was hungry, and beholding a fig tree by the way which had no fruit, He pronounced a curse against it.	Matt. xxi. 18, 19. Mark xi. 12–14.
Proceeding to the city, He enters the temple and purifies it. He heals there the blind and lame, and the children cry, "Hosanna to the Son of David." His reproofs enrage the priests and scribes, who seek how to destroy Him. In the evening He departs, and returns to Bethany.	Matt. xxi. 12–16. Mark xi. 15–19. Luke xix. 45–48.

Both Matthew and Mark relate that the Lord was hungry as He returned into the city; but upon what ground He had abstained from food that morning, does not appear. It could not well have been from the early hour of His departure from Bethany, but was probably a self-imposed

[1] Whitby, Greswell, Alford, Wieseler.

fast. It has been inferred from this circumstance that He could not have spent the night with His friends. It may have been spent in solitude and prayer.

Into an examination of the supposed moral difficulties connected with the cursing of the fig tree, we cannot here enter.[1] It is plain that this miracle is narrated because of its symbolic teachings. The fig tree was the type of the Jewish people, (Luke xiii. 6–9.) They had the law, the temple, all rites of worship, the externals of righteousness; but bore none of its true fruits. Christ found nothing but leaves.

Matthew relates the withering of the fig tree as if it took place, not only on the same day on which it was cursed, but within a few moments, (vs. 19, 20.) Mark, on the other hand, speaks as if the withering was not seen by the disciples till the next day, (xi. 20.) Greswell, who supposes that the malediction instantly took effect, and that the tree began at once to wither, would make Matthew and Mark refer to two distinct conversations between the Lord and the disciples; one that day, and the other upon the next. More probably, Matthew brings together all that occurred upon both days, in order to complete his narrative.[2]

That this purification of the temple is distinct from that at the beginning of His ministry, (John ii. 13–17,) has been already shown. That the latter was passed over by the Synoptists, is explained from the fact that they begin their account of Jesus' ministry with His departure to Galilee after John the Baptist's imprisonment. That John should omit the former, is wholly in keeping with the character of his Gospel. The first cleansing and rebuke had wrought no permanent results, and the old abuses were restored in full vigor.

After cleansing the temple, or that part of the court of

[1] See Trench on Miracles, p. 346.

[2] So Alford, Trench, Krafft, Wieseler.

the Gentiles called "the shops," where every day was sold wine, salt, oil, as also oxen and sheep,[1] He permits the blind and lame, probably those who asked alms at the gates, to come to Him, and He healed them. These healings, and the expressions of wonder and gratitude which they called forth, joined to the remembrance of the acclamations that had greeted Him the day before, led the children in the temple, who may have been members of the choir of singers employed in the temple service, to cry, "Hosanna to the Son of David," greatly to the displeasure of the priests and scribes. It is remarkable that children only are mentioned, and may indicate that already the multitude, overawed by the firm and hostile bearing of His enemies, had begun to waver, and dared no more openly express their good will. (See, however, Mark xi. 18.)

Some, from the fact that the children are here mentioned as crying Hosanna, and that in the temple, make it to have been on the day of the Lord's entry.[2] But there is no difficulty in believing that the children might now re-echo what they had heard a few hours before.[3]

Tuesday, 4th April, 12th Nisan, 783. A. D. 30.

Returning into the city in the morning with His disciples, they saw the fig tree dried up from the roots, and this leads Jesus to speak to them respecting faith. As	Mark xi. 20–26. Matt. xxi. 20–22.
He entered the temple, the Pharisees ask Him by what authority He acts. He replies by a question respecting the baptism of John, and adds the parables of the two sons and of the wicked husbandmen. The Pharisees wish to arrest Him, but are afraid of the people. He speaks of the parable of the king's son. The Pharisees and Herodians propose to Him the question concern-	Matt. xxi. 23–46. Mark xi. 27–33. Luke xx. 1–18. Mark xii. 1–13. Matt. xxii. 1–14. Matt. xxii. 15-46. Mark xii. 13–40.

[1] See Lightfoot on Matt. xxi. 12. [2] Alford, Newcome, Robinson.
[3] Krafft, Wieseler, Lichtenstein, Ellicott.

ing the lawfulness of tribute to Cæsar. The Sadducees question Him respecting the resurrection of the dead; and a lawyer, Which is the chief commandment in the law? He asks the Pharisees a question respecting the Messiah, and puts them to silence, and addressing the disciples and people denounces their hypocrisy. LUKE xx. 19–47. MATT. xxiii.

After this He watches the people casting in their gifts, and praises the poor widow who casts in two mites. Some Greeks desiring to see Him, He prophesies of His death. A voice is heard from heaven. He speaks a few words to the people and leaves the temple. As He goes out, the disciples point out to Him the size and splendor of the buildings, to whom He replies that all shall be thrown down. Ascending the Mount of Olives He seats Himself, and explains to Peter, James, John, and Andrew, the course of events till His return. He adds, that after two days was the Passover, when He should be betrayed. He goes to Bethany, and the same evening, His enemies hold a council and agree with Judas respecting His betrayal. MARK xii. 41–44. LUKE xxi. 1–4. JOHN xii. 20–36. MARK xiii. 1–37. LUKE xxi. 5–36. MATT. xxiv. xxv. MATT. xxvi. 1–5. MARK xiv, 1, 2. MAT. xxvi. 14–16. Mark xiv. 10, 11.

The withering of the fig tree seems to have begun as soon as the Lord had spoken the curse against it. Matthew says, "presently the fig tree withered away." Mark says, "it was dried up from the roots." In twenty-four hours it was completely dead. That the disciples did not at evening, upon their return to Bethany, see that it had withered, may be owing to the late hour of their return, or that they did not pass by it.

The people assembling at an early hour in the temple, Jesus goes thither immediately upon His arrival in the city, and begins to teach. Very soon the chief priests and elders of the people, and scribes, came to Him, demanding by what authority He acted. It seems a question formally put to Him, and probably by a deputation from the Sanhedrim.[1] It differs essentially from the question put to Him after the first purification, (John ii. 18,) "What sign shew-

[1] So Alexander, Meyer.

est thou unto us, seeing thou doest these things?" Now it is, "By what authority doest thou these things? And who gave thee this authority?" Then, they desired that He should work miracles as signs or proofs of His divine mission. But His miracles had not been sufficient to convince them. Now, he must give other vouchers. He must show himself to be authorized by those who, sitting in Moses' seat, were alone able to confer authority. But they had not authorized Him, and He was therefore acting in an arbitrary and illegal manner. To this question He replies by another respecting the baptism of John. The Baptist had borne his testimony to Him when, three years before, they had sent a deputation to him, (John i. 26.) If John was a prophet, and divinely commissioned, why had they not received his testimony? This was a dilemma they could not escape. They could not condemn themselves; they dare not offend the people; they must remain silent.

Although thus repulsed, yet, His enemies continuing in the temple, He begins to speak to them in parables, (Mark xii. 1;) "the second beginning," says Stier, "as before in Galilee, so now in Jerusalem." It is to be noted that now, for the first time, the Lord utters plainly the truth in the hearing of the Pharisees, that they shall kill Him, and that in consequence the kingdom shall be taken from them.[1] The point of these parables was not missed by the Pharisees, but they dare not arrest Him.

The parable of the marriage of the king's son is related by Matthew only, for that in Luke (xiv. 16–24) was spoken much earlier.[2] It set forth more distinctly than the parables preceding, the rejection of the Jews, those bidden of old; the bidding of others in their place; and the destruction of their city.

[1] See Matt. viii. 11, 12. These words seem to have been spoken to the disciples.

[2] Meyer, Alford, Robinson, Tischendorf, Lichtenstein, Trench.

Stung by these parables, so full of sharp rebuke, the Pharisees now consult together how "they may entangle Him in His talk." Never were their craft and inveterate hostility more strikingly shown, than in these attempts to draw something from His own mouth which might serve as the basis of accusation against Him. The first question would have been full of peril to one less wise than Himself, for it appealed to the most lively political susceptibilities of the people. No zealous Jew could admit that tribute was rightly due to Cæsar, and much less could one who claimed to be the Messiah admit this; for it was to confess that He was the vassal of the Romans, a confession utterly incompatible with Messianic claims. Yet if He denied this, the Herodians were at hand to accuse him of treason, an accusation which the Romans were always quick to hear. But He avoided the artfully contrived snare by referring the question to their own discernment. God had chosen them for His people, and He alone should be their king, and therefore it was not right for them to be under heathen domination. Yet, because of their sins, God had given them into the hands of their enemies, and they were now under Roman rule. This fact they must recognize, and in view of this they must fulfil all duties, those to Cæsar as well as those to God.

The question of the Sadducees was in keeping with the sceptical, scoffing character of that sect. Apparently, it was not so much designed to awake popular hatred against Him as to cast ridicule upon Him, and also upon their rivals, the Pharisees, by showing the absurd consequences of one of their most cherished dogmas, the resurrection of the dead. Perhaps, also, they were curious to see how He would meet an argument to which their rivals had been able to give no satisfactory answer.[1]

The question of the lawyer seems to have been without

[1] See Meyer in loco.

any malicious motive on his part.[1] It referred to a disputed point among the schools of the Rabbis, and which he, admiring the wisdom of Jesus, wished to hear solved. Some, however, suppose (see Matt. xxii. 34) that the lawyer was sent by the Pharisees, who had gathered together to devise a new attack.[2] But these two views are not really inconsistent. The lawyer, a man of ability and reputation, and on these grounds chosen to be their representative and spokesman, may have had a sincere respect for that wisdom that had marked Christ's previous answers. He proposes this question respecting the comparative value of the commandments, rather to test His knowledge in the law than to array the people against him. Had the answer been erroneous, doubtless advantage would have been taken of it to His injury, although it is not obvious to us in what way; but it so commended itself to the intelligence of the lawyer, that he honestly and frankly expresses his approbation. (See Mark xii. 32–34.)

All his adversaries being silenced, the Lord proceeds in His turn to ask a question that should test their own knowledge, and inquires how the Messiah could be the Son of David, and yet David call Him Lord? Their inability to answer Him shows us how little the truth that the Messiah should be a divine being, the Son of God, as well as Son of man, was yet apprehended by them; and how all Christ's efforts to reveal His true nature had failed, through their wickedness and unbelief.

It is questioned whether the Lord's words to the scribes (Mark xii. 38–40; Luke xx. 45–47) are to be distinguished from those recorded by Matthew, xxiii. Greswell (iii. 121) gives ten reasons for distinguishing between them, which, however, have no great weight. Most regard them as identical.[3] Wieseler (395) supposes Mat-

[1] Greswell, Alford. [2] Meyer, Ebrard.

[3] Ebrard, Meyer, Alford, Robinson, Krafft.

thew to have included the address to the Pharisees, recorded by Luke xi. 39–52. The attempts of the Pharisees to entrap Him, their malice and wickedness veiled under the show of righteousness, awaken the Lord's deepest indignation, and explain the terrible severity of His language. They had proved that "they were the children of them which killed the prophets;" and as the old messengers of God had been rejected and slain, so should they reject and slay those whom He was about to send. Thus should all the righteous blood shed upon the earth come upon them.

It is not certain who was the "Zacharias son of Barachias," to whom the Lord refers as slain between the temple and the altar. Many identify him with the Zechariah son of Jehoiada, who was "stoned with stones, at the commandment of the king in the court of the house of the Lord," (2 Chron. xxiv. 20, 21.) In this case, Barachias may have been another name of Jehoiada, as the Jews had often two names; or Barachias may have been the father, and Jehoiada the grandfather; or, as it is omitted by Luke xi. 51, some, as Meyer, infer that it was not mentioned by Christ, but was added from tradition, and erroneously given, perhaps confounding him with the Zechariah son of Berechiah, (Zech. i. 1.) But if this Zacharias was meant, why is he called the last of the martyrs, since there were others later? The explanation given by Lightfoot is at least probable, that it was the last example in the Old Testament as the canon was then arranged, and therefore the Lord cites the first, that of Abel, and this as the last. Both have also another circumstance in common; a call of the murdered for vengeance. "The requiring of vengeance is mentioned only concerning Abel and Zacharias. 'Behold the voice of thy brother's blood crieth unto me,' (Gen. iv. 10.) 'Let the Lord look upon it and require it,'"

(2 Chron. xxiv. 22.[1]) Others make this Zechariah to be prophetically spoken of, and identify him with the Zecharias son of Baruch mentioned by Josephus,[2] who was slain by the Zealots in the midst of the temple, and the body cast into the valley of the Kidron. But the Lord does not speak of blood to be yet shed, but of that which had been shed; and as the death of Abel was a well-known historical event, so also was that of Zacharias. Others refer to a tradition that Zacharias, father of John the Baptist, was murdered by the Jews.[3]

Many make this discourse to the Pharisees to have been spoken just before He left the temple, and His last words there. "It is morally certain," says Greswell, "that our Lord immediately left the temple, and never returned to it again." But most follow the order of Mark, (xii. 41–44,) who places the visit of Jesus to the treasury after this discourse.[4] Seating Himself by the treasury, or treasure chests in the court of the women, in which offerings were placed, He watches those who come to bring their gifts.

The visit of the Greeks to Him is mentioned only by John, (xii. 20–36.) Some place it upon the evening of the triumphal entry.[5] But the Lord's language fits better to the final departure from the temple than to the time of the entry. Beside, if He was now in the court of the women, it explains the request of the Greeks to see Him; for if He had been in the outer court, all could have seen Him; but into the inner court they could not come. Upon these, and other grounds, it is placed here by many.[6] It is not

[1] So Meyer, Alford, Lange; see Winer, ii. 711.

[2] War, 4. 5. 4.

[3] Thilo, Codex Apoc. i. 267; Hofmann, Leben Jesu, 134; Jones on the Canon of the N. Test., ii. 134. According to the latter, this tradition was very generally credited in early times, as by Tertullian, Origen, Epiphanius. See also Baronius, who defends it.

[4] Krafft, Friedlieb, Robinson, Wieseler, Ellicott, Tischendorf.

[5] Greswell, Krafft, Ebrard, Townsend, Stier.

[6] Robinson, Lichtenstein, Tischendorf, Wieseler, Ellicott.

certain whether these Greeks did actually meet the Lord. His words (vs. 23–27) were not addressed directly to them, but they may have been within hearing. Their coming is a sign that His end is nigh, and that the great work for which He came into the world, is about to be fulfilled. Stier sets this visit of the Greeks from the west, in contrast to the visit of the Magi from the east; the one at the end, the other at the beginning of His life.

In reply to the Lord's prayer—"Glorify Thy name," (v. 28)—there "came a voice from heaven, I have both glorified it, and will glorify it again." These words, according to most interpreters, were spoken in an audible voice. It is said by Alford, "This voice can no otherwise be understood than as a plain articulate sound, miraculously spoken, heard by all, and variously interpreted." This would imply that all present heard the words plainly articulated. But this is not said. They heard a voice; yet some said, "It thundered;" and others, "An angel spake to Him;" which could not have been the case if the words had been distinctly spoken.

Probably, the capacity to understand the voice was dependent upon each man's spiritual condition and receptivity. To Jesus, and, perhaps, to the apostles and disciples, it was an articulate voice; to others it was indistinct, yet they recognized it as a voice, perhaps of an angel; to others still, it was mere sound, as if it thundered.[1] Townsend would make it an answer to the Greeks who desired to see Jesus, or, at least, spoken in their hearing. We find, however, its true significance if we compare it with those other testimonies of the Father to Him at His baptism and at His transfiguration. (Matt. iii. 17; xvii. 5.)

After Jesus had finished His words in the temple, He "departed, and did hide Himself from them," (v. 36.) His departing and hiding are not to be understood of a night's

[1] See Luthardt in loco.

sojourn in Bethany, but of His final departure from the temple, and His sojourn in retirement till His arrest. His public work was over. He appears no more in His Father's house as a preacher of righteousness. Henceforth all His words of wisdom are addressed to His own disciples. The statements (vs. 37–43) are those of the Evangelist. But when were the Lord's words (vs. 44–50) spoken? Most regard them as a citation by the Evangelist from earlier discourses, and introduced here as confirming his own remarks.[1]

The allusion of the disciples to the size and splendor of the temple buildings, seems to have been occasioned by His words to the Pharisees foretelling its desolation, (Matt. xxiii. 38.) That so substantial and massive a structure could become desolate, was incredible to them, for they had as yet no distinct conception that God was about to cast off His own covenant people, and bring the worship He had appointed to an end. This manifestation of incredulity led Him to say, with great emphasis, that the buildings should be utterly destroyed, not one stone being left upon another. This was literally fulfilled in the destruction of the temple, though some of the walls enclosing it were not wholly cast down. It was a prediction that, made public, would have greatly angered the Jews, and hence the apostles came to Him "privately" to learn its meaning.

It was probably at the close of the day, perhaps in the twilight, that He sat down on the Mount of Olives over against the temple. The city lay in full view before Him. Mark (xiii. 3) speaks of only four of the apostles, Peter and James, and John and Andrew, who asked Him privately when these things should be. Matthew (xxiv. 3) states that "the disciples came unto Him privately;" Luke (xxi. 7) that "they asked Him." There can be little doubt that

[1] Lichtenstein, Meyer, Alford, Tholuck, Tischendorf. Luthardt and Wieseler make them to have been spoken to the disciples.

Mark gives the more accurate account, and that these four only were present.[1] The remainder of the Twelve may have preceded Him on the way to Bethany. Alexander supposes that all were present, and that "the four are only mentioned as particularly earnest in making this inquiry, although speaking with and for the rest."

If His words were spoken to these four only, it implies that the predictions He uttered could not at that time be fittingly spoken to the body of the apostles.

The announcement to the disciples (Matt. xxvi. 1, 2) that "after two days was the Passover, when the Son of man should be betrayed to be crucified," was probably made soon after His discourse upon the Mount of Olives, and so upon the evening of Tuesday. Perhaps, He wished distinctly to remind them that His coming in glory must be preceded by His death and resurrection. Whether it was made to all the disciples or to the four, is not certain, but probably to all. Alford thinks that "it gives no certainty as to the time when the words were said: we do not know whether the current day was included or otherwise." If, however, Thursday was the 14th Nisan, or the Passover, according to the rule already adopted, excluding one of the extremes and including the other, the announcement was made on Tuesday.[2] The meeting of the chief priests and the scribes and elders at the palace of Caiaphas for consultation, was upon the same evening. This may be inferred, at least, from Matthew's words, (xxvi. 3,) "Then assembled together," &c., the assembly being on the same day when the words were spoken, (v. 2.)[3] From the fact that the council met at the palace of Caiaphas, and also that its session was in the evening, we may infer that it was an

[1] Lichtenstein, Alford, Lange, Greswell.
[2] Meyer, Lichtenstein, De Wette.
[3] Meyer; Ellicott places it on Wednesday.

extraordinary meeting, held for secret consultation.[1] It may readily be supposed that the severe language of the Lord had greatly enraged His enemies, and that they felt the necessity of taking immediate steps against Him. But they dared not arrest him during the feast, because of the people, and determined to postpone it till the feast was past. Thus, it may be, at the same hour when Jesus was foretelling that He shall suffer at the Passover, His enemies were resolving that they would not arrest Him during the feast.[2] But the divine prediction was accomplished in a way they had not anticipated. Judas, one of the Twelve, coming to them, offers, for money, to betray Him into their hands. They at once make a covenant with him, and he watches for an opportunity. Still it does not appear that he designed to betray Him during the feast; and his action on the evening following the Paschal supper was, as we shall see, forced upon him by the Lord. Whether Judas presented himself to the council at their session, is not said; but it is not improbable that, hearing the Lord's rebukes of their hypocrisy, and seeing how great was their exasperation against Him, he had watched their movements, and learned of their assembly at the high priest's palace. This gave him the wished-for opportunity to enter into an agreement with them. Some, as Ellicott, put this visit of Judas to the priests and elders on Wednesday.

[1] Tradition makes the bargain with Judas to have been entered into at the country house of Caiaphas, the ruins of which are still shown upon the summit of the Hill of Evil Counsel. The tradition is not ancient; but it is mentioned, as a singular fact, that the monument of Annas, who may have had a country-seat near his son-in-law, is found in this neighborhood. Williams, H. C. ii. 496.

[2] Some understand that they proposed to arrest Him before the feast. So Neander, Ewald; see, contra, Meyer in loco.

WEDNESDAY, 5TH APRIL, 13TH NISAN, 783. A. D. 30.

During this day the Lord remained in seclusion at Bethany.

The Lord left the temple for the last time on Tuesday afternoon. His public labors were ended. There remained, however, a few hours before the Passover. How was this period spent? We can well believe that some part of it was spent alone, that He might enjoy that free communion with God which He had so earnestly sought in the midst of His active labors, and which was now doubly dear to Him in view of His speedy death. Some part of it, also, was doubtless devoted to His disciples, giving them such counsel and encouragement as was demanded by the very peculiar and trying circumstances in which they were placed. That Wednesday was spent in retirement, is generally admitted.[1]

THURSDAY, 6TH APRIL, 14TH NISAN, 783. A. D. 30.

From Bethany He sends Peter and John into the city to prepare the Passover. He describes a man whom they should meet, and who should show them a room furnished, where they should make ready for	MATT. xxvi. 17-19. MARK xiv. 12-16. LUKE xxii. 7-13.
the supper. He remains at Bethany till toward evening, when He enters the city, and goes to the room where the supper was to be eaten.	MATT. xxvi. 20. MARK xiv. 17. LUKE xxii. 14.

At this feast the Jews divided themselves into companies, or households, of not less than ten nor more than twenty persons; and these together consumed the paschal lamb.[2] One of the number, acting as the representative of

[1] Wieseler, Robinson, Ellicott.

[2] Exod. xii. 3, 4; Josephus, War, 6. 9. 3.

all, presented the lamb in the court of the temple, and aided the Levites in its sacrifice. The victim was then carried away by the offerer to the house where it was to be eaten, and there wholly consumed. On this occasion Peter and John acted as the representatives of the Lord and of His apostles at the temple, and provided the bread, wine, bitter herbs, and all that was necessary for the proper celebration of the feast. It appears that, up to this time, the disciples did not know where the Lord would eat the Passover, and, as the hour drew nigh, inquired of Him, (Matt. xxvi. 17.) According to Mark and Luke, the two apostles were to go to the city, and a man should meet them bearing a pitcher of water, whom they should follow into whatsoever house he entered. There they should find a guest-chamber, furnished and prepared, which the master of the house should place at their disposal. Matthew says nothing of their meeting the man with the pitcher, but makes the two to have gone directly to the house. Meyer supposes that Matthew follows the early tradition, which represents the master of the house as a disciple of Jesus, who had, earlier in the week, arranged with Him for the use of the guest-chamber; and that Mark and Luke follow a later tradition, which represents the Lord as ignorant of the man, but giving directions to the two through prophetic foresight. There is no need of thus supposing two traditions. Matthew passes over in silence the incident of the man with the pitcher, upon what grounds we cannot state, (Alford supposes, perhaps from ignorance;) but this silence is no way inconsistent with the statements of the other Evangelists. From Mark and Luke it is apparent that no agreement had been made by the Lord for the room; else He would not have given such directions to the two apostles, but have sent them directly to the house.[1] Whether the master of the house were an entire stranger to Jesus, or a concealed

[1] Alford, Alexander.

disciple, like Joseph or Nicodemus, or an open follower, is not certain.[1] The Lord's message to him, "My time is at hand. I will keep the Passover at thy house, with my disciples," seems, however, to presuppose some previous acquaintance; as also the phrase, "the Master saith." This, however, is not necessary, if, as said by Alexander, "the whole proceeding be regarded as extraordinary, and the result secured by a special superhuman influence."

It is at this point that we meet the difficult questions connected with the last Passover. For the sake of brevity and clearness, we shall pursue the following order in our inquiries: I. State the real or supposed discrepancies between the statements of Matthew, Mark, and Luke, on the one hand, and of John on the other. II. Give an outline of the various attempts to harmonize them. III. State the results.

I. We consider the real or supposed discrepancies between the Synoptists and John. The day on which the Lord sent Peter and John to prepare the Passover was, according to Matthew, (xxvi. 17,) "the first day of the feast of unleavened bread." Mark and Luke use similar language. From these statements, it appears that Jesus partook of the paschal supper at the same time with the Jews in general, and at the time appointed in the law, which was upon the evening following the 14th Nisan. Upon the next day, Friday, the 15th, He was crucified.

If we now turn to John, we find that he speaks as if the paschal supper was legally upon the evening of Friday; and that, consequently, the Lord, who ate it upon the evening of Thursday, ate it before the time. Referring (xviii. 28) to the unwillingness of the Jews to enter the judgment hall on the day of the crucifixion, he says: "They themselves went not into the judgment hall, lest they should

[1] See Bynaeus, i. 480, who gives an account of early opinions.

be defiled, but that they might eat the Passover." From this it follows that, if the Passover was yet to be eaten, and upon the day of His crucifixion, the supper eaten by Jesus and His disciples the evening previous, was not the legal paschal supper. Friday, as the day when the lamb was slain, was the 14th Nisan, and Thursday was the 13th. So, also, John (xix. 14) calls the day on which He was crucified, not the Passover itself, but "the preparation of the Passover," from which it follows that the Passover was yet to come.

It is admitted on all sides, upon grounds to be hereafter stated, that Jesus died on Friday, in the afternoon.[1] The eating of the supper, on the evening previous, was, therefore, on Thursday evening; His resurrection was on the Sunday following. The point in question is respecting the day of the month: Was Friday the 14th or 15th Nisan? It is said that John asserts the former, the Synoptists the latter. We give the discrepancy in tabular form:

St. John.	Synoptists.
Supper eaten, evening of Thursday, 13th Nisan.	Evening of Thursday, 14th Nisan.
Jesus crucified, Friday, 14th Nisan.	Friday, 15th Nisan.
Was in the grave, Saturday, 15th Nisan.	Saturday, 16th "
Resurrection, Sunday, 16th Nisan.	Sunday, 17th "

This difference as to the time of the paschal supper eaten by the Lord, was early noted by Christian writers.[2] Modern criticism has brought it very prominently forward, and attached to it great importance, and it demands, therefore, our careful attention.

II. The attempts to harmonize the Synoptists and John.

1st. That the Jews kept the Passover on two distinct days, both of which were legal. It is said by some that

[1] See, however, Westcott, 320. [2] Wichelhaus, 187.

there were two ways of determining the first day of the month, and consequently the day of the feast, by astronomical calculation and by ocular observation; and thus the paschal lamb might be slain on the 14th Nisan of real, or the 14th of apparent time. One of these modes was followed by the Sadducees, and the other by the Pharisees, and thus the discrepancy between the Synoptists and John is explained. Jesus, with the Sadducees, kept the true day; the Pharisees and most of the Jews the apparent day. If, however, such a difference in the mode of computation did actually exist between the Rabbinites and Karaites after the destruction of Jerusalem, there is no proof that it did before.[1] The only way of determining the beginning of the month practised by the Jews before the capture of the city by Titus, A. D. 70, was the appearance of the new moon. Thus there could not have been, during the Lord's ministry, two legal days for the observance of the Passover; and the supposition that He, with one part of the Jews, rightly observed Thursday, as astronomically correct, and that another part rightly observed Friday, as determined by the appearance of the new moon, is without any foundation.

A modification of this view has lately been presented by Serno.[2] He supposes, that, as the moon in some sections of the country might be seen at its first appearance, and in others be hidden by the clouds, and thus a difference in computation arise, the first day of the feast was doubled, and the paschal supper was lawfully eaten on either. But of this there is no proof. When the authorities at Jerusalem had determined the first of the month, all succeeding days were reckoned from it; and if a Jew from any distant part of the land had mistaken the day of the month through ignorance of the appearing of the moon, he must make the

[1] Winer, ii. 150; Paulus, iii. 486.

[2] Berlin, 1859.

feast days to conform to those fixed upon by the Sanhedrim. Even if the latter had erred, their decision was final. There is not the least evidence that the Passover could be, or ever was, observed upon two successive days.

It has been said by Cudworth,[1] that, the Jews having erred in the day, placing it too late, the Lord corrected the error, and directed the supper to be prepared at the legal time, on Thursday evening. He, also, affirms that it was "a custom among the Jews, in such doubtful cases as these, which oftentimes fell out, to permit the feasts to be solemnized, or passovers killed, on two several days together." He quotes Scaliger to the same effect. But all this is without any historic basis. The language of Mark, (xiv. 12,) "And the first day of unleavened bread, when they killed the passover," &c., plainly implies that He ate the paschal supper on the same day as the Jews in general.[2]

It has been said, also, that, according to the law, the Passover should be killed on the evening following the 13th, or at the beginning of the 14th Nisan. Jesus, in common with a few of the Jews, kept the law; but most of them killed it on the afternoon, or at the close of the 14th, twenty-four hours later than the legal time. This rests upon an untenable construction of the law.

We find, then, no good grounds for believing that the Jews recognized two distinct days as equally legal for the paschal solemnities; or that, through error of computation, they observed the wrong day, and the Lord the right one.

2d. That the Lord kept the Passover on Thursday, at the appointed time, but that the Jews purposely delayed it. The ground of this delay is found in the fact, that when the 15th Nisan, the first day of the feast, and so a sabbath,

[1] True Notion of the Lord's Supper, ii. 528. [2] Wichelhaus, 205.

(Lev. xxiii. 7, 8,) fell upon Friday, and thus two sabbaths, the feast sabbath and week Sabbath, would immediately follow each other, the Jews united them in one, and the sacrifice of the paschal lamb on the 14th was postponed to the 15th. Thus the Lord, according to the law, ate the paschal supper on Thursday evening, but the Jews on Friday evening.[1] But this explanation has no sufficient basis, as there is no room for doubt that such changes of the feasts, and the rule forbidding that the Passover should fall on Friday, were posterior to the destruction of Jerusalem, probably about 400 A. D.[2]

Another ground of delay was given early by Eusebius and others, that the Jews were so busy with their accusations against Christ, that they postponed the feast till His trial and crucifixion should be over. This is so intrinsically improbable that it now finds no defenders. A modification of this is still supported by some: that those most active against Him, and who are specially alluded to (John xviii. 28) as not willing to enter the judgment hall, did delay their paschal supper on this account.[3] This view will be hereafter noticed.

We do not thus find any proof that the Jews delayed the Passover after the legal time.

3d. That the Lord anticipated the day and ate, not the true paschal supper, but one of a sacramental character, and corresponding to it. That He anticipated the day, was very early affirmed by some of the fathers, supposing, that as the true Paschal Lamb, the Antitype, He must have suffered at the hour when the typical lamb was slain, and so upon the 14th Nisan. The supper He observed must,

[1] So Calvin, on Matt. xxvi. 17, who remarks that the Jews affirm that this was done by them after their return from Babylon, and by God's express direction.

[2] Wichelhaus, 203; Paulus, iii. 487, note; Cudworth, ii. 524.

[3] Fairbairn, Her. Mam., 382.

therefore, have been on the evening following, the 13th. This point had in the first days of the church a special importance, because of the controversy with some of the Christian Jews in regard to the binding force of the Mosaic laws. It was asserted by them, that as Jesus kept the legal Passover, the paschal sacrifice and supper, these were still binding, and to be kept in the Church. In reply, it was asserted by many of the Christians that He did not eat the paschal supper, but, as the true Paschal Lamb, was slain at the hour appointed for the sacrifice of the Passover. In the Greek Church this became by degrees the ruling opinion, and is generally defended by her writers.[1] In the Latin Church, on the other hand, it was generally denied; but in neither is it made an article of faith. The question as to the use of leavened or unleavened bread in the Eucharist, may have had some influence upon the matter; the Greeks, using the former, were led to say that the Lord used it at the institution of the rite, and that, therefore, it was not the true paschal supper, at which only unleavened bread was used. The Latins, using unleavened bread, maintained that the Eucharist was instituted at the true paschal supper.

This view, that the Lord anticipated the paschal supper, has, besides its antiquity, much in its favor, and is now supported by many.[2] But the objections against it are very strong. First, the language of the Synoptists leaves little room to question that the Lord kept the Passover at the same time with the Jews in general. "The first day of unleavened bread, when they killed the Passover;" "the day of unleavened bread, when the Passover must be killed." Second. It is difficult to believe that the Lord, who said that He came not to destroy, but to fulfil the law, should have set it aside. If He observed the Passover at

[1] Wichelhaus, 190.

[2] So Krafft, 129; Greswell, iii. 133; Ellicott, 322; J. Müller, in Herzog's Real. Encyc., i. 22; Clinton, ii. 240; The author of "The Messiah."

all, He would observe it at the legal time. In this, most Protestant writers agree with the Latins.[1] Third. Such a sacrifice would not have been permitted by the priests. They would not have aided in the sacrifice of the lamb upon a day which they did not recognize as the legal one. To avoid this difficulty, Greswell quotes Philo, (iii. 146,) to show that each man was then his own priest, and could slay the lamb, if he pleased, in his own dwelling. But the weight of authority is against him. The lamb must be slain in the temple, and the blood be sprinkled on the altar.

By some, however, it is said that the supper of Thursday evening was not the true paschal supper, but such an one as the Jews, who could not be present at the feast, observed at their own homes, when all the forms of the Passover were kept, except the eating of the lamb.[2] But such a supper could only be eaten out of Jerusalem, and upon the legal day, not in the city, and upon the day previous. Nor is there any evidence that this Memorial Passover was ever observed till after the destruction of Jerusalem, when it became impossible that the lamb could be slain in the temple, and the supper was necessarily limited to unleavened bread and bitter herbs.

We do not then find sufficient grounds to believe that the Lord anticipated the Passover.

Some peculiar solutions, that have found no general reception, need only be mentioned. Such is that of Rauch,[3] that the paschal lamb was legally slain, not on the 14th, but on the 15th Nisan. And of Schneckenburger,[4] that Jesus was crucified on Wednesday, and was four days in the grave.

If none of these solutions satisfies us, we are compelled either to admit that the statements of the Synoptists are

[1] Wichelhaus, 202.

[2] So Grotius on Matt. xxvi. 11.

[3] Bib. Repertory, Jan., 1834.

[4] Wieseler, 338.

irreconcilable with those of John, or to deny, what we have hitherto assumed, that a discrepancy really exists.

Let us therefore examine the point as to the existence of any discrepancy between the Synoptists and John. And before considering the statements of the several Evangelists, it will be well to keep before us the origin and design of the Passover, and the peculiarities of its observance.

1st. Its origin and design. It was instituted in commemoration of the deliverance of the Jews in Egypt from the destroying angel, when all the first-born of the Egyptians were slain, (Exod. xii. 14, &c.) This remarkable deliverance was ever afterward to be commemorated by a feast. This was introduced by the paschal supper. The people being divided into households or families, of not less than ten or more than twenty, a lamb was slain for each family, and eaten immediately after with unleavened bread and bitter herbs. Now followed a feast of seven days' continuance, during which only unleavened bread was eaten. There is no reason for attributing to this feast any earlier origin than the historical deliverance it commemorated.[1]

2d. The manner of its celebration. The lamb or goat was to be selected on the 10th Nisan, a male without blemish. On the 14th, "between the evenings," it must be slain, (Exod. xii. 6; Lev. xxiii. 5; Num. ix. 3.) The expression "between the evenings," was generally understood by the Jews of the period from the decline of the sun to its setting, or from 3 to 6 P. M. This was, without doubt, the ruling mode of computation.[2] The Karaites and Samaritans, however, referred it to the period between sundown and dark, or from 6 to 7 P. M.[3] Wieseler refers it to a period a little before and a little after the going down of the sun, say from 5 to 7 P. M., citing Deut. xvi. 6 in proof.

[1] See Bähr, Symbolik, ii. 640; Ewald, Alterthürmer, 391.

[2] Josephus, War, 6. 9. 3; Antiq., 14. 4. 3.

[3] Winer, ii. 198.

Ewald makes it to include three hours before and three hours after the sun set.

The paschal lamb was originally slain by the head of each family, (Exod. xii. 6;) but this seems later to have been done by the Levites, and always in the court of the temple where stood the brazen altar, (Ezra vi. 20; Deut. xvi. 2–6.) After the sacrifice came the supper. This was upon the evening following the 14th Nisan, or, as the Jews began the day at sundown, upon the beginning of the 15th. The lamb was to be wholly consumed before morning, either by eating or by fire.

Besides the paschal lamb, other offerings were made, which were eaten at the paschal supper and upon the following day. These are mentioned (Deut. xvi. 2) "as the Passover of the flock and herd," and embraced the sacrifices of sheep or bullocks voluntarily added, and called by the Jews, chagigah, or feast-offering. Concerning these, Maimonides (quoted by Ainsworth in loco) says: "When they offer the Passover in the first month, they offer it with peace-offerings on the 14th day, of the flock and of the herd, and this is called the chagigah, or feast offering, of the 14th day. And of this it is said, (Deut. xvi. 2,) that thou shalt sacrifice the Passover to the Lord thy God of the flock and the herd."

To understand the relation of the chagigah to the Passover in general, we must remember that this feast was the commemoration of a great national deliverance, and, as such, to be kept with thanksgiving and joy. The paschal supper, strictly speaking, seems to have had much less of the joyous element in it than the rest of the feast. As said by Lightfoot, "the eating of the lamb was the very least part of the joy; a thing rubbing up the remembrance of affliction, rather than denoting gladness and making merry." The lamb, which constituted the chief part of the supper, reminded them of that fearful night when all the first-born of Egypt died; the bitter herbs with which it was eaten, reminded them of the bitterness of their Egyptian bondage; and all the attendant circumstances would tend to beget seriousness and reflection. The festival character of the season appeared much more plainly upon the succeeding day, when the peace offerings voluntarily presented to God in token of thankfulness, were eaten, (Exod. xxiii. 15.) That these peace offerings were sometimes offered on the 14th Nisan, and eaten at the paschal supper, appears from Maimonides; but, according to Lightfoot, (on John xviii. 28,) only when the lamb was not sufficient for the company. The usual time for the chagigah was on the 15th, and with these offerings the rejoicing was more directly connected.

We thus see that no sharp line of distinction can be taken between the paschal supper and the feast of unleavened bread. The former served as the introduction to the latter, but had peculiar to itself the eating of the lamb and of the bitter herbs. Still it was but the beginning of the feast, for none but unleavened bread was used during its continuance, (Exod. xii. 18.)

The ceremonies of the second day of the feast, the 16th Nisan, were peculiar, and important to be noted. Upon this day the first fruits of the barley harvest were brought to the temple, and waved by a priest before the Lord, to consecrate the harvest; and not till this was done might any one begin his reaping, (Lev. xxiii. 10–12.)[1]

The removal of the leaven from their houses, the preparations for the paschal supper, and the sacrifice of the lamb, taking place on the 14th Nisan, this day was popularly called the first day of the feast, thus extending it to eight days.[2] The Evangelists follow this popular usage,

[1] Josephus, Antiq., 3. 10. 5. As to the connection of this rite with the Passover, see Winer, ii. 201; Bähr, ii. 638.

[2] Josephus, Antiq., 2. 15. 1.

(Matt. xxvi. 17; Mark xiv. 12; Luke xxii. 7.) Upon each of the seven days of the feast was offered a sacrifice for the whole people, (Num. xxviii. 19–24.) The first and last days of the feast, or the 15th and 21st, were holy days, or sabbaths, (Lev. xxiii. 7, 8.) But these feast sabbaths do not seem ever to have been regarded as equal in sacredness to the week Sabbaths. And it is important that the distinction between them should be clearly seen, as it has an important bearing upon several points to be hereafter discussed.

Besides the weekly Sabbath, there were seven days of the year that had a sabbatical character: the first and seventh of the feast of unleavened bread; the day of Pentecost; the first and the tenth of the seventh month; and the first and eighth of the feast of Tabernacles. Of these, one, the tenth of the seventh month, the day ot atonement, was put on the same footing as the weekly Sabbath in respect to labor. No work at all could be done upon it; but on the other six feast sabbaths they could do no servile work, (Lev. xxiii. 3–39.) These were called by the Talmudists "good days." It is not wholly clear what kind of work was not servile, but the preparation of food was expressly permitted, (Exod. xii. 16.) Maimonides (quoted by Ainsworth) says: "All work needful about meat is lawful, as killing of beasts, and baking of bread, and kneading of dough, and the like. But such work as may be done in the evening of a feast day they do not on a feast day, as they may not reap, nor thrash, nor winnow, nor grind the corn, or the like. Bathing and anointing are contained under the general head of meat and drink, and may be done on the feast day." The penalty for doing servile work on these days was, according to Maimonides, to be beaten; but the penalty for working on the Sabbath was death, (Num. xv. 32–35.)

To these feast sabbaths we find few allusions in Jewish

history. They are not mentioned at all in the Gospels. All the violations of the Sabbath with which the Lord was charged were those of the weekly Sabbath. Nor is there any distinct allusion to them in the Old Testament, or in Josephus. Before the weekly Sabbath was a time of preparation, because no labor of any kind could then be done, but it is not probable that there was such a period of preparation before the feast sabbaths, as then all labor but servile labor was permitted. This point, however, will be hereafter more particularly examined.

A special mark of distinction was shown to the weekly Sabbath in the doubling the usual offerings, (Num. xxviii. 9,) and the renewal of the show bread, (Lev. xxiv. 8.)

Thus we find in the paschal festival three distinct solemnities: 1st. The killing of the paschal lamb on the afternoon of the 14th Nisan, and the eating of it the evening following. 2d. The feast of unleavened bread, beginning with the paschal supper, and continuing to the close of the 21st day of Nisan. 3d. The offering of the first fruits of the barley harvest on the 16th Nisan, or second day of the feast. To the latter no distinct allusion is made by the Evangelists.

With these preliminary observations upon the origin and observance of the Passover, we pass to the consideration of the terms applied to it, first in the Old Testament and then in the New. The Hebrew pesach, or Aramaic pascah, refers primarily to the paschal lamb. "Draw out and take you a lamb, and kill the Passover," (Exod. xii. 21.) To kill the Passover, and to eat the Passover, is to kill and eat the paschal lamb, (see Exod. xii. 11; Num. ix. 2–6; 2 Chron. xxx. 15.) But, as has been said, often with the flesh of the lamb the flesh of other sacrifices offered as peace offerings was eaten; and hence, naturally, the term was made to embrace these also; and then the whole seven days of the feast. "Thou shalt sacrifice the Passover to the

Lord thy God of the flock and the herd; thou shalt eat no leavened bread with it; seven days shalt thou eat unleavened bread therewith," (Deut. xvi. 2, 3.) That the Passover is here used as a general term, embracing the sacrifices of both flock and herd, is generally admitted.[1] "They did eat the feast seven days offering peace offerings," (2 Chron. xxx. 22.) In the days of Josiah he and his princes gave small cattle and oxen for passovers—pesachim, (2 Chron. xxxv. 7–9; see also xxx. 17, where the same word seems to be limited to paschal lambs.) Thus made to include all the special sacrifies of the feast, it became a designation of the feast in general. "To keep the Passover," was to observe all the solemnities of the feast without distinction of specific acts, unless through the force of the context the meaning must be limited to the paschal supper. It is thus used Deut. xvi. 1; 2 Kings xxiii. 21; 2 Chron. xxx. 1; 2 Chron. xxxv. 1; Ezek. xlv. 21.

From this examination of the terms in the Old Testament, we find that there is no exact discrimination in their use. Sometimes the Passover and the feast of unleavened bread are expressly distinguished, and the former limited to the paschal supper, (Lev. xxiii. 5, 6; Num. xxviii. 16, 17.) At other times they are used interchangeably. The precise meaning in each case must be determined by the connection in which it stands.

We proceed to consider the usage of these terms in the New Testament. And first their usage by the Synoptists. Here also the term Passover, *το πασχα*, is used in its narrowest sense, of the paschal lamb. Thus in Mark xiv. 12, "when they killed the Passover;" in Luke xxii. 7, "when the Passover must be killed." It is used in the large sense, including both the sacrifice of the lamb and the supper, Matt. xxvi. 17; Mark xiv. 14; Luke xxii. 11. It is used

[1] So Bleek, Beiträge, 111. See other constructions in Cudworth, ii. 522.

as a designation of the feast in its whole extent, Matt. xxvi. 2; Luke xxii. 1. (See also Mark xiv. 1.) That the phrase, "feast of unleavened bread," τα αζυμα, embraced the paschal supper, appears from Matt. xxvi. 17; Mark xiv. 12; Luke xxii. 7.

Turning from the Synoptists to John, it is at once apparent that he generally uses the term Passover, το πασχα, in its largest sense, as embracing the whole feast. So ii. 13 and 23; vi. 4; xi. 55; xii. 1; xiii. 1. So in the references to it as the feast, εορτη, iv. 45; xi. 56; xii. 12 and 20; xiii. 29. In xviii. 28 and 39, and in xix. 14, its meaning is in dispute.

We are now prepared to enter upon a more particular examination of the statements of the Evangelists; and first, those of the Synoptists. Their language is very express: "Now the first day of the feast of unleavened bread—τη δε πρωτη των αζυμων—the disciples came to Jesus, saying, Where wilt Thou that we prepare for Thee to eat the Passover?" (Matt. xxvi. 17.) "And the first day of unleavened bread—Και τη πρωτη ημερα των αζυμων—when they killed the Passover, His disciples said unto Him," &c., (Mark xiv. 12.) "Then came the day of unleavened bread, when the Passover must be killed,"—η ημερα των αζυμων, (Luke xxii. 7.) That this was the 14th Nisan seems beyond reasonable doubt, for on the afternoon of this day the paschal lamb was slain, and all preparations made for the feast that began at evening with the paschal supper. As has been already remarked, this was not, strictly speaking, the first day of the feast, for this began with the 15th, but was, in popular language, so called; and the circumstance that the lamb was yet to be slain, sufficiently determines what day was meant. (Compare Exod. xii. 18.)

The attempts so to interpret these statements as to make them refer to a supper on the 13th Nisan, are very forced and unsatisfactory. Krafft (129) bases his interpretation upon the Jewish mode of beginning the day at sunset. The 13th Nisan was from the eve of Wednesday to the eve of Thursday; the 14th, from the eve of Thursday to the eve of Friday. The Synoptists thus count the 14th, beginning at sunset of Thursday, as the first of the feast. Upon Thursday, the 13th, the Lord gave directions that the Passover should be prepared, and the lamb was killed the same afternoon, and eaten during the evening following, or at the beginning of the 14th. Greswell (iii. 171) presents the same view: "From sunset on Thursday to sunset on Friday was considered, and might be called, the first day of unleavened bread. We have but to suppose that the disciples came with their inquiry at sunset on Thursday, and were sent at that time accordingly, and the assertion would be strictly correct."[1] The great, and as it seems, insuperable objection to this, is, that the Lord must then have killed and eaten the Passover twenty-four hours earlier than the Jews in general. Krafft (130) admits this of most of the Jews, but supposes, from the language of the Synoptists, and from the multitude of sacrifices to be offered, that some of them must have eaten the supper on the 13th, at the same time with the Lord. But there is no proof that it was ever eaten by any portion of the people, except on the evening following the 14th. The arguments that the Lord did so, drawn from the language of the Synoptists, are by no means conclusive. From the message sent by him to the master of the house, (Matt. xxvi. 18,) "My time is at hand, I will keep the Passover at thy house," it has been inferred, that "the Passover about to be celebrated was something out of course," or before the usual period.[2] But this is not a necessary inference. "My time is not 'the time of the feast,' but *my time*, i. e. for suffering."[3] This interpretation is much the most obvious

[1] See also Journal Sac. Lit., Oct. 1861.
[2] Greswell, iii. 144.
[3] Alford in loco.

and natural. Some, as Ellicott, have inferred from His words at the beginning of the supper, (Luke xxii. 15,) "With desire I have desired to eat this Passover with you before I suffer," that He designs to designate the Passover as a peculiar one. But its peculiarity did not necessarily consist in its being celebrated earlier than was usual, but in the fact that it was the last.

None of the advocates of this view meet in any satisfactory way the statement of Luke, "Then came the day of unleavened bread, when the Passover must be killed;" and of Mark, "And the first day of unleavened bread when they killed the Passover, His disciples said," &c. We cannot, without doing great violence to this language, make it refer to the 13th of Nisan, since neither according to the law nor to usage, was the paschal lamb slain on that day. And the difficulty is increased since, according to the law, (Deut. xvi. 5, 6,) the lamb could not be sacrificed anywhere else than in the temple.[1] It is incredible that the priests would have permitted the time to have been anticipated by a day in this single instance. The supposition of Ellicott,[2] that the time specified for killing the lamb, viz., "between the evenings," may be understood to mean between the eves of Nisan 14th and Nisan 15th, is wholly without proof.[3] The whole tenor of the synoptical narratives makes irresistibly upon us the impression, that the disciples prepared, and the Lord ate, the Passover, at the same time when it was prepared and eaten by the people at large. The truth is well expressed by Robinson:[4] "Their language is full, explicit, and decisive, to the effect that our Lord's last meal with His disciples was the regular and ordinary paschal supper of the Jews, introducing the festival of unleavened bread on the evening after the 14th day of Nisan."

[1] See Ainsworth in loco; Friedlieb, Arch. 47.

[2] 322, note 3.

[3] See Godwyn, Moses and Aaron, 108; De Wette, Archaölogie, 224; Ewald Alterthürmer, 397.

[4] Har., 214.

Taking, then, as established, that the Synoptists make the supper eaten by the Lord to have been the true paschal supper, let us consider in detail the statements of John that bear upon the point. The first of these we find in xiii. 1: "Now before the feast of the Passover, when Jesus knew that His hour was come," &c. The chronological value of this passage depends upon the relation in which the clause, "before the feast of the Passover," stands to the supper subsequently mentioned, at which the Lord washed the feet of the disciples. But before we can examine this point, we must consider the opinion of those who make this a supper previous to the paschal supper, and one not mentioned at all by the Synoptists.

The chief arguments urged by those who would make the supper of John distinct from the paschal supper of the Synoptists, are, 1st, that it is not described by him as a paschal meal; 2d, that it is said to have been "before the feast of the Passover;" 3d, that the interpretation of the Lord's words to Judas, (v. 29,) by the disciples, shows that the Passover was still future; 4th, that the language of Jesus at this supper, (xiv. 31,) "Arise, let us go hence," refers to His departure to Jerusalem to keep the feast upon the following day; 5th, that the act of washing the feet was incongruous with the paschal supper; 6th, that the statement, (John xiii. 27,) that Satan, after the sop, entered into Judas, is identical with Luke's statement, (xxii. 3,) and must therefore have been previous to the paschal supper.[1] But those, who, upon the above grounds, deny the supper of John to be the paschal meal, are by no means agreed when it took place. Some put it upon Wednesday evening.[2] Lightfoot puts it on Tuesday evening, identifying it with that supper at Bethany when the Lord was

[1] See Bengel in loco; Krafft, 125; Jarvis, 442; Wichelhaus, 154.

[2] So Bengel, Krafft, Wichelhaus. See Bynaeus, De Morte Jesu Christi, i. 386, for an elaborate defence of this view.

anointed, (Matt. xxvi. 6,) which he distinguishes from that in John xii. 2.

Upon the other hand, it is said that this supper was the paschal supper, and so to be identified with that of the Synoptists, upon the following grounds: 1st. Through the designation of Judas by the Lord as he that should betray Him. (Compare John xiii. 21–30 with Matt. xxvi. 21–25, Mark xiv. 18–21, Luke xxii. 21–23.) 2d. Through the prophecy that Peter should thrice deny Him, and of the crowing of the cock. (Compare John xiii. 38 with Matt. xxvi. 34, Luke xxii. 34.) 3d. Through the connection between the Lord's words recorded in John, chaps. xiv. xv. xvi., showing that they were all spoken at once. 4th. Through the statement, (Luke xxii. 24,) that at the paschal supper there was a strife among them, who should be accounted greatest, and which serves to explain His conduct in washing His disciples' feet. (Compare John xiii. 13–17).

Upon these grounds most of the modern commentators have arrayed themselves in favor of the identification of this supper in John with the supper of the Synoptists.[1] A careful examination of the arguments justifies this conclusion. That the supper is not expressly named as the paschal supper, does not show that it was a common meal. Rather it is supposed to be something well known and familiar to the reader; the supper by way of eminence.

Returning now to the interpretation of John xiii. 1–4, we ask to what does the introductory chronological notice, "before the feast of the Passover," refer? Our answer must depend upon the relation in which v. 1 stands to the verses following. That it forms a sentence complete in itself, and grammatically independent upon what follows, is generally admitted.[2] If so, the words, "before the feast of

[1] Tholuck, Greswell, Alford, Meyer, Tischendorf, Robinson, Friedlieb, and others.

[2] Meyer, Lange, Robinson, Alford, Tischendorf.

the Passover," would seem to qualify either the participle ειδως, or αγαπησας. If the former, the meaning would be, that Jesus, knowing before the feast that His hour was come, and, having loved His own, continued to love them to the end; and at the feast, i. e. the paschal supper now present, gives them a new proof of His love. This interpretation is in perfect harmony with the whole narrative. Before Jesus left Galilee, He announced His departure as at hand, (Matt. xvii. 22,) and again after He left Ephraim, (xx. 17.) Two days before the feast, He repeated that at the Passover He should be betrayed, (Matt. xxvi. 2.) And now the feast had come, and with it "His hour." He, knowing all this, gives at this introductory supper of the feast, a new and last proof of the love with which He had loved them. With the full knowledge that the hour of His arrest and death had come, and that He no more should thus meet His disciples, He shows them, in the most expressive way, how great and unchangeable His affection for them. In this way the abrupt and incidental mention of the supper (v. 2) is readily explained; and that it was the paschal supper follows from the whole connection of the thought.

The meaning is thus given by Norton in his translation: "But Jesus, before the feast of the Passover, knew that the hour had come for Him to pass from the world to the Father; and having loved His own who were to remain in this world, He loved them to the last."[1]

If we connect the clause, "before the feast of the Passover," with αγαπησας, the meaning is, Jesus, having loved His own down to this time, or to the Passover which was now come, and knowing that the hour of His death was at hand, continues to love them, even to the end; and now gives a fresh proof of it at the paschal supper. Here, as before, it is implied that this supper, at the beginning of the

[1] See also Luthardt, ii. 274.

feast, was the last opportunity He should have of manifesting His love. In this construction the antithesis between "before the feast" and "to the end," is most clearly brought out. The love which He had felt to His own before the feast, continued firm to the end, and was shown in the act of washing the disciples' feet.[1] Still, the former explanation is to be preferred.

This clause is, however, said by many to qualify the whole narrative, and not to belong to ειδως or αγαπησας; thus making the supper, and all that then took place, to have been before the Passover.[2] It is said that it could not have been the paschal supper on the evening following the 14th Nisan, but a supper probably on the previous evening, or that following the 13th.[3] But of this, Norton (note in loco) justly says: "It is a very forced interpretation to regard the words 'before the feast of the Passover,' as intended to fix the date of what follows. Supposing the night to which the succeeding narrative relates not to be the night of the Passover, St. John has in the second verse abruptly introduced the mention of a supper in a manner in which it cannot readily be believed that any writer would." From the preposition "before," προ, we conclude, then, that nothing definite in regard to the time of the supper can be determined. Supposing all between v. 1 and v. 4 to be stricken out, and the statement to read, "Now before the feast of the Passover, &c., He riseth from supper and laid aside his garments," it would still remain probable that the paschal supper was meant. The presumption is very strong, that this meal, thus incidentally

[1] See Wieseler, 379; Tholuck in loco; Robinson, Har. 217.

[2] Meyer and Alford.

[3] That the form of expression, "Before the feast of the Passover," denotes the day before the Passover, *pridie Paschatis*, is affirmed by Bynaeus; who, however, does not make this the Paschal supper. See Wieseler, 379, who denies that the expression can be thus understood.

mentioned, must have been that so prominently and inseparably associated with the feast.

An additional proof that this was not the paschal supper is found by many[1] in the fact mentioned, (John xiii. 29,) that none of the disciples knew what the Lord had said to Judas at the table, but some of them supposed He had told him to buy what was necessary for the feast, or to give something to the poor. It is said, if the disciples were now eating the feast, no one could have thought that Judas went out for this purpose. Besides, the day following the paschal supper, or 15th Nisan, was a feast sabbath, when nothing could be bought; nor could any purchases be made upon that evening, as all shopkeepers would be engaged keeping the feast; nor could gifts then be given to the poor. Thence it follows that this supper was previous to the beginning of the feast. But this inference is not well grounded. The feast continued seven days, and embraced various sacrifices and offerings other than the paschal lamb. It is not at all improbable that a master of a family, speaking at this first meal, should thus refer to the provision to be made for the further keeping of the feast. Judas, as the treasurer of the body of apostles, was in this case the person to make such provision. And the fact, that he went out immediately after the Lord had spoken to him, would naturally suggest to others that something necessary to the feast was to be at once procured. The statement that nothing could be purchased upon a feast sabbath, is by no means certain. It appears rather, that the purchase and preparation of food were allowable on all feast days, though not on the fast of the Atonement.[2] That Judas should go out, as some supposed, to give something to the poor, indicates a special urgency, which may be best

[1] Meyer, Bleek, Alford.

[2] Tholuck in loco; Wieseler, 344 and 366; Luthardt, ii. 286.

explained as referring to some gifts to be sacrificially used on the morrow, and therefore to be made at once.

A careful examination of this passage seems rather to prove that this was the paschal supper, than to disprove it. The disciples heard the Lord say to Judas, "That thou doest do quickly." He immediately arises and goes out, and "it was night." Supposing this to have been a supper on the night of the 13th Nisan, and a full day before the paschal supper, would they connect his departure with any preparations for the feast? The next day would give him abundant time to buy all that was necessary. Why hasten out at that hour of the night? So also he had then ample time to give to the poor. But if we suppose that this was the paschal supper, and that the next day, the 15th, was the first day of the feast, we can readily explain their conjectures as to the cause of Judas' sudden departure. What he was to do must be done at once.

The next passage in John, and that most relied on to prove that the Lord could not have eaten the paschal supper, is found xviii. 28: "Then led they Jesus from Caiaphas unto the hall of judgment; and it was early; and they themselves went not into the judgment hall lest they should be defiled, but that they might eat the Passover." This, it is said, plainly proves that the Jews had not yet eaten the Passover; and that the supper which Jesus had eaten on the previous evening, could not have been the paschal supper, as the Synoptists state.[1]

Two solutions of this difficulty are given: First, that those who would not go into the judgment hall, were those Scribes and Pharisees who had been engaged during the night, while the other Jews were keeping the feast, in directing the proceedings against Jesus, and thus had had no time to partake of the paschal supper. Second, that John uses the expression, "eat the Passover," in its larger

[1] Meyer, Bleek, Alford.

meaning, not referring to the paschal lamb, but to the offerings eaten on the second day of the feast. The former of these solutions has never found many defenders, though not in itself impossible. So great was the hate against Jesus, and so little scrupulous His enemies, that we cannot doubt, that to compass His death, they would have postponed for a time the paschal supper, or even have neglected it altogether. There are, however, other obvious difficulties, which this explanation does not fully meet.

We must then consider the second of these solutions. It is admitted, that as the Synoptists use the phrase "to eat the Passover," φαγειν το πασχα, it always means to eat the paschal supper, (Matt. xxvi. 17; Mark xiv. 12 and 14; Luke xxii. 11 and 15.) If John uses it in the same sense, then the paschal supper was eaten by the Jews on the day when Jesus was crucified, and He must have anticipated it. But the usage of the Synoptists does not decide the usage of John. We must determine its meaning from the way in which he uses the phrase elsewhere, and from the general character of his writings. It has already been shown, that out of the nine times in which he uses the word πασχα, Passover, in six it is applied to the feast generally, and not to the paschal supper only. The meaning in the other three passages is in dispute. Only in the passage before us does the phrase "eat the Passover" occur. The simple point is, does John here use it in its wider or narrower meaning?

Some considerations, drawn from the character of John's Gospel, as influenced by the period of time at which he wrote, may serve to show how this marked distinction in the use of terms between him and the Synoptists, is to be explained. John wrote toward the close of the century,[1] and after the destruction of Jerusalem. To him the Jews were no more the holy people of God. Rejecting Jesus,

[1] Meyer, about 80 A. D.

and afterwards His apostles, they had themselves been rejected. Everywhere he speaks of them distinctly as "The Jews," formerly the Church of God, but now cut off, and standing in a hostile attitude to Christ, and to that new, universal Church, composed both of Jews and Gentiles, of which He was the Head.[1] Jewish institutions had, in his eyes, been emptied of their significance and value, since Christ, in whom all the law was fulfilled, had come. Hence he speaks of them commonly as the institutions of a people between whom and himself was a broad line of distinction. Their purification is spoken of as that "of the Jews;" the Passover as "a feast of the Jews;" Nicodemus, as "a ruler of the Jews." The Synoptists, on the other hand, writing before the total rejection of Judaism, and whilst it still stood side by side with Christianity as of divine authority and sanctity, show, by their mode of allusion, that no such line of distinction then existed. To them, the Jews are not as aliens, but still the chosen people of God.

Placing ourselves in the position of John, we shall readily understand why he speaks in such general and indefinite terms of Jewish rites, as of things now superseded. Since Jesus, the true Paschal Lamb, had been slain, the true paschal supper was kept only in the Christian church. To Christians he could say, with Paul, (1 Cor. v. 7, 8,) "Christ, our Passover, is sacrificed for us; therefore, let us keep the feast," &c. The Jews, in their Passover, had only the shell or shadow; the Church had the kernel or substance. Hence, it is not to be expected that he would refer to any rites of the Jews at this feast with the care that marks the Synoptists. He does not distinguish, as do they, its several component parts, but speaks of it only in general terms, as one of the Jewish feasts. There is not,

[1] See Meyer on John i. 19; Bleek, 247.

in the many times in which he mentions the Passover, any clear proof that he means to distinguish the paschal supper from the solemnities of the following days. Why, then, in the passage before us, are we forced to believe that the Passover which the Jews were to eat on the day of the crucifixion was the paschal supper, and that only? Why may he not mean the subsequent sacrifices? Standing, as he does, to the Jews, in a position so unlike that of the Synoptists, it seems most arbitrary to assert that he must use language with precisely the same strictness; and that "to eat the Passover" must mean to eat the paschal lamb.

As has been said, upon the first day of the feast, or the the 15th, thank offerings of the flock and herd were slain and eaten. There is certainly no intrinsic reason why John may not have meant these. At the time of Hezekiah, (2 Chron. xxx. 22,) "they did eat the feast seven days, offering peace offerings." But it is said in reply,[1] that if the phrase "to eat the Passover" may be used of the other offerings, inclusive of the paschal lamb, it cannot be exclusive of it. But this is by no means obvious. Passover, with John, is a term denoting the whole festival; and why, if the paschal supper was past, might he not employ it to designate the remaining feasts? To affirm that he could not is mere affirmation. Norton,[2] referring to the oft-repeated remark that the term Passover is never used "absolutely" to denote the thank offerings considered apart from the paschal supper, observes: "This remark has been repeatedly praised for its acuteness by Kuinoel and Strauss. But, in fact, it only implies a forgetfulness of a very common metonymy, by which the name of a whole is given to a part. If, when the paschal festival were half over, it had been said that certain Jews desired to avoid pollution, that they might keep the Passover, every one perceives that the expression

[1] Meyer and others, after Mosheim.

[2] Notes 2, 466.

would be unobjectionable, though no one would think of applying the name Passover 'absolutely' to the last three or four days of the festival."

The exact nature of the defilement to which the Jews would be exposed by entering the judgment hall does not appear. (See Acts x. 28.) In the law, defilements are mentioned which were only for a day, and which could be cleansed by ablution, (Lev. xv. 5–11, and xxii. 5–7.) It is supposed by some that contact with the heathen was of this class, and that, therefore, if the day of the crucifixion had been the 14th Nisan, the Jews could still have cleansed themselves by evening, and been ready to eat the paschal supper. If, however, it was the 15th, during which day the thank offerings were sacrificed and eaten, they could not have partaken of them. Hence it is inferred that the thank offerings, rather than the paschal supper, were meant, and that this day was the 15th rather than the 14th.[1] Much stress, however, in the present state of our knowledge of Jewish customs, cannot be laid upon this argument.[2]

This passage, then, affords no data for the final determination of the question as to the time of the paschal supper. If any think that John could not have used the phrase "to eat the Passover" in any other sense than the Synoptists used it, such must admit a chronological difference between him and them which we find no satisfactory way to reconcile. But if, on the other hand, we find it not only possible, but also probable, that he should thus speak of the festival apart from the supper, the supposed difference disappears.

The next important passage we find xix. 14: "And it was the preparation of the Passover, and about the sixth hour; and he saith unto the Jews, Behold your King." A

[1] So Bynaeus, iii. 13. [2] See Friedlieb, Arch. 102; Bleek, 113.

different punctuation of this passage has been proposed, making it to read thus: "And it was the preparation. The hour of the Passover was about the sixth."[1] Though some plausible reasons may be given for this change, yet it involves considerable difficulties. We shall follow the generally received punctuation.

Our first inquiry relates to the meaning of the term "preparation," παρασκευη. It occurs in the Gospel five times besides the text: Matt. xxvii. 62, Mark xv. 42, Luke xxiii. 54, John xix. 31, John xix. 42. In all these cases there is no doubt as to its meaning. It was, as Mark explains it, "the day before the Sabbath;" or the day in which preparation was made for the Sabbath. Such preparation, though not expressly commanded in the law, was yet made necessary by the strictness of the commands respecting the Sabbath, which forbade all labor, even to prepare food, on that day. (Compare Exod. xvi. 5.) Hence it became the habit of the Jews to observe Friday afternoon, from three o'clock, as a time of getting ready for the Sabbath, which began at sunset.[2] As they came more and more under bondage to that legal spirit which so characterized the Pharisees, and the rigor of the original Sabbath laws was augmented by burdensome additions, of which many examples are to be found in the Evangelists and in Josephus, this period of preparation became more and more important. Thus, by degrees, Friday, or the προσαββατον, became known as the παρασκευη, or preparation; as Saturday, the day of rest, was known as the Sabbath, all other days being distinguished only as the first, second, third, &c. As the preparation was made in the afternoon of Friday, or during that part of it which was known as "the evening," this term was generally applied to it in Hebrew and Chaldee, as by the Germans the day before the Sabbath is

1 So Hofmann, followed by Lichtenstein, 359.

2 Josephus, Antiq., 16. 6. 2.

called Sonnabend, or Sun-evening. Thus the sixth day of the week received its current name from its peculiar relations to the Sabbath; and παρασκευη became equivalent to Friday, and is uniformly so rendered in the Syriac.[1]

From this origin of the term, and from the fact that it was generally used to designate the sixth day of the week, and that it is so used both by the Synoptists and by John, we are disposed to infer, that in the passage before us, it means the preparation day before the Sabbath, or Friday. But it is said, on the other hand, that this is here inadmissible, because it is not simply said, "it was the preparation," but it was "the preparation of the Passover." It must, therefore, denote a day of preparation, not for the Sabbath, but for the feast; and this day must have been the 14th Nisan, as the first day of the feast was the 15th.[2] This of course implies, that there was a preparation day for the feasts as well as for the Sabbath. And this first demands our attention.

It is admitted by all that the proofs of such a preparation day are very indistinct. To meet the difficulty, that there is no mention in Jewish writings of such a preparation day in connection with any of the feasts, some would confine it to those feast days that had a sabbatical character, in this case, the first and seventh.[3] As such, preparation was to be made for them as for the weekly Sabbath. But the main reason that made a time of preparation necessary for the weekly Sabbath, was, that on that day no food could be prepared, whereas it could be upon a feast sabbath. Nor anywhere in Jewish history does the latter appear as equal to the former in sanctity and dignity. All labor but servile labor was then lawful. There seems, then, no good reason why every feast sabbath should have had its day of preparation; nor is there any proof of the fact. If there

[1] Michaelis, 44. [2] So Meyer, Alford, Winer, Bleek.
[3] Bleek, Beiträge, 120.

was, on the afternoon of the 14th Nisan, a period thus set apart and designated as "the Passover eve," Robinson[1] maintains that the expression did not "arise until after the destruction of the temple, and the consequent cessation of the regular and legal Passover meal, when of course the seven days of unleavened bread became the main festival." To such a Passover eve the expression in the text, "preparation of the Passover," could not apply.

Thus we reach the result, that the term "preparation," παρασκευη, is never applied, so far as we know, to any day preceding a feast, but is applied by the Evangelists, by Josephus, and by the Rabbis, to the day before the Sabbath. Recurring weekly, this would readily become the current designation of the sixth day, and equivalent to its proper name, or to our Friday.

But we have still to meet the grammatical difficulty. It is insisted that the nature of this preparation is expressly defined by the addition "of the Passover," and cannot therefore refer to the weekly Sabbath. But if παρασκευη is used as equivalent to Friday, it would simply mean, this was the Friday of the Passover, or the preparation day for that Sabbath that occurred during the paschal week. It is thus translated by Campbell: "Now it was the preparation of the paschal Sabbath;" by Norton: "The preparation day of the paschal week." The latter observes, "that the 14th of Nisan, whenever it began and ended, was the day of the Passover; that it was ordained to be so in the Old Testament; that it is so designated by Josephus; that there is no question that it was universally recognized as such; that it was consequently so recognized by John; and that therefore it is utterly incredible that he should, in this solitary instance, have gone out of his way to call the 14th of Nisan, the proper day for the Passover, by the name of the 'preparation for the Passover,' even if any

1 Har. 220.

ground can be imagined for giving it that name." There is much force in these observations. The law (Exod. xii. 18) says, "In the first month, on the fourteenth day of the month, at the evening, ye shall eat unleavened bread," &c. If then the 14th was universally regarded as the Passover, (see Matt. xxvi. 17; Mark xiv. 12,) how could John speak of it as the day of preparation for the Passover? This expression would lead us rather to look upon it as the 13th, which only could be properly called the day before the Passover.[1]

Some light may be gained by asking what was the object of the Evangelist in mentioning, that it was "the preparation of the Passover" when Jesus was brought before Pilate. Was it chronological simply? This is possible; but he seems to have had a higher purpose. It was the time when the Jews should have been engaged in making themselves ready for the holiest services of God, in His temple; but their preparation consisted in putting His Son to the shameful death of the cross. The incongruity of their labors with the character of the day, is thus brought into the clearest contrast.[2]

The phrase, "preparation of the Passover," as used by John, does not then, we conclude, compel us to regard the day of the crucifixion as the day before the Passover.

Still another passage is found, (John xix. 31:) "The Jews, therefore, because it was the preparation, that the bodies should not remain upon the cross on the Sabbath day, (for that Sabbath day was an high day, μεγαλη,) be-

[1] Wieseler; 335, note 3; contra, Bleek, 122.

[2] An attempt has been made to show (Journal Sac. Lit., July, 1850) that παρασκευη means properly "preparation time," and comprises the interval between mid-day or the sixth hour, and sunset or the twelfth. Translated according to this view, the passage before us would read: "For about the sixth hour, the preparation time on Passover day commenced." This makes it necessary to read ωρα εκτη with the iota subscript. This is hardly satisfactory.

sought Pilate," &c. The ground upon which this Sabbath is designated as a high day, is supposed by many[1] to be, that the first day of the feast, or 15th Nisan, which was a feast sabbath, (Exod. xii. 16,) fell upon the weekly Sabbath, and thus it was a double Sabbath, and "an high day." This, in itself considered, would be a sufficient and satisfactory explanation. But no weight can be attached to it, as showing that this was actually the case. If the weekly Sabbath fell upon the 16th Nisan, or the second day of the feast, a day distinguished from the other days as the time for the waving of the sheaf of first fruits, it would, with equal propriety, be called a high day.[2] "It was an high day, first, because it was the Sabbath; second, it was the day when all the people presented themselves in the temple; third, it was the day when the sheaf of first fruits was offered."[3] There are no data for a positive decision of the question; and whether the weekly Sabbath fell on the 15th or 16th Nisan, it might in either case be called an high, or great day. In point of fact, this question is always decided according as the day of the crucifixion, for other reasons, is placed upon the 14th or 15th Nisan. Cudworth's assertion, that "great day," in the Greek of the Hellenists, is used for the first or the last day of every feast, in which there was a holy convocation to the Lord, is not sustained by the passage to which he refers, (Isa. i. 13.) Every weekly Sabbath, as well as every feast sabbath, there was a holy convocation, (Lev. xxiii. 3.)

Having now examined all the disputed passages in John usually cited to show that he puts the crucifixion upon the 14th Nisan, let us notice some of the objections made to the 15th. 1st. The improbability of such a trial and execution upon a feast sabbath. It is said, that, according to Rabbinical precepts, the Sanhedrim could not upon that

[1] Meyer, Alford, Bleek. [2] So Wieseler, Robinson, Lichtenstein.
[3] Lightfoot in loco.

day have held a session; that they could not have sent armed men to arrest Jesus; that no judicial proceedings were lawful, nor any public execution.[1] All here depends upon the degree of sanctity that was ascribed to a feast sabbath. It appears upon the face of it very remarkable, that Matthew, Mark, and Luke, whom we cannot suppose to have been ignorant of Jewish customs, should have so expressly put these events on a feast sabbath, if they were so clearly forbidden by the Rabbis. They could not but know that all their Jewish readers would at once perceive the inconsistency. The very fact, then, that these Evangelists do place the arrest, trial, and execution of Jesus upon a feast sabbath, together with the judicial sessions of the Sanhedrim and the subsequent purchase of spices and preparations for His embalming, gives the strongest presumptive proof that these were not incompatible with the character of the day. As against their statements, any Rabbinical precepts of a later age cannot be considered as decisive. But, in point of fact, it does not appear from the Rabbins themselves, that Jesus could not have been crucified on that day. Bleek (140) admits that criminals were often arrested on the Sabbath, and of course, if necessary, by men bearing arms.[2] That the Sanhedrim held its sessions on feast days and Sabbaths, is proved from the Gamara; and also, that on those days sentence of death could be passed.[3] That the execution of criminals was purposely reserved till the feasts, in order to produce a greater impression upon the people, appears from Maimonides, quoted by Ainsworth, on Deut. xvii. 13: "They put him not to death in the judgment hall, that is, in his city, but carry him up to the high Synedrion in Jerusalem, and keep him until the feast, and strangle him at the feast, as it is said,

[1] Ebrard, Bleek.

[2] See Winer, ii. 537; also John vii. 32; Acts xii. 3.

[3] See the citations in Lightfoot, and in Tholuck in loco.

'all the people shall hear and fear.'" It seems, also, to have been the custom of Pilate and of other governors, who always went up to Jerusalem at the feasts, then to try and punish criminals; and thus it was that the two malefactors were crucified at the same time with Jesus. The crucifixion itself was performed, not by the Jews, but by Pilate and his soldiers. The following observations of Tholuck seem well founded: "We consider it, therefore, as certain, that judicial proceedings were also held on the feast days, perhaps under certain legal provisos, and that this very period, when large assemblages of the people came together, was, for the reason mentioned Deut. xvii. 13, selected for the execution of notorious criminals."

But if we admit that, as a rule, the Jews did not arrest, and try, and execute, criminals during the feasts, still the case of Jesus may have been an exception. How great was the hate of the Pharisees and chief priests and elders to Him, we have already had abundant opportunities to observe. They stuck at nothing, if they could but accomplish His death. Here, if ever, the end would in their eyes have justified the means; and when the long-desired opportunity of getting their dreaded enemy into their power came, they were not likely to be prevented from using it by any conscientious scruples respecting the sanctity of the day. That even the sanctity of the weekly Sabbath was no barrier against popular passion, appears from Luke iv. 16–30, where the inhabitants of Nazareth attempted to put Jesus to death on that day. So also the Jews at Jerusalem, at the feast of Dedication, attempted, first to stone Him, and afterward to arrest Him, (John x. 22–39.) Upon the last day of the feast of Tabernacles, "the great day of the feast," the Sanhedrim was in session, and officers were engaged in the attempt to take Him, (John vii. 37–52.) Upon the weekly Sabbath the chief priests and Pharisees did not hesitate to go to Pilate to take measures for sealing the sepulchre, (Matt. xxvii. 62–66.)

2d. It is said, that no one after the paschal supper could leave the city till the next morning, and that therefore Jesus, upon this evening, could not have gone to the garden of Gethsemane. (See Exod. xii. 22.) It seems evident, however, that this direction was not designed to be permanently observed, any more than the command (v. 11) to eat it standing, with loins girded, shoes on the feet, and staff in the hand. We know, in point of fact, that the Jews in the Lord's time did not observe these and other directions, regarding them as peculiar to its first institution.

3d. It is said, that the preparation of spices and ointments for the Lord's embalming, upon the afternoon of the day of the crucifixion, (Luke xxiii. 56; John xix. 38–40,) implies that it was not a feast sabbath. Here, also, all depends upon the strictness with which the Jews observed the feast sabbaths. As we have seen, Maimonides mentions bathing and anointing, as things that might be done on the feast days; and, in the very nature of the case, every thing necessary to prepare the dead for burial would then be permitted. That purchases could be made even on the Sabbath, is shown by Tholuck, (on John xiii. 1,) if the price was not agreed upon, and no money paid. But with whatsoever strictness the feast sabbath was usually observed, we cannot question that both Joseph and Nicodemus would have regarded themselves as fully warranted to perform, during its hours, the last offices of love to one who had taught them in express words, and shown by His example, that He was Lord of the Sabbath.

That Luke (xxiii. 54) should designate the day following the crucifixion as a Sabbath, "And that day was the preparation, and the Sabbath drew on," has been explained as showing that the day of the crucifixion could not have been a feast sabbath.[1] But it proves only that the Evangelists, in conformity with Jewish opinion, regarded the weekly Sabbath as more sacred than the feast sabbath.

4th. It is said that the account given of Simon of Cyrene, (Mark xv. 21; Luke xxiii. 26,) who, coming out of the country at the time Jesus was on His way to the place of crucifixion, was compelled to bear His cross, is additional evidence that this was not a feast sabbath, he having probably been at work. But if this were so, we have still to inquire respecting the nature of the work. Lightfoot supposes him to have come from the field, bearing wood, which was lawful on a feast day. But it is not said that he had been out in the fields at work, nor that he had travelled any distance; and to come from the country into the city upon a feast sabbath was no violation of any law. For aught that we know, he was a resident of Jerusalem, who was casually without the wall, and was entering the gate when he met Jesus; or he may have been a pilgrim, who had come up to the feast.

5th. It is said that the Synoptists, in their mention of the day of crucifixion, give no hint that it had a sabbatical character. It is true that they do not do this in express terms, but they plainly imply it. According to them, the Lord ate the Passover at the legal time, on the 14th Nisan; the day therefore of His death was the 15th, or the first feast sabbath. That they designate it as the preparation day, without making prominent its sabbatical character, simply shows what great importance they attached to the fact that the Lord died and was buried before the weekly Sabbath began. This was of far more moment to them, as illustrating the relation of the Jewish Sabbath to the Christian, than to make prominent the sabbath character of the first day of the feast.

We thus reach the result that there is no real discrep-

[1] So Meyer.

ancy between the Synoptists and John. The Lord ate the true paschal supper at the appointed time—the time when it was eaten by the Jews in general, on the evening following the 14th Nisan.

Thursday Eve, 14th Nisan, 6th April.

As the disciples are about to take their places at the table, Jesus observes a strife among them for	Luke xxii. 24–30.
precedency and seats of honor. To rebuke them, He	John xiii. 2–20.
arose and girded Himself, and proceeded to wash their	Luke xxii. 15–18.
feet. Afterward, while they were eating, He declares	Matt. xxvi. 20–24.
that one of them should betray Him. The declara-	Mark xiv. 18–21.
tion creates great excitement among the apostles,	Luke xxii. 21–23.
and they begin to ask anxiously, Is it I? The Lord describes the traitor as one that was eating with Him,	John xiii. 21, 22.
but without designating him further. Peter makes a sign to John to ask Him who it was, which he does, and Jesus gives him privately a sign; and dipping	John xiii. 23–30.
the sop, gives it to Judas, who asks, Is it I? Jesus answers him affirmatively, and he immediately goes	Matt. xxvi. 25.
out, to the surprise of those apostles who do not un-	Matt. xxvi. 26–29.
derstand the cause. After the departure of Judas,	Mark xiv. 22–25.
the Lord proceeds to the institution of the eucharistic supper.	Luke xxii. 19, 20.

It is very difficult to arrange the events of this supper in a chronological order, as no one of the Evangelists has so narrated them. There are four points that especially demand our attention: the strife for precedency; the washing of the disciples' feet; the announcement of Judas' treachery and his departure; and the institution of the eucharist.

Luke alone mentions that there was "a strife among them, which of them should be accounted greatest." When during the supper did this occur? This Evangelist narrates in the following order: first the Passover and institution of the Lord's supper; second, the announcement of

Judas' treachery; third, the strife for precedency. Many of the earlier harmonists follow this order as the chronological one, and some of the moderns.[1] But this has great *intrinsic difficulties. It* is scarce possible that, after the discovery of the treason of Judas, and with the solemn impression which the Lord's words respecting the traitor must have made upon them, and after they had eaten His sacred supper, any such strife could have occurred. And the improbability is increased if, before this, He had taught them humility by washing their feet. Upon these grounds most affirm that Luke's order is not chronological.[2] Shall we then place the strife at the beginning of the feast? This is most probable; though some, as Calvin, would identify it with the incident mentioned in Matt. xx. 24, and suppose it related here out of its place. The strife may have arisen respecting their places at the table, each wishing to be as near the Lord as possible; the degree of nearness being an index of rank in the future kingdom.[3]

Luke does not mention the feet washing, nor John this strife; but the two accounts combined form a consistent whole. The Lord, after rebuking the disciples in words, proceeds to teach them in a symbolic manner in what their real greatness should consist, by girding Himself, and taking a towel to wash their feet. Both events are thus to be placed at the beginning of the feast. Some, however, would place the washing of the feet at the close of the supper, and this has a seeming support in our English version, John xiii. 2: "And supper being ended, He riseth," &c.[4]

[1] Patritius, Alford. [2] Calvin, Newcome, Ebrard, Oosterzee.

[3] Lightfoot supposes the strife to have been between Peter, James, and John, and that Peter began it. As to the degrees of honor attached to the various places at the table, see Becker's Gallus, Eng. trans., 472.

[4] The text is disputed. The received text is δειπνου γενομενου; so Alford. Tischendorf has γινομενου; so Meyer. It is rendered by Norton, "during supper;" by Campbell, "while they were at supper;" by Alford, "supper being prepared, or going on."

There can be little doubt that the commencement of the meal is meant. Some, however, would put the feet washing at the close of the paschal supper, and before the eucharistic supper; and others still after the eucharist. That it was at the close of the meal is affirmed by Thomson, (i. 183,) on the ground of oriental usage, it being customary to wash the hands and mouth after eating. "The pitcher and ewer are always brought, and the servant, with a napkin over his shoulder, pours water on your hands. If there is no servant, they perform this office for one another." In this case, however, Jesus must have washed both hands and feet; but it is plain from Peter's words, (v. 9, compare v. 5,) that He washed their feet only. It has been said that washing of the feet before a meal was an act of customary cleanliness, and that, no servant being present to perform it, each shrank from doing it, as implying inferiority.[1] The references, however, to the Old Testament show only that it was customary to wash the feet after a journey, and not always before a meal. The hands were usually washed three times during the paschal supper: after the first cup of wine; after the bitter herbs and the second cup; and after the eating of the lamb. It is possible that the feet were washed after the first cup, (Luke xxii. 17.)

It does not appear with what disciple the Lord began the feet washing. "If He did observe any order," says Lightfoot, "He began with Peter, who sat in the next place immediately to Himself." This commentator supposes that He washed the feet of Peter, James, and John only, thus avoiding the washing of Judas. Chrysostom affirms that He began with Judas; Greswell that He began with Peter and ended with Judas. It seems evident from vs. 5 and 6 that Peter was not the first, and from vs. 10 and 11 that the feet of Judas were washed.

[1] Bengel, Ebrard, Da Costa.

Some have found proof that this was not the paschal supper in the fact that Jesus "sat down with the Twelve," and did not eat standing, as directed, (Exod. xii. 11.) Calvin, who regarded this command as binding, supposes, therefore, that He ate the Passover standing, and afterward sat down. But, as there is no doubt that the Jews generally sat at this feast, either because this was the posture of freemen, or because they regarded the command of Moses as limited to its first observance, there is no good reason why He should not have followed the general custom.[1]

The third point is the announcement by the Lord of the treachery of Judas, and the departure of the traitor. In His reply to Peter, (John xiii. 10,) He had said, "Ye are clean, but not all." Probably no one then knew the meaning of these words but Judas. Afterward, v. 18, He spoke more openly; still His words do not seem to have made any special impression upon their minds. He, therefore, soon after declares in plain words that one of them should betray Him, (Matt. xxvi. 21; Mark xiv. 18; John xiii. 21.) This at once attracts their deepest attention, and they all begin to ask Him, "Lord, is it I?" In reply, He says that it is one of the Twelve, and one who was then eating with Him, (Matt. xxvi. 23; Mark xiv. 20; Luke xxii. 21.) In this designation of the traitor, He does not seem to refer to any present act of eating, but to the fact that he was sitting and partaking with Him at the same table. From these words, therefore, the apostles could not tell which of them was meant.[2] It is to the fulfilment of the prophecy (Ps. xli. 9) that He has special reference: "Yea, mine own familiar friend, in whom I trusted, which did eat of my bread, hath lifted up his heel against me." (See John xiii. 18.) This prophecy was now finding its accom-

[1] As to the early customs of the Jews in this respect, see Bynaeus, i. 204.

[2] Some would render Matt. xxvi. 23: "He that dippeth his hand," "He that has dipped his hand." So Meyer, Conant.

plishment in one sitting and eating at the same table with Him. The same truth is expressed by Luke: "Behold, the hand of him that betrayeth me is with me on the table." Some, however, find in the language of Mark, xiv. 20, "One of the Twelve that dippeth with me in the dish," a specific designation of Judas. "The expression seems to describe the traitor as particularly near to Christ at table, and in some peculiar sense partaking with Him."[1] It is possible that Judas may have been sitting near to Jesus, and both have dipped in the same dish; but, if so, it is plain that the others did not yet know who was meant.

At this point, when all had doubtless suspended eating, and their anxiety was at its height, and all were looking upon one another, doubting of whom He spake, and asking, Is it I? Peter beckons to John to ask Him who it was.[2] To John's question, "Lord, who is it?" which, probably, from his position as lying on Jesus' breast, was unheard by the others, He replied, "He it is to whom I shall give a sop when I have dipped it."[3] It is not probable that this reply was heard by any one but John. Taking a piece of the bread and dipping it in the broth, He gives it to Judas, and thus he is revealed as the traitor to John, but to none of the others. It may be that, on receiving the sop, Judas saw that his treachery was known not only to Jesus but also to John; and, knowing that all longer concealment is useless, he now asks, as the rest had done, but mockingly, "Lord, is it I?" (Matt. xxvi. 25.) To his question the

[1] Alexander in loco; Meyer.

[2] The text, as given by Tischendorf, (John xiii. 24,) makes the question to have been addressed by Peter to John, *νευει ουν τουτῳ Σιμων Πετρος και λεγει αυτῳ, Ειπε τις εστιν περι ου λεγει.* So Alford, Meyer. The received text is defended by Stier. Peter first beckons to John to gain his attention, and then asks him, supposing that he may know, but he, being ignorant, asks Jesus. "Then Simon Peter made a sign to this disciple, and said to him, Tell us who it is of whom He speaks?" Norton's trans.

[3] Tischendorf and Alford read *βαψω*, Meyer *βαψας*.

Lord replies, "Thou hast said," or in other words, Thou art the man.

There is some difficulty in determining when Judas asked this question and the Lord replied, from the fact that when the former went out none of the apostles seems to have known the cause of his departure, (John xiii. 28, 29.) Grotius supposes it to have been asked before Peter beckoned to John, the Lord's reply not being heard by him; and Friedlieb puts it before the sign of the sop given to John. In the general agitation and confusion the Lord's reply was unnoticed. According to Ebrard, (518,) the Lord answered John's question, "Who is it?" openly, so that all knew who was meant, and then Judas asks, "Is it I?" According to some, as Stier, all heard the question of Judas, but none specially marked it, as all had asked the same, and no suspicion seems to have attached to him in particular. The difficulty, however, is not with the question of Judas, which might easily have passed unnoticed, but with the Lord's reply, which, if heard, was too direct to have been misunderstood. If Judas had been thus openly designated as the traitor, how could the other apostles suppose that he was sent out to execute some official commission? Some, therefore, suppose that both question and reply were in a whisper, or very low tone of voice, and inaudible to the others. This is possible if Judas was very near the Lord, perhaps upon one side as John was upon the other, as some have inferred from Mark xiv. 18. In this case what was said might easily have escaped the ears of the other apostles; and it seems that Judas must have been near Him when he received the sop. According to some, both question and reply were not by words, but by signs. Others still suppose that both were heard and understood by all present, but that the apostles, looking forward to the betrayal as not imminent, did not imagine that His words, spoken immediately after, "That thou doest, do quickly," (John xiii. 27--29,) had any reference to the execution of his treacherous project. This is not intrinsically improbable. Notwithstanding the express terms in which He had spoken of His betrayal and death at this Passover, none of the disciples seems to have taken His words literally; and thus the designation of Judas as the betrayer by no means aroused them to a just apprehension of the treachery he was meditating—much less that it was to take effect that night.[1] They might, therefore, suppose that Jesus had given him some command connected with his official position as the treasurer of the band of apostles.

Before considering when, during the meal, the Lord instituted the eucharist, it will be necessary to have before us the order of the paschal supper.[2] 1. The supper opens with a glass of wine mingled with water, preceded by a blessing, and followed by washing of the hands. 2. Giving of thanks, and eating of the bitter herbs. 3. Bringing in of the unleavened bread, the sauce, the lamb, and the flesh of the chagigah, and thank offerings. 4. Benediction. The bitter herbs dipped in the sauce are eaten. 5. The second cup is mixed, and the father explains to his children the origin of the feast. 6. The first part of the Hallel (Psalms cxiii. and cxiv.) is sung, prayer offered, and the second cup drank. 7. The father washes his hands, takes two loaves of bread, breaks one and blesses it, takes a piece, and, wrapping it in the bitter herbs, dips it in the sauce, and eats it with thanksgiving. Giving thanks, he then eats of the chagigah, and, again giving thanks, eats of the lamb. 8. The meal continues, each eating what he pleases, but eating last of the lamb. After this was consumed, no more was eaten. 9. He washes his hands and takes the third cup,

[1] Lichtenstein, 404; Luthardt, ii. 283.

[2] For this, see Lightfoot and Meyer on Matt. xxvi. 26; Friedlieb, Arch. 54; Brown, Antiq. i. 450.

after giving thanks. 10. The second part of the Hallel (Psalms cxv.–cxviii.) is sung. 11. The fourth cup is taken, and sometimes a fifth. 12. The supper concludes with singing the great Hallel, (Psalms cxx.–cxxvii.)

Upon several of these points there is dispute among the Jewish writers, but the order, as here given, is substantially according to the paschal ritual of the Talmudists. Whether this order was generally followed in our Saviour's time, is very doubtful; nor, if so, is it by any means certain that He strictly followed it.

The order may be most clearly seen in its relation to the evangelical narratives, if we consider it in connection with the several cups of wine. "Four cups of wine," says Lightfoot, "were to be drank up by every one." The first introductory with thanksgiving. This was followed by the bringing in of the bitter herbs and eating of them; the bringing in of the bread, the sauce, the lamb, and the chagigah; the explanation of the meaning of the feast; and the first part of the Hallel. The second cup, followed by the eating of the unleavened bread, of the chagigah, and of the lamb. The third cup, commonly called the cup of blessing, and the second part of the Hallel sung. The fourth cup drank. If the great Hallel was sung, a fifth cup. All that took place between the first and second cups was introductory to the meal. The feast proper began with the second cup and ended with the third. Except the partial eating of the bitter herbs, the object of which was to awaken the interest of the children preparatory to their instruction, nothing was eaten before the second, and nothing at all was eaten after the third. The singing of the second part of the Hallel, and the fourth cup, generally closed the feast.

If we now turn to the Evangelists, we find that Luke only (xxii. 17 and 20) mentions two cups of wine. To which of the four customary cups of the paschal supper shall these be referred? Many identify the first of Luke with the first of the supper.[1] But against this are the Lord's words, vs. 16 and 18, that He would no more eat or drink of the Passover till the kingdom of God should come, which imply, that He had already eaten and drunken, and that the paschal supper was over.[2] The words, however, may mean no more than that He would partake of no Passover after the present. Meyer insists that the words, "Take this and divide it among yourselves; for I say unto you, I will not drink of the fruit of the vine until the kingdom of God shall come," show conclusively that He did not Himself drink of the cup; which abstinence, if this were the first cup, is most improbable, and that therefore these words, which were later spoken, (Matt. xxvi. 29,) Luke has erroneously inserted here. But it is by no means certain that the words, "Take this and divide it among yourselves," do exclude His own participation in the cup. He greatly desired to eat the Passover with them, and it is not questioned that He did so. Why then should He not partake of the wine, which, though not divinely commanded, was yet regarded as a regular part of the supper? Luke's language does not at all forbid the supposition that He had Himself partaken of the cup ere He gave it to the disciples.[3]

The similarity of Matt. xxvi. 29 and Mark xiv. 25 with Luke xxii. 18, may best be explained by supposing that the latter was spoken in reference to the paschal supper, the former in reference to the eucharistic supper. He kept the Passover with His disciples according to the law, and thus fulfilled it. He would no more partake of it, till it should be observed in its new and higher form in the kingdom of God. He established the eucharistic supper, and

1 So Robinson, Stier, Alford.

2 So Paulus in loco, who makes this the fifth cup.

3 See Alford in loco.

henceforth would no more partake of it, till all should be made new in the kingdom. It may be, that in this are references to two distinct ordinances in the age to come: that of the paschal supper for the Jews, and of the Lord's supper for the Church.

Some, however, make the first cup of Luke to have been the third of the paschal supper.[1] The supper was then, so far as eating the Passover was concerned, fully over; and His words, "With desire have I desired to eat this Passover with you before I suffer," refer to His own supper, which He was about to establish. Bucher (742) refers these words, vs. 15–18, to the paschal supper just ended; but Matt. xxvi. 29, and Mark xiv. 25, to the eucharistic supper.

The second cup of Luke (v. 20) was that "after supper," *μετα το δειπνησαι*, (see also 1 Cor. xi. 25,) and is the same as that mentioned by Matt. xxvi. 27 and Mark xiv. 23. To which of the four cups of the supper does this correspond? Many refer it to the third.[2] Of this cup, Brown remarks: "It was emphatically called 'the cup of blessing,' because, while it stood before them, the president did what we commonly do at the end of a feast—he returned thanks to the Father of all for every temporal and spiritual blessing, but especially that of the Passover." To this some suppose St. Paul to refer, (1 Cor. x. 16:) "The cup of blessing which we bless, is it not the communion of the blood of Christ?" If this be correct, then, after the eating of the paschal lamb was ended, and the law had thus been fulfilled, and the supper finished, Jesus, before proceeding to take the cup after supper, the cup of blessing, takes bread, probably the unleavened bread upon the table, and gives thanks, and declaring it to be His body, gives them to eat. It had been a rule that the paschal lamb should be the last thing eaten; but He now sets this aside, and gives them the flesh

[1] Brown, Antiq. 465.

[2] So Lightfoot, Lange, Robinson, Lichtenstein.

of "the Lamb slain from the foundation of the world." He now takes the cup, and giving thanks, gives it to them, that all might drink. By thus placing the taking of the eucharistic bread immediately after, and in connection with, the eating of the paschal lamb, we best meet the statements of Matthew and Mark, that "as they were eating, *εσθιοντων αυτων*, He took bread," &c.

Some, however, make this to have been the fourth cup.[1] The chief argument for this is, that if it was the third cup, the fourth cup must have been wholly omitted, which is not probable. Of this fourth cup, Brown remarks: "We are not particularly informed whether it immediately succeeded the third, or that a certain interval was between them. But we know that it was called the cup of the Hallel, because the president finished over it the Hallel which he had begun over the second cup."[2] Still, as this observance respecting the four cups of wine was not commanded in the law, Jesus might not have regarded it, and have sung the hymn after the third. If, however, a cup was taken after the sacramental cup, which is not probable, it is not mentioned.

It has been a point much discussed, whether Judas departed before or after the institution of the eucharist. Matthew, (xxvi. 25,) who alone relates his question, "Master, is it I?" and the Lord's reply, "Thou hast said," says nothing of his departure, but mentions the eucharistic supper as taking place after the question and reply. John, (xiii. 26–30,) who mentions his departure immediately after receiving the sop, says nothing of the eucharistic supper. The Evangelists Mark and Luke do not speak of Judas by name. Where then, in Matthew's narrative, shall we insert his departure? Probably between vs. 25 and 26. From the expression, v. 26, "And as they were eating, Jesus took

[1] Meyer, Brown. Bynaeus hesitates between the third and fourth.

[2] See Friedlieb, Arch. 58.

bread," &c., some infer the presence of Judas, the paschal supper not being yet ended.[1] But the expression may mean no more than that, while yet at the table, Jesus took bread; or if the eating was even of the lamb, of which all were bound to partake, the peculiar position of Judas would justify his exclusion. The argument from the Lord's words, v. 27, "Drink ye all of it," as implying that Judas was to drink with the others, is thus stated by Alford: "It is on all accounts probable, and this account confirms the probability, that Judas was present, and partook of both parts of this first communion. The expressions are such throughout as to lead us to suppose that the same persons, the Twelve, were present." But Matthew uses the same expression: "All ye shall be offended in me this night," (v. 31, so vs. 33 and 35,) when only eleven were present. According to many, this command that all should drink, is a prophetic warning against the custom of the Romish Church in withholding the cup from the laity.[2] Perhaps the right explanation may be that given by Buxtorf,[3] who says, that it is the law among the Jews, that all who were present at the paschal supper, should drink of the four cups, whether men or women, adults or children; and especially of the fourth or last cup.

If we turn to the narrative of John, we read that, after Jesus gave Judas the sop, Satan entered into him, and "he went immediately out." Some have attempted to determine, from the mention of the "sop," to what period of the meal this event is to be referred. But it is uncertain whether this sop, ψωμιον, literally bit, or morsel, was of flesh or bread.[4] If of bread, as is most probable, it may have been given immediately after the second cup, when

[1] Bengel; *ergo Judas aderat.*

[2] Calvin, Alexander.

[3] Cited by Bynaeus, i. 624.

[4] The opinion of Origen and others, that this was the bread consecrated to be the Lord's body, and now given to Judas, is refuted by Augustine.

each of the company, wrapping a piece of unleavened bread in bitter herbs, dipped it in the sauce and ate it. This was before the paschal lamb was eaten. But, as both the bread and sauce continued on the table to the end of the meal, the Lord may have given him the sop at a later period, and no definite inference can be drawn from this circumstance.

If Judas went out immediately after receiving the sop, and yet were present at the Lord's supper, this supper must have been prior to the dipping of the sop. But where in John's narrative can it be placed? According to Stier, it may find place between vs. 22 and 23. But there is the greatest intrinsic improbability, that after Jesus had solemnly announced to them, "Verily, verily, I say unto you, that one of you shall betray me," and "all were looking on one another, doubting of whom He spake," He should have proceeded at once to the institution of this holy rite. It is to be noted, also, that in announcing the treachery of Judas, v. 21, "He was troubled in spirit," but that after the departure of Judas, v. 31, He said, "Now is the Son of man glorified, and God is glorified in Him." There seems to be in John's narrative no possible place for inserting the institution of the eucharist prior to the departure of Judas. Where, after that, it is to be placed is disputed. Some place it between vs. 30 and 31; some between vs. 32 and 33; some after v. 33; some after v. 38; and others find no place wholly satisfactory.

Some would make a distinction between the two parts of the Lord's supper, an interval elapsing between the consecration of the bread and that of the wine.[1] Hence it is said that Judas partook of the bread, but went out before the distribution of the cup. There is no sound basis for this distinction.

[1] Greswell, iii. 181. "The bread was ordained during the supper, the use of the cup was prescribed after it."

Upon these grounds, we conclude that Judas left the paschal supper before the Lord instituted the eucharist. This point has been connected with questions respecting the spiritual efficacy of the sacrament, into which it would be foreign to our purpose to enter. The weight of authority down to recent times, is in favor of the view that he was present, and partook with the other apostles of the bread and wine.[1]

Evening following Thursday, 14th Nisan, 6th April.

After the supper Peter makes protestations of fidelity, but the Lord announces to him that before the cock should crow he should deny Him. He teaches the disciples of the perils that await them, and they bring to Him two swords.	Luke xxii. 31–38. John xiii. 36–38. Matt. xxvi. 30–35. Mark xiv. 26–31.
He proceeds to address to them words of encouragement, and answers questions of Thomas and Philip. He adds the promise of the Comforter, and calling upon them to arise and depart with Him,	John xiv. 1–31.
He continues His address to them as they stand around Him, and ends with a prayer.	John xv., xvi., xvii.

Matthew and Mark narrate the Lord's conversation with Peter, as if it took place after they had left the supper room, and were upon their way to the Mount of Olives; Luke and John, as taking place before they had left the

[1] Wichelhaus (257) enumerates as its defenders, Cyprian, Jerome, Augustine, Chrysostom, the two Cyrils, Theodoret; and later, Bellarmine, Baronius, Maldonatus, Gerhard, Beza, Bucer, Lightfoot, Bengel. Calvin is undecided. *Probabile tamen esse non nego Judam affuisse.* It is affirmed by the Lutherans, but denied by the Reformed. Of the later commentators affirming it, are McKnight, Krafft, Patritius, Stier, Alford; denying it, Meyer, Tischendorf, Robinson, Lichtenstein, Friedlieb, Bucher, Ebrard, Lange, Wieseler, Riggenbach, Ellicott. For an interesting discussion of the point, see Bynaeus, i. 443.

room. Hence, some suppose that the conversation began before they left it, and was renewed by the way; and that His declaration respecting the crowing of the cock was twice spoken: once as recorded by the former, and once as recorded by the latter.[1] Others, however, who agree with these, that Jesus twice uttered the prediction respecting the denials of Peter, would identify Matthew, Mark, and Luke. Luke does not narrate in chronological order. This identification is defended on internal grounds, and especially that the Lord's words to Peter, as given by Luke, "When thou art converted, strengthen thy brethren," seem plainly to point to His words respecting all the apostles, as given by Matthew and Mark, "All ye shall be offended because of me this night."[2] That the prediction respecting Peter's denials was twice spoken, is intrinsically probable, and wholly in accordance with Peter's character. Jesus had said (John xiii. 33) that He must go whither His disciples could not follow Him. This leads Peter to ask whither He was going, and why he could not now follow Him; and he adds, "I will lay down my life for thy sake." Now the Lord declares to him, that ere the cock crow he shall deny Him thrice. (At this time, probably, were also spoken the words given by Luke xxii. 31–34.) Later, perhaps as they were approaching the garden of Gethsemane, Jesus, addressing them as a body, declares that "they all shall be offended in Him this night." This leads Peter to repeat his protestations of fidelity, and to affirm that though all others should be offended, yet he would not. The Lord therefore repeats, and more emphatically, "Verily I say unto thee, this day, even in this night, before the cock crow twice thou shalt deny me thrice."

According to some, the Lord three times predicted Peter's denials, once as given by John, once by Luke, and

[1] Meyer, Alford, Oosterzee. [2] See Bynaeus, ii. 9.

once by Matthew and Mark.[1] Others still make but one prediction, which John and Luke relate in its place, and Matthew and Mark by retrospection.[2] Townsend makes two predictions, of which one occurred at the paschal supper, and one on the way to the Mount of Olives.[3]

The words the "cock shall not crow," may be understood as referring, not to a literal cock, but to that watch of the night known as the "cock-crowing," (see Mark xiii. 35,) or the third watch, that from 12–3 A. M. "Within the time of cock-crowing," says Lightfoot, "the short space of time between the first and second crowing." This would be equivalent to saying, before early dawn thou shalt deny me. But the Lord seems to include the actual crowing of the cock, as the event shows, (Mark xiv. 66–72.) The second crowing was probably about 3 A. M. That Mark should say, "Before the cock crow twice thou shalt deny me thrice," while the other Evangelists say, "Before the cock crow thou shalt deny me thrice," makes no real discrepancy. The latter speak generally of the cock-crowing as a period of time within which the three denials should take place; Mark more accurately says, that during this period the cock should not crow twice ere the denials were made.[4] The assertion that no cocks were permitted at Jerusalem has no basis.[5]

The allusion to the swords is found only in Luke. Some, as Stier, make this incident to have taken place on the way to Gethsemane, and just before the entrance into it. As, however, it seems to be directly connected with the words spoken to Peter, it may have occurred in the supper room.[6]

[1] So Augustine, Greswell. [2] Newcome, Robinson, Riggenbach.

[3] So substantially Patritius.

[4] See Friedlieb, Archaöl. 79; Greswell, iii. 211.

[5] See Alford on Matt. xxvi. 34. "It is certain that there were cocks at Jerusalem as well as at other places." Lightfoot.

[6] So Da Costa, Ebrard, Oosterzee.

After thus warning His disciples of the twofold danger from invisible temptation and external violence, and encouraging them to trust in Him, and giving them the promise of the Comforter, He offers His farewell prayer, the hymn is sung, and the paschal solemnity ended. We may, however, connect this hymn with His words, (John xiv. 31,) "Arise, let us go hence," or place it before the discourse. Norton supposes that He rose from the table to pray, but continued for a time His address. That the discourse in chaps. xv. and xvi., with the prayer in chap. xvii., was spoken in the supper room, appears very clearly from chap. xviii. 1, where it is said, "When Jesus had spoken these words He went forth—εξηλθε—with His disciples over the brook Cedron," which can scarcely refer to a departure from any other place, although referred by some to His going out of the city. It appears, also, from this, that after His words, "Arise, let us go hence," no change of place is mentioned till the prayer is ended; and from the improbability that such a discourse would be spoken by the way. We conclude, therefore, that the Lord, after the disciples had arisen, and while still standing in the room, continued His discourse and ended it with the prayer.[1] Many, however, suppose it to have been spoken on the way to Gethsemane.[2] Conversation with His disciples while journeying with them was indeed not unusual, but that He should deliver so long a discourse at night, and under these circumstances, is most improbable. Those who deny this supper in John xiii. 2 to be the paschal supper, but make it one previous at Bethany, place its close at xiv. 31, when Jesus arose to go to Jerusalem. Bynaeus finds three distinct discourses: the first, John xiii., at the supper on the evening of Wednesday preceding the paschal supper; the second, John xiv., on Thursday, just before Jesus left Bethany to go to Jerusa-

[1] Meyer, Stier, Alford, Norton, Tholuck, Ellicott.

[2] Lange, Da Costa, Ebrard, Patritius.

lem to the paschal supper; the third, John xv. xvi. xvii., on the night following the paschal supper.

EVENING FOLLOWING THURSDAY, 14th NISAN, 6TH APRIL.

After His prayer was ended, Jesus went with His disciples over the brook Cedron to the garden of Gethsemane, where He would await the coming of Judas. This apostate, after leaving the supper room, had gone to the priests, and with them made arrangement for the immediate arrest of the Lord.	JOHN xviii. 1, 2. MATT. xxvi. 36. LUKE xxii. 39. MARK xiv. 32. JOHN xviii. 3.
Coming to the garden, Jesus takes with Him Peter and James and John, and retires with them to a secluded spot. Here He begins to be heavy with sorrow, and, leaving the three, goes alone to pray. Returning, He finds them asleep. Leaving them, He again prays, and in His agony sweats a bloody sweat, but is strengthened by an angel. Again returning to the three disciples, He finds them asleep. He goes a third time and prays, and returning, bids them sleep on, but soon announces the approach of Judas.	MATT. xxvi. 37–46. MARK xiv. 33–42. LUKE xxii. 40–46.

The hour when Jesus left the supper room to go to Gethsemane, cannot be exactly determined. Lichtenstein (411) puts it at midnight; first, because usually at this hour the supper was ended; second, because if He had left earlier, there would have been too great delay at Gethsemane. Greswell puts it between eleven and twelve o'clock; Morrison at nine or ten; Fairbairn at eight or nine; Jarvis at eight. Supposing the paschal supper to have commenced about 6 P. M., or sundown, the several incidents of the feast, and the Lord's discourse and prayer, must have occupied them till near midnight. The only datum of time bearing on it is the crowing of the cock (Mark xiv. 68 and 72,) and this gives no definite result. Of the situation of the house where the supper was eaten, we know nothing. Greswell supposes it to have been in the eastern part of the city; and, wherever it was, it could not have been very far distant from the garden.[1] We cannot be far wrong if we suppose the Lord to have reached Gethsemane about midnight.

The garden of Gethsemane, "valley of oil," or "oil press," to which the Lord went, was a place He was accustomed to visit, (John xviii. 2,) and a little way out of the city. It seems to have been an olive orchard, and not connected with any private residence. If, however, this was a private garden, still, as at the feasts all the houses and gardens were thrown open to the public, Jesus could visit it at this time without hindrance, or attracting to Himself any special attention. Greswell hints that the family of Lazarus might have had possessions there. From a comparison of Luke xxi. 37 with xxii. 39, it appears that the Lord had spent some part of the previous nights there, perhaps alone in prayer.

Whether the site of the modern Gethsemane is to be identified with the ancient garden, is doubtful. It is first mentioned by Eusebius as at the Mount of Olives, and afterward more definitely by Jerome as at the foot of the Mount.[2] Several of the most recent inquirers are disposed to deny the identification. Thomson (ii. 483) says: "The position is too near the city, and so close to what must have always been the great thoroughfare eastward, that our Lord would scarcely have selected it for retirement on that dangerous and dismal night." He finds a better site several hundred yards to the northeast, on the Mount of Olives. Barclay (63) thinks it evident that the present enclosure, from its narrow dimensions, can occupy only in part the site of

1 As to the traditional site of the "Upper Room," now shown in the pile of buildings surrounding the tomb of David, see Williams, H. C., ii. 507.

2 Robinson, i. 235.

the ancient garden, and finds a better position higher up in the valley. Stanley (415) is undecided. But whether the present garden occupies precisely the old site or not, it is certain that it must be near it. It lies a little east of the valley of Cedron, at the intersection of two paths, both leading in different directions over the Mount of Olives. Descending from St. Stephen's gate into the valley, and crossing a bridge, it is easily reached, being distant but nine or ten rods from the bridge. Formerly it was unenclosed, but recently the Latins have built a high wall around it. There are within eight venerable olive trees, undoubtedly of great age, their trunks much decayed, but branches flourishing. "The most venerable of their race on the face of the earth," says Stanley, "their gnarled trunks and scanty foliage will always be regarded as the most affecting of the sacred memorials in or about Jerusalem." The Greeks, envious of the Latins, have recently enclosed a piece of ground a little north, beside the Virgin's tomb, and contend that this is the true garden.[1]

The words of Jesus at the paschal supper, (John xiii. 27,) "That thou doest, do quickly," forced Judas to do at once what he had apparently not designed to do till the feast was over. Perhaps he feared that if the arrest was was not made the same night, Jesus would next day leave the city. Of the movements of Judas after he left the supper, none of the Evangelists give us an account till he reappears at the garden of Gethsemane; but we can readily picture them to ourselves in their outline. Going immediately to Caiaphas, or to some other leading member of the Sanhedrim, he informs him where Jesus is, and announces that he is ready to fulfil his compact, and at once to make the arrest. It was not, as we have seen, the intention to arrest Him during the feast, lest there should be a popular tumult, (Matt. xxvi. 5;) but now that an opportunity of-

[1] Porter, i. 177

fered of seizing Him secretly at dead of night, when all were asleep or engaged at the paschal meal, and therefore without danger of interference or uproar, His enemies could not hesitate. Once in their hands, the rest was easy. A hasty trial, a prejudged condemnation, an immediate execution, and the hated Prophet of Galilee was forever removed out of their way. All perhaps might be done by the hour of morning prayer and sacrifice.[1] With great despatch all the necessary arrangements are made. Some soldiers the Sanhedrim had under its own direction, the guards of the temple, commanded by "the captains of the temple," or, as translated by Campbell, "officers of the temple guard," (Luke xxii. 52;) and to these they added some of their own servants, armed with staves. But they must be attended by Roman soldiers, in case a disturbance should arise; and to this end Pilate was persuaded to place at their command the cohort, or a part of it, under its captain, χιλιαρχος, that during the feast was stationed at Fort Antonia for the preservation of order.[2] Some of the chief priests and elders were also themselves to be present, to direct the proceedings, and if necessary to control the people.[3] The soldiers, or some portion of them, were to be provided with lanterns and torches, probably to search the garden if any attempt were made to escape. That at this time the moon was at the full presents no objection. "They would," says Hackett, (140,) "need lanterns and torches, even in a clear night and under a brilliant moon, because the western side of Olivet abounds in deserted tombs and caves." It is possible that they thought to surprise Him asleep. It was agreed that Judas should precede the others, and, approaching Him in a friendly way, kiss Him, and thus make Him known. This indicates that no resistance was anticipated.

[1] Lichtenstein, 414. [2] John xviii. 3 and 12. See Meyer in loco.
[3] Luke xxii. 52. Lichtenstein, 415.

Of the events at Gethsemane prior to the arrival of Judas, John says nothing. Luke is brief, and, omitting the choice of the three apostles to accompany Jesus, mentions but one prayer. On the other hand, he alone mentions the bloody sweat and the presence of the angel, (xxii. 40–46.) In Matthew and Mark we find the fullest details.

Whether all the apostles entered the garden does not appear; but if so, all, except Peter, James, and John, remained near the entrance. How long time He was with the three in the recesses of the garden, can but be conjectured, for the words given by Matthew, xxvi. 40, "What, could ye not watch with me one hour?" do not imply, as said by Greswell, that this was the time actually occupied in His prayer, but are a proverbial expression, denoting a brief interval. Some place the visit of the angel between the first and second prayer, to strengthen Him for that more terrible struggle when He sweat drops of blood.[1] Others make the agony and bloody sweat to have taken place before the appearance of the angel, and its cause, although narrated after it. That the grief and heaviness were greatest during the first prayer, may be inferred from Matthew and Mark. The language of Luke does not permit us to think of sweat falling in large, heavy drops like blood, but of sweat mingled with blood.[2]

The Lord's words to the three apostles, after His last return to them, (Matt. xxvi. 45; so Mark,) "Sleep on now, and take your rest," are understood by some as giving them permission and opportunity to sleep, and thus refresh themselves to meet the coming peril. "The obvious objection to this explanation is that in the same breath He tells them to awake; but even this is not unnatural, if taken as a sort of after thought, suggested by the sight or sound of the

[1] Meyer, Alford.

[2] Meyer, Alford, De Wette. For cases having points of similarity, see Stroud on Death of Christ, 85, and note iii.

approaching enemy."[1] Others understand them as ironically spoken.[2] Others still, as interrogatively: "Sleep ye on still, and take ye your rest?"[3] The first explanation is to be preferred. "The former words," says Ellicott, "were rather in the accents of a pensive contemplation—the latter in the tones of exhortation and command." It was the sudden appearance of Judas and his band that caused the words, "Rise, let us be going; behold, he is at hand that doth betray me," and explain their apparent abruptness.[4] Hackett (254) connects them with the local position of the garden, from which Jesus could survey at a glance the entire length of the eastern wall, and the slope of the hill toward the valley. "It is not improbable that His watchful eyes at that moment caught sight of Judas and his accomplices, as they issued from one of the eastern gates, or turned round the northern or southern corner of the walls, in order to descend into the valley."

Evening following Thursday, 14th Nisan, 6th April.

John xviii. 3–12.
Matt. xxvi 47–56.
Mark xiv. 43–52.
Luke xxii. 47, 48.

Upon the arrival of Judas and those with him, Jesus, accompanied by the apostles, goes forth from the garden to meet him. Judas, coming forward before the others, kisses Him as a sign to them. Addressing Judas, with the words, "Betrayest thou the Son of man with a kiss," He advances to the multitude and demands of them whom they seek? At their reply, "Jesus of Nazareth," He answers, "I am He," and they go backward and fall to the ground. Again He asks the same question, and receives the same reply. He

[1] Alexander. See Lichtenstein, 414.

[2] Calvin, Campbell, Meyer.

[3] Greswell, iii. 194; Robinson, Har. 151. The former would refer Luke xxii. 45, not to the three disciples, but to the eight whom He found also asleep near the entrance of the garden. There seems no basis for this.

[4] See Mark xiv. 41. "It is enough;" i. e., "Ye have slept enough."

now requests that the apostles may go free. As they proceed to take and bind Him, Peter smites a servant of the high priest, but the Lord heals the wound. Beholding their Master in the power of His enemies, all the apostles forsake Him and flee, and also a young man who had followed Him. He reproaches the multitude that they had come to arrest Him as a thief.

LUKE xxii. 49–53.

The time spent in the garden was probably more than an hour, so that, if they entered it about midnight, it was between one and two in the morning when Judas came.[1] The Lord seems to have met him near the entrance of the garden—whether without it or within it is not certain. "He went forth," (John xviii. 4;) "out of the garden," (Meyer;) "out of the circle of the disciples," (Lange;) "from the shade of the trees into the moonlight," (Alford;) "from the bottom of the garden to the front part of it," (Tholuck.) The matter is unimportant. According to his arrangement with the priests, Judas, seeing the Lord standing with the disciples, leaves those that accompanied him a little behind, and, coming forward, salutes Him with the usual salutation, and kisses Him. To this Jesus replies, "Friend, wherefore art thou come?" (Matt. xxvi. 50.) "Betrayest thou the Son of man with a kiss?" (Luke xxii. 48.) Appalled at these words, Judas steps backward, and Jesus goes toward the multitude, who were watching what was taking place, and who, beholding Him advance, await His approach. It may be that Judas had advanced so far before his companions that he was not seen by them to kiss the Lord, and that they were still awaiting the sign. He asks, "Whom seek ye?" They reply, "Jesus of Nazareth." His words, "I am He," spoken with the majesty that became the Son of God, so overawed them that they went backward and fell to the ground. After a like ques-

[1] Jones, Notes, 331, makes the arrest to have been about 10 P. M., and Jesus taken to Caiaphas about 11 P. M. It must have been later than this.

tion and reply, He requests them to let the apostles go free, thus implying his own willingness to be taken; and they, thus emboldened, now lay hands upon Him. At this moment Peter draws his sword and smites one of the band. Jesus orders him to put up his sword, and declares that He gives Himself up to them voluntarily, and that, if He needed help, His Father would send Him legions of angels. The healing of the servant's ear is mentioned only by Luke, (xxii. 51.) He now addresses a few words to the chief priests and captains and elders, who had probably to this time been standing behind the soldiers, and now came forward; and, as He finished, the apostles, seeing Him wholly in the power of His enemies, forsook Him and fled. It does not appear that there was any design to arrest them. If their Master was removed out of the way, the Sanhedrim doubtless thought that they would soon sink into obscurity. There was no attempt to seize them, and in the darkness and confusion they could easily escape. Peter and John, however, continued lurking near by, watching the progress of events. The incident of the young man "having a linen cloth cast about his naked body," is mentioned only by Mark, (xiv. 51, 52.) From the linen cloth or cloak, Lightfoot infers that he was a religious ascetic, and not a disciple of Jesus, but a casual looker-on. Lichtenstein (395) makes him to have been the Evangelist Mark himself, and son of the man at whose house Jesus ate the paschal supper; others, John; others, James the Just.[1]

The circumstances connected with the arrest are put by some in another order. The incidents narrated by John, (xviii. 4–9,) the going forth of Jesus to the multitude; His questions to them; and their prostration; took place before Judas approached Him to kiss Him.[2] According to Stier,

[1] See Alexander in loco. The matter is elaborately discussed by Bynaeus, ii. 228.

[2] So Robinson, Alford, Stier.

(vii. 277,) Judas was with the band, but stood irresolute as the Lord came to meet them. He with the others fell to the ground, but, reviving, goes forward to give the kiss. But why give the kiss to make Jesus known, when He already avowedly stood before them? It was not needed as a sign. Stier affirms that it was given in "the devilish spirit to maintain his consistency and redeem his word." This may be so, but the order before given is more probable.[1]

Friday Morning, 15th Nisan, 7th April.

From the garden Jesus is taken first to the house of Annas, and, after a brief delay here, to the palace	John xviii. 13–15.
of Caiaphas, the high priest; Peter and John following Him. Here, whilst the council is assembling, He	Matt. xxvi. 57, 58. Mark xiv. 53, 54.
is subjected to preliminary examination by Caiaphas	Luke xxii. 54, 55.
respecting His disciples and doctrine. The council	John xviii. 19–23.
having assembled, He is put on trial. As the witnesses disagree and no charge can be proved against	Matt. xxvi. 59–66. Mark xiv. 55–64.
Him, He is adjured by Caiaphas to tell whether He	
be the Christ. Upon His confession He is condemned	Matt. xxvi. 69–75.
as guilty of blasphemy. During this period, Peter,	Mark xiv. 66–72.
who had followed Him with John to the high priest's	Luke xxii. 56–62.
palace, there denies Him, and, reminded of His words	John xviii. 15–18.
by the crowing of the cock, goes out to weep.	" 25–27.

That Jesus was led from Gethsemane to Annas first, and then sent by Annas to Caiaphas, is mentioned only by John. According to Matthew, He was led to Caiaphas, the high priest, and in his palace, before the priests and scribes and elders, the trial took place. Mark and Luke say merely that He was led away to the high priest, without naming him. The preliminary examination mentioned by John, they all pass over in silence. Our first inquiry

[1] So Lichtenstein, Krafft, Ebrard, Luthardt, Meyer, Patritius.

therefore concerns this preliminary examination, before whom it was held, and its relations to the formal trial.

The Jews led Jesus away to Annas first. Various causes have been assigned why He should have been taken to Annas, as that his house was near at hand, and here the Lord might be kept safely till the council assembled; that he was president or vice-president of the Sanhedrim, and so had a legal right to examine Him; that he occupied the same palace with Caiaphas; that he was father-in-law to Caiaphas, and therefore this mark of respect was shown him. To this latter relationship the Evangelist gives special emphasis, (v. 13,) and seems to make it the cause why Jesus was led before him.[1] It is apparent from Josephus,[2] as well as from the Evangelists, that he was for many years a man of great influence, and virtually the ecclesiastical head of the nation. It is in this personal reputation and authority, that we find the explanation of the fact that Jesus was taken to him first. As the former high priest, as father-in-law of Caiaphas, as an experienced and able counsellor, a wish on his part to see so noted a prisoner, aside from other reasons, would sufficiently explain why the Lord was led before him.

But all this still leaves undetermined the point whether the Lord was examined by Annas. If so, he is designated by John as high priest, (v. 19:) "The high priest then asked Jesus," &c. But does he so designate him, or is Caiaphas meant? That Annas is so called by Luke (iii. 2, Acts iv. 6) is not conclusive, for the question turns not on this fact, but on John's meaning. Nowhere in his Gospel does this Evangelist call Annas the high priest. This office was held by Caiaphas, (xi. 49 and 51.) That a distinction, based upon official position, is taken in the passage before us between Annas and Caiaphas, is apparent. Of the latter it is expressly said that he was high priest, (see also v. 24;) of

[1] Ellicott, 333, 1. [2] Antiq., 20. 9. 1.

the former that he was father-in-law of the high priest. When he then, immediately after, speaks of the palace of the high priest, whose palace is meant? Obviously that of Caiaphas. This seems the only natural and unforced interpretation of the language. The remark of Neander, repeated by Stier, that, by being styled the "high priest *of that year*," Caiaphas is not designated as *the* high priest, and is distinguished from other high priests, has little force.

The argument that tends most strongly to show that Annas is called high priest, is drawn from the statement (v. 15) that Simon Peter was following Jesus with John, and that they went in with Him into the palace of the high priest. As they led Him to Annas first, it is inferred that the disciples followed Him thither, and that what is said in vs. 15–23 must be the account of what there took place.[1] But if this visit to Annas was brief, and had no important bearing on what followed; and was to gratify his curiosity, or to get his advice, or to find a place of temporary security, we can readily see why it is so briefly mentioned, and why the disciples are not said to have entered his palace.

If we turn to the examination itself, all the circumstances indicate that it was before Caiaphas, the legal high priest: the mention of his palace, the character of his questions, the fact that the Lord answers him, and the conduct of the officer. But does not the statement (v. 24) that "Annas sent (απεστειλεν) Him bound unto Caiaphas, the high priest," show that this sending was after the examination previously mentioned? (vs. 19–23.) All here depends upon the point whether απεστειλεν can be translated, as in our version, "had sent."[2] It is easily comprehensible that

[1] So Luthardt, ii. 385.

[2] Winer (Gram. 246) leaves the point undecided; so Buttman, New Test. Gram. 173. In favor of this translation, Tholuck, De Wette, Krafft, Robinson, Norton, Greswell, Campbell.

John, not having explicitly mentioned this sending to Caiaphas, should give this supplementary statement. Still, some find the key to this verse in the word "bound," as referring back to vs. 22, 23. Annas had sent Him to Caiaphas bound; yet the high priest permits Him, thus helpless, to be smitten in his presence. In this way the statement comes in parenthetically, and in its right place. "The fact is mentioned here because this indignity and prejudgment of the case of Jesus led to, and countenanced, the indignity just before mentioned."[1] Perhaps the more natural position of v. 24 would be after v. 13, where some would place it. If, however, we translate it, "Annas sent Him bound to Caiaphas," the difficulty of its present position is not thereby removed. Why is this fact mentioned here? No account is given of what took place before Caiaphas, but v. 25 resumes the narrative of Peter's denials in the palace of the high priest, and v. 28 simply announces that they led Jesus from Caiaphas to the hall of judgment. In whatever point of view we regard it, the position of v. 24 is peculiar; but its reference to what had taken place seems best to explain the narrative.

We reach the same result by comparing the statements of the Evangelists respecting the place where Peter was when he thrice denied the Lord. It was, according to John, (xviii. 15,) in the palace of the high priest, or, more properly, in the court—αυλη—where a fire of coals had been made, (vs. 18 and 25.) Mark (xiv. 54 and 67) mentions the same court and fire; and so Luke, (xxii. 55, 56.) From Matthew (xxvi. 57) it appears that this palace was that of Caiaphas, and from vs. 69–75 that here Peter made the denials. If, then, all these denials were made in the same court, and this was that of Annas, they must have been made during the preliminary examination, and before

[1] Norton, ii. 463. See also Bengel in loco.

Jesus was led to Caiaphas. But this is in opposition to Matthew, who makes the court to have been that of Caiaphas. Hence some[1] find an irreconcilable discrepancy between Matthew and John. To avoid this difficulty, many would make this palace, which in all probability was the high priest's official residence, to have been occupied by Annas and Caiaphas in common. The first examination may thus have been before Annas in one apartment, and the formal trial before Caiaphas and the Sanhedrim in another—Peter remaining all the while in the court.[2] In this supposition of a common residence, there is nothing at all improbable in itself. Still, the statement that He was taken to Annas first, and then sent by Annas to Caiaphas bound, seems to imply more than that He was taken to their joint residence, and then transferred from one apartment to another. We conclude, therefore, that they had distinct palaces, and that what John relates (xviii. 15–27) took place in that of Caiaphas.

The order of those[3] who suppose that Annas and Caiaphas occupied different palaces, and yet that the first examination was before Annas, and that the denials of Peter were during this examination, and before Jesus was sent to Caiaphas, cannot be reconciled with the statements of Matthew; nor can we accept their solution that these statements are corrected by John, who saw their inaccuracy. That, after Jesus was led to Caiaphas, Peter did not remain behind and complete his denials, appears plainly from Luke xxii. 61, where it is said that the Lord turned and looked upon him after the third denial. Jesus must then have remained in the court of Annas till the second cock-crowing. This would put the sending to Caiaphas, and subse-

1 Meyer, Bleek.
2 So Stier, Lange, Ebrard, Lichtenstein, Alford, Ellicott.
3 So Olshausen, Wieseler.

quent proceedings, much later than the tenor of the narrative warrants.

The assertion of many, that Luke, who does not mention his name, intends to designate Annas as the high priest, (xxii. 54,) has no sufficient basis. That he does (iii. 2) speak of both Annas and Caiaphas as high priests, and in Acts (iv. 6) names Caiaphas without any official title, but calls Annas the high priest, does not show that Annas is here meant. There is no question that Caiaphas was the legal and acting high priest. As such he is designated by Matthew and Mark, and as such he takes the lead in all the judicial proceedings against Jesus. Of these facts Luke could not be ignorant. He himself names Caiaphas high priest. The presumption is therefore very strong that he alludes to him here, and that all he relates (vs. 54–65) was in his palace.

We conclude, then, that Jesus was sent to Annas first, but not examined by him; that He was soon sent from Annas to Caiaphas; that the two had distinct palaces; that the examination (John xviii. 19–23) was before Caiaphas; that to this palace Peter followed; that here were all his denials; and that thus the Evangelists are harmonized.[1]

We may then arrange these events in the following order:—Jesus, being arrested, is led first to Annas. Here He remains but a short period, and is sent by Annas to Caiaphas, in whose palace the trial was to take place.[2] Because this sending to Annas had no important bearings on the trial itself, it is passed over by the Synoptists. But as some interval necessarily elapsed ere all the members of the Sanhedrim could be assembled, Caiaphas takes upon himself to ask Him some questions respecting His disciples

[1] Lightfoot, Lardner, Bynaeus, Grotius, Whitby, Newcome, Norton, Robinson, Greswell, Krafft, Friedlieb, Da Costa.

[2] As to the traditionary site of the palace of Caiaphas, see Porter, i. 173; Barclay, 171; Raumer, 258, note 21.

and doctrines. There is nothing here like a regular judicial examination; the judges are not present, and no witnesses are called or testify. Still, as Caiaphas was the high priest, Jesus pays him the respect which his office demanded, and answers him. That his object was evil is apparent. He would learn from Him how many, and who, had become His disciples, that he might hereafter use this knowledge against them. But upon this point Jesus kept perfect silence. In regard to His doctrine He had always and everywhere spoken openly. Let Caiaphas ask those who had heard Him in the synagogues and temple, and let them testify. An officer present, declaring that this answer is insulting to the high priest, smites Him with the palm of his hand. Caiaphas seems now to have withdrawn, probably to meet the Sanhedrim, and to have left Jesus to the mockery and abuse of His captors.

Let us now consider more fully the three denials of Peter. After the arrest, he, with "another disciple," followed Jesus to the high priest's palace. It is disputed who this other disciple was. Most regard it as a modest designation of John himself; others, of some unknown disciple. A. Clarke approves Grotius' conjecture that it was the person at whose house Jesus had supped. Some have thought of Judas. This disciple, being known unto the high priest, was permitted to enter with those who were leading Jesus, but Peter was shut out. Perceiving this, he turns back, and persuades the woman that kept the door to admit Peter also. They seem then, or soon after, to have separated, as no mention is afterward made of the other disciple. Either before or soon after Peter's entrance, the officer and soldiers made a fire of coals in the court.

To understand the details that follow, it is necessary to have in mind the ordinary construction of oriental houses, which is thus described by Robinson:[1] "An oriental house

[1] Har. 225.

is usually built around a quadrangular interior court, into which there is a passage (sometimes arched) through the front part of the house, closed next the street by a heavy folding gate, with a smaller wicket for single persons, kept by a porter. In the text the interior court, often paved and flagged, and open to the sky, is the αυλη, (translated 'palace,' 'hall,' and 'court,') where the attendants made a fire; and the passage beneath the front of the house, from the street to this court, is the προαυλιον or πυλων, (both translated 'porch.') The place where Jesus stood before the high priest may have been an open room or place of audience on the ground floor, in the rear or on one side of the court; such rooms, open in front, being customary." In Smith's Bible Dictionary, (i. 838,) the writer speaks of "an apartment called makad, open in front to the court, with two or more arches and a railing; and a pillar to support the wall above. It was in a chamber of this kind, probably one of the largest size to be found in a palace, that our Lord was arraigned before the high priest, at the time when the denial of Him by St. Peter took place." That the trial of Jesus actually occurred in such an apartment seems plain from Matt. xxvi. 69, where Peter is spoken of as sitting "without in the palace," εξω—εν τη αυλη, or court, implying that the Lord and His judges were in an inner room.[1] Mark (xiv. 66) speaks of Peter as "beneath in the palace," εν τη αυλη κατω, "in the court below." "Not in the lower story of the house or palace," says Alexander, "as the English version seems to mean, but in the open space around which it was built, and which was lower than the floor of the surrounding rooms."

For convenient inspection, we give the denials of Peter in tabular form:

[1] See Meyer in loco.

First Denial.

	Matthew.	Mark.	Luke.	John.
Questioner	Maid servant.	Maid servant.	A certain maid.	Portress.
Time	Indefinite.	Indefinite.	Indefinite.	Soon after entering.
Place	Court.	By fire in court.	By fire in court.	Court.
Question	"Thou also wast with Jesus of Galilee."	"Thou also wast with Jesus of Nazareth."	"This man was also with Him."	"Art thou not also one of this man's disciples?"
Denial	"I know not what thou sayest."	"I know not, neither understand I, what thou sayest."	"Woman, I know Him not."	"I am not."

Second Denial.

	Matthew.	Mark.	Luke.	John.
Questioner	Another maid.	The maid.	Another.	They.
Time	Indefinite.	Indefinite.	After a little while.	Indefinite.
Place	Porch.	Porch.	Indefinite.	By the fire.
Question	"This was also with Jesus of Nazareth."	"This is one of them."	"Thou art also of them."	"Art not thou also one of His disciples?"
Denial	With an oath, "I do not know the man."	He denied it again.	"Man, I am not."	"I am not."

Third Denial.

	Matthew.	Mark.	Luke.	John.
Questioner	They that stood by.	They that stood by.	Another.	A servant of the high priest, kinsman of Malchus.
Time	After a while.	A little after.	About the space of an hour after.	Indefinite.
Place	Indefinite.	Indefinite.	Indefinite.	Indefinite.
Question	"Surely thou art also one of them, for thy speech betrayeth thee."	"Surely thou art one of them, for thou art a Galilean, and thy speech agreeth thereto."	"Of a truth this fellow also was with Him, for he is a Galilean."	"Did I not see thee in the garden with Him?"
Denial	With cursing and swearing, "I know not the man."	"I know not the man of whom you speak."	"Man, I know not what thou sayest."	Peter then denied again.

In regard to the first denial there are no special difficulties. How soon after Peter entered the court he was addressed by the damsel who kept the door, or portress, does not appear. It is probable that, as her attention had been specially drawn to him when he was admitted, she watched him as he stood by the fire; and that something in his appearance or conduct may have excited her suspicions. The attention of all who heard her must now have been directed to Peter, but no one seems to have joined her in her accusation.

In regard to the second denial, there are several apparent discrepancies both as to the persons and the place. The former are described as "another maid," "the (same) maid," "another person," "they." But in the several narratives it is plain that it is not deemed important to specify who addressed Peter; the important point is his denials. The matter may very naturally be thus arranged: The damsel who first accused him, silenced for the time, but not satisfied with his denial, speaks to another maid servant, and points out Peter to her as one whom she knew, or believed, to be a disciple. Seeing him soon after in the porch, for, in the agitation of his spirit, he cannot keep still, she renews the charge that he is a disciple; and the other maid repeats it. Others, hearing the girls, also join with them, perhaps dimly remembering his person, or now noting something peculiar in his manner. That, under the circumstances and in the excitement of the moment, such an accusation, once raised, should be echoed by many, is what we should expect. During the confusion of this questioning, Peter returns again to the fire, where most were standing, and there repeats with an oath his denial. There is no necessity for transposing, with Ellicott, the first and second denials as given by John.

The second denial, so energetically made, seems to have finally silenced the women, and there is no repetition of the charge for about the space of an hour. During this interval, Peter, perhaps the better to allay suspicion, joins in the conversation, and is recognized as a Galilean by his manner of speech.[1] As most of the disciples of Jesus were Galileans, this again draws attention to him. Perhaps the kinsman of Malchus, who had been with the multitude, and had seen him in the garden, and now remembers his person, begins the outcry, and the bystanders join with him; and the more that his very denials betray his Galilean birth. The charge, thus repeated by so many, and upon such apparently good grounds, threatens immediate danger; and Peter therefore denies it with the utmost vehemence, with oaths and cursings.

The exact relations in which the denials of Peter stand in order of time to the examination and trial of the Lord, it is impossible to determine. Probably the first denial, and perhaps also the second—for there seems to have been but a short interval between them, (Luke xxii. 58)—may have been during the preliminary examination before Caiaphas, or at least before the assembling of the Sanhedrim; and the third during the trial or at its close. The incident recorded by Luke, (xxii. 61,) that immediately after the third denial, as the cock crew, the Lord turned and looked upon Peter, is supposed by some to show that Jesus was now passing from one apartment to another, and, as He passes, turns and looks upon Peter, who was standing near by. But, if so, when was this? Those who put the preliminary examination before Annas, and Peter's denials there, make this the departure to Caiaphas after the examination; others, His departure after the trial from Caiaphas to Pilate; others still, the change from the apartment in Caiaphas' palace, where He had been examined, to that in which He was to be tried. But it is by no means necessary to

[1] As to the pronunciation of the Galileans, see Friedlieb, Archäol. 84.

suppose any change of place on the part of the Lord. As we have seen, the Sanhedrim probably assembled in a large room directly connected with the court, and open in front, and therefore what was said in the one could, with more or less distinctness, be heard in the other. There is, then, no difficulty in believing that Jesus had heard all the denials of Peter; and that now, as he denied Him for the third time, and the cock crew, He turned Himself to the court and looked upon the conscience-stricken apostle. Meyer, indeed, finds it psychologically impossible that he should have made these denials in the presence of Jesus.[1] Few will deem such a psychological impossibility, which exists only in the mind of the critic, of much weight against the word of an Evangelist; but, in fact, Peter was not in His presence, though not far removed.

We have no datum to determine at what hour of the night these denials took place, except we find it in the cock-crowings. Mark (xiv. 68) relates that after the first denial the cock crew. All the Evangelists mention the third denial in connection with the second cock-crowing. Greswell (iii. 216) makes the first cock-crowing to have been about 2 A. M., the second about 3 A. M.[2] But we do not know whether this second cock-crowing was at the end of the first examination, or during the formal trial, or at its close, and have therefore no datum to determine when the Sanhedrim began its session. We cannot, however, well place it later than 3 A. M. How long it continued we shall presently see.

We have still to inquire as to the legality of the Lord's trial. As to the competency of the court, no reasonable doubt can exist. The Sanhedrim had lawful and exclusive jurisdiction in all cases where capital punishment

[1] Note, Luke xxii. 61.
[2] So, in substance, Wieseler, 406; Lichtenstein, 422.

could be inflicted;[1] and among the offences punishable with death, were false claims to prophetic inspiration, and blasphemy. Several instances are mentioned in the Acts of the Apostles, where the disciples were arraigned before it: iv. 5–21; v. 17–40; vi. 12–15; xxiii. 1–10. Although its origin cannot easily be traced, it was at this time the recognized tribunal for the trial of all the more important offences.[2] That usually the trials were fair, and the judgment equitable, there seems no good reason to doubt.

Whilst the Sanhedrim had power to try those charged with capital offences, it had no power to execute the sentence of death. It is generally agreed that from the time Judea became a Roman province, or from the deposition of Archelaus (759) the authority to punish capitally, the *jus gladii*, had been taken away from the Jewish tribunals. Lightfoot (on Matt. xxvi. 3) gives as a tradition of the Talmudists: "Forty years before the temple was destroyed, judgment in capital cases was taken away from Israel." He elsewhere remarks, (on John xviii. 31:) "It cannot be denied but that all capital judgment, or sentence upon life, had been taken from the Jews for above forty years before the destruction of Jerusalem, as they oftentimes themselves confess." It seems to have been the custom of the Romans to take into their own hands, in conquered provinces, the power of life and death, as one of the principal attributes of sovereignty.[3] That the Sanhedrim lost this power by its own remissness, and not by any act of the Romans, as affirmed by Lightfoot from the Talmudists, is wholly improbable.[4]

1 Josephus, Antiq. 14. 9. 3.

2 Friedlieb, Archäol. 20; Winer, ii. 552.

3 See Dupin, Jesus devant Caiphe et Pilate. Paris, 1855, p. 88.

4 See Winer, ii. 553, note 1. Friedlieb, Archäol., 97. Bynaeus (iii. 19) affirms that the Jews had judgment in capital cases other than that of treason; but, from fear of the people, they charged Him with this offence to throw the odium and danger of His execution upon Pilate.

It has been inferred by some, from Pilate's words to the Jews, (John xix. 6,) "Take ye Him and crucify Him," that the right to inflict capital punishment in ecclesiastical cases, though not in civil, was still continued to them.[1] But these words seem to have been spoken in bitter irony. Crucifixion was not a Jewish punishment, nor could they inflict it.[2] Krafft (142) explains their language, (John xviii. 30,) "If He were not a malefactor, we would not have delivered Him up unto thee," as meaning that He was guilty of a civil offence. Were this man a spiritual offender, we would have punished Him ourselves. They accused Him of civil crime in order to throw the responsibility of His death upon Pilate. But against this is the fact that Pilate refused to punish Him for any such offence, and that the Jews were at last obliged to charge Him with violation of ecclesiastical law, (John xix. 7.) It is certain that if they had had power to punish Him upon this ground, he would at once have given the case into their hands, and thus thrown off all responsibility from himself. Their words, (xviii. 31,) "It is not lawful for us to put any man to death," seem plainly to cover the whole ground, and to embrace ecclesiastical as well as civil cases.[3] The view supported by some,[4] that the Jews had authority to put Jesus to death, but did not dare exercise it because of the holiness of the day, and yet did not dare retain Him in prison lest it should provoke insurrection, and so sought Pilate's help, seems without any good basis.

It thus appears that all capital offences must be reserved to the cognizance of the procurator. The Sanhedrim could try and convict, but must obtain his assent ere the sentence

[1] So A. Clarke, Krafft. [2] Meyer in loco.

[3] As to the death of Stephen, (Acts vii. 58,) and its bearings on this point, see Meyer and Lechler in loco, who maintain that it was an act of violence, and illegal: contra, Alexander in loco; Winer, ii. 553, note 2.

[4] Early by Augustine; see Godwyn, Moses and Aaron, 200.

could be executed. These reserved cases Pilate seems to have been in the habit of hearing when he went up from Cæsarea to Jerusalem at the feasts.[1] The case of Jesus, then, must necessarily come before him, and he could confirm or set aside their verdict as he pleased. "It appears," says Lardner, "from the sequel, that Pilate was the supreme judge in this case, and the master of the event. For he gives the case a fresh hearing, asks the Jews what accusation they had brought, examined Jesus, and when he had done so, told them that he found in Him no fault at all. Thus his conduct is full proof that he was the judge, and that they were only prosecutors and accusers."

Let us now inquire what was the actual accusation brought against the Lord before the Sanhedrim. None of the Evangelists mention specifically of what He was accused. We are told that the council sought false witness against Him. But to what did these witnesses testify? Their testimony is not given, except in one instance, and that a perversion of His words, (John ii. 19:) "Destroy this temple, and in three days I will raise it up." If the statements of the witnesses had been concordant and true, this language could be regarded at most as only a vainglorious boast; and if deserving of any punishment, certainly not of death. So far as appears, no charges were brought against Him that could be proved, and He was at last condemned upon His own confession that He was the Christ and Son of God. This fact is very remarkable, and demands our attentive consideration.

It is evident, from the Evangelists, that the rulers of the Jews were early resolved to put Jesus to death, so soon as they could find any sufficient ground of accusation. That He had broken the Sabbath, according to their construction of the law, by the healing of the sick, (Luke vi. 6–11,)

[1] Ewald, v. 16; Friedlieb, Archäol. 104.

and perhaps in other ways, and that He had assumed to forgive sins, which was, by implication, blasphemy, (Matt. ix. 3,) was beyond question; but for offences of this kind they did not dare arrest Him.[1] But when they learned that in His teaching He "made Himself equal with God," (John v. 18,) this was a flagrant transgression of the law, and a capital offence. The first of the ten commandments was, "Thou shalt have no other gods before me," and for a man to make himself God, the equal of Jehovah, was a violation of this command, and a crime of the deepest dye. It was both blasphemy and treason, and hence the attempt of the Jews to kill Him upon the spot. A few months later they "murmured at Him, because He said, I am the Bread which came down from Heaven," (John vi. 41.) When, a little later, He said, "Before Abraham was, I am," (viii. 58,) thus implying a divine preëxistence, they took up stones to stone Him; and when afterward (x. 30) He still more plainly affirmed, "I and my Father are one," they again sought to stone Him. They expressly declared, "We stone thee for blasphemy, and because that thou, being a man, makest thyself God."

There can be little doubt that it was to this point, the assertion by Jesus of an equality with God, that the testimony of the "many false witnesses" was turned. His other and minor offences were well known and undisputed. He had wrought many miracles, He had wrought some on the Sabbath, He had claimed to be the Lord of the Sabbath, He had assumed the power to forgive sins. All these things were well known, and witnesses testifying to them would not have testified falsely. It may be that attempts were made to prove that He had spoken against Jehovah, that He had denied the authority of the law, that He had

[1] In John v. 16, where it is said, "The Jews sought to slay Him because He had done these things on the Sabbath day," the clause "sought to slay Him," is omitted by Tischendorf. So Alford, Meyer.

prophesied falsely, that He had been a disturber of the public peace. But if these charges were made, they must have been subordinate to the higher one, that, "being a man, He made Himself God." Could not, then, this charge be proved against Him? Probably not. If any witnesses could be found to report what He had said, still His words were mysterious, and there was room for great difference of interpretation. That He did assume to be something more than man was the current belief, but one by no means easy to establish by legal evidence.

Whether the mere claim to be the Messiah, if proved false, was regarded by the Jews as a capital offence, is very questionable; but if so, there was the same difficulty in finding proof against Jesus in regard to His Messianic claims as in regard to His divinity. In no instance recorded, except that of the Samaritan woman, (John iv. 26,) did He avow Himself to be the Christ when other than His disciples were present. Nor did He permit evil spirits to proclaim Him as the Messiah, (Mark i. 34.) To the direct question of the Jews (John x. 24) He answers by referring them to His works. He permitted the apostles to confess their faith in Him as the Christ, (Matt. xvi. 16,) but He gave them strict command that they should tell it to no man, (v. 20.) Probably no two witnesses could be found, out of the ranks of the disciples, who had ever heard out of His own lips an avowal of His Messiahship. Had, then, such an avowal been blasphemy, they could not on this ground condemn Him.

It has been said that the Jews found cause to charge Jesus with blasphemy in that He had wrought miracles in His own name. "He had performed many miracles, but never in any other name than His own."[1] It is said that He had thus violated the law, (Deut. xviii. 20,) "He that

[1] Greenleaf, Test. of Evangelists, 524.

shall speak in the name of other gods, even that prophet shall die;" for if to prophesy in the name of another god deserved death, equally so to perform any miracle or supernatural work in his name. But it may well be questioned whether, on this ground, He could have been tried for blasphemy. If He did not work His miracles expressly in the name of Jehovah, yet He ever affirmed that the power was not in Himself, but from God. (Compare John v. 19, viii. 18.) Nor was He ever understood to work them by virtue of His own deity. Beholding what He did, the multitudes "marvelled and glorified God, who had given such power unto men," (Matt. ix. 8.) And at His final entry into Jerusalem the cry of the people was, "Blessed is He that cometh in the name of the Lord."

We conclude, then, that upon no ground could the Jews, through their witnesses, convict Him of any ecclesiastical offence punishable with death. Neither as the Son of God, nor as the Messiah, nor as a false prophet, could He be legally convicted of blasphemy. His violations of the Sabbath were not such as they could punish with severity, if at all. If He had disturbed the public peace, punishment of this offence properly belonged to the Romans. Thus, upon the rule which He had Himself laid down, (John xviii. 21,) "Ask them which heard me what I have said unto them," He could not have been convicted. Only by His own confession was He brought within the scope of the law.

A Jewish writer, Salvador, in his "Histoire des Institutions de Moïse,"[1] commenting upon the trial of Jesus, attempts to show that He was tried fairly, and condemned legally. He speaks of Himself as God, and His disciples repeat it. This was shocking blasphemy in the eyes of the citizens. It was this, not His prophetic claims, which ex-

[1] Cited by Greenleaf, Test. 529, and by Dupin, Refutation, 41.

cited the people against Him. The law permitted them to acknowledge prophets, but nothing more. In answer to Caiaphas, He admits that He is the Son of God, this expression including the idea of God Himself. "The Sanhedrim deliberates. The question already raised among the people was this: Has Jesus become God? But the senate, having adjudged that Jesus had profaned the name of God by usurping it to Himself, a mere citizen, applied to Him the law of blasphemy, (Deut. xiii., and xviii. 20,) according to which every prophet, even he who works miracles, must be punished when he speaks of a God unknown to the Jews and their fathers; and the capital sentence was pronounced."

Had the accusation against Jesus, as asserted by Salvador, had respect simply to His assertion that He was the Son of God, and He been condemned upon this ground only, however great the blindness and guilt in not recognizing His divine character, it could not be said that the court acted illegally. Such an assertion from the lips of any mere man was blasphemous. If a false prophet deserved to die, how much more he who made himself equal with God! Was it for this that He was, in fact, condemned? When nothing worthy of death could be proved against Him by the witnesses, Caiaphas adjures Him by the living God, "Tell us whether thou be the Christ, the Son of God."[1] We cannot certainly determine how these two expressions, "the Christ," and "the Son of God," were connected in the mind of Caiaphas. It may be that he regarded them as of substantially the same meaning, though it may be questioned how far the title, Son of God, was one of the customary titles of the Messiah at this time. Still, it had been so often, and openly, applied to Him, that we can-

[1] Matt. xxvi. 63. According to Mark, "Art thou the Christ, the Son of the Blessed?" This adjuration, according to Jewish custom, was equivalent to putting the Lord under oath. Friedlieb, Archäol. 91.

not well suppose Caiaphas ignorant of it. At the time of His baptism, John Baptist testified of His Divine Sonship, (John i. 34:) "I saw, and bare record that this is the Son of God." Very soon after, (v. 49,) Nathanael thus avows his faith: "Rabbi, thou art the Son of God; thou art the King of Israel." Often was He thus addressed by evil spirits whom He cast out, (Matt. viii. 29; Mark iii. 11, v. 7; Luke iv. 41, viii. 28.) After the stilling of the tempest, (Matt. xiv. 33,) those in the ship said, "Of a truth thou art the Son of God." So was He addressed by Martha, (John xi. 27,) "I believe that thou art the Christ, the Son of God." During the crucifixion, His enemies, mocking Him, cried, (Matt. xxvii. 40–43,) "If thou be the Son of God, come down from the cross." At His death the centurion and guard said, (v. 54,) "Truly this was the Son of God." Only in one instance, however, did Jesus directly claim for Himself this title, (John ix. 35–37,) although He often indirectly applied it to Himself. (So John xi. 4.) In like manner He repeatedly speaks of God as His Father, (John v. 17.)

Granting that this phrase, "Son of God," was currently applied to men of great wisdom and piety, still, as Salvador admits, it could not have been so used by Caiaphas. If it did not, in its ordinary usage, imply participation of the Divine nature, it nevertheless was, and was designed to be, a designation that distinguished Him from all other men.

That the Jews, generally, did not suppose that the Messiah was to be a Divine Person, God manifest in flesh, seems fairly inferable from the perplexity into which the Lord's question cast them, (Matt. xxii. 42–45,) "What think ye of the Christ? Whose Son is He?" Only a few, as Nathanael, seem to have had a higher perception of the truth.[1] Hence, when Jesus was presented to Pilate, (John xix. 7,) as one who "made Himself the Son of God," he evidently looked upon Him as one of much higher preten-

[1] Luthardt, i. 344.

sions than a mere "king of the Jews." Perhaps Caiaphas, in his adjuration, purposely selected both titles, that in this way the Lord's own conceptions of His Messianic dignity might be drawn out, and the way opened for further questions. The answer of Jesus, "Thou hast said," was an express affirmation, as if He had said, "I am;" and was regarded as blasphemy. It could have been so only as it implied equality with God, or an assumption of the power and authority that belonged to Jehovah alone. That the Jews so understood it, is plain from their language to Pilate.[1]

But if we admit that the Lord, regarded as a mere man who claimed equality with God, was justly condemned by the Sanhedrim, as Salvador affirms, still it by no means follows that the trial was fair and impartial. He had long been prejudged, and His death predetermined. Almost from the beginning of His ministry, spies had been sent to watch His actions; and afterward it was agreed that if any man did confess that He was Christ, he should be put out of the synagogue, (John ix. 22.) After the resurrection of Lazarus, it was determined in council, by the advice of Caiaphas, that He should be put to death, and that without regard to His guilt or innocence, (John xi. 47–53.) After His public entry into Jerusalem, several attempts were made to entangle Him in His talk; then a consultation was held how they might take Him by subtlety and kill Him; then one of His apostles was bribed to betray Him; and at last He was arrested at dead of night. At the trial itself, the usual forms were not observed; no one appeared as advocate for Him, no witnesses were called to testify in His favor; and when the witnesses against Him could not agree in their testimony, He Himself was put under oath.[2] The abuse which He suffered, both before and after the trial,

[1] As to the argument for the Lord's divine nature, drawn from this trial, see Whately, Kingdom of Christ, Essay I.

[2] See Friedlieb, Archäol. 87; Dupin, 75.

and in the very presence of His judges, sufficiently shows how bitter and cruel was their enmity toward Him.

FRIDAY MORNING, 15TH NISAN, 7TH APRIL, 783. A. D. 30.

After the Sanhedrim had pronounced Him guilty of blasphemy, and so worthy of death, it suspends its session to meet at break of day. During this interval Jesus remains in the high priest's palace, exposed to all the ridicule and insults of His enemies, who spit upon Him, and smite Him.	MATT. xxvi. 67, 68. MARK xiv. 65. LUKE xxii. 63–65.
As soon as it was day the Sanhedrim again assembles, and, after hearing His confession that He is the Christ, formally adjudges Him to death. Binding Him, they lead Him away to the Roman governor Pontius Pilate, that he may execute the sentence.	MATT. xxvii. 1, 2. MARK xv. 1. LUKE xxii. 66–71. LUKE xxiii. 1.
Judas Iscariot, learning the issue of the trial, and that Jesus was about to be put to death, returns the money the chief priests had given him, and goes and hangs himself.	MATT. xxvii. 3–10. ACTS i. 18, 19.

Condemned to death as a blasphemer, Jesus was now given up by the council to the abuse of His captors and of the crowd; and cruel personal violence was added to most contemptuous speech. Salvador denies that the council would have permitted Him to be so treated in its presence; but it is to be remembered that most of its members cherished the most bitter and vindictive feelings against Him, and in their fierce fanaticism thought that no mercy should be shown to one guilty of such a crime. (Compare Acts xxiii. 2.) According to Matthew, the judges themselves seem to have taken part in this abuse; but Luke confines it to those that held Jesus.

It has been inferred from Matt. xxvii. 1, and Mark xv. 1, that there was a second and later session of the Sanhedrim than that at which Jesus was tried.[1] Others suppose

[1] Greswell, iii. 203; Friedlieb, 326.

that the Sanhedrim continued its session after the trial proper had ended, having as the special subject of consultation how the sentence pronounced against Jesus could be carried into effect.[1] The language of these two Evangelists is not decisive as to the point. That which most implies a new and distinct session is the designation of time. Matthew: "When the morning was come, πρωιας δε γενομενης, all the chief priests," &c. Mark: "And straightway in the morning," ευθεως επι το πρωι, &c. This allusion to the fact that it was morning, seems to have some special significance, and may refer to the fact that capital cases could not be legally tried in the night; and hence a morning session was necessary. "Capital cases were only to be handled by day."[2] This is affirmed by Salvador, (quoted by Greenleaf:) "One thing is certain, that the council met again on the morning of the next day, or of the day after, as the law requires, to confirm or to annul the sentence; it was confirmed." Neither Matthew nor Mark states that the place of session had been changed, though perhaps their language may intimate a meeting more largely attended.[3]

Our decision as to a second and distinct session of the Sanhedrim will mainly depend upon the place we give to the account in Luke, (xxii. 66–71.) Is this examination of Jesus identical with that of Matt. xxvi. 57–68, Mark xiv. 53–65?[4] Against this identity are some strong objections: 1st. The mention of time by Luke: "As soon as it was day." This corresponds well to the time of the morning session of Matthew and Mark, but not to the time when Jesus was first led before the Sanhedrim, which must have been two or three hours before day. 2d. The place of meeting: "They led Him into their council," ανηγαγον

[1] Meyer, Ellicott, Lichtenstein.

[2] Lightfoot; see Friedlieb, Arch. 95.

[3] Compare Mark xiv. 53 with xv. 1. In the latter case, "the whole council" being expressly mentioned.

[4] Meyer, Alford, Lichtenstein, Ebrard.

αυτον εις το συνεδριον εαυτων. This might better be rendered, "they led Him up into their council chamber," or the place where they usually held their sessions.[1] Whether this council chamber was the room Gazith, at the east corner of the court of the temple, is not certain. Lightfoot (on Matt. xxvi. 3) conjectures that the Sanhedrim was driven from this its accustomed seat half a year or thereabout before the death of Christ. But if this were so, still the "*Tabernæ*," where it established its sessions, were shops near the gate Shusan, and so connected with the temple. They went up to that room where they usually met.[2] 3d. The dissimilarity of the proceedings, as stated by Luke, and which shows that this was no formal trial. There is here no mention of witnesses—no charges brought to be proved against Him. He is simply asked if He is the Christ; and this seems plainly to point to the result of the former session. Then, having confessed Himself to be the Christ, the Son of God, He was condemned to death for blasphemy. It was only necessary now that He should repeat this confession, and hence this question is put directly to Him: "Art thou the Christ? tell us." His reply, "If I tell you ye will not believe. And if I also ask you, ye will not answer me, nor let me go," points backward to His former confession. To His reply they only answer by asking, "Art thou then the Son of God?" The renewed avowal that He was the Son of God, heard by them all from His own lips, opens the way for His immediate delivery into Pilate's hands.[3] 4th. The position which Luke gives (xxii. 63–65) to the insults and abuse

[1] See Meyer in loco; Rob. Lex., Art. *συνεδριον*: here "as including the place of meeting; the Sanhedrim as sitting in its hall."

[2] So Krafft, Greswell. See, however, against this, John xviii. 28, which implies that Jesus was led, not from the temple, but from the palace of Caiaphas, to Pilate. This would not disprove the fact of a second session of the Sanhedrim, but shows that it was held at the same place as the first.

[3] See Stier, vii. 336; Greswell, iii. 204.

heaped upon Jesus. There can be no doubt that they are the same mentioned by Matthew and Mark as occurring after the sentence had been pronounced, and before the second session to ratify it.

From all this it is a probable, though not a certain conclusion, that Luke (xxii. 66–71) refers to the same meeting of the Sanhedrim mentioned by Matthew (xxvii. 1) and Mark, (xv. 1,) and relates, in part, what then took place. Alford thinks that Luke has confused things, and relates as happening at the second session what really happened at the first. This meeting was, then, a morning session, convened to ratify formally what had been done before with haste and informality. The circumstances under which its members had been convened at the palace of Caiaphas, sufficiently show that the legal forms, which they were so scrupulous in observing, had not been complied with. The law forbidding capital trials in the night had been broken; the place of session was unusual, if not illegal; perhaps the attendance, so early after midnight, had not been full. On these accounts it was expedient that a more regular and legal sitting should be held as early in the morning as was possible. At this nothing was to be done except to hear the confession of Jesus, to pronounce sentence, and to consult in what manner it could best be carried into effect.

One object of this morning session was to consult how they might put Him to death; for, although they had condemned Him, they had no power to execute the sentence. To put Jesus to death, they must then have at least the assent of Pilate. Their plans for obtaining this will appear as we proceed. Being again bound, He was led early in the morning before Pilate.

So soon as Judas learned what the Sanhedrim had done, he knew that the Lord's fate was decided, and bitterly repented of his treachery.[1] Taking the money, the price

[1] That this was upon the same day, seems fairly inferable from Matt. xxvii. 3, τοτε ιδων, &c.

of his crime, he carried it back to the chief priests and elders, confessing his sin in betraying innocent blood. It is not said where he found them, whether at the palace of Caiaphas or at their own council chamber in the temple. If the latter was the case, we have a ready explanation of the fact that "he cast down the pieces of silver in the temple and departed."[1] That part of the temple in which he cast them, is defined as εν τῷ ναῷ, which, according to the uniform usage of the term in the Gospels, cannot mean any thing else than the inner court, or court of the priests, or holy place.[2] Into this it was not lawful for him to enter; but he could approach the entrance and cast the silver within; or, in his remorse and despair, entering the holy place, he casts it down at the feet of the priests, who, it may be, were there, preparing to offer the morning sacrifice. From thence he departs and hangs himself. But how is this statement to be reconciled with that of Peter, (Acts i. 18,) that, "falling headlong, he burst asunder in the midst —και πρηνης γενομενος ελακησε μεσος—and all his bowels gushed out." De Quincey[3] finds here only a figurative statement that "he came to utter and unmitigated ruin," and died of a "broken heart." The language is obviously to be taken in its literal sense; and the bursting asunder of Judas may readily have happened after he had hung himself. Such a thing as the breaking of a cord, or a beam, or bough of a tree, is not unusual; or, at the moment when the body was about to be taken down, it may by accident or carelessness have fallen. Hackett,[4] referring to a suggestion that he may have hung himself upon a tree overhanging the valley of Hinnom, says: "For myself, I felt, as I stood in the valley and looked up to the rocky terraces which hang over it, that the proposed explanation was a perfectly natural one. I was more than ever satisfied with

[1] See Greswell, iii. 219.
[2] Meyer, Alford.
[3] Essay upon Judas Iscariot.
[4] Ill. Scrip., 266.

it." He found the precipice, by measurement, to be from twenty-five to forty feet in height, with olive trees growing near the edges, and a rocky pavement at the bottom, so that a person who fell from above would probably be crushed and mangled, as well as killed.[1]

Meyer finds proof that Matthew, in his statement that Judas "hanged himself," and Luke, in his report of Peter's statement that he "burst asunder," followed different traditions, in the fact that, as self-murder was very unusual amongst the Jews, Peter could not have passed it by in silence. But, as the falling and bursting asunder were subsequent to the hanging, and presupposed it; and as the event had taken place but a few days before, and was well known to all present; there was no necessity that he should give all the details.

Probably the money which had been paid to Judas, had been taken from the treasury of the temple; and the priests and elders, unwilling to return to it the price of blood, determine to buy a field to bury strangers in. Peter (Acts i. 18) speaks as if Judas had himself bought it: "Now this man purchased a field with the reward of iniquity." Perhaps he may be here understood as speaking oratorically, and as meaning only to say that the field was bought, not by himself in person, but with his money, the wages of his iniquity.[2] If so, the actual purchase of the field was doubtless made after the Lord's crucifixion, as the time of the priests and elders was too much occupied upon that day to attend to such a transaction. Matthew narrates it as taking place before the crucifixion, in order to finish all that pertained to Judas. Others make Judas to have purchased

[1] As to the various traditional accounts of Judas' death, see Hofmann's Leben Jesu, 333. Bynaeus (ii. 431) gives a full statement of the various opinions up to his day. Arculf, (Early Travels, 4,) A. D. 700, speaks of being shown the large fig tree from the top of which Judas suspended himself.

[2] Alexander in loco; Lechler.

a field before his death with part of the money he had received; and in this field he hanged himself; and the priests, after his death, with the remainder of the money, to have purchased another.[1] Thus there were two fields, both called "the field of blood," but for different reasons: one as bought with the price of blood, the other as the place where Judas hanged himself. It is said that "ecclesiastical tradition appears from the earliest times to have pointed out two distinct, though not unvarying spots, as referred to in the two accounts." Early travellers mention Aceldama as distinct from the spot where Judas hanged himself.[2] Maundrell also (468) mentions two Aceldamas; one on the west side of the valley of Hinnom, and another on the east side of the valley of Jehosaphat, not far distant from Siloa. To the latter Saewulf (42) refers as at the foot of Mount Olivet, a little south of Gethsemane. That two fields are referred to by the Evangelists, is doubtful; and the former solution of the discrepancy is to be preferred.

The field of blood is still pointed out in the eastern part of the valley of Hinnom. "The tradition which fixes it upon this spot reaches back to the age of Jerome, and it is mentioned by almost every visitor of the Holy City from that time to the present day. The field or plat is not now marked by any boundary to distinguish it from the rest of the hillside."[3] Hackett[4] observes: "Tradition has placed it on the Hill of Evil Council. It may have been in that quarter, at least; for the field belonged originally to a potter, and argillaceous clay is still found in the neighborhood. A workman, in a pottery which I visited at Jerusalem, said that all their clay was obtained from the hill over the valley of Hinnom." A charnel house, now in ruins, built over a cave in whose deep pit are a few bones

[1] See Greswell, iii. 220; Smith's Bib. Dict., i. 15.
[2] So Maundeville, Early Trav. 175.
[3] Robinson, i. 354.
[4] Ill. Scrip., 267.

much decayed, is still shown. Some would identify it with the tomb of Ananias mentioned by Josephus.[1]

Our purpose does not lead us to inquire into the motives that impelled Judas to betray his Lord. The theory, however, advocated by many,[2] that, sharing the general Jewish expectations as to the Messianic kingdom, and fully believing Jesus to be the Messiah, he had no intention of imperilling His life, but wished only to arouse Him to direct and positive action, cannot be sustained. If, knowing the supernatural powers of Jesus, he had no fears that He could suffer evil from the hands of His enemies; and delivered Him into the power of the Jewish authorities in order that He might be forced to assert His Messianic claims, why should he bargain with them for thirty pieces of silver? He could in many ways have accomplished this end, without taking the attitude of a traitor. The statements of the Evangelists about his covenant with the chief priests, his conduct at the arrest, his return of the money, the words of Peter respecting him, and especially the words of the Lord, "Good were it for that man if he had never been born," conclusively show that he sinned, not through a mere error of judgment, while at heart hoping to advance the interests of his Master, but with deliberate perfidy, designing to compass His ruin.[3]

Friday Morning, 15th Nisan, 9th April, 783. A. D. 30.

The members of the Sanhedrim who led Jesus to Pilate, refuse to enter the judgment hall, lest they should be defiled; and thereupon he comes out to them and asks the nature of the accusation. They charge — John xviii. 28–33.

[1] War, 5. 12. 2. So Barclay, De Saulcy. [2] De Quincy, Whately.
[3] See Winer, i. 635; Ebrard, 524; Christian Review, July, 1855.

Him with being a malefactor, and Pilate directs them
to take Him and judge Him themselves. As they
cannot inflict a capital punishment, they bring the LUKE xxiii. 2–4.
charge of sedition; and Pilate, reëntering the judg- MARK xv. 2.
ment hall, and calling Jesus, examines Him as to His JOHN xviii. 33–38.
Messianic claims. Satisfied that He is innocent, Pilate MATT. xxvii. 11.
goes out and affirms that he finds no fault in Him.
The Jews renewing their accusations, to which Jesus MATT. xxvii. 12–14.
makes no reply, and mentioning Galilee, Pilate sends MARK xv. 3–5.
Him to Herod, who was then at Jerusalem; but Jesus LUKE xxiii. 5–12.
refuses to answer his questions, and is sent back to
Pilate. The latter now resorts to another expedient. MATT. xxvii. 15–18.
He seats himself upon the judgment seat, and calling MARK xv. 6–10.
the chief priests and elders, declares to them that nei- LUKE xxiii. 13–17.
ther himself nor Herod had found any fault in Him.
According to custom, he would release Him. But the JOHN xviii. 39, 40.
multitude beginning to cry that he should release Barabbas, not Jesus, he leaves it to their choice. During MATT. xxvii. 19.
the interval whilst the people were making their choice,
his wife sends a message to him of warning. The
people, persuaded by the priest and elders, reject Je- MATT. xxvii. 20–23.
sus and choose Barabbas, and Pilate in vain makes MARK xv. 11–14.
several efforts to change their decision. At last he LUKE xxiii. 18–25.
gives orders that Jesus be scourged previous to cruci- MATT. xxvii. 26–31.
fixion. This was done by the soldiers with mockery MARK xv. 15–20.
and abuse; and Pilate, going forth, again takes Jesus JOHN xix. 1–4.
and presents Him to the people. The Jews continue JOHN xix. 5–12.
to demand His death, but upon the ground that He
made Himself the Son of God. Terrified at this new
charge, Pilate again takes Jesus into the hall to ask
Him, but receives no answer. Pilate still strives earnestly to save Him, but is met by the cry that he is
Cæsar's enemy. Yielding to fear, he ascends the tribu-
nal, and, calling for water, washes his hands in token MATT. xxvii. 24–25.
of his innocence, and then gives directions, that He be JOHN xix. 13–16.
taken away and crucified. As He comes forth he pre-
sents Him to them as their King. They cry, Crucify
Him, and He is led away to the place of crucifixion.

It is not easily determined whether the Pretorium or judgment hall, to which Jesus was taken, was in the palace of Herod the Great, and now occupied by Pilate; or in the fortress Antonia. That the Roman governors sometimes used this palace as head-quarters, appears from Josephus,[1] where Florus is said to have done so; and afterward (2. 15. 5) mention is made of his leading out the troops from the royal residence. The palace of Herod at Cæsarea was used in like manner, (Acts xxiii. 35.) The palace at Jerusalem was situated on the north side of Mount Sion, and was a magnificent building of white marble, with which, according to Josephus, the temple itself bore no comparison.[2] It is to be distinguished from the palace of Solomon, which was lower down on the side of the mount, and near the temple, and where Agrippa afterward built.[3] That it was used by Pilate when he visited Jerusalem is very probable.[4] Those who place the judgment hall at the fortress Antonia refer in proof to John xix. 13, where it is said that Pilate "sat down in the judgment seat, in a place that is called the Pavement, but in the Hebrew, Gabbatha."[5] This Pavement is supposed to have been between the fortress Antonia and the western portico of the temple, identifying it with one mentioned by Josephus.[6] Pilate was thus sitting upon the highest point of the large temple area, where what he did was plainly visible to all present. But the fact that the outer court of the temple was "paved throughout"[7] does by no means show that Pilate here erected his tribunal. Lightfoot (in loco) argues at some length to show that this Pavement was the room Gazith in the temple, where the Sanhedrim sat, and, as the Jews would not go to Pilate's judgment hall, he went to theirs.

[1] War, 2. 14. 8.
[2] War, 1. 21. 1; 5. 4. 4.
[3] Josephus, Antiq. 8. 5. 2; 20. 8. 11.
[4] So Meyer, Winer, Alford, Friedlieb, Lewin. Ewald (v. 14) supposes this palace to have been reserved for the use of Herod's heirs, when they came to the capital.
[5] Wieseler, 407.
[6] War, 6. 1. 8; and 6. 3. 2.
[7] Josephus, War, 5. 5. 2.

Greswell observes that "to suppose that the tribunal of Pilate could have been placed in any court of the temple would be palpably absurd." We must then conclude that this Pavement was a movable one, like that which Suetonius mentions, when he says that Julius Cæsar took with him pieces of marble ready fitted, that they might be laid down at any place, and the judgment seat be placed upon them; or, which is more probable, that it was the open paved space before the palace of Herod. The latter view is confirmed by Josephus,[1] for Florus, when he had fixed his quarters in the palace, erected his tribunal in front of it, and there gathered the chief men of the city before him. The judge seems to have been at liberty to place his tribunal where he pleased, and Pilate on one occasion did so in the great circus.[2] We consider it then most probable that all the judicial proceedings before Pilate were at the palace of Herod upon Mount Sion.[3]

Pilate, being informed that members of the Sanhedrim had brought a criminal before him, and of their unwillingness to enter the palace, goes out to meet them.[4] It was plainly the purpose of the priests and elders to obtain at once from Pilate a confirmation of their sentence, without stating the grounds upon which He had been condemned; but this plan was wholly baffled by his question, "What accusation bring ye against this man?" Whether Pilate asked this question from a sense of justice, not thinking it right to condemn any man to death without knowing his offence; or whether he already knew who the prisoner was, and that He had been condemned upon ecclesiastical

[1] War, 2. 14. 8.

[2] Josephus, War, 2. 9. 3.

[3] Winer, ii. 29; Greswell, iii. 225; Tobler, Top. i. 222. Many, however, place the judgment hall in the castle Antonia; so Williams, Barclay. The point is important only in its bearings on the site of the sepulchre, and the direction of the Via Dolorosa.

[4] Jones (Notes, 3 and 9) puts the arrival of the Jews about five o'clock, or a little before sunrise; Ewald (v. 483) an hour before sunrise.

grounds, we cannot determine. We can scarce doubt, however, that he had some knowledge of Jesus, of His teaching, works, and character. Without troubling himself about ecclesiastical questions, he would closely watch all popular movements; and he could not overlook a man who had excited so much of public attention. If, as is most probable, he was in Jerusalem at the time of the Lord's public entry, he must have heard how He was hailed by the multitude as King of the Jews; and the fact that he placed a part of the Roman cohort at the disposal of the priests when about to arrest Him, shows that they must have communicated to him their design. But, however this may have been, it is plain that he was by no means disposed to be a mere tool in the hands of the priests and elders to execute their revengeful plans. Vexed at his question, they reply, almost contemptuously, "If He were not a malefactor, we would not have delivered Him up unto thee." It is as if they had said, 'We have tried Him, and found Him to be a malefactor; there is no need of any further judicial examination. Rely upon us that He is guilty, and give us without more delay the power to punish Him.'

It is not certain what force is to be given to the word "malefactor,"[1] but apparently His accusers design to designate Jesus as one who had broken the civil laws, and therefore was amenable to the civil tribunals. By the use of this general term they conceal the nature of His offence, which was purely ecclesiastical. They had condemned Him for blasphemy, but for this Pilate would not put Him to death —probably would not entertain the case at all; and as they knew not what other crime to lay to His charge, they present Him as a malefactor. This vague and artful reply displeases Pilate, who is, beside, touched by the cool effront-

[1] Κακον ποιων, Tischendorf, Alford.

ery of the council in demanding that he shall, without examination, ratify their sentence; and he answers tartly, "Take ye Him and judge Him according to your law." It is as if he had said, If you can judge, you can also execute; but if I execute, I shall also judge. This answer forces them to confess that they had no power to put Him to death; and shows them that, if they would accomplish their purpose, they must bring some direct and definite charge, and one of which Pilate would take cognizance. They therefore now begin to accuse him of perverting the nation, of forbidding to give tribute to Cæsar, and of saying that He was Christ, a king, (Luke xxiii. 2.) These were very serious accusations, because directly affecting Roman authority, and such as Pilate was bound to hear and judge.

Up to this time Jesus and His accusers, and Pilate, had been standing without the Pretorium. According to Roman law, the examination might take place within the Pretorium, but the sentence must be pronounced in public without. Entering it, Pilate calls Jesus and demands of Him, "Art thou the King of the Jews?" The Synoptists give simply this reply: "Thou sayest," or "I am;" but John relates the reply in full, in which Jesus describes the nature of His kingdom, (xviii. 33–38.) The effect of this conversation upon Pilate was very great. He saw at once that Jesus was no vulgar inciter of sedition, no ambitious demagogue or fanatical zealot, and that the kingdom of which He avowed Himself to be the king was one of truth, and not of force. At worst, He was only a religious enthusiast, from whose pretensions Cæsar could have nothing to fear; and he determines to save Him, if possible, from the hands of His enemies. Taking Jesus with him, he goes out and declares to them that he finds no fault in Him. This, probably unexpected, exculpation on his part only makes them "the more fierce," and they renew the charge that He stirred up the people throughout all Judea and Galilee, (Luke xxiii. 5.) Mark, xv. 3, says: "And the chief priests accused Him of many things." Galilee may have been thus mentioned because the Galileans were prone to sedition. To all these accusations Jesus answers nothing, so that His silence makes even Pilate to marvel. The incidental mention of Galilee suggests to the governor that he might relieve himself from responsibility by sending Him to Herod, who was then in the city, and unto whose jurisdiction, as a Galilean, He rightfully belonged. He accordingly sends Him to Herod, and hopes that he is now quit of the matter; or, if Herod should decline jurisdiction, that he would express some opinion as to His guilt or innocence. The chief priests and scribes follow Him, that they may renew their accusations before the new judge.

By Herod the Lord was gladly received, as he had long desired to see Him, and hoped that He would now work some miracle before him. But to all the king's questions He answered nothing, nor did He reply to the accusations of His enemies. Angry at His continued silence, and doubtless interpreting it as a sign of contempt, Herod and his soldiers mock Him with pretended homage, and, clothing Him in a gorgeous robe, send Him back to Pilate.[1] His return so attired was a very intelligible sign to Pilate that Herod, who, from his position, must have known His history, had no knowledge of any seditious practices in Galilee; and regarded Him as a harmless man, whose Messianic pretensions were rather to be ridiculed than severely punished. This sending of Jesus by Pilate to Herod was understood by the latter, and probably designed by the former, as a mark of respect and good will, and was the means of restoring friendship between them, which had been broken, per-

[1] Some would make this a white robe, such as candidates for office were accustomed to wear, and chieftains when they went into battle. Thus robed, He appeared as a candidate for the honor of king of the Jews. So Friedlieb, Archäol. 109; contra, Meyer. In Vulgate, *veste alba*.

haps by some question of conflicting jurisdiction.[1] Where Herod took up his residence, when in the city, is not known. If Pilate occupied the fortress Antonia, Herod would doubtless occupy his father's palace. It is not probable that both occupied the latter together, as some suppose.[2] Possibly he made his abode at the old palace of the Maccabees.[3] In either case, the distance was not great, and but little time was spent in going to and returning from Herod.

After Jesus was brought back to Pilate, the latter calls together "the chief priests and the rulers and the people," (Luke xxiii. 13.) He now designs to pronounce Him innocent and end the trial, and therefore seats himself upon his judgment seat, (Matt. xxvii. 19.) There was a custom that at this feast a prisoner chosen by the people should be released from punishment. As to the origin of this custom nothing definite is known. From the language of the Synoptists, κατα εορτην, it has been inferred that at each of the feasts a prisoner was released.[4] John, however, confines it to the Passover, and it might have had some special reference to the release of the people from Egyptian bondage. No traces of it are to be found in later Jewish writings. It may possibly have been established by the Romans as a matter of policy, but more probably it was of Jewish origin, and continued by the Roman governors.[5] Whether Pilate had this custom in mind when he took his seat upon the tribunal, is not certain; but his words (Luke xxiii. 16) strongly imply this, as well as the fact that he had gathered the people together with the chief priests and rulers. Ascending the tribunal, he formally declares that, having examined Jesus, he had found no fault in Him, neither had Herod, to whom he had sent Him; and after chastising

[1] Some would trace the origin of this quarrel to the incident mentioned by Luke xiii. 1. See Greswell, iii. 26.

[2] Lichtenstein, 432.

[3] Josephus, Antiq. 20. 8. 11.

[4] Friedlieb, Archäol. 110.

[5] Winer, ii. 202; Hofmann, 360.

Him, he will therefore release Him. It seems from the scope of the narrative that he intended to chastise Jesus, thus to propitiate the priests, and then to release Him under the custom without further consulting the people. In this way, apparently, Pilate thought to satisfy all: the people, by releasing Him; the priests and elders, by chastising Him; and himself, by delivering Him from death. But he satisfied none. The people, reminded of their claim, began to clamor for it, but they did not demand that Jesus should be released. To satisfy the priests and rulers, His chastisement was far too light a punishment The cry is raised, "Away with this man, and release unto us Barabbas." Pilate, who knew how well affected the people at large had been to Jesus, cannot believe that they will reject Him and choose Barabbas; and he therefore accepts the alternative, and leaves them to elect between the two.

Of this Barabbas, son of Abbas, little is known. According to some authorities, the true reading (Matt. xxvii. 16 and 17) is Jesus Barabbas.[1] From the statements of the Evangelists respecting him, it appears that he was one of that numerous and constantly growing party who detested the Roman rule, and who afterward gained such notoriety as the Zealots. In company with others, he had stirred up an insurrection in the city, and had committed murder, (Mark xv. 7; Luke xxiii. 19.) John speaks of him as a robber also; but this crime was too common to attract much attention, or bring upon its perpetrator much odium. Josephus,[2] speaking of Florus, says that "he did all but proclaim throughout the country that every one was at liberty to rob, provided he might share in the plunder." It is remarkable that this man was confessedly guilty of the very crime with which the priests and rulers had falsely charged Jesus—that of sedition; and no plainer proof of their hypocrisy could be

1 So Meyer, Ewald; and, formerly, Tischendorf: contra, Alford.
2 War, 2. 14. 2.

given to the watchful Pilate than their efforts to release the former and to condemn the latter. And this it was easy for them to effect; for the tide of popular feeling ran very strong in favor of national independence, and one who had risen up against the Romans, and had shed blood in the attempt, was deemed rather a hero and a patriot than a murderer. On the other hand, Jesus, so far from encouraging the rising enmity to Roman rule, had always inculcated obedience and submission—teachings ever unpalatable to a subject nation. It is probable, too, that most of those present were the citizens of Jerusalem, rather than the pilgrims from other parts of the land; and, if there were some from Galilee, that they did not dare, in opposition to the rulers, to express openly their wishes.

Whilst waiting for the people to come to a decision, he receives the message from his wife mentioned by Matt. xxvii. 19. Nothing is known of her but her name, which tradition gives as Procla, or Claudia Procula.[1] This dream was generally regarded by the fathers as supernatural, and by most ascribed to God, but by some to Satan, who wished to hinder the Lord's death.[2] This message would naturally tend to make Pilate more anxious to release "that just man," even if he did not ascribe to the dream a divine origin.[3]

The Synoptists agree that Pilate made three several attempts to persuade the people to release Jesus, though the order of the attempts is not the same in all. The events may be thus arranged: Pilate presents to the people the two, Jesus and Barabbas, between whom they were to choose. A little interval followed, during which he received

[1] Winer, ii. 262; Hofmann, 340. [2] See Jones, Notes, 359.

[3] Lewin (129) finds in this circumstance a proof that the locality was Pilate's ordinary residence, the palace of Herod; and that the charge against Jesus was brought at so early an hour that he was aroused from his slumbers to hear it.

his wife's message. He now formally asks the people whom they wished to have released, (Matt. xxvii. 21; Mark xv. 9; Luke xxiii. 16–18.) They answer, Barabbas. Pilate, hoping that by changing the form of the question he could obtain an answer more in accordance with his wishes, says, "What shall I do then with Jesus, which is called Christ?" (Matt. xxvii. 22; Mark xv. 12. Luke, xxiii. 20, does not give the question; but the answer shows that it must have been the same as in Matthew and Mark.) To this they reply, "Let Him be crucified." Alexander (on Mark xv. 13) suggests that the cry "Crucify Him" arose from the fact that, as Barabbas, by the Roman law, would have been crucified, Jesus should now stand in his stead and bear his punishment. Bynaeus (iii. 118) explains it on the ground that crucifixion was the usual punishment of sedition, of which He was accused. Pilate now sees that not only do the people reject Jesus, but that they insist upon the most severe and ignominious punishment. He had proposed chastisement; they call for crucifixion. He had not anticipated this, and will reason with them. He therefore asks, "Why, what evil hath He done?" (Matt. xxvii. 23; Mark xv. 14.) Luke (xxiii. 22) adds: "I have found no cause of death in Him; I will therefore chastise Him and let Him go." This judicial declaration of His innocence, and attempt to substitute the milder punishment, only cause the people to cry out the louder, "Let Him be crucified."

John (xviii. 39, 40) sums up the narrative very briefly, and gives no details. He omits the sending to Herod, and states only the result of the popular election.

The great and rapid change in public feeling in regard to Jesus which four or five days had brought, would appear incredible, did we not find many analogous cases in history. The thoughtlessness and fickleness that characterize a populace, are proverbial. Besides, we here find special causes in operation to bring about this change. The multitude, that shouted " Hosanna to the son of David " on the day of His triumphal entry, doubtless expected that He would immediately assert His kingly claims, and take a position before the public corresponding to His high dignity. But so far from this, He reappears the next day, not as a prince, but as a teacher; He does nothing answering to their expectations; He passes much of His time in seclusion at Bethany, and the excitement of His entry dies away. Still, He has a powerful hold on the popular mind as a prophet and worker of miracles; and this is recognized by the rulers in the manner in which they effect His arrest, and the haste with which they press on the trial. It was His conviction as a blasphemer that turned the heart of the people against Him. The chief priests, the elders, the scribes, all those in whom they trusted, and who guided public opinion, were busy in declaring that He had blasphemed in the presence of the whole Sanhedrim. He assumed to be something more than the Messiah whom they expected—to be even the Son of God. All His teachings, all His miracles are straightway forgotten. He is a blasphemer; He must die.

It may be, also, as has been said, that most of those who cried " Crucify Him " were citizens of Jerusalem, who, under the influence of the hierarchy, had never been well inclined toward him, and do not seem to have joined in the hosannas and rejoicings upon the day of His entry.

From the Synoptists it would appear that, after the failure of the attempts to induce the multitude to release Jesus, Pilate, despairing of success, washed his hands before the people, and then gave Him up to be scourged and crucified. But John (xix. 4–12) relates other and apparently subsequent attempts to save Him, placing them after and in connection with the scourging. Was He, then, twice scourged? This is affirmed by some, who regard the scourging of John (xix. 1–3) as designed to gratify the elders and priests, and to excite popular compassion; but that mentioned by the Synoptists as the scourging usually inflicted before crucifixion. But this is improbable. That scourging generally preceded the crucifixion, appears from Josephus.[1] This scourging was excessively severe, the leathern thongs being often loaded with lead or iron, and cutting through the flesh even to the bone, so that some died under it.[2] But the Lord having been once scourged, there seems no reason why it should be repeated; nor is it likely that Pilate would have permitted it.

If, then, Jesus was scourged but once, and the accounts of the Synoptists and of John refer to the same event, why did Pilate now permit it? Was it that, finding himself unable to save Jesus, and having no further expedient, he gives up the struggle, and sends Him away to be scourged as preliminary to His death?[3] Or did he permit it, hoping that through the milder punishment he might awaken pity, and thus rescue Him from death?[4] It is not easy to decide as to Pilate's motives. He had early offered to chastise Jesus, and then release Him; but this the multitude refused, and demanded His crucifixion. It does not, then, seem probable that He could hope that the mere sight of Jesus suffering this punishment could so awaken their pity as to change their determination.[5] And why, if this were his purpose, should Jesus be taken into the common hall, or Pretorium, and subjected to the insults and mockery of the soldiers? We infer, then, that Pilate, having yielded to the priests and rulers, sent Him to be scourged as preliminary to His crucifixion, which was done by the

[1] War, 2. 14. 9, and 5. 11. 1. See Winer, i. 677; Friedlieb, Arch. 114.

[2] As to flagellation among the Jews, see Ainsworth on Deut. xxv. 1–3.

[3] Bynaeus, Stier, Krafft, Ellicott.

[4] Meyer, Sepp, Alford, Jones, Tholuck.

[5] It is not certain whether He was scourged in the Pretorium or without it. The words of Matthew and Mark imply the latter; so Meyer, Lange. But if He was scourged but once, it would seem from John xix. 4 that it was done in the Pretorium; so Bynaeus.

soldiers in their usual cruel way; that, beholding Him bloody from the scourge, clothed with the purple robe, and wearing the crown of thorns, his own compassion was awakened, and he resolved to make one last effort to deliver Him from death. He therefore leads Him forth, and after an emphatic declaration for the third time that he finds no fault in Him, presents Him to the people, saying, "Behold the man." He hoped that the sight of one so meek, so helpless, so wretched, would touch the hearts of all as it had touched his own. Stier gives rightly the meaning of his words: "Is this man a king? An insurgent? A man to be feared, or dangerous? How innocent, and how miserable! Is it not enough?" It is probable, as said by Jones, that as He wore the crown of thorns and purple robe, so He also bore in His hand the reed. But nothing could touch the hearts of His imbittered enemies. As they saw Him, the chief priests and officers raised anew the cry, "Crucify Him, crucify Him." It is not said that the people at large joined in it; and perhaps for a time, through fear or pity, they were silent.

Angry at the implacable determination of the rulers that Jesus should be crucified, Pilate tauntingly responds to the cry, "Take ye Him and crucify Him, for I find no fault in Him." Lardner (i. 54) paraphrases these words: "You must crucify Him, then, yourselves, if you can commit such a villany, for I cannot. He appears to me innocent, as I have told you already, and I have now punished Him as much as He deserves." The Jews now perceived that Pilate, knowing that the charge of sedition was baseless, and deeply sympathizing with Jesus, would not put Him to death; and are compelled to return to the original charge of blasphemy. "We have a law, and by our law He ought to die, because He made Himself the Son of God." This mention of the fact that Jesus made Himself the Son of God, had a power over Pilate, who now heard of it for the first time, which the Jews little anticipated. Was then his prisoner, whose appearance, words, and conduct had so strangely and so deeply interested him, a divine being? Full of fear he returns to the judgment hall, and commands Jesus to be brought, and demands, "Whence art thou?" His silence at first, and still more His answer afterward, confirmed Pilate in his determination to release Him; and he may probably have taken some open step toward it. But the rulers will not thus give up their victim. They begin to threaten that if he release Him he thereby shows that he is Cæsar's enemy, and that they will accuse him before the emperor. Pilate now perceives the danger of his position. Such an accusation he must, at any cost, avoid. His administration would not, in many respects, bear a close scrutiny; and the slightest suspicion that he had shown favor to a claimant of the Jewish throne, falling into the ear of the jealous and irritable Tiberius, would have endangered, not only his office, but his life. Such peril he could not meet. The shrewd elders and priests, who knew the selfish weakness of his character, pressed their advantage, and Pilate dared do no more. Jesus must be crucified. He now prepares to give final sentence. But he will first clear himself of the guilt of shedding innocent blood. He takes water and washes his hands before all, to show that he is clean.[1] "Then answered all the people, His blood be on us and on our children." At this moment, about to give sentence, Pilate could not give up the poor satisfaction of mocking the Jews in what he knew well to be a most tender point: their Messianic hopes. He cries out, "Behold your king." His contemptuous words only bring back the fierce response, "Away with Him; crucify Him." Still more bitterly he repeats, "Shall I crucify your king?" The answer

[1] Many place this after the words of the Jews, "We have no king but Cæsar," (John xix. 15;) so Stier. Some before the scourging of Jesus; so Jones.

of the chief priests, for the people are not said to have joined in it, "We have no king but Cæsar," was an open renunciation of their allegiance to Jehovah, and of the covenant which He had made with the house of David, (2 Sam. vii. 12.) Thus had the Jews been led, step by step, not only to reject their Messiah, to prefer a robber and murderer before Him, to insist mercilessly that He should be put to a most shameful death, but even to accept and openly proclaim the Roman emperor as their king. This was the culminating point of national apostasy.

Some points presented by the narrative demand further consideration. Brief reasons have been given for supposing that Jesus was scourged but once. Some, however, would make the scourging mentioned by John (xix. 1) a kind of judicial torture, or *quaestio per tormenta*, for the purpose of forcing a confession if the prisoner were really guilty. To this torture by scourging Pilate subjected Jesus, not that he had any doubt of His innocence, but that if no confession of guilt were extorted, he might have stronger grounds for setting Him free.[1] Torture was customary with the Romans, (Acts xxii. 24,) and was practised by Herod the Great.[2] But that Pilate should now have recourse to it, when he himself knew Jesus to be innocent, merely that he might say to the Jews that He had made no confession, is most improbable. Sepp (vi. 241) supposes that the soldiers regarded the scourging as intended to extort a confession, and acted accordingly, though Pilate had other designs.

The person to be scourged was bound to a low pillar, that, bending over, the blows might be better inflicted. The pillar to which the Lord was bound is mentioned by Jerome and Bede, and others.[3] There is now shown in the church of the Holy Sepulchre a fragment of a porphyry

[1] Hug, cited by Tholuck; Bucher, 777; Kirchen, Lex. vi. 271; Friedlieb, 331. See, however, contra, his Archäol. 116.

[2] See Josephus, Antiq. 16. 10. 3 and 4.

[3] Hofmann, 365.

column called the Column of the Flagellation, and a rival column is preserved at Rome.

The traditional site in the Via Dolorosa of the place where Pilate presented Jesus to the people, or the Arch of the *Ecce Homo*, has been recently defended by Saulcy, (ii. 291.) This writer makes Pilate to have led Jesus forth upon the gallery, βημα, (John xix. 13,) which was situated in the Pavement, and there, for the second time, to have shown Him to the people.

The form of Pilate's sentence is not given. The customary form was, *Ibis ad crucem.* Friedlieb (Arch. 125) gives a sentence pretended by Adrichomius to be genuine, but rightly rejects it. Another sentence, said to have been found in Aquila in Italy, has been often printed. Another was found at the same place a few years since.[1] Both are obvious fabrications.

It has been much disputed whether Pilate transmitted to the emperor at Rome any account of Christ's trial and death. In itself this is intrinsically probable, for it seems to have been the custom of governors of provinces to send thither records of the more important events occurring during their administration. Thus Philo speaks of the "acts," *acta*, transmitted to Caligula from Alexandria. That Pilate did send such records, appears from Justin Martyr's address to the Emperor Pius, in which he appeals to them as proving Christ's miracles and sufferings. Tertullian, in his Apology, also appeals to them. Eusebius, in his History, (ii. 2,) relates, upon the authority of Tertullian, that Tiberius, receiving these acts of Pilate, containing an account of the Lord's resurrection, and of His miracles, proposed to the senate that He should be ranked among the gods. If, however, Pilate really sent such an account, we obtain from it no additional particulars respecting the trial

[1] See both, given by Hofmann, 366–369.

and death of the Lord. No writer gives any quotation from it; from which it may be inferred that none, even of those who refer to it, had ever seen it. The supposition that Pilate's records had been destroyed by the senate or emperor before the time of Constantine, in order to remove this proof of Christianity, is not very probable.[1]

Some have attempted to cast additional light upon the evangelical narratives by referring to the Apocryphal Gospel of Nicodemus. But from it very little of value can be drawn.[2]

Friday, 15th Nisan, 783. A. D. 30.

Delivered by Pilate into the hands of soldiers, He is led without the city to a place called Golgotha, bearing His cross. Falling exhausted under the burden, the soldiers compelled Simon of Cyrene, whom they met, to bear it with Jesus. To some women following Him and weeping, He speaks words of admonition, and foretells the judgments about to come upon Jerusalem. After He had been affixed to the cross, they gave Him wine mingled with gall, but He would not drink. Two malefactors were crucified with Him, one on the right hand and one on the left. As they were nailing Him to the cross, He prays to His Father to forgive them. The inscription placed over His head displeased the Jews, but Pilate refused to change it. The soldiers who kept watch at the foot of the cross, divide His garments among themselves.

John xix. 16–24.
Matt. xxvii. 32–38.
Mark xv. 21-27.
Luke xxiii. 26–34.

It was, according to John, (xix. 14,) "about the sixth hour," *ωρα δε ωσει εκτη*, when Pilate sat down in the judgment seat to pronounce final sentence. But this seems in

[1] See Jones, Canon N. Test. ii. 330; Pearson on Creed, art. 4; Jarvis, 375.
[2] See Tischendorf's Pilati Circa Christum Judicium. Lipsiae, 1855.

direct opposition to Mark, (xv. 25,) "And it was the third hour, and they crucified Him." Against John's statement, is that also of all the Synoptists, that there was darkness from the sixth hour over all the land till the ninth hour, (Matt. xxvii. 45; Mark xv. 33; Luke xxiii. 44.) This darkness did not begin till Jesus had been for some time nailed to the cross. Many efforts have been made to harmonize this discrepancy.[1] That change of punctuation which places a period at the word "preparation," (in John xix. 14,) and joins "of the Passover" with "hour," making it to read, "And it was the preparation, and about the sixth hour of the Passover," has been already spoken of in another connection. It is forced and untenable. Some would change "sixth" into "third," and thus bring John into harmony with Mark, regarding the former as an error of copyists.[2] But the weight of authority is in favor of the present reading.[3] Lightfoot finds a solution in his interpretation of Mark, who does not say, "it was the third hour *when* they crucified Him," but "it was the third hour *and* they crucified Him." It notes that the fathers of the Sanhedrim should have been present at the third hour in the temple, offering their thank offerings. "When the third hour now was, and was passed, yet they omitted not to prosecute His conviction." This is wholly unsatisfactory. Some would make the "preparation" of John, παρασκευη, to denote not the whole day, but that part of it immediately preceding the Sabbath, or from 3–6 P. M. Thus John's meaning would be, it was the sixth hour before the commencement of the preparation, or about 9 A. M., which would agree with Mark. Others would read it, "about the sixth hour, or noon, the preparation time of

1 For a full account of early opinions, see Bynaeus, iii. 178.

2 Bynaeus; Robinson, Har. 226, who refers to Griesbach and Wetstein; Luthardt, Bloomfield.

3 Tischendorf, Alford, Greswell, Wieseler, Meyer.

Passover day commenced." Both these constructions are arbitrary. Some would make the term hour, ωρα, to be used by John in a large sense. The day was divided into four periods of three hours each, and to each of these periods was the term hour applied. Thus the first hour was from 6–9, the third from 9–12, the sixth from 12–3, the ninth from 3–6. The third hour of Mark was from 9–12. During this period, and probably at the beginning of it, Jesus was crucified. John, in his statement, refers to the end of it.[1] But this is unsupported by usage. Many suppose that John reckons the hours according to the Roman mode, from midnight. Thus his sixth hour would be 6 A. M. Some, as Jones, so modify this as to make the sixth hour to continue till nine. In regard to this, Newcome remarks,[2] "That the Romans ever reckoned their hours in the manner that we do, from midnight or from midday, is destitute of proof. Though other matters were regulated by the civil computation, the hours were counted according to the natural day, from six in the morning to six in the evening, and again from six in the evening to six in the morning." Wieseler, (414,) who admits that the Romans in general reckoned from sunrise, yet finds an exception in this case, because the 15th Nisan, as distinguished from the Passover, began at midnight, (Exod. xii. 29.) Upon this one day John could reckon the hours from midnight. But this is certainly most improbable, and the Roman computation being the same with the Jewish, nothing is gained. Greswell, therefore, after Townson, makes John to reckon after our own mode, from midnight; but this does not fit the other notices of time in his Gospel, and it is scarcely possible that all could have been done by so early an hour.[3]

[1] So Godwyn, Moses and Aaron, 81; Campbell, notes in loco; Krafft, 147.

[2] Har. notes in loco.

[3] See, however, Ewald, (v. 483), who makes Jesus to have been brought

We conclude, then, that the sixth hour of John was the twelfth hour with us, or midday. But it is to be noted that he says, "about the sixth hour," ως εκτη,[1] which implies that he gives no exact note of the time. It is rendered by Norton, "it was toward noon," and this very well expresses the meaning. Mark's words, "It was the third hour, and they crucified Him," need not be taken as a specific designation of the hour when He was nailed to the cross, but as marking the time when, the sentence having been pronounced, He was given up to the soldiers, and the preparatory steps to the crucifixion began. Our exact divisions of time were wholly unknown to the ancients.[2]

If the Sanhedrim held its second session about sunrise, as the statements of the Evangelists lead us to suppose, the events subsequent down to the crucifixion, must have occupied several hours. The time when Jesus was led to the hall of judgment is noted by John, (xviii. 28,) "and it was early," ην δε πρωι. If this denote the fourth watch of the night, it was from 3–6 A. M. The usual hour for opening judicial proceedings among the Romans was 9 A. M., and probably Pilate now a little anticipated the time. The crucifixion itself was during the interval from nine to twelve.

The place of the crucifixion will be hereafter considered when we inquire where the Lord was buried. From Heb. xiii. 12 it appears that the cross was placed without the gate; and from the Evangelists, that it was called Calvary, or in the Hebrew, Golgotha, meaning the place of a skull; and that it was not far from the public street. Jesus was conducted thither by the soldiers, Pilate not having lictors, to whom such duty specially belonged. According to

to Pilate an hour before sunrise, (John xviii. 28, πρωι,) the sentence given at 6 A. M., (John xix. 14,) and the crucifixion at 9, (Mark xv. 25.)

[1] Tischendorf. [2] See Pauly, Real. Encyc., ii. 1017, art. Dies.

Roman custom, He bore his own cross; but, wearied by the labors of the night, and faint from the scourging and abuse of His enemies, He sank beneath the burden. At this juncture, meeting a man of Cyrene, named Simon, they compelled him to assist Jesus in bearing it, (Luke xxiii. 26.) According to some, he bore it alone. Probably he was met just as they were going out of the city gate, and he was entering in, (Matt. xxvii. 32.) Of this Simon little is known, except that he was a Cyrenian, and the father of Alexander and Rufus, (Mark xv. 21.) Many suppose him a slave from the fact that, while so many Jews must have been present, they were passed by, and he was seized upon to perform this degrading office.[1] The reason, however, of his selection may simply have been that, chancing to be close at hand when Jesus sank down from weariness, they compel him to assist. Others suppose him to have been a disciple, and on that account selected; but this fact could scarcely have been known to the soldiers. That he subsequently became a disciple is more probable. Following the Lord upon the way to the place of crucifixion was "a great company of people and of women, which also bewailed and lamented Him," (Luke xxiii. 27.) These women do not seem to have been those who followed Him from Galilee, but those of the city, or the parts adjacent, who had seen Him, or heard Him, and now sympathized with Him.[2]

[1] So Meyer.

[2] For a minute account of the Lord's progress from the judgment hall to the cross, along the Via Dolorosa, and the traditionary incidents, see Hofmann, 371. "Whether the Via Dolorosa receives a right designation or not, we do not know. It was up part of its ascent, or that of its neighborhood, that, in all probability, Christ bore His cross," (Wilson, i. 425.) Robinson finds in the fourteenth century the earliest allusion to the Via Dolorosa, (i. 233, note.) For full details as to the traditional stations along this way, see Tobler, Top. i. 262, &c. But if the trial of the Lord was at the palace of Herod on Mount Sion, He could not have passed along the Via Dolorosa.

It is uncertain whether the cross was placed in the ground before the victim was nailed to it, or after; but the former is most probable.[1] With Jesus were crucified two malefactors, respecting whom we know nothing, but who may have been companions of Barabbas.[2] An early tradition makes them to have been two robbers, named Titus and Dumachus, whom Jesus met in Egypt; and it is said that He then predicted that both should be crucified with Him.[3] His position between the two was probably owing to the malice of the priests; though the soldiers may have done it in mockery of his kingly claims. Greswell, (iii. 246,) from John xix. 32, 33, conjectures that the crosses of the two malefactors looked to the west, but that of Jesus to the east. Tradition makes His to have looked to the west.[4]

The offering of vinegar mingled with gall (Matthew and Mark) seems to have been before the nailing to the cross. The object of this was to stupefy the victim, so that the pain might not be so acutely felt. This, however, was a Jewish, not a Roman custom, though now permitted by the Romans.[5] Lightfoot (on Matt. xxvii. 34) quotes from the Rabbins, "To those that were to be executed they gave a grain of myrrh, infused in wine, to drink, that their understanding might be disturbed, or they lose their senses, as it is said, 'Give strong drink to them that are ready to die, and wine to them that are of sorrowful heart.'" This mixture the Lord tasted, but, knowing its purpose, would not drink it. He would not permit the clearness of His mind to be thus disturbed, and, in the full possession of consciousness, would endure all the agonies of the cross. Meyer and Alford find a contradiction between Matthew

[1] Friedlieb, Arch. 142; Greswell, iii. 245.

[2] As to the abundance of thieves and robbers at this time, and its causes, see Lightfoot on Matt. xxvii. 38.

[3] Hofmann, 176. [4] Hofmann, 376. [5] Friedlieb, Archäol. 140.

and Mark, because the former speaks of "vinegar mingled with gall;" the latter, of "wine mingled with myrrh." But it is well said by Alexander, that "as the wine used by the soldiers was a cheap sour wine, little, if at all, superior to vinegar, and as myrrh, gall, and other bitter substances are put for the whole class, there is really no difference in these passages."[1]

Lightfoot supposes that it was not the usual mixture, wine and frankincense, or myrrh, but, for greater mockage, and out of rancor, vinegar and gall. Townsend[2] supposes that three potions were offered him: the first, vinegar mingled with gall, in malice and derision, which He refused; then the intoxicating draught, which He also refused; then the sour wine, or posca, which He drank. Another supposition is, that benevolent women gave him the wine and myrrh, and at the same time the soldiers brought the vinegar and gall.

Crucifixion was a punishment used by the Grecians, Romans, Egyptians, and many other nations, but not by the Jews. It was indeed permitted by the law to hang a man on a tree, but only after he had been put to death, (Deut. xxi. 22, 23.) Upon this, Maimonides, quoted by Ainsworth, remarks: "After they are stoned to death, they fasten a piece of timber in the earth, and out of it there crosseth a piece of wood; then they tie both his hands one to another, and hang them near unto the setting of the sun." The form of the cross varied. Sometimes it was in the shape of the letter X. This was called *crux decussata.* Sometimes it was in the shape of the letter T. This was called *crux commissa.* Sometimes it was in the form following: †. This was called *crux immissa.* Tradition affirms that the cross on which the Lord suffered was of the latter

[1] That χολη, gall, is used in the Septuagint for various kinds of bitter stuffs, see Winer, i. 350; Friedlieb, Arch. 141.

[2] Part vii. note 23

kind; and early painters have so represented it.[1] The upright post, or beam, was by no means lofty, generally only so high as to raise the person a few inches from the ground. Midway upon it was a little projection, *sedile*, upon which the person sat, that the whole weight of the body might not fall upon the arms, and they thus be torn from the nails. The arms were sometimes tied with cords, perhaps to prevent this pressure upon the nails, or that the nailing might be the more easily effected. The head was not fastened. Whether the feet were generally nailed, has been much disputed.[2] That the Lord's feet were thus nailed, may be inferred from Luke xxiv. 39, 40. Appearing to the Eleven upon the evening following His resurrection, He said to them: "Behold my hands and my feet, that it is I myself; handle me and see, for a spirit hath not flesh and bones, as ye see me have. And when He had thus spoken, He showed them His hands and His feet." This showing of the hands and feet could not be simply to convince them that His body was a real body, and not a mere phantasm; but had also the end to convince them of His identity. "It is I myself; and in proof of this, look at the prints of the nails remaining in my hands and my feet." John (xx. 20) says, "He showed unto them His hands and His side." From both narratives, it follows that He showed them the wounds in His hands, His side, and His feet. That, at his second appearing to the Eleven, He spake to Thomas only of His hands and His side, is to be explained as giving all the proof that that sceptical apostle had demanded, (v. 25.) Alford gives a little different explanation: "He probably does not name the feet,

[1] Hofmann, 372. See Bynaeus, (iii. 225,) and Didron's Christian Iconography, (Trans. i. 374,) for a discussion of the various forms of the cross.

[2] In neg., see Paulus, (Handbuch, iii. 669,) who discusses this point at great length; Winer, i. 678; aff., Friedlieb, 144; Meyer on Matt. xxvii. 35. Alford, "not always, nor perhaps generally, though certainly not seldom."

merely because the hands and side would more naturally offer themselves to his examination than the feet, to which he must stoop." That the feet were nailed, has been the current view of commentators.[1]

It has been questioned whether the feet of the Lord were separately nailed, or one nail was used for both. According to Hofmann, most of the painters have represented the feet as lying one over the other, and both penetrated by the same nail.[2] Didron (Christian Iconography) observes: "Previous to the thirteenth century, Christ was attached to the cross by three or four nails indifferently. After the thirteenth century, the practice of putting only three nails was definitively in the ascendant." On the other hand, early tradition speaks of four nails.[3] It is possible that the crown of thorns remained upon His head, as represented by the painters. Matthew and Mark, who both speak of taking off the purple robe, say nothing of the soldiers removing the crown of thorns.

The prayer, "Father, forgive them, for they know not what they do," given only by Luke, (xxiii. 34,) was probably spoken while the soldiers were nailing him to the cross, or immediately after. It doubtless embraced all who took part in His crucifixion—not only the soldiers, who were compelled to obey the orders given them, but the Jewish priests and elders, and the Roman governor—all who had caused His sufferings. The garments of the crucified belonged to the soldiers as their spoil. After the four appointed to this duty had divided His garments, they sat down to watch the body.

It was customary among the Romans to affix to the cross an inscription, *τιτλος*, *αιτια*, in order to point out to all the nature of the offence. Whether it was borne before

1 Tholuck, Stier, Lange, Ebrard, Ewald, Olshausen.

2 See, however, Friedlieb, Archäol. 145, note.

3 See Winer, i. 678; Sepp, vi. 333; Ellicott, 353.

the criminal, or upon his neck, or was attached to the cross, is uncertain; but, on reaching the place of execution, it was set up over his head. As this inscription is differently given by the Evangelists, it has been conjectured that it was differently written in the Greek, Latin, and Hebrew.[1] Pilate, who as judge prepared the inscription, took occasion to gratify his scorn of the Jews, who had so thwarted him; and his short and decisive answer, when he was requested by them to change it, shows the bitterness of his resentment. Jones sees in this a providential acknowledgment of Jesus, by public authority, as King of the Jews. Greswell supposes this request may have been made before the arrival at Calvary.

Friday, 15th Nisan, 7th April, 783. A. D. 30.

While hanging upon the cross, the multitudes, as they passed by, reviled and derided Him. In this mockery the high priests and scribes and elders, and even the two malefactors, joined.	Matt. xxvii. 39–44. Mark xv. 29–32. Luke xxiii. 35–43.
From the cross, beholding His mother standing near by with John, He commends him to her as her son, and her to him as his mother; and John takes her to his own house.	John xix. 25–27.
Darkness now overspreads the land from the sixth to the ninth hour, and during this period He suffers in silence. Afterward drink is given Him, and after He had drunk He commends His spirit to God, and dies. At this moment the veil of the temple is rent, the earth shakes, the rocks are rent, and graves opened. The centurion bears witness that He was the Son of God, and women of Galilee go home smiting their breasts.	Matt. xxvii. 45–56. Mark xv. 33–41. Luke xxiii. 44–49. John xix. 28–30.

The place of crucifixion being near the city, and great multitudes being gathered at the feast, it was natural that

[1] See Pearson on Creed, art. 4; A. Clarke on Matt. xxvii. 37.

many should come to look upon Him, whom all knew by reputation, and most in person. From the time of the crucifixion to the time when the darkness began, sufficient time elapsed to allow His enemies, who hastened to the spot, to behold Him upon the cross. Matthew (xxvii. 39–44) divides those who reviled Him into three classes: the rabble, or passers by; the chief priests, elders, and scribes; and the malefactors. (So Mark xv. 29–32.) Luke says, that "the rulers with the people derided Him," which implies that the rulers began the mockery. He adds, that the soldiers also "mocked Him, coming to Him, and offering Him vinegar." Some, as Stier, would identify this with the offer to Him of the mixed wine as He was about to be nailed to the cross; some, as Lichtenstein, to the giving of vinegar just before His death. Most probably, however, it is to be distinguished from these, and refers to something done a little before the darkness began; perhaps, as the soldiers were eating their dinner near the cross.[1] The vinegar was doubtless the sour wine, or posca, which they usually drank. Their offers were in derision, no wine being actually given.

It is not certain whether both of the malefactors reviled Him, or but one. Matthew and Mark speak of both; Luke of but one. According to some, both joined at first in the general derision; but, beholding the godlike patience and forbearance of Jesus, and knowing on what grounds He was condemned, one repents, and begins to reprove his more wicked companion.[2] The obvious objection, however, to this is, that the first act of one so converted could scarcely be to reprove in another what he had but a few moments before been guilty of himself. This, perhaps, is more plausible than sound. Most, after Augustine, suppose that Matthew and Mark speak in general terms of

[1] Greswell, Alford.

[2] So, early, many; recently, Lange.

them as a class of persons that joined in deriding Jesus, but without meaning to say that both actually derided Him.[1] At what time the words were spoken by the Lord to the penitent thief, we are not told. Most place them before His words to His mother and to John, (John xix. 25–27.)[2] They were thus the second words spoken from the cross.

We cannot determine whether the mother of Jesus, or any of the women that followed Him from Galilee, or any of the apostles, were present at the time He was nailed to the cross; but if not there, some of them soon after came, doubtless hoping to comfort Him by their presence. For a time, they would naturally stand at a distance, till the first outbreaks of anger and mockery were past, and His chief enemies, satiated with the spectacle, had withdrawn. The statement of the Synoptists, (Matt. xxvii. 55, 56; Mark xv. 40, 41; Luke xxiii. 49,) that His acquaintance and the women that followed Him from Galilee stood afar off, seems to refer to a later period, and after the darkness; perhaps, to the moment of His death. The incident narrated by John may thus have been a little before the darkness began; and after this the disciples, terrified by it and the signs that attended His death, did not dare approach the cross. Krafft, however, (150,) supposes that it was after the darkness that His mother and John, with the other women, approached Him, and that the Synoptists refer to an earlier period.

According to many, John at once took Mary to his home, or the house he was occupying during the feast; for it does not appear otherwise that he had any house in Jerusalem of his own.[3] A confirmation of this is found in

[1] Ebrard, Da Costa, Lichtenstein. Meyer finds two traditions; and Alford, that Matthew and Mark report more generally and less accurately than Luke. For a statement of opinions, see Bynaeus, iii. 367.

[2] Ebrard, Stier, Da Costa, Greswell.

[3] Townson, Greswell, Stier, Meyer.

the fact that the Synoptists do not mention her name among those that beheld afar off at the hour of His death. It has, therefore, been inferred that Jesus, in his compassion, would spare her the pain of seeing His dying agonies, and so provides that she be taken away.[1] But it may be questioned whether the words, "And from that hour that disciple took her unto his own house," mean any more than that ever after this she was a member of John's household, and was treated by him as a mother.[2] But if John then led Mary away from the place of crucifixion, he must afterward have returned, as he declares himself to have been an eye-witness of the piercing of the side, and the flowing out of the blood and water, (xix. 35.) Whether he was the only apostle present at the Lord's death, is matter of conjecture. This is supposed by Stier; but there is no good reason why others, if not daring to approach near, should not have looked on from a distance.

That the darkness was no natural darkening of the sun, but a supernatural event, is recognized by all who do not wholly deny the supernatural element in the Gospel narratives. The attempt to bring it into connection with the eclipse mentioned by Phlegon of Tralles, has been already mentioned; and that it could have been caused in such a way is disproved by the fact that it was then full moon. The attempt of Seyffarth to show that the Jews might then have kept the Passover on the 25th March, finds no defenders.[3] Some, however, would connect it with the earthquake, and explain it as the deep gloom that not unfrequently precedes such convulsions of nature.[4] But this supposes that the earthquake was a mere natural event, whereas this also was plainly extraordinary. The darkness began at the sixth hour, or twelve A. M., and continued till the ninth, or three P. M. The forms of expression, "over

[1] Bengel.
[2] Luthardt, ii. 421; Lichtenstein, 448.
[3] See Winer, ii. 482.
[4] Paulus, Handbuch, iii. 764.

all the land," πασαν την γην, (Matthew,) "over the whole land," ολην την γην, (Mark and Luke,) do not determine how far the darkness extended. Many would confine it to the land of Judea, as our version does, except in Luke, where it is rendered, "over all the earth."[1] If, however, it extended beyond Judea, the phrase "whole earth" need not be taken in its most literal sense, but is to be regarded as a general expression, embracing the countries adjacent.[2] Some, however, would extend it over all that part of the earth on which the sun was then shining.[3]

That during this period of darkness many of the bystanders should have left the place of crucifixion and returned to the city, is probable, though not stated. Stier, however, affirms, "No man dares to go away, all are laid under a spell; others, rather, are attracted to the place." But when we consider that the Lord's enemies would naturally construe this darkness as a sign of God's anger against Him, if they gave it any supernatural character, any such fear can scarce be attributed to them; nor does it appear in their subsequent conduct. That some of the spectators remained, appears from Matthew's words, (xxvii. 47,) that there were some standing there when He called for Elias. (See also Luke xxiii. 48.) It is probable, though not explicitly stated, that the darkness dispersed a few moments before the Lord's death, and that the returning light emboldened His enemies to renew their mockeries.[4]

The cry of Jesus, "My God, my God, why hast thou forsaken me?" was about the ninth hour; either a little before the cessation of the darkness,[5] or just after its cessation.[6] So far as appears, during the three hours of gloom,

[1] So Ebrard, Olshausen, A. Clarke; Norton, who renders it, "over the whole country."

[2] Meyer, Lange.

[3] So Alford, who makes the fact of the darkness at Jerusalem all that the Evangelists testify to as within their personal knowledge.

[4] Stier, Lichtenstein. [5] Stier, Ellicott. [6] Greswell

the Lord was silent, and doubtless all were silent around Him. But by whom were His words understood, as a call for Elias? From the similarity of sound, the Roman soldiers might have so misunderstood Him; but it is not probable that they knew much of the current Jewish expectations respecting Elias as the forerunner of the Messiah. Lightfoot explains it, that the word "Eli" is not properly Syriac, and thus was strange to the Syrian ear, and deceived the standers by. But such a misunderstanding on the part of the Jews, whether they were from Judea or from other lands, is not easily credible. Some, however, affirm that the Jews, terrified by the darkness, now began to fear that the day of God's judgment was actually at hand; and, in their superstitious terror, naturally interpreted Christ's words as a call for him, the prophet, whose coming was closely connected in their minds with the great day of God.[1] But this is not consistent with what follows. The general view, therefore, seems to be the right one, that they wilfully perverted His meaning, and made the cry of distress an occasion of new insult and ridicule.[2]

In immediate connection with the words of the bystanders, "this man calleth for Elias," one of them is said by Matthew and Mark to run and, taking a sponge and filling it with vinegar, to give Him to drink. This act, which in those Evangelists seems unexplained, may have followed from His words, which are recorded only by John, (xix. 28,) "I thirst." We may thus arrange the events: Immediately after His exclamation, "My God, why hast thou forsaken me?" He adds, "I thirst." One of those present, perhaps a soldier, perhaps a spectator, moved by a sudden feeling of compassion, prepares the vinegar, which was at hand, and makes ready to give Him to drink. Whilst doing this, the others call upon him to

[1] Olshausen, Lange, Jones.

[2] Meyer, Alexander, Alford, Friedlieb, Ellicott.

wait a little, that they might see whether Elias would come to save Him, (Matt. xxvii. 49.) He, however, gives Jesus the drink, and then, having satisfied his compassionate impulse, mockingly adds, "Let alone, now we will wait for Elias," (Mark xv. 36.) Thus the words of Matthew will be those of the spectators; those of Mark, the words of the giver of the drink. John (xix. 29) omits this mockery, and merely says, in general terms, "they filled a sponge with vinegar," &c. Luke (xxiii. 36) may be referred to earlier mockeries.[1]

After Jesus had received the vinegar, He cried out with a loud voice, "It is finished." The Evangelist adds, "And He bowed His head, and gave up the ghost," (John xix. 30.) Luke (xxiii. 46) narrates that "When He had cried with a loud voice, He said, Father, into Thy hands I commend my spirit: and having said thus, He gave up the ghost." Matthew and Mark both mention that He cried with a loud voice, but do not relate what He said. There can be little doubt that His words given by John, "It is finished," were spoken before those given by Luke, "Father, into Thy hands I commend my spirit."[2] Having taken the vinegar, which gave Him a momentary relief from His thirst, He says, feeling that the end was at hand, "It is finished." He now turns to God, and, addressing to Him His dying prayer, bows His head and dies.

The order of the words spoken by our Lord from the cross may be thus given:—Before the darkness: 1st. His prayer for His enemies. 2d. His promise to the penitent thief. 3d. His charge to His mother and to John. During the darkness: 4th. His cry of distress to God. After the

[1] See Stier, viii. 14–18; Alexander in loco. As to the kind of drink given Him, and the motive with which it was given, see various suppositions in Bynaeus, iii. 423. As to the hyssop branch on which the sponge was put, see Royle, Jour. Sac. Lit., Oct. 1849.

[2] Meyer, Stier, Da Costa, Alford.

darkness: 5th. His exclamation, "I thirst." 6th. His declaration, that "It is finished." 7th. The final commendation of His spirit to God.[1] Ebrard would thus arrange the first three: 1st. His prayer for His enemies. 2d. His charge to His mother and John. 3d. His promise to the penitent thief. Krafft's order is as follows: 1st. His prayer for His enemies. 2d. His promise to the penitent thief. 3d. His cry of distress to God. 4th. His charge to His mother and John. 5th. His exclamation, "I thirst." 6th. "It is finished." 7th. Commendation of His spirit to God.

The quaking of the earth, and the rending of the veil of the temple and of the rocks, appear from Matthew and Mark to have been at the same instant as His death. Luke, (xxiii. 45,) who mentions only the rending of the veil, speaks as if it took place when the sun was darkened; but his language is general. Meyer's interpretation of the statement that "there was a darkness over all the earth until the ninth hour," as denoting only a partial obscuration of the sun, but that at the ninth hour it "was darkened" and wholly disappeared from sight; and that at the same moment the veil of the temple was rent, has little substantial in its favor. Darkness, in which the sun was still visible, could scarcely be so called. The first statement, v. 44, is the effect; the second, v. 45, the cause.[2] Perhaps the darkness may have deepened in intensity to its close. That the rending of the veil could not be ascribed to an earthquake, however violent, is apparent. There were two veils, one before the holy and one before the most holy place, (Exod. xxvi. 31–36.) It is generally agreed that the latter is here meant.

The account given by Matthew only (xxvii. 52, 53) of the opening of the graves and appearing of many bodies of the saints, some, as Norton, have rejected as an interpolation. There is, however, no doubt as to the genuineness of

[1] Stier, Greswell, and many.

[2] Oosterzee in loco.

the text. The graves seem to have been those in the immediate vicinity of Jerusalem. That those who arose are called "saints," αγιοι, does not determine who are meant; whether some who had died recently, perhaps since Christ began His ministry, or some who died long before, and had been buried there, perhaps patriarchs and prophets. From the fact that they appeared to many, the presumption is, that they had not long been dead, and thus were recognized by those to whom they appeared. That their resurrection was after Christ's resurrection, although the opening of their tombs was at His death, best harmonizes with the scope of the narrative. This, however, is questioned by Meyer, who supposes the Evangelists to say that they came out of the graves at His death, but did not enter the holy city till after His resurrection.[1] After He had arisen, they appeared openly, their resurrection thus giving force and meaning to His. But it was the Lord's resurrection, not death, that opened the gates of Hades. Dying, the rocks were rent and the doors of the sepulchres were opened; but, rising, He gave life to the dead.[2] Da Costa (429) places, however, the opening of the graves also subsequent to the resurrection. Whether those thus raised were raised in the immortal and incorruptible body, and soon ascended to heaven; or whether, like others, they died again, we have no means of determining. In favor of the former is the language, they "appeared unto many," ενεφανισθησαν πολλοις; which implies that they, like the Lord Himself, after His resurrection, were not seen by all, but only by those to whom they wished to manifest themselves.[3]

The impression made upon the centurion by all the

[1] So Bynaeus.

[2] Calvin, Lightfoot, Whitby, A. Clarke, Calmet, Greswell, Krafft, Ebrard, Bengel, Alford.

[3] For early opinions, see Calmet, translated in Journal Sac. Lit. 1848, vol. i. See also Lardner, ix. 328; Sepp, vi. 401.

wonderful events accompanying the Lord's death, was such that he openly testified his conviction, as given by Matthew and Mark, that Jesus was "the (a) Son of God;" as given by Luke, "Certainly, this was a righteous man." The latter words are explained by Alford thus: "Truly, this man was truthful;" that is, He had asserted Himself to be, and He was, the Son of God. Thus the expressions of the Evangelists are made identical. More probably He uttered at different times both expressions.

FRIDAY, 15TH NISAN, 7TH APRIL, 783. A. D. 30.

Soon after the Lord's death, the chief priests came — JOHN xix. 31–37.
to Pilate, requesting that the bodies might be taken
down before sunset, because the next day was the
Sabbath. Obtaining their request, the legs of the two
malefactors are broken to hasten their death; but Jesus, being found already dead, is pierced with a spear
in the side. At this time, Joseph of Arimathea goes — MATT. xxvii. 57–60.
to Pilate, and informing him that Jesus was already — JOHN xix. 38–42.
dead, asks His body for burial; and Pilate, after satis- — MARK xv. 42–46.
fying himself that He was actually dead, orders the — LUKE xxiii. 50–54.
body to be given him. Aided by Nicodemus, Joseph
took the body, and winding it in linen cloths with
spices, laid it in his own sepulchre, in a garden near
the cross; and shut up the sepulchre. Some women — LUKE xxiii. 55, 56.
beheld where He was laid, and, returning home, pre- — MATT. xxvii. 61.
pared spices and ointments, that they might embalm — MARK xv. 47.
Him after the Sabbath was past. During the Sabbath
the council obtains permission from Pilate to seal up — MATT. xxvii. 62–66.
the sepulchre and to place a watch, lest the disciples
should steal the body.

It was the custom of the Romans to permit the body to remain on the cross till it was consumed by the birds and beasts, or wasted by corruption.[1] But it was an express

[1] Pearson on Creed, art. 4.

command of the law, (Deut. xxi. 23,) that the body should not remain all night upon the tree, but must be taken down and buried the same day.[1] Aside from this command of the law, it was probably thought desirable by the rulers, that the body of Jesus should be, as early as possible, removed from public sight. It is not certain whether the Jews who came to Pilate knew that He was actually dead; but their request that the legs of the crucified might be broken, implies that they did not. If so, they must have come to Pilate about three P. M., or a little before His death. If, however, they did know that He was dead, as is not improbable from the marked circumstances that attended the act of dissolution, their request had reference to the two malefactors, who were still living; and perhaps also was designed to make the death of Jesus certain.[2] That the natural effect of the breaking of their legs would be to hasten death is plain, and this was the end the Jews sought. Usually the Romans did not in this, or any other way hasten it; though sometimes the crucified were subjected to personal injuries, as pounding with hammers or breaking of limbs, in order to increase their sufferings. The term *crurifragium*, though literally applicable only to the breaking of the legs, and which sometimes constituted a separate punishment, seems to have been applied to various other acts, which tended to increase the pain, and so to shorten life; and may have included the use of the spear. The Jews wished not to increase their sufferings, but to hasten death; and we may well suppose that the soldiers were directed, if the breaking of the legs should not prove sufficient, to use other means.[3] Whether, in addition to the breaking of the legs of the two malefactors, other violent means were used, is not certain; but the narrative does not imply it.

The object of piercing the Lord's side was not so much

[1] Josephus, War, 4. 5. 2; Josh. x. 26. [2] So Meyer.
[3] Friedlieb, Archäol. 164.

to cause death as to make sure that He was already dead. Which side was pierced, is not said; and the painters, as well as commentators, have been divided in opinion: most, however, suppose the left side. With what intent does the apostle mention the flowing out of the blood and water? Does he mention it as a simple physiological fact, and in proof of the Lord's death; or as a supernatural event, to which some special significance is to be attached? As this point has an important bearing upon the question respecting the physical cause of the Lord's death, it deserves our consideration.

Lying at the basis of all inquiries respecting the Lord's death, physiologically regarded, is the question whether He died as other crucified persons died, death being the natural consequence of His physical sufferings; or whether He gave up His life by an immediate act of His own will, or by an immediate act of His Father in answer to His prayer. The latter opinion seems to have prevailed in the early Church, though by no means universally.[1] Of recent writers may be mentioned Tholuck: "By an act of power the Redeemer actually separated His spirit from His body, and placed it, as a deposit, in His Father's keeping." Alford: "It was His own act,—'no feeling the approach of death,' as some, not apprehending the matter, have commented, but a determined delivering up of His spirit to the Father." Stier: "He dies, as the act of His will, in full vigor of life."[2] If this opinion be correct, and Jesus died by His own act, it is not easy to see how it can be said that He was slain by the Jews. His death was in consequence of His own volition, and not of any sufferings inflicted upon Him by His enemies. We therefore conclude, that though He voluntarily gave Himself to death, and submitted to be nailed to the cross, yet that death came to

[1] See Stroud, Physical Cause of Christ's Death. London, 1847, p. 47.

[2] In like way speak Greswell, Alexander, Jones, Baumgarten.

Him as to the two malefactors, naturally, not supernaturally; and was the consequence of His physical sufferings, aggravated by mental distress.[1]

Many, however, have found difficulty in explaining, in this way, the quickness of the Lord's death. He was not upon the cross, at the longest, more than six hours; while it is well known that the great majority of the crucified live at least twelve hours; many, one or two days; and some, three or four days. But there seems no valid reason why we may not attribute this speedy decease to the great physical weakness caused by His previous bodily and mental sufferings, superadded to the ordinary agonies of crucifixion. That those sufferings were most intense we know from the account given of the hour passed at Gethsemane; and that the Lord, already exhausted by His great spiritual conflicts with the power of darkness, by the excitement and fatigue of that awful night, and by the scourging inflicted upon Him, should have died so much sooner than was usually the case, can excite no surprise. Nor do the objections of Stroud, based upon the natural vigor and healthfulness of the Lord's body; the short duration of His mental agony in the garden; and the proof of unabated physical strength shown by the loudness of voice with which He uttered His last words upon the cross, seem of much weight.[2]

Those who regard the Lord's death as a natural event, yet one whose quick consummation is not adequately explained by the pains attendant upon His crucifixion, are forced to give another explanation. Of these, several have been presented. One is that of Stroud, that the immediate physical cause was rupture of the heart, caused by the great mental suffering He endured, (pp. 74 and 143.)

[1] So, in substance, Pearson, Bloomfield, Stroud, Ellicott.

[2] As to the pains of crucifixion, and their natural effects in destroying life, see Richter in Friedlieb, Archäol. 155.

Another, that attributes His death to the piercing of the spear, is so directly at variance with the evangelical narrative, that it may be at once dismissed, (John xix. 30 and 33.) As the incident of the flowing of the blood and water from His side furnishes the chief ground upon which Stroud rests his explanation, we turn to its consideration.

The first question that arises is, does the Evangelist narrate here a natural or a supernatural event? That he attached some special importance to it, is apparent from His words, (v. 35,) which seems to refer chiefly to it,[1] though the reference may be to all related, vs. 32–34. Commentators are by no means agreed in opinion.[2]

If the former view be correct, and the flowing of the blood and water was without any miraculous features, why is it here mentioned? Some reply, to prove the reality of the Lord's body as against the Docetæ.[3] But the reality of His body had been proved, in a thousand ways, during His life; and if His body, sensible to touch and sight, was a phantasm, so might much more easily be this seeming blood and water. According to Alford, it was to show that the Lord's body was a real body, and underwent real death, "not so much by the phenomenon of the water and blood, as by the infliction of such a wound." But the Evangelist had distinctly stated that Jesus was dead before this wound was inflicted; and none of the other Evangelists mention the piercing, though all speak of His death. But, granting this to be the intention of St. John, how is the reality of His death thus shown? Are proper blood and

[1] So Meyer.

[2] On the one side may be mentioned Calvin, who says, *Hallucinati sunt quidam, miraculum hic fingentes*; A. Clarke, Tholuck, Ebrard, Ewald, Alford; on the other, Lightfoot, Bengel, Greswell, Luthardt, Meyer.

[3] So Coleridge in Stroud: "The effusion showed the human nature. It was real blood, composed of lymph and crassamentum, and not a mere celestial ichor, as the Phantasmatists allege."

water here meant, *aqua pura et vera, sanguis purus et verus*, as said by Bengel? No, for this would remove it into the region of the supernatural. Have we, then, in these terms, merely a hendiadys for reddish lymph, or bloody water? This is inadmissible. Does the apostle then mean blood that had decomposed, and was thus resolved into crassamentum and serum, or the thick red part of the blood and the aqueous transparent part? This is the view taken by many; and it is said that we have in this, conclusive proof not only of His death, but that He had also been some time dead, since the blood had begun to decompose. Thus Neander says: "I must believe that John, as an eye-witness, meant to prove that Christ was really dead from the nature of the blood that flowed from the wound."

Admitting, for the moment, that the blood and water were the constituent parts of blood now decomposed, whence came they? According to Stroud, from the pericardium, into which, through the rupture of the heart, there was a great effusion of blood, and which was there decomposed. The pericardium, being pierced by the spear, it flowed in crassamentum and serum, "a full stream of clear watery liquid, intermixed with clotted blood, exactly corresponding to the clause of the sacred narrative." Ebrard (563) supposes it to have been extravasated blood, that, flowing into some of the internal cavities of the chest, there decomposed, and these cavities being opened by the spear, the constituent parts made their escape.

Against all these explanations which are based upon the coagulation of the blood, and aside from the physiological objections to which they are open, we find an invincible difficulty in the words of the Psalmist, that God would not suffer His Holy One to see corruption; and in the declaration of St. Peter, that "His flesh did not see corruption." His body was not to see corruption; or, in other words, the usual processes of decay were not to commence in it. Decomposition of the blood can scarcely be considered as other than the initial step of corruption. The full separation of His soul and His body must take place; but, after this, he "that had the power of death" had no more power over the Holy One.

The explanations of the Grüners and of the Bartholines[1] are free from this difficulty, since they do not affirm a coagulation of the blood. The former suppose that both pericardium and heart were pierced by the spear; and that from the former came the water, and from the latter the blood. The statement of the elder Grüner, that "the pericardium is full of water when a person dies after extreme anxiety," does not seem to be sustained by facts. That there must have been a considerable quantity of water as well as of blood flowing forth, appears from the fact that the apostle, standing doubtless at some distance from the cross, was able to distinguish them. It is in a high degree improbable that any such quantity of serum should have been found in the pericardium as to be visible to him. It is also difficult to explain, in this way, the flowing of the blood, since the heart of a dead person is usually emptied of its blood; or, if any remains, it would flow very slowly: and to say that Jesus was not wholly dead when pierced with the spear, is contrary to the sacred narrative.

The second explanation, that of the Bartholines, supposes that the water and blood came from one or both of the pleural sacs. It is said that, during the sufferings of crucifixion, a bloody serum was effused in these sacs, from which, when pierced by the spear, it flowed out. But aside from the fact that such an effusion of bloody serum or lymph as the narrative demands, is not proved in cases of crucified persons, if indeed in any case whatever; there is

[1] See Stroud, 135–137.

the further objection that such bloody serum does not answer to the Evangelist's "blood and water."

We conclude, then, that the attempts to explain this phenomenon as a merely natural event, and upon physiological grounds, are by no means satisfactory. They are wholly unable to explain how so much clear serum, as the narrative plainly implies, could have been found in the pericardium, or in the pleural sacs, or in any of the internal cavities which the spear could have reached. Against the view that it was coagulated blood, stands the fact that the Lord's body saw no corruption; nor would any unlearned reader understand the terms "blood and water" of decomposed blood. We therefore infer, that the event was something supernatural. It is not here the place to inquire into its special significance. It may have been a sign to all beholders that the body was not subject to the common law of corruption. The spirit of Jesus had departed, and with it that vital energy which held together the constituent elements of the body; yet disorganization and dissolution did not begin. According to Lange,[1] it was a sign that the change in the body, preparatory to the resurrection, had already begun; the power of God was already working in it, to prepare it for immortality and incorruptibility.

It was in the power of governors of provinces to grant private burial to criminals when requested by friends; and this was usually done, except they were very mean and infamous.[2] But for the request of Joseph of Arimathea, the body would probably have been buried in some place appropriated to criminals, and where the two malefactors were actually buried. "They that were put to death by the council were not to be buried in the sepulchres of their fathers; but two burying places were appointed by the

[1] Note in loco. [2] Pearson, Creed, 332.

council, one for those slain by the sword and strangled, the other for those that were stoned or burnt."[1] Pilate could have no objection to granting Joseph's request; as, on the one hand, his position as a member of the Sanhedrim entitled him to a favorable hearing; and, on the other, he was not unwilling that the innocent victim should have an honorable burial. (Mark xv. 45. He gave the body to Joseph; or, more literally, made a gift or present of the body to him.) According to Mark, xv. 44, Pilate was surprised that He was already dead; and, calling the centurion, made inquiries how long He had been dead. How is this coming of Joseph related to that of the Jews, (John xix. 31,) who asked that the bodies might be taken down? We may suppose that the Jews came about 3 P. M., before the coming of Joseph, and were ignorant of the Lord's death. Joseph may have stood near the cross, and heard His last words, and thus have known of His death so soon as it occurred. He went to Pilate "when the even was come," (Matt. xxvii. 57,) or from 3–6 P. M. Going at once to Pilate he informs him of it; and the latter, knowing that sufficient time has not elapsed for the execution of the order respecting the breaking of the legs, or at least for their death after their legs were broken, is surprised. The Jews, indeed, may have preferred their request after Joseph had preferred his, and Pilate have given the soldiers orders to make sure that Jesus was really dead, ere He was given up for burial; but the former order is most probable. It is not necessary to suppose that Joseph knew of the purpose to have the bodies taken down, though he might have done so.

Joseph, having received permission to take the body, is aided by Nicodemus; and, taking it down, they wrap it in linen cloths, with "myrrh and aloes about an hundred pound weight," which the latter had brought, and lay it in a new sepulchre in a garden near at hand, which belonged to Jo-

[1] Lightfoot on Matt. xxviii. 58.

seph.[1] It has been questioned whether the spices were actually used, because of the shortness of time. But John's words are express that the spices were used. It, however, remains doubtful whether the customary embalming was then perfected. Lardner (x. 368) remarks, that "all was done, as may reasonably be supposed, after the best manner, by the hands of an apothecary or confectioner, or perfumer, skilled in performing funeral rites. There must have been many such at Jerusalem." Norton[2] makes the transactions of anointing and burying the body, to have occupied many hours, and the dawn of the Sabbath to have appeared ere all engaged in them had left the tomb. But it is more probable that Joseph and Nicodemus were themselves able to do all that was necessary to be done; for there is no reason to suppose that the body was embalmed in any proper sense of that term. "The Egyptians filled the interior of the body with spices; but the Jews, who buried on the day of decease, only wrapped the body round with spices."[3] It is probable that all was finished before the Sabbath began. If, however, the body was then properly prepared for its burial, why did the women, who "beheld the sepulchre and how the body was laid," prepare additional spices and ointments? It could not well have been from ignorance of what Nicodemus had done. We must, therefore, suppose that this further anointing was something customary;[4] or that the first was imperfect, and this therefore necessary; or that it was a mark of love.[5]

[1] It is not certain that Nicodemus came till the body had been taken from the cross.

[2] Notes, 317.

[3] Michaelis on Resurrection, 93; Greswell, iii. 260, note.

[4] Friedlieb, Arch. 172.

[5] Meyer, Greswell; Alex. on Mark xvi. 1. Lange regards the first as only for the preservation of the body, and the second as the proper anointing. Jones affirms, that, as Joseph and Nicodemus were secret disciples, the women had no acquaintance with them, and did not know their purpose.

The Lord was crucified at a place called in the Hebrew, Golgotha, and His body was laid in a sepulchre in a garden near by. The site of this sepulchre has been much discussed, and with great learning and ingenuity, but without leading to any certain result. For many centuries the Christian Church received, without question, the traditionary tomb beneath the dome of the present church of the Holy Sepulchre as that to which He was borne, and from which He arose. Of this belief is still the great body of Christians. But a large number of modern travellers have been led, by a personal inspection of the spot, to doubt the tradition, and have brought very cogent arguments against it. Fortunately, here, as often, it is of little importance whether the traditionary site be, or be not, the true one. The fact of the Lord's resurrection is a vital one, but not whether He arose from a tomb in the valley of Jehosaphat, or on the side of Acra. Nor is, as affirmed by Williams,[1] "the credit of the whole Church for fifteen hundred years in some measure involved in its veracity." Few will so press the infallibility of the Church as to deny the possibility of a topographical error. The little value attached by the apostles to the holy places, appears from the brevity with which they speak of them when they allude to them at all. Not to the places of His birth and of His burial would they turn the eyes of the early Christians, but to Himself—the ever-living One, and now the great High Priest at the right hand of God.

But however unimportant in itself, either as confirmatory of the Gospel narratives, or as illustrating the Lord's words, still, as a point that has so greatly interested men, it may not be wholly passed by. A brief statement of the question will therefore be given, that the chief data for a judgment may be in the reader's possession. It naturally presents itself, first, as a question of topography; and, sec-

[1] Holy City, ii. 2.

ond, of history. But before we consider it from either of these points of view, let us note what is said respecting the places of crucifixion and of burial by the Evangelists.

From their statements it appears, First, that the place of crucifixion was out of the city, (John xix. 17; Matt. xxviii. 11; Heb. xiii. 12.) Second, it was near the city, (John xix. 20.) Third, the sepulchre was near the place of crucifixion, (John xix. 41.) Fourth, it was in a garden and hewn in a rock, (Matt. xxvii. 60; Mark xv. 46; John xix. 41; Luke xxiii. 53.) It may, perhaps, be inferred from Mark xv. 29, "And they that passed by railed on Him," that the cross stood near some frequented street, but much weight cannot be laid upon it. The name of the place where He was crucified was Golgotha, which Alexander calls "an Aramaic form of the Hebrew word for skull." "The proper writing and pronunciation of the word," says Lightfoot, "had been Golgolta, but use had now brought it to be uttered Golgotha." Some suppose it so called from its resemblance to the shape of a skull—a little hill so shaped;[1] others, because it was the usual place of execution. "They come to the place of execution commonly called Golgotha, not the 'place of graves' but the place of skulls; where, though indeed there were some buried of the executed, yet was it in such a manner that the place deserved this name rather than the other."[2]

If the first interpretation of the name be taken, it is still possible that it was the common place of execution. That it was a well known spot, appears from the use of the article, (Luke xxiii. 33; John xix. 17;) but it is doubtful whether the Jews had any one place set apart as a place of execution;[3] and if so, would a rich man like Joseph have had a

[1] So Reland, Meyer, Alexander, Winer.

[2] Lightfoot, iii. 164; so early, Jerome, *locum decollatorum;* Greswell, iii. 243; Ewald, v. 484.

[3] See Kitto, Bib. Cyc., i. 779; Herzog's Cyk., v. 308.

garden there? If, then, we reject this, we may suppose that the Lord was taken to the nearest convenient place in the suburbs of the city. In regard to the epithet "mount," applied to Calvary, Robinson denies that Eusebius, or Cyril, or Jerome, or any of the historians of the fourth or fifth centuries, use it; and ascribes its origin to the fact that the rock of Golgotha was left in the midst of the large open court, formerly the garden, on one side of which a Basilica was erected. "From this rock or monticule of Golgotha was doubtless derived the epithet 'mount' as applied to the present Golgotha or Calvary."[1] According to Willis, the rock of Calvary was part of a little swell of the ground forming a somewhat abrupt brow on the west and south sides. "This would afford a convenient spot for the place of public execution. For the southwestern brow of the rock has just sufficient elevation to raise the wretched sufferers above the gazing crowd, that would naturally arrange itself below and upon the sloping ridge opposite."[2]

We come now to the consideration of the topographical question; and as this has been most fully discussed by Robinson in his "Biblical Researches" on the one side, and by Williams in his "Holy City" on the other, our references will be chiefly to them. As we have seen, the place of crucifixion was without the city. The site of the Holy Sepulchre is within the present city wall. If, therefore, the present wall were the same that existed at the death of Jesus, this site could not be the true one. But it is admitted that the present wall is not the same; and the point in dispute is, Where did that wall stand? Josephus mentions three walls.[3] With the first, built by David and Solomon, and

[1] i. 376, note 3.

[2] Holy City, ii. 240. Ewald (v. 485, note) identifies it with "the hill Gareb," Jer. xxxi. 39; Lewin, (130,) following Krafft, with Goath: "In the time of the prophets, Calvary appears to have been called Goath, and was without the city." See p. 35, where Gareb is identified with Bezetha.

[3] War, 5. 4. 2.

embracing Mount Sion, and with the last, built by Agrippa after Christ's death, we have no concern. The question concerns only the position of the second wall, which began at the gate Gennath in the first wall, and reached to Antonia, encircling the northern part of the town. Did this include or exclude the present church of the Holy Sepulchre?

Into the intricate discussions respecting the position of Acra, and of the valley of the Tyropoeon, it is not necessary here to enter. Acra may be, as maintained by Robinson and others, on the north side of Sion, and the valley of the Tyropoeon lie between it and Sion; and yet the position of the second wall be not thereby determined.[1] To determine the position of the second wall, Josephus gives us the two termini—the gate Gennath in the first wall and the tower Antonia; and implies that it ran not in a straight line but in a circle, *κυκλουμενον δε το προσαρκτιον κλιμα*, &c., "encircling the northern part." Where was the gate Gennath? The name indicates that it was a gate leading to a garden, or near one. By Robinson it is placed in the first wall, near the tower Hippicus, which both Robinson and Williams agree to have been upon, or very near, the site of the modern citadel El Kalah, not far south or southeast from the present Jaffa gate.[2] By others it is placed farther to the east, near the Bazaars, which lie midway upon the street running from the Jaffa gate to the temple wall, and close to the traditional "Iron Gate, (Acts xii. 10.)[3] The arguments upon either side are not conclusive; nor which-

[1] Much importance is, indeed, given by many in this controversy to the exact locations of Acra and the Tyropoeon; so Williams and Robinson. Schaffter makes the whole controversy to turn upon it. Raumer, on the contrary, who agrees upon these points with Robinson, does not find that they decide the course of the second wall.

[2] So Raumer. According to Lewin, this is not Hippicus but Phasaelus.

[3] So Williams, Schaffter. Lewin puts it east of the three great towers of Herod, and due south from the southwest corner of the Pool of Hezekiah.

ever point be selected, does it decide the question; since it is admitted by Robinson, (i. 410,) that if the second wall ran in a straight line from Hippicus to Antonia, it would leave the Holy Sepulchre without the city. Still, the nearer was this gate to Hippicus, the less the probability that it ran east of the present sepulchre; and the probability diminishes as the northern terminus is carried westward. It is, however, to be noted that all are not agreed as to the position of Hippicus. Schwartz places it on a high rocky hill, north of the so-called Grotto of Jeremiah; Fergusson identifies it with the present Kasr Jalud; Bonar denies that it is the citadel of David, but assigns no site.

As to the general position of Antonia, there is no doubt. It was on the north of the temple area, and probably on the northwest corner.[1] Robinson, however, makes it to have occupied the whole northern part of the present Haram area. In this discussion the difference is unimportant.

With this knowledge of the termini, we now ask as to the course of the wall. It was not straight, but curved. Are there any ruins by which it may be traced? Robinson discovered in the present wall, at the Damascus gate, some ancient remains, which he identifies with the guard houses of a gate of the second wall; and the identification is accepted by Williams. This narrows down the question to the course of the wall from the gate Gennath to the Damascus gate. Are there any remains that indicate its position between these points? West of the Damascus gate, for about 300 feet, Robinson finds traces of an old wall, which he supposes may be the ancient second wall.[2] If correct, this would remove its northern terminus so much farther westward; and here it is placed by Williams. Similar remains have been found in an angle of the present

[1] Raumer, 389; Williams, 409.

[2] So Wilson.

wall, near the Latin Convent.[1] If it is true that these remains mark the course of the second wall, it is apparent that the present site of the sepulchre would be embraced within it, and is thus disproved.

On the other side, Williams (ii. 51) finds remains of two ancient gateways, as he supposes, of the second wall; one on the south side of ruins of the Hospital of St. John, and another farther to the north, and known by tradition as the "Porta Judicii," or Gate of Judgment. In these remains Robinson, however, finds no traces of the second wall. Of the first he says, it may have been one of the piers of a portal, but not more ancient than the hospital; of the second, that a single column furnishes no evidence of a gateway; and that the tradition respecting the Judgment Gate goes no farther back than the end of the Crusades.[2]

All defenders of the present site of the sepulchre do not admit, with Williams, that the present gate of Damascus is a gateway of the second wall. Some make it to turn easterly from the Gate of Judgment to Antonia.[3]

The objection[4] to the present site, drawn from the fact that the distance from it to the western wall of the Haram area is less than a quarter of a mile, thus making the city much too small for the number of inhabitants, is of weight, but not decisive, since we know that the ancient city extended much farther south than the present.[5]

Much stress has been laid by some upon the fact that within the present Church of the Sepulchre is a "rock-tomb, formed long before the church was built, and which probably belonged to an old Jewish sepulchre of an age prior to the destruction of Jerusalem by the Romans."[6] "The existence of these sepulchres," says Stanley, (452,) "proves,

[1] Robinson, iii. 219; Porter, i. 109.
[2] See Schaffter, 46; Barclay, 226; Lewin, 119.
[3] See Raumer, 396; Lewin, Map.
[4] Robinson, i. 410.
[5] See Ritter, Theil xvi. 426.
[6] Willis on Holy City, ii. 194.

almost to a certainty, that at some period the site of the present church must have been outside the walls of the city; and lends considerable probability to the belief that the rock excavation, which perhaps exists in part still, and certainly once existed entire, within the marble casing of the chapel of the Holy Sepulchre, was at any rate a really ancient tomb, and not, as is often rashly asserted, a modern structure intended to imitate it." The antiquity of this rock-tomb is, however, denied by Robinson; and if this could be proved, he denies the conclusion that the second wall must have been to the east of the sepulchre.

Into a consideration of the novel view propounded by Fergusson, that the sepulchre was in the rock now under the dome of the Mosque of Omar, and that this building is the identical church erected by Constantine, we are not called to enter. It is stated by himself, in Dict. of Bible, i. 1018, &c., and rests mainly on architectural grounds.[1]

A new method of proving the genuineness of the present site was presented by Finlay, "On the Site of the Holy Sepulchre," 1847. He supposes that the Roman government had, from time to time, accurate surveys made of its territories, and that "maps were constructed indicating not only every locality possessing a name, but so detailed that every field was measured;" and that this was done throughout the provinces. Thus it was in the power of Constantine to trace the garden of Joseph, from the day of the crucifixion down, through its successive owners, and at any time to identify it. He was therefore able to find it, even though hidden under rubbish and covered over by the temple of Venus. All depends here upon the facts whether such minute and accurate measurements were made at intervals; and if made, whether they had been preserved

[1] For replies, see Williams, Holy City, ii. 90; Willis, same, ii. 196, note; Schaffter, 77; Robinson, iii. 263; Lewin, 146; Edinburgh Review, Oct. 1860. See also Fergusson's Answer to the Review, London, Murray, 1861.

from the day of the crucifixion to the reign of Constantine. Either of these is intrinsically improbable, and anything like demonstrative proof seems to be wanting.[1]

We now come to the historical question. It is certain that the places of crucifixion and burial must have been known, not only to the disciples, but to the priests and rulers, and to many of the inhabitants. It is in the highest degree improbable that they could have been forgotten by any who were witnesses of the Lord's death, or knew of His resurrection. As the apostles, according to a commonly received tradition, continued for a number of years after this at Jerusalem, there could be no doubt that each site was accurately known. Besides, the Evangelists, writing from twenty to fifty years after His death, mention distinctly Golgotha and the garden. Down to the destruction of Jerusalem by Titus, A. D. 70, there can be no question that these places were well known. During the siege of the city, most or all of the Jewish Christians retired to Pella, but they seem soon to have returned.[2] Was the city so destroyed that the former site of the sepulchre could not be recognized? This is not claimed by any one. Robinson (i. 366) speaks of it as "a destruction terrible, but not total."

If, then, the site was known to the Jewish Christians after the destruction of Jerusalem by Titus, it could not well have been forgotten before its second destruction by Hadrian, A. D. 136. Whether up to this period it had been marked by any monument, does not appear. This is possible, although we cannot believe, as assumed by Chateaubriand, that a church was erected upon it. That the city was not wholly destroyed by Hadrian, and that the work of rebuilding began immediately after the close of the war, is historically proved. It became in many respects a new city, taking the name of Aelia Capitolina, by which it was

[1] So Williams, Holy City, ii. 66; contra, Schaffter, 56.

[2] Giesseler, i. 98.

generally known for many years. It was at this period that the Jewish Christian Church at Jerusalem first elected a Gentile bishop; and Eusebius gives a list of his successors, twenty-three in number, down to the time of Constantine.[1] From this time, 136 to 324 A. D., a period of about 190 years, we know nothing of the sepulchre except what we learn from a statement of Eusebius, that impious men had erected over it a temple to the goddess Venus, first covering it with earth.[2] When this temple was erected, or by whom, we do not know. Jerome, at a later period, speaks of a statue of Venus standing upon the spot, and ascribes it to the time of Hadrian. That Hadrian erected upon the site of the Jewish temple a temple to Jupiter, is well known.[3] It is then possible, at least, that at this time a temple to Venus may have been also erected upon the site of the sepulchre; the latter being in the eyes of the Christians a sacred spot, as was the former in the eyes of the Jews, and therefore both alike dishonored by the Romans. How far the Roman government made a distinction between the Jews and the Christians, is not clear; but that Hadrian was so friendly to the latter that he would not erect a temple over the sepulchre, is not shown.[4] But whether erected by Hadrian or not, there seems no good reason for doubting the statement of Eusebius. The objection of Robinson, that his language implies that Constantine learned the site by immediate revelation, and that therefore it could not have been previously known, is hypercritical. Eusebius plainly means that the thought of building a church over the sepulchre, was through divine impulse. This had long been "given over to forgetfulness and oblivion" in the purpose of its enemies; it was buried out of sight, and nothing existed to bring it to mind as the place of the Lord's burial; but he does not say that it was actually thus

[1] Williams, i. 215.
[2] Robinson, iii. 257; Williams, ii. 239.
[3] Robinson, i. 370.
[4] See Giesseler, i. 125.

forgotten. "In the days of Constantine not the least doubt was entertained where the sepulchre was situate; but the only hesitation was, whether, by removing the temple, the sepulchre itself could be recovered."[1]

That Constantine erected a church where the temple of Venus stood, is admitted; that this temple actually stood on the site of the sepulchre, must rest upon the authority of Eusebius. This is supposed to find some support in the fact that a coin of Antoninus Pius contains a figure of Venus standing in a temple with the inscription, C. A. C.: Colonia Aelia Capitolina.[2] The fables related by Cyril and others, in connection with the Invention of the Cross, do by no means show that the site of the sepulchre is fictitious.[3] We cannot well doubt, that if its true position was wholly unknown, and, for purposes of pious fraud, a new one was to be selected, one would have been taken free from such obvious topographical difficulties as encompass the present site.

In concluding this brief statement, it may be added that, as the topographical argument now stands, it seems to make against the genuineness of the present sepulchre. Further excavations and researches may, however, wholly change the aspect of the question. The historical argument in its favor has not yet been set aside. Modern opinions are about equally divided. While most of the Roman Catholic writers defend its genuineness, some deny it; and on the other hand, many Protestants defend it.[4]

The next day, that which followed the day of preparation, or the Sabbath, the chief priests and Pharisees came

[1] Lewin, 155.

[2] See Williams, i. 240.

[3] See Winer, i. 437, note 6. Isaac Taylor (Ancient Christianity, ii. 277) argues more forcibly than fairly that the whole was a stupendous fraud.

[4] Among those not already cited, who deny it, may be mentioned: Wilson, Barclay, Bonar, Stewart, Arnold, Meyer, Ewald. Among those who defend it: Tischendorf, Olin, Prime, Lange, Alford, Friedlieb, Lewin. Among those who are undecided: Ritter, Raumer, Winer, Bartlett, Stanley, Ellicott.

to Pilate, desiring that the door of the sepulchre might be sealed, and a watch set, to prevent the disciples from stealing the body; alleging, as the ground of their fear, His words, "After three days I will rise again." Whether the request was made on the Sabbath itself, or upon the evening following, is uncertain.[1]

Meyer regards all this account as unhistorical, chiefly for the reason that the Pharisees could not have heard Christ's predictions respecting His resurrection; or, at least, could not have thought them worthy of attention. If the disciples did not understand or believe these predictions, much less would His enemies. But this by no means follows. He had openly spoken of His death and resurrection to His disciples, (Matt. xvi. 21; xvii. 22, 23.) This was then unintelligible to them, because they truly believed that He was the Christ; and when He was actually crucified, in their grief and despair all remembrance of His words seems to have escaped them. To the Pharisees He had spoken of the sign of the prophet Jonah as to be fulfilled in Himself, (Matt. xii. 40;) and now that He was dead, they must have thought of its actual fulfilment. Besides, it is scarce possible that they should not, through some of the disciples, have heard of His words respecting His resurrection spoken to them. Judas must have known what his Lord said, and may have told the priests. They were far too sagacious not to take precautions against all possible contingencies. Even if they did not believe His resurrection possible, and had no faith in His words, still it was wise to guard against the stealing of the body. But it is not certain that they did not fear that He would rise. Did they not know of the resurrection of Lazarus? and might not He who then bade the dead arise, Himself come

[1] For the former, Friedlieb; for the latter, Alford. Bucher puts it on the evening following the crucifixion, or the beginning of the Sabbath; so Jones.

forth? In their state of mind, to seal the stone and set the watch was a very natural precaution.

But why was not the body at once taken charge of by the Pharisees, and not delivered into the hands of His disciples? Very likely the request of Joseph for the body was something unknown and unexpected to them; but as it was given to him by permission of Pilate, they could not interfere. It was of no importance in what sepulchre it was placed, provided it was secure; and doubtless they knew that it was in the sepulchre ere they sealed the stone. When the stone was sealed, is not said: many suppose, upon the evening following the crucifixion. "They went to Pilate that same evening, which now no longer belonged to Friday, but formed part of the Sabbath."[1] But let us suppose, with Alford, that it "was done in the evening after the termination of the Sabbath." This delay presents no real difficulty. "The prediction of our Lord was that He would rise the third day; and till it was approaching they would give themselves no concern about His body. The absence of it from the tomb before the commencement of that day, would rather falsify the prediction than show the truth of it."[2] Perhaps they relied on the sanctity of the Sabbath as a sufficient preventive against His disciples, and thought no guard necessary till the day was past. Perhaps they supposed at first that with His death all cause of apprehension had vanished, and that afterward they began to reflect, and this step occurred to them. Of course it was in itself wholly unimportant when the stone was sealed, provided only that the body was then there.

That the account is given by Matthew only, is readily explained from the fact that he wrote specially for the Jews, among whom the report of stealing the body had been put in circulation. It was omitted by Mark and Luke, who wrote for another class of readers.[3]

[1] Michaelis on Resurrection, 100; so McKnight, Bucher.

[2] Townson, 93.

[3] See Michaelis on Resurrection, 98.

PART VII.

FROM THE RESURRECTION TO THE ASCENSION; OR FROM SUNDAY, 9TH APRIL, (17TH NISAN,) TO THURSDAY, MAY 18TH, 783. A. D. 30.

SUNDAY, 17TH NISAN, 9TH APRIL.

As the day began to dawn there was a great earthquake; and an angel of the Lord, descending, rolled away the stone from the door of the sepulchre, and sat upon it. For fear of him, the soldiers be-	MATT. xxviii. 2–4.
came as dead men. Immediately after came Mary	MATT. xxviii. 1.
Magdalene, and other women, to embalm the body.	MARK xvi. 1.
As they approach the sepulchre, Mary Magdalene,	LUKE xxiv. 1.
beholding the stone rolled away, and supposing that the body had been removed by the Jews, runs to find	JOHN xx. 1, 2.
Peter and John, to inform them. The other women	MARK xvi. 2–8.
proceed to the sepulchre, and there meet an angel,	LUKE xxiv. 2–8.
(or angels,) who tells them of the Lord's resurrection, and gives them a message to the disciples.	MATT. xxviii. 5–8
Soon after they had departed, Peter and John,	JOHN xx. 3–10.
who had heard the story of Mary Magdalene, come in haste to see what had occurred; and Mary follows them. Entering the sepulchre, they find it empty, and the grave clothes lying in order; and John then believes. They leave the tomb to return, but Mary	LUKE xxiv. 12 & 24.
remains behind weeping. Looking into the sepulchre, she sees two angels, and immediately after, the	JOHN xx. 11–18.

Lord appears to her, and gives her a message to bear to the disciples. The accounts of the women seem to the disciples as idle tales, and are not believed. Upon the return of the soldiers from the sepulchre into the city, the priests and elders, learning what had taken place, bribe them to spread the report that the disciples had stolen the body away.

MATT. xxviii. 9, 10.
MARK xvi. 9–11.
LUKE xxiv. 9–11.
MATT. xxviii. 11–15.

IN our attempts to put in order the events from the resurrection to the ascension, it is necessary to bear constantly in mind that the Lord now appears under new physical conditions. Up to His death He had been under the usual limitations of our humanity. Now He is the Risen One. Without entering into any inquiries as to the nature of His body after the resurrection, it is certain that it was in many respects unlike what it had been before. During this period of forty days, He came and went, appeared and disappeared, in a most mysterious and inscrutable manner. He passes, seemingly in an instant, from place to place; He is seen by His disciples, and converses with them, and yet is not recognized; He enters the room where they are assembled while the doors are shut. Hence, in examining the narrative of His various appearances during this period, we must remember that He is no more under the ordinary laws of nature; and that we are in the highest sense in the region of the supernatural. Also the angels, of whose modes of existence we know so little, now appear as His attendants, and manifest themselves from time to time to the disciples.

Before attempting to form a connected and complete narrative, let us examine the statements of the several Evangelists separately, and critically compare them with each other. We begin with John. This Evangelist mentions that early on the first day of the week, when it was yet dark, Mary Magdalene came to the sepulchre. He speaks of her only, but his silence respecting others is no certain proof that she was alone. Incidental evidence that others were with her, is found in the use of the plural, (xx. 2,) "We know not where they have laid Him."[1] How many constituted the party, must be learned from the Synoptists. Seeing the stone taken away from the door of the sepulchre, she naturally supposed that the body of Jesus had been removed by the Jews; and in her alarm, without entering it, runs to announce the fact to Peter and John. It is not said where she found them; but hearing her message, they hasten with all speed to the tomb, and entering it, see that it is empty, except the linen clothes and napkin. It is said by John of himself, (v. 8,) "And he saw, and believed." By many this is understood as meaning no more than that he believed what Mary had said about the removal of the body;[2] but this is inconsistent with the general use of this word by John, and with the context, which clearly implies that he believed that Jesus was risen.[3] The two apostles return home, or go to find others of their number. Mary Magdalene, who had followed them back to the sepulchre, remains to weep. Bending down and looking into it, but not entering it, she sees two angels, who address her, asking why she weeps. Absorbed in her grief, she does not seem to have noticed the strangeness of their appearance in such a place, and hastily answers them. Turning backward she sees Jesus, but supposes Him to be the gardener, and not till He calls her by name is He recognized. His words, (v. 17,) "Touch me not, for I am not yet ascended to my Father," seem to point to some movement on her part to embrace Him, which He forbids. (See Matt. xxviii. 9.) He then gives her a message to His brethren; and she, returning to the disciples, told them of all that had occurred. Townson (121) regards this mes-

[1] Compare v. 13, where the singular is used; so Norton, Luthardt, Stier.

[2] Ebrard, Stier, Newcome.

[3] Townson, Luthardt, Robinson.

sage, which is very unlike that given by Matthew, (xxviii. 10,) as a voucher to the apostles that Mary Magdalene had actually seen Him, for He had spoken these very words to them on the evening before His death, (John xvi. 16, 17.) Hearing them repeated from her lips, they could not doubt that He had appeared to her; but, notwithstanding this, her testimony was not at first believed, (Mark xvi. 11.)

This narrative presents several questions that demand examination. Was this appearance to Mary Magdalene the first after Christ's resurrection? Was she alone when He appeared to her? With what intent had she gone to the sepulchre? These questions will be answered as we examine the accounts of the Synoptists.

Matthew's account of the resurrection stands in close connection with what he had said of the burial, and of the guarding of the sepulchre. He wishes to show how all the efforts of the Pharisees "to make the sepulchre sure," by setting a watch and sealing the stone, were made of no effect by the mighty power of God. He sends His angel, and the guards become as dead men; the seal is broken, and the stone rolled away. Let us examine his narrative in detail.

The two women, "Mary Magdalene and the other Mary," who were left on Friday evening "sitting over against the sepulchre," now reappear at the dawning of the first day of the week, going "to see the sepulchre." Were these two alone? If we turn to the other Evangelists, we find that Mark mentions Mary Magdalene, Mary mother of James, and Salome. Luke mentions Mary Magdalene, Mary mother of James, and Joanna, "and other with them." John mentions Mary Magdalene only. What shall we conclude from these discrepancies? Do the Evangelists speak in general terms, giving the names of certain prominent members only of the party, without designing to enumerate all; or do they refer to two or more distinct parties, who visited the sepulchre at different times? The former is much the more probable. A scrupulous exactness in regard to the number of the persons witnesses of an event, is by no means characteristic of the Gospels. The Evangelists do not write as men who are fearful that their statements will be discredited, and therefore anxious to confirm them by heaping up evidence. Each uses the facts connected with the visit of the women to the sepulchre in such manner as will best serve the purpose of his special narrative. How many women went, and who they were—circumstances important indeed in a court of justice—were to them a minor matter, not at all affecting the central fact of the resurrection, which was established by quite other evidence. Each Evangelist mentions certain of the women by name, and passes by others: the grounds of this mention and silence are not known to us, but in no degree affect the truth of the narrative. John mentions Mary Magdalene only; but this does not exclude others; and her language, as has been said, plainly implies that others were present. Matthew had spoken of Mary Magdalene and Mary mother of James as being at the tomb on Friday evening; and he now mentions the same two as going thither on Sunday morning. These two Mark also had mentioned as at the burial; and he now adds to them Salome. Luke had spoken in general of the women from Galilee, as beholding how the body was laid; and now mentions by name Mary Magdalene, and Joanna, and Mary mother of James; and adds, "and other women that were with them."

We conclude, then, that of the Galilean women, or those who came up with the Lord from Galilee, and whose number seems to have been considerable, all, or certainly most of them, came on the morning of the first day of the week to assist in embalming the body. That four are mentioned by name, is very probably owing to the fact that they were especially prominent. Whether all came together to the sepulchre, does not appear; but it is more likely that they lodged in different places, and met near the tomb by agreement.

Matthew speaks of the two Marys as coming "to see the sepulchre;" John does not mention the object for which Mary Magdalene came; but Luke and Mark speak of the women as coming to anoint the body. Beyond question, this was the chief object. Affection, or a melancholy curiosity, might indeed have led them to wish to behold where the Lord was laid; but here was a duty to be performed of a most sacred character. That Matthew passes by in silence the facts that Nicodemus brought spices on Friday, and that the women brought more on Sunday morning, is explained from the scope of his narrative. In pursuance of his purpose to show how vain were all the precautions of the priests and Pharisees, in sealing the stone and setting a watch, he relates, and he only, that there was a great earthquake; for an angel, descending from heaven, rolled back the stone from the door and sat upon it; and for fear of him the keepers did shake, and became as dead men. The connection between the descent of the angel and rolling away of the stone, and of the resurrection of the Lord, is not defined. It was the general opinion of the fathers, that He rose and left the tomb before the stone was rolled away; the object of this act by the angel being, not to give the Lord a way of exit, but to open the way for the women to enter. There is no indication that the soldiers saw Jesus as He left the sepulchre, and their terror is expressly ascribed to the sight of the angel. Still, the general tenor of the narrative makes on us the impression that the Lord did leave the sepulchre at the time when the stone was rolled back, even if the act of revivification was some time earlier.

Whether by the "earthquake," σεισμος, we are to understand a literal earthquake, has been questioned. Some would refer it to the confusion, or commotion, which the sudden appearance of the angel made among the soldiers keeping watch; others to the shock made by the rolling away of the stone, which was very great; others to a tempest, or tempest and earthquake. If, however, as is most probable, it was a literal earthquake, it is doubtful whether it was felt throughout the city; for such an event, taken in connection with what occurred at the crucifixion, could scarce have passed unnoticed by the disciples. "The first earthquake," says Stier, "extended all over Jerusalem to the temple and graves; the second only moves the stone in Joseph's garden, and scares the guards away."

It has been inferred by some, from Matt. xxviii. 2–5, that the descent of the angel, and rolling away of the stone, were after the women had reached the sepulchre. "'Behold there was,'" says Alford, "must mean that the women were witnesses of the earthquake, and that which followed."[1] But the language does not compel us to this conclusion; and indeed the more natural interpretation is, that these events had taken place while they were on their way, or just before their arrival.[2] That Mary Magdalene saw this angel, and the rolling away of the stone, and the opening of the sepulchre, is not consistent with John xx. 1, 2. She obviously saw no more than that the door was open, and was afraid that the Jews had taken the body away. It may be questioned whether any of the women approached the sepulchre so long as the angel, in that terrible glory with which he affrighted the keepers, was still sitting upon the stone. (Compare Mark xvi. 5 and Luke xxiv. 4.) Whether the keepers had departed ere the women came, is uncertain. On the one hand, the angel's address to the latter, v. 5, "Fear not ye," where the "ye" is emphatic, implies

[1] So Meyer.

[2] "There was (εγενετο) a great earthquake," is translated by Campbell and Norton, "there had been," &c. See De Wette in loco. Ellicott supposes that "they beheld it partially, and at a distance."

their presence; yet, on the other hand, they would hardly have approached the door if they had seen the Roman soldiers.

Mark says that the women "entering into the sepulchre, saw a young man sitting on the right side." Did they see two angels, one without and one within? This is affirmed by Greswell, and also that each addressed them in the same terms. But this is intrinsically improbable. There is nothing in Matthew's narrative that forbids us to suppose that the angel, whose first appearance had special reference to the soldiers and the opening of the door, was not seen by the women at all till they were about to enter, or had actually entered, the sepulchre. Then he addresses them, and invites them "to come and see the place where the Lord lay." It may be that the sepulchre had a porch or entrance, from which all the interior could be seen. "There is no allusion in the Scripture to a vestibule or outer cave; but, on the other hand, there is nothing to contradict its existence; and the common arrangement of the Jewish sepulchres make it probable that there was one."[1]

The mention of the two angels by Luke (xxiv. 4) will be considered when his account comes before us.

After receiving the message, Matthew adds that the women "departed quickly from the sepulchre with fear and great joy: and did run to bring His disciples word." This is seemingly at variance with Mark's statement, (xvi. 8,) that "They went out quickly and fled from the sepulchre, for they trembled and were amazed; neither said they any thing to any man, for they were afraid." Alford affirms that the two accounts cannot be reconciled. But the discrepancy is more apparent than real. According to

[1] Willis in Holy City, ii. 196; see Townson, 80; Lichtenstein, 466. The distinction sometimes taken between μνημειον and ταφος—the former as the name of the whole sepulchre, including the porch or anteroom; the latter as the place where the body was deposited—does not seem well supported.

Mark, the women were afraid and amazed, or, more literally, "trembling and ecstasy held them;" a form of expression nearly parallel to Matthew's, "with fear and great joy." They said nothing to any one. What does this mean? That they never told any one what they had seen? This is contrary to Luke xxiv. 9, and intrinsically improbable. The obvious meaning is, that they did not tell it to any one but the disciples. They said nothing to the strangers whom they met by the way, but hastened to find those for whom their message was intended. That on finding the apostles they continued silent, is neither implied in the narrative, nor supported by the circumstances of the case. No such overpowering fear seized them at the sight of the angel as seized the keepers, and yet the latter, speedily recovering themselves, went to the city and showed to the priests all that had been done.

Matthew adds, (vs. 9, 10,) "Behold Jesus met them, saying, All hail.[1] And they came, and held Him by the feet, and worshipped Him. Then said Jesus unto them, Be not afraid: go, tell my brethren that they go into Galilee, and there shall they see me." When, and with whom, was this interview? Apparently the Lord met the women as they were going from the sepulchre into the city to find the disciples. But this has been often questioned. Newcome, and many, suppose that the women bore to the disciples the message of the angel, (v. 7,) and then returned to the tomb, and that upon their second departure Jesus appeared to them.[2] Greswell puts this meeting several days after the day of the resurrection. Rejecting these constructions as forced, we hold to the obvious tenor of

1 The received text has, "And as they went to tell His disciples," &c., but this clause is omitted by Tischendorf; so Alford and Meyer.

2 See Ellicott, 390, note, who says: "After the delivery of the first tidings to the apostles, they directed their steps back again to the sepulchre, and that it was on their way there that the Lord vouchsafed to appear to them."

the narrative, and place this meeting while the women were returning from the sepulchre, soon after the vision of the angel. But who were these women? Apparently Mary Magdalene and the other Mary. Were there then two appearances the same morning to Mary Magdalene; or, are this and that mentioned by John (xx. 14–18) one and the same? The point is one of importance, and needs careful examination.

While from John's language it would appear that Mary Magdalene visited the sepulchre alone, from the Synoptists it appears that she was accompanied by others. Leaving these, she ran to call Peter and John, and followed them back to the sepulchre; and here Jesus appeared to her. Was she now alone? This is the natural construction of the language. Every circumstance indicates that she alone saw him. This is confirmed by Mark's words, (xvi. 9,) "He appeared first to Mary Magdalene." If she had not been alone, this could not have been said. Taking then as certain that Jesus appeared first to Mary Magdalene, and that no others were present, can the account of Matthew be referred to this appearance? We have seen that the mention of the two, Mary Magdalene and Mary mother of James, does not show that others did not accompany them to the tomb. If Mary Magdalene separated herself from this party, and, returning to the sepulchre after the others had left it, then beheld Jesus, could Matthew speak of it in the general terms which he uses? From his words it would appear that more than one were present. The plural is used throughout: "ye," "they," "them"; but this is not conclusive, since we may say, with Krafft, that the plural is here rather a generic than a numerical designation. Also, the circumstances mentioned by Matthew seem in many points unlike those mentioned by John, both as to the place where Jesus appeared, the words which He spake, and the demeanor and language of the women. Still, the tenor of the narrative leads us to the result that Matthew states in general what John gives in detail. The purpose of the latter leads him to give special prominence throughout his Gospel to the words of Jesus; and His words here to Mary Magdalene are of peculiar interest, and are therefore recorded. The former, whose account is adapted to meet the report current among the Jews, that the disciples had stolen the body away, contents himself with saying generally that the Lord first appeared to certain women, and that they held Him by the feet and worshipped Him. The important facts in Matthew's account are, that to the women a vision of angels appeared, announcing the Lord's resurrection; and that afterward the Lord himself appeared to them. How many there were of the women, and whether the two whom he mentions as having seen the angels, saw also the Lord, are but incidental and unimportant circumstances.

We conclude then that, although a number of women visited the sepulchre, and several of them saw the angels, or an angel, to Mary Magdalene alone did Jesus himself appear. We thus make the accounts of Matthew and John refer to the same event.[1]

There are some, who, making two appearances of the Lord to the women, attempt to avoid the difficulty that, according to Matthew, the women must have reached the disciples before Mary Magdalene returned to the sepulchre, and therefore could not have seen Jesus at this time, by denying that the first appearance was to Mary Magdalene, as is generally assumed. It is said that the words of Mark, (xvi. 9,) "Now when Jesus was risen early the first day of the week, He appeared first to Mary Magdalene," do not mean that His first appearance, absolutely speaking, was to her, but that the first of the appearances related by Mark was to her. It is remarked by Robinson[2]: "Mark narrates

[1] So Lightfoot, Krafft, Lichtenstein, Wieseler, Da Costa.
[2] Har. 232.

three, and only three, appearances of our Lord; of these three that to Mary Magdalene takes place first, and that to the assembled disciples the same evening occurs last." Thus interpreted, the Lord may have appeared first of all to the women departing from the sepulchre, and then, a few minutes later, to Mary Magdalene. But the great body of commentators interpret Mark's words as referring to His first appearance to any one after His resurrection.[1]

In immediate connection with the departure of the women to announce the resurrection to His friends, Matthew relates the departure of the soldiers to announce it to His enemies. The latter incident will be considered by and by.

From Matthew's narrative we turn to that of Mark.[2] The main points in which the two differ have been already noticed, but Mark adds some interesting particulars. The subject of conversation with the women as they approach the sepulchre, is, how the stone shall be rolled away; but advancing, they see that it is already rolled away.[3] In mentioning the fact that Jesus appeared first to Mary Magdalene, Mark adds, "out of whom He had cast seven devils." This may be to designate her in distinction from others, but more probably is explanatory of the high honor that was given her. Her faith had been great, and here was her reward.

We turn now to Luke. He had related (xxiii. 55, 56)

[1] So West, Greswell, Newcome, Krafft, Ellicott, Wieseler; Alexander is undecided.

[2] Many regard the latter portion of the sixteenth chapter of this Evangelist, vs. 9–20, as not his own, but as added by another at a later period; so Tischendorf, Alford, Meyer. Some, as Ebrard, make it a later addition of Mark himself. Alexander defends the present conclusion as the original one of the Evangelist.

[3] Lewin (159) infers from the narratives that the stone was a large circular one, moving in a groove, cut laterally in the front of the sepulchre. A specimen of this kind of stone door is still to be seen at the "Tombs of the Kings," at Jerusalem.

that the women which came with Jesus from Galilee, followed His body to the tomb, and beheld the sepulchre, and how the body was laid. Returning, they prepared spices and ointments, and, resting the Sabbath, went early the next morning, (xxiv. 1,) taking the spices they had prepared.[1] The names of these women were, (v. 10,) Mary Magdalene, Joanna, and Mary mother of James; but others were with them, whose names are not mentioned.[2] In what relation does this visit stand to that of Matthew and Mark? Some have supposed them to be wholly distinct.[3] It is said that there were two parties of women; the first of which consisted of the two Marys and Salome, the second of Joanna and others, among whom was probably Susanna. In proof that there were two parties, several points of difference in the narrations of Matthew and Mark on the one hand, and of Luke on the other, are made prominent: 1st. That, according to the former, the women prepared their spices after the Sabbath; according to the latter, before the Sabbath. 2d. That, according to the former, they saw but one angel; according to the latter, they saw two; and also that the angelic messages are unlike. 3d. That, according to the latter, Peter, hearing the report of the women, runs to the sepulchre; but of this the former makes no mention.

Before considering these points of difference, let us note the character of Luke's narrative. Is he giving a particular account of what happened to a certain party or number of women; or is he summing up what happened to the women generally, without distinction of parties or individuals? The latter is most probable. If, as is claimed,

[1] Tischendorf omits, "And certain with them," which is in the received text; so Alford.

[2] The form of expression, αι λοιπαι, seems to embrace all the Galilean women.

[3] West, 50; Greswell, iii. 264.

there were two distinct parties, what happened to one did not to the other; and the account here must refer to one party only. But if this relates merely to what Joanna and her companions saw and heard, why is the name of Mary Magdalene mentioned? She was not present with them, and did not see these angels, or hear their message. The mention of her name shows that Luke is giving a summary of what occurred, a general statement of the facts, without distinction of witnesses. A number of women go to the sepulchre; find the stone rolled away, and the tomb empty; are in perplexity to know what has become of the body; see a vision of angels, who give them a message; return and tell the disciples, and are not believed, only Peter and others (see xxiv. 24) go to see for themselves: this is the substance of Luke's narrative. It is an outline of what occurred in the early part of the day to the women, but without entering into any details. Why he omits all mention of the fact that Jesus appeared to Mary Magdalene, and narrates His appearance to the two disciples on their way to Emmaus, as if it were the first, we can but conjecture. That he does not mention it here, may be explained as springing from the scope of the narrative, which represents that the two disciples, leaving the city before the appearance to her was known, had heard only of the angelic announcement that He was alive.

If this be a correct view of Luke's narrative, all the supposed discrepancies between him on the one side, and Matthew and Mark on the other, are readily removed. The first, in regard to the time of the preparation of the spices, has already been considered. The second, in regard to the number of angels, finds its explanation in the fact that if the women in Matthew and Mark saw but one, according to John, Mary Magdalene saw two; and Luke gives the greater number. He simply says that "two men stood by them (επεστησαν) in shining garments," but without any details. The message given by them is substantially the same in the three Evangelists. The third, in regard to the running of Peter to the sepulchre, is a brief statement of the same fact that John (xx. 3, 4) relates more at length. That Luke was aware that Peter was not alone appears from v. 24: "And certain of them which were with us, went to the sepulchre." There is no necessity to say, as West and Townson do, that Luke refers to another and later visit.

No notice has yet been taken of the time when these various events are said by the several Evangelists to have taken place. For the sake of convenience we bring together here their statements. Our main inquiry concerns the time when the women first visited the sepulchre. In Matthew, (xxviii. 1,) it is spoken of as "In the end of the Sabbath, as it began to dawn toward the first day of the week."[1] As the Sabbath ended at sunset, this may be understood, as by Patritius, of its last hours, or those just before sunset.[2] But most agree that the natural day, commencing at sunrise and ending at sunset, is spoken of; and that the coming of the women was at the dawn of the day following the Sabbath.[3] Mark (xvi. 2) says: "And very early in the morning, the first day of the week, they came unto the sepulchre, at the rising of the sun," *ανατειλαντος του ηλιου*. Luke (xxiv. 1) says: "Now upon the first day of the week, very early in the morning, *ορθρου βαθεος*, they came," &c. John (xx. 1) says: "The first day of the week cometh Mary Magdalene early, when it was yet dark," *πρωι, σκοτιας ετι ουσης*. Let us note the exact force of each of these statements. "The beginning of the dawn," in

[1] This is translated by Greswell: "Now late in the week, at the hour of dawn, against the first day of the week." By Norton: "And the Sabbath being over, in the dawn of the first day of the week."

[2] See Luke xxiii. 54, where the Greek term *επιφωσκω* is the same.

[3] See Alford and Meyer in loco.

Matthew, was about 5 o'clock A. M., it being then early in April.[1] The "very early" of Mark is somewhat indefinite. If πρωι be taken here as in xiii. 35, for the "morning watch," it would embrace 3–6 A. M.; if used indefinitely, it denotes simply the early morning. Taken in connection with λιαν, "very," as here, it is parallel to the "day dawn" of Matthew, or "while it was yet dark" of John.

But how can this be reconciled with that further note of time which Mark gives, "at the rising of the sun," or "the sun having arisen"? If both expressions be strictly taken, the Evangelist is inconsistent with himself.[2] Various solutions have been proposed. Townsend would make a period at sepulchre, and connect the "rising of the sun" with the clause following, making it to read: "At the rising of the sun they said among themselves," &c. But this is indefensible. West, (42,) followed by Greswell, would make the women to have reached the sepulchre at the rising of the sun, but to have left their homes much earlier. This, however, does not meet the difficulty, the verb "they came" being qualified by both marks of time. Ewald (vi. 73, note) regards "at the rising of the sun" an addition to the original Gospel. This is to cut the knot. Newcome would change the reading, but without authority. But, in truth, no solution is necessary. It is most unreasonable to suppose that Mark should not know what he designed to say, and contradict himself in the compass of a single sentence. He evidently speaks in general terms. If, then, "very early" be understood as the dawning day, as is most probable, the phrase "at the rising of the sun" denotes the same period which we designate as the sun-rising, or that period from the first illumination of the sky till the sun is above the horizon.[3]

[1] Winer, ii. 560.

[2] So Meyer, Alford.

[3] See Robinson, Har. 230, who cites several passages from the Old Testament in which a like form of expression is used: Judges ix. 33; Psalms civ. 22; 2 Kings iii. 22. So Hengstenberg and Alexander.

Thus Mark is both in harmony with himself, and with the other Evangelists. The "very early in the morning" of Luke, the early morning twilight, or deep dawn, is plainly identical with "the dawning" of Matthew, and the "very early" of Mark. The "early" of John is more exactly defined by the addition "when it was yet dark," or before it was yet clear day. It was at least sufficiently light for Mary Magdalene to see that the stone was rolled away.

Thus it appears that the only discrepancy in regard to the time of the women's visiting the sepulchre, arises from Mark's statement that they came "at the rising of the sun." If this phrase should be pressed to the letter, as skeptical critics for the most part do, he would not only contradict himself, but also the statement of John that Mary Magdalene came "while it was yet dark." It should, however, be noted, that some interval must have elapsed between the departure of the women from their homes and their arrival at the sepulchre, and that the Evangelists may speak of one or the other period without special discrimination.

We may, without violence, take Mark's expression in the large sense, as embracing the whole period from early dawn till actual sunrising. The women, however early they may have left their homes, could scarcely expect to begin their work of embalming the body till it was broad daylight. Lightfoot (on Mark xvi. 2) mentions a fourfold distinction of twilight among the Rabbins: 1st. "The hind of the morning, or first appearance of light." 2d. "When one may distinguish between purple color and white." 3d. "When the east begins to lighten." 4th. "Sunrise." He would apply these four periods to the statements of the four Evangelists—the first to Matthew, the second to John, the third to Luke, the fourth to Mark. There seem no good grounds for this.

All the Evangelists imply that the Lord's resurrection

was *very early, for the* women find the sepulchre empty; but none give any note of time except Mark (xvi. 9:) "Now when Jesus was risen early the first day of the week," &c. Here it is seen that Mark speaks only indefinitely, for the Lord arises "early," πρωι, whilst the women came "very early," λιαν πρωι. Some, however, would make this define the time when the Lord appeared to Mary.[1]

This examination of the several narratives shows us how many of the data are wanting which are necessary to enable us to form a regular, harmonious, and complete history of this eventful morning. Each of the Evangelists gives us some particulars which the others omit, but no one of them aims to give us a full and connected account; and for us to supply the missing links in the chain, is impossible. To a superficial examination there seem many discrepancies, not to say contradictions, but a thorough investigation shows that the points of real difference are very few; and that in several ways even these differences may be removed. Whilst thus we cannot say of any order which we can frame that it is certain, we can say of several that they are probable; and if they cannot be proved, neither can they be disproved. This is sufficient for him who finds in the moral character of the Gospels the highest vouchers for their historic truth.

To bring before the reader some of the many possible arrangements of these events, and to show what the special difficulties in the way of the harmonist are, we select the following, which have found many adherents. It will be noted that the point which chiefly determines the order, is whether Jesus appeared once or twice to the women. We begin with—

Lightfoot. 1. Earthquake, and resurrection of Christ. 2. Visit of Mary Magdalene and other women to the tomb, which they reach just as the sun is up. They are told

[1] See Meyer in loco.

of His resurrection by the angels, and go back to the disciples. 3. Peter and John go to the sepulchre, followed by Mary Magdalene. They return, and she remains. 4. Christ appears to her, and she takes Him for the gardener. She afterward embraces His feet, kissing them. Thus Matthew xxviii. 9 and John xx. 14 refer to the same appearance.

Lardner. 1. The women, with Mary Magdalene, go to the sepulchre and find it empty. 2. Mary, with others, goes to the apostles Peter and John. 3. They come to the tomb, and then return home. 4. Mary Magdalene and the others follow the two apostles back to the tomb, and remain there after Peter and John are gone. 5. Jesus appears to them all there. 6. Mary Magdalene and the others go and announce all to the disciples. 7. Jesus appears to the two disciples. 8. He appears to Peter. 9. He appears to the Eleven. Here, also, the appearance to Mary Magdalene mentioned by John, and that to the two Marys mentioned by Matthew, are made the same.

West. 1. The two Marys and Salome visit the tomb, the angel having before rolled away the stone, and the guards being gone. 2. Mary Magdalene, seeing the stone rolled away, runs to find Peter and John. 3. Mary, mother of James, and Salome, remaining, see an angel, and receive his message. Greatly terrified, they depart. 4. Peter and John visit the sepulchre, and depart. 5. Mary Magdalene, having followed them, sees the two angels, and then the Lord himself. 6. The Lord appears to the other Mary and Salome. 7. Joanna and her party of women come to the sepulchre, see two angels, and hear from them that Jesus is risen. They depart and announce to the disciples that they had seen a vision of angels. 8. Peter runs a second time to the sepulchre, but sees only the linen clothes. 9. The two disciples having heard the report of Joanna and her party, set out for Emmaus. Here the appearances mentioned by John and Matthew are distinguished.

Townson. 1. The two Marys and Salome go to the tomb, and while they are on the way the angel descends and rolls away the stone. They reach it at the rising of the sun. 2. Mary Magdalene goes for Peter and John. 3. The other Mary and Salome enter the porch of the sepulchre, see an angel, receive his message, and depart in great fear. 4. Peter and John come and visit the tomb. 5. Mary Magdalene returns and sees first the angels, and then the Lord. 6. Mary Magdalene departing, falls in with the other Mary and Salome, and to them together Jesus appears the second time. 7. Joanna and her party now come, and, entering the tomb, see two angels. They return, and confirm to the disciples what the other women had already reported. 8. Peter goes a second time to the sepulchre, and finds only the clothes. 9. The two disciples set out for Emmaus. 10. The Lord appears to Peter. Here are made two successive appearances to Mary Magdalene: first when alone, second to her in company with the other Mary.

Newcome. 1. The two Marys, Salome, Joanna, and others, go to the sepulchre, and, finding the stone removed, enter the tomb. Two angels appear to them, and one gives them a message. 2. They return to Jerusalem, and Mary Magdalene communicates the message to Peter and John, and the other women to the other disciples. 3. Peter and John go to the sepulchre, and return. 4. The two disciples, having heard the report of the women and of Peter and John, depart for Emmaus. 5. Mary Magdalene and the other women follow Peter and John to the tomb. She, arriving before them, or following after them, sees the angels, and afterward the Lord. 6. She joins the other women who were near by, and, as they were returning to Jerusalem, Jesus meets them. 7. He appears to Peter. 8. He appears to the two at Emmaus. Here Mary Magdalene alone first sees the Lord, and afterward she sees Him the second time in company with others.

Da Costa. 1. The two Marys, Joanna, Salome, and others, start before daybreak for the sepulchre, and find the stone rolled away. 2. Mary Magdalene runs to find Peter and John. 3. The other women enter the sepulchre, see the angels, receive their message, and return to the disciples. 4. Peter and John visit the sepulchre and depart home. 5. Mary Magdalene, who had followed them, sees first the angels, and then the Lord, and returns to the disciples. 6. Jesus appears to the two at Emmaus. 7. He appears to Peter. Here the Lord appears to Mary Magdalene only.

Greswell. 1. Two parties of women—one the two Marys and Salome, the other, Joanna and some with her—set out from different quarters to go to the sepulchre. While on their way, the stone is rolled away and the Lord rises. 2. The Marys and Salome arrive first at the sepulchre about sunrise. Mary Magdalene runs to find Peter and John. The other two enter the sepulchre, see an angel, receive a message, and depart. 3. The party of Joanna arrives, sees two angels, and returns to the disciples. 4. Peter and John visit the sepulchre. 5. Mary Magdalene, who had followed Peter and John, sees two angels, and then Christ. 6. The two disciples depart for Emmaus, before Mary Magdalene reports the appearance of Jesus to her. Upon the way the Lord meets them. 7. He appears to Peter. 8. He appears to the Eleven. 9. He appears the second time to the Eleven, a week after. 10. Soon after this He appears to the other Mary and Salome, and perhaps also to Mary Magdalene. Here the Lord is seen first by Mary Magdalene, and does not appear to the other women till a week after.

Ebrard. 1. Mary Magdalene visits the sepulchre early, while it is yet dark. She finds the stone rolled away, and runs to find Peter and John. 2. Mary, mother of James, Joanna, Salome, and the other women go to anoint the body, and looking into the tomb, see an angel, who gives them a message. They depart, but dare not report to any one what had occurred. 3. Peter and John come to the grave and return home. 4. Mary Magdalene, who had followed them, sees two angels, and then the Lord. She returns, and tells the disciples. 5. The Lord appears to the two on the way to Emmaus. 6. He appears to Peter. Here the appearance to Mary Magdalene of John, and that to the two Marys of Matthew, are identified.

Lange. 1. The two Marys and Salome go to the grave. Another party—Joanna, and others with her—was to follow with the spices and ointments. The former see the stone rolled away, and Mary Magdalene runs to find Peter and John. 2. The other Mary and Salome approach and see one angel sitting upon the stone, and afterward another within the sepulchre, who gives them a message, and they depart. 3. Peter and John visit the sepulchre, and return. 4. Mary Magdalene sees two angels, and then the Lord. 5. Jesus appears to the other Mary and Salome, on their way to the disciples. 6. These two fall in with Joanna and her party, and together return to the sepulchre and see two angels. 7. He appears to the two disciples. 8. He appears to Peter. Here the Lord appears first to Mary Magdalene, then to the other Mary, and Salome.

Robinson. 1. The two Marys, Joanna and Salome, and others, go to the sepulchre to embalm the body, and find the stone rolled away. 2. Mary Magdalene runs to find Peter and John. 3. The other women see two angels in the tomb, who give them a message to the disciples, and they depart. 4. Jesus meets them on the way, and renews the message. 5. Peter and John come to the sepulchre, and return home. 6. Mary Magdalene sees the two angels, and then the Lord. 7. Jesus appears to Peter. 8. He appears to the two going to Emmaus. Here the Lord first appears to the other women, and then to Mary Magdalene.

Let us now attempt to frame a continuous narrative from the accounts of the several Evangelists. Very early in the morning the women from Galilee, to the number of five or more, who had been present at the crucifixion and burial, start for the sepulchre to embalm the body. Whether all went from one place, and at the same moment, is uncertain; but under the circumstances it is more probable that they came from different parts of the city, and met by agreement. Perhaps Mary Magdalene alone, or with the other Mary and Salome, may have a little preceded the others. They knew, for some at least were eye-witnesses, that a great stone had been rolled to the door of the sepulchre, and it was therefore a question with them how they could roll it away. But they did not know of the sealing of the stone, and the setting of the watch, which took place at the eve of the Sabbath. As they approach the sepulchre they see that the stone is rolled away; and Mary Magdalene, who naturally inferred that the Jews had removed the body, in deep excitement runs to inform the two chief apostles, Peter and John, of this fact. The other women continue to approach the sepulchre. That the angel was not now sitting upon the stone, and visible to them, and that the guards were not lying as dead men before the door, seem most probable, as otherwise their fears would have deterred them from advancing. Seeing nothing, they enter the sepulchre, or its vestibule. An angel now appears to them, and, after bidding them not be afraid, shows them the empty niche where the body was laid, and gently reproves them for coming to find the Lord there, the living with the dead. He proceeds to announce to them that He is risen, and will meet the disciples in Galilee, as He had said to them while He was with them there. Greatly agitated by what they had seen and heard, fear contending with joy, they leave the sepulchre.

Soon after their departure—but how soon is uncertain, as we do not know where Mary Magdalene found Peter and John—the two apostles come running with all speed to determine the truth of her account. John, who reaches the tomb first, only looks in, but Peter enters, and is followed by John. The body is gone; but, examining carefully, they see the grave clothes arranged in order, and the napkin lying by itself. John is convinced, by all that he sees, that the Lord is indeed risen; but Peter only marvels. They seem to have departed very quickly again, perhaps to inform the other disciples that the body was truly gone; or perhaps they were afraid lest they should be found by their enemies at the tomb. Mary Magdalene, who had followed them back to the sepulchre, did not depart with them, but remained standing without, weeping. It is plain from the whole narrative that she was under the power of most intense grief, believing that the body of her Lord had been borne away by His enemies. Whilst weeping, she stoops down to look in, as if a faint hope still lingered that she should see Him there. She sees two angels sitting, one at the head and one at the feet, where the body had lain. Unlike the other women, who had been greatly terrified at the angelic apparition, she seems scarce to have noticed them; and to their question, "Woman, why weepest thou?" she answers in words showing how wholly her heart was filled with her one great sorrow. Lifting her head, for she was now looking into the tomb, she sees Jesus, but does not recognize Him. He addresses her with the inquiry, "Woman, why weepest thou?" Supposing Him to be the gardener, probably because it was natural that he should be there, and thinking that he might possibly have taken away the body, she asks Him, in words full of passionate earnestness. The Lord's reply, "Mary," spoken in His own familiar voice, recalls her to herself. She recognizes Him, and, prostrating herself, would hold Him by the feet to worship Him. He forbids her to touch Him, and gives her a message to His brethren. She departs, and tells the disciples, but they believe not.

Thus we find most probable that there were two visions of angels, the first to the women, the second to Mary Magdalene; and one appearance of the Lord, that to Mary Magdalene; all closely following each other. As yet, these supernatural manifestations were vouchsafed only to the women. Peter and John saw at the sepulchre neither angels nor the Lord. They found, indeed, the sepulchre open and the body gone; but the fact that He had risen rested solely on the testimony of the women. It is not, in one point of view, at all strange that all their words should have seemed to the disciples as idle tales; for it is plain that, notwithstanding His most explicit declarations that He would rise on the third day, none were expecting, or even hoping for, His resurrection. The women went to the grave to anoint the body, and Mary Magdalene's grief was caused by the thought that she could not show it the last sad tokens of regard. She does not once allude to His resurrection as if it were possible. Perhaps the fact that He had not appeared to any of the apostles, had something to do with the incredulity of the latter, for it was natural to suppose that He would first manifest Himself to them, (Mark xvi. 11.) Accordingly, we find that it was the testimony of Peter that he had seen Him, that convinced them, (Luke xxiv. 34,) though even then they seemed to have doubts whether it was a real resurrection.

Rumors that the sepulchre was empty, must have become current among the disciples early in the day, and probably most or all of them, or at least of the apostles, visited it, though we have no record of their visits.

The historical accuracy of the account of the bribing of

the soldiers by the priests and elders, has been often questioned,[1] but on insufficient grounds. The watch came, reporting what had taken place at the sepulchre, and that Jesus had actually risen. The priests and elders may have believed this or may not, but they doubtless ascertained to their own satisfaction that the body was actually gone. What should they do? Arrest and punish the soldiers? But to what end? since all the facts of the affair must thus necessarily come to the ears of Pilate, and become more generally known. As it could not be concealed that the body was gone, some plausible explanation must be given. What could answer the purpose so well as to admit this fact, and affirm that the disciples had done what they attempted to guard against when they set the watch—had stolen away the body. But this the soldiers would naturally contradict, as exposing them to military punishment. They therefore must be bribed to admit that the story set afloat by the priests, was true. They would not affirm the absurdity that they knew what the disciples were doing while they were sleeping; but merely keep silence as to what they had actually seen, and not deny that they might have been asleep, and that what the rulers said, might have occurred. Of course this report would soon become current, and by most of the Jews be believed.[2]

Sunday, 17th Nisan, 9th April, 783.

Early in the afternoon two of the disciples leave Jerusalem for Emmaus. As they go, Jesus joins Himself to them, and converses with them till they reach the village. At their urgent request He sits down to eat with them, and as He was breaking the bread, their eyes, which were holden that they should not know Him, were opened, but He immediately vanished out of their sight. They return at once to Je-	Luke xxiv. 13–32. Mark xvi. 12. Luke xxiv. 33

1 See Meyer in loco.

2 See the excellent observations of Jones, Notes, 483.

rusalem, and find the Eleven and others gathered together, who meet them with the announcement that the Lord is indeed risen, and has appeared to Simon. But the account of the two disciples that they had also seen Him at Emmaus, was disbelieved. While yet speaking together, Jesus Himself stood in the midst of them, although the doors were shut, and saluted them. He convinces them of the reality of His bodily presence by showing them His hands and His feet, and by eating before them. He breathes upon them, and gives them the power to remit sins, and opened their understanding to understand the Scriptures.

MARK xvi. 13, 14.
LUKE xxiv. 34, 35.
1 COR. xv. 5.

LUKE xxiv. 36–48.
JOHN xx. 19–23.

The name of one of the disciples going to Emmaus was Cleopas, (Luke xxiv. 18.) Many identify him with Cleophas, Clopas, or Alphaeus, the husband of Mary. It is most probable that he was a different person. The name of the other disciple is not given. Lightfoot supposes him to have been Peter himself; and it was early a very common opinion that he was Luke, and that the Evangelist through modesty did not mention his own name. Wieseler, (431,) who makes Cleopas to have been Alphaeus, makes the other the apostle James, his son.

Josephus mentions three places by the name of Emmaus.[1] Of one of these he speaks as "sixty furlongs distant from Jerusalem." This coincides so exactly with the statement of Luke, (v. 13,) that no reasonable doubt can exist that both refer to the same place. The name itself signifies warm water, and indicates that there was a hot spring in the neighborhood. The site of the old Emmaus has been for a long period supposed to be a village now called El Kubeibeh, which lies about seventy furlongs, or nine miles, north-westerly from Jerusalem, and is reached by the road running near Mizpeh. Schwartz (117) finds its site in some ruins about seven and a half miles from Jerusalem,

[1] War, 4. 1. 3; 7. 6. 6. Antiq. 14. 11. 2.

now called by the Arabs Baburaia. The identification with Kubeibeh, Robinson denies, (ii. 255 and iii. 147,) and attempts to identify it with that Emmaus which lay in the plain of Judah, more than one hundred and seventy stadia from Jerusalem, or about twenty-two Roman miles, and ten from Lydda. It received the name of Nicopolis in the third century, and both names were in use for many centuries. It is now known as Amwas.

The ground upon which Robinson asserts that this village is the Emmaus of Luke, is, that "for thirteen centuries did the interpretation current in the whole Church regard the Emmaus of the New Testament as identical with Nicopolis." He disposes of the statement of Luke, that it was "about threescore furlongs from Jerusalem," (v. 13,) by questioning the correctness of this reading, several manuscripts having one hundred and sixty furlongs. He questions also the reading, sixty stadia, in Josephus, several manuscripts having thirty. The correctness of the received reading in both cases seems too well supported to be shaken. But aside from this it is scarcely possible that Emmaus could have been so far distant from Jerusalem. According to Robinson himself, it now requires six to six and a half hours to pass from the former to the latter, and if the two disciples had left Jerusalem at 12 A. M., they would have reached their home about 6 P. M. Allowing that only a very brief interval was spent in preparation for the evening meal, (v. 30,) and that they returned with all haste, they could not have reached Jerusalem till near midnight. But considering the habits of the orientals, it is very improbable that the disciples were assembled together at that hour; nor is it likely that the Lord would have selected it to make His first appearance to them. Besides, some marks of the time when they met the Eleven are given us. John (xx. 19) states that when Jesus made His appearance to them it was evening. This was probably the first evening, which began at 3 P. M. and ended at 6, or at sunsetting. This is confirmed by Mark, (xvi. 14,) who says that "He appeared to the Eleven as they sat at meat." This could not well have been late in the evening.

Upon these grounds we believe that the Emmaus of Luke cannot be placed at a greater distance than he has placed it. Whether it can be identified with Kubeibeh or not, is unimportant. Robinson[1] says rightly, although in opposition to his present opinion, that "the distance (of Nicopolis) one hundred and sixty stadia, or six hours, is too great for the disciples to have returned the same evening. We must therefore abide by the usual reading."[2]

The time when the two disciples left Jerusalem is not mentioned, but it was probably early in the afternoon, as the distance was about eight miles, and they seem to have reached Emmaus about sundown.[3]

When the Lord met the two He was not recognized by them. Luke says (v. 16) "Their eyes were holden that they should not know Him." This some have thought discrepant with Mark's statement (xvi. 12) that "He appeared in another form—εν ετερᾳ μορφῃ—unto two of them." The latter expression may refer to His previous appearance to Mary Magdalene, by whom He had been mistaken for the gardener;[4] or to another form than that before the resurrection. That His bodily aspect was in many points after the resurrection unlike what it had been before, we cannot doubt, though it is impossible for us to tell wherein those distinctions consisted. (See John xxi. 4.) Still the language of Luke implies that there was no such distinction as to hinder His recognition; and that, in this case, except the

[1] In Bib. Sacra, 1845, p. 181. [2] See Winer, i. 325; Raumer, 169.

[3] See v. 29: "For it is toward evening, and the day is far spent;" and it was about the time of the evening meal. "They arrived at Emmaus about 3 P. M.," (Lardner;) between 3 and 4 P. M., (Jones.) But this is too early.

[4] So Lardner.

eyes of the disciples had been specially holden, they would have known Him. "And their eyes were opened and they knew Him," (v. 31.)

It was probably early in the evening that the two reached Jerusalem on their return, joy at again beholding their Lord adding wings to their feet. They find the eleven apostles gathered together, and others with them, but the doors were closed for fear of the Jews. As they enter they are greeted by the cry, "The Lord is risen indeed, and hath appeared unto Simon."[1] They proceed to tell that He has also appeared to them, but their words are not believed, (Mark xvi. 13.) Why was this? If the disciples believed Peter's word, that He had appeared to him, and thus the fact of His resurrection was established, how easy to believe the report of the two that they also had seen Him. Upon this ground, and because Luke does not mention the fact that the Eleven disbelieved, it is said that the two Evangelists are at variance.[2] But the silence of Luke does not disprove Mark's statement. Nor is it difficult to understand why, after having given credit to Peter, they should deny it to the two disciples. It was in the supposed incompatibility of their respective statements. The two reported that He had been with them on their journey and at Emmaus; yet He had also been seen by Peter at Jerusalem. If we now suppose that immediately after He vanished from their sight He appeared to the apostle, into what perplexity would all be cast! Ignorant of the properties of His resurrection body, and its power of sudden transition from place to place, they would either deny the reality of the resurrection, and say that they had seen a spirit or ghost; or deny their testimony, and the fact that they had seen Him at all. Probably the former opinion was the more general

[1] Some would make this an interrogation: "Has the Lord risen, and has He appeared to Simon?" So Townsend; but there is no ground for this.

[2] So Meyer, Alford.

one; for when the Lord immediately afterward stood in the midst of them, "They were terrified, and thought that they had seen a spirit."

Under what circumstances the Lord appeared to Peter we are not informed: it is probable that it was the same appearance to which Paul alludes, (1 Cor. xv. 5.) The circumstance mentioned by John, (xx. 19,) that the doors were shut when Jesus appeared to the disciples, seems designed to show that He had now entered a new stage of being; and that that, which was a barrier against the intrusion of the Jews, was no barrier against Him. How He entered we cannot say. The doors were shut—they were not seen or heard to open, yet He stood among them. As He had suddenly vanished from the two at Emmaus, so did He now suddenly appear to the apostles at Jerusalem. And these sudden appearances and disappearances seem to have marked all His interviews with His disciples during the forty days. The first work of the Lord, after He saw the terror of the Eleven and their superstitious fears, was to convince them of His true bodily presence. He shows them His hands and His feet, in which they might see the prints of the nails, and even proceeds to eat before them. He afterward, when their minds were tranquillized, and they were fully convinced that He was indeed with them, breathes on them, and gives to them the Holy Ghost, with power to remit and retain sins. Into the special significance of this gift, or its relations to the descent of the Spirit at Pentecost, our purpose does not lead us to enter. He also opened their understanding that they might understand the Scriptures.

Some would refer the statement of Mark (xvi. 14) not to His first, but to His second appearance to the Eleven. It is said that neither Luke nor John in their accounts of the first interview intimates that He upbraided their unbelief. It was their continued incredulity that brought down upon them His reproof. But it does not appear that any of the apostles except Thomas, who was not present at His first appearance, did disbelieve after they had actually seen Him; and He may have used language of reproof, although it is not specially reported by Luke or John. Indeed, His words and acts during that interview necessarily imply reproof.[1]

SUNDAY, 24th NISAN, 16th APRIL, 783.

After eight days Jesus again appeared to the assembled apostles, Thomas, who had been before absent, now being with them. By showing him the prints of the nails and the spear, as he had demanded, and desiring him to touch them, the Lord convinces him of the reality of His resurrection; and Thomas acknowledges Him as his Lord and his God.

JOHN XX. 26–29.
JOHN XX. 24, 25.

The place where the apostles were assembled, was in all probability the same in which Jesus had before met them, and may have been the upper room in which the paschal supper was eaten, and to which they returned from the Mount of Olives. Why they continued so long in Jerusalem, when the Lord had bidden them go to Galilee, is not stated; and some have inferred that they waited for the expiration of the feast, which lasted seven days. "The Lord's command," says Stier, "presupposed their tarrying through the eight days, according to the rules of the feast." Lightfoot affirms that, on the first day, no one should exceed the limits of a sabbath-day's journey; on the second, no one might go home, because of the "appearance before the Lord" which then took place; on the third, one might go if necessary, though it was better to stay through the whole feast. But the feast had been some days ended, yet they remain. Luthardt

[1] Clericus refers to this occasion all of Mark xvi. 14–18; Luke xxiv. 36–49. Bucher would place this meeting after the return from Galilee, and just before the ascension: Mark xvi. 14–19; Luke xxiv. 44–53; Acts i. 4–13.

(in loco) supposes that they may have assembled to keep the day in commemoration of His resurrection, and with the hope that He would appear to them again. It seems, however, more probable that it was the unbelief of the apostles which kept them at Jerusalem. Just before His arrest, and while on His way from the Passover supper to the garden, Jesus had said to them that "After He was risen He would go before them into Galilee," (Matt. xxvi. 32; Mark xiv. 28.) Probably also at the same time He specified the place where He would meet with them there, (Matt. xxviii. 10 and 16.) This direction, in the first moments of their grief, they seem utterly to have forgotten; and the Lord, first by the angels, and then from His own mouth, reminded them of it, and incited them to obedience. Had their faith been strong, they would have gone at once to Galilee, and waited for Him there. This they did not do. Even after He had by the most convincing proofs established the fact of His resurrection to others of the Eleven, still Thomas disbelieved; and perhaps many among the disciples. Whilst this fact was in dispute they could not go into Galilee, for this implied that they no longer had any doubts that He was risen and would meet them there. It thus became necessary that He should manifest Himself to them again and again, and tarry for them at Jerusalem till the unbelief of all was overcome. And yet it is said that some which had gathered at the mountain in Galilee, doubted, (Matt. xxviii. 17.) It is most probable, however, that these were not of those who had seen Him in Judea.

Why Thomas was not present at the first meeting of the apostles is not stated, and we can but conjecture. It can scarcely, however, have been accidental. That the Lord should appear the second time to the Eleven on the eighth day after His resurrection, is of deep significance.

April—May, 783. A. D. 30.

The apostles having returned to Galilee, the Lord appears to seven of them whilst engaged in fishing upon the lake. The miracle of the great draught of fishes is repeated, and He feeds the seven with fish and bread. After they had dined, He commands Peter three times to feed His sheep, and signifies his future death and the protracted life of John.	John xxi. 1–23.
After this He appears upon a mountain to a great body of disciples, and commands that the Gospel be preached and disciples baptized throughout the world.	Matt. xxviii. 16–20. 1 Cor. xv. 6. Mark xvi. 15–18.

That the appearance of the Lord at the lake of Galilee was before His appearance upon the mountain, may be inferred from the fact that "This was now the third time that He showed Himself to His disciples after that He was risen from the dead," (John xxi. 14.) This order is followed by most.[1] In this threefold enumeration the Evangelist plainly refers to the apostles as constituting the most important part of the disciples, although not perhaps to them exclusively. Thus the first appearance was to the "Eleven gathered together and them that were with them," (Luke xxiv. 33.) Mark (xvi. 14) says "The Eleven." John speaks simply of "The disciples," (xx. 19.) At this time Thomas was absent. The second was to the disciples, including Thomas, (John xx. 26.) The third "To the disciples at the sea of Tiberias." Of these, five at least were apostles; the names of the remaining two are not given, and it is not certain, though probable, that they also were of the apostles. Lightfoot supposes them to have been Philip and Andrew. Meyer (in loco) thinks it impossible that these three appearances can be made to harmonize with the statements of Paul, (1 Cor. xv. 5.) But this depends upon the point whether Paul is

[1] So Lightfoot, Robinson, Lichtenstein, Ebrard, Krafft, Newcome.

designing to a give a chronological outline of all the appearances. This is generally and with good reason denied.[1] Luthardt supposes that Paul, in the words "Then of the Twelve," (v. 5,) may embrace all the three appearances to them, and thus his order be made chronological.

Perhaps at this time the Lord gave them more specific directions respecting the meeting upon the mount. If we identify this meeting upon the mount with that when the 500 brethren were present, as most do, such a number of disciples could not have been gathered unless the notice had been early given, and widely spread. Both the time and place must have been definitely known.

The name of the mountain where the disciples met the Lord according to His appointment is not given. Many suppose it to be the same where He delivered the sermon, (Matt. v. 1.) Others identify it with the Mount of Transfiguration; others still with Tabor. It was a tradition current during the middle ages that it was the northern peak of the Mount of Olives. Saewulf[2] speaks of a chapel called Galilee of Mount Sion, where the Lord first appeared to His apostles after His resurrection, according to His words, "After I am risen again I will go before you into Galilee." "That place was called Galilee, because the apostles, who were called Galileans, frequently rested there."[3] This tradition has recently been defended by Hofmann,[4] but is wholly untenable.[5]

This meeting, having been appointed by the Lord before His death, and recalled to the memory of the disciples by the angels, must be looked upon as the chiefest and most significant of all His manifestations. There can be little doubt that it was identical with that mentioned by Paul, (1 Cor. xv. 6:) "After that He was seen of above five

[1] Lichtenstein, 476; Hodge in loco; Wieseler, 432.
[2] A. D. 1102. Early Travels, 42.
[3] See also Maundeville, Early Travels, 177. [4] Leben Jesu, 395.
[5] See Meyer on Matt. xxviii. 16; Ewald, Jahrbuch, 1856, p. 196.

hundred brethren at once." Although Matthew speaks only of the eleven disciples as present at the mountain, yet his silence respecting others would not exclude them, as in his introduction to the sermon on the mount, he speaks only of the disciples as His auditors, although great multitudes beside were present. That he should mention only the Eleven, is wholly consistent with his general purpose, and with the peculiarities of his Gospel. But in his own brief account there is a hint that others were there beside the Eleven. He says, "And when they saw Him they worshipped Him; but some doubted." Who were these that doubted? Meyer insists that it could only have been some of the Eleven. But when we recollect His prior appearances to them; how that none of them after the first interview, except Thomas, seem to have had any doubts as to the reality of His resurrection; how the unbelief of Thomas was wholly overcome at the second interview; how He had given to them the first fruits of the Spirit; and that they had now gathered expressly to meet Him—we find it very difficult to believe that any of these doubters were apostles. If not, then others must have been present; and as most of these had not seen Him since His resurrection, it will not appear surprising if some among them should doubt.[1] This is confirmed by the fact that the angel, speaking to the women, does not confine his direction to go into Galilee to the apostles, but makes it general, embracing all the disciples, and perhaps also the women.

Some, however, though admitting that others were present with the apostles, make some of the latter to have doubted. If so, of what did they doubt? Whether they should offer to Him worship?[2] It is not indeed anywhere said that He had before been worshipped by them; and now something new and divine in His aspect may have

1 So Lightfoot, Norton, Robinson, Ebrard, Stier, Alford.

2 So Wetstein, quoted in Meyer; De Wette, Lange.

impelled them to the act. (See Matt. xxviii. 9.) But their doubts could scarce refer to this. Did they doubt of His personal identity? Some have thought that He was so far from them that all could not at first distinctly see Him; others refer their doubts to the changed appearance of His body, either as already glorified, or as in an intermediate condition, midway between the earthly and heavenly. Some, as Newcome, would translate it "had doubted," and refer it to the earlier doubts of the apostles. "Some had doubted before; but all were now convinced." But if this was the interview when the 500 were present, many of whom must have been from Galilee, and had not seen Him since His resurrection, this fact best explains the circumstance that some doubted even now.

Upon this occasion, the words seem to have been spoken which are recorded by Matthew xxviii. 18–20, and Mark xvi. 15–18.[1] Some, however, suppose His words in Mark to have been spoken to the Eleven, as they sat at meat, on the evening of the day of the resurrection.[2] Alford would refer v. 15 to this occasion, but doubts respecting vs. 16–18. Townson makes all to have been spoken in Jerusalem, after the return from Galilee. He would place here also His words, Luke xxiv. 44–48.[3] Ebrard considers all that Luke records from v. 44 on, a resumé of all that Jesus had spoken after His resurrection, in His various interviews with His disciples. We shall consider the point more fully in connection with the ascension.

THURSDAY, MAY 18TH, 783. A. D. 30.

A few days after the meeting upon the mountain in Galilee, the apostles return to Jerusalem, accompanied by Jesus' mother and brethren. Upon the fortieth day after His resurrection, Jesus gathers the	LUKE xxiv. 49. ACTS i. 1–3. ACTS i. 4–8.

[1] So Lichtenstein, Tischendorf, Krafft, Ebrard.

[2] So Newcome, Robinson.

[3] So Wieseler, Bengel, Tischendorf.

Eleven at the Mount of Olives, and, leading them toward Bethany, ascends to heaven. Whilst they were gazing after Him, two angels appear to them, and remind them that He is to return. The apostles go back to Jerusalem, and there wait for the promised baptism of the Holy Spirit. After Pentecost they begin their labors.	LUKE xxiv. 50, 51. MARK xvi. 19. ACTS i. 9–12. LUKE xxiv. 52, 53. MARK xvi. 20.

That Luke, in his statement (Acts i. 3) that Jesus "Showed Himself alive after His passion by many infallible proofs, being seen of the apostles forty days, and speaking of the things pertaining to the kingdom of God," includes more interviews than are specifically recorded by any of the Evangelists, cannot well be doubted. But whether these interviews occurred in Galilee, before the apostles went up to Jerusalem, or in Jerusalem, or in both, can only be conjectured. In favor of Galilee it may be said, that here the apostles were at home and among friends, and that amidst the scenes of His former teachings His present words would come with double power and meaning; whilst in Jerusalem they would be among His enemies, and in a state of disquietude, if not of positive fear. We may, then, suppose that it was near the fortieth day ere they went up to Jerusalem. That they went in obedience to some special direction, is probable, and not simply to be present at the feast of Pentecost; but that they knew for what end He had gathered them there, may be doubted. Indeed it may be fairly inferred from Acts i. 6, that so far from supposing that He was then about to depart from them into heaven, they rather hoped and expected that He was about to reveal Himself in glory, and to commence His reign with the baptism of the Holy Ghost, conformably to His promise, (v. 5.) Olshausen would refer v. 4 to one assembling of the disciples, and v. 6 to another and later, but his reasons are not strong.

The exact spot of the ascension upon the Mount of

Olives has been preserved by tradition; and a chapel now stands upon it, of modern erection, and in the hands of the Mohammedans. But it is certain that Helena, mother of Constantine, erected a church upon the summit, and probably near the present site; though Stanley (448) claims that she did not mean to honor the scene of the ascension itself, but a cave, in which, according to Eusebius, Jesus initiated His disciples into His secret mysteries. "There is, in fact, no proof from Eusebius that any tradition pointed out the scene of the ascension."[1] As to the rock within the present chapel, which has been pointed out to pilgrims since the seventh century as bearing the imprint of the Lord's footsteps, he says, "There is nothing but a simple cavity in the rock, with no more resemblance to a human foot than to any thing else."

As Luke alone of the Evangelists mentions the place of the ascension, we must turn to his statements. He says in his Gospel, (xxiv. 50:) "And He led them out as far as to Bethany," εως εις Βηθανιαν; in the Acts of the Apostles, (i. 12:) "Then returned they unto Jerusalem from the mount called Olivet, which is from Jerusalem a sabbath-day's journey." There is thus the topographical objection to the traditional site of the ascension, that it is but about half a mile from the city wall; and if Jesus was separated from the disciples here, He did not lead them out as far as to Bethany. There is also another objection, in the fact of its publicity, being in full view from the city. But if we construe the statement, "as far as to Bethany," to mean the village of Bethany, we on the other hand make Luke inconsistent with himself, since this is a mile below the summit of Olivet, and much more than a sabbath-day's journey.

Several solutions of the difficulty have been proposed. Lightfoot would distinguish between Bethany, a tract of

[1] See, however, Porter, i. 177.

the mount, and the town Bethany. The former was distant from the city but seven furlongs, or one mile; the latter, fifteen furlongs, or two miles. Between the two lay Bethphage, and He ascended "in that very place where He got upon the ass when He rode into Jerusalem." Wieseler (435, note) supposes that Bethphage was regarded by the Jews as if it constituted a part of the city, and that, reckoning from it eastward, Bethany was but a sabbath-day's journey. He refers to John xii. 9–11, that the Jews did go as far as Bethany upon the Sabbath. Robinson [1] affirms that Bethany and the Mount of Olives are used by Luke "interchangeably, and almost as synonymous." With him many agree. "As far as to Bethany, not quite to the village itself, but over the brow of the Mount of Olives, where it descends on Bethany." (Alford.) "Not altogether into Bethany, but so far as the point where Bethany came into sight." (Stier.) "The secluded hills which overhang that village on the eastern slope of Olivet." (Stanley.) That the "Mount of Olives" is a general designation, embracing the eastern as well as the western slopes, and the villages upon them, is apparent from various passages in the Evangelists. (Compare Mark xi. 1; Luke xix. 29; Mark xi. 11, 12; Luke xxi. 37.) We have, then, to seek a site somewhere upon the mount, in the neighborhood of Bethany, and distant about a sabbath-day's journey from Jerusalem.[2] Such a site Barclay thinks he finds in a hill which overhangs Bethany, that lies about five hundred yards below. This hill is a mile from St. Stephen's gate,

[1] Har. 234.

[2] Meyer would make, not the place of the ascension, but the mountain, to be so far distant. But the mountain, at its base and lower slopes, is within a few rods of the city. "The mean distance," says Barclay, (59,) "of that portion of its summit opposite the city, is about half a mile. But by the nearest pathway it is 918 yards from St. Stephen's gate to the Church of the Ascension; by the longer footpath, 1310 yards; and by the main camel road, is perhaps a little farther."

and within a hundred yards of the direct footpath from Bethany to Jerusalem. However it may be with this particular spot, there is little doubt that from some one of the heights a little below the summit of Olivet, that look to the east, and overhang the village of Bethany, He ascended to sit at the right hand of His Father.[1]

In regard to the hour of the day when the ascension took place, nothing definite can be said. By some it is supposed to have been early morning, by others midday. That others were present beside the Eleven, is probable, though not expressly said.

The difficulties connected with the statements of the Evangelists respecting the ascension demand that we examine their respective narratives in some detail. Matthew does not say that Jesus ascended into heaven after His resurrection, but closes his Gospel with the departure of the Eleven from Jerusalem to Galilee, where Jesus met them at the mountain, as He had appointed them. There, as it would seem, He gave them the commission to go and teach all nations, promising to be with them to the end of the world.[2] That these words were spoken at this interview in Galilee is intrinsically probable; and there is an especial fitness in it if we suppose that, not only the Eleven, but the great body of the disciples were present. But the assertion that this was the final interview, and these the last words of Jesus to His apostles, and therefore that the ascension was from Galilee, is without proof. Here, as often, the brevity of our Evangelist must be complemented by the fuller narratives of the others. Had we the account of Matthew only, we could not know that Jesus ascended

[1] In favor of the traditional site, see Williams, ii. 440; Ellicott, 413. Jones, (Notes, 451,) who supposes several ascensions, makes the first to have taken place on the evening of the day of the resurrection, (Luke xxiv. 50, 51,) and to have been at Bethany, nearly two miles from Jerusalem; and the last, (Acts i. 12,) from Olivet, about five furlongs distant.

[2] Tischendorf, Lichtenstein, Robinson.

from the mountain in Galilee, since he does not mention the ascension at all. But as he was not ignorant of the fact, so he could not have been of the time and place.

The narrative of Mark (xvi. 14–20) presents greater difficulties. He records the command of the Lord to go into all the world and preach the Gospel, and the promise that certain signs should follow them that believe. From the connection in which His words stand it would seem that they were spoken to the Eleven as they sat at meat on the evening of the day of the resurrection, and that immediately after He ascended into heaven. This, however, is wholly irreconcilable with the statements of Luke; and it is also intrinsically improbable that upon the occasion of His first meeting with the apostles after He had risen, and while their minds were in so great excitement, He should give them this commission. We give some of the solutions that have been proposed: 1st. That which takes Mark's narrative as strictly chronological, and makes the Lord's words to have been spoken to the Eleven, on the evening of the day of the resurrection, and His ascension to have immediately followed. This is affirmed by those who, as Kinkel and Jones, maintain that He repeatedly ascended to heaven; and, indeed, that He departed thither after each appearance to His disciples. The ascension on the fortieth day (Acts i. 9) was the last, and as such visible, and marked with especial solemnity.[1] This view of several ascensions may remove some difficulties, but involves others greater, both historical and dogmatic. Others affirm, as Meyer and Alford, that Mark, intending to relate what took place at one and the same time, brings together here by mistake what really took place on several distinct occasions. He supposed that the Lord spake these words to the Eleven

[1] See Kinkel, Studien u. Krit., 1841, translated in Bib. Sacra, Feb. 1844. Jones, (Notes, 480:) "He was during the forty days ordinarily an inhabitant of the heavenly world." See, contra, Robinson, in Bib. Sacra, May, 1845.

on the evening of the day He rose, and the same evening ascended to heaven. The same rule of interpretation seems also to show that He was received up from the room in which they were eating, and that the Eleven, going immediately forth from this room, began at once to preach the Gospel. Of course the writer, whether Mark or some one else, could have known nothing of the several appearances of Jesus during the forty days, of the ascension from Bethany, or of the ten days' waiting for the Spirit ere the disciples began to preach. The supposition of such ignorance itself presents a greater difficulty than that it is intended to remove.

2d. That which makes Jesus to have spoken these words to the Eleven on the evening of the day of the resurrection, but defers the ascension itself to the fortieth day following. In this case the phrase *μετα το λαλησαι*, "After the Lord had spoken to them," (v. 19,) is not to be confined to the few words just recorded, but embraces His discourses in general, down to the time He ascended.

3d. That which places His interview with the Eleven on the evening of the day of the resurrection, (v. 14,) but the words following upon some subsequent occasion, perhaps upon the mount in Galilee; and the ascension at a still later period.

4th. That which makes this interview with the Eleven to have been after the return of Jesus and the disciples from Galilee to Jerusalem, and immediately before the ascension at Bethany.

The obvious and natural interpretation of the narrative is this: The Evangelist, wishing to give in the briefest way the substance of the Lord's missionary commission to the Church, with its accompanying promises, connects it with a meeting of the eleven apostles, which may have been on the evening of the day of the resurrection, or more probably at some subsequent period. All the instructions of the forty days upon this point, are summed up in these few words. In the same concise way it is said, that after the Lord had spoken to them, or after He had finished His instructions, He was received up. To press this brevity as indicating ignorance on his part of the real order of events, is hypercritical.

Substantially the same difficulties meet us in the narrative of Luke as in that of Mark. In his Gospel, (xxiv. 33–51,) he seems to represent the ascension as taking place the evening after Jesus rose from the dead. He meets the Eleven and others as they were gathered together, and after convincing them that He was really risen, by eating before them, and discoursing to them, He leads them out to Bethany, and, blessing them, is carried up into heaven. In the Acts of the Apostles, however, the Evangelist states explicitly that He was seen of them forty days, and full details respecting His ascension at the end of this period, are given. Do these two accounts conflict with each other? This is affirmed by Meyer. According to him, there were two traditions, one of which represented the Lord as ascending upon the day of the resurrection; the other, after forty days. In his Gospel, Luke follows the former; in the Acts, the latter. With Meyer, Alford agrees. "Luke, at the time of writing his Gospel, was not aware of any Galilean appearances of the Lord, nor indeed of any later than this one. That he corrects this in Acts 1, shows him to have become acquainted with some other sources of information, not however, perhaps, including the Galilean appearances." All this is arbitrary conjecture. There is not the slightest hint that the Evangelist wished to correct in the later account an error in the earlier. Had he made so gross a mistake, common honesty toward his readers would have demanded an explicit statement of it, and a retraction. On the contrary, he says that his former treatise embraced all that Jesus did and taught "Until the day in which He was taken up," which day, as he says, was the fortieth after His resurrection. This is a plain averment that in his Gospel he placed the ascension on the fortieth day, although he did not then give any specific designation of time.[1]

Those who, like Jones, make the Lord to have often ascended, refer these accounts of Luke to different events. In the Gospel he speaks of the ascension on the evening following the resurrection; in Acts, of the last ascension. And as the time, so the place was different; the former ascension being from Bethany, the latter from the summit of the Mount of Olives.[2] But Luke's language, in his Gospel, plainly shows that he cannot speak of an ascension upon the evening of the day when Jesus arose. The day was far spent when He was with the two disciples at Emmaus, and they returned to Jerusalem, and probably were some time with the Eleven, ere Jesus joined them. Some time passed in convincing them of His actual resurrection, and in discoursing to them. It must therefore have been late in the evening ere He led them out to Bethany, two miles distant, and the ascension itself must have been in the dead of night. This is intrinsically improbable, or rather incredible.

When the words recorded by Luke (xxiv. 44–48) were spoken, is not certain. Some would put them in immediate connection with what precedes; others refer them to a later period; to the second interview with the Eleven, or to the meeting upon the mount in Galilee, or to the day of the ascension. That the Evangelist gives here a summary of Jesus' teachings during the forty days, is made doubtful by the fact of His opening their understanding, v. 45, which seems to refer to some special act rather than to a gradual process of enlightening. We therefore connect this with

[1] See Ebrard, 596.

[2] In this way Jones explains the statement of Barnabas, that the Lord ascended on the eighth or Sabbath day. See Heferle, Patrum Apostolicorum Opera, 42.

the reception of the Holy Ghost, John xx. 21–23, which was on the evening following the resurrection. Possibly vs. 46–48 may have been spoken later. That the command, v. 49, to tarry in the city of Jerusalem was spoken after they had returned hither from Galilee, and is identical with the command Acts i. 4, needs no proof.

Thus comparing the several Evangelists, we find that the Lord, during the forty days, first manifested Himself to His disciples in Judea, and, going thence to Galilee, returned again to Judea. So far as we can learn, it was not His purpose to have shown Himself to them in Jerusalem, for He had commanded them to go into Galilee, and there they should see Him. But their unbelief in His words respecting His resurrection, made it necessary that He should manifest Himself to them there; yet even after they had seen Him, the unbelief of one seems to have detained them some days at Jerusalem. As in Galilee He had gathered His disciples, so here He appoints a place of general meeting. But He cannot ascend to His Father from Galilee. As He went up to Jerusalem to die, He now goes up thither again, that from the Mount of Olives, overlooking the Holy City and the temple, He may ascend to His Father's right hand to receive the kingdom, and to await the hour when His enemies shall be made His footstool, and the Lord shall be King over all the earth.

"Ye men of Galilee, why stand ye gazing up into Heaven? This same Jesus which is taken up from you into Heaven, shall so come in like manner as ye have seen Him go into Heaven."

GENERAL INDEX.

CHRONOLOGICAL INDEX.

PASSAGES OF SCRIPTURE REFERRED TO IN THE HISTORY.

MATTHEW.

MARK.

LUKE.

JOHN.

ACTS.

1 CORINTHIANS.

PASSAGES OF SCRIPTURE REFERRED TO IN THE CHRONOLOGICAL ESSAYS.

MATTHEW.

LUKE.

JOHN.

NUMBERS.

DANIEL.

ISAIAH.

THE END.

www.ingramcontent.com/pod-product-compliance
Lightning Source LLC
LaVergne TN
LVHW021058110826
845150LV00001B/105